Holy Communion
in the Piety of the Reformed Church

Hughes Oliphant Old, D.théol.

Edited & Introduced
by
Jon D. Payne

Tolle Lege Press
Powder Springs, Georgia

HOLY COMMUNION
IN THE PIETY OF THE REFORMED CHURCH
by Hughes Oliphant Old

Edited and Introduced by Jon D. Payne

© 2013 Hughes Oliphant Old. All rights reserved. No part of this publication may be reproduced, stored in a retrieval system or transmitted in any form or by any means, electronic, mechanical, photocopy, recording or otherwise, without the prior permission of the publisher, except as provided by the copyright laws of the United States of America.

Produced and Distributed by:

TOLLE LEGE PRESS
3150-A Florence Road
Powder Springs, GA 30127

www.TolleLegePress.com
800-651-0211

Unless otherwise indicated, Scripture quoted from the Revised Standard Version of the Bible, copyright 1952 [2nd edition, 1971] by the Division of Christian Education of the National Council of the Churches of Christ in the United States of America. Used by permission. All rights reserved.

Jacket design by Jennifer Tyson

Typeset by Michael Minkoff, Jr.

ISBN: 978-1-938139-27-7

Printed in the United States of America.

Excerpts from *The Book of Common Worship*. Philadelphia: Published for the Office of the General Assembly by the General Division of Publication of the Board of Christian Education of the Presbyterian Church in the United States of America, 1946. Used by permission of the Office of the General Assembly of the Presbyterian Church (USA).

Excerpts from *The Constitution of the Presbyterian Church: Part I, The Book of Confessions*. Louisville: The Office of the General Assembly, 2004. Used by permission of the Office of the General Assembly of the Presbyterian Church (USA).

Excerpts from *The Confession of Faith: The Larger and Shorter Catechisms*. Edinburgh: The Free Church of Scotland, 1976. Used by permission of the Moderator of the Free Church of Scotland.

From *Institutes of the Christian Religion* by John Calvin. © 1960 Westminster Press, Philadelphia. Used by permission of Westminster John Knox Press. www.wjkbooks.com.

Edwards, Jonathan. *Sermons and Discourses 1723–1729*. The Works of Jonathan Edwards, volume 14. Edited by Kenneth Minkema. New Haven: Yale University Press, 1997. Used by permission of Yale University Press.

Edwards, Jonathan. *Sermons on the Lord's Supper*. Edited by Don Kistler. Orlando, Florida: The Northampton Press, 2007. Used with permission of Don Kistler.

Nevin, John Williamson. *The Mystical Presence: A Vindication of the Reformed or Calvinistic Doctrine of the Holy Eucharist*. Philadelphia: J. B. Lippincott & Co., 1846: reprint edited by Augustine Thompson. Eugene, OR: Wipf and Stock, 2000. Used by permission of Wipf and Stock Publishers. www.wipfandstock.com.

Old, Hughes Oliphant. "Gilbert Tennent and the Preaching of Piety in Colonial America." In *Princeton Seminary Bulletin*, 10/2 (1989): 132–137. Used by permission of Princeton Theological Seminary.

Old, Hughes Oliphant. "*Eutaxia, or, The Presbyterian Liturgies: Historical Sketches* by Charles W. Baird." *American Presbyterians* 66/4 (Winter, 1988): 260–263. Used by permission of the Presbyterian Historical Society and the *Journal of Presbyterian History*.

Old, Hughes Oliphant. *The Reading and Preaching of the Scriptures in the Worship of the Christian Church*. Volume 4, *The Age of the Reformation*. Grand Rapids, MI: Wm. B. Eerdmans Publishing Co., 2002, chapter 7. Reprinted by permission of the publisher; all rights reserved.

Old, Hughes Oliphant. *The Reading and Preaching of the Scriptures in the Worship of the Christian Church*, vol. 5, *Moderatism, Pietism, and Awakening* (Grand Rapids, MI: Wm. B. Eerdmans Publishing Co., 2004), sections on Robert Walker and Andrew Thomson from chapter 8. Reprinted by permission of the publisher; all rights reserved.

Robertson, George W. *Sacramental Solemnity: Gilbert Tennent, the Covenant and the Lord's Supper*. PhD dissertation. Westminster Theological Seminary, 2007. Used with permission of George W. Robertson.

Von Allmen, Jean-Jacques. *The Lord's Supper*. London: Lutterworth Press, 1969. Used by permission of Lutterworth Press. A modern reprint is available from James Clarke.

To my doctor father, Jean-Jacques von Allmen

TABLE OF CONTENTS

Editor's Introduction by Jon D. Payne xv

Introduction 3

1: CALVIN'S COMMUNION LITURGY 13

    Lord's Day Observance 16
    Praise and Thanksgiving 19
    Prayer of Confession 22
    The Reading and Preaching of the Gospel 24
    The Pastoral Prayer 26
    The Confession Of Faith 28
    The Communion Invocation 29
    Invitation 31
    The Sharing of the Meal 33
    The Prayer of Dedication 36
    The Communion Psalmody 38
    The Benediction 39
    Collection of Alms 40

2: CALVIN ON COMMUNION
THE COVENANTAL AND SACRAMENTAL DIMENSIONS . . . 41

    THE COVENANTAL DIMENSION 45
        A. The Basic Concept 49
            1. *Institutes* IV, xiv, 1–6 49
            2. *Institutes* IV, xvii, 1f. 51
            3. Commentary on Mark 14:24 54
            4. Commentary on 1 Corinthians 11 55
            5. Commentary on 1 Corinthians 10:16–18 58
        B. The Supper As Memorial 64
        C. The Supper As Communion 68
        D. The Supper as Proclamation 70
    THE SACRAMENTAL DIMENSION 71

3: CALVIN ON COMMUNION
THE WISDOM DIMENSION 81

    A. Calvin's Appreciation of Wisdom Theology 82
        1. Prologue to the Gospel of John 83
        2. The First Epistle of John 88
        3. The Epistle of James 90
        4. The Wisdom Psalms 92
    B. Calvin's Interpretation of the Bread of Life Discourse . . . 97
        1. Feasting on Wisdom 97

    2. The Manna. 101
    3. The Feast of Passover. 103
  C. Wisdom Concepts in Calvin's Teaching on the Supper . . . 106
    1. The Supper Empowers 107
    2. The Supper Enlightens 112
    3. The Supper Enlivens 115

4: CALVIN ON COMMUNION:
THE PNEUMATIC AND EVANGELISTIC DIMENSIONS   125

THE PNEUMATIC DIMENSION 125
THE EVANGELISTIC DIMENSION 136
  A. Sermons 138
  B. The Liturgy 151

5: CALVIN ON COMMUNION:
THE EUCHARISTIC AND ESCHATOLOGICAL DIMENSIONS   157

THE EUCHARISTIC DIMENSION 157
THE ESCHATOLOGICAL DIMENSION 173

6: HOLY COMMUNION
IN THE REFORMED CHURCH OF ENGLAND   181

KING EDWARD'S PRAYER BOOK . . . .

THOMAS CRANMER 189
  A. Cranmer's Eucharistic Theology 192
  B. Cranmer's Attempt at a Reformed Canon 194
NICHOLAS RIDLEY AND *THE ALTARS OF BAAL* 199
MARTIN BUCER, *CENSURA* 203
THE THIRTY-NINE ARTICLES 214
JOHN JEWEL 217
  A. John Jewel's "Challenge Sermon" 219
  B. John Jewel and the Patristic Witness 224
RICHARD HOOKER AND THE BEGINNINGS OF ANGLICANISM . . . 227
WILLIAM PERKINS:
  UNION WITH CHRIST AND COMMUNION WITH THE BRETHREN . . 230

7: JOHN KNOX
AND THE SCOTTISH TRADITION   239

JOHN KNOX'S LITURGY 239
  A. Prayers of Lamentation, Confession, and Repentance . . . 241
  B. Pastoral Prayer 244
  C. Invitation 246

    D. Sitting at the Table 248
    E. The Eucharistic Prayer 249
    F. Prayer of Dedication 255
ROBERT BRUCE *THE MYSTERY OF THE LORD'S SUPPER*, **1589** 259
    A. Meeting the Polemic of the Counter-Reformation 262
    B. The Whole Christ 271
    C. The Work of the Holy Spirit 275
    D. Real Presence 278
    E. The Call for Repentance and Restoration
       in the Covenant Community 280
SAMUEL RUTHERFORD 282
    A. Communion with the Christ to Come 285
    B. Communion with the Smitten Christ 287
    C. The Lord's Supper and the Parable of the Great Feast . . . 291
    D. The Lord's Supper and the Presence of the Risen Christ . . 293
    E. The Lord's Supper and the Wedding Feast of the Lamb . . 296

8: URSINUS, BULLINGER,
AND THE SECOND GENERATION   305

    URSINUS AND *THE HEIDELBERG CATECHISM* 306
    BULLINGER AND *THE SECOND HELVETIC CONFESSION*. 313
        A. *The Second Helvetic Confession* on the Sacraments 315
           1. Affirmation 169 316
           2. Affirmation 170 317
           3. Affirmation 171 317
           4. Affirmation 172 317
           5. Affirmation 173 318
           6. Affirmation 175 318
           7. Affirmation 178 319
           8. Affirmation 180 319
        B. *The Second Helvetic Confession* on the Lord's Supper. 320
           1. Affirmation 193 320
           2. Affirmation 195 320
           3. Affirmation 198 321
           4. Affirmation 200 322
           5. Affirmation 201 322
           6. Affirmation 203 322
           7. Affirmation 205 323

9: THE ROOTS OF ENGLISH PURITANISM   325

    ADMONITION, **1570** 327
    EDWARD REYNOLDS 330
        A. The Covenantal Dimension 332
        B. Divine Origin of the Sacrament of Communion 333

    C. Scholastic Terminology. 334
    D. Mystical Union with Christ 338
    E. The Real Presence 341
    F. The Operations of the Holy Spirit 344
  JEREMIAH BURROUGHS 346
    A. Worship as Sanctifying God's Name. 347
    B. Fencing the Table 349
    C. Worship as Meditation on the Cross. 352

10: THE PURITANS AT WESTMINSTER   355

    A. Frequency of Celebration 357
    B. Preparation for the Sacrament 358
    C. Sunday Celebration 359
    D. Arrangement of and at the Table 360
    E. Liturgical Elements 362
  RICHARD BAXTER'S *REFORMED LITURGY*, **1661** 365
    A. Collect for Pardon 369
    B. Epiclesis 369
    C. Prayer of Consecration. 371
    D. Eucharistic Prayer 373
  THOMAS DOOLITTLE'S *A TREATISE CONCERNING THE LORD'S SUPPER* . . 377
    A. Frequency of Celebration 378
    B. Preparation for the Lord's Supper 380
    C. Preoccupation with Worthiness 381
  JOHN OWEN'S *SACRAMENTAL DISCOURSES* **(1669–1682)** 384
    A. The Supper as Memorial of the Gospel. 388
    B. The Supper as Invitation 391
    C. The Supper as Profession of Faith 393
    D. The Supper as Covenant 395
    E. The Supper as Communion 397

11: THE AGE OF PROTESTANT ORTHODOXY   405

  JEAN DAILLÉ AND THE HUGUENOT TRADITION. 405
    A. Outside the Gates of Paris 406
    B. The Sacrament as Agapé 407
    C. The Sacrament as Commemoration 409
    D. The Sacrament as Sign and Seal of the Covenant . . . 411
    E. The Sacrament as Communion 412
    F. The Uniqueness of Christ's Sacrifice. 414
    G. The Nature of the Real Presence. 416
    H. Preparation for Receiving the Sacrament 417
    I. The Frequency of Communion 419
  THE NETHERLANDS IN ITS GOLDEN AGE 420
    A. Willem Teellinck 422

    B. Jodocus van Lodenstein. 429

12: MATTHEW HENRY   441

A Communicant's Companion, 1704 442
    A. The Names of The Lord's Supper 443
        1. "Sacrament" 443
        2. "The Lord's Supper". 444
        3. "Communion". 445
        4. "Eucharist" 447
        5. "Feast" 449
    B. The Nature of the Lord's Supper. 451
        1. A Commemorative Ordinance 452
        2. A Confessing Ordinance. 454
        3. A Communicating Ordinance 455
        4. A Covenanting Ordinance 457
    C. Henry's Eucharistic Piety 459
        1. Proclaiming the Feast 459
        2. Self-Examination 461
        3. Renewing Our Covenant 462
        4. Meditation and Prayer 463
        5. The Affecting Sights 465
        6. The Benefits of the Sacrament. 467

13: COMMUNION SEASONS
IN EIGHTEENTH-CENTURY SCOTLAND   473

JOHN WILLISON 474
    A. *Five Sacramental Sermons*, 1722 477
    B. Action Sermon 487
    C. *A Sacramental Catechism*, 1720 495
        1. Covenantal Dimension 496
        2. Sacramental Dimension 499
        3. The Communion Dimension 503
        4. The Sacrament as Sign 506
        5. Meditation 515
        6. Thanksgiving 522
        7. Pneumatic Dimension 525

14: THE ERSKINE BROTHERS
AND THE COVENANTER TRADITION   531

EBENEZER ERSKINE 533
    A. A Sermon on the Beauty of Holiness 534
    B. Communion as Union with Christ 536
    C. Communion as Delight in the Divine Presence 539
    D. Communion as Embracing Christ 543

RALPH ERSKINE 549
   A. Mounting Up on Eagles' Wings 550
   B. The Bethel Experience. 553
   C. Communion as Tasting the Wedding Feast of the Lamb . . 559
ROBERT WALKER 563
ANDREW THOMSON 573

15: DUTCH PIETISM   585

WILHELM À BRAKEL. 587
PETER IMMENS 590
   A. A Day of Reparation 591
   B. The Invitation. 594
   C. Communion Meditation 596
   D. Covenant Renewal 599
   E. Appropriate Thanksgiving 600
THEODORUS JACOBUS FRELINGHUYSEN 603

16: THE GREAT AWAKENING
AND JONATHAN EDWARDS   605

JONATHAN EDWARDS 606
   A. Communion as Self-Examination 608
   B. Communion as Feast 611
   C. Communion as the Memorial of Christ's Atoning Sacrifice . 617
   D. Communion as Glorying in the Savior 621
   E. Communion as Union with Christ 624
   F. Communion as Seal 625
   G. Communion with Christ's Body and Blood 627
   H. Communion with Christ 629

17: THE GREAT AWAKENING
OTHER VOICES   633

GILBERT TENNENT 634
   A. Preaching Piety in Colonial America 636
   B. The Sacrament as Assurance of the Love of Christ 642
   C. The Sacrament as Mystical Experience. 646
SAMUEL DAVIES 651
   A. Memorial 654
   B. Sacrament 656
   C. Covenant 658
   D. Communion 661
   E. Evangelism. 666

18: NEW SCHOOL CONGREGATIONALISM   673

TIMOTHY DWIGHT 674
NATHANIEL WILLIAM TAYLOR. 688

19: OLD SCHOOL PRESBYTERIANISM   693

CHARLES HODGE 693
   A. Princeton's Systematic Theologian 694
   B. The Means Of Grace 695
   C. The Rite of Communion 700
   D. Controversies Over Eucharistic Doctrine 711
   E. Review Of Nevin's *Mystical Presence* 715
JAMES WADDEL ALEXANDER 716
   A. The Supper as the Hallowing of God's Name. 719
   B. The Supper as the Memorial of the Incarnation 722
   C. The Supper as Memorial of Christ's Redemptive Sacrifice . 725
   D. The Supper as *Agapé*. 730
   E. The Supper as Sign and Seal of the New Covenant . . . 733
   F. The Supper as Foretaste of the Wedding Feast of the Lamb . 737
BENJAMIN BRECKINRIDGE WARFIELD 739
   A. "Communion in Christ's Body and Blood". 741
   B. The Sacrificial Feast 744
   C. Sitting at the Lord's Table 746

20: THE AGE OF ROMANTICISM   751

JOHN WILLIAMSON NEVIN 751
CHARLES WASHINGTON BAIRD'S *PRESBYTERIAN LITURGIES*. 767

21: VICTORIAN EVANGELICALISM   777

THOMAS CHALMERS. 777
   A. Holy Communion as Covenant Renewal 779
   B. Holy Communion as Invitation to Accept Christ 780
   C. Holy Communion as Eucharist 781
   D. Holy Communion as Sitting at the Father's Table 783
   E. Holy Communion and the Sign of the Lord's Day 785
ROBERT DALE 786
CHARLES HADDON SPURGEON 787
   A. The Lord's Table 789
   B. Communion with Christ 791
   C. Communion with the Brethren 793
   D. The Paschal Psalms 795
   E. The Real Presence of Christ 797
   F. Christ's Presence and the Work of the Holy Spirit 799
   G. Presence and Mysticism 800

22: HENRY VAN DYKE
AND THE BOOK OF COMMON WORSHIP 805

HENRY VAN DYKE: A MAN OF LETTERS. 805
    B. Van Dyke's Communion Service:
        The High Tide of Romanticism 809
    C. An Alternative Order for Liberal Protestantism 823
    D. *The Book Of Common Worship* in Retrospect 830

23: JEAN-JACQUES VON ALLMEN
AND THE ECUMENICAL APPROACH 835

A BORDER THEOLOGIAN 836
THE ECUMENISM OF TAIZÉ 840
ESSAY ON THE LORD'S SUPPER 842
    A. The New Biblical Philology 845
    B. The Byzantine Doctrine of the Holy Spirit 846
    C. Baptismal Discipline. 847
    D. Episcopacy. 848
    E. The Supper as Fraternal Communion 849
    F. Spiritual Food 851
    G. Eucharistic Sacrifice. 853
WILLY RORDORF. 855

CONCLUSION 857
BIBLIOGRAPHY 867
SCRIPTURE INDEX 909
SUBJECT INDEX 911

EDITOR'S INTRODUCTION

Holy communion is at the heart of Reformed worship and piety. Sixteenth and seventeenth-century Reformed confessions, catechisms, liturgies, and church orders, from Geneva to Westminster, give primary attention to the doctrine of the Lord's Supper. Along with baptism and the preached Word, communion is viewed by the Reformed as a primary means whereby Christ imparts the benefits of Christ's mediation to the elect.

For the Reformed, then, the Lord's Supper is more than symbolic memorialism. It is an objective means of grace through which a believer's faith is mysteriously and yet truly nourished and strengthened in Christ. It is a spiritual (not corporeal) partaking of Christ's body and blood, a holy feasting which occurs as the Spirit works through genuine faith. It is also a confirmation and pledge of God's steadfast love for his redeemed children—a sign and seal of His covenant fidelity. Those who come to the Table with penitent hearts and sincere faith in the gospel receive divine comfort and blessing. Therefore, to trivialize the role of the Lord's Supper in the worship and piety of the church is to stand outside of the Reformed tradition.

According to the *Belgic Confession* (1561) the Lord's Supper is a "spiritual table at which Christ communicates Himself, with all His benefits to us, and gives us there to enjoy both himself and the merits of His sufferings and death, nourishing, strengthening, and comforting our poor comfortless souls" through his body and blood (Article 35). In similar fashion the *Heidelberg Cat-*

echism (1563) states that "as bread and wine support this temporal life, so His crucified body and shed blood are the true meat and drink whereby our souls are fed to eternal life . . . visible signs and pledges to assure us that we are really partakers of His true body and blood (by the operation of the Holy Ghost)" (Q. 79). The *Westminster Shorter Catechism* (1647) teaches that, at the Lord's Table, believers are "partakers of [Christ's] body and blood, with all his benefits, to their spiritual nourishment, and growth in grace" (Q. 96). Confessional formulations such as these remind us why the Lord's Supper has always been essential to Reformed spirituality.

This strong emphasis on the Lord's Supper in the piety of the Reformed church did not vanish in the mid seventeenth century. It continued in various measure in Reformed churches throughout the expanding world, and in the rich eucharistic preaching and writings of notable pastors such as John Owen, Willem Teellinck, Matthew Henry, Jonathan Edwards, Thomas Chalmers, and the famous Calvinistic Baptist preacher, Charles Spurgeon. Like Calvin and Owen before him, Spurgeon's high view of the Lord's Supper led him to advocate a weekly observance of the Supper.

The Reformed have always confessed that it is in the verdant pastures of the divinely appointed means of grace that true piety flourishes. Notwithstanding, there is a kind of sacramental anemia that exists in our churches today. In my experience, pastors rarely take time to reflect on the nature and spiritual benefits of holy communion, thus providing very little instruction for their flocks on these crucial matters. Consequently, church members do not approach the table as they ought nor benefit from the table as they should. Moreover, most students who enter my classes at Reformed Theological Seminary admit to only a scant consideration of the connection between the sacraments and godly piety. Surprisingly, a majority of these students are from Reformed backgrounds.

As a young seminary student, I too was among the uninitiated as it concerned the doctrine of the Lord's Supper— that is, until

Editor's Introduction

I had the privilege of taking Dr. Hughes Oliphant Old's magnificent course on Christian Worship. In his class I was introduced to the regulative principle of worship, the *lectio continua* reading and preaching of Scripture, Psalm singing, biblical prayer, and the nature and spiritual benefits of the sacraments. Not only is his instruction on worship firmly rooted in the theology of the sixteenth-century Reformation, so is his appearance! Indeed, his long, Calvin-like beard only adds to the aura of his captivating lectures. Like some of you, I have been profoundly impacted by Dr. Old's scholarship. Therefore, it is an honor to edit and introduce this outstanding and illuminating volume on the Lord's Supper. Dr. Old is arguably the greatest living authority on the subject of Protestant and Reformed worship. Pastors, seminary students, and laypersons, therefore, would do well to get acquainted with his writings in this age of doxological and liturgical confusion.

In *Holy Communion in the Piety of the Reformed Church*, Hughes Oliphant Old leads his readers through the lives and eucharistic writings of several key Reformed ministers from the Reformation to the present. He introduces us to Reformed pastor-theologians from around the world who may not have agreed on every aspect of the Lord's Supper, but who thought deeply about its application to Christian living, church unity, and biblical mission. In so doing Old challenges the sacramental anemia of our day, calling the church to consider afresh the ordinance that our Good Shepherd instituted for the blessing, growth, assurance, and comfort of His sheep.

Rev. Dr. Jon D. Payne
Christ Church Presbyterian
Charleston, South Carolina
August, 2013

Holy Communion
in the Piety of the Reformed Church

INTRODUCTION

The Reformed communion liturgy has come to flower over the centuries. It is not as though its first efforts back in the early years of the Reformation were its best or that the clandestine Huguenot celebrations in the Cevennes Mountains at the end of the seventeenth century reached an ultimate purity which we have never since attained. The *Strasbourg German Mass* of 1524 and the *Zurich Service Book* of 1525 were only beginnings. The intense celebrations of the sacrament told by Jonathan Edwards in Northampton, Massachusetts, exemplify Reformed sacramental piety every bit as much as the communion sermons of Jodocus van Lodenstein in the Dutch city of Utrecht. The piety of Reformed churches has often come to expression in its simple and disciplined way in one land or another, century after century. The purpose of this work is to show both the continuity and the diversity in the attempt of Reformed Christians to be obedient to the command of our Lord to "do this as often as you do it in remembrance of me" (cf. Luke 22:19 and 1 Cor. 11:24–25).

From the very beginning the Reformed churches took a collegial approach both to their doctrine and their liturgical practice. Luther had, of course, been a pivotal inspiration and yet in the upper Rhineland, Alsace, and the Swiss city states there had been those who preached reform at least a generation before him. There had been pastoral reforms and attempts at moral and doctrinal reforms. The worship of the Reformed churches has been shaped by many hands.

The Reformers of Strasbourg were especially prominent. Bucer in particular developed the prayers which Calvin took to Geneva. Bucer's prayers had been shaped by his study of the Hebrew Psalter on one hand and the prayer life of the Fathers of the ancient Church on the other. Wolfgang Capito did much of the research behind the deep appreciation for the Lord's Day as the Christian Sabbath so characteristic of Reformed piety. John Oecolampadius was the foremost patristic scholar of the Reformation, opening up the preaching of the Greek Fathers so attractively that they became a continuing influence on Protestant preaching.

The teaching of Ulrich Zwingli on the nature of Christ's presence at the sacrament of the Lord's Supper was soon amplified by Heinrich Bullinger, Zwingli's successor, in such a way that John Calvin was able to agree with the pastors of Zurich in the *Consensus Tigurinus* of 1549.

Then there were the hymn writers of Constance, Ambrosius Blaurer and Johannes Zwick, who did so much to develop a popular hymnody. Clément Marot, the great Huguenot psalmodist, gave Reformed worship a lyrical, poetic quality that was tremendously appreciated not only in its early days but even down to our own day. The reform of worship in the early sixteenth century was hardly the work of a single Reformer, but the creative effort of a whole school of reformers.

Calvin's *Genevan Psalter* of 1542 represents a certain stage in the development of Reformed worship. It summarizes the first attempts and experiments of a generation which tried to recast the shape of Christian worship through a careful study of the principles, directions, and examples of Scripture. As will become evident from time to time it was not so much what Calvin thought of as ideal, but what he could get the city council to go along with. Only in a limited sense did the worship of the Reformed Church of Geneva during the pastorate of Calvin (1542–1564) become a normative pattern of Reformed worship for following generations.

INTRODUCTION

The basic principles were still unfolding. A century later the *Westminster Directory for Public Worship* had unfolded Reformed worship in a very different way.

What has intrigued me over the years is that some of the best insights of Reformed worship come quite a bit later than the *Genevan Psalter* of 1542 and the period of Calvin's pastoral leadership in Geneva. Often Reformed piety reached far greater heights in the seventeenth and eighteenth centuries than it did in the early days of the Reformation. Even at that, most of the roots of this maturity were clearly to be found in the earlier days.

The insights of the Puritans, so rich and so profound, need to be looked at more intently. Matthew Henry has left us important works on the Lord's Supper which reflect the best of seventeenth century eucharistic doctrine. John Willison—pastor in Dundee, Scotland, early in the eighteenth century (1668–1750)—left us a treasury of sacramental meditations which deserves careful reading. The American Great Awakening fathomed some surprising depths of Reformed eucharistic theology. This is especially the case regarding the relation of the sacraments to evangelism.

In the pages ahead we will look at a few examples of how Reformed eucharistic faith and worship have unfolded, starting with Calvin and continuing during the period of Protestant Orthodoxy. Then we will look at how the sacrament was celebrated among the Puritans. The *Westminster Directory* will claim our attention as well as communion sermons from several prominent Puritans, such as John Owen and Edward Reynolds. The communion meditations of Matthew Henry will be given special attention because they are of the highest value. Following that we will look at some of the devotional manuals and eucharistic sermons of the eighteenth century, giving particular attention to the Old School Presbyterianism of Willison. Then we will turn our attention to several American pastors, well known for their leadership in the Great Awakening. We will look first at Jonathan Edwards (1703–1758) who was not as helpful on this subject as we might have hoped, but whose contemporary Gilbert Tennent was a real find. Tennent (1703–1764) with his colleague Theodorus Jacobus Frelinghuysen (1692–1747), pastor of the Dutch Reformed Church in New Brunswick, sparked the Great Awakening in New Jersey's Raritan Valley. We will study the communion sermons of Samuel Davies (1723–1761), who introduced the Great Awakening to Virginia. Finally we will look at James W. Alexander (1804–1859), who provides us with a good insight into the theology of Old Princeton.

Both in my doctoral thesis, *The Patristic Roots of Reformed Worship*, and in my work on baptism, *The Shaping of the Reformed Baptismal Rite in the Sixteenth Century*, my attention was focused on the development of Reformed worship from the first attempts at liturgical reform in the early sixteenth century to the publication of the *Genevan Psalter* of 1542. We looked particularly at the reforms of the Upper Rhineland, but also at the attempts at reform in France, especially in the circle of Jacques Lefévre d'Étaples and Guillaume Briçonnet, the Bishop of Meaux. These two works concentrated on the sources of the reform, on the roots of Reformed worship. Now my interest is to continue the story.

One reason for this approach is that the seventeenth and eighteenth centuries produced remarkable works on both eucharistic doctrine and eucharistic piety. To understand the Lord's Supper in Reformed faith and worship, it is not enough simply to go back to John Calvin. Helpful as that undoubtedly is, it is not sufficient. Nor is it enough to go back to John Calvin set in the context of the other Reformers, namely Martin Luther on one hand and Ulrich Zwingli on the other. Martin Bucer, Heinrich Bullinger, Peter Martyr Vermigli, John Knox, and John Oecolampadius must be brought into the discussion in order to get the true picture.

What we have in mind for this study goes much further. In regard to the observance of the Lord's Supper especially it needs to be said that there were aspects of eucharistic observance which remained unachieved during the pastorate of Calvin in Geneva. There was a hundred years between the *Genevan Psalter* of 1542 and the *Directory for Public Worship* of the Westminster Assembly in 1646. The Reformed Communion liturgy had changed considerably. We need to look at these changes and ask why they took place. Were these changes an unfolding of nascent Reformed insights or did they come from elsewhere—from John Wycliffe, for instance, or from the Anabaptists, or from the continuing influence of late Medieval pietism? Perhaps much of the *Westminster Directory* was nothing more than the resistance of a contrary spirit to the state-sponsored *Book of Common Prayer*. That, of course, was the charge of the Anglican Archbishop of Canterbury, John Whitgift.

It has long been my experience that the most nourishing spiritual food is not found so much in the controversial literature as in the devotional literature of the Church. The meditations of Matthew Henry, the sacramental catechism of John Willison, and the communion sermons of Gilbert Tennent are in the end much more edifying than the disputations of John Calvin and Joachim Westphal.

In the nineteenth century a number of Congregational, Presbyterian, as well as Dutch and German Reformed churches, began to re-evaluate their worship practices. Alexander Campbell (1788–1866), of Scottish Covenanter background, began to demand a strict application of the regulative principle. He refused to baptize infants and demanded the celebration of communion each Lord's Day. In the other direction, John Williamson Nevin (1803–1886), very much under the influence of Romanticism, reacted strongly against the emotionalism of frontier religion. Then, in an effort to give balance to the discussion, Charles Washington Baird (1828–1887) published Calvin's communion liturgy as well as that of John Knox in an attempt to cultivate greater reverence, decency, and order to public worship.

How it is that I have not pressed on further into the eighteenth and nineteenth centuries I have a hard time justifying. It is, however, easy to explain. In the first place it is that for one reason or another I happened on the devotional writings of these masters, and I found them so attractive that I got hooked. It is a good number of years ago that I first began to realize the devotional riches treasured up in the writings of Matthew Henry. Then one day in a second hand bookstore I discovered a volume of the eucharistic writings of John Willison. I took the book home and could hardly put it down. On another occasion my friend Bill Harris, the now retired archivist at Princeton Seminary's Speer Library, asked me to read the rediscovered autograph sermons of Gilbert Tennent.

At some point I began to realize that in Scotland especially it became the practice to collect the sacramental sermons of a particular preacher. Communion sermons apparently became a genre of preaching in Reformed circles. It must have been shortly after this that I heard Iain Maclean's paper on van Lodenstein's eucharistic sermons at the Calvin Colloquium at Davidson College. I was amazed at the eucharistic piety I found in these sermons and began to realize that there was a similarity in these different sermons. They had the same ardent devotion and treated many of the same themes. Only slowly did I begin to see how these themes had grown out of the Reformed eucharistic faith of the early sixteenth century. Something very beautiful began to appear, and it is that which I want to report in this work. At the time it seemed only happenstance that I ran into these documents, but now as I have applied more disciplined study to them it all seems more providential than circumstantial. This, I am sure, will not come as a surprise to my regular readers.

It has always seemed such a pity to me that the doctrine of the Lord's Supper has been so controversial. Studying eucharistic doctrine usually starts by drawing up the lines of battle. First one has to define the basic points of contention between the Reformers and late medieval Catholicism. Even in the High Middle Ages the

Western Church had not been sure about its sacramental teachings and John Wycliffe had not been alone in his objections. Then one has to listen to the differences between Luther and Zwingli and the attempts of Bucer to reconcile the two. These controversies had barely calmed down when the controversies between Calvin and the Genesio-Lutherans broke out. My years in Tübingen made me a Lutheran sympathizer. Even the Lutheran Scholasticism of the seventeenth century wins my warmest admiration. It embarrasses me terribly when Lutherans and Calvinists disagree, but that is the pain of our humanity, I suppose. Those who know me understand I may be very conservative but I am not a hardliner.

With teachers like Matthew Henry, Samuel Davies, and John Willison it is possible to get beyond the controversies. There is an obvious reason for this; we are no longer dealing with theological treatises, but rather with pastoral literature. Here we are reading the sermons of a pastor preparing his congregation to observe the sacrament. We are looking over the shoulder of a minister teaching the young people in his congregation on the occasion of their first participation in the Lord's Supper, or we are listening to a minister describing a celebration of communion at the consummation of a revival when the communicants made their covenant vows and were received into the household of faith. This is not the place for doctrinal controversy.

We don't want to belittle doctrinal debates and discussions in our saying this. They have their place in the Christian life. Nothing stagnates Christian thought more than the artificial compromises which have so often been forced upon us in the name of political expediency or ecumenism. In fact, our research in this field shows us that the debates over eucharistic theology in the sixteenth century bore rich fruit in the seventeenth and eighteenth centuries. The Reformers opened up trails that had been closed for a long time, and their disciples in later generations followed them out with profit.

What about the twentieth century? Have I nothing to say about more recent times? As a matter of fact I do. I very much admire some of the twentieth century biblical scholarship which has helped us understand the important biblical texts. One thinks of the words of Gerhard von Rad on the nature of true thanksgiving, or Brevard Childs on memorial, or Joachim Jeremias on the subject of Christ's celebration of Passover. One thinks of Oscar Cullman's studies on the worship of the ancient church as well as Willy Rordorf's study *Sunday*. Twentieth century biblical scholarship has given us valuable insights into the nature and use of the sacraments.

Alas, I have to admit that the book before you is unfinished. I wanted to do a chapter on the celebration of Communion in the German Reformed churches of the nineteenth century. Surely Friedrich Wilhelm Krummacher has left us something! Even more, what I wouldn't give for the chance to report on the celebration of Communion in the house churches of China. But my traveling days are over; besides that, my eyes are giving out on me. My daughter and my son both read to me. I have a good assistant, Rev. Glen Clary, pastor of Immanuel Orthodox Presbyterian Church in West Collingswood, New Jersey. He gets things out of the library for me and my wife puts it on the computer, but there is no question about it, I can't do the research I once did.

My readers have come to expect long treatments from me. I have been writing about preaching for seven volumes now. To be sure, I would love to be able to tell a comprehensive story of the Lord's Supper from the Upper Room in Jerusalem to Calvary Chapel in Costa Mesa, California, but I have already had my three score years and ten. I am grateful for that. If I am able to finish up what I have started, I will consider myself blessed. One multi-volume project in a lifetime is enough.

I was very glad to know that the editing of this volume would be supervised by Jon Payne. I am very happy to have the opportu-

INTRODUCTION 11

nity to work with him once again. I remember him as my student at Reformed Theological Seminary in Charlotte many years ago. He was captain of the Charlotte professional soccer team at the time, and gave me an autographed poster of him in his uniform to give to my son. My family had spent a winter in the south of France, where my son had learned to play soccer. The poster was proudly displayed on the wall of his room for several years. We still have it. I believe that Jon took several courses from me over time, and I was impressed with his considerable abilities as a student in the subject of Reformed worship.

Originally I thought I would end this volume with my study of Henry van Dyke (1852–1933) and the *Book of Common Worship*. Professor Edward Dowey was right; one should not try to write the history of his own time. But I kept getting requests to write something on Jean-Jacques von Allmen (1917–1994), my doctor father at the University of Neuchâtel. It suddenly occurred to me that I should write a chapter on him and dedicate the entire volume to him. The more I thought about it the more I liked the idea, so that is what I have done.

Hughes Oliphant Old
White River Junction, Vermont
June, 2012

1
CALVIN'S COMMUNION LITURGY

As is widely known, the communion liturgy of Geneva from 1542 until well after the death of Calvin was not Calvin's work.[1] For the most part, Calvin borrowed it from Strasbourg.[2] Luther's influence was very strong. The liturgical traditions of Zurich and Basel had come into play as well. The *Genevan Psalter* of 1542 was the product of a generation of liturgical reform.[3] There

[1] On the development of the Reformed communion liturgy up to Calvin see: Hughes Oliphant Old, *The Patristic Roots of Reformed Worship* (Zurich: Theologische Verlag Zurich, 1975; American edition, Black Mountain, NC: Worship Press, 2004). See also Brian A. Gerrish, *Grace and Gratitude: The Eucharistic Theology of John Calvin* (Eugene, OR: Wipf & Stock Publishers, 2002); Markus Jenny, *Die Einheit des Abendmahlsgottesdienstes* (Zürich and Stuttgart: Zwingli Verlag Zürich, 1968); Gottfried W. Locher, *Huldrych Zwingli in neuer Sicht* (Zürich and Stuttgart: Zwingli Verlag Zürich, 1969); Gottfried W. Locher, *Zwingli's Thought: New Perspectives* (Leiden: E. J. Brill, 1981); and Bard Thompson, *Liturgies of the Western Church* (Philadelphia: Fortress Press, 1961).

[2] One of my students, Walter Taylor, recently brought to my attention the existence of an English translation of Bucer's *Grund und Ursach*, a most important document on the reform of worship in Strasbourg in the sixteenth century. Ottomar Frederick Cypris, *Basic Principles: Translation and Commentary of Martin Bucer's Grund und Ursach, 1524* (Ann Arbor: UMI Dissertation Services, 2003). For an English translation of the communion service of the Reformed Church of Strasbourg, see Thompson, *Liturgies of the Western Church*, pp. 159–181. The original French text can be found at René Bornert, *La réforme protestante du culte à Strasbourg au XVIe siècle (1523–1598): approche sociologique et interprétation théologique* (Leiden: E. J. Brill, 1981).

[3] For the liturgical texts of the Reformed Church of Geneva, see: John Calvin, *Opera selecta*, ed. Petrus Barth and Dora Scheuner, 5 vols. (Munich: Chr. Kaiser, 1952), volume 2; John Calvin, *Short Treatise on the Lord's Supper*, Library of Christian Classics, vol. 22 (Philadelphia: Westminster Press, 1954); John Calvin, *A Treatise on the Sacraments of Baptism and the Lord's Supper* (Edinburgh: John Johnstone, 1837); John Calvin, *Treatises on the Sacraments, Catechism of the Church of Geneva, Forms of Prayer, Confessions of Faith*, trans. Henry Beveridge (Fearn, UK: Christian Heri-

were certain changes, to be sure, but essentially it was a French translation of Bucer's German service of 1537. The attempt at a French version of the Strasbourg service had been made to provide the congregation of French Evangelical refugees in Strasbourg with Protestant worship in their own language.

The fact that Calvin introduced the Strasbourg service to the Church of Geneva would certainly indicate that he was satisfied with it, but we must be careful not to assume that it was a perfect expression of Calvin's ideals for an evangelical celebration of the sacrament of the Lord's Supper. It was far more about what he could get through the city council at the time. Most pastors will understand the problem. There were many in Geneva who had a strong resentment against the liturgical superstitions and clerical pretensions of the past, as well as the fetid piety of folk religion. They wanted a religious service that was simple, direct, and serious. The communion service which was celebrated at the first, right after the Reformation, was extremely simple and direct. When Calvin first arrived in Geneva the observance of the sacrament had been severely curtailed. To a large extent preaching services had replaced the Mass. The annual Easter Communion had been preserved, but in Geneva, at least, there had been little of the orderly reshaping of the service of worship that there had been in Strasbourg or Zurich. In Geneva the Reformation had at first taken the form of an iconoclastic riot. It had been led by revolutionaries rather than reformers, and, sad to say, it was as much political as it was religious. Clever politicians had been able to use the spiritual frustrations of the community to fuel their revolution.

When Calvin returned to Geneva in 1541 he had a mandate to give the city an ecclesiastical constitution. Central to this was

tage, 2002); Kilian McDonnell, *John Calvin, the Church, and the Eucharist* (Princeton, NJ: Princeton University Press, 1967); Old, *Patristic Roots*, pp. 93–95; Thompson, *Liturgies of the Western Church*, pp. 185–210; and Ronald S. Wallace, *Calvin's Doctrine of the Word and Sacrament*. Reprint (Portland: Wipf and Stock, 1997).

1: CALVIN'S COMMUNION LITURGY 15

a collection of liturgical forms to guide the Church of Geneva. Within a few months Calvin produced a catechism, a polity, and the *Genevan Psalter*, or, as its title appears in French, *La Forme des Prieres et Chantz ecclesiastiques*.[4] It is the communion liturgy of this *Genevan Psalter* of 1542 that we would like to study.[5]

Calvin's first stay in Geneva had been difficult. It had not lasted very long, and it ended with Calvin's banishment. The problem was that religious affairs in the City of Geneva were completely in the hands of the city council. The city council had ordered the Mass to be discontinued. It was to be replaced by the Lord's Supper; presumably to be celebrated much the same way as it was in Bern. Even before Calvin's rupture with the city council in 1537 the Reformer had complained about the manner of celebrating the Lord's Supper:

> Seeing that the Supper was instituted by our Lord to be used more frequently by us and also that it was the same way in the ancient church until the devil upset things and set up the Mass in its place, the infrequency of our current celebration is a fault which ought to be corrected, so that the Supper be celebrated more often.[6]

Today one wonders why there was so much opposition to a more frequent celebration of the Lord's Supper. There were several reasons. First, the Mass had become a symbol of the superstitious rites which had burdened medieval worship and from which so many Christians in the sixteenth century wanted to extricate themselves. Second, before the Reformation even the most devout

---

[4] For an English translation, see Thompson, *Liturgies of the Western Church*, pp. 211–224. For the original French text, see Calvin, *Opera selecta*, 2:1–58.

[5] For a study of the origins of the worship forms found in the *Genevan Psalter* of 1542, see Old, *Patristic Roots*.

[6] "Puys que la cene a este instituee de nostre seigneur pour nous estre en usage plus frequent, et aussi quil a ainsi este observe en lesglise ancienne, iusques a ce que le dyable a tout renverse, erigeant la messe au lieu dicelle, cest ung deffault quon doibt corriger, que de la celebrer tant peu souvent." Calvin, *Opera selecta*, 2:344. All translations from the *Opera selecta* are by the author.

were accustomed to receiving the communion but once a year, at Easter, perhaps at Christmas or Pentecost as well, but not more than that. They came to Mass to watch the clergy participate. The Reformers vigorously criticized these clergy-centered celebrations and many people saw the justice of their criticism. They did not like clergy-dominated worship, but were tentative about approaching the Lord's Table too frequently. Third, the long tradition of eucharistic discipline had made people think twice about whether they were worthy to approach the Table. The most devout were hesitant to approach the Table but the less devout often disregarded the moral commitments implied by participation. The immediate cause of Calvin's expulsion from Geneva in 1537 had been over this very issue. Reformers such as Calvin were not willing to go to the extreme of admitting the scandalous or the casually committed to the Table.

One of the compromises which Calvin was able to win from the city council upon his return was that each of the parish churches celebrated the Supper on different Sundays so that the Church of Geneva had at least somewhat more frequent communion.

With these brief introductory remarks let us look at some of the features of Calvin's eucharistic liturgy.

Lord's Day Observance

The *Genevan Psalter* is quite specific that the Lord's Supper is to be observed on the Lord's Day. In French one does not have the problem that the first day of the week is called "Sunday." The French name for the first day of the week is *dimanche*, that is, "The Lord's Day." The *Genevan Psalter* makes a clear distinction between weekday worship and Lord's Day worship:

> On work days, the minister exhorts the people to pray, as seems most appropriate to him, taking into consideration the times and the matters to be treated in the sermon.

1: Calvin's Communion Liturgy

On Lord's Day mornings, however, one uses the following form.[7]

This distinction between the worship of the Lord's Day and the other days of the week is much more significant than might at first appear. Calvin never really gave a treatise on the observance of the Lord's Day. If the Reformed Church has given particular attention to the observance of the Lord's Day it is not because of Calvin's interest in the subject.[8] It was the Strasbourg Reformers who gave most attention to the subject, and among them particularly was Wolfgang Capito. At one point the Anabaptists at Strasbourg had advocated a return to Sabbath worship. They claimed Sunday worship was an invention of Constantine. Capito was charged by the city council with looking into the question. Capito supplied the council with a thorough study of the question, underlining the Lord's Day as the weekly celebration of the resurrection.[9]

Calvin had two points to make about the Lord's Day. First, it was a sign of salvation by grace. The Sabbath rest was meant to remind us that salvation was not a matter of our works or exertion but was a gift, a repose granted by heaven. Second, the Lord's Day was a day of rest from the standpoint of its humanitarian value. One should take pity on those who have heavy burdens to bear, especially the underprivileged. These were not liturgical considerations but were the things which seemed to catch Calvin's interest

---

[7] "*Les iours ouvriers, le Ministre fait telle exhortation à prier, que bon luy semble: l'accomodant au temps et à la matiere, qu'il traicte en sa predication. Pour les Dimanches au matin, on use communement de la forme qui s'ensuit.*" Calvin, *Opera selecta*, 2:18. Italics in original.

[8] For more on Calvin's view of the Sabbath see Richard B. Gaffin, *Calvin and the Sabbath: The Controversy of Applying the Fourth Commandment* (Fearn, UK: Christian Focus Publications, 1997).

[9] Capito, who had earned a doctorate in law as well as in theology, had been able to give the Reformers of Strasbourg a rather clear picture of the role of Christ in the origins of the observance of the Sabbath. Cf. Willy Rordorf, *Sunday* (Philadelphia: Westminster Press,1968); and James M. Kittelson, *Wolfgang Capito, from Humanist to Reformer* (Leiden: E. J. Brill, 1975).

when he preached or commented on the fourth commandment.

Yet, Calvin must have had some of the traditional liturgical concerns which are so traditionally part of Reformed piety. For instance, we read in the *Ecclesiastical Ordinances* of 1541 that the communion is to be observed four times a year: the Lord's Day closest to Christmas,[10] at Easter, at Pentecost, and on the first Lord's Day of September.[11] This meant communion was always to be celebrated on the Lord's Day even if it meant that the Christmas Communion might fall on a date two or three days away from December 25th. This, of course, was exactly what the early second century Church did with the Christian celebration of Passover. Traditionally it was celebrated on the 14th of Nisan according to the Jewish calendar. Some Christians wanted to follow the traditional Jewish date. Other Christians wanted to celebrate on the Lord's Day following the Jewish Passover. This, of course, was the position which prevailed, the reason being that it was the Lord's Day which was the day of Christ's resurrection. This whole story was well known to the sixteenth century Reformers, because it is discussed at length in the *Ecclesiastical History* of Eusebius, a patristic work very popular among the Reformers.[12]

We need to say something about the fact that such a large portion of the communion services were celebrated in connection with Christmas, Easter, and Pentecost. This was done in Geneva as it was done in Zurich and other Swiss churches. Two things need to be said here. First, Calvin inherited from earlier Reformed churches the observance of the so-called evangelical feast days: Christmas, Good Friday, Easter, Ascension, and Pentecost. The

---

[10] The *Ecclesiastical Ordinances* of 1542 reads simply at Christmas, at "noel", while that of 1561 reads, "on the Sunday nearest Christmas," "le plus prochain Dimanche de noel." Calvin, *Opera selecta*, 2:344.

[11] "*(Toutesfoys pour au present y avons advise et ordonne, que Elle soyt administree quatre foys l'annee, assavoyre a noel, pasques, penthecoste et le premier dymenche de septembre en aulthone.)*" Calvin, *Opera selecta*, 2:344. Italics in the original text.

[12] Old, *Patristic Roots*, p. 29.

1: Calvin's Communion Liturgy

other Reformers had discussed this at length. My theory is that Oecolampadius had supported this list.[13] Second, we should notice that it tended to give a festal character to the sacrament. It may be true that the strong tendency to understand the sacrament as "showing forth the Lord's death" (1 Cor. 11:26) had firm biblical foundations. This tendency has been strong down through the whole history of the Church. When the celebration is reserved to the Lord's Day and when its most conspicuous celebrations are on Christmas, Easter, and Pentecost, this tendency is moderated. The celebration clearly becomes a feast, a joyful occasion, which remembers not only the Lord's death, but his birth, his resurrection, and the sending forth of his Spirit as well.

As we will see, Reformed churches rarely celebrated communion on weekdays. This insistence was well established before Calvin began to shape Reformed worship. Calvin follows the trend, but to my knowledge never developed nor discussed this prominent feature of the Reformed eucharistic liturgy.

Praise and Thanksgiving

A prominent characteristic of Calvin's liturgy for the Lord's Supper is the way it is framed by psalms of praise and thanksgiving. Again this is something which Calvin borrowed from Strasbourg and, to be sure, Wittenberg. At the beginning of the service one or more metrical psalms were sung in the place of the Introit. There was psalmody as the minister entered the pulpit, as well as during the distribution of the bread and wine, and then again at the conclusion of the service. We will have more to say about the communion psalmody, but for the moment we will focus on the psalms at the beginning of the service.[14] There were a number of psalms which

---
[13] See Hughes Oliphant Old, *The Reading and Preaching of the Scriptures in the Worship of the Christian Church*, vol. 4, *The Age of the Reformation* (Grand Rapids, MI: Eerdmans, 2002), pp. 53–65.

[14] On Calvin and Psalm singing, see the two articles of Ross J. Miller, "Calvin's Understanding of Psalm Singing as a Means of Grace," and "Music and the

would be appropriate: Psalm 8, Psalm 19, Psalm 32, Psalm 42, Psalm 84, Psalm 96, Psalm 98, Psalm 100, Psalm 104, and Psalm 121. These psalms in particular express the themes of praise and adoration appropriate to the beginning of the communion service. Calvin gave great attention to the development of psalmody. He viewed it as an element of the service of worship which the Word of God directs the Church to observe. The singing of the psalms, as Calvin understood it, is particularly valuable to express our praise to God:

> When it has to do with public prayers, there are two types. The one is offered in simple words; the other is sung. And this is not something invented only recently, for it was found from the first origins of the Church as we find in the church histories. Even as far back as the Apostle Paul we find that he speaks not only of praying with the mouth but also of praying in song.[15]

Calvin believed that the singing of the psalms exercised the people of God in the praise and adoration of God and was therefore very valuable in promoting worship that was in Spirit and truth:

> And in truth, we know by experience that song has great power and vigor in moving and inflaming the human heart, for invoking and praising God with a zeal both vehement and ardent.[16]

The doxological nature of worship was very important to Calvin.

Spirit: Psalm Singing in Calvin's Liturgy," found in *Calvin Studies VI*, ed. John H. Leith, Papers presented at the sixth Colloquium on Calvin Studies at Davidson College (Davidson, NC: Colloquium on Calvin Studies, 1994), pp. 35–58.

[15] "Quant est des prieres publiques, il y en a deux especes. Les unes se font par simple parolle: les aultres avec que chant. Et n'est pas chose inventee depuis peu de temps. Car des la premiere origine de l'Eglise, cela a esté; comme il appert par les histoires. Et mesmes sainct Paul ne parle pas seulement de prier de bouche, mais aussi de chanter." Calvin, *Opera selecta*, 2:15.

[16] "Et à la verité, nous congnoissons par experience, que le chant a grand force et vigueur d'esmouvoir et enflamber le coeur des hommes, pour invoquer et louer Dieu d'un zele plus vehement et ardent." Calvin, *Opera selecta*, 2:15.

1: Calvin's Communion Liturgy

This was true in general, but it was particularly true regarding the celebration of the sacrament of the Lord's Supper. This has remained true for Reformed worship ever since. It is to be celebrated with profound seriousness and exultant joy:

> It should always be remembered, however, that the songs of the church should not be flighty or frivolous, but rather they should have weight and majesty, as St. Augustine said. And also one should remember, there is a big difference between the music one plays at home for entertaining friends and the psalms which are sung in church in the presence of God and his angels.[17]

For Calvin there was obviously a difference between secular music and church music. The purpose of church music was to inspire us to the praise and adoration of God. It is with praise that one enters into the courts of the Lord.

The psalmody which has been so important to Reformed worship cannot help but lead to a typological understanding of worship. The type for the worship of the Church is the worship of Solomon's Temple. "Enter his gates with thanksgiving, and his courts with praise!" (Psa. 100:4). To sing this psalm at the beginning of the communion service helps us understand worship in terms of that glorious picture of the worship of ancient Israel. Psalm 84 would lead us in the same direction: "How lovely is thy dwelling place, O Lord of Hosts!" (Psa. 84:1). And, of course, the typology leads even further. It leads us to think of the transcendent worship of the heavenly Jerusalem. A Christian can hardly sing Psalm 121:1—"I lift up mine eyes to the hills. From whence does my help come?"—without thinking of the Jerusalem on high.

---

[17] "Il y a tousiours à regarder, que le chant ne soit pas legier et volage: mais ait pois et maiesté, comme dit sainct Augustin. et ainsi il y ait grande difference entre la musicque qu'on faict pour resiouyr les hommes à table et en leur maison: et entre les psalmes, qui se chantent en l'Eglise, en la presence de Dieu et de ses anges." Calvin, *Opera selecta*, 2:15.

Prayer of Confession

A prominent characteristic of the Genevan communion liturgy is the Prayer of Confession. Here, again, Calvin has followed the lead of Strasbourg. Written by Bucer, the prayer developed rather slowly, but was a rather comprehensive Prayer of Confession and Supplication by the time he finished with it.

Down through the history of Christian worship it has been recognized that believers should approach the Lord's Table in humility and repentance. In the Middle Ages it was expected that individuals would go to confession, examine their conscience with the aid of a confessor, confess their sin, do penance, and receive absolution before approaching the sacrament. After these elaborate penitential rites, the Prayer of Confession, as we find it in the Genevan communion liturgy, seems rather informal and yet direct and sincere.

The prayer begins with a sense of the divine majesty and an expression of our humility before that majesty:

> Lord God, Father eternal and almighty: we confess and recognize without hesitation, before your holy majesty, that we are poor sinners, conceived and born in iniquity and corruption: inclined to do evil, inept at any good: and out of our depravity transgress, never ceasing nor relenting, your holy commandments.[18]

Classical Reformed piety has always fostered reverence in worship and here is a good case in point. This confessional prayer never flinches at a realistic recognition of the human condition. It is a lamentation over the troubles of life, as are many of the psalms. In fact, this prayer of confession was often followed with

---

[18] "Seigneur Dieu, Pere eternel et tout puissant: nous confessons et recongnoissons sans feinctise, devant ta saincte Maiesté, que nous sommes paovres pecheurs, conceuz et nez en iniquité et corruption: enclins à mal faire, inutiles à tout bien: et que de nostre vice, nous transgressons, sans fin et sans cesse, tes sainctz commandemens." Calvin, *Opera selecta*, 2:18.

the singing of psalms of lamentation. Several of the classics of the *Genevan Psalter* were psalms of lamentation, particularly Clément Marot's version of Psalm 6, "Je te supply, O Sire, ne reprendre en ton ire."[19]

This prayer is not only a confession, it is a supplication as well. Crying out to the Lord has always been a significant component of worship. In fact, this prayer of lamentation was often accompanied by the singing of the Ten Commandments. This was the case particularly for Calvin's French-speaking congregation in Strasbourg. The *Genevan Psalter* of 1542 contained a metrical version of the Ten Commandments, and no doubt was used the same way as in Strasbourg. This was done to encourage the examination of the conscience.

Then came an Assurance of Pardon, following the practice of Calvin's French-speaking congregation in Strasbourg:

> Let each one of you truly recognize that he is a sinner and humble himself before God and believe that the heavenly Father wants to be gracious to him in Jesus Christ. To all those who repent in this manner and turn to Jesus Christ for their salvation, I declare absolution in the name of the Father, of the Son and of the Holy Spirit. Amen.[20]

The point was that the self-examination, the lamentation over our troubles and frustrations, the confession of sins, and the repentance for our faults and misdeeds was elaborated in the course of the service of worship, rather than developed as a special service of worship or turned into a separate sacrament.

---

[19] For Marot's contributions to the *Genevan Psalter*, see Old, *Patristic Roots*, pp. 93 and 324.

[20] "Ung chascung de vous se recognoisse vrayement pecheur s'humiliant devant dieu, et croye que le pere celeste luy veult estre propice en Jesus Christ. A tous ceux qui en ceste manyere se repentent et cerchent Jesus Christ pour leur salut, ie denonce labsolution au nom du pere du filz et du sainct esperit, amen." Calvin, *Opera selecta*, 2:19.

THE READING AND PREACHING OF THE GOSPEL

The preaching of the Gospel was essential to a true celebration of the sacrament of the Lord's Supper as the Reformers understood it. This was the common view of all the Reformers whether in Wittenberg, the Rhineland, or Great Britain. The rubrics of Calvin's Strasbourg liturgy indicate that while the church sings the minister enters the pulpit and offers prayers appropriate for the beginning of the sermon.[21] The rubrics of the *Genevan Psalter* of 1542 say that after the assembly sings a psalm, the minister begins again to pray, asking of God the grace of his Holy Spirit to the end that his Word be faithfully expounded to the honor of his name and the edification of the Church, and that it be received in humility and obedience. The form is left to the discretion of the minister.[22]

On Sunday mornings the Church of Geneva preached through the Gospels. This meant that at a communion service the sermon was always on a Scripture lesson from the Gospels. It is not clear whether this was usually done on a harmony of the Gospels, but at certain points this seems to be suggested. It was the practice in Geneva to preach through the passion narrative the week before Easter and we assume something similar was done at both the Christmas and Pentecost communions. One thing at play here is the concern, especially on the part of the city council, to follow the practice of the other Reformed Churches of Switzerland which did observe the Evangelical feast days: Christmas, Good Friday, Easter, Ascension, and Pentecost. Calvin may not have been completely happy about the observance of the Evan-

---

[21] "**Icy ce pendant que leglise chante, le Ministre va en la chaire et a lors se font pryeres en la sorte qui sensuyt par le ministre au commencement du sermon.**" Calvin, *Opera selecta*, 2:19. Bold in original.

[22] "*Cela faict, on chante en l'assemblee quelque Pseaulme: puis le Ministre commence derechef à prier, pour demander à Dieu la grace de son sainct Esprit: afin, que sa parolle soit fidelement exposée à l'honneur de son Nom, et à l'edification de l'Eglise: et qu'elle soit receue en telle humilité et obeissance, qu'il appartient. La forme est à la discretion du Ministre.*" Calvin, *Opera selecta*, 2:20. Italics in original.

gelical feast days, but it is not immediately clear.

The point here is that the reading and preaching of the Scriptures was essential to the celebration of the sacrament because the sacrament was understood as sealing the Word. Word and sacrament were kept together. During the Middle Ages they had come apart, particularly in the case of the innumerable votive masses, which were said at countless side altars and cluttered every church building. All too often Mass was one thing and the sermon something else. Mass was for Sunday morning and preaching for Sunday afternoon, or, as was often the case, Mass was celebrated first and then came the sermon. What the Reformers wanted was a dynamic relation between the two. Despite their best attempts the Reformers could not get the people to receive communion each Lord's Day.

Bucer had made a valiant effort to do this in Strasbourg. It was his original plan to gather the whole Christian community into the cathedral each Lord's Day to hear the preaching of the Word of God and to celebrate the sacrament of the Lord's Supper as the sealing of the promises of the Gospel and the renewal of the covenant of grace. The Supper was to be understood as a confirmation of the covenant community. This proved too radical a reform, but Calvin seems to have been won to this ideal; in fact, it seems to be an underlying assumption that appears and reappears through the Reformed liturgical tradition. There was weekday preaching, both morning and evening, which was not followed by the Supper and there were Sundays where the dominical service was truncated and the Supper was not observed, but the ideal was that both, Word and sacrament, were the two foci of the service of the Lord's Day.

The Supper was the sign and the seal that God's Word is really offered to us. It is God's sign and God's seal that his Word is true and is true for us. It is offered to us; it is put into our hands as a sign of God's gracious acceptance and hospitality, his kindly providence and fatherly care. But it is also our sign. We take the bread and eat it and we take the wine and drink it to signify that we accept God's grace. We affirm the faith that is being proclaimed to us. If nothing is proclaimed—if there is no sermon—then what is being accepted? There must be a sermon in order for something to be received by faith. This, at least, is the way it looked in Geneva in the middle of the sixteenth century.

THE PASTORAL PRAYER

While the dynamic between Word and sacrament is basic to Reformed worship, there is another necessary dimension, which is prayer. There is an interplay between Word and prayer, just as there is between Word and sacrament. It is not a dichotomy between Word and sacrament or, even less, a dialectic between Word and sacrament. In the same way there is neither a dialectic nor a dichotomy between Word and prayer, but rather an interplay. The covenantal relationship is much more complex.

The *Genevan Psalter* gives us a long series of intercessions, much like the prayers of intercession found in many of the liturgies of the ancient church. The pastoral prayer of Geneva is similar to the *Apostolic Constitutions*, the worship of the Church of Antioch in the late fourth century, or the pastoral prayer of St. Basil from about the same time.[23] Calvin never tires of saying toward the end of his sermons that the study of the Scriptures moves us to bring to God the problems of this world, the leaders of the church, the church itself, and those undergoing special trials and tribulations. Scripture helps us to see the problems; Scripture helps us turn to God in time of need. God's Word often leads us through our temptations and suggests a way out of our troubles.

Even more, the Lord's Table, in the words of Psalm 23, is prepared for us in the presence of our enemies. Even though we walk in the shadow of death, it is a sign and a promise of the presence of the Good Shepherd. The Lord's Table is spread before us even when we are in the midst of troubles, just as the Last Supper was

---

[23] On the sources of these intercessions see Old, *Patristic Roots*, pp. 240–250.

shared with Jesus and his disciples on the way to the cross. Jesus maintained a ministry of intercessory prayer in the Upper Room as he offered the High Priestly Prayer. He continued that ministry in his vigil in the Garden of Gethsemane, and even on the cross he interceded for those who crucified him, "Father, forgive them; for they know not what they do" (Luke 23:34).

It could be said that the prayers of intercession gather us around the Lord's Table. It is here that we join with the whole Church in the whole world. It is here that we share one another's burdens.

In Strasbourg, Calvin concluded the Pastoral Prayer with a recitation of the Lord's Prayer.[24] The congregation began to sing the Apostles' Creed while the minister prepared the bread and the wine on the table. When the singing of the Creed concluded, the minister offered the Communion Invocation. In Geneva this Communion Invocation had to be added to the Prayers of Intercession. Apparently the city council wanted nothing that even resembled the canon of the Mass. We suspect that Calvin was much happier with the Strasbourg arrangement.

One thing to notice is that the canon of the Mass has been completely eliminated. We find no *Sursum corda*, no preface, no *Sanctus*, no formula of consecration, no oblation and no *Agnus Dei*. While a trace of the *Sursum corda* may remain in the Communion Exhortation, it is quite clear that it is in no way understood as part of a formula of consecration that magically produced a miracle. All these incantations were thought of as part of the hocus pocus of sacramental magic that had seduced the medieval church. It was formulae such as these that infuriated the young reform-minded pastors of the sixteenth century. Let us now notice what the Reformers put in the place of the canon.

---

[24] Calvin, *Opera selecta*, 2:45.

The Confession Of Faith

In the *Genevan Psalter* of 1542 we find the following rubric:

> Having finished the prayers and the confession of Faith to testify in the name of the people that all wish to live and die in the teaching of the Christian Religion, the minister delivers the Invitation in a loud voice.[25]

Here again Calvin is following the lead of Bucer and the usage of the Reformed Church of Strasbourg. In the liturgy of the French Church of Strasbourg we read very specifically that the congregation sang the Creed.[26] The *Genevan Psalter* of 1542 contained a metrical version of the Creed which could have been sung by the whole congregation. This is probably another example of Calvin having to settle for what the city council would approve. Zwingli apparently had the same problem with the singing of the Creed.

This recitation of the Creed, however, was of great theological significance for Calvin. It is recited, according to the rubric, "to testify in the name of the people that all wish to live and die in the teaching of the Christian Religion."[27] What we have here is the vows of the covenant. Calvin, as Bucer and Zwingli before, was mindful of what Tertullian and Augustine said about the Creed as the sacrament of our faith.[28] The *sacramentum* had been the oath of allegiance a Roman soldier made on entering military service. This Latin word, while taken from pagan Roman culture, beautifully expressed the covenantal theology of the Lord's Supper so clearly found in the New Testament. We will have more to

---

[25] "*Puis apres avoir faict les prieres et la confession de Foy, pour testifier au nom du peuple, que tous veulent vivre et mourir en la doctrine et Religion chrestienne, il dit à haulte voix:*" Calvin, *Opera selecta*, 2:46. Italics in original.

[26] "**. . . on chante le symbole des Apostres, . . .**" Calvin, *Opera selecta*, 2:45. Bold in original.

[27] "*. . . pour testifier au nom du peuple, que tous veulent vivre et mourir en la doctrine et Religion chrestienne, . . .*" Calvin, *Opera selecta*, 2:46. Italics in original.

[28] Cf. Old, *Patristic Roots*, pp. 286f.

say about this, but for the present the point must be made that the reciting of the Creed in the liturgy of both the French church in Strasbourg and the *Genevan Psalter* of 1542 makes particularly clear the covenantal theology of the Supper in the early Reformed churches. Both Zwingli and Bucer had set a clear example, and Calvin is following it closely.

THE COMMUNION INVOCATION

The communion table was prepared during the singing of the Creed, as we are told by the rubrics of the Strasbourg service, and presumably the ministers were now standing behind it. The *Genevan Psalter* of 1542 is less precise, but the procedure must have been similar. It was at this point that Calvin would probably have preferred to offer the Communion Invocation he had borrowed from Strasbourg. As it worked out, he put the Communion Invocation at the end of the Prayers of Intercession. There was a certain logic to this, but it did make for a very long prayer.

The Communion Invocation adopted by Calvin is both pastorally sensitive and theologically perceptive.[29] This prayer, from a liturgical standpoint, serves three functions: it is an invocation, it is a prayer of thanksgiving, and it is a vow of the covenant. In good biblical form, the prayer invokes God's grace in the present by remembering his grace in the past:

> Heavenly Father full of all goodness and mercy, we pray that as our Lord Jesus Christ not only offered up on the cross his body and his blood for the remission of our sins, but also wished to communicate them to use for our nourishment unto eternal life . . .[30]

---

[29] For an analysis of this prayer from the standpoint of its sources, see Old, *Patristic Roots*, pp. 289f.

[30] "Pere celeste plain de toute bonté et misericorde, nous prions que comme nostre Seigneur JesusChrist non seullement a une foys offert en la croix son corps / et son sang, pour la remission de noz pechez / mais aussi le nous veult communicquer pour nourriture en vie eternelle / . . ." Calvin, *Opera selecta*, 2:45.

This is both thanksgiving and memorial. It is a thanksgiving which leads to a supplication. Here we have basic biblical theology. This is one of the things that the theologians of the early sixteenth century were learning from their Hebrew Bible. Bucer had been a pioneer in this. His commentary on the Hebrew text of the Psalms had opened new windows for the theology of worship.

The petition of this Communion Invocation is highly developed. First, the prayer asks:

> Grant us this grace, that with true sincerity of heart and ardent zeal we receive of him such great favor and blessing, and that in sure faith we receive his body and his blood, that is, that we receive Christ wholly and entirely, that we receive him who is true God and true man, the holy bread of heaven which makes us truly alive.[31]

The petition here is basically one of sanctification, that we be given true faith and the sincerity of heart we need in order to receive the gift of God's grace. In the end this gift is Christ—true God and true man—offered as a sacrifice for our sin. The petition is explicit that the gracious gift we receive at the communion is to be made alive as God created us to be alive.

This Communion Invocation is analogous to the *epiclesis* so important to the liturgies of the Eastern Orthodox churches. It is a prayer that in our receiving this bread and wine we are made holy as Christ is holy:

> Grant that we no longer live to ourselves and according to our nature, which is evil and corrupt, but rather that he live in us so that we be brought to a life that is

---

[31] ". . . fais nous ceste grace que de vraye sincerité de cueur / de d'un zele ardant nous recepvions de luy ung si grand don et benefice, et que en certaine foy nous recepvions son corps et son sang / voire luy tout entierement / comme luy estant vray Dieu et vray homme est veritablement le sainct pain celeste pour nous vivifier." Calvin, *Opera selecta*, 2:45.

1: Calvin's Communion Liturgy

> holy, blessed, and eternal . . .[32]

This may not be a prayer for the transubstantiation of the bread and wine, but it is, as it were, a prayer for the transformation of the congregation.

The petition goes further. It asks for our inclusion in the covenant. It asks that we be received into the covenantal community. It is an invocation of covenantal grace:

> Grant that we be made true participants in the new and eternal testament, that is to say, the covenant of grace.[33]

Again we notice that the covenantal theology of the sacrament of the Lord's Supper is made explicit.

One thing must be made clear. This is not a eucharistic prayer, but rather a communion invocation. It is not a eucharistic prayer in the sense that we find it in Psalm 78, Psalm 105, Psalms 114–115, Deuteronomy 26:5–11, or in the prayer over the cup of blessing which we find in the Passover liturgy. It was, however, a step in that direction. It is certainly much more than the communion invocation we find in the *Westminster Directory*, which asks no more than the setting apart of the bread and wine from a common to a sacred use.

Invitation

There were undoubtedly those in the early sixteenth century who would happily have left the sacrament of the Lord's Supper aside. They saw it as a demonstration of all that was superstitious and magical in religion. Those with theological training and a solid knowledge of the Bible realized this would be a radical departure from historic Christianity. Jesus had, after all, instituted the sacra-

---

[32] "Affin que nous ne vivions plus en nousmesmes et selon nostre nature / laquelle est toute corrumpue et vivieuse, mais que luy vive en nous pour nous conduire à la vie saincte bienheureuse et sempiternelle . . ." Calvin, *Opera selecta*, 2:45.

[33] ". . . par ainsi que nous soyons faictz vrayement participans du nouveau et eternel testament asscavoir l'alliance de grace /. . ." Calvin, *Opera selecta*, 2:45.

ment of the Lord's Supper, and one needed to return to the Bible to see how Jesus intended it to be observed. In the early days of the Reformation it was necessary to explain to the congregation how the church was going to observe this institution of Christ. This is why the Words of Institution were carefully read at the beginning of the communion proper. With the reading there was an appropriate explanation to the congregation. This explanation was probably more drawn out at first, but became less so as the Reformation began to settle in.

One of the things that required explanation was communion discipline. Throughout the Middle Ages the Lord's Supper had been closely related to church discipline. In the late Middle Ages the ban had been used indiscriminately, often with petty political motives. People were hesitant to approach the sacrament for fear of violating its sanctity, participating in an unworthy manner and thereby bringing judgment upon oneself. They needed to be encouraged to receive communion. Too many thought it safer to quietly observe the liturgy rather than to actually participate. The invitation had to be made clear. This seems to be the primary purpose of the Communion Exhortation that appears so frequently in the Reformed communion liturgies of the sixteenth century.

But there was another problem. The Reformers were not willing to cut the sacrament loose from church discipline completely. Geneva had a group of prominent loose-living citizens who wanted to go in that direction. In fact there had been an incident which had led to Calvin's dismissal from Geneva. The story is well known and we do not need to repeat it here, but the point was that those living scandalously should not be presenting themselves at the Lord's Table. And while the point of the exhortation was to invite and encourage the faithful to take part in the sacrament, it also needed to be made clear that participation implied a moral commitment to live the Christian life. The commitment was both moral and theological. Participation in the sacrament of the

Lord's Supper was an affirmation of membership in the church, just as being baptized was a sign of membership. Here again the covenantal theology comes through very clearly. The church is the covenant community. To participate in the covenant is, to put it in more usual terms, to join the church. Each time we receive communion we are reaffirming our membership in the church.

The liturgical function of reciting the Words of Institution was to recount, in the words of Jesus himself, the invitation to participate in the covenant community: "Take, eat. This is my body broken for you. Do this in remembrance of me. . . . This cup is the New Testament in my blood. Do this as often as you drink it in remembrance of me."[34] While the Invitation discourages unbelievers and those who deny Christ with their lives, its primary purpose is to make clear the gracious invitation of Christ. The Lord's Table offers all the promises of the Gospel, that we may receive them by faith.

The Sharing of the Meal

At the heart of the Reformed understanding of the Lord's Supper is the sharing of the sacred meal. The medieval Mass put the emphasis on reciting the canon through which the miracle of transubstantiation took place and the consecrated host was offered up as a sacrifice for the living and the dead. As the Reformers taught it, the communion was the focal point of the service. The sign Jesus gave was the sharing of a meal and as the Reformers understood it the visual sign should look like a meal shared by the communicants. Various approaches were taken by churches to make the celebration look more like the sharing of a meal. In Strasbourg, right from the start, the altar was replaced with a table. People came forward and stood around the table as the ministers passed the bread and the wine to them. In Zurich a table

---

[34] "Prenez, mengez, cecy est mon corps, qui est rompu pour vous: faictes cecy en memoire de moy . . . Ce Calice est le nouveau Testament en mon sang. Faictes cecy toutes fois et quantes que vous en beuvrez, en memoire de moy." Calvin, *Opera selecta*, 2:46.

was set in the middle of the church in front of the pulpit. While the people remained in their seats the bread and the wine were passed to them. The church was centered around the baptismal font, the pulpit, and the table. In the Rhineland, the Netherlands, and Scotland special tables were set up in the front of the church and the people left their seats, sat down at these tables, and passed trays of bread and the cups from one to another.

While the local variety was obvious, certain aspects were fairly consistent. In the first place, altars were replaced with tables and altar rails were eliminated. The ministers stood behind the table to officiate rather than in front of it. In the second place, kneeling to receive communion was generally discontinued. It was replaced by standing, or even more often, by sitting about the table. As time went along, setting up large tables became the more usual practice, especially in the Netherlands and in Scotland.

An important feature of the Mass, especially as it was watched, was the use of the sign of the cross again and again during the celebration. Particularly prominent was the tracing of the cross on the bread and over the chalice as a sign of its consecration. The sign of the cross was discontinued in Reformed churches because it came to symbolize superstition and the most primitive forms of magic. It was exactly this kind of thing that offended the thoughtful sixteenth century Christian. Signing the cross was a perfect example of an outward religious rite that was done in a mechanical, unthinking way.

During the sharing of the meal appropriate passages of Scripture were read and psalms were sung. The prologue to the Gospel of John, the eighth chapter of Romans, Paul's writings on love in 1 Corinthians 13, or perhaps Isaiah 53 were all thought to be especially significant at this point. Psalm 23, Psalm 116, or Psalm 138 were favorite psalms for singing during Communion. We will have more to say about the communion psalmody in a moment. What is important to note now is that these texts, whether read or sung, prompted the thankful remembering that was so fundamental to the sacrament.

Here the *anamnesis* comes into play. When John 1:1–18 was read, a memorial was made of the incarnation. When Isaiah 53 was read, a memorial of Christ's sacrifice was observed. In reading 1 Corinthians 15, there was a memorial of the resurrection. When John 14 was read, a memorial of our Lord's ascension was celebrated.

In time great importance was given to the breaking of the bread and the pouring of the wine. If the making of the sign of the cross over the bread and the wine had been an important visual sign for the Middle Ages, its place was soon taken by the breaking of the bread, sharing it with a neighbor, pouring the cup, receiving it from a neighbor, and passing it on. We do not immediately find these ideas, but more and more the visual elements of sharing the meal began to show the meaning intrinsic in the sign Jesus had instituted. Artificial signs such as the sign of the cross began to fall away and the natural signs involved in the sharing of a meal began to assert their significance.

We do not find the Words of Administration in the *Genevan Psalter* of 1542, but we do find them in Calvin's Strasbourg service: "Take, eat, the body of Jesus, who was offered up to death for you."[35] Then, in administering the cup: "This is the cup of the New Testament which is poured out for you."[36] These words are no doubt to be taken the same way as the words at the beginning of the Invitation. Although here they are in the mouth of the minister, they still mean the same thing. They are an invitation to participate in the life of the covenant community, inviting us to receive Christ and offering all the promises of the Gospel. Here Calvin, as Luther before him, sees the proclamation of the Gospel in its shortest and most concise form. The Gospel is presented in the Words of Administration to be received by faith.

---

[35] "Prenez, mangez, le corps de Iesus, qui a esté livré à la mort pour vous." Calvin, *Opera selecta*, 2:49.

[36] "C'est le Calice du nouveau Testament au sang de Iesus, qui a esté respandu pour vous." Calvin, *Opera selecta*, 2:49.

THE PRAYER OF DEDICATION

Thanksgiving is at the very heart of a Reformed eucharistic theology. We find this already with Zwingli, but we find it even more with Calvin.[37]

In my earlier studies of Calvin's communion liturgy I called this prayer the Post-Communion Thanksgiving.[38] I don't remember where I got this term, but in time I began to prefer the term Prayer of Dedication because it intimates an important theological dimension of early Reformed eucharistic theology. The term Post-Communion Thanksgiving is accurate enough, but it is theologically neutral. From the standpoint of a biblical theology of prayer two things should be said: (1) Recount the story of God's saving acts, as we find in Psalms 78, 105, and 136, and (2) dedicate our lives to his service in recognition of his grace. We owe our lives to God's saving acts; a full Prayer of Thanksgiving should confess the obligation this entails. This is fundamental, of course, to covenant theology. The prayer that concludes the communion service of the *Genevan Psalter* gives a very clear expression of this second moment in a true Prayer of Thanksgiving. The invocation of the prayer is a masterpiece:

> Heavenly FATHER, we return to you praise and eternal thanks, that you have prospered us with such manifold blessing. You have lifted us up from our poverty and futility and brought us into the communion of your Son JESUS Christ, our Savior. For our sake you offered him up to death and even now you have given him to us for our food and nourishment.[39]

---

[37] This has been brought out with admirable clarity by Brian A. Gerrish, *Grace and Gratitude: The Eucharistic Theology of John Calvin* (Eugene, OR: Wipf & Stock Publishers, 2002).

[38] See Old, *Patristic Roots*, pp. 319f.

[39] "Pere celeste, nous te rendons louenges et graces eternelles, que tu nous as eslargy un tel bien, à nous paovres pecheurs, de nous avoir attiré en la communion de ton Filz Jesus Christ, nostre Seigneur, l'ayant livré, pour nous, à la mort, et le nous donnant en viande et nourriture de vie eternelle." Calvin, *Opera selecta*, 2:25–26.

1: Calvin's Communion Liturgy

The hand of Bucer is immediately apparent, for it is clearly a French translation of the prayer in the *Strasbourg Psalter* of 1537.[40] The saving work specifically mentioned is the atoning sacrifice of the Father in the person of his Son. It is the eternal sacrifice made once and for all, but now in our time, through the work of the Holy Spirit, the benefits of it are offered and applied to us by faith. Notice particularly the trinitarian nature of the invocation. The prayer is addressed to the Father in the name of the Son. Here the application of God's saving acts in Christ is the principle subject. We have been brought "into the communion of your Son JESUS Christ." The observance is not merely a memorial of God's saving acts of Christ. Rather, it is a participation in the communion of Christ; it is entering into his presence and enjoying his fellowship.

The prayer continues with dedicating ourselves to the exaltation of God's glory and the service of our neighbor:

> Now grant us also this further blessing, that we not ever be allowed to forget these things, but have them engraven upon our hearts. Grant that we grow and diligently increase in the Faith; that we abound in all kinds of good works. Grant that we live out our whole lives in the exaltation of your glory and the edification of our neighbor, through the same JESUS Christ your Son, who in the unity of the Holy Spirit, lives and reigns eternally with you, O Father. Amen.[41]

Again we find a strong allusion to covenantal theology in that the prayer asks that these things be engraven upon our hearts. This

---

[40] Thompson, *Liturgies of the Western Church*, pp. 178–179.

[41] "Maintenant aussi octroye nous ce bien, de ne permettre, que iamais nous ne mettions en oubly ces choses: mais plustost les aiant imprimees en noz coeurs, nous croissions et augmentions assiduellment en la Foy, laquelle besogne en toutes bonnes oeuvres: et en ce faisant, ordonnions et poursuyvions toute nostre vie à l'exaltation de ta gloire, et edification de nostre prochain, par iceluy Jesus Christ ton Filz, qui en l'unité du sainct Esprit, vit et regne, avec toy Dieu eternellement, Amen." Calvin, *Opera selecta*, 2:26.

is what was so unique about the new covenant, as envisioned by Jeremiah: "Behold, the days are coming, says the LORD, when I will make a new covenant with the house of Israel.... I will put my law within them, and I will write it upon their hearts..." (Jer. 31:31–33). In this prayer the congregation dedicates itself to living the life of the new covenant community. Having been saved from the perishing world, we are obligated to nothing less than a life well-pleasing to God.

This is not a misplaced eucharistic prayer, but a thanksgiving for having received the communion. It is a prayer which points the way to the life that is opened up by the gift of communion.

THE COMMUNION PSALMODY

One of the most beloved aspects of the worship of the early Reformed churches was its psalmody. Already in the time of Calvin certain traditions were beginning to develop regarding which psalms were appropriate for the communion service. We have already made a few remarks, but there is more to say. We have only a few passages on which to base our thoughts, but we can make a number of guesses about which psalms or canticles were used.

In the German-speaking congregation of Strasbourg the communion service regularly concluded with the singing of Luther's metrical version of Psalm 138. A French version of this psalm was made available to evangelical worship by Clément Marot. Calvin's commentary on this psalm is particularly noteworthy.

In Zurich the Passover psalms were favorites for the communion even if they were read responsively rather than sung. The *Zurich Service Book* of 1525 indicates the use of Psalm 113. This was one of the psalms Calvin tried to render into French himself. It may well have been his desire to use it for communion, which prompted him to attempt his own metrical version. Psalms 114 and 115 were available in his first *Genevan Psalter*. Psalms 116 and 118 are not found in the *Genevan Psalter* of 1542, but do appear later.

1: Calvin's Communion Liturgy

The Song of Simeon is specifically indicated in the *French Evangelical Psalter* of 1542, but we assume this was not the only selection used. The *Genevan Psalter* of 1542 simply indicates a psalm, but we can imagine that Psalm 138 or Psalm 113 might have been used as well.

John Knox, as we will see later, found Psalm 103 especially appropriate for the conclusion of the communion service. "He has filled our mouth with good things to eat" (Psalm 103:5), would, of course, make this selection obvious and the psalm as a whole is most suitable to a celebration of the sacrament. In Scotland, Psalm 23 was always thought of as a good psalm for the beginning of the service, and Psalm 24 was often used when the table was being prepared and as the bread and wine were brought out.

THE BENEDICTION

It was Martin Luther who restored the Benediction to Reformed worship. In his *German Mass* of 1523, very early in the Reformation, he suggested that the service be concluded with the giving of the Aaronic Benediction as found in Numbers 6:24–26. As Luther interpreted the text, it was in this way that Christ had concluded his ministry on earth. In the Gospel of Luke's account of the ascension, Jesus led his disciples out of Jerusalem as far as Bethany, "and lifting up his hands he blessed them" (Luke 24:50). Luther's suggestion was very favorably received by the other Reformers. Whereas the Mass had been concluded with the sign of the cross, the more ancient biblical gesture was recovered and put in its place.[42] Other benedictions have been used in Protestant Churches from time to time, but this has always been the favorite. No doubt it is the majesty of its language that has made it so popular; it can hardly be improved.

---

[42] For a study of the liturgical origins of the Benediction, see, Old, *Patristic Roots*, pp. 330f.

COLLECTION OF ALMS

Calvin understood the collection of alms to be a significant element in Christian worship. He makes this explicit in his preface to the *French Evangelical Psalter* of 1542, where he recounts that Christian worship should include the reading and preaching of Scripture, the offering of prayers, the observing of the sacraments, and the opportunity to give alms to the poor. In his *Grund und Ursach,* Bucer draws the same point from Acts 2:42: "And they continued in the teaching and fellowship of the Apostles, the breaking of the bread, and the prayers." As Bucer interpreted this text, part of the fellowship of the Apostles was their sharing with those who were in need. We know that very early in the Reformation large chests were put at the doors of the churches so that those leaving the service might deposit their alms. In fact, these alms chests are still to be found in some of the old "evangelical" churches of the Upper Rhineland.

According to Professor Elsie McKee, Calvin was not able to get this practice established in Geneva.[43] The city council of Geneva apparently had enough of the constant collections of the medieval clergy. More than likely, however, Calvin would have preferred the practice of his French-speaking congregation in Strasbourg.

---

[43] Elsie Anne McKee, *John Calvin on the Diaconate and Liturgical Almsgiving* (Geneva: Librairie Droz, 1984).

2

CALVIN ON COMMUNION
The Covenantal and Sacramental Dimensions

Perhaps the best introduction to Calvin's theology of the sacrament of Holy Communion is his *Short Treatise on the Lord's Supper* of 1541.[1] True to its title it is short and simple, intending to serve a pastoral purpose. The work begins with a few basic statements, which help set the course of our study:

> First it needs to be pointed out that it has pleased the good Lord to receive us by baptism into his Church as into his own house. There he wishes to train and direct us. He has therefore received us not that we be his servants but rather that we be his own children. God wishes to be our devoted Father, nourishing us with spiritual food, supplying us with everything we need in life.[2]

---

[1] John Calvin, *Petit traité de la Sainte cène de notre Seigneur Jésus Christ* (La Haye: Imprimerie de J. Roering, 1844). For modern editions, see John Calvin, *Theological Treatises*, Library of Christian Classics, vol. 22 (Philadelphia: Westminster Press, 1954); and John Calvin, *Treatises on the Sacraments, Catechism of the Church of Geneva, Forms of Prayer, and Confessions of Faith*, trans. Henry Beveridge (Fearn, UK: Christian Heritage, 2002). On Calvin's theology of Holy Communion see: Ulrich Beyer, *Abendmahl und Messe: Sinn und Recht der 80. Frage des Heidelberger Katechismus* (Neukirchen-Vluyn: Neukirchener Verlag des Erziehungsvereins, 1965); Brian A. Gerrish, *Grace and Gratitude* (Minneapolis: Fortress Press, 1993); Kilian McDonnell, *John Calvin, the Church, and the Eucharist* (Princeton, NJ: Princeton University Press, 1967); "Calvin, John," in *The Oxford Encyclopedia of the Reformation*, 4 vols. (New York and Oxford: Oxford University Press, 1996), 1:234–240; Ronald S. Wallace, *Calvin's Doctrine of the Word and Sacrament*. Reprint (Portland: Wipf and Stock, 1997); and Edward David Willis, *Calvin's Catholic Christology: The Function of the So-called Extra Calvinisticum in Calvin's Theology* (Leiden: E. J. Brill, 1966).

[2] "Quant est du premier article: Puis qu'il a pleu à nostre bon Dieu de nous recevoir par le baptesme en son Esglise, qui est sa maison, laquelle il veult entretenir et gouverner: et qu'il nous a receuz non seullement pour nous avoir comme ses domestiques, mais comme ses propres enfans: il rest que pour faire l'office d'un bon

Here we discover something fundamental about Calvin's theology of the Lord's Supper. He sees the Supper in terms of the typology of the Father's house. This was a major typology for Jesus. He used it in his Upper Room Discourse, "In my Father's house are many rooms . . ." Again he used it in the parable of the prodigal son, "How many servants in my Father's house have food enough . . ." This should remind us of the patriarchs of Genesis who provided a full supply of all the necessities of life for their whole households. The Supper is, above all else, the provision of a loving father for his children; it is a sacrament of the love of God.

Through the sacrament of Holy Communion, God provides us with the food and drink of the household of faith. But Calvin declares that this food and drink is nothing other than a living fellowship with Jesus himself. To be received into the house of the Father is to be received into fellowship with the Son. In fact, it is by receiving the Son that we enter into the house of the Father. This fellowship is experienced in prayer, in the study of Scripture, and in a particularly vivid way in the Supper. Additionally, the Word of the Lord, which is called both the Bread of Life and the water welling up within us, distributes it: "That which is said of the Word is said as well of the sacrament of the Lord's Supper, for it is by means of the sacrament, just as it is by means of the Word, that we are brought into communion with Jesus Christ."[3] Here we find a fundamental assumption of Calvin's eucharistic theology: the purpose of the Lord's Supper is to bring us into communion with Jesus Christ.

Further on in this short essay, Calvin gives another statement of the fundamentals of his eucharistic theology. The first statement was more of a typology but now Calvin gets more doctrinal:

---

pere, il nous nourrisse et pourvoye de tout ce qui nous est necessaire à vivre." John Calvin, *Opera selecta*, ed. Petrus Barth and Dora Scheuner, 5 vols. (Munich: Chr. Kaiser, 1926–1959), 1:504. Translations from the *Opera selecta* are by the author.

[3] "Or, ce qui est dict de la parolle il appartient aussi bien au Sacrement de la Cene, par le moyen duquel le Seigneur nous meine à la communication de Iesus Christ." Calvin, *Opera selecta*, 1:505.

> It is for this cause that our Lord has established his Supper, that it might sign and seal in our consciences the promises contained in his Gospel.[4]

Here is a strong statement of the covenantal dimension of Calvin's eucharistic theology. Here, significantly, the covenantal dimension of the Supper is primary. Although the word "covenant" does not appear in the text, the idea of signing and sealing the promises of the Gospel is the heart of the covenantal theology of the sacraments. This is followed by an equally strong statement of the eucharistic dimension of Calvin's doctrine of the Supper:

> Secondly, the Lord has instituted this sacrament in order to excite a recognition of his great goodness toward us that we might all the more praise and magnify him.[5]

The Lord's Supper is a public memorial and thanksgiving for God's mighty acts of salvation. It is a witness to the world that God is gracious. At its heart, the Supper is both eucharistic and kerygmatic and this is what makes it worship. As Calvin understood it, one of the purposes of public worship is to exercise God's people in praise and thanksgiving. The sacraments, because of their visual and tactile character, are especially helpful in stimulating the devotion of the faithful. As the Word made visible, the Supper speaks to our deepest emotions and stirs up thanksgiving. The Supper acts out the central messages of the Christian Gospel in visual signs and tactile experience. It presents an opportunity to experience the truth, to learn it by doing it. As we continue we will notice that the eucharistic dimension is characteristic of a covenantal understanding of the Supper.

At this point Calvin gives a third purpose for the institution of the sacrament:

---

[4] "Pour ceste cause le Seigneur nous a institué sa Cene, à fin de signer et seeller en noz consciences les promesses contenues en son Evangile." Calvin, *Opera selecta*, 1:505.

[5] "Secondement, à fin de nous exerciter à recongnoistre sa grande bonté sur nous, pour la louer et magnifier plus amplement." Calvin, *Opera selecta*, 1:505.

> Thirdly, the Lord's Supper has been established to exhort us to all holiness and innocence, seeing that we are members of Jesus Christ. In a special way we are exhorted to be united to our fellow Christians and live in the bond of fraternal love.⁶

Here, again, the covenantal dimension of the sacrament comes to the surface. The Lord's Supper is understood as communion, but here Calvin points more to the communion with other Christians than to communion with the Father and the Son. For Calvin the two directions of communion—communion with God and communion with our brothers and sisters in Christ—are intimately connected. In fact, to refer to the sacrament as "communion" comes very naturally to the Reformer of Geneva.

There is one more thing to be noted in this succinct little essay, and that is the future. The Lord's Supper seals the Gospel promises for the future. Here then is the eschatological dimension of Calvin's theology:

> We are to understand that not only are we called to receive a heavenly heritage at some time off in the future, but rather through hope we are already in this life granted a foretaste of it. Not only are we promised eternal life, but somehow in the celebration of this sacrament we are transferred into it . . ."⁷

As the Jewish Passover was a celebration both of God's mighty acts of redemption in the past as well as a celebration of the messianic hope for a consummate redemption in the world to come, so the Christian sacrament is also a celebration and a foretaste of

---

⁶ "Tiercement, à fin de nous exhorter à toute saincteté et innocence, entant que nous sommes membres de Iesus Christ: et singulierement à union et charité fraternelle, . . ." Calvin, *Opera selecta*, 1:505.

⁷ "Car nous debvons entendre que non seullement il nous a appellez à posseder une foys son Heritage celeste: mais que par esperance il nous a desia aucunement introduictz en ceste possession: que non seullement il nous a promis la vie, mais nous a desia transferez en icelle, nous retirant de la mort." Calvin, *Opera selecta*, 1:504.

the kingdom of God yet to come.

Having taken these broad opening statements of Calvin's *Short Treatise on the Lord's Supper* as an introduction, let us turn now to spreading out these different dimensions of Calvin's eucharistic theology in a more systematic way.

THE COVENANTAL DIMENSION

The covenantal dimension of Calvin's eucharistic theology is rarely recognized, at least for the importance it indeed has. By the covenantal dimension we mean that Calvin's eucharistic theology seeks to understand worship in terms of the covenantal relationship between God and his people. Worship is one of the primary responsibilities of the covenant people. We have been called out of the world to serve God's glory (Ephesians 1:12). The first four of the Ten Commandments have to do with worship (Exodus 20:3–8), and these four were summed up by Jesus as the first and greatest commandment: "You shall love the Lord your God with all your heart, and with all your soul, and with all your mind" (Matt. 22:37–38).[8] It is through worship that we obey this commandment.

A covenantal understanding of the Lord's Supper implies that it is an experience of love. Put another way, to celebrate the sacrament of the Lord's Supper is to have communion with God, and not only with God but with the people of God. It is an event in which we experience God's love toward us, in which we exercise our love toward one another, and in which we express our love toward God. It is in worship that we enter into the covenant and that the covenantal relationships are sustained, nourished, and renewed. Christian worship can be understood as the exercising of the covenantal relationships. It is to live the life of the household of faith, to exercise

---

[8] This section is the text of a paper given at the Colloquium on Calvin Studies at Erskine Theological Seminary in January of 2006. It has been previously published as, Hughes Oliphant Old, "The Covenantal Dimension of Calvin's Eucharistic Theology," *Calvin Studies XII*, ed. Michael D. Bush (Due West, SC: Calvin Colloquium, 2006).

being children of God in our Father's house (Exod. 24:1–11, Deut. 26, Psa. 105, 1 Cor. 10:16–17 and 11:25). Interestingly, Ignatius of Loyola in his classic *Spiritual Exercises* also develops the idea of worship as exercise. A covenantal understanding of the Lord's Supper particularly implies that this sacrament is to be understood as a sign of the covenant, that this sacrament signs and seals the covenantal promises. A covenantal understanding of the sacrament regards the Lord's Supper above all as Holy Communion.

Calvin was not the originator of the covenantal theology of worship. His covenantal understanding of worship was inherited from the Rhenish Reformers who were busily working out this approach to worship around the same time Calvin arrived on the theological scene.

Even further back, Luther suggested that the sacraments might be understood better in terms of a covenantal theology rather than in terms of Scholastic theology. The Scholastics sought to interpret the Christian faith in terms of the logic of classical antiquity. In fact, using the philosophical terminology of Plato and Aristotle, the Schoolmen had made considerable progress toward the development of a distinctly Christian theology. By the end of the Middle Ages, however, Scholastic theology began to lose its effectiveness, or at least so it seemed to many. The recovery of the Biblical languages had shifted the whole theological ground. In light of this Luther very early in the Reformation suggested that the Church begin to think out the sacraments in terms of the biblical concept of covenant, rather than in terms of Scholastic theology. What led Luther to make this suggestion was the text of the words of institution: "This cup is the new covenant in my blood." Luther's suggestion was certainly reasonable and straightforward.

Luther launched his attack on the Scholastic understanding of the sacraments in his famous *Babylonian Captivity of the Church*, published in 1520. In another work, published in 1522, Luther made an attempt to present an alternative to Scholastic theology. This inten-

2: Calvin on Communion
The Covenantal and Sacramental Dimensions

tion is made clear in its title, *A Treatise on the New Testament, that is the Mass*.⁹ Luther is obviously pointing to the fact that Jesus had called the rite the sign of the New Covenant, "New Testament" being another translation for the term "New Covenant." In this work Luther outlines the basic points of a covenantal understanding of the Lord's Supper. God leads his people by giving them promises for the future. When these promises are accepted by faith we begin to move toward them. The sacraments are the signs of these promises, just as the rainbow was the sign of the covenant with Noah and circumcision was the sign of the covenant with Abraham. Luther's primary concern was to show that we are saved by faith. The sacraments are significant because in them the promises of God are offered to us to be believed. As the discussion developed, Luther apparently changed his mind on the covenantal understanding of the sacraments; he simply never developed the idea any further.

The following Maundy Thursday, in the year 1523, John Oecolampadius celebrated the Lord's Supper in such a manner that the covenantal aspects of the sacrament were emphasized. He published the text of this celebration and titled it *The Testament of Jesus Christ*.¹⁰ He had obviously followed Luther's suggestion. Not long after this the Reformers in Strasbourg began to pick up on the covenantal dimensions of the Lord's Supper. This is particularly evident in the prayers of the Strasbourg service. Luther's suggestion that a more biblical eucharistic theology be developed out of the concept of covenant was generally followed in the Upper Rhineland. Undoubtedly one of the reasons for this was that the Christian Humanists¹¹ in the Rhineland were well advanced in the

---

⁹ A translation of these two documents can be found in Martin Luther, *Works*, 6 vols. (Philadelphia: Muhlenberg Press, 1930–1943).

¹⁰ The title in German is *Das Testament Jesu Christi*. For a discussion of this work, see Hughes Oliphant Old, *The Patristic Roots of Reformed Worship*, American edition (Black Mountain, NC: Worship Press, 2004), pp. 15–16.

¹¹ The term "humanists" here refers to members of a Renaissance intellectual movement who were concerned with recovering and understanding ancient and

recovery of Biblical Hebrew. The Rhenish Reformers had sharper tools for rediscovering Hebrew concepts such as covenant because of their knowledge of Hebrew.

Zwingli understood the sacraments as signs and seals of the covenant quite early in the discussion. In his treatise, *On the Lord's Supper*, written early in 1526, he turns his attention to the text, "This cup is the new covenant in my blood."[12] He figures this should make clear that the Lord's Supper is a covenant meal like the Passover. To participate in it makes one a member of the covenant community. The Supper is a covenantal sign much like circumcision is in Genesis 17; it makes the recipient a part of the community.[13] For Zwingli, the Passover typology was critical for explaining the Christian sacrament. But equally important was the story of the sealing of the covenant on Mt. Sinai, found in Exodus 24. It was there that Moses sprinkled the blood on the people and said, "This is the blood of the covenant." It was a sign of the covenantal bond between God and his people.

It was also about this same time that the Anabaptists began to advance their views of reform for the sacrament of baptism. The biblical concept of covenant became an important issue in this discussion. Both Zwingli and Oecolampadius relied heavily on the concept to defend the baptism of infants. Not to be outdone the Anabaptists developed a covenantal theology of their own. This led Zwingli's successor, the young Heinrich Bullinger, to elaborate covenantal theology more fully. Consequently it is usually Bullinger who is thought of as the architect of covenant theology. As Charles McCoy put it, Bullinger became the fountainhead of Federalism. When we speak of Calvin's covenantal theology we do

---

classical learning. This "humanism" is not to be confused with the secularist anti-Christian philosophical movement which often goes by the same name.

[12] Ulrich Zwingli, *On the Lord's Supper*, found in *Zwingli and Bullinger*, Library of Christian Classics, vol. 24, ed. G. W. Bromiley (Philadelphia: The Westminster Press, 1953), pp. 185–238.

[13] Zwingli, *On the Lord's Supper*, pp. 225–230.

not mean that Calvin understood the Lord's Supper in terms of Federal theology. Bullinger made it an all-embracing approach to Christian theology, but originally it was much more specifically intended as the Reformed approach to sacramental theology.

Calvin adopted this rapidly developing tradition when he became involved with the Rhenish Reformation between 1536 and 1542. During this period Calvin lived and studied in Basel for well over a year and there must have become thoroughly acquainted with the work of Oecolampadius, who had been the city's leading Reformer and had died five years earlier. Between 1538 and 1541 Calvin lived in Strasbourg and there became familiar with the Anabaptist claims, which had been advanced so forcefully in that city. We have discussed Calvin's use of Rhenish covenantal theology in regard to baptism in another work; here we will concentrate on Calvin's use of covenantal theology to explain the Lord's Supper.

A. THE BASIC CONCEPT

Let us look at several passages where Calvin's covenantal understanding of the Lord's Supper comes to expression.

1. *INSTITUTES* IV, XIV, 1–6

We begin with the chapter of the *Institutes* where Calvin discusses the sacraments in general.[14] Our theologian opens up his discussion with a definition of sacrament:

> An outward sign by which the Lord seals on our consciences the promises of his good will toward us in order to sustain the weakness of our faith; and we in turn attest our piety toward him in the presence of the Lord and of his angels and before men.[15]

---

[14] *Institutes* IV, xiv, 1–6. Quotations will be taken from John Calvin, *Institutes of the Christian Religion*, ed. John McNeill, trans. Ford Lewis Battles, Library of Christian Classics, vols. 20–21 (Philadelphia: The Westminster Press, 1960).

[15] *Institutes* IV, xiv, 1.

Surely, even though the word "covenant" does not appear, this definition makes abundantly clear the covenantal framework through which Calvin thinks out his theology of Holy Communion. Notice the emphasis on the promises of God; what God promises are his good will and love toward us.[16] These are, to be sure, the promises of the covenant of grace. Also, notice that the relationship the covenant people have to God is one of faith and faithfulness. Finally, notice that the celebration of the sacrament takes place in a solemn assembly gathered in the presence of the Lord and his angels.

Because the High Rhenish Reformers understood the sacraments in terms of their function in the covenant relationship, Calvin goes on to speak of the way sacraments seal God's promises from his Word. The Word of God proclaims the covenant promises and delineates the terms of the covenant. This delineation is important because it makes clear how to live within the bonds of the covenant. The promises and benefits of the covenant are in fact closely related to the quality of life demanded by the covenant. This must be understood to live life in the covenantal community. Calvin consents that there are many who speak of the sacrament in terms of Word and sign, but by Word mean some magical formula or incantation. The Word, however, must be more than that. It must set forth the promises of the covenant of grace, so that believers receive them as seals of those promises. A true sacrament, then, must have both: the setting forth of the promises and the sealing of the promises. This is at the center of a covenantal understanding of worship, and this is what we have here in Calvin's definition of a sacrament.

Calvin picks up on the Apostle Paul's explanation of how the sacrament of circumcision sealed the promises of God's covenant with Abraham. Here "covenant" is used explicitly.

> Paul expressly argues that Abraham's circumcision was not for his justification but for the seal of that cov-

---

[16] *Institutes* IV, xiv, 6.

enant by faith in which he had already been justified.[17]

The Apostle explains this at length in the fourth chapter of the Epistle to the Romans. There, as Calvin points out, it is clearly stated that Abraham was justified by faith and that circumcision was given as a sign and a seal of the covenant which had already been granted in the word of promise and received by faith. It was this explanation of the function of sacramental signs which had commended a covenantal theology of the sacraments to the Reformers to begin with. When the Reformers realized that salvation did not come through the sacramental system, but rather by faith in the crucified and risen Christ, they also realized that they needed to understand how the sacraments did fit in. Paul's explanation of circumcision and how it sealed the old covenant became a paradigm for the Reformers of how both baptism and the Lord's Supper are related to the new covenant. Salvation came by the grace of God through faith in Christ. The sacraments of baptism and the Lord's Supper seal the promises of the Gospel, which we have received by faith.

2. *INSTITUTES* IV, XVII, 1F.

Let us turn now to another important passage on the Lord's Supper where Calvin used the concept of covenant as the framework for his eucharistic theology: the beginning of his chapter on the Lord's Supper in Book Four of the *Institutes*.[18] Calvin begins by speaking in terms of the persons of the Trinity.[19] The Lord's Supper eloquently reveals God as Father, who nourishes at his table the very children he received into his household by baptism.

> God has received us, once for all, into his family, to hold us not only as servants but as sons. Thereafter, to fulfill the duties of a most excellent Father concerned for his

---

[17] *Institutes* IV, xiv, 5.

[18] *Institutes* IV, xvii, 1f.

[19] Most theologians emphasize the Lord's Supper in terms of our relation to Christ. The Supper expresses the presence of Christ.

offspring, he undertakes also to nourish us throughout the course of our life. And not content with this alone, he has willed, by giving his pledge, to assure us of this continuing liberality. To this end, therefore, he has, through the hand of his only-begotten Son, given to his church another sacrament, that is, a spiritual banquet, wherein Christ attests himself to be the life-giving bread, upon which our souls feed unto true and blessed immortality [John 6:51].[20]

The key words here are "by giving his pledge." The Lord's Supper gives us God's pledge, his promise to bring us through the trials of this life well supplied by his grace until at last we enter his eternal presence. This spiritual banquet attests that Christ is indeed our Savior.

When the God who has granted us the covenant is revealed to be our Father, then we are revealed to be the children of God. With paternal love and generosity God the Father nourishes his beloved sons and daughters to eternal life.[21]

The prayer of Jesus, commonly called the Lord's Prayer, reveals that God is our Father. It invokes God as "our Father in heaven." This is the center of Christian worship. It defines the relationships in which Christian prayer takes place. Prayer, too, takes place in the covenantal relationships and the Lord's Prayer makes this explicit. It is the same way with the Lord's Supper; when we sit at his table, we discover God to be our Father. Calvin often speaks of worship as an exercise of our faith. In the celebration of Communion we exercise our relation to the Father. We experience his paternal love as well as the fraternal love of fellow Christians. Calvin has a strong sense of the sacrament as communion, that is, as fellowship with God and fellowship with the brethren. This is the essence of a covenantal approach to the sacrament; it is an exercise of Christian fel-

---

[20] *Institutes* IV, xvii, 1. Brackets in original.

[21] In very similar words Calvin makes the same point at the beginning of his *Petit traité de la sainte Cène*. It is obviously a central theme in his eucharistic piety.

lowship.[22] Calvin often speaks of this and we get the impression that the celebration of the Lord's Supper was a profound experience for him. It must have been a time when he felt very near to God, when the eternal realities of God's kingdom deeply affected him. Surely this is what he means when he speaks of the Supper as the place where the richness of God's grace is manifested. Passages like this one should cause us to question whether Calvin's religion was really as austere and abstract as we have been led to believe.

The heart of a covenantal understanding of the Lord's Supper is that through the sacrament God establishes, sustains, and exercises the covenantal relationships between God and his people. These are the relationships of mercy and love, faith and faithfulness, paternal care and thankfulness. The relationships of the new covenant were established by the sacrifice of Christ. "This mystery of Christ's secret union with the devout is by nature incomprehensible,"[23] and yet, "By giving guarantees and tokens he makes it as certain for us as if we had seen it with our own eyes."[24] The broken bread and spilled wine assure us that the broken body and poured out blood of Christ nourish us to eternal life. They nourish us in the covenant relationship we have with our Savior, who has established this covenant as the eternal covenant. The relationships are both redemptive and eternal. To this end, the words of promise are added to the sacrament: "'Take, this is my body which is given for you.' We are therefore bidden to take and eat the body which was once for all offered for our salvation, in order that when we see ourselves made partakers in it, we may assuredly conclude that the power of his life-giving death will be efficacious in us."[25] It is the same way with the words of promise

---

[22] Physical exercise was a significant metaphor for worship. We find it used often in Calvin's commentary on the Psalms. It is interesting to compare Calvin with Ignatius of Loyola and his famous work, *The Spiritual Exercises*.

[23] *Institutes* IV, xvii, 1.

[24] *Institutes* IV, xvii, 1.

[25] *Institutes* IV, xvii, 1.

which accompany the cup: "This cup is the new covenant in my blood." With these words, says Calvin, Christ "renews, or rather continues, the covenant which he once for all ratified with his blood . . . whenever he proffers that sacred blood for us to taste."[26]

What is most interesting about this first section of Calvin's chapter on the Lord's Supper in the *Institutes* is the way it shows the covenant to be essentially a relationship to the Father through the Son. This is something revealed in regard to the new covenant which had been only foreshadowed by the old covenant. In the old covenant the promise is: I shall be your God and you shall be my people. In the new the promise becomes much more profound and personal: I shall be your Father and you shall be my sons and daughters.[27]

3. Commentary on Mark 14:24

Let us turn now from the *Institutes* to several important passages in the Commentaries. We begin with Calvin's commentary on the Last Supper found in his *Commentary on the Harmony of the Gospels*:

> He had no other reason for calling the bread His body than to make a lasting Covenant with us; that offering the sacrifice once for all we should now feast spiritually. There are two points worthy of note. From the word Testament or Covenant we infer that a promise is included in the holy Supper. This refutes the error of those who say that faith is not aided, fostered, supported, and increased by the Sacraments, for between God's Covenant and men's faith there is always a mutual relation. By the word "New" He wishes to teach that the old images are at an end and give place to a stable and eternal settlement. There is an indirect contrast between this mystery and the legal foreshadowings: evidently our state is far better than the Fathers', for after the sacrifice concluded on the cross we enjoy the solid truth.[28]

---

[26] *Institutes* IV, xvii, 1.

[27] *Institutes* IV, xiv, 13.

[28] Commentary on Mark 14:24 in John Calvin, *A Harmony of the Gospels Matthew, Mark and Luke, vol. 3, and The Epistles of James and Jude*, trans. A. W. Morrison, Cal-

2: CALVIN ON COMMUNION
THE COVENANTAL AND SACRAMENTAL DIMENSIONS

Here Calvin is unmistakable that by participating in the Supper we enter into the covenant. In giving us the bread and the cup God gives us a place in the covenant fellowship. The covenant was ratified by the sacrifice of Christ's body. We partake of the covenant by participating in the feast. It is by sharing in the covenant meal that we receive the benefits of the covenant sacrifice. Already in the passage we sense a play on words. The body of Christ is the body of the Church. The Supper is the sign of the new covenant, which is the fulfillment of the old covenant. In the end there is but one covenant—the eternal covenant.

4. COMMENTARY ON 1 CORINTHIANS 11

Another passage mentioning the covenantal framework of Calvin's eucharistic theology is his commentary on the Words of Institution, as we find them in Paul's First Epistle to the Corinthians. This lengthy commentary treats a number of eucharistic themes which are fundamental to a covenantal theology of the sacrament. Early on in the Latin text, Calvin refers to the Supper as a "covenant-seal;" the French text simply says "sacrament." There is no unfolding of a covenantal theology of the sacrament here, but the use of this term—covenant-seal—makes Calvin's basic patterns of thought obvious; he understands the sacrament as a seal of the covenant.

Further on, commenting on the text "and when he had given thanks," Calvin reveals that this is far more than the usual table blessing.

> This thanksgiving goes deeper than that, for Christ is giving thanks to His Father for His mercy towards the human race, and His priceless gift of redemption; and He encourages us, by His example, so that, as often as we approach the Holy Table, we may lift up our hearts in acknowledgment of the boundless love of God towards

---

vin's New Testament Commentaries (Grand Rapids, MI: Eerdmans, 1989), p. 139.

us, and be inflamed with true gratitude to Him.[29]

For Calvin the Supper speaks of God's love in sending his Son to atone for our sin. The breaking of the bread and the pouring out of the wine are a visible word that speaks of the Father's sacrifice of his Son, and of the suffering of the Son who willingly offered himself. When we taste of the broken bread and poured out wine the love of God is manifested to us very specifically and personally. When this manifestation occurs the covenantal relationships are nourished as hearts are kindled to respond to God's love by returning thanks to him. It is here that we experience communion.

As we would expect, Calvin's commentary on the text "This cup is the New Covenant in my blood," makes our theologian's covenantal understanding of the Supper explicit. This text implies that what is true of the cup is true of the loaf, that is:

> . . . a covenant which has been once for all ratified by the sacrifice of His body, and is now confirmed by eating, viz. when believers eat that sacrifice . . . For the blood was poured out to reconcile us to God, and now we drink it spiritually in order to have a share in that reconciliation. Therefore, in the Supper we have both the covenant (*foedus*) and a reinforcing pledge of the covenant.[30]

As Calvin apparently understands it, there are two moments in the sacramental celebration. There is the word of promise and the sign which confirms the promise. The covenant is a testament, that is, it is a witness. This is certainly an important aspect of covenant which has not yet been brought out. The sacrament gives witness to the atoning sacrifice of Christ, but it is a witness which is sealed. It is a confirmed, sworn-to witness. As a lawyer, Calvin appreciates the importance of these two moments. Before a trial

---

[29] Commentary on 1 Cor. 11:24, found in John Calvin, *The First Epistle of Paul to the Corinthians*, trans. John W. Fraser, Calvin's New Testament Commentaries (Grand Rapids, MI: Eerdmans, 1989), p. 234. Hereinafter, Calvin, *Commentary on First Corinthians*.

[30] Commentary on 1 Cor. 11:25 in Calvin, *Commentary on First Corinthians*, p. 249.

there are those who give testimony that is undoubtedly helpful in ascertaining the truth, but when a witness takes the stand and confirms his testimony with an oath before the court, then the testimony is accepted as valid.

This should make it clear why the use of the Apostles' Creed at the celebration of the Lord's Supper was so important to Calvin. As we find it in the *Genevan Psalter*, the service of the Lord's Supper proper began with the reciting of the Creed as a vow of the faith in which we intend to live and die. This certainly heightened the covenantal impact of the service. It is not surprising therefore that we find this passage in Calvin's commentary on 1 Corinthians 11:26:

> Paul now adds a description of the way in which the memorial ought to be kept, viz. with thanksgiving. It is not that the memorial depends completely upon the confession of our lips, for the main point is that the power of the death of Christ should be sealed in our consciences. But this knowledge ought to move us to praise Him openly, so as to let men know, when we are in their company, what we are aware of within ourselves in the presence of God. The Supper, is therefore, if I may say so, a kind of memorial (*quoddam memoriale*) which must always be maintained in the Church until the final coming of Christ; and which was instituted for this purpose, that Christ may remind us of the benefit of His death, and that we, on our part, may acknowledge it before men. That is why is it called the *Eucharist*. Therefore, in order that you may celebrate the Supper properly, you must bear in mind that you will have to make profession of your faith.[31]

We might put Calvin's thought this way: the Supper is a pledge of God's faithfulness and steadfast love. This is the very nature of God's love as we experience it in the bonds of the covenant—it is steadfast. The Supper is also our pledge of faith responding to God in thanksgiving as we find it so often in the worship of the

---

[31] Commentary on 1 Cor. 11:26 in Calvin, *Commentary on First Corinthians*, p. 250.

Temple. "O give thanks unto the LORD, for he is good, for his steadfast love endures for ever." In the covenant relationship our love for God is expressed in thanksgiving, that is, it is expressed in the exercise of our thanksgiving. Such exercising strengthens and nourishes the covenant relationship. It is in this way that thanksgiving is essential to a covenantal understanding of worship.

There is another point to be made and that is the importance of remembrance. The High Rhenish Reformers understood the biblical concept of memorial much better than we usually imagine. For example, they understood how the Hebrew Old Testament treated the celebration of Passover as a memorial, that the service was to be done "in remembrance of me" (1 Cor. 11:24–27). The thanksgiving is a memorial which recounts the mighty acts of God in the death and resurrection of Christ for our salvation.

One of the most lamentable modern deformations of typical Protestant eucharistic prayers is how we briefly give thanks for Christ's death on the cross and the forgiveness of our sins and then move on to other things. Often there is no mention of either the resurrection or the incarnation. It would be far better if the eucharistic prayer had a full recounting of the history of salvation, that is, the mighty acts of God for our salvation.

5. COMMENTARY ON 1 CORINTHIANS 10:16–18

Another place where Calvin discusses the general covenantal framework of eucharistic theology is in his commentary on 1 Corinthians 10:16–18. It is here that the Apostle Paul most clearly expresses his own covenantal understanding of the Lord's Supper. "The cup of blessing which we bless, is it not a participation in the blood of Christ? The bread which we break, is it not a participation in the body of Christ? Because there is one bread, we who are many are one body, for we all partake of the one bread. Consider the people of Israel; are not those who eat the sacrifices partners in the altar?" The idea, which Calvin so obviously understands, is that just as those who participated in the covenant meals of ancient Israel were united in the religious body of God's people, so Christians who participate in the Lord's Supper become one body with Christ and members of the new covenant people of God, that is, the Church.

Calvin observes that believers are united together in the blood of Christ, so as to become one body. A union "of that kind is properly called a κοινωνία."[32] This word, κοινωνία (koinonia), is the one Calvin seems to prefer to describe the union believers have with Christ and with each other in the Lord's Supper. He usually translates it with the Latin word *communio*. The Reformer apparently understood that this κοινωνία, or communion, was a sacred fellowship. The word speaks of the relationship appropriate to members of a covenant community. Κοινωνία is a uniquely biblical concept which speaks of the bond of the covenant community, a sacred bond that binds God's people together in community. It speaks of a sharing community and for Calvin this sharing is evidently one of its more fundamental characteristics. This sharing did not, however, erase the identity or compromise the integrity of the individual members. The sacramental union that many Christian writers from centuries before had imagined was an ontological fusion. Chalcedonian Christology should have guarded them against this, but it apparently did not. Calvin understood that κοινωνία was not fusion. Covenantal union is not a fusion, it is a union characterized by faith, hope, and love. This is the whole drift of Paul's argument in 1 Corinthians 10–14. It is faith, hope, and love that the service of worship exercises. The memorial of the mighty acts of redemption inspires our faith, the proclamation of the promises strengthens our hope, and the sharing of the loaf and the cup with thanksgiving exercises our love.

Having said this Calvin plunges into a line of thought which tends in the opposite direction. He begins to discuss the Lord's Supper not as communion or fellowship with Christ but as incorporation into the body of Christ. Is this not fusion? Referring to Ephe-

---

[32] Commentary on 1 Cor. 10:16 in Calvin, *Commentary on First Corinthians*, p. 216.

sians 5:30,[33] Calvin says, "But, I would ask, what is the source of that κοινωνία or communion, which exists among us, but from the fact that we are united to Christ so that 'we are flesh of His flesh, and bone of His bones'?"[34] It is like the union between husband and wife. It would be difficult to imagine that Calvin has simply a physical sexual union in mind. He calls it a spiritual union. He goes on to say:

> For it is necessary for us to be incorporated, as it were, into Christ in order to be united to each other. Besides, Paul is discussing here not a mere human fellowship (*non tantum de mutua inter homines communicatione*), but the spiritual union between Christ and believers (*sed de spirituali Christi et fidelium unione*). . . . Therefore from the context of this verse we can conclude that κοινωνία or communion of the blood is the alliance (*societatem*) which we have with the blood of Christ when He ingrafts all of us into His body, so that He may live in us, and we in Him.[35]

Exactly what Calvin means here is not as clear as we might like, and no doubt the reason is that Calvin, as he repeatedly insists, is talking about a mystery. He insists, however, on holding fast to both sides of the dilemma. The sacramental union is both a fellowship and an incorporation. As much as we would like to break the dilemma, Calvin himself seems to resist this by seeing the incorporation in terms of a fellowship. He calls on the Johannine phrase, "that he may live in us and we in him," which only strengthens the dilemma.[36] Because these parallel passages, Ephesians 5 and John 17, are so obviously important to Calvin's understanding of 1 Corinthians 10:16–17, let us look at them separately.

---

[33] Calvin follows the text of the *Bezae-cantatrigiensis*.

[34] Commentary on 1 Cor. 10:16 in Calvin, *Commentary on First Corinthians*, p. 216.

[35] Commentary on 1 Cor. 10:16 in Calvin, *Commentary on First Corinthians*, p. 216.

[36] In his commentary on John 17:23, Calvin does not seem to have in mind a material unity, but rather a unity of faith and obedience worked out by the Holy Spirit. In John 17, this unity is a matter of love. On the other hand, Calvin's commentary on Ephesians 5:30–32 indicates a very different opinion.

Incorporation into the body of Christ is, strictly speaking, a very particular image for our communion with Christ. Students of Pauline thought have studied this at considerable length, and there are widely differing opinions as to what Paul meant by this imagery. Checking Calvin's own commentary on Ephesians we find a most interesting interpretation of the passage. His entire section on Ephesians 5:21–33 is rich in sacramental teaching and should be studied as a whole. Calvin speaks at length of the bonds of love that hold society together. For the Christian, the love of Christ for the Church, which creates the bond uniting the Church to him, is the example for all these other relationships. The most sacred of these social relationships is the bond uniting husband and wife. According to Calvin, the fact that Eve was made of the substance of Adam is significant. She is bone of his bone and flesh of his flesh.

> What does this mean then? As Eve was formed out of the substance of her husband Adam, and thus was a part of him, so, if we are to be true members of Christ, we grow into one Body by the communication of His substance. In short, Paul describes our union to Christ, a symbol and pledge of which is given to us in the holy Supper. Some assert that it is a twisting of this passage to refer it to the Lord's Supper, when no mention is made of the Supper, but only of marriage; but they are very mistaken. Although they teach that the death of Christ is commemorated in the Supper, they do not admit a communication such as we assert from the words of Christ.[37]

Here Calvin uses the word "substance." For the Scholastic theologian, it is a technical term and Calvin, like many other young Christian Humanists of his day, had turned from Scholasticism and its technical terminology. Here this term seems to creep back in, though not with its technical definition.

---

[37] Commentary on Eph. 5:30 in John Calvin, *Galatians, Ephesians, Philippians and Colossians*, trans. T. H. L. Parker, Calvin's New Testament Commentaries (Grand Rapids, MI: Eerdmans, 1965), pp. 208–209.

First of all we want to underline the two words "commemorated" and "communicated" in this passage. The Lord's Supper is not merely a commemoration of Christ's saving death but a communication of it as well. What did Calvin mean by the substance of Christ being communicated to us? The bread and wine given at the supper is not to be confused with the substance, but are the sign and seal of that substance, which is given to those who receive them in faith. At this point Calvin does not say that this substance is the new life of the Kingdom of God. Further on in our discussion of the Wisdom dimension of Calvin's thought we will suggest that this is indeed what he had in mind. Calvin speaks of this substance in Johannine terms; as life, the life of a new humanity in fellowship with God; as light, the illumination of the inner witness of the Holy Spirit; and as power, the power which makes us able to do the works of God and nourishes us to eternal life. This is the substance of Christ which is communicated to us by means of the Supper. These blessings of the new covenant are communicated when we participate in the Supper.

The second passage Calvin uses to explain 1 Corinthians 10:16–17 is the High Priestly Prayer in which Jesus prays that we would live in him and he in us. Commenting on John 17:20–23 Calvin says our redemption unites us to God by joining us to the body of Christ in the unity of faith. This is the beginning of a blessed life where we all live by the one Spirit of Christ. What Calvin does here is explain the covenantal union experienced in the Lord's Supper first in terms of the Pauline figure of the unity of the body of Christ and second by the Johannine figure of the mutual indwelling of Christ and believers. Calvin's understanding of the Johannine figure is dependant upon his Christology.

> Again, we must learn that, whenever Christ declares in this chapter that He is one with the Father, He does not speak simply of His divine essence, but that He is called one in His person as Mediator and inasmuch as

2: CALVIN ON COMMUNION
THE COVENANTAL AND SACRAMENTAL DIMENSIONS

He is our Head . . .[38]

For Calvin it is important that the whole Christ, both in his divinity and his humanity, is one with the Father.

> To comprehend aright what it meant that Christ and the Father are one, take care not to deprive Christ of His person as Mediator. But consider Him rather as He is head of the Church, and join Him to His members. Thus the connexion will best be preserved; that, if the unity of the Son with the Father is not to be fruitless and useless, its power must be diffused through the whole body of believers. From this, too, we infer that we are one with Christ; not because He transfuses His substance into us, but because by the power of His Spirit He communicates to us His life and all the blessings He has received from the Father.[39]

This suggests a contradiction. The unity, we are told, must be diffused through the whole body, but Christ's substance is not transfused into us. There also seems to be a contradiction between this and the passage above from the Ephesians commentary, which states that a Christian is joined to Christ by the communication of his substance.[40] There is no contradiction if Calvin is distinguishing between Christ communicating his substance to us and transfusing it.[41] This appears to be a place where the *extra Calvinisticum* comes into play, which would mean that the passage from Calvin's commentary on John implies that the covenantal union with Christ brings the blessings of the new covenant. Covenantal union

---
[38] Commentary on John 17:21 in John Calvin, *The Gospel According to St. John, part two 11–21, and the First Epistle of John*, trans. T. H. L. Parker, Calvin's New Testament Commentaries (Grand Rapids, MI: Eerdmans, 1988), p. 148. Hereinafter, Calvin, *Commentary on the Gospel of John (2)*.

[39] Commentary on John 17:21 in Calvin, *Commentary on the Gospel of John (2)*, p. 148.

[40] The translation may be at fault. I hope the problem is with the word "diffused" (Fr. trans. *repande*), and "transfused" (Fr. trans. *transmit*).

[41] From *Institutes* IV, xvii, 32 it appears that Calvin does not like the term "transfuse." See further on this subject, *Second Defense . . . to Westphal*, in Calvin, *Theological Treatises*, pp. 248, 270, and 276.

is not achieved by a transfusion of Christ's flesh any more than a transfusion of Christ's divinity comes by eating divinized food.

A part of Calvin's final reply to Westphal is remarkable here:

> What do Luke and Paul affirm to be given in the cup? A covenant in the blood. As the same thing must be true of the body, it follows that nothing else can be inferred from the words of Christ, than that under the bread there is the ratification of a covenant in the body of the Son of God which was crucified for us. We are ordered to eat the body which was crucified for us; in other words, to become partakers of the sacrifice by which the sins of the world were expiated. If they insist that the two things are conjoined, viz., the fruit of the sacrifice and the communion of the flesh, I myself press the very same point--that since by the same law and the same words the Son of God offers his body, and the covenant in the body, the one is not to be taken without the other. As it was said, Eat, this is my body, they insist that the body of Christ is eaten substantially by all men whatsoever. Why might not I, on the other hand, insist that all men whatsoever receive the covenant by drinking of the cup? From this it would follow, that all who approach the table truly and spiritually communicate with Christ.[42]

Notice that participation in the covenant comes about through participation in Christ's sacrifice. The covenant is established by the vicarious sacrifice of Christ. By divine intention the sacrifice was for us, and we lay hold of it by sharing in the feast.

B. THE SUPPER AS MEMORIAL

There are several corollaries to the covenantal dimension of the Lord's Supper. The first is that the Lord's Supper is a memorial. In regard to both the breaking of the bread and the sharing of the wine Jesus said, "Do this in remembrance of me" (1 Cor. 11:24–25; cf. Luke 22:19).

---

[42] Calvin, *Theological Treatises*, pp. 481–482.

2: Calvin on Communion
The Covenantal and Sacramental Dimensions

Much had been said about the Lord's Supper as memorial early in the Reformation. Zwingli, one of the principal pastors of the city of Zurich, was a capable young scholar who had mastered the new tools of Renaissance scholarship. Little more than a year after Luther published his ninety-five theses, Zwingli was called to be preacher at the Great Minster in the center of Zurich. He began preaching through the Gospel of Matthew every day— chapter by chapter, verse by verse. His preaching caused a sensation. Everyone for miles around came to hear this brilliant young scholar explain the Scriptures as he read them from the original Greek text, which had been published only a few months earlier in nearby Basel, the university town where Zwingli had studied. Along with Luther and Bucer, Zwingli was at the vanguard of the Reformation. In 1523 he published a study of the text of the Roman Mass in which he showed that it was in no way an ancient text going back to the days of Christ and the Apostles, but was largely the invention of much more recent times.

One thing was very clear to Zwingli: the Lord's Supper, as instituted by Jesus and observed by the Apostles, was not a sacrifice. In this, of course, all the Reformers—Luther, Bucer, Calvin, Knox, and Cranmer—were in agreement. The doctrine of the eucharistic sacrifice was foreign to the New Testament; not only was it not found in the New Testament, it was in direct contradiction to the New Testament. The Lord's Supper, Zwingli's *De canone* concluded, was not a sacrifice, but rather a memorial of a sacrifice.

In 1525 Zwingli published his essay on the Lord's Supper, a popular work in which he set forth his interpretation of the basic biblical texts on the Supper. The *Zurich Service Book* of 1525 was published shortly afterward.[43] It contains the text of the service of the Lord's Supper as it was celebrated at Easter that year. The

---

[43] The official name for the *Zurich Service Book* of 1525 is *Action or Use of the Lord's Supper*, written by Ulrich Zwingli, the English text of which is found in Bard Thompson, *Liturgies of the Western Church* (Philadelphia: Fortress Press, 1980), pp. 149–156. Citations will be given to Thompson.

preface of this liturgy gives considerable importance to understanding the Lord's Supper as memorial. We read:

> This memorial is a thanksgiving and rejoicing before Almighty God for the benefit which He has manifested to us through His Son; and whoever appears at this feast, meal or thanksgiving bears witness that he belongs to those who believe that they are redeemed by the blood of our Lord Jesus Christ.[44]

Here we clearly see that although the Lord's Supper was understood as a memorial, it was not only a memorial. The sacrament is to be understood as a thanksgiving. In ancient times it was called the Eucharist. Beyond this, the Reformers of Zurich preferred to call the sacrament a witness, drawing attention to the covenantal dimension of the Supper.

"This memorial is a thanksgiving and a rejoicing before Almighty God."[45] Oecolampadius' first attempt at an evangelical Lord's Supper was entitled *The Memorial of the New Covenant*. In the *Grund und Ursach* the pastors of Strasbourg tell us that the Lord's Supper is a memorial.

In his commentary on 1 Corinthians 11:24 Calvin treats the subject. Commenting on the phrase "This do in remembrance of me" we read:

> The Supper is therefore a memorial (μνημόσυνον) provided to assist our weakness; for if we were otherwise sufficiently mindful of the death of Christ, this help would be superfluous. This applies to all the sacraments, for they help us in our weakness. But we shall soon learn what sort of memorial of Himself Christ wanted us to keep in the Supper.[46]

As Calvin understands the word, a "memorial" is something done

---

[44] Thompson, *Liturgies of the Western Church*, p. 150.

[45] Thompson, *Liturgies of the Western Church*, p. 150.

[46] Calvin, *Commentary on First Corinthians*, p. 248.

that the community might not forget. He claims it to be a memorial in the same sense that Passover was a memorial in Exodus 12:14, "This day shall be for you a memorial day." There is no question that Calvin sees such a memorial as more than an aid to the memory. It is an act of affirming the covenant that was established by the redemptive acts of God—first in the Passover and the redemption from Egypt and then finally in the ministry of Jesus and his atoning death and triumphant resurrection. The saving acts of God established the covenant. Participation in the memorial feast of these events affirms our place in the covenant community.

Calvin makes this clear further on when he says that being reminded of God's mighty acts of salvation should first move us to thanksgiving, and second to witnessing before the world our allegiance to his kingdom. To celebrate the memorial is an act of homage, a pledge of allegiance. "Paul now adds a description of the way in which the memorial ought to be kept, viz. with thanksgiving."[47] Prayers of thanksgiving and singing psalms of thanksgiving at the observance of the Supper is part of this, but even more important is the inward thanksgiving of the heart. The story of these saving acts is recounted that we might remember.

> But this knowledge ought to move us to praise Him openly, so as to let men know, when we are in their company, what we are aware of within ourselves in the presence of God. The Supper is, therefore, if I may say so, a kind of memorial (*quoddam memoriale*) which must always be maintained in the Church until the final coming of Christ.[48]

That is, the memorial not just a remembering, it is a public commitment. "Therefore, in order that you may celebrate the Supper properly, you must bear in mind that you will have to make profes-

---

[47] Commentary on 1 Cor. 11:26 in Calvin, *Commentary on First Corinthians*, p. 250.
[48] Commentary on 1 Cor. 11:26 in Calvin, *Commentary on First Corinthians*, p. 250.

sion of your faith."[49] In this sense it was a sacrament as Tertullian understood the word. Observing the memorial was to be recognized as an oath of allegiance.

As Reformed theologians began more and more to realize, the feast of Passover had been a memorial. The Exodus text was quite specific about this. If the rainbow which appeared to Noah was a sign of God's covenant and if circumcision was a sign of the covenant God gave to Abraham, so Passover was, in a very similar way, a sign of the covenant granted to the children of Israel. It was to be a memorial of God's sovereign act of redemption in bringing his people out of Egypt. The Passover typology was very important to the Reformers as they sought to understand the sacrament in terms of a more biblical theology.

C. The Supper As Communion

A second corollary to the covenantal theology of the sacrament is that the Supper is a communion with God—the God and Father of our Lord Jesus Christ—as well as communion with God's people. Behind the word "communion" is the New Testament word *koinonia*. It is a very rich word in the New Testament; it is used to speak of covenantal relationships. In addition to what we have already said about this passage, several things should be noticed. Calvin discusses the meaning of this word, inserting the actual Greek into his text. Calvin is fully aware of its uniqueness, as it is found in the New Testament.

> Paul says that the cup blessed in this way is κοινωνία, a communion in the blood of Christ. "What exactly does that mean?" someone asks. Keep controversy out of it, and everything will be quite clear! It is true that believers are bound together by the blood of Christ, so that they become one Body. It is also true that a unity of that kind is properly called a κοινωνία or communion.[50]

---

[49] Commentary on 1 Cor. 11:26 in Calvin, *Commentary on First Corinthians*, p. 250.
[50] Commentary on 1 Cor. 10:16 in Calvin, *Commentary on First Corinthians*, p. 216.

2: CALVIN ON COMMUNION
THE COVENANTAL AND SACRAMENTAL DIMENSIONS

Calvin insists on the closeness of this bond, which the Apostle Paul calls κοινωνία. We read further:

> But, I would ask, what is the source of that κοινωνία or communion, which exists among us, but the fact that we are united to Christ so that "we are flesh of His flesh and bone of His bones"? For it is necessary for us to be incorporated, as it were, into Christ in order to be united to each other.[51]

The whole point of fellowship with Christ is that we would be crucified and rise with him. The whole point of the covenant is that we would have communion with the God and Father of our Lord Jesus Christ. Calvin says, "Therefore from the context of this verse we can conclude that κοινωνία or communion of the blood is the alliance *(societatem)* which we have with the blood of Christ when He ingrafts all of us into His body, so that He may live in us, and we in Him."[52] What Calvin is essentially doing here is explaining the Pauline text with Johannine theology.

What we need to notice is that there is tension between understanding the Lord's Supper as memorial and the Lord's Supper as communion. Celebrating the Lord's Supper as memorial assumes Christ's absence, while celebrating the Lord's Supper as communion assumes his presence. The way Reformed piety comes to reconcile the two will be by means of typology. In one case we are dealing with the Passover typology (Exodus 12 and 13); while in the other we are dealing with the Sinai typology (Exodus 24), the meal up on the top of the mountain.

Calvin sees the problem clearly. In his commentary on 1 Corinthians 11:24 he says, "This do in remembrance of me ... Some draw the inference from this phrase that, in these circumstances, Christ is not present in the Supper, because there can only be a memorial

---

[51] Commentary on 1 Cor. 10:16 in Calvin, *Commentary on First Corinthians*, p. 216.
[52] Commentary on 1 Cor. 10:16 in Calvin, *Commentary on First Corinthians*, p. 216.

(memoria) of something that is absent."[53] Calvin admits this to be true in a certain sense. Christ is not visibly present. He does not leave his place in heaven, and yet when he is remembered the efficacy of his saving work is established among us.[54] This is a kind of presence implied by the word "memorial," but this is not the last word. As Calvin presents it, we must think of the Supper as communion as well as memorial. We find both words used in the New Testament to speak of the Supper, and as we have been saying, there are a number of words given by Scripture to explain the sacrament.

D. THE SUPPER AS PROCLAMATION

The third corollary of a covenantal theology of the Supper is that the celebration of the Lord's Supper is proclamation—a witness to the world. It is καταυγελιον, to use the biblical term (cf. 1 Cor. 11:26).

At the heart of a covenantal theology of worship is the idea that when God has heard our cry for help and delivered us from our misery, then we owe to God a witness to his mercy and his mighty acts for our salvation. We have often spoken of this, for it is a motivating obligation to tell to the congregation, as well as to the whole of creation, what God has done for us. This is why the recounting of holy history is essential to worship. We tell the story as both memorial and thanksgiving, which is a witness. This witness not only strengthens the faith of the faithful but also inspires the faith of the doubtful. The giving of the witness is essential to evangelism because it is a proclamation.

Commenting on the text, "For as often as you eat this bread and drink this cup you proclaim the Lord's death until he comes," Calvin says:

> Paul now adds a description of the way in which the memorial ought to be kept, viz. with thanksgiving. It is not that the memorial depends completely upon the

---

[53] Calvin, *Commentary on First Corinthians*, p. 248.
[54] Calvin, *Commentary on First Corinthians*, p. 248.

confession of our lips, for the main point is that the power of the death of Christ should be sealed upon our consciences. But this knowledge ought to move us to praise him openly, so as to let men know, when we are in their company, what we are aware of within ourselves in the presence of God. The Supper is, therefore, if I may say so, a kind of memorial (*quoddam memoriale*) which must always be maintained in the Church until the final coming of Christ; and which was instituted for this purpose, that Christ may remind us of the benefit of His death, and that we, on our part, may acknowledge it before men. That is why it is called the *Eucharist*. Therefore, in order that you may celebrate the Supper properly, you must bear in mind that you will have to make profession of your faith.[55]

In other words, the very act of participating in the sacred feast is a profession of faith.

From the very beginning the covenant community had a responsibility to the world outside the covenant. The covenant promised God's blessing to the seed of Abraham, with the goal that the blessing of the covenant people would issue in the blessing of all the peoples of the earth (cf. Genesis 12:2). Covenant theology has always had a kerygmatic corollary.

THE SACRAMENTAL DIMENSION

A second dimension of Calvin's eucharistic theology might be called the sacramental dimension. The Lord's Supper had been considered a sacrament in the Latin-speaking Church since its beginning. Strictly speaking, the word "sacrament" is not biblical. Tertullian, the founder of Christian Latin, is said to have coined the word and it has been defined and redefined through theological discussion. Scholastic theology had developed a very specific understanding of the word and it was one of the fundamental concepts of the entire Scholastic system. The medieval approach to worship was built on

---

[55] Commentary on 1 Cor. 11:26 in Calvin, *Commentary on First Corinthians*, p. 250.

this understanding of sacrament. When Beatus Rhenanus discovered a number of lost works of Tertullian, he rescued this earliest of major Latin Christian writers from obscurity. It soon became clear that the meaning of "sacrament" had shifted over the centuries. This could not help but affect the way the Christian Humanists and their students at the beginning of the sixteenth century began to look at their sacramental theology. As far as the students were concerned the rug had been pulled out from under the whole sacramental system. It might be said that the patristic roots of Reformed worship began to tap some unexpected sources.

Zwingli was one of these students, as were Melanchthon, Bucer, and Calvin. Certainly Luther should be included as well. He had availed himself of much material the Christian Humanists had brought to light, but it was the Rhenish Reformers who really took the lead. In fact, Zwingli's close associate, Konrad Pellikan, wrote the preface to the famous edition of Tertullian which Beatus Rhenanus produced. As was plain to anyone who read the Rhenanus edition, Tertullian had taken the word *sacramentum* from the oath of allegiance sworn by Roman soldiers when entering military service. In the first line, Tertullian understood the confession of faith made at baptism to be a *sacramentum*. The Apostles' Creed was the oath of allegiance sworn by when becoming a Christian. Baptism, in the second line, was called a *sacramentum* because it was the rite at which the oath was made. For Tertullian the profession of faith made at baptism was clearly of the essence of baptism. Tertullian's insight fit well into a covenantal understanding of the sacrament. It would be difficult to overestimate the importance of Tertullian's explanation of baptism as a sacrament for the Reformers, particularly for those of the Rhineland. For those putting a strong emphasis on justification by faith, the idea that sacraments were signs and seals of faith would have an obvious appeal.

Zwingli's early attempts to take this new discovery into account in his writings on the sacraments were not well balanced. This is to be expected; it is what generally happens when new information is brought into any discussion. Calvin's use of this new information is much more balanced, but it is still noticeably significant.

While Zwingli was influenced by Tertullian's use of the Latin word *sacramentum* his fellow Reformer in Basel John Oecolampadius became interested in looking into the meaning of the word the Greeks used for the sacraments, *mustêrion* (μυστήριον). In his preface to the eucharistic liturgy of the *Basel Service Book* of 1525, he carefully outlines the significance of the word *mustêrion* as used in the New Testament. This sort of careful philological analysis was the very thing the students of the Christian Humanists did best. The sort of education they gave themselves led to a profound sense of the use of language and a wide perspective in the variety of ways words can be used.

Though the Reformers may have revised their understanding of sacrament in light of what they learned from Tertullian about how the word came into currency, they never gave up the basic insight of Scholastic theology on the subject, namely, that a sacrament is an outward and visible sign of an inward and spiritual grace. This definition had, of course, come from Augustine. The medieval theologians had taken it a long way from Augustine but for Calvin and most of the other Reformers it rang true, especially as Augustine had originally meant it. Calvin pressed hard to understand the original meaning by consulting Augustine's other writings. From this it was clear that a sacrament entailed not only a profession of faith but also a visible figure or symbol. Sacraments are figures; they speak figuratively. The very concept of sacrament implied metonymy even if that involved a visible symbol or sign. Here Calvin sticks very closely to Augustine's *De doctrina christiana*.

Despite their best intentions the Reformers never could leave behind the Scholastic discussion of *res* and *signum*. This was particularly the case in England where the influence of Wycliffe was still strong. We can never really understand the Reformers on the subject of the Lord's Supper until we take seriously their intentions to carry out their reform according to Scripture. Biblical concepts were fundamental to their understanding.

Several passages from Calvin's works show how the concept of sacrament functioned in his approach to the Lord's Supper. The chapter in the *Institutes* devoted to the sacraments in general is where we would expect to find a full discussion of the concept. Any systematic theology from the Middle Ages would contain a treatise on the sacraments in general as well as a specific discussion of the matter. Quite traditionally, Calvin begins his chapter on the sacraments in general with his interpretation of Augustine's famous definition of a sacrament being a visible sign of an invisible grace. Calvin then gives the following explanation of why the word "sacrament" is used:

> The reason why the ancients used this word is clear enough. For wherever the old translator wished to render into Latin the Greek word μυστήριον, especially where it refers to divine things, he translated it "sacrament." For example, in Ephesians: "That he may make known the 'sacrament' of his will" [Eph. 1:9].[56]

Three more quotations from the New Testament are given and then Calvin remarks:

> He did not wish to use the word "secret," lest he seem to say something beneath the greatness of the matter. Therefore he wrote "sacrament" for "secret" but in reference to a sacred thing. In this sense it repeatedly occurs among church writers. And it is sufficiently known that what the Latins call "sacrament" the Greeks call "mysteries." The identity of meaning banished all controversy. And from this it came to be applied to those signs which reverently represented sublime and spiritual things. Augustine, too, notes this

---

[56] *Institutes* IV, xiv, 2.

> somewhere: "It would be tedious," he says, "to argue over the variety of signs which, when they apply to divine things, are called 'sacraments.'"[57]

What is striking here is that Calvin insists on defining the word in terms of what might be called biblical philology. A sacrament is a sign which reverently represents sublime and spiritual things. For Calvin the use of the term *sacramentum* is understandable, if it is understood to refer to the biblical concept of sign, *sêmeion* (σημεῖον). This is a particularly rich biblical concept. As both Calvin and Augustine well understood, there are many things in Scripture referred to as signs. There are passages in the Pentateuch which speak of various signs of the covenant. There are the signs which Jesus performed in the Gospel of John. There are profound events which God has used to reveal his eternal purposes. In fact, all creation can be regarded as a sign or sacrament of God's glory.

Further on, Calvin sets himself against those who stick too closely to Tertullian's use of the word and do not take into consideration the meaning which the word *sacramentum* picked up in the ancient Church.

> Some derive an argument from the very term "sacrament," but one that is far from convincing. Sacrament, they say, although it has many senses among reputable authors, has only one that accords with "signs." That is, it signifies the solemn oath that the soldier took to the commander when he entered military service. For as recruits bind their fealty to their commander by this military oath and make profession of military service, so by our signs do we profess Christ our commander, and testify that we serve under his ensign.[58]

Augustine had obviously tapped in on Tertullian in the use of the word *sacramentum*, and this is not surprising because both were North African theologians. Augustine's modification of Tertul-

---

[57] *Institutes* IV, xiv, 2.
[58] *Institutes* IV, xiv, 13.

lian's meaning of the word is significant. For Tertullian it is the new Christian who gives the oath; for Augustine it is God who makes the promise implied in the sacraments. Calvin sees no reason to abandon the traditional terminology because he sees it as an attempt to understand Scripture. In fact, Calvin tries to understand the traditional terminology in terms of Scripture. All through Scripture Calvin finds signs that God gives as seals of his promises, which he assumes is what the North African theologians had in mind when they used the word *sacramentum*.

It would be hasty to jump to the conclusion that this passage is directed against Zwingli. It seems more probable that Calvin has the arguments of the Anabaptists in mind, who may have gotten their basic information about Tertullian's use of the word from Zwingli. The Anabaptists of Zurich carefully followed the preaching of Zwingli—at least in the early days—but the way they developed this information was to make the sacraments, particularly baptism, symbolic professions of faith. Zwingli did not follow the argument to this extreme. Tertullian's use of *sacramentum* was prone to a Pelagian understanding, which appealed to neither Zwingli nor Calvin. It was another matter with the Anabaptists.

Another passage which illuminates Calvin's use of the term *sacramentum* is found in this same chapter:

> The term "sacrament," as we have previously discussed its nature so far, embraces generally all those signs which God has ever enjoined upon men to render them more certain and confident of the truth of his promises. He sometimes willed to present these in natural things, at other times set them forth in miracles.[59]

As an example of a natural sacrament, Calvin points to the rainbow given to Noah by God as a sign of the covenant in which God promised to maintain the order of nature. We could regard many things as natural sacraments, Calvin says, if God had imprinted

---

[59] *Institutes* IV, xiv, 18.

such promises upon them. The sun, the stars, the earth, the stones all point to the glory of God but they do not have a divine promise attached to them as the rainbow does. Calvin gives an important distinction here between those who would approach the sacraments from the standpoint of revelation and those who would approach them from the standpoint of natural theology. He gives a striking example of the distinction:

> Why are crude and coined silver not of the same value, though they are absolutely the same metal? The one is merely in the natural state; stamped with an official mark, it becomes a coin and receives a new valuation. And cannot God mark with his Word the things he has created, that what were previously bare elements may become sacraments?[60]

It was for this reason that Calvin rejected so many of the auxiliary rites which had grown up around the Christian sacraments, such as baptismal anointings, the liturgical calendar, the use of lights, symbolic colors, and other things which may have a certain natural appropriateness, but which do not bear a divine promise. For Calvin it is the divine word of promise that distinguishes a mere symbol from a sign in the true biblical sense of the word. It is these signs—on which are imprinted the promises of God, like the silver minted by royal authority—that are the legitimate sacraments.

Calvin also sees a second kind of biblical sign, or *sêmia* (σημία), which signs can legitimately be called sacraments. These signs are miraculous rather than natural: the smoking pot of fire which God showed to Abraham (Gen. 15:17), the sign of the fleece given to Gideon (Judges 6:37–38), and the sign on the sundial which God gave to Hezekiah to strengthen his faith in God's promise. As Calvin sees it, the fact that these signs were given to support and confirm faith makes them sacraments. Those influenced by the

---

[60] *Institutes* IV, xiv, 18.

Enlightenment may not like the idea of miraculous signs, but this is certainly an important element for a biblical sign.

Calvin knows much about the religious rites of Greek and Roman paganism. Just how much may be surprising until we remember the amount of Greek and Latin literature the students of the Christian Humanists had read. Calvin knew all about the Hellenistic mystery religions and not surprisingly regarded them the same way the fathers of the ancient Church regarded them; they were but degraded forms of the rites God had given to his people. He agrees with Augustine that any religious community must be held together by such rites. It is natural for men to have rites of initiation but, as Justin Martyr, Calvin sees these rites as corruptions of the more ancient rites given by God to the fathers, to Abraham and the patriarchs before him. In good Ciceronian style Calvin says that he wants to pass over such debased matters, but he says enough to show that he was knowledgeable on the subject. For Calvin, the mysteries of Greek and Roman antiquity were corrupted by superstition; they no longer witnessed to the truth.

It was quite different with the sacraments of the Old Testament. This high regard for the sacraments of the old covenant is typical of the Reformed theologians of the early sixteenth century. They confirmed faith and pointed to Christ just as the sacraments of the Gospel did. Calvin recognized that a certain prophetic dimension was inherent in the concept of sacrament. Many of the old covenant sacraments foreshadowed Christ and the sacraments of the new covenant. They were signs of the future. In due time we will speak at length of the eschatological nature of the sacraments. There was a distinction, of course, between the sacraments of the old covenant—such as circumcision, the various rites of purification, the sacrifices, various covenantal meals, and the Passover meal—on the one hand, and typological foreshadowings of the saving work of Christ on the other. The Great Flood, Abraham's sacrifice, the passage through the Red Sea, and the story of Jonah and the whale, could be called sacraments of the future, which is what the Fathers of the early Church called them. All these preliminary sacraments laid the foundation for appreciating the Christian sacraments. They enriched their meaning and pointed the way to the sacraments of the Gospel. Calvin's understanding of the nature of the sacraments emphasized the importance of this typological background of Christian worship.

3
CALVIN ON COMMUNION
The Wisdom Dimension

Biblical wisdom theology significantly shaped Calvin's understanding of the Lord's Supper, but the wisdom dimension of Calvin's eucharistic theology is only one dimension of his thought.[1] We have already mentioned the covenantal dimension, the kerygmatic dimension, the eucharistic dimension, and several others. We will have more to say about these different dimensions. In these next few pages we will focus on the wisdom dimension. The biblical Wisdom School had developed a particular temper of piety that went along certain tendencies in worship, tendencies which profoundly influenced Calvin. In recent years biblical scholars have made considerable progress in elucidating the theology of the Wisdom School.[2] Calvin, in the middle of the sixteenth

---

[1] This chapter is the text of a paper given at the Colloquium on Calvin Studies at Davidson College in January, 1992. It has been previously published as, Hughes Oliphant Old, "Biblical Wisdom Theology and Calvin's Understanding of the Lord's Supper," *Calvin Studies VI* (Davidson, NC: Calvin Colloquium, 1992).

[2] Among the most important works on the wisdom theology, Felix Christ, "Jesus Sophia," *Abhandlungen zur Theologie des Alten und Neuen Testaments*, 57 (1960); Hans Conzelmann, "Wisdom in the N. T.", *The Interpreter's Dictionary of the Bible*, supplementary volume (Nashville: Abingdon Press, 1984), pp. 956–960; James L. Crenshaw, ed., *Studies in Ancient Israelite Wisdom* (New York: Ktav Publishing House, 1976); James L. Crenshaw, "Wisdom in the O. T.", *The Interpreter's Dictionary of the Bible*, supplementary volume (Nashville: Abingdon Press, 1984), pp. 952–956; Burton Mack, *Logos und Sophia, Untersuchungen zur Weisheitstheologie im hellenistischen Judentum*, SUNT, 10 (Göttingen: Vandenhoeck und Ruprecht, 1973); Robert Balgamie Young Scott, *The Way of Wisdom in the O. T.* (New York: Macmillan, 1971); Gerhard von Rad, *Wisdom in Israel*, trans. James D. Martin (Nashville and New York: Abingdon Press, 1972); Ulrich Wilckens, "SOPHIA", *Theologisches Wörterbuch zum Neuen Testament*, eds. Gerhard Kittel and Gerhard Friedrich, 9 vols. (Stuttgart: W. Kohlhammer Verlag, 1964), 7:465–475.

century, was hardly aware of all that modern scholars have been able to show about this school, but he was aware of many of the characteristic insights of the school.[3]

A. Calvin's Appreciation of Wisdom Theology

Let us begin with a look at Calvin's grasp of some of the basic insights of the Wisdom School aside from any relation these insights might have to the Lord's Supper. We would expect to find an indication of Calvin's awareness of this particular dimension of biblical theology from his commentaries. This approach has some limitations even if in the end it yields the information we need. Calvin did not leave commentaries on Proverbs, Ecclesiastes, Job, or the Song of Solomon.[4] We cannot say as much as we might like, therefore, on how he may or may not have recognized the wisdom theology of these major statements of the school. He has, on the other hand, treated the wisdom psalms in his commentary on the Psalms,[5] and

---

[3] The renaissance of learning in the early sixteenth century was especially interested in the biblical concept of Wisdom. Cf. Eugene F. Rice, *The Renaissance Idea of Wisdom* (Cambridge, MA: Harvard University Press, 1958); and Lewis W. Spitz, *The Religious Renaissance of the German Humanists* (Cambridge, MA: Harvard University Press, 1963). Among the Reformers it was Melanchthon who produced the great commentary on Ecclesiastes.

[4] It should be noticed that while there is not a commentary on Job, there is a series of sermons. In addition to these sermons we can get a number of ideas of how Calvin would have regarded these works from the notes to the Geneva Bible.

[5] Calvin's commentary on the Psalms first appeared in the Latin version, *In librum Psalmorum, Iohannis Caluini commentarius*, published by the famous printer Robert Stephanus in 1552. A few months later the French version appeared under the title, *Le Livre des Pseaumes exposé par Iehan Caluin* . . . . It was issued by the equally famous printer Conrad Badius. As early as 1571 an English translation was made by Arthur Golding, one of the best known translators of classical literature during the reign of Elizabeth I. It is interesting to note that this translation was dedicated to the Earl of Oxford, whom many today believe to have been the true author of the dramas of Shakespeare. The translation quoted in this paper is John Calvin, *Commentary on the Book of Psalms by John Calvin, Translated from the original Latin and collated with the Author's French Version*, by James Anderson (Edinburgh: The Calvin Society, 1845, photolithographic reproduction, Grand Rapids, MI: Eerdmans, 1949). Hereafter Calvin, *Commentary on the Book of Psalms*.

3: Calvin on Communion
The Wisdom Dimension

his commentary on James, as we shall see, shows a certain recognition of its relation to the Solomonic tradition.[6] Calvin's greatest appreciation of biblical wisdom theology, however, is discovered in his commentaries on the Johannine writings where the wisdom theology is found in its Christian form.[7] There the Old Testament wisdom concepts are developed into the logos theology of the early Church. Let us look at some specific passages.

1. Prologue to the Gospel of John

Calvin's appreciation of biblical wisdom theology is especially evident in his commentary on the prologue to the Gospel of John[8] where Calvin begins by saying that Christ is called the Word of God because he is the eternal Wisdom of God, the holy Wisdom from above.

I think he calls the Son of God 'the Word' (sermo) simply because, first, He is the eternal wisdom and will of God, and sec-

---

[6] Calvin originally composed his commentary on James in French. It was published by Jean Crespin in 1550 under the title *Commentaire de M. Jean Calvin sur l'Epistre de sainct Iaques*. The following year Crespin published Calvin's Latin version, together with his commentaries on 1 and 2 Peter, I John, and Jude: *Commentarii in Epistolas Canonicas, unam Petri, unam Joannis, unam Iacobi, Petri alteram. Iudae unam*. The most recent English translation is that of A. W. Morrison found in *Calvin's Commentaries*, 12 vols. (Grand Rapids, MI: Eerdmans, 1989), hereafter Calvin, *Commentaries*. Translations of *Calvin's Commentaries*, unless otherwise noted, are taken from this edition.

[7] Calvin's Latin commentary on the Gospel of John appeared at the publishing house of Robert Stephanus in 1553 with the title, *In Evangelium secundum Iohannem Commentarius*. Calvin's French translation appeared in the same year, *Commentaire de M. Iean Calvin sur l'Evangile selon sainct Iean, Traduit du latin*. The translation quoted in this article is that of T. H. L. Parker in Calvin, *Commentaries*, vols. 4 and 5. For Calvin's *Commentary on the First Epistle of John*, see note 20 (p. 88).

[8] On the Gospel of John as a Christian interpretation of the wisdom theology, see Raymond Brown, *The Gospel according to John* (Garden City, N. Y.: Doubleday Company, 1966), pp. cxxii-cxxviii; François-Marie Braun, *Jean le théologien: les grandes traditions d'Israël et l'accord d'Écritures selon le quatrième évangile* (Paris: Gabalda, 1964); G. Ziener, *Weisheitsbuch und Johannesevangelium*, Bib 38 (1957), 395–418; and 39 (1958), 37–60.

ondly because he is the express image of his purpose.⁹

Throughout the remainder of the commentary on the prologue the word "Wisdom" is used as a synonym of "Word."¹⁰ This is a crucial insight. As Calvin understands it, when John was speaking about the Word he had in mind the divine Wisdom.¹¹ Calvin had a rather surprising grasp of the wisdom theology. This passage alone should be sufficient to make the point, but there is more.

In the first book of the *Institutes* where he is developing his doctrine of the incarnation, Calvin calls attention to the logos theology of the prologue to the Gospel of John.¹² There, too, he tells us that "Word" basically means Wisdom.¹³ What is even more interesting

---

⁹ Calvin, *Commentaries*, 4:7.

¹⁰ The Latin text is of interest here. "Quod sermonem vocat Dei filium, haec mihi simplex videtur esse ratio, quia primum aeterna sit Dei sapientia et voluntas, deinde expresse consilii eius effigies." John Calvin, *Ioannis Calvini opera quae supersunt omnia*, ed. William Baum, Edward Cunitz, and Edward Reuss, 59 vols., Corpus Reformatorum, vols. 29–87 (Brunswick and Berlin: C. A. Schweiske, 1863–1900), hereinafter *Corpus Reformatorum*, 47: col. 1. It was Erasmus who had translated the Greek *logos* with *sermo*. A few paragraphs further on Calvin discusses the translation of Erasmus.

¹¹ Calvin's French version of his commentary on the Gospel of John is of particular interest here. "Quant à ce qu'il appelle le Fils de Dieu *Parole* il me semble que c'est pour la simple raison qu'en premier lieu il est la sagesse et la volunté éternalles de Dieu; . . ." John Calvin, *Commentaires de Jean Calvin . . . tome deuxième, Évangile selon saint Jean*, ed. M. Réveillaud (Geneva: Labor et Fides, 1968), p. 12. According to those who are knowledgeable in the history of the French language, it is to none other than John Calvin that the credit goes for having coined the modern French word for wisdom, *la sagesse*.

¹² *Institutes* I, xiii. The English text used in this study is John Calvin, *Institutes of the Christian Religion*, ed. John T. McNeill, trans. Ford Lewis Battles, Library of Christian Classics, vols. 20 and 21 (Philadelphia: The Westminster Press, 1960). The Latin text of the *Institutes* used in this study is that found in Calvin, *Opera selecta*, vols. 3 and 4, Petrus Barth and Dora Scheuner, eds. (Munich: Chr. Kaiser, 1926–1959).

¹³ ". . . 'Word' means the everlasting Wisdom, residing with God, from which both all oracles and all prophecies go forth." *Institutes* I, xiii, 7. The original Latin text reads, "Certe quum Dei verbum nobis proponitur in Scriptura absurdissimum fuerit imaginari fluxam duntaxat et evanidam vocem, quae in aerem emissa prodeat extra ipsum Deum: cuiusmodi et oracula Patribus edita, et prophetiae omnes fuerunt: quum perpetua magis Sapientia indicetur apud Deum residens, unde et oracula et prophetiae omnes prodierunt." Calvin, *Opera selecta*, 3:117.

3: Calvin on Communion
The Wisdom Dimension

is that he draws this idea out of two very important passages of what today we recognize as wisdom literature—namely, the eighth chapter of Proverbs and the twenty-fourth chapter of Ecclesiasticus.

> . . . "Word" means the everlasting Wisdom, residing with God, from which both all oracles and all prophecies go forth. For, as Peter testifies, the ancient prophets spoke by the Spirit of Christ just as much as the apostles did [1 Peter 1:10–11; cf. 2 Peter 1:21], and all who thereafter ministered the heavenly doctrine. . . . And Moses clearly teaches this in the creation of the universe, setting forth this Word as intermediary. For why does he expressly tell us that God in his individual acts of creation spoke, Let this or that be done [Gen. 1] unless so that the unsearchable glory of God may shine forth in his image? . . . And indeed, sane and modest men do not find obscure Solomon's statement, where he introduces wisdom as having been begotten of God before time [Ecclus. 24:14, Vulgate], and presiding over the creation of things and all God's works [Prov. 8:22ff.]. . . . But John spoke most clearly of all when he declared that that Word, God from the beginning with God, was at the same time the cause of all things, together with God the Father [John 1:1–3]. For John at once attributes to the Word a solid and abiding essence, and ascribes something uniquely His own, and clearly shows how God, by speaking, was Creator of the universe. Therefore, inasmuch as all divinely uttered revelations are correctly designated by the term "word of God," so this substantial Word is properly placed at the highest level, as the wellspring of all oracles. Unchangeable, the Word abides everlastingly one and the same with God, and is God himself.[14]

Calvin may not have produced a commentary on Proverbs or on some of the other wisdom books, but there is no question he had considerable insight into their meaning; the fact that he related them to the logos theology of the Gospel of John is almost startling. Calvin anticipated some of the best scholarship of our day on the

---
[14] *Institutes* I, xiii, 7.

relationship of the wisdom tradition to the Gospel of John.

At this point the wisdom theology is primarily of interest to Calvin because it helps him understand the Johannine Christology. According to Calvin, understanding Christ as the Wisdom of God aids in understanding how the Father has a certain priority to the Son, but at the same time that there was never a time when the Father was without the Son, since there was never a time when God was without wisdom. This thought was hardly original to Calvin. The most obvious place for Calvin to have found this idea is Augustine's *De trinitate*.[15] It goes back to the logos theology of the early Fathers and beyond that to the wisdom theology of Israel. Calvin, as is becoming more and more clear, was a thorough student of the church Fathers.[16] He had a particular appreciation of the logos theology of the Greek Fathers who developed Old Testament wisdom theology in a Christian way. Calvin clearly understood what today we call the Wisdom Christology.

There is something more to be noted. The chief point that Calvin wants to make in his exposition of the prologue to the Gospel of John is that the Word of God is the source of life and light; it is a saving power: "The power of God unto salvation." It is the Word—the divine Wisdom—who was with God from the beginning, whom the Gospel of John proclaims to be incarnate in the flesh of Jesus. This Jesus, as Son of the Father, is Savior of the world. He is the divine Wisdom, as Calvin understands it, who empowers, enlightens, and enlivens those who receive him by faith. Christ is the divine Wisdom who imparts wisdom; because of his Word—the Word of grace and truth—believers are brought from darkness to light. From a study of Calvin's commentary on the

---

[15] Augustine, *De trinitate*, VI, 1. An English translation of this work can be found in Augustine, *On the Holy Trinity*, The Nicene and Post-Nicene Fathers, first series, vol. 3 (Grand Rapids, MI: Eerdmans, 1976), pp. 1–228.

[16] On Calvin's interest in patristic literature see Luchesius Smits, *Saint Augustine dans l'oeuvre de Jean Calvin*, 2 vols. (Assen: Van Gorcum, 1957); Jan Koopmans, *Das altkirchliche Dogma in der Reformation* (Munich, 1955); and Old, *Patristic Roots*.

prologue to the Gospel of John we gather that Calvin understands in that crucial passage the sapiential bent of the fourth Gospel which modern scholarship has begun to point out.

This sapiential approach to religion places a high value on teaching and preaching in the life of devotion. Wisdom theology is characterized by its emphasis on the Word. The Judaism in which Jesus was brought up gave a tremendous amount of time to the study of the sacred text, the scholarly exposition of the Scriptures, and the hearing of sermons which applied this scholarly work to the life of the community. The Wisdom School engendered a scholarly sort of piety; it practiced a very devout sort of scholarship. The same was true of the early Christian church. Studying Scripture, memorizing it, meditating on it, and interpreting it were regarded as the most sacred of tasks. They were among the most essential devotional disciplines. The study of Scripture was understood as worship in its most profound sense. This sapiential approach to religion, so characteristic of the biblical Wisdom School, obviously had a profound influence on Calvin. And, of course, Calvin was not the only sixteenth-century Reformer to have received this influence.

Calvin's sapiential approach to Christian faith and life is particularly clear in his commentary on the prologue to the Gospel of John when he says:

> For the knowledge of God is the door by which we enter into the enjoyment of all blessings. Since, therefore, God reveals Himself to us by Christ alone, it follows that we should seek all things from Christ. This doctrinal sequence should be carefully observed. Nothing seems more obvious than that we each take what God offers us according to the measure of our faith. But only a few realize that the vessel of faith and of the knowledge of God has to be brought to draw with.[17]

From this passage it should be clear how important the knowledge of the truth is to our salvation. This saving knowledge, received by

---
[17] Calvin, *Commentaries*, 4:25.

faith, is far from the same thing as being saved by education. For both the Wisdom School and for Calvin, the divine Wisdom is a rich and comprehensive wisdom. The divine Wisdom is filled with every blessing, with power and vitality, with all the holiness and righteousness for which we hunger and thirst.[18] According to the wisdom theology, as we find it in the Gospel of John and as we find it in Calvin, the imparting of the divine Wisdom—in all its power, all its illumination, and all its vitality—is of the essence of God's saving work in Christ.

2. The First Epistle of John

A second place where Calvin's appreciation of the wisdom theology is apparent is in his commentary on the beginning of the First Epistle of John.[19] Here we discover one of the marks of the wisdom theology, namely, its appreciation of the transcendent nature of the Word of God.[20] For Calvin the Word of God is ultimately Christ. The Word which believers have heard and believed is the same Word who is from the beginning the divine Wisdom. We find this very clearly in Calvin's comments.

> Furthermore, "Word" can be explained in two ways, either of Christ or of the teaching of the Gospel, by which salvation is brought to us. But since its substance is Christ and it contains nothing but that He who had been always with the Father was at last revealed to men, the first explanation seems to me more simple

---

[18] Calvin, *Commentaries*, 4:23.

[19] The first edition of the commentary on I John appeared in the volume *Commentarii in epistolas Canonicas* mentioned above in note 7 (p. 83). In the same year, 1551, a French edition of this commentary appeared separately in Geneva at the publishing house of Girard, *Commentaire sur l'epistre Canonique de S. Iean*. The translation quoted in this article is that of T. H. L. Parker in Calvin, *Commentaries*, vol. 5.

[20] While the older literature spoke at great length of wisdom as a hypostasis, e.g., Oliver Shaw Rankin, *Israel's Wisdom Literature* (Edinburgh: T. & T. Clark, 1936), pp. 222–264, recent literature is more cautious, e.g., Hans Conzelmann, *Der erste Brief an die Korinther* (Göttingen: Vandenhoeck & Ruprecht, 1969), pp. 53–64, and von Rad, *Wisdom in Israel*, pp. 144f.

and natural. Moreover, it is established more fully from his Gospel that the Wisdom dwelling in God is called the Word.[21]

In substance the Word is Christ—God of God, light of light, very God of very God. Just as he did in the prologue of the Gospel of John, Calvin finds here in the beginning of the First Epistle of John that the Word of God is the divine Wisdom. The Word of God is a transcendent reality. In fact, it is the fundamental transcendent reality of our salvation. If nothing else, this passage makes it clear that Calvin has understood the wisdom theology not only of the Johannine literature, but also of the logos theologians of the patristic age.

Another thing we notice here is the Word of God's capacity to enliven. Wisdom as it is understood in Scripture is obviously far removed from the sort of abstract intellectualism that many associate with an education in philosophy, the humanities, and the sciences. Wisdom is a way of life, but more than that, it is a power, a sacred vitality. This, too, is a mark of the wisdom theology. When the text speaks of "the Word of life," Calvin interprets this to mean the "vivifying Word."[22] This vivifying "Word of life" was with the Father, according to the text. Calvin comments:

> This is true, not only from the foundation of the world, but also from all eternity; for always He was God, the fountain of life. And the power and capability of giving life was in the power of His eternal Wisdom.[23]

As Calvin sees it, the eternal Wisdom is a creative wisdom, a redemptive wisdom, and even a sanctifying wisdom, and therefore it is a fountain of life. Wisdom is a power, a redemptive, transform-

---

[21] Calvin, *Commentaries*, 5:235.

[22] Calvin, *Commentaries*, 5:235.

[23] Calvin, *Commentaries*, 5:235.

ing power.²⁴ The ability of the Word to transform human life is the basis of its authority. It is, in fact, its glory. It is this saving Word, this Word of life, this divine Wisdom which brings us into fellowship with God and restores the bond of love between believers and God, and between believers one with another.²⁵

As Calvin notes in his preface, First John is an epistle that, above all, teaches about love. The whole book teaches and exhorts us to love God and each other. It is appropriate, therefore, that First John begins with such a strong statement of the divinity of the Word, because this Word establishes the bond of love and is therefore recognizable as the divine Wisdom—the revelation of the secret counsel of God's will.²⁶

3. THE EPISTLE OF JAMES

A very different aspect of the biblical wisdom theology is found in the Epistle of James.²⁷ Calvin's recognition of this is rather startling. James, like the book of Proverbs in the Old Testament, is a collection of wise sayings on good conduct. Neither of these books tells a story nor develops a systematic line of thought. Typical of the wisdom writers is this delight in collecting proverbs on living the godly life. As is well known, Luther had little appreciation for the moral concerns of James. It seemed to him to be bogged

---

[24] Mack's *Logos und Sophia*, p. 179f., gives us a helpful excursus on the doctrine of power found in Philo's Wisdom theology.

[25] Calvin, *Commentaries*, 5:237.

[26] Calvin, *Commentaries*, 4:7.

[27] Our understanding of the Epistle of James has changed considerably in the last few years. Recent research has shown its strongly Semitic character. The attempt, for example, of Martin Debelius to explain James from the popular philosophy of the Hellenistic world has not succeeded, Martin Debelius, *Der Brief des Jakobus*, ed. H. Greaven, 11th edition (Göttingen: Vandenhoeck & Ruprecht, 1964). It has even been claimed that it is the oldest book in the New Testament. Even if it is written in good *koine* Greek it was written by a Christian of strong Palestinian Jewish background. For the more recent discussion, see: Klaus Beyer, *Semitische Syntax in Neuen Testament*, SUNT I (Göttingen: Vandenhoeck & Ruprecht, 1962); Bo Reicke, *The Epistles of James, Peter, and Jude*, Anchor Bible (New York: Doubleday, 1964).

down in works righteousness. Calvin was of a different mind, as he relates in the introduction to his commentary on the epistle. Without mentioning Luther by name Calvin refers to the fact that in his day there were those of the opinion that James was not as clear on the subject of the grace of Christ as an apostle ought to be. Calvin's response to this was that there was no reason all the New Testament writers should have to go over the same ground.

> See how the writings of Solomon differ widely from the style of David. The former was concerned with the training of the outward man, and with handing down rules of social behaviour, while the latter is noted for his profound attention to the spiritual worship of God, peace of mind, God's loving-kindness, and the free promise of salvation. Such diversity does not make us praise one and condemn the other.[28]

What is surprising here is that Calvin, back in the sixteenth century, recognized a Solomonic theology, that is, a wisdom theology. It is a distinct style of theology.[29] While Calvin does not use the term "wisdom theology," the substance is certainly conveyed when he calls attention to the difference between the writings of Solomon and David. By saying that James is to the rest of the New Testament as the writings of Solomon were to the Old Testament, we discover that the sixteenth century Reformer recognized in substance what modern biblical scholarship has so beautifully identified. Again we see Calvin significantly anticipating more recent biblical scholarship.

The whole nature of Calvin's piety was positively disposed

---

[28] Calvin, *Commentaries*, 3:259.

[29] The Latin text of the introduction to Calvin's commentary on the Epistle of James needs to be quoted here. "Multum a stylo Davidis distant Solomonis scripta. Nam quum hic posterior formando externo homini, et tradendis politicae vitae praeceptis magis sit intentus: illum assidue de spiritali tum Dei cultu, tum conscientiae pace, Deique misericordia, et gravita salutis promissione concionari, notum est. Atqui non facit haec diversitas ut alterum probando, alterum damnemus." *Corpus Reformatorum*, 55: col. 381.

toward those beautiful passages in the Epistle of James which speak of the character of wisdom—for example, James 3:13-18:

> Who is wise and understanding among you? By his good life let him show his works in the meekness of wisdom. But if you have bitter jealousy and selfish ambition in your hearts, do not boast and be false to the truth. This wisdom is not such as comes down from above, but is earthly, unspiritual, devilish. For where jealousy and selfish ambition exist, there will be disorder and every vile practice. But the wisdom from above is first pure, then peaceable, gentle, open to reason, full of mercy and good fruits, without uncertainty or insincerity. And the harvest of righteousness is sown in peace by those who make peace.

Calvin's comments on this passage show a sympathy with this kind of piety. He appreciated wisdom that was calm and well composed, the kind of wisdom that was learned but without pretension.[30] Calvin admired simplicity, sincerity, and sobriety. The Epistle of James taught exactly the sort of piety that he so much admired. It was this kind of life which he hoped to live in Basel or Strasbourg when Farel challenged him to labor beside him in Geneva. Perhaps the pressure of the times made him admire the calm and peaceful nature of heavenly wisdom.

4. The Wisdom Psalms

Let us turn our attention now to Calvin's commentary on several of the wisdom psalms to get yet another impression of how sen-

---

[30] Calvin would no doubt have been of much the same mind as Ulrich Wilckens who in regard both to the Apostle Paul's understanding of wisdom and that found in the Epistle of James stresses the fact that the biblical writers distanced themselves from the wisdom philosophy of Hellenism. Biblical wisdom theology was not some sort of rationalism which spiritualized the biblical as well as the Greek religious traditions. That sort of wisdom was "earthly, unspiritual, and devilish," in spite of its claims. Wilckens, "SOPHIA", *Theologisches Wörterbuch zum Neuen Testament*, 7:519-523 and 526.

sitive Calvin was to the thought world of the wisdom writers.[31] In his commentary on the first psalm, Calvin says that the sum of this psalm's teaching is that "they are blessed who apply their hearts to the pursuit of heavenly wisdom."[32] We notice here that even without the prompting of modern scholarship Calvin uses the terminology of the Wisdom School. This psalm is one of the classic statements of the wisdom piety and Calvin gets the spirit of it easily enough.[33] One would hardly expect otherwise, for Calvin lived the same kind of scholarly piety exemplified by the scribes, teachers, and biblical scholars of the Wisdom School.[34] When the psalmist writes that "his delight is in the Law of the LORD in which he doth meditate day and night," Calvin immediately recognizes a kindred spirit. Though separated by the centuries, they practiced the same kind of bookish piety. Calvin's comments indicate not only an understanding of the kind of delight to which the psalm refers but that he has found the same kind of blessing as well. Calvin delighted in studying the Bible day and night. One senses a word of personal testimony when Calvin tells us about the fruit produced in the lives of those who constantly study the Scriptures. "The children of God constantly flourish, and are always watered

---

[31] On the wisdom psalms see the following: John Kenneth Kuntz, "The Canonical Wisdom Psalms of Ancient Israel, their Rhetorical, Thematic, and Formal Dimensions," *Essays in Honor of James Muilenberg*, ed. Jared T. Jackson and Martin Kessler (Pittsburg: The Pickwick Press, 1974); Sigmund Mowinckel, *The Psalms in Israel's Worship*, trans. D. R. Ap-Thomas, 2 vols. (New York and Nashville: Abingdon Press, 1962), 2:104–125; Roland E. Murphy, "A Consideration of the Classification 'Wisdom Psalms'," *Vetus Testamentum*, Sup. 9, pp. 156–167; Roland E. Murphy, *Seven Books of Wisdom* (Milwaukee: Bruce Publishing Co., 1960), pp. 28–52; von Rad, *Wisdom in Israel*, pp. 47f. See also Herman J. Selderhuis, *Calvin's Theology of the Psalms* (Grand Rapids, MI: Baker, 2007).

[32] Calvin, *Commentary on the Book of Psalms*, 1:1.

[33] For the various themes of wisdom theology found in this psalm, see: Hans-Joachim Kraus, *Psalmen*, 2 vols., Biblischer Kommentar altes Testament (Neukirchen Kreis Moers: Neukirchener Verlag, 1961), 1:1–10; and Artur Weiser, *The Psalms, A Commentary* (Philadelphia: The Westminster Press, 1962), pp. 102–103.

[34] On the scholarly piety of the Wisdom School, see von Rad's chapter, "Centers and Transmitters of the Didactic Traditions," *Wisdom in Israel*, pp. 15–23.

with the secret influences of divine grace."³⁵ Calvin found a life devoted to the service of the Word to be very satisfying, just as the *hakhamim* of Israel so many centuries before him.

Let us turn our attention now to another psalm, Psalm 19. Here is a passage of Scripture of which Calvin seems particularly fond, and it was also one of the most characteristic expressions of the Wisdom School. From the enthusiastic comments Calvin makes on this psalm we gather that it well expresses his own piety,³⁶ albeit it in a different way. The psalm begins with the familiar line, "The heavens are telling the glory of God." Calvin comments:

> As soon as we acknowledge God to be the supreme Architect, who has erected the beauteous fabric of the universe, our minds must necessarily be ravished with wonder at his infinite goodness, wisdom and power.³⁷

Calvin was deeply moved by both the beauty of creation and the wonder of providence. It may come as a surprise to some, but Calvin often speaks of the spiritual benefits of meditating on the glory of God in creation. Of the next verse, "Day unto day uttereth speech," Calvin says:³⁸

> Philosophers who have more penetration into those matters than others, understand how the stars are arranged in such beautiful order, that notwithstanding their immense number there is no confusion; . . . David, therefore having spoken of the heavens, does not here descend from them to other parts of the world; but, from an effect more sensible and nearer our apprehension, he confirms what we just now said, namely, that the glory of God not only shines, but resounds in the heavens.³⁹

---

[35] Calvin, *Commentary on the Book of Psalms*, 1:6.

[36] Calvin, *Commentary on the Book of Psalms*, 1:307f.

[37] Calvin, *Commentary on the Book of Psalms*, 1:309.

[38] Calvin, *Commentary on the Book of Psalms*, 1:310. It should be noted here that when Calvin uses the word "philosophers" he means natural philosophers or what today we would call natural scientists.

[39] Calvin, *Commentary on the Book of Psalms*, 1:310.

What is interesting here, and is quite typical of the wisdom theology of the Old Testament, is that the glory of God is not only seen but heard. It was even more typical of the logos theology of the New Testament. The wise men of Israel and the saints of the early Church were inspired by what we might call the intellectual beauty of creation. They perceived in it a certain divine law, a certain order or purpose. The creation is understandable and this understandable order is beautiful because it teaches about the order and purpose of life. The creation has a didactic structure which witnesses to the Creator and his righteousness. It has both an intellectual and a moral beauty. One has only to look at creation to feel its beauty. Its glory is that it speaks to us of divine things.

> The heavens are telling the glory of God;
>   and the firmament proclaims his handiwork.
> Day to day pours forth speech,
>   and night to night declares knowledge.
> There is no speech, nor are there words;
>   their voice is not heard;
> yet their voice goes out through all the earth,
>   and their words to the end of the world.
> (Psalm 19:1–4)

Glory is usually thought of as being seen, but in this instance it is being heard.[40] What the Psalmist says of the Creation he goes on to say of the Law. The Law of God is the glory of God heard rather than seen. The beauty of the heavens, the order of nature, according to Calvin, is "a visible language."

> David here metaphorically introduces the splendor and magnificence of the heavenly bodies, as preaching the glory of God . . . [It is] a visible language . . . which addresses itself to the sight; for it is to the eyes of men that the heavens speak, not to their ears, and thus David justly compares the beautiful order and

---

[40] On the relation of seeing and hearing to faith, see the perceptive study of Walter Ong, S. J., *The Presence of the Word, Some Prolegomena for Cultural and Religious History* (Minneapolis: University of Minnesota Press, 1981).

arrangement, by which the heavenly bodies are distinguished, to a writing.[41]

This is an astonishing statement.[42] It is immediately reminiscent of Augustine's famous phrase, so often used by the Reformers, which referred to the sacraments as the Word made visible. That Calvin spoke of both the sacraments and creation as the visible Word of God is certainly an indication of how fully Calvin followed the teaching of the wisdom theology. According to the biblical Wisdom School it is in hearing the Word that we are related to God. Seeing God's glory in creation is understood in terms of hearing the Word, as is made clear from this particular psalm. However, the psalm goes on to speak of the Law of the Lord and its perfection, and quite typically of the Wisdom School, we learn that the Word is an even more profound revelation of God's glory than the glories of nature. This, to be sure, is just what the Gospel of John is so carefully teaching. It is the Word, received by faith, which saves us. "No one has ever seen God" (John 1:18), but seeing God is not really necessary. "Blessed are those who have not seen and yet believe" (John 20:29). Since the wisdom we encounter in Christ is the fundamental structure of reality, seeing—although useful to the life of faith—is secondary to hearing.

---

[41] Calvin, *Commentary on the Book of Psalms*, 1:313.

[42] The Latin text is as follows: "Sed quum metaphorice coelestis machinae splendorem David hic instar doctoris de gloria Dei concionatem inducat, frigida esset ista loquutio, lineam coelorum exire in ultimos usque terrae fines. Adde, quod statim proximo membro verba ubique exandiri subiicit, quid autem verbis affine cum specie aedificii? Quod si vetamus scripturam, haec duo optime convenient, in coelis, tanquam volumine omnibus conspicuo, descriptam esse Dei gloriam, et simul inditam illis esse sonoram vocem quae ad omnium aures perveniat. Atque ita monemur, visualem (ut ita loquar) esse sermonem illum, cuius facta prius fuit mentio. Oculis enim, non auribus loquuntur coeli: ut merito eorum speciem tam distincte ordinatam scripturae comparet David." *Corpus Reformatorum*, 31: col. 196–197. We notice here that Calvin speaks of *visualem sermonum* rather than *visualem verbum*. As we have already noted, Calvin consistently follows the Latin translation of Erasmus which in translating the Greek *logos* in John 1:1 uses *sermonum* rather than *verbum*.

3: CALVIN ON COMMUNION
THE WISDOM DIMENSION

The Apostle Paul puts it this way: "So faith comes from what is heard" (Romans 10:17). A fundamental principle of the wisdom theology is that we relate to God primarily by means of the Word. This Calvin understands quite thoroughly, and, as we shall see, it seems to have significantly set the temper of his worship.

These passages should be sufficient to show that Calvin had an appreciation for biblical wisdom theology; in fact, he seems to have a surprising insight into the wisdom theology of biblical antiquity. Let us now look at several places where this wisdom theology seems to have influenced his understanding of the Lord's Supper.

B. CALVIN'S INTERPRETATION OF THE BREAD OF LIFE DISCOURSE

When Calvin speaks of sharing the Supper with Christ, covenantal concepts naturally come into play, most notably when Calvin is discussing the tenth and eleventh chapters of 1 Corinthians. But when he deals with passages about feeding on Christ, particularly those in the sixth chapter of the Gospel of John which present Christ as the bread of life, then we discover the influence of the Wisdom School. Calvin frequently emphasizes that in the Supper we enjoy both the presence and the benefits of Christ. It should be recognized that these are distinctly different lines of thought. They are two fundamental dimensions of Calvin's eucharistic theology. These two sections of Scripture—the one Pauline, the other Johannine—convey very different ideas about the Lord's Supper and these ideas use very different imagery. The sixth chapter of John is filled with the sapiential themes so typical of the wisdom writers of the Old Testament. Let us take a moment to look at how Calvin interpreted the sapiential themes of the Bread of Life Discourse.

1. FEASTING ON WISDOM

Eating to be enlightened is rather strange imagery to modern minds. It would be considered far-fetched if not for the fact that this point is so clearly made in the wisdom tradition. There are several prominent examples. Very important to the development of the ideas found in the sixth chapter of the Gospel of John is surely a passage in the book of Proverbs where Wisdom invites the faithful to a feast.[43]

> Wisdom has built her house,
> she has set up her seven pillars.
> She has slaughtered her beasts, she has mixed her wine,
> she has also set her table.
> She has sent out her maids to call
> from the highest places in the town,
> "Whoever is simple, let him turn in here!"
> To him who is without sense she says,
> "Come, eat of my bread
> and drink of the wine I have mixed.
> Leave simpleness, and live,
> and walk in the way of insight."
> (Proverbs 9:1–6)

The wisdom theology understood this banquet as a figure for the delight of sacred learning.[44] Wisdom, according to this passage, has built her house, set up her seven pillars, arranged her table and now invites all to come and eat of her bread and drink of her wine. The Bread of Life Discourse picks up on this figure to show

---

[43] That Proverbs 9:1–6 stands behind John 6 is recognized by a number of commentators. See Brown, *The Gospel According to John*, 1:273; Bruce K. Waltke, *The Book of Proverbs, Chapters 1–15* (Grand Rapids, MI: Eerdmans, 2004), p. 438; and C. H. Dodd, *The Interpretation of the Fourth Gospel* (Cambridge: At the University Press, 1958), p. 336.

[44] As yet I have not found any passage where Calvin treats Proverbs 9:1f. except perhaps a few passages where the Supper is referred to as a banquet. On the wisdom theology of Proverbs 9:1–6, see: Derek Kidner, *An Introduction To Wisdom Literature: The Wisdom Of Proverbs, Job & Ecclesiastes* (Downers Grove, IL: IVP, 1985); André Barucq, *Le livre des Proverbs* (Paris: Gabalda, 1964), pp. 97–100; Charles T. Fritsch, *The Book of Proverbs*, The Interpreter's Bible, volume IV (New York & Nashville: Abingdon Press, 1955), pp. 834–835; Berend Gemser, *Sprüche Solomons*, in *Handbuch zum alten Testament*, 2nd edition (Tübingen: J. C. B. Mohr (Paul Siebeck), 1963), pp. 48–49; and William McKane, *Proverbs, a New Approach* (Philadelphia: Westminster Press, 1975), pp. 360–365.

3: CALVIN ON COMMUNION
THE WISDOM DIMENSION

that Jesus is the Word of God upon whom the Christian feasts. All are invited to eat of this bread of life and thereby be taught by God, where Jesus is offering himself as the divine teaching to be received by faith. Besides this passage in Proverbs, we find much the same idea in Ecclesiasticus.[45]

> "Come to me, you who desire me,
>   and eat your fill of my produce.
> For the remembrance of me is sweeter than honey,
>   and my inheritance sweeter than the honeycomb.
> Those who eat me will hunger for more,
>   and those who drink me will thirst for more.
> Whoever obeys me will not be put to shame,
>   and those who work with my help will not sin."
> (Ecclesiasticus 24:19–22)

Several sayings of Jesus seem to play off this passage.[46] This imagery, obviously, was well understood in Jesus' day and it is not at all surprising that it should find its way into the Bread of Life Discourse.[47] A passage of Scripture that may have been more important for Calvin, however, would have been the fifty-fifth chapter of Isaiah.

> Ho, every one who thirsts, come to the waters;
>   and he who has no money, come, buy and eat!

---

[45] Ecclesiasticus, or, as it is more often called today, the Wisdom of Jesus Son of Sirach, is a book which the Reformers may not have regarded as canonical, but which they would have studied nevertheless. For Calvin's appreciation of the wisdom character of Ecclesiasticus, see his allusion to this chapter, *Institutes* I, xiii, 7. For a contemporary commentary on Ecclesiasticus, see Alexander A. DiLella and Patrick W. Spehan, *The Wisdom of Ben Sira*, The Anchor Bible Commentary, volume 39 (New York: Doubleday, 1987), particularly pp. 31–39 and 327–338. See also M. Gilbert, "L'Eloge de la Sagesse (siracide 24)," *Revue théologique de Louvin* V (1974): 326–348.

[46] Matthew 11:28, "Come unto me all ye that labor . . . "; John 4:14, "Whoever drinks of the water I will give will never thirst"; and then again, John 6:35, "I am the bread of life; he who comes to me shall not hunger." We notice that while the language and imagery of Jesus is similar, what Jesus says with it is quite different.

[47] Even in more conservative rabbinic circles it was common to speak of the Torah as bread. Cf. Dodd, *The Interpretation of the Fourth Gospel*, pp. 333–345.

> Come, buy wine and milk
>   without money and without price.
> Why do you spend your money for that which is not bread,
>   and your labor for that which does not satisfy?
> Hearken diligently to me, and eat what is good,
>   and delight yourselves in fatness . . .
> (Isaiah 55:1–3)

What Calvin noticed here is how eating and drinking are taken as a figure for receiving divine teaching and thereby entering into an everlasting covenant.[48] The idea that the Word of God should be understood as spiritual food and that the bread and wine were signs of that spiritual food is embedded in the biblical wisdom tradition.[49] This obviously makes sense to Calvin because near the beginning of his commentary on the Bread of Life Discourse he says that its simple meaning is "our souls are fed by the teaching of the Gospel."[50] If we find this imagery awkward we can hardly blame Calvin. As Isaac, he was only digging the wells that had been dug before him.

There have always been those who have interpreted the Bread of Life Discourse exclusively in terms of Christian teaching and preaching. They have insisted that the Discourse presents Jesus as the Word of God, the teacher of heavenly wisdom, on whom the Christian feeds by faith. According to them the sixth chapter

---

[48] In his commentary on Isaiah Calvin tells us the words water, wine, bread, and milk refer to all that is necessary for spiritual life. As our bodies are nourished by these ordinary foods so our souls are fed and supported by the teaching of the Gospel, the inner work of the Holy Spirit and all other gifts of Christ.

[49] While this passage is not from one of those books of the Bible which we usually regard as a wisdom book, it clearly shows the influence of the Wisdom School. Cf. Mack, *Logos und Sophia*, p. 97. As early as 1938 Joachim Begrich pointed out the influence of wisdom theology on Isaiah 55, *Studien zu Deuterojesaja*, reprint (Munich: Theologische Bücherei, 1963). That Isaiah 55 is an expression of the Wisdom School seems to be commonly accepted in more recent commentaries. See James Muilenburg, "The Book of Isaiah," Chapters 40–66, *Interpreters Bible*, vol. 5 (New York and Nashville: Abingdon Press, 1956), pp. 642–646; and Claus Westermann, *Isaiah 40–66, A Commentary* (Philadelphia: The Westminster Press, 1969), pp. 280–286.

[50] Calvin, *Commentaries*, 4:154.

of the Gospel of John has nothing to do with the Lord's Supper.[51] Calvin is not to be counted among them. As the Genevan Reformer understands it, John 6 does tell about feeding on the Word of God by faith, but

> At the same time, I confess there is nothing said here that is not figured and actually presented to believers in the Lord's Supper. Indeed we might say that Christ intended the holy Supper to be a seal of this discourse.[52]

If it is true that the Word of God is a sacred food and drink which nourishes unto eternal life, it is also true that this food is given both in the reading and preaching of Scripture and in the celebration of the Lord's Supper. In fact, Calvin goes even further. He says that the Supper is a sign and seal that Christ is the Bread of Life for us today, just as it was a sign for the multitude of Galileans whom Jesus fed with loaves and fishes so long ago. When Calvin speaks of the sacraments as signs and seals of the Word, he has in mind that they are signs in the same pregnant sense of John's Gospel.

2. THE MANNA

Even more important to the Bread of Life Discourse in the Gospel of John is the story of the feeding of the manna.[53] The rabbis of New Testament times had richly embroidered the story of the feeding of the children of Israel with manna in the wilderness. We already find this in the Old Testament itself where manna is called the grain of heaven and the bread of angels (Psalm 78:24–25). Already in Deuteronomy the manna is understood sacramentally as a sign of the Word of God delivered on Mt. Sinai. We are told

---

[51] For a list, see Brown, *The Gospel According to John*, 1:272.

[52] Calvin, *Commentaries*, 4:170.

[53] For further information, see: Peder Borgen, *Bread from Heaven: An Exegetical Study of the Concept of Manna in the Gospel of John and the Writings of Philo* (Leiden: Brill, 1965); Brevard Childs, *The Book of Exodus* (Philadelphia: Westminster Press, 1975), pp. 271–304; Ulrich W. Mauser, *Christ in the Wilderness*, SBT 39 (1963); Rudolf Meyer, "MANNA," *Theologisches Wörterbuch zum neuen Testament*, 4:466f.

that God fed Israel with manna to teach them that man does not live by bread alone but by everything that proceeds out of the mouth of the Lord (Deuteronomy 8:3). The idea was well understood in New Testament times; the manna was a sign that the Word of God is a spiritual food.

Philo of Alexandria, commenting on the story of the manna, says: "Of what food can he rightly say that it is rained from heaven, save of the heavenly wisdom which is sent from heaven above on souls which yearn for virtue by Him who sheds the gift of prudence in rich abundance."[54] Philo is concerned to make the point that the manna was a sign of *sophia*, the higher kind of wisdom, which unlike the philosophical education of the Greeks acquired through rigorous study is graciously bestowed by God. Philo believed in revelation. The Law of Moses came down from heaven as a gracious gift from God to enlighten the people of Israel with sacred wisdom.[55] Of this the manna was the divinely given sign. In his *Allegorical Interpretation*, Philo has yet another point to make on the subject of the manna: "The food of the soul is not earthly but heavenly. . . . The soul is fed not with things of the earth which decay, but with such words as God shall have poured like rain out of . . . 'heaven.'"[56] The Word of God is clearly a heavenly or spiritual food. A sapiential interpretation of the story of the manna comes quite easily for Philo. The teachings of Scripture are a spiritual food. The story of the manna was of special importance to the Wisdom School, particularly as the school began to develop in the direction of a logos theology. As we see from Philo, these ideas were connected with each other among

---

[54] Philo of Alexandria, *On the Change of Names*, as found in *The Works of Philo*, 10 vols., The Loeb Classical Library, Greek text with English trans. F. H. Colson and G. H. Whitaker (Cambridge, MA: Harvard University Press, 1971), 5: paragraphs 259–260.

[55] On Philo as a Wisdom theologian, see Mack, *Logos und Sophia*, pp. 110f.

[56] Philo of Alexandria, *Allegorical Interpretation*, as found in *The Works of Philo*, 1: paragraph 162.

Jewish thinkers at the same time Christians began to understand Jesus as the logos, the divine wisdom from above.

As one would expect, there was no single standard interpretation of the manna in New Testament times, either among the rabbis or the apostles. Modern commentators have pointed out the difference between John's interpretation of the manna and Paul's.[57] Calvin noticed the difference as well. He says that the Pauline interpretation compares the manna to the Lord's Supper as a type of spiritual food. The Johannine interpretation contrasts the manna which fed the bellies of the murmuring children of Israel with the spiritual food believers receive from Christ in the ministry of Word and sacrament.[58] Whether following the Pauline line or the Johannine, Calvin still interprets the Supper as spiritual food.

What should be abundantly clear at this point is that when Calvin says that the bread and wine of the Lord's Supper is spiritual food, he is following closely in the tradition of the Wisdom School.

3. THE FEAST OF PASSOVER

Another central theme of the Bread of Life Discourse is the Feast of Passover.[59] That Christ is the Lamb of God on whom believers feast is obviously an important teaching of the Gospel of John. This Calvin understands quite well. At the very beginning of the Gospel of John, Jesus is introduced as the Lamb of God. Noting this, Calvin suggests this to be an identification of Christ as the paschal lamb, whose sacrifice will atone for the sin of the world.[60] This theme—Christ as the paschal lamb—runs throughout the Gospel. The Johannine passion narrative has Jesus dying at the same time

---

[57] Childs, *The Book of Exodus*, p. 296.

[58] Calvin, *Commentaries*, 4:157 and 9:201f.

[59] On the history of interpretation of the Passover and particularly on its relation to the sixth chapter of John, see: Brown, *The Gospel According to John* 1:268–294; Childs, *The Book of Exodus*, pp. 178–214; and Bertil E. Gärtner, *John 6 and the Jewish Passover* (Lund: C. W. K. Gleerup, 1959).

[60] Calvin, *Commentaries*, 4:32.

when the Passover lambs were being sacrificed in the Temple. In fact the whole passion is understood in the imagery of Passover (John 13:1). At the beginning of the sixth chapter, when the story of the feeding of the multitude is recounted, John indicates that this event took place around the time of Passover. If we are to understand the sacrifice of Jesus in terms of Passover imagery, speaking of feeding on the Passover lamb comes quite naturally. Toward the end of his commentary on the Bread of Life Discourse, Calvin again recognizes the paschal theme: "For it would be of no use to us that the sacrifice was once offered, if we did not now feed upon that sacred feast."[61] This should make it clear that Calvin's understanding of the Lord's Supper had a place for feeding on Christ. At the Supper, as Calvin sees it, we feed on the paschal lamb whose sacrifice atoned for the sin of the world.

The Christian interpretation of the wisdom theology was at certain points quite radical. In the wisdom hymn of the eighth chapter of Proverbs we read that Wisdom is the first of God's creations; the prologue to the Gospel of John identifies Wisdom with God. "The Word was God . . . all things were made through him and without him was not anything made that was made" (John 1:1–3). The Christian interpretation of the Gospel of John understands Wisdom not as the first of God's creations but as the Creator. This is certainly a major reinterpretation of the wisdom theology on the part of the early church. Just as major is the Christian insistence that in the death of Christ the ultimate wisdom of God is revealed. The Apostle Paul's major passage on wisdom—namely, 1 Corinthians 1:18–2:9—contrasts the divine Wisdom and human wisdom.[62] It may be true, Paul says, that in the wisdom of this world the cross is folly but in the wisdom of God the preaching of the cross saves those who believe. At this point Paul makes his

---

[61] Calvin, *Commentaries*, 4:168.
[62] On the Apostle Paul's distinction between the wisdom of this world as exemplified by some of the Corinthians and the wisdom of God, see Wilckens, "SOPHIA", *Theologisches Wörterbuch zum neuen Testament*, 7:519–523.

strongest statement of Christian wisdom theology, for Christ is the power of God and the Wisdom of God.[63] For Paul, the cross is the ultimate revelation of the Wisdom of God. As he puts it a few verses later: "I have decided to know nothing among you except Jesus Christ and him crucified." This is another example of how radical was the Christian interpretation of the wisdom theology.

We find the same thing in the Gospel of John. It is put quite differently but it means the same thing. The Wisdom of God is revealed in the cross. "For God so loved the world that he gave his only begotten son . . ." Calvin's comment on this text is that to behold the cross in faith "is placing Christ before one's eyes and beholding in Him the heart of God poured out in love."[64] In other words, as Calvin understands this central Johannine passage, the cross reveals that the height and depth of the Wisdom of God is sacrificial love. The Word of God is the Lamb of God, the paschal lamb, who by his sacrifice takes away the sin of the world. The paschal themes alluded to in the story of the feeding of the multitude and the Bread of Life Discourse become patent in John 6:51–58, which insists: "The bread which I shall give for the life of the world is my flesh . . . He who eats my flesh and drinks my blood has eternal life, and I will raise him up at the last day." Calvin says that this "denotes that unique giving which was made on the cross when he [that is, Christ] offered Himself to the Father as a sacrifice."[65] That is, the Supper reveals that the wisdom which nourishes to eternal life is the cross. Here the Passover imagery is essential for an understanding of this passage.[66] The vicarious suffering of the Lamb of God is the sacred food which enables those who believe to pass from death to life. In Johannine theology, as in Pauline theology, the proclamation that the Lamb of God who

---

[63] Cf. Conzelmann, *Der erste Brief an die Korinther*, pp. 53–64. Conzelmann's exposition of Paul's Wisdom theology in this passage is particularly well balanced.

[64] Calvin, *Commentaries*, 4:74.

[65] Calvin, *Commentaries*, 4:168.

[66] Cf. Gärtner, *John 6 and the Jewish Passover*.

died for the sin of the world and is alive forevermore is the Gospel of salvation, the divine wisdom which unmasks the wisdom of this world. When this Word is received by faith it is a sacred food that nourishes unto eternal life. This is the great feast of the children of God—to feed upon the Lamb of God. It is a feast kept in faith and by faith, for it is faith that feeds upon the divine Word, the holy Wisdom from on high. The Lord's Supper is not only a symbol of this truth. It is, to use Calvin's words, "actually presented;" it is promised and sealed.[67] When the bread and wine of the sacrament is offered, Christ is truly offered for salvation. When we accept it, the promise is sealed. The sermon and the Supper both proclaim the Lord's death until Christ comes, and yet they are two distinct moments in our receiving God's gracious gift of salvation. In the sermon it is presented; in the Supper it is sealed.

To briefly sum up: Calvin understands the Bread of Life Discourse to mean that in the worship of the Church, both in the sermon and the Supper, we feast upon the divine Wisdom—the wisdom revealed in the cross.

C. Wisdom Concepts in Calvin's Teaching on the Supper

Feeding on Christ by hearing the Word and in sharing the Supper is central to the Bread of Life Discourse. This was, at least, the way Calvin interpreted it, and he was not the first or the last to understand it that way. The image of feeding on the divine Wisdom had been highly developed by the biblical wisdom literature, as we have shown. The question is how Calvin understands the Lord's Supper to be "spiritual food." This is surely one of the most characteristic features of Calvin's teaching on the Supper, and it is here where we find the most obvious influence of the biblical wisdom theology. First let us look at it as an empowering food, then as an enlightening food, and finally as an enlivening food.

---

[67] Calvin, *Commentaries*, 4:170.

3: Calvin on Communion
The Wisdom Dimension

1. The Supper Empowers

The first theme of Calvin's eucharistic theology which appears to be suggested by the wisdom theology is that feeding on Christ at the Supper empowers the Christian to live the Christian life. This empowering is the work of the Holy Spirit.[68] The Supper is spiritual nourishment that we might live in the Spirit. It is spiritual nourishment promised by the sign of bread and wine and realized by the Holy Spirit.[69] If this empowering is the work of the Holy Spirit, it must also be said that the Spirit works through faith. The wisdom theology so strong in the prologue to the Gospel of John reveals that to those who received Christ he gave power to become children of God. This empowering comes through believing the Gospel, both as it is preached and as it is offered to us in the sacraments. What the empowering does, as the prologue to the Gospel makes so clear, is enable believers to live the life of the children of God.

In a passage from the *Institutes*, Calvin makes the point very clear:

> For though he has taken his flesh away from us, and in the body has ascended into heaven, yet he sits at the right hand of the Father—that is, he reigns in the Father's power and majesty and glory. This Kingdom is neither bounded by location in space nor circum-

---

[68] The role of the Spirit in the Wisdom writers is discussed by Mack, *Logos und Sophia*, pp. 176f. See as well Hermann Kleinknecht, "PNEUMA," *Theologisches Wörterbuch zum neuen Testament*, 6:343–357; Werner Bieder, "PNEUMA in Sapientia," *Theologisches Wörterbuch zum neuen Testament*, 6:369–70; and Eduard Schweizer, "PNEUMA bei Johannes," *Theologisches Wörterbuch zum neuen Testament*, 6:436–443.

[69] The marrow of Calvin's doctrine of the Lord's Supper is his understanding of the work of the Holy Spirit. A particularly good statement of this is given by Wilhelm Niesel, *The Theology of Calvin*, Eng. trans. Harold Knight (Philadelphia: The Westminster Press, 1956), pp. 223–228. See further, Wilhelm Niesel, *Calvins Lehre vom Abendmahl* (Munich: Chr. Kaiser, 1930); François Wendel, *Calvin, the Origens and Development of his Religious Thought*, trans. Philip Mairet (New York and Evanston: Harper & Row, 1963), especially the chapter, "The Hidden Work of the Holy Spirit," pp. 233–290; and Werner Krusche, *Das Wirken des Heiligen Geistes nach Calvin* (Göttingen: Vandenhoeck und Ruprecht, 1957).

scribed by any limits. Thus Christ is not prevented from exerting his power wherever he pleases, in heaven and on earth. He shows his presence in power and strength, is always among his own people, and breathes his life upon them, and lives in them, sustaining them, strengthening, quickening, keeping them unharmed, as if he were present in the body. In short, he feeds his people with his own body, the communion of which he bestows upon them by the power of his Spirit. In this manner, the body and blood of Christ are shown to us in the Sacrament.[70]

This makes the point that the sort of local presence experienced by the disciples is transcended by another kind of presence experienced by believers after the ascension. This is an experience of the glorified Christ who dwells in us through the Holy Spirit. It is an experience of power that dwells within us. It is a sort of experience which is not limited to any space or location, but it is real and effective, nevertheless. In fact it is more real and effective because it is not merely beside us, but within us. It is not a presence simply to aid but a presence to transform, so that we are empowered to live as children of God.

At this point Calvin is obviously following the Johannine line of thought which understands the ascension of Jesus to be necessary that Christ might live within the hearts of his disciples: "He who believes in me will also do the works that I do; and greater works than these will he do, because I go to the Father" (John 14:12). The crucifixion, death, resurrection, ascension, and the pouring out of the Spirit were all necessary for our redemption. "Unless a grain of wheat falls into the ground and dies it remains alone; but if it dies it bears much fruit" (John 12:24). This fruit-bearing presence experienced by Christians after the ascension is not the same as the presence before the ascension, although to be sure it is grounded in that presence. Christ's presence with us after the ascension is, according

---

[70] *Institutes* IV, xvii, 18.

to the Gospel of John, experienced in the spiritual power of bearing fruit. It is in this way that Calvin understands the empowering.[71]

Another passage that should be pointed out is found in the *Commentary on First Corinthians*. In the course of Calvin's remarks on Paul's report of the Words of Institution, we find the following:

> But I myself maintain that it is only after we obtain Christ Himself, that we come to share in the benefits of Christ. And I further maintain that He is obtained, not just when we believe that He was sacrificed for us, but when He dwells in us, when He is one with us, when we are members of His flesh, when, in short, we become united in one life and substance (if I may say so) with Him. Besides, I am paying attention to the implication of the words, for Christ does not offer us only the benefit of His death and resurrection, but the self-same body in which He suffered and rose again. My conclusion is that the body of Christ is really (*realiter*), to use the usual word, i.e. truly (*vere*) given to us in the Supper, so that it may be health-giving food for our souls. I am adopting the usual terms, but I mean that our souls are fed by the substance of His body, so that we are truly (*vere*) made one with Him; or, what amounts to the same thing, that a life-giving power from the flesh of Christ (*vim ex Christi carne vivificam*) is poured into us through the medium of the Spirit, even although it is at a great distance from us, and is not mixed with us (*nec misceatur nobiscum*).[72]

Calvin speaks here of empowering in terms of the covenantal themes, so strong in the Apostle Paul's discussion of the Lord's Supper in the tenth and eleventh chapters of 1 Corinthians. For Calvin the covenantal union with the incarnate Christ, crucified and risen, is essential to the Christian. It would seem that while Calvin distinguishes between being united to Christ in the Supper and being nourished by the blessing of Christ displayed in the

---

[71] Cf. Calvin's commentary on John 14:8–14, in Calvin, *Commentaries*, 5:78–81.

[72] Calvin, *Commentaries*, 9:247.

Supper, he nevertheless recognizes that they cannot be separated. He makes it clear that the covenantal union is the basis of the empowering and we assume he meant that the empowering is the means of experiencing the presence.

The perplexing question in this passage is what Calvin means by the substance of Christ. We get the impression that Calvin is trying to accommodate himself to the theological terminology which had been used by medieval Scholasticism to insist that Christ is in substance present at the Supper. On the other hand, Calvin probably does not want to use the word "substance" as it was defined by Scholastic theology. Why, then, does he use the word when he and the other Reformers were usually careful to distance themselves from Scholastic theology? We can only guess. Perhaps he used the word because it conveyed that Christ was present in a special or unique sense. He was obviously not present in the usual sense. Scholastic theology understood this and taught that the substance of bread and wine were transformed into the body and blood of Christ, but the accidents of the bread and wine remained. However we understand this, it is clear that even for Scholastic theology Christ is present at the Supper only in a certain sense. Calvin had read enough theology to realize that different theologians have meant very different things by "the eucharistic presence" down through history. We might wish Calvin to be more explicit on the subject, but apparently what he meant was that Christ was present in his bestowing the power of God and the wisdom of God. This is the substance of Christ. "He is the power of God and the wisdom of God" (cf. 1 Cor. 1:24).

We still need to say something about what Calvin meant by a life-giving power being poured into us by the Spirit. It seems that what he means is no less than the changing of the heart—the central miracle of our redemption. This miracle comes about when the Spirit of Christ—the Holy Spirit, the Spirit of the crucified and risen Son of God—dwells within us. This happens when from the Son of God we become sons of God.

In Calvin's sermon for a communion service celebrated at the Feast of Ascension, we find these words:[73]

> It is, that since Jesus, having ascended on high, has dominion over everything, indeed, so that even the Angels are subject to Him, they and all creatures will serve us by that token. . . . It is necessary to join this glorious power with the knowledge that He is here with us. Not that it was here for a time, but that His power extends to us, as it is spread through heaven and through earth. . . . That is also how we are certain of His presence, and that by His Holy Spirit He will maintain us. (Otherwise what would happen? We could do nothing else but fail, for we are too frail to do anything else. On the contrary we see the devil who is armed with all kinds of ammunitions against us. It is, then, very needful that God give us strength by His Holy Spirit in order that we may be able to resist him.) That is how being far from Jesus Christ, with respect to His body, we are near Him with respect to His power. [74]

This is a significant idea. The presence of Christ is experienced in his sanctifying power. We feel his presence as we are transformed into his likeness, as we are made holy as he is holy. What is important here is that the power of God is to the end of holiness. The Wisdom School always sharpened its arrows so as to aim them at the living of a godly life. Wisdom was to the end of righteousness. This may seem moralistic today, but it was as characteristic of biblical wisdom theology as it was of Calvin's whole theological endeavor.[75]

---

[73] John Calvin, *Sermons on the Saving Work of Christ*, selected and trans. Leroy Nixon (Grand Rapids, MI: Baker Book House, 1980), pp. 206–207. Hereafter referred to as Calvin, *Sermons*.

[74] Calvin, *Sermons*, pp. 206–207.

[75] Calvin's great concern for holiness and the cultivation of the Christian life has attracted the attention of many scholars. Of particular interest for our study is: J. Todd Billings, *Calvin, Participation, and the Gift: The Activity of Believers in Union with Christ* (Oxford: Oxford University Press, 2007); Jean Boisset, *Sagesse et sainteté dans la pensée de Jean Calvin* (Paris: Presses universitaires de France, 1959); Albert

The charge is often made that Calvin's eucharistic theology is dynamistic, but it is not some philosophy of dynamism which is at work here. Rather, it is biblical wisdom theology, which understands Christ as both the power of God and the Wisdom of God (1 Cor. 1:24).

2. THE SUPPER ENLIGHTENS

Enlightenment for those who participate in the Lord's Supper is a frequent theme found in Calvin's writings on the sacrament.

> There, Word and sacraments confirm our faith when they set before our eyes the good will of our Heavenly Father toward us, by the knowledge of whom the whole firmness of our faith stands fast and increases in strength. The Spirit confirms it when, by engraving this confirmation in our minds, he makes it effective. Meanwhile, the Father of Lights [cf. James 1:17] cannot be hindered from illumining our minds.[76]

The Word being known to the eyes as well as to the ears is a persistent theme of the wisdom literature. The heavens declare the glory of God. That is, the heavens as seen, declare his glory. The commandment of the Lord is pure; enlightening the eyes is clearly a related thought. The Word enlightens by means of the eyes, and yet it is the Word—the Word of life, as the First Epistle of John tells us—which is known, be it through the sense of hearing, the sense of touch, or the sense of sight.[77] For John, just as for Paul, faith comes by hearing: "Blessed are those who have not seen and yet believe." To know God, for mortal beings, is to know his Word, and yet the

---

Goehler, *Calvins Lehre von der Heiligung* (Munich, 1934); Wilhelm Kolfhaus, *Christusgemeinschaft bei Johannes Calvin* (Neukirchen: Krs. Moer, 1939); John H. Leith, *Calvin's Doctrine of the Christian Life* (Louisville: Westminster John Knox, 1989), especially pp. 95f.; and Ronald S. Wallace, *Calvin's Doctrine of the Christian Life* (Edinburgh: Oliver and Boyd, 1959).

[76] *Institutes* IV, xiv, 10.

[77] On the priority of hearing over seeing in our innermost communion with others, and especially in our religious experience, see Ong, *The Presence of the Word*.

Word can be seen as well as heard. We can see the Word in the glory of the heavens; we can see the Word in the incarnate Christ, at least the Apostles did; and we can see the Word in the sacraments. As Calvin tells it, this is what Augustine was referring to when he spoke of the sacraments as the visible Word.

Of particular interest in this quotation is Calvin's allusion to the Epistle of James where God is called the "Father of Lights." Calvin understands this title as the wisdom writers understood it, that is, God—by his very nature—is one who enlightens, by both the gift of the Law and the Gospel. God is one who reveals himself. The Word is of his very essence; he is the "Father of Lights," that is, the God who enlightens. The Word of the Father is both the light of the world and the bread of life. Calvin even goes so far as to say that God cannot be hindered from illumining our minds. To have communion with God necessarily involves being enlightened.[78]

In the end, however, it is neither the sense of hearing nor the sense of sight that enlightens us; it is the work of the Holy Spirit which opens our minds and hearts to hear, or to see, the Word. It is the Holy Spirit who works faith in us so that what we hear and what we see is received by faith. When the Holy Spirit opens our ears and our eyes we feed upon Christ in both Word and sacrament so that we are nourished unto eternal life.

Calvin is most eloquent on this subject in his commentary on the Bread of Life Discourse. As he understands it, Christ is presented as the bread of life which the Father has given to us as food

---

[78] On the subject of illumination or enlightenment in the theology of Calvin, see Niesel, *The Theology of Calvin*, pp. 30–39. There were plenty of those in Calvin's day who pushed an illuministic understanding of Scripture and Calvin was careful to push for a full appreciation of the objective nature of God's self-revelation in Scripture. The Anabaptists particularly tended to be illuministic. On the other hand any kind of literalistic or mechanistic approach to revelation Calvin significantly transcended with his teaching on the inward illumination of the Holy Spirit. See further: Donald K. McKim, "Calvin's View of Scripture," *Readings in Calvin's Theology* (Grand Rapids, MI: Baker Book House, 1984), pp. 43–68; and Richard Muller, "The Foundation of Calvin's Theology: Scripture as Revealing God's Word," *The Duke Divinity School Review* 44 (1979).

for eternal life. As Israel fed on the manna, so the Church now feeds on Christ presented to us in both Word and sacrament. Primarily, the Discourse has Christ in mind as teacher. The bread the Father gives us to feed on is the Word. Commenting on the text, "They shall all be taught by God" (John 6:45), Calvin insists that this is a reference to the inward illumination of the Spirit.

> The only way in which the Church can be restored is by God undertaking the office of schoolmaster, and bringing believers to Himself. The way of teaching which the prophet speaks of consists not only in the outward word but also in the secret operation of the Holy Spirit. In short, this teaching of God is the inward illumination of the heart.[79]

The didactic nature of the Christian faith could hardly be put more strongly or more profoundly. The teaching received by those who learn from God is the saving Lordship of Christ. Those who are taught by God accept Christ. This is the enlightenment they receive. In fact at this point Calvin calls it wisdom.

> It is impossible that any of God's disciples shall not submit to Christ, and that those who reject Christ will not be taught by God, since the only wisdom that all the elect learn in the school of God is to come to Christ.[80]

This remark, almost parenthetical, makes abundantly clear that Calvin perceived the full implications of the Johannine interpretation of Old Testament wisdom literature. As a matter of course Calvin's approach to worship in general and to the ministry of Word and sacrament in particular is didactic, just as the piety of the Wisdom School was didactic. What needs to be sensed is that this didacticism is very, very profound. It is not arid learning; it is a hearty wisdom.

We must be careful to notice that when Calvin talks about enlightenment he has far more in mind than the absorbing of mere

---

[79] Calvin, *Commentaries*, 4:164.
[80] Calvin, *Commentaries*, 4:165.

information. He means the opening of our hearts to divine Wisdom, which is the work of the Holy Spirit.[81] By receiving Christ we acquire the divine Wisdom and Calvin has learned from the biblical wisdom tradition that this is what it means to feed on Christ.[82]

3. THE SUPPER ENLIVENS

The third theme suggested by the wisdom theology we find in Calvin's teaching on the Lord's Supper is that when we are at the Lord's Table we feed on Christ. That is, we are thereby enlivened by the sacred meal. Jesus Christ is the Bread of Life, who makes us spiritually alive.

For the wisdom theology the divine wisdom is a creative wisdom. In the beginning, God's creative Word was spoken and all things came thereby into existence.[83] As Psalm 33 puts it:

> By the word of the LORD the heavens were made,
> and all their host by the breath of his mouth.

---

[81] Calvin, *Commentaries*, 4:164.

[82] It is here that we should point out the evangelistic dimension of Calvin's eucharistic doctrine. See chapter 4, pp. 157–172, for a closer analysis. Calvin, particularly in his sermons for Holy Week, was accustomed to preach on the Passion Narrative from the Gospels in such a way that it had an evangelistic thrust. Calvin, leading up to Easter Communion, preached Christ as crucified for us and risen for us. This made the receiving of the bread and wine at Communion the accepting of Christ as Lord and Savior. It was in this way that the sacrament sealed the covenant. This idea was seminal for Reformed piety as it developed in the Scottish communion seasons. On this topic, see chapter 13 of this volume. See also John Willison, *A Sacramental Directory* (1716); *Five Sacramental Sermons* (1722); and *Sacramental Meditations* (1747), found in a collection of Willison's works edited by W. M. Hetherington (Glasgow, Edinburgh, and London: Blackie and Son, [1830]). The *Sacramental Meditations* has been reprinted under the title, John Willison, *A Sacramental Catechism*, ed. Don Kistler (Morgan, PA: Soli Deo Gloria Publications, 2000). The same evangelistic approach to the sacrament is found in the communion sermons of Gilbert Tennent, *The Espousals, or a Passionate Perswasive to a marriage with the Lamb of God* (New York: J. Peter Zenger, 1735).

[83] On Calvin's understanding of the creative nature of the Word, see my article, "John Calvin and the Prophetic Criticism of Worship" in *John Calvin and the Church, A Prism of Reform*, ed. Timothy George (Louisville: Westminster John Knox Press, 1990), pp. 234f.

The wisdom theology had meditated deeply on the fact that God created the world through his Word.[84] It found significance in the fact that God guided Israel by his Word as it was known in the Law and that it was also by his Word that he had created all things. The Word of creation was the same Word they heard in the Law—it was a Word of life. A profound appreciation for the creative nature of the Word is found through the whole of biblical Wisdom literature. This understanding of the Word helps to explain why the ancient Jews gave such an important place to the reading of the Law in worship.[85] The Law of the Lord was creative and therefore it was constantly read and preached. For Calvin the Word was far more than just words. Commenting on the text, "I am the living bread which came down from heaven" (John 6:51), he says,

> Since this secret power of bestowing life of which He is speaking might be referred to His divine essence, He now comes to the second step and tells them that this life resides in His flesh so that it may be drawn from it. It is a wonderful purpose of God that He has set life before us in that flesh, where before there had only been the material of death.[86]

---

[84] Calvin's commentary on Psalm 33:6 speaks of the Wisdom of God both in creation and in providence. At some length Calvin speaks of the vitality of the Word of God, the same Word who is incarnate in Jesus Christ. Quoting Isaiah 11:4, "And he shall smite the earth with the rod of his mouth and with the breath of his lips he shall slay the wicked," Calvin insists on the power of divine wisdom. Apparently for Calvin the Pauline phrase "the power of God and wisdom of God" refers to the same Word. The Word of truth is a powerful word. Calvin, *Commentary on the Book of Psalms*, 1:542f.

[85] On the importance of Scripture reading in the synagogue, see: David Hedegard, *Seder R. Amran Gaon* (Lund: A. B. Ph. Lindstedts Universitetsbokhandel, 1951), especially chapter VIII, "The Synagogue Service a Bible Service;" Jacob Mann and Isaiah Sonne, *The Bible as Read and Preached in the Old Synagogue*, 2 vols. (New York: KTAV Publishing House, 1971, and Cincinnati: Hebrew Union College, 1966); George Foot Moore, *Judaism in the First Centuries of the Christian Era*, 2 vols. (New York: Schocken Books, 1971), vol. 1, chapter 6 and vol. 2, chapter 3; and Eric Werner, *The Sacred Bridge, Liturgical Parallels in Synagogue and Early Church* (New York: Schocken Books, 1970), pp. 50–101.

[86] Calvin, *Commentaries*, 4:167.

The Gospel of John is careful to avoid the spiritualist tendencies of Greek philosophy. Calvin, as Luther, well understands the problem and is equally careful to avoid spiritualism.[87] Further on, commenting on this same text, Calvin says,

> For as the eternal Word of God is the fountain of life, so His Flesh is a channel to pour out to us the life which resides intrinsically, as they say, in His divinity. In this sense it is called life-giving, because it communicates to us a life that it borrows from elsewhere. This will not be at all obscure if we consider what is the reason for life, namely, righteousness. Although righteousness flows from God alone, we shall not have the full manifestation of it anywhere else than in Christ's flesh. For in His flesh was accomplished man's redemption; in it a sacrifice was offered to atone for sins, and an obedience yielded to God to reconcile Him to us; it was also filled with the sanctification of the Spirit; finally, having overcome death, it was received into the heavenly glory.[88]

Christian salvation is not a matter of liberation from the flesh, but rather the sanctification of the flesh. We were created flesh and blood, and by that same creative Word we were made good and in God's image. In that same flesh and blood we must now be made righteous. We must be made righteous as Christ is righteous. And it is from his righteousness, that is, the righteousness which he manifested in the flesh, that we become righteous. Here

---

[87] There were numerous attempts early in the Reformation to develop a spiritualist interpretation of the Lord's Supper. Andreas Bodenstein von Carlstadt, Luther's senior colleague at Wittenberg, developed a spiritualist interpretation of the Lord's Supper which Luther rejected uncompromisingly. See George Hunston Williams, *The Radical Reformation* (Philadelphia: Westminster Press, 1962), pp. 39–44. Caspar Schwenkfeld von Ossig developed a thoroughly spiritualistic interpretation of the Lord's Supper which he presented both to Luther and to the Strasbourg Reformers. Living in Strasbourg between 1529 and 1533 he had the effect of alienating Bucer, and the Rhenish Reformers generally, from a spiritualist interpretation of the sacraments. On Schwenkfeld's eucharistic teaching, see Williams, *The Radical Reformation*, pp. 106–117.

[88] Calvin, *Commentaries*, 4:167.

again we detect Calvin's Cyrillian Christology. Calvin, as Cyril, is determined to give full justice to the flesh of Christ. Christ in his full human nature is ascended and seated at the right hand of the Father.[89] Calvin's understanding of the Lord's Supper reflects his understanding of the person and work of Christ. It was only natural, then, that the Johannine interpretation of the wisdom tradition would show up in his understanding of the Lord's Supper. To feed on the Bread of Life is to be vivified or enlivened.

> First of all, we are taught from the Scriptures that Christ was from the beginning that life-giving Word of the Father [John 1:1], the spring and source of life, from which all things have always received their capacity to live. Therefore, John sometimes calls him "the Word of life" (1 John 1:1], sometimes writes that "in him was life" [John 1:4], meaning that he, flowing even into all creatures, instilled in them the power to breathe and live.[90]

Fallen humanity, hearing and believing the Gospel, comes to the Lord's Table to feed on the Bread of Life and in so doing returns to the source of life from which its creation came in the beginning.

Calvin understands Christ to be the Bread of Life, not only in terms of creation but in terms of the incarnation as well.[91] He finds in John 6 that Christ is the Bread of Life which came down from heaven and gives life to the world. He tells us in the *Institutes*:

> The same John afterward adds that life was manifested only when, having taken our flesh, the Son of God gave himself for our eyes to see and our hands to touch [1 John 1:2]. For even though he previously poured out his power upon the creatures, still, because man (estranged from God through sin and having lost participation in life) saw death threatening from every side, had to be received into communion of the Word in

---

[89] Cf. Willis, *Calvin's Catholic Christology*.

[90] *Institutes* IV, xvii, 8.

[91] On Calvin's doctrine of the incarnation, see Paul van Buren, *Christ in Our Place* (Edinburgh: Oliver and Boyd, 1957).

order to receive hope of immortality.... But when the source of life begins to abide in our flesh, he no longer lies hidden far from us, but shows us that we are to partake of him. But he also quickens our very flesh, in which he abides, that partaking of him we may be fed unto immortality.... By coming down he poured that power upon the flesh which he took in order that from it participation in life might flow unto us.[92]

The Christ we feed on at the Lord's Supper is the incarnate Christ. Calvin calls on Cyril of Alexandria to make the point that it is not only in the divinity of Christ but also in his humanity that fullness of life dwells.[93] Calvin recalls that according to the Gospel of John Christ's flesh is truly food and his blood is truly drink. It is because Christ has entered into our humanity—our flesh and blood, and made that flesh and blood spiritually alive—that we can enter into the blessed life. Christ's incarnation nourishes us unto eternal life:

> ... and by these foods believers are nourished unto eternal life. It is therefore a special comfort for the godly that they now find life in their own flesh. For thus not only do they reach it by an easy approach, but they have it spontaneously presented and laid out before them. Let them but open the bosom of their heart to embrace its presence, and they will obtain it.[94]

It is Christ's incarnation—that is, his incarnation in our flesh and blood—which enlivens us, or nourishes us, to eternal life. It is not so much that faith enlivens us, nor even that faith in the incarnation enlivens us, as it is that the incarnate Christ, whom we receive by faith, enlivens us. Christ always remains the Word of life. When we receive that Word we are enlivened. The sacrament is not just an auxiliary way of hearing the Word, it is not just seeing the Word instead of hearing it. It is that, to be sure, but beyond that,

---

[92] *Institutes* IV, xvii, 8.

[93] *Institutes* IV, xvii, 9. Calvin had a particular appreciation for Cyril of Alexandria.

[94] *Institutes* IV, xvii, 8.

it is the way in which we receive the Word and thereby the way in which the Word is sealed unto us. If Calvin makes a point that in the Supper we feed on the incarnate Christ and are thereby enlivened, so he also makes the point that in the Supper we feed on Christ crucified and risen and thereby pass from death to life.[95] From the Bread of Life Discourse Calvin had gotten the point that the flesh which is food indeed and the blood which is drink indeed is the sacrificed body and blood of the Lamb of God. In the *Institutes*, Calvin writes:

> . . . the sacraments send us to the cross of Christ, . . . For we do not eat Christ duly and unto salvation unless he is crucified, when in living experience we grasp the efficacy of his death . . . When, offering himself as a sacrifice, he bore our curse in himself to imbue us with his blessing; when by his death, he swallowed up and annihilated death [cf. 1 Pet. 3:22, Vulgate; 1 Cor. 15:54]; and when, in his resurrection, he raised up this corruptible flesh of ours, which he had put on, to glory and incorruption [cf. 1 Cor. 15:53–54].[96]

Feeding on Christ at the Supper, according to Calvin, is to be joined to the Lamb of God who was slain and lives forevermore.[97]

---

[95] Cf. Robert Paul, *The Atonement and the Sacraments* (Nashville: Abingdon, 1960).

[96] *Institutes* IV, xvii, 4.

[97] Note the Latin text: "Non ergo praecipuae sunt sacramenti partes, corpus Christi simpliciter et sine altiori consideratione nobis porrigere: sed magis promissionem illam qua carnem suam vere cibum testatur, et sanguinem suum potum, quibus in vitam aeternam pascimur, qua se panem vitae affirmat, de quo qui manducaverit vivet in aeternum: illam (inquam) promissionem obsignare et confirmare: et quo id efficiat, ad Christi crucem mittere, ubi ae promissio vere praestita et numeris omnibus impleta fuit. Neque enim Christo rite et salutariter vescimur nisi crucifixo, dum efficaciam mortis eius vivo sensu apprehendimus. Nam quod se panem vitae nuncupavit, non eam a sacramento sumpsit appellationem, ut quidam perverse interpretantur: sed quia talis a Patre datus nobis fuerat talemque sese praestitit, quum humanae nostrae mortalitatis particeps factus nos divinae suae immortalitatis consortes fecit: quum in sacrificium se offerens, maledictionem in se nostram sustulit, ut sua nos benedictione perfunderet:

In that historic event, which happened once and for all at a particular time and place, Christ performed the sacrifice that reconciles us to God.[98] It was a full, complete, and perfect sacrifice which needs no repetition or representation.[99]

Because the Reformers insisted on the uniqueness and the completely historical genuineness of the death and resurrection of Christ, the Supper became an important means of uniting believers to that event. If Christ's sacrifice were something to be repeated again and again in every age in every land, whenever and wherever Christians gathered, the whole idea of sealing would be unnecessary. Similarly, if the Supper were treated as a cultic myth to be constantly repeated one would seriously compromise its historical reality. It is upon this that the Epistle to the Hebrews so carefully insists: Christ was sacrificed once for all. Uniting us to this event, therefore, is the essential function of the sacrament. It is from that sacrifice—then and there—that we in our time and our place—here and now—are enlivened with eternal life. Christ's

---

quum morte sua mortem de glutivit et absorbuit: quum in sua resurrectione carnem hanc nostram corruptibilem, quam induerat, in gloriam et incorruptionem suscitavit." Calvin, *Opera selecta*, 5:345.

[98] The attempt of certain Reformed theologians such as Donald Baillie and Max Thurian to "recover" a doctrine of eucharistic sacrifice for the Reformed churches is contrary to the whole direction of Protestant theology be it Lutheran or Reformed. See Donald Baillie, *The Theology of the Sacraments* (New York: Charles Scribners and Sons, 1957); Max Thurian, *L'Eucharistie, mémorial du Seigneur, Sacrifice d'action de grâce et d'intercession* (Neuchâtel: Delachaux et Niestlé, 1959); and Pierre-Yves Emery, *Le sacrifice eucharistique selon le théologiens réformés français du XVIIe siècle* (Neuchâtel: Delachaux et Niestlé, 1959).

[99] It is here that the eucharistic theology of the Reformation departed most radically from that of medieval Scholasticism. It was the doctrine of the eucharistic sacrifice far more than the doctrine of the real presence to which the Reformers so vehemently objected. Both Luther and Calvin insisted on some kind of real presence. It was another matter with the doctrine of the eucharistic sacrifice. See Ulrich Beyer, *Abendmahl und Messe, Sinn und Recht der 80. Frage des Heidelberger Katechismus, Beiträge zur Geschichte und Lehre der Reformierten Kirche* (Neukirchen: Verlag des Erziehungsvereins, 1965); and Carl F. Wisloff, *The Gift of Communion: Luther's Controversy with Rome on Eucharistic Sacrifice*, trans. Joseph M. Shaw (Minneapolis: Augsburg Publishing House, 1964).

sacrifice saves us; the Supper joins us to that sacrifice. The Supper "shows forth" the sacrifice and the benefits of the sacrifice. In the Supper we experience restored communion with God and with each other, both of which flow from that sacrifice. The main purpose of the Supper is to seal upon our consciences the power of that sacrifice so that we live in its power. Living in its power, we witness to the glory of God before the world. Living in its power we give thanks to God and recount the story of God's mighty acts of salvation. This is how Calvin understands 1 Corinthians 11:26, "For as often as you eat this bread and drink the cup you proclaim the Lord's death."[100] At the Supper, therefore, it is upon the sacrificed Lamb, risen and reigning in heaven, that we feed. This is the paschal feast which nourishes us to make the passage from this world to the Father. It is at the Supper that "in living experience we grasp the efficacy" of the Gospel.

Biblical wisdom theology, as we find it in the Gospel of John, led Calvin to understand the Supper not only in covenantal terms—as communion with Christ in the bonds of the new covenant—but as feeding on Christ as well. The covenantal aspect is probably to be considered the basic understanding. We come to the Lord's Table to share a meal with Christ and are thereby united to him and each other in the new covenant. For Calvin though, there is another dimension. We come to the Lord's Table to feed on him who is the Bread of Life. It is in the sapiential terms of the biblical wisdom tradition that Calvin understood this. Those who feed on the bread and wine of the Lord's Table in true faith are nourished by the flesh and blood of Christ—our incarnate, crucified, risen, and ascended Lord. It is not a matter of symbolism. We are really nourished; we are empowered, enlightened, and enlivened. This nourishing is accomplished by the work of the Holy Spirit who produces faith in us so that we might chew and digest this spiritual nourishment in a spiritual way.

---

[100] Calvin, *Commentaries*, 9:250.

3: Calvin on Communion
The Wisdom Dimension

The wisdom theology understands our relation to God primarily in terms of the Word. It is not surprising therefore that one strongly influenced by the wisdom theology—whether in the first century, as the author of the Gospel of John; whether in the fourth century, as Augustine; or whether in the sixteenth century, as Calvin—would even think of the sacraments in terms of the Word. The sacraments are the Word made visible: they proclaim the Word; they confirm the Word; they seal the promises made in the Word. But even more, it is important to see that for the wisdom theology this Word, which is so basic to our relationship to God, is a life giving power. The Word enlightens us to the end that we are empowered to live the life of the Kingdom of God. The Word, for those who have been shaped by the wisdom theology, is never dissolved into merely words, intellectualism, or bookishness. The beauty of the wisdom theology is its appreciation of the surprising power of the Word to sanctify life. In the end, the wisdom theology does not stress the primacy of the Word in our relating to God, so much as it does the vitality of the Word.

4

CALVIN ON COMMUNION
The Pneumatic and Evangelistic Dimensions

The importance of the pneumatic dimension of Calvin's eucharistic theology has long been recognized. It did not receive full liturgical expression in Reformed churches, however, until the seventeenth century when the Puritans began to emphasize the invocation of the Holy Spirit in their celebrations of the Supper. Nevertheless, the theology was clearly there in Calvin and in the early Reformed churches generally.

Calvin's emphasis on the work of the Holy Spirit is said to have been influenced by Martin Bucer on one hand, and by the highly developed theology of the Holy Spirit and his role in the ministry of the sacraments developed in the Byzantine church on the other. Both these sources must be recognized, but the fact that the theology of the late Middle Ages gave an important place to the work of the Holy Spirit should also be mentioned.

The influence of the Byzantine church is a complicated subject. It came to Calvin by different routes. He would have been well aware of the importance of the discussion of the invocation of the Holy Spirit at the councils of Basel and Florence during the previous century. Calvin spent quite a bit of time in the rich libraries of Basel during his years as a wandering student, and it may have been in the libraries of Basel that he learned of the Byzantine perspective.

Let us now look at several significant passages in Calvin's works on the role of the Holy Spirit in the celebration of the Lord's Supper. In the *Institutes*, writing on the sacraments in general, Calvin tells that the purpose of the sacraments is to inspire, confirm, and nourish faith. For Calvin it is important, however, to realize that the sacraments do this ministerially. We must distinguish between the outward, public, and ministerial role of the sacraments and the more intimate and personal role of the Holy Spirit. From an inward standpoint, it is the Holy Spirit who sparks and inflames faith in our hearts:

> But the sacraments properly fulfill their office only when the Spirit, that inward teacher, comes to them, by whose power alone hearts are penetrated and affections moved and our souls opened for the sacraments to enter in. If the Spirit be lacking, the sacraments can accomplish nothing more in our minds than the splendor of the sun shining upon blind eyes, or a voice sounding in deaf ears. Therefore, I make such a division between Spirit and sacraments that the power to act rests with the former, and the ministry alone is left to the latter—a ministry empty and trifling, apart from the action of the Spirit, but charged with great effect when the Spirit works within and manifests his power.[1]

This was an important point for the Reformers to make since they believed that salvation was by faith in Christ, rather than by the sacramental system. The Reformers did not want to throw out the sacraments. They obviously had their place in the Christian life; Scripture is quite clear about this. By insisting that they were not magic and had no power in themselves, but rather had power in so far as God's Spirit used them to inspire and strengthen faith, the Reformers could show that they did truly belong to genuine Christianity. One of the major concerns of the Reformation was to show that salvation came through faith in Christ, following in the ways of Christ, and being joined to Christ in faith, hope, and love. Therefore, the Reformers very strongly objected to the idea that one is

---

[1] John Calvin, *Institutes of the Christian Religion*, ed. John T. McNeill, trans. Ford Lewis Battles, Library of Christian Classics, vols. 20 and 21 (Philadelphia: The Westminster Press, 1960) IV, xiv, 9.

4: Calvin on Communion
The Pneumatic and Evangelistic Dimensions

saved by participating in a series of ceremonies such as baptism, confirmation, penance, communion, and extreme unction.

Calvin develops this analogy between the work of the Holy Spirit and the ability of seeing and hearing still further. He tells us that just as the eyes can only see by the brightness of the sun and just as the ears can only hear by the sound of another human voice, so it is also true that this brightness can only be detected because the seer has been endowed with sharpness of vision, having the capability of being illumined. In the same way, the ears of the hearer would never be struck by any noise unless they were created and fitted for hearing. What the facility for sight does for our eyes and what the capacity of hearing does for our ears are both analogous to what the Holy Spirit does in our hearts that faith be conceived, sustained, nourished, and established in our hearts. What this means is, first, being blessed by the sacraments is primarily a matter of the objective act of blessing on God's part, namely God's redemptive work in Christ. Second, being blessed is a matter of subjective appropriation of that divine act of blessing. This subjective appropriation is a matter of the work of the Holy Spirit who gives us the ability to hear and see spiritually. In the final edition of the *Institutes*, Calvin adds this sentence:

> There is only this difference: that our ears and eyes have naturally received the faculty of hearing and seeing; but Christ does the same thing in our hearts by special grace beyond the measure of nature.[2]

Calvin is very much concerned to make clear that the subjective appropriation is a work of divine grace, every bit as much as the objective redemptive act of Christ is a work of divine grace. For Calvin the pneumatic dimension of the eucharist is the subjective dimension. It was a way of embracing the subjectivity of Nominalist pietism while avoiding its Pelagianism.

Further on in this same chapter is another passage on the

---
[2] *Institutes* IV, xiv, 9.

work of the Holy Spirit in the sacraments. Calvin discusses the sacraments having the same office as the Word of God, namely, to offer Christ and the treasures of heavenly grace he promises.[3] Calvin recounts that the treasures of grace, the gifts of the Holy Spirit, and all the blessings of the Christian life come to us by receiving Christ. To be united to Christ in covenantal fellowship is how we receive the gifts of grace. It is the faith relationship to Christ which brings everything else. Word and sacrament offer Christ and his blessings. Faith accepts the offer. As Calvin sees it, there is a danger in regarding this offer too objectively. Some of the church Fathers spoke much too objectively in this matter. They spoke of the sacraments conveying grace as a cup conveys wine. The sacraments do not contain grace. Unless the Holy Spirit opens our hearts they are like corked bottles; no amount of wine poured over them will avail. It will simply splash over onto the ground. The sacraments are of no benefit unless the Holy Spirit accompanies them:

> For he it is who opens our minds and hearts and makes us receptive to this testimony. In this also, varied and distinct graces of God brightly appear. For the sacraments (as we have suggested above) are for us the same thing from God, as messengers of glad tidings or guarantees of the ratification of covenants are from men. They do not bestow any grace of themselves, but announce and tell us, and (as they are guarantees and tokens) ratify among us, those things given us by divine bounty. The Holy Spirit (whom the sacraments do not bring indiscriminately to all men but whom the Lord exclusively bestows on his own people) is he who brings the graces of God with him, gives a place for the sacraments among us, and makes them bear fruit.[4]

Sacraments confer grace the same way preaching does; grace is not conferred simply because the sacrament is performed. A merely *opus operandi* approach to the sacraments is no more sufficient than

---
[3] *Institutes* IV, xiv, 17.

[4] *Institutes* IV, xiv, 17.

an *opus operandi* approach to preaching. Preaching conveys grace in so far as the Holy Spirit opens the ears of those listening, in so far as the Holy Spirit inclines the hearts of those to hear, so that what is preached is received. It is the same with the sacraments. If that were not the case and the sacraments conveyed grace willy-nilly, without any regard to the receptivity of the individual, then one would have a magical concept of the sacraments. For the Scholastic theologian, of course, the sacraments did not convey grace willy-nilly. They were simply effective if not obstructed by mortal sin. The sacraments conferred grace if the recipient maintained the disciplines of the Christian life. According to the Reformers, this explanation was both too Pelagian and too close to magic.

Calvin was aware that there would be many who found his approach too subjective. He hastens to assure therefore that God is present in the sacraments. He has, after all, instituted these very sacraments. He is there by "the very present power of the Holy Spirit."[5] What Calvin is concerned about is that the objectivity of the sacraments not be stressed to the point that they lose their fruitfulness because the faithful have not cultivated a sensitivity to the subjective dimension of the sacrament. Both Calvin's doctrine of the Lord's Supper and the eucharistic liturgy of the early Reformed church demanded a highly developed interiority. One was expected to approach the table well instructed and well prepared. We will notice this as we watch the eucharistic piety of the Reformed churches unfold. The ministers conducting the service did not do everything; the intellectual, imaginative, and emotional participation of the faithful was essential. The subjective aspect of worship was indeed emphasized by Calvin. Without religious affections, as Jonathan Edwards would later call them, there was no true worship. This is what Calvin has in mind when he says:

> We do not deny that God himself is present in his institution by the very-present power of his Spirit. Nev-

---
[5] *Institutes* IV, xiv, 17.

ertheless, that the administration of the sacraments which he has ordained may not be unfruitful and void, we declare that the inner grace of the Spirit, as distinct from the outward ministry, ought to be considered and pondered separately. God therefore truly executes whatever he promises and represents in signs; nor do the signs lack their own effect in proving their Author truthful and faithful. The only question here is whether God acts by his own intrinsic power (as they say) or resigns his office to outward symbols. But we contend that, whatever instruments he uses, these detract nothing from his original activity.[6]

The pneumatic dimension of Calvin's doctrine of the Lord's Supper insists on putting the heavy weight of the celebration not on the outward forms but on the inward communion between Christ and the faithful. Beyond the symbols, Christ is immediately present to those who believe his Word. He is present by the power of and in the person of the Holy Spirit, who is both the power of God and the bond of love between the Father and the Son. That is, believers are united to Christ in the same way the Son is united to the Father—by the bond of love who is the Holy Spirit.

The same theme is taken up later in the *Institutes*. In his chapter devoted to the Lord's Supper, Calvin writes:

> . . . the Lord bestows this benefit upon us through his Spirit so that we may be made one in body, spirit, and soul with him. The bond of this connection is therefore the Spirit of Christ, with whom we are joined in unity, and is like a channel through which all that Christ himself is and has is conveyed to us.[7]

Calvin was a most attentive student of Augustine throughout the whole course of his theological studies and was particularly aware of Augustine's highly developed doctrine of the Holy Spirit being the bond of love between the Father and the Son. This insight is

---

[6] *Institutes* IV, xiv, 17.

[7] *Institutes* IV, xvii, 12.

4: Calvin on Communion
The Pneumatic and Evangelistic Dimensions

surely at play in Calvin's understanding of union with Christ at the Lord's Supper. Even more important than Augustine's insight is the teaching of the Apostle Paul on the Holy Spirit's role in uniting us to Christ.

In Calvin's eyes, the eighth chapter of the Epistle to the Romans was one of the prime cuts in the feast of Holy Scripture. Being united to Christ by the bond of the Holy Spirit is one of the principle teachings of this exceedingly meaty passage:

> But you are not in the flesh, you are in the Spirit, if in fact the Spirit of God dwells in you. Any one who does not have the Spirit of Christ does not belong to him. But if Christ is in you, although your bodies are dead because of sin, your spirits are alive because of righteousness. If the Spirit of him who raised Jesus from the dead dwells in you, he who raised Christ Jesus from the dead will give life to your mortal bodies also through his Spirit which dwells in you. (Romans 8:9–11)

Calvin comments: "For Paul, in the eighth chapter of Romans, states that Christ dwells in us only through his Spirit. Yet he does not take away that communion of his flesh and blood which we are now discussing, but teaches that the Spirit alone causes us to possess Christ completely and have him dwelling in us."[8] A few paragraphs later, we read that a serious wrong is done to the Holy Spirit unless we believe that it is through his incomprehensible power that we come to partake of Christ's flesh and blood.[9] Calvin's teaching on the spiritual presence of Christ is unsatisfactory to many simply because they do not have Calvin's highly developed doctrine of the Holy Spirit. Calvin believed our participation in Christ is always through the Holy Spirit. Our union with Christ is spiritual and feeding on Christ is spiritual as well. Feeding on Christ must be *manducatio spiritualis*. Spiritual union with Christ is not merely an ephemeral union. Quite to the contrary, it is even

---
[8] *Institutes* IV, xvii, 12.
[9] *Institutes* IV, xvii, 33.

more real than a merely carnal union. Calvin puts it succinctly: "For us the manner is spiritual because the secret power of the Spirit is the bond of our union with Christ."[10]

In his *Short Treatise on the Lord's Supper* of 1541, Calvin gives another insight into the relation of the Holy Spirit to the Lord's Supper, even though the remark is specifically made about baptism. Calvin recalls the baptism of Jesus and the fact that the Holy Spirit descended on Jesus in the form of a dove. No one thought that the Holy Spirit was the dove, but because the Holy Spirit by his very essence is invisible, the dove was given as a sign that the invisible might be made visible. In the same way, at the Lord's Supper, the essence of what is happening is the work of the Holy Spirit and therefore cannot be seen. Since what happens at the Lord's Supper is essentially a work of the Holy Spirit, God has given us a visible sign of what the Spirit is doing, that is, feeding us with spiritual food. The most natural visible sign for this is the Lord's Supper—a meal of bread and wine. The nature of our participation in the sacraments is spiritual and, according to Calvin, this is made particularly evident by the sign of the descent of the dove at Christ's baptism.

In the *Consensus Tigurinus* is yet another facet of the relation of the Holy Spirit to the Lord's Supper.[11] In Article 15 we read that while the sacraments are called seals (see Rom. 4:11, 2 Cor. 1:22, and Eph. 1:13) and are said to nourish, confirm, and advance faith, it is more proper to say that the Holy Spirit is the seal, and the beginner and finisher of our faith.[12] What is specifically meant by the seal of the Spirit has been discussed frequently down through

---

[10] *Institutes* IV, xvii, 33.

[11] For a discussion of the *Consensus Tigurinus*, see Paul E. Rorem, *Calvin and Bullinger on the Lord's Supper* (Bramcote, England: Grove Books Limited, 1989).

[12] The most important passages of Scripture in regard to this are Romans 4:11, 2 Corinthians 1:22, Ephesians 1:13, and 4:30. It is not always clear in these passages whether the sealing is the objective experience of receiving the sacraments or the subjective experience to which the sacraments point. No doubt there is some extent to which both are indicated in the *Consensus Tigurinus*.

the centuries. This may be one of the places where Calvin weakened his position for the sake of peace with the pastors of Zurich.

Finally, it is in one of his sermons that we find some of Calvin's most profound thoughts on the subject of the pneumatic dimension of Calvin's eucharistic theology. His sermon for the Pentecost communion service in 1549 gives a good example of how he understood the work of the Holy Spirit in general, as well as how he related it to the Lord's Supper.[13] Calvin's sermons had a way of winning the hearts of his congregation, which is a surprising facet of his ministry. The last century looked at Calvin with several rather strange presuppositions. Because of this, the last thing we expect to find is an interest in experiential religion. However, when it comes to the doctrine of the Holy Spirit, Calvin's own interiority begins to show through. Further, this sermon reveals his theology as having a very clear place for personal religious experience. This is true whether Calvin is making a point of the role of the Holy Spirit in our reading, preaching, and hearing the Word of God, or whether he is speaking of his doctrine of prayer, or his doctrine of the ministry, or his doctrine of baptism and the Lord's Supper. It has often been pointed out that where we would expect Calvin to speak at great length on the Holy Spirit, namely at the beginning of Book IV of the *Institutes*, we find very little. On the other hand, when Calvin speaks of the church, the ministry, or the sacraments he has a great deal to say about the Holy Spirit. All this makes clear that Calvin's doctrine of the Holy Spirit is found in terms of experiential religion.

The sermon begins by speaking of the need for Christians to have the Word of God sealed in their heart.[14] We have already noted that "sealed" is a hot word for theologians who make a special study of worship. In this sermon it becomes clear that what Calvin understands by this sealing of our hearts is a personal

---

[13] John Calvin, *Sermons on the Saving Work of Christ*, Leroy Nixon, ed. and trans. (Grand Rapids, MI: Baker Book House, 1980), pp. 243–257.

[14] Calvin, *Sermons*, p. 243.

appropriation of Christ's redemptive work. The outward sign of the tongues of fire assured the infant church that its witness would catch fire and inflame the hearts of the people of God. On the day of Pentecost the hearts of the first disciples were warmed with an inward fire of devotion toward God. This was the work of the Holy Spirit. Calvin tells his congregation that they need the same experience of sealing: "We need, then, to be set on fire with the love of God."[15] Have the great authorities on Calvin of the last few generations ever read these lines?

Calvin goes on to speak of experiential religion in such a way that, to put it a bit anachronistically, he might have fallen under the influence of Jonathan Edwards:

> Let us learn, then, to note why God wished that His Holy Spirit appeared in tongues of fire. It was so that believers might know that they needed to be touched to the quick, even in such a manner that God change them and renew them. That, then, is what we have to bear in mind, in summary, to properly apply this account to our use.[16]

At this point Calvin seems almost evangelistic. As we shall see further on, Calvin was evangelistic; in fact, this was especially the case when he was preaching at the Lord's Table. What could be more evangelistic than this?

> Thus, then, let us take the side of our Lord Jesus Christ, if we wish to experience to our salvation the profit and the fulfilment of what is here narrated by St. Luke: namely, not only may God speak to our ears, and may His doctrine pierce our hearts, may we be inflamed, may we be remade and renewed, in such a way that the corruptions of this world may be put down, and, as we wish to be owned and acknowledged as His people, may we be able to claim in truth our God in the Name of our Lord Jesus Christ, to Whom

---

[15] Calvin, *Sermons*, p. 249.

[16] Calvin, *Sermons*, p. 250.

we are joined in order that He may unite us in perfection to God His Father.[17]

Calvin was indeed concerned with experiential religion. He was concerned with the outward formal ministry of preaching, public prayer, and the administration of the sacraments. He was, after all, not an academic theologian, but a practicing pastor of a rather difficult congregation. He knew from his own pastoral experience that a perfunctory performance of the ministry of Word, prayer, and sacraments accomplished very little in itself. It had to be sealed in the experience of the believer, and this was what Pentecost was all about. It was the inward work of the Holy Spirit which sealed these outward formal ministries. Anything less would be a mere *opus operandi* approach to worship. For Calvin the *opus operandi*, that is, the doing of the thing to be done, was of the greatest importance, but without the anointing of the Holy Spirit, it lacked life. The sermon concludes with these words:

> So then, today, . . . let us not doubt: that the Son of God displays the power of His Holy Spirit over us, that He makes us to experience His gifts, according to our need; and let us content ourselves with this inestimable benefit, . . . indeed, in this union which we have by means of the Gospel, and by means of Jesus Christ, Who is the Fountain of every benefit and of life and Who has in Himself all perfection of joy.[18]

With this the celebration of the Supper itself begins. Calvin believes it is of the greatest possible importance for the outward form of the celebration to push for a breakthrough to the inward reality. He was confident that Christ was present at that sacred moment to those who received the sacrament in faith. God's faithfulness could be counted on. Calvin makes clear that the congregation before him—like the congregation at Pentecost—would be

---
[17] Calvin, *Sermons*, p. 254.
[18] Calvin, *Sermons*, p. 257.

anointed with all the blessings of redemption and gifts of the Holy Spirit they would need to carry out the service God was calling them to perform. Christ is a fountain of blessings and it is God's will that these blessings be richly poured out upon his people.

One might call Calvin a theologian of the "third article," a term used by Jean-Jacques von Allmen. It is on the third article of the Creed—the faith in the Holy Spirit—that Calvin had some of his most important insights. He carefully worked out his doctrine of the Holy Spirit in terms of his doctrine of the church, the ministry, and the service of Word, prayer, and sacraments.

THE EVANGELISTIC DIMENSION[19]

Calvin's celebration of the Lord's Supper had a very distinct evangelistic dimension. In other words, it was at the Lord's Supper, and the services in the preparation for the Lord's Supper, that the evangelistic appeal was made.

Some may prefer to speak of the *kerygmatic* dimension of the sacrament because, for them, the word "evangelism" has been hopelessly compromised by revivalism. Whatever word we choose, it must do justice to the text: "for as often as you eat this bread and drink this cup you proclaim the Lord's death until he comes." Call it proclamation or call it evangelism; it amounts to the same thing.

The locus of evangelistic preaching was the celebration of the Eucharist. There was certainly nothing original about this. When we study the preaching of the Patristic Age we discover that evangelistic preaching often took place in preparation for Easter and the baptism of new converts on Easter Sunday morning. In the late Middle Ages the mendicant orders often organized their evangelistic campaigns around Easter communion.

---

[19] For a paper related to the same subject see Hughes Oliphant Old, "Calvin as Evangelist: A Study of the Reformer's Sermons in Preparation for the Christian Celebration of Passover," *Calvin Studies VII*, ed. John H. Leith (Davidson, NC: Calvin Colloquium, 1994).

4: Calvin on Communion
The Pneumatic and Evangelistic Dimensions

In fact, the city of Geneva had for several generations been accustomed to having an annual series of revival sermons the week before Easter. This had been conducted by the Franciscans at Rive, the strongest monastic community at Geneva. This community belonged to the Spiritual Franciscans who were especially influenced by Bernardino da Siena, whose preaching of revival seasons were among the most serious and most devout attempts at true evangelism attempted in the late Middle Ages.[20] There was something very natural about this. At Easter, Pentecost, and Christmas the central verities of the faith are proclaimed. To do this truly, an evangelistic dimension must, of necessity, be included. This evangelistic dimension of Calvin's doctrine of the Supper is noticeable more in the actual liturgical documents themselves than in the doctrinal discussion. And for some of us, this makes them even more significant.

Those who study Calvin's eucharistic theology devote most of their attention to the *Institutes* and after that they study the Commentaries. The controversial works have to be gone over by a careful student, but Calvin is not at his best in controversy. His *Short Treatise on the Lord's Supper*, the most irenic of his writings on the subject, is his best work, and this has been recognized by many. What is surprising is that so few scholars have focused their attention on the actual liturgical texts, the prayers, the psalms, and the sermons which Calvin used in the celebration of the Lord's Supper. In speaking about the evangelistic dimension of Calvin's understanding of the Supper we will have to focus on the liturgical texts themselves, particularly the sermons. When we have done this we will discover the basic insights which have shaped the eucharistic faith and practice of the Reformed Church ever since.

---

[20] See my study of Bernardino's evangelistic preaching: Hughes Oliphant Old, *The Reading and Preaching of the Scriptures in the Worship of the Christian Church*, volume 3, *The Medieval Church* (Grand Rapids, MI: Eerdmans, 1999), pp. 547–564.

A. Sermons

There are several dozen sermons preached by Calvin either at Communion services or in the days preceding or following Communion which have come down to us. The various Reformed psalters and directories of worship in Calvin's day usually made the point that when Communion was celebrated the preacher should take this into account and in his preaching prepare the congregation to receive the sacrament worthily. This seems to have been particularly cultivated in Strasbourg. The eucharistic sermon needed to present the covenant promises that were sealed in the covenant meal; it needed to offer Christ so that the faithful might receive him and pledge themselves to him in the covenant vows. It is not at all surprising therefore that eucharistic preaching began to take on a special character. This happened slowly as the Reformed eucharistic piety began to emerge, but its appearance is unmistakable already in Calvin's pulpit. This is obvious in several of Calvin's eucharistic sermon series.

The most obvious place we find this new approach to eucharistic preaching is in a series of sermons published in 1558, that is, at the height of Calvin's ministry in Geneva.[21] This series preaches through the passion narrative from the Gospel of Matthew, starting the Sunday morning before Easter, continuing Sunday at Vespers, then each morning through Holy Week until Easter Sunday morning. This made nine sermons. The series comes to a climax with an exposition of the story of the resurrection and concludes with an invitation for the faithful to participate in the sacrament. Reading through these sermons, it is clear that there is a pastoral integrity to the whole series. Calvin has obviously set aside his usual preaching schedule in order to devote the pulpit to preparing the congregation for Communion on Easter Sunday.

---

[21] This edition of Calvin's sermons was published to make the point that Calvin did preach on the fundamental events of evangelical history. See Calvin, *Sermons*.

The first sermon of this series reminds the congregation that the following Lord's Day, that is, Easter Sunday, the Lord's Supper is to be celebrated and that to this Supper Christ invites them to himself that they might participate in his passion and in the salvation which flows from it.[22] The series of sermons as a whole is an invitation to receive Christ:

> For we see that our Lord Jesus calls us to it to be partakers of His death and passion that we should enjoy the benefit He acquired for us and by this means we should be fully assured that God declares that we are His children and that we can claim him openly as our Father.[23]

The same theme is picked up at the end of the series when Calvin concludes his sermon for Easter Sunday:

> Now, since our Lord Jesus condescends to acknowledge us as His brothers so that we may have access to God, let us seek Him, and come to Him with full confidence, being so cordially invited.[24]

For Calvin, these sermons are an invitation to enter the Kingdom. "The gate of paradise has been opened to us, so that we may boldly approach our God."[25] Already Calvin is beginning to think of these sermons as preparatory sermons. Here we easily recognize the progenitor of the Scottish communion season with its preparatory services.

As the series develops, Calvin goes through the story of Christ's journey to the cross, giving particular attention to those who participated in the story. He treats the disciples who fell asleep in the garden, Pilate, the cynical politician, the corrupt priests, the converted thief, and the faithful women. Calvin knew that he had every one of them in his congregation. For each of

---

[22] Calvin, *Sermons*, pp. 51–65; *Corpus Reformatorum*, 46: col. 845f.

[23] Calvin, *Sermons*, p. 65, *Corpus Reformatorum*, 46: col. 846.

[24] Calvin, *Sermons*, p. 195.

[25] Calvin, *Sermons*, p. 196.

them Calvin pointed the way to salvation. The saving work of Christ is sufficient for the salvation of every kind of sinner. Calvin puts particular emphasis on the vicarious nature of Christ's sacrifice. Christ died for our sins and rose for our salvation. He did for us what we cannot do for ourselves, but the atonement which he vicariously accomplished we can receive by faith. It is by faith that we participate in that atonement and therefore our preacher offers his congregation their savior that he might be received by faith.

This is one sense, at least, in which for Calvin Christ is present at the Lord's Supper. Christ is present in that he is displayed as Savior; he is present in that he is offered to be received by faith. He is presented as having suffered and risen for our sake. He is presented as the ascended and glorified Lord and, for those who receive that presentation, Christ is indeed present. At the Supper, he is to be encountered as Lord and Savior. It is for this reason that the story of Christ's obedient suffering unto death and his victorious resurrection unto life is recounted in such detail. It happened for us. When we hear this story, faith is kindled in our hearts and we are assured that God loves us to the point of offering his uniquely beloved Son. Again Calvin makes this clear at the beginning of the series. The passion story is recounted to assure us of God's sacrificial love toward us.[26] When we receive Christ at the Lord's Table he is redemptively present. We are united to him by the bonds of the new covenant. It is this which is expressed by sharing a meal with him.

One notices this series of sermons draws out the meaning of the Lord's Supper by explaining the typology of the Passover. Not only do we eat with the risen and ascended Christ in the covenant meal, but we eat the Passover Lamb.

> And that is also why St. Paul says that our Paschal Lamb has been crucified and sacrificed, so nothing

---

[26] *Corpus Reformation*, 42: col. 833.

4: Calvin on Communion
The Pneumatic and Evangelistic Dimensions

more remains but that we keep the feast and that we take part in the sacrifice.[27]

Christ is present as Passover Lamb in that his sacrificed flesh and blood, although in heaven at the right hand of the Father, nourish us here and now. It is not something that takes place merely in our imagination, as Calvin makes clear. What we see in the signs truly takes place in the lives of those who receive the signs in faith. God is faithful in his promises and the broken bread and poured out wine are divinely given signs which seal the promises of God. The body and blood of Christ which we receive here in this life nourish us unto eternal life. The transcendent is immanent! That is the miracle of the Lord's Supper. The Lamb who was slain and lives ever more is to be tasted here and now. The invitation to the Lord's Supper is an invitation to the transcendent Passover Feast, the Wedding Feast of the Lamb.

There is another series of sermons on the passion narrative in the Gospel of Matthew which was never published but has been nevertheless preserved in manuscript form in the library of Geneva.

One sermon for Christmas communion has been published.[28] The title of the sermon indicates that it was preached on Christmas Day and that the Lord's Supper was celebrated. Several of the Reformers were opposed to a celebration of the birth of Christ on the 25th of December because, even in those days, historians were beginning to discover the pagan origins of the feast. Christmas Day, therefore, was not always observed in Geneva. At one point during Calvin's ministry in Geneva the practice seems to have been to celebrate Christmas on the Lord's Day nearest December 25th. At this point in my research it is not clear to me what Calvin really thought on the subject. This sermon could have been preached on a Christmas that fell on the Lord's Day. It may be, on the other hand, that by the time this sermon was pub-

---

[27] Calvin, *Sermons*, pp. 195–96.
[28] See Calvin, *Sermons*, pp. 35–50.

lished Calvin had changed his mind on the subject of observing Christmas or had simply acquiesced to the practice of the other Swiss churches such as Bern, Basel, and Zurich. The sermon is based on the nativity narrative in Luke. It is in fact a fine sermon. Focusing on the song of the angels, "Glory to God in the highest, peace on earth, good will toward men," Calvin invites Christians to enter into the heavenly joy of the angels and the peace of God which passes all understanding. Calvin makes the point that the true song of the Christian is to live a life in accord with our praises. The reason that we come to the Lord's Table is to praise God and to be assured of God's love. This assurance is the basis of praise; it gives us both peace and joy. The sermon is an invitation to come to Christ. Calvin's purpose is to invite the Christians of Geneva to come to the Lord's Table on Christmas Day that they might experience the reality of Christ with us, but, even more, Christ *within* us.

Calvin's highly developed Christology is particularly evident in this sermon. His doctrine of the incarnation is unfolded in several different directions. Truly the incarnation is a mystery and it is the whole of this mystery that we experience when we participate in the Supper. Toward the end of the sermon Calvin turns to the subject of how we are to experience the incarnation. Christ is not only incarnate in human flesh so that he is God with us, but when we receive him as Lord, that which is true *generally* becomes true *personally*. Christ comes to dwell within each individual Christian.

> Since this is so, may we not doubt when Jesus Christ invites us to this table, although we perceive only bread and wine, that He really dwells in us, and that we are so joined to Him there is nothing of Himself that He is not willing to communicate to us. May we recognize, I say, that in order that we know how to profit from this Sacrament which has been established for us from Him. However and whenever we receive it, may we know assuredly that God might have delivered us from the depth of condemnation in which we were by another means if He had so willed. But He willed

4: Calvin on Communion
The Pneumatic and Evangelistic Dimensions

> to give us more assurance of the love which He bears toward us when we have Jesus Christ for a Guarantee, so that we seek all our good in Him. May we know that we cannot fully appreciate what this is, until He be given, as it were, in the midst of us and he be so approached by us that by means of Him we are led into the Kingdom of heaven.[29]

The invitation to receive Christ by participation in the Supper is quite obviously evangelistic. The final words of the sermon are, "May our true joy be to serve Him in all fear and humility, and to give ourselves entirely to His obedience."[30] The evangelistic appeal is presented in terms quite appropriate to Christmas. It is presented in terms of "God with us," just as we read in the nativity narratives of the Gospels. The theme of "God with us" is unfolded very personally in the Johannine terms of God within us and we in him. It is to this relationship that we are invited. It is a love relationship. The Supper assures us of God's redemptive love toward us in Christ and invites our love toward him.

Though we know of only one Christmas sermon, we have abundant evidence that Calvin regularly preached sermons for Ascension and Pentecost. What has apparently been preserved is a series of sermons on the first two chapters of the Acts of the Apostles which was begun with the celebration of communion on Ascension Day. One gets the impression that the series of sermons is only partially preserved by the editor of a collection of sermons published in 1557. The sermons probably fit on the calendar something like this:

Ascension Day (Communion)	Acts 1:1–4
Friday after	Acts 1:4–5
Saturday after	Acts 1:6–8

---

[29] Calvin, *Sermons*, p. 49.

[30] Calvin, *Sermons*, p. 50.

Sunday after Ascension	Acts 1:9–11
Monday	There may have originally been six sermons on verses 12–26 preached during this week. These sermons, if they were preached, were not published in this collection.
Tuesday	
Wednesday	
Thursday	
Friday	
Saturday	
Pentecost Sunday (Communion)	Acts 2:1–4

There is a gap in this series as we have reconstructed it. It occurs in the week following the Sunday after Ascension. Two different explanations suggest themselves. The first is that Calvin preached on Acts 1:12–26 during that week, but since those sermons were not on subjects appropriate to the feast days, the editor of the collection of sermons left them out of the series. The second explanation is that Calvin normally preached on weekdays only every other week. If that system was followed consistently and Calvin had preached the daily morning sermons during Holy Week he would have preached the week in which Ascension Day fell but not the week preceding Pentecost. During the weeks he did not preach, another preacher filled the pulpit. We do not know who might have been charged with preaching the daily morning sermons at Saint Pierre the week before Pentecost, but it would be quite consistent with the way things were done in those days that another preacher would have preached a short series on another passage of Scripture appropriate to the week before Pentecost. The passage which immediately suggests itself is the fourteenth chapter of the Gospel of John in which Jesus promises the disciples to send the Holy Spirit as the Paraclete. Certain chapters of the Epistle to the Hebrews might have been thought equally appropriate, as would Psalm 110.

The more one studies the material, the more plausible it

4: CALVIN ON COMMUNION
THE PNEUMATIC AND EVANGELISTIC DIMENSIONS

would appear that toward the end of Calvin's ministry in Geneva, the traditional Reformed communion seasons were beginning to appear. The most obvious was the season around Easter, but the season of Ascension and Pentecost was also beginning to develop.

Let us look for a moment at the content of the Ascension-Pentecost sermons. What do they tell us about Calvin's understanding of the Lord's Supper and how it is to be celebrated? The first thing we notice is of no surprise to any Calvinist theologian. Christ's ascension was of the greatest possible significance to Calvin's eucharistic theology. The ascension teaches us that the bodily presence of Christ is, since the ascension, at the right hand of the Father. For the Christian still on earth, Christ's presence is a spiritual reality to be experienced by faith. It is an experience mediated by the Holy Spirit. By faith we lift up our hearts to the risen and ascended Christ enthroned in glory.

> But how shall we come to seek Him in the Supper? . . . We must, then, seek Him on high, and knowing that he is in heaven let us not doubt at all however that He is with us by His grace, so that just as we see and touch the symbols, likewise Jesus Christ truly accomplishes in us what the symbols signify to us: namely, that he dwells in our souls. . . . He wishes to make us sharers of this life eternal. . . . Our affections must ascend to heaven, or otherwise we would not be at all united to Jesus Christ.[31]

For Calvin the feasts of Ascension and Pentecost were especially significant times for the celebration of communion. The two are so closely linked to Calvin's deepest insights into the nature of the sacrament.

Also of particular interest, we find here the beginnings of the thanksgiving sermons which in the traditional Reformed communion season of later centuries became such an important part of the service. This is particularly the case with the sermons preached

---
[31] Calvin, *Sermons*, p. 208.

on the second and third day after Ascension where Calvin treats at length the life which the Christian, assured of salvation, lives in thanksgiving to God. In the fourth sermon on the Ascension we find these words:

> Do we wish, then, to be sharers in this ascension? We must not be separated from Him. But how shall we be joined to Him? We must put off these earthly members and things which hold us here below. Some are given to luxury, others to vengeance, others to gluttony, and others to other vices. Although faith raises us on high, our affections must follow it, in order that we may renounce all the world and all things which could hinder us from being united to our Head. This is why it is said that He will come just as He was seen to go to heaven—in order that we may learn to unite ourselves to Him through the affection of our hearts.[32]

A covenantal understanding of the Lord's Supper emphasizes that, by participating in the covenant meal, we commit our lives to Christ. We do not commit only to serve him but to love him as well. It is a commitment both to Christian worship and to living the Christian life.

A number of sermons for Pentecost communion have been preserved. The one most commonly available is supposed to have been preached in 1549.[33] It is an exposition of the first four verses Acts 2, which recounts the Day of Pentecost when the Apostles received the gift of the Holy Spirit.

Great attention is given to explaining the "visible signs" which the passage records, the mighty wind, the gift of tongues, and, above all, the descent of the tongues of fire. These signs show us that the establishment of the Church is far more than a human achievement. It is an act of God's grace. The Apostles could never have done what they did if it had not been for the gifts of the Holy

---

[32] Calvin, *Sermons*, p. 239.

[33] Calvin, *Sermons*, pp. 243–257.

Spirit which were poured out upon them. Their preaching would never have accomplished what it did if it had not been anointed by the Holy Spirit. By this visible sign we understand that the Apostles were set on fire by the love of God. One notices here that Calvin understands that the secret of the success of their preaching was that the Apostles were set on fire by the love of God. This is something, Calvin tells us, we need to experience today: "We need, then, to be set on fire with the love of God."[34]

The covenantal dimension of the sign of Pentecost is of special interest. Calvin presents the gift of tongues on Pentecost as the undoing of the curse of Babel. Where once the nations of the earth were divided up by the confusion of different languages, now with the miracle of tongues all nations are united in the wondrous works of God:

> How then were the Apostles, having always been isolated as foolish and unlearned people in this corner of Judea, able to publish the Gospel to all the world, unless God accomplished what He had previously promised: namely, that He would be known by all tongues and by all nations? It is true that it is said that all will speak the Hebrew language in order to join in a true faith, but the truth is better declared to us when it is said that all believers, from whatever region they may be, will cry, "Abba, Father," invoking God with one accord; although there may be diversity of language. That, then, is how the Spirit of God wished to display His power in these tongues, in order that the Name of God might be invoked by all and that we might together be made partakers of this covenant of salvation which belonged only to the Jews until the wall was torn down.[35]

The new covenant, unlike the old covenant, was to embrace all the peoples of the earth. In it we see the wonderful goodness of God who will not permit that any difference of tribe or tongue hinder

---

[34] Calvin, *Sermons*, p. 249.
[35] Calvin, *Sermons*, p. 248.

the proclamation of his Word throughout the whole of the world. For it is of the nature of his fatherly love that he wishes to receive those who were separated from him "and to gather them all, as it were, into His bosom."[36] As we have often pointed out before, at the center of Calvin's theology of worship is the perception that it is in worship above all that we exercise that first and greatest commandment that we love God with all our hearts, all our minds, and all our wills.

It is to this end that the Lord's Supper was established—to call all the children of God into the house of their Father. Here, again, Calvin returns to the typology of the Father's house. This is the evangelistic call, to invite all peoples into the household of faith. In the house of the Father we are to be seated at the sacred Supper together with Christ. It is there, united to Christ in covenantal fellowship, that we, too, receive the gifts of the Holy Spirit.

> That is also why this Holy Table is now prepared for us. For, as I have already said, we cannot communicate any grace from the Holy Spirit without being members of our Lord Jesus Christ. How can we arrive at that condition unless He presents Himself to us and He lives with us in such a manner that everything that is His belongs to us, and we enjoy the benefits which have been given to Him in our name? It is said in the eleventh chapter of Isaiah that the Spirit of God has rested upon Him, but not for any necessity He had of it, nor for His private use; it was for the profit of all of His body, that is to say, of all of the Church.[37]

In this passage we find two important themes joined together: the Supper as covenantal fellowship and the Supper as spiritual nourishment. As Calvin understood it, we are invited to the Lord's Table that we might enter into covenantal fellowship with Christ and then, by virtue of that covenantal fellowship, we gain spiritual

---

[36] Calvin, *Sermons*, p. 248.

[37] Calvin, *Sermons*, p. 254.

nourishment by the gifts of the Holy Spirit. It is by virtue of our being united to Christ in the covenantal fellowship that the benefits of the covenant are offered to us. Just as Calvin's eucharistic preaching invites us to the table to be joined to Christ, so it also offers to us spiritual nourishment.

> So then, let us recognize, when now the Supper is offered to us, that our Lord Jesus wishes that we might find all our good in Him, He draws near to us through His goodness. It is true that He does not leave His heavenly glory, He need not descend here below (as the Papists imagine) to communicate to us His body and His blood, but although we are far away from Him, yet He does not cease to feed us with His body and His blood.[38]

From this it is patent that Calvin's understanding of the Lord's Supper gives wide berth to the dimension of wonder and mystery. During the Age of the Enlightenment there might have been those who claimed Calvin to be a rationalist, but from this passage it should be evident that Calvin had a high respect for the miraculous nature of the Lord's Supper.

> Let us know that what cannot be conceived of by men is accomplished, nevertheless, by the secret and invisible grace of the Holy Spirit; for this is how we are made partakers of the body and of the blood of Jesus Christ.[39]

In speaking of the gifts of the Holy Spirit Calvin is obviously very much guided by the passage from Isaiah 11 which speaks of the Messiah being anointed by the gifts of the Spirit, the Spirit of wisdom and understanding, counsel and might, knowledge, and the fear of the Lord. This was a favorite text of the Middle Ages as many monuments of Christian art can testify. There are sev-

---

[38] Calvin, *Sermons*, pp. 254–255.
[39] Calvin, *Sermons*, p. 255.

eral other texts which speak of the gifts of the Spirit. One thinks immediately of the list given in Galatians 5, "Now the gifts of the Spirit are love, joy, peace . . ." This sermon has already made a strong point about the gift of love. For Calvin it is love which is the Pentecostal fire. We have noticed in the eucharistic sermon for Christmas, the spiritual gifts of joy and peace were emphasized. One also thinks of the spiritual gifts of ministry mentioned by the Apostle Paul in 1 Corinthians 12—the gifts of apostleship, the gifts of prophecy, evangelism, teaching, administering, healing, and even speaking in tongues. While Calvin makes the point that God bestows his gifts upon us as we need them, both from the standpoint of their variety and their perfection, he seems primarily interested in the gifts of wisdom and power. At least that is the case in this passage. The gifts of wisdom and power are no doubt emphasized here because Calvin has been thinking about Isaiah 11, which specifically mentions these gifts. The gifts of the Holy Spirit are the substance of this spiritual nourishment which is so important for Calvin's understanding of the Supper.

In the Pentecost sermon, the invitation to accept Christ is given in terms of receiving Christ and being united to him in covenant fellowship in order to receive the spiritual gifts which follow from our union with Christ. Covenant theology often made the point that κοινονία, or sharing, is of the essence of the covenant relationship. It is because we are united to Christ in the covenant relationship that we are entitled to the spiritual gifts poured out on Christ in his messianic anointing. It is in these terms, then, that the evangelistic appeal is made to participate in the Supper and thereby renew the covenantal relation to Christ.

All Calvin's eucharistic sermons which have been preserved make a point of inviting the faithful to come to the Lord's Table to receive Christ and the blessings of our redemption. One notices that depending on whether the celebration of communion is at Christmas, Easter, Ascension, or Pentecost the invitation is put a bit differently. However that may be, the evangelistic dimension of these sermons is clear.

B. The Liturgy

If Calvin's eucharistic sermons make clear that in the Lord's Supper the crucified and risen Christ is presented to us that we might receive him by faith, the actual service itself makes equally clear that in sharing the bread and the cup we receive Christ and commit ourselves to him as his disciples. Already in the eucharistic rites of the earliest sixteenth century Reformed churches, such as those of Strasbourg and Zurich, the liturgy was shaped to express this fundamental understanding of the sacrament: to receive the bread and wine is to receive Christ. This was understood as making a covenantal commitment to Christ by sharing in the covenantal meal. It was understood as a profession of faith in that sharing in the meal was to take one's place in the fellowship of believers. It was understood as accepting the obligations of the new covenant, receiving the precepts of the Christian faith, and living the Christian life. To receive the Lord's Supper was to receive Christ.

Nothing made the evangelistic dimension of the sacrament more clear than the fact that at the Reformed celebration of the Lord's Supper the communion of the people became the central liturgical action. Neither the offertory, the prayer of consecration of the host, nor the oblation was given the emphasis it had come to have in the Middle Ages. The communion of the faithful, on the other hand, which for centuries had been losing the attention of the liturgists, once more became the center of the service. The whole focus of the service was shifted. The preaching of the central themes of the Gospel became essential to the service because it was here that the invitation was given to receive Christ as Savior. The promises of the Gospel were expounded and the people exhorted to receive them with faith. The congregants signaled their acceptance of this offer by taking part in the sacred meal.

The actual sharing of the bread and the cup by the congregation was the central act of the service toward which all else moved.

An important implication of the evangelistic dimension was that to receive the Lord's Supper was to receive the Lord himself. This was Calvin's approach to what we call "joining the Church." Young people who had been baptized in infancy were to receive catechetical instruction and, when they had completed this, they were to make the vows of faith and be admitted to the Lord's Supper. In a very concrete way, then, to be invited to the Lord's Supper was to be invited to join the Church.

Quite understandably the reciting of the Creed played an important role in emphasizing the evangelistic dimension of the Lord's Supper. An important part of accepting Christ is making a confession of faith. For centuries, the reciting of the Creed had been the way one made a profession of faith. This reciting of the Creed logically took place after the preaching and at the beginning of the communion service proper. The sixteenth-century Reformers knew that Tertullian had used the word *sacramentum* for the Creed as well as for what we usually call sacraments. The vows of faith were of the essence of the sacrament and that was the reason Tertullian had used the word. To come to the Lord's Table was to make a faith commitment, to use a phrase popular in our day. The words with which Calvin introduces the Creed ask us to make profession of our faith in the Christian religion, and to agree by God's grace to live and die in that faith. When the Creed is presented this way, it is clear that it is not only a commitment, but a life commitment. In the worship of the early Reformed churches, the saying of the Apostles' Creed at both baptism and the Lord's Supper functioned as the covenant vows.

For those who approached the Lord's Table for the first time, this profession of faith had been, to be sure, entailed by their baptism. It was part of the life-long unfolding of their baptism. Their catechetical instruction had prepared them to understand the Creed as the Church had always understood it, so that their recital of the Creed would, in fact, be their own profession of faith. The sacrament of the Lord's Supper, unlike baptism, is constantly renewed. That goes together with the basic sign of the meal. One needs to eat repeatedly. For both those approaching the Lord's Table for the first time and those who came to renew their covenant vows, reciting the Creed played an important role in the celebration of the sacrament.

What we have called the evangelistic nature of the Lord's Supper is further shown by the Communion Invocation in the *Genevan Psalter*. Let us look at this prayer once again, emphasizing several points not looked at previously.

> Most gracious GOD! we beseech thee, that as thy Son hath not only once offered up his body and blood upon the cross for the remission of our sins, but hath also vouchsafed them unto us, for our meat and drink unto life eternal: So thou wilt grant us grace, with sincere hearts and fervent desires, to accept this great blessing at his hands. May we by lively faith partake of his body and blood, yea, of himself, true GOD and man, the only bread from heaven, which giveth life unto our souls. Suffer us no longer to live unto ourselves, according to a corrupt and sinful nature; but may He live in us, and lead us to the life that is holy, blessed, and unchangeable for ever. Thus make us true partakers of the new and everlasting testament, which is the covenant of grace. And thus assure us of thy willingness ever to be our gracious Father; not imputing unto us our sins, but that we may magnify thy name by our words and works, providing us as thy beloved children and heirs with all things necessary for our good. Fit us, O heavenly FATHER! so to celebrate at this time the blessed remembrance of thy beloved Son. Enable us profitably to contemplate his love, and show forth the benefits of his death: That receiving fresh increase of strength in thy faith and in all good works, we may with greater confidence call thee our FATHER, and evermore rejoice in thee: Through JESUS CHRIST,

our Redeemer. Amen.[40]

This Communion Invocation begins by giving thanks that Christ once for all offered up his body and blood upon the cross for the remission of our sins, and then prays that we might accept this sacrifice for our salvation. "Grant us grace . . . to accept this great blessing." The prayer continues to ask that we may "by lively faith partake of his body and his blood, yea, of himself." Nothing could be clearer: to partake of the sacred food is to accept Christ himself. The same petition is again made in another idiom, ". . . May he live in us and lead us to a life that is holy . . ." What more is this than acceptance of the Lordship of Christ? Finally the acceptance of the evangelistic invitation is expressed in covenantal terms: "Thus make us true partakers of the new and everlasting testament which is the covenant of grace." From this it is clear that those who receive the sacrament do so as the acceptance of Christ as their Savior. They are to receive his redemptive work for their salvation. They are to partake of Christ's body and blood in the sense that they receive him to live within their hearts and lead them into a new and holy life. This is what it is to participate in the covenant of grace. It is to be joined to Christ; by his Spirit we live in him and he in us. It is a love relationship. At the sacrament, God's love is shown forth and we are to contemplate his love, and not only contemplate it at the Supper but demonstrate it in the whole of life.

This is what is meant by *manducatio spiritualis*, the spiritual eating mentioned so often in Calvin's controversial writings on the Lord's Supper. It is to contemplate the love of God portrayed by the sacramental action, to recognize that it is offered to us. It is to be assured that the Father has received us as his well beloved children. At the Lord's Supper the faithful meditate on these eternal verities and are thereby transformed. They are enabled to live the Christian life. The *manducatio spiritualis* is the appropriation of the spiritual food to

---

[40] Charles Washington Baird, *Eutaxia, or The Presbyterian Liturgies: Historical Sketches* (Grand Rapids, MI: Baker Book House, 1957), pp. 50–51.

the spiritual life. It is that necessary action on the part of the believer which accepts the food that is offered and uses it as it was intended. It is the way the believer uses the spiritual food.

At the center of the Reformed celebration of the Lord's Supper is the invitation to come to the wedding feast of the Lamb. This is the evangelistic dimension. When we accept that invitation we make evident both to the world and to ourselves that we are the children of God.

5
CALVIN ON COMMUNION
The Eucharistic and Eschatological Dimensions

The early Reformed theologians had all noticed that the church Fathers had often called the sacrament of the Lord's Supper the Eucharist, that is, the thanksgiving.[1] Calvin was, to be sure, no exception. In the 1536 edition of the *Institutes of the Christian Religion* (i.e., the first edition), he begins his discussion of the sacrament of the Lord's Supper by telling us that sometimes the sacrament is called the Lord's Supper and sometimes it is called the Eucharist. When it is called the Eucharist it is because in it we give thanks to God for his lovingkindness.[2]

The Lord's Supper is a holy and solemn feast of praise and thanksgiving. In 1541 Calvin published an irenic essay on the Lord's Supper which theologians have ever since regarded as his simplest and most straightforward statement on the subject. In this *Short Treatise on the Lord's Supper,* Calvin tells us that one of the principal functions of the sacrament of the Lord's Supper is that it brings us to the adoration and praise of God. The sacrament moves us to render thanksgiving to God for his infinite goodness.[3]

---

[1] This chapter is the text of a paper which I read at the Fourteenth Calvin Colloquium at Due West, SC, in January 2010, entitled, "The Eucharistic and Eschatological Dimensions of Calvin's Doctrine of the Lord's Supper."

[2] John Calvin, *Institutes of the Christian Religion, 1536 Edition*, trans. and ed. Ford Lewis Battles (Grand Rapids, MI: Eerdmans, 1986), p. 102.

[3] "Le second fruict qu' elle nous apporte est qu' elle nous admonneste et incite à mieux recongnoistre les biens que nous avons receuz et recevons iournellement du Seigneur Iesus, à fin que nous luy rendions telle confession de louange quelle luy est deue. Car de nous mesmes nous sommes tant negligens que c'est merveilles, à mediter la bonté de nostre Dieu, sinon qu'il reveille nostre paresse,

A few lines further on in his *Short Treatise* he says much the same thing. Calvin tells us that one of the most helpful things about the Lord's Supper is that it helps us recognize the grace which God has so generously poured out on us. It refreshes our memory of all that God has done for us and leads us to magnify before others his mighty acts of salvation. In all this there is a mutual edification as all of us together give thanks to God for his love and grace toward us. The Supper keeps us from sinking into ingratitude, not permitting us to forget the good which our Lord Jesus has done in dying for us. We are here led to render thanksgiving as a public profession of our devotion to our Savior.[4]

One notices in these words from the *Short Treatise* how thoroughly Calvin has understood the distinctive biblical concept of thanksgiving. The Hebrew word *yadah* means to give thanks but it also means to witness or confess. A cognate form of the word was used to speak of the thank offering as we find it in the heading of Psalm 100, for example. In a biblical theology of worship, thanksgiving was a matter of recounting the story of how God had delivered one in a time of need. Telling this story was a testimony or a witness before the congregation as well as before the world. This witness both glorified God and edified the neighbor. Beyond that it was a confession of the obligation which one therefore had to serve one's redeemer.

This biblical concept of thanksgiving is a fundamental constituent of a covenantal theology of worship. This is particularly obvious in those words from the institution of the sacrament, "Do this in remembrance of me." Remembering God's mighty acts of

---

et nous poulse à faire nostre debvoir." John Calvin, *Opera selecta*, Petrus Barth and Dora Scheuner, eds. (Munich: Chr. Kaiser, 1926–1959), 1:510.

[4] "Si c'est doncq une chose tant requise à salut, de ne point mescongnoistre les graces que Dieu nous a faictes, mais les reduire diligemment en memoire et les magnifier envers les autres, à fin de nous edifier mutuellement: en cela nous voyons une aultre singuliere utilité de la Cene, qu'elle nous retire d' ingratitude, et ne permet pas que nous oublions le bien que nous a faict le Seigneur Iesus en mourant pour nous: mais nous induict à luy rendre action de grace, et quasi par confession publique protester combien nous sommes attenus à luy." Calvin, *Opera selecta*, 1:510.

creation and redemption is fundamental to the sacrament. A true celebration of the sacrament should recount the history of salvation. It should tell again how God brought us from sin to salvation. It should recall the sacrifice of Christ, his victory over death, and his reign in heaven. True thanksgiving remembers the gracious gift of one's benefactor. Some theologians have been very quick to deplore the Reformed emphasis on memorial, forgetting that the early Reformed theologians were rather good at their Hebrew. The early Reformed theologians discovered early in the discussion the liturgical significance of the memorial of God's mighty acts of creation and redemption. The eucharistic memorial was quite simply the recounting of the mighty acts of God for our salvation. It is when we are mindful of this that we are moved to dedicate ourselves to God's service. This is the giving that is thanksgiving.

Returning to the *Institutes* we find another place where Calvin speaks about the eucharistic dimension of the sacrament.[5] In this passage our theologian is arguing against the doctrine of the eucharistic sacrifice. Calvin points out that in the Law of the Old Testament there were different kinds of sacrifices. This whole sacrificial system which indeed intimated Christ's sacrifice was fulfilled by Christ's sacrifice on the cross and has now been set aside. All this is made quite clear in the Epistle to the Hebrews. Referring to Hebrews 9 he writes,

> For among the Jews the Levitical priests were commanded to prefigure the sacrifice that Christ was to perform; the victim was brought forward to take the place of Christ; there was an altar on which it was to be sacrificed; thus, in short, all things were carried out in order that there might be set before the people's eyes a likeness of the sacrifice that was to be offered to God in expiation. But after Christ's sacrifice was

---

[5] John Calvin, *Institutes of the Christian Religion*, ed. John T. McNeill, trans. Ford Lewis Battles, Library of Christian Classics, vols. 20 and 21 (Philadelphia: The Westminster Press, 1960) IV, xviii, 13. This passage was in the first edition of the *Institutes*, but it was considerably expanded in the second edition.

> accomplished, the Lord instituted another method for us, that is, to transmit to the believing folk the benefit of the sacrifice offered to himself by his Son. He has therefore given us a Table at which to feast, not an altar upon which to offer a victim; he has not consecrated priests to offer sacrifice, but ministers to distribute the sacred banquet.[6]

In the Old Testament Law the priests stood daily at the altar offering sacrifices which could never really take away sin, but now Christ has come and has on the cross offered the perfect sacrifice. This one sacrifice has once and for all atoned for our sin.

> The sacrificial victims which were offered under the law to atone for sins [Ex. 19:36] were so called, not because they were capable of recovering God's favor or wiping out iniquity, but because they prefigured a true sacrifice such as was finally accomplished in reality by Christ alone; and by him alone, because no other could have done it. And it was done but once, because the effectiveness and force of that one sacrifice accomplished by Christ are eternal, as he testified with his own voice when he said that it was done and fulfilled [John 19:30].[7]

No more sacrifices are needed to atone for sin. The only kind of sacrifice which now makes any sense is the sacrifice of praise and thanksgiving. This sacrifice is "to testify gratefulness of heart for benefits received."[8] It is an "exercise of simple piety, to renew the confirmation of the covenant."[9] For Calvin a sacrifice of praise and thanksgiving "consists in veneration and worship of God, which believers owe and render to him, . . . It is given to God only by those who, laden with innumerable benefits from him, pay

---

[6] *Institutes* IV, xviii, 12.
[7] *Institutes* IV, xviii, 13.
[8] *Institutes* IV, xviii, 13.
[9] *Institutes* IV, xviii, 13.

5: Calvin on Communion
The Eucharistic and Eschatological Dimensions

back to him their whole selves and all their acts."[10] The sacrifice of thanksgiving is quite different from "a sacrifice of propitiation or expiation."[11] While a sacrifice of thanksgiving is appropriate to the Christian, an attempt at making a sacrifice of propitiation only mocks the uniqueness of Christ's sacrifice. "Whatever was necessary to recover the Father's favor, to obtain forgiveness of sins, righteousness, and salvation—all this was performed and completed by that unique sacrifice of his. And so perfect was it that no place was left afterward for any other sacrificial victim."[12]

A bit further on in this same chapter of the *Institutes* Calvin returns to the subject of the Christian thank offering. This Christian thank offering is the worship spoken of in the Psalms:

> Let my prayer be counted as incense before thee,
>   And the lifting up of my hands as an evening sacrifice!
> (Psalm 141:2)

or again:

> "He who brings thanksgiving as his sacrifice honors me;
>   to him who orders his way aright
>   I will show the salvation of God!"
> (Psalm 50:23)

The Christian thank offering is the prayer or hymn of thanksgiving.[13] As we find it in the Epistle to the Hebrews, Christians are to worship God by continually offering up through Christ, ". . . a sacrifice of praise to God, that is, the fruit of lips that acknowledge his name" (Heb. 13:15). It is in acts of mercy toward our neighbor and in maintaining fellowship with the brethren that we perform the sacrifices that are pleasing to God (Heb. 13:16). It is in the reading and preaching of Scripture, in the prayers and hymns of

---

[10] *Institutes* IV, xviii, 13.
[11] *Institutes* IV, xviii, 13.
[12] *Institutes* IV, xviii, 13.
[13] *Institutes* IV, xviii, 17.

thanksgiving, and in good works, that we offer to God the "spiritual sacrifices" of the "royal priesthood" (1 Pet. 2:4–10). Christian worship in all its forms is a sacrifice of thanksgiving. It is a sacrifice of thanksgiving, to be sure, but not a sacrifice of propitiation. For just as the Christian life is lived not in order to win God's favor but because we have received God's favor, so Christian worship is offered to God not to *win* his love but in grateful *recognition* of his love. We love him because he first loved us.

Let us turn now to Calvin's commentary on the harmony of the Gospels. This commentary was published in 1555, fairly late in Calvin's career, and reflects the controversies which arose with Westphal and the Gnesio-Lutherans. In the midst of a discussion on the Last Supper in the different Gospels, Calvin comments on the prayer of thanksgiving which Jesus offered over first the bread and then the wine, "As they were eating Christ took bread, to invite them to share the new Supper. He gave thanks, which made a preparation and transition to reflect upon the mystery."[14] This comment would lead one to think that Calvin saw in this prayer over the bread and the wine an opportunity to meditate on the mighty acts of God for our salvation, those mighty acts in which the mystery of God's love was revealed. The bread and the wine on the table, the breaking of the bread and the sharing of the cup, were the signs of that mystery. The prayer that was offered there would only naturally be a reflection or meditation upon that mystery.

Calvin has more to say in his commentary on this passage. He has particularly in mind the fact that Matthew and Mark speak of the *blessing* of the elements while Luke speaks of *giving thanks*.

> Mark and Matthew use the word *blessed*, but as Luke employs in its place the word "give thanks" (εὐχαριστήσας) there is no ambiguity in sense. Since

---

[14] John Calvin, *A Harmony of the Gospels, Matthew, Mark and Luke, and the Epistles of James and Jude*, 3 vols., trans. A. W. Morrison, *Calvin's New Testament Commentaries*, eds. David W. Torrance and Thomas Forsyth Torrance, (Grand Rapids, MI: Eerdmans, 1989), 132.

over the cup they use the word "giving thanks" they are interpreting the first saying clearly enough. This makes the papists' ignorance more ridiculous, expressing the blessing with the sign of the cross as if Christ has used an exorcism. Remember what I just remarked, that the giving of thanks is linked to the spiritual mystery. Nor does Christ have regard to ordinary eating where the faithful are told to give thanks to God who sustains them in this frail life, for He was turning to the sacred action, to give thanks to God for the eternal salvation of the human race.[15]

We need to notice two things here—first what this blessing is not, and second, what it is. This prayer of thanksgiving is not some sort of "magical incantation."[16] In the Latin mass, the priest blessed the bread and the cup, making the sign of the cross over them as if, according to Calvin, he were casting out a demon. Calvin is, of course, aware that a well-trained Scholastic theologian had a much more sophisticated explanation of how the bread and wine were blessed. Calvin's point, however, is clear. The liturgical practice had for a long time invited a magical understanding of the sacrament. Whatever origins the sign of the cross might have had, by the time of the Reformation, it had become a magical gesture to ward off evil spirits.

Understandably, good Catholics today are insulted by the Reformers' reaction to their liturgical gestures, but that was part of the agony of the Reformation. More and more the Christians of Europe had begun to regard the medieval rites as superstitious. The sign of the cross was particularly seen this way. The Reformers were determined to move worship beyond the superstitious performance of magical rites. The Reformers were sure that there was something very true and worthy in the blessing of the bread and wine. Their study of Scripture helped them recover a biblical understanding of blessing and even of consecration.

---

[15] Calvin, *A Harmony of the Gospels*, 3:133.
[16] Calvin, *A Harmony of the Gospels*, 3:134.

As Calvin saw it, Luke explains what Matthew and Mark meant by saying that Jesus blessed the bread and wine. Luke tells us that this blessing was a prayer of thanksgiving. Calvin understood the biblical concept of thanksgiving very well. When we receive God's gifts and give thanks for them, we acknowledge that they come from God and thereby consecrate them to our use. The Reformers understood this from 1 Timothy 4:4–5, "For everything created by God is good, if it is received with thanksgiving; for then it is consecrated by the word of God and prayer." To give thanks for the bread and wine is to bless it or consecrate it. But even beyond that, we must understand that it was not just a common table blessing thanking God for our ordinary food. This prayer of thanksgiving is a prayer which thanks God "for the eternal salvation of the human race."[17]

Turning to Calvin's commentary on the Apostle Paul's account of the institution of the sacrament in 1 Corinthians 11:24f., we find the following remark on the text, "When he had given thanks . . ."

> Paul says in I Tim. 4.5 that every gift we receive from God's hand is sanctified to us through the Word of God and prayer. Nowhere, therefore, do we read of our Lord eating with His disciples, without the fact that He gave thanks being recorded. There is no doubt that He has taught us, by His own example, to do the same thing. Yet this thanksgiving goes deeper than that, for Christ is giving thanks to His Father for His mercy towards the human race, and His priceless gift of redemption; and He encourages us, by His example, so that, as often as we approach the Holy Table, we may lift up our hearts in acknowledgment of the boundless love of God towards us, and be inflamed with true gratitude to Him.[18]

Several things are clear from this passage. First, Calvin recognizes

---

[17] Calvin, *A Harmony of the Gospels*, 3:133.

[18] John Calvin, *The First Epistle of Paul to the Corinthians*, trans. John W. Fraser, *Calvin's New Testament Commentaries* (Grand Rapids, MI: Eerdmans, 1989), p. 243.

the importance of a common table blessing to true piety. Such a prayer was a fundamental act of devotion not only for Jesus but the whole people of God, Jewish and Christian alike. Calvin even goes so far as to say that Jesus taught this practice by his example. When we approach the Lord's Table, however, there is something more. When Jesus gave thanks at the last Supper he gave "thanks to His Father for His mercy towards the human race, and His priceless gift of redemption."[19] In other words, this prayer should be a prayer of thanksgiving for God's mercy in his mighty acts of creation and redemption. According to Calvin, we should follow Christ's example by being filled with gratitude when we approach the Table.

Rather strangely, Calvin does not make the application that the minister ought to follow the example of Jesus by offering a prayer of thanksgiving for the works of creation and redemption over the bread and the wine. Calvin seems to be much more concerned here about how the *congregation* is to worship God in the celebration of the sacrament than he is about what constitutes a valid celebration on the part of the *ministers*. The ministers perform the sacramental action of breaking the bread and giving the cup to the faithful. They perform the visible word and the congregation, perceiving the meaning of these signs, is moved to gratitude and thanksgiving. It is, therefore, with genuine praise and adoration that the church enters into the prayer of thanksgiving and which concludes the service. Presumably that is the way one would understand the Genevan eucharistic liturgy. Yet, the Post-Communion Prayer of Thanksgiving is something quite different. Perhaps the best way to understand it is that the Genevan communion liturgy was, practically speaking, incomplete. The liturgical form had not yet achieved the full vision which the theologians perceived. The liturgical practice lagged behind the theological understanding.

The eucharistic dimension of the Supper is fundamental to Calvin. It is, however, the second fruit of the sacrament, as Calvin

---

[19] Calvin, *Commentary on First Corinthians*, p. 243.

said in his *Short Treatise on the Lord's Supper*. The first fruit of the sacrament is that God feeds us, and that with spiritual food. First the sacrament is something God does and second it is something we do and that is that we give thanks. The action of the congregation is above all to give thanks to God.

What Calvin has to say in his *Short Treatise on the Lord's Supper*, what he has to say in the *Institutes*, and what he has to say in his commentaries must now be complemented by what we find in the actual celebration of the Supper in the worship of the Church of Geneva during Calvin's pastorate.

Surely, one of the most puzzling things about the Genevan communion service is that it did not have a full scale eucharistic prayer. This does not mean that the eucharistic dimension was neglected in the communion service. There were, in fact, a number of ways in which the eucharistic dimension was expressed in the service. The communion psalmody was very important in the celebration of the sacrament. The meditation of the congregation during the celebration was another important element, especially the meditation of the congregation during the distribution of the bread and wine. While this was being done, appropriate passages of Scripture were read, such as the passage from Isaiah 53 concerning the vicarious suffering of the servant of the Lord, or the prologue to the Gospel of John, or the discourse on Christ being the resurrection and the life (John 11). These passages were read during the distribution to inspire the gratitude of the faithful and to lift up their prayers of thanksgiving with genuine adoration. The singing of the Psalms and the reading of Scripture did much to foster the general air of solemn thanksgiving with which the service was celebrated.

More specifically, however, there was the Genevan communion invocation which stood at the beginning of the eucharistic liturgy proper. The prayer might easily be understood as a eucharistic prayer, for it certainly has elements of praise and thanksgiving, as the text shows:

5: Calvin on Communion
The Eucharistic and Eschatological Dimensions

> Most gracious God! we beseech thee, that as thy Son hath not only once offered up his body and blood upon the cross for the remission of our sins, but hath also vouchsafed them unto us, for our meat and drink unto life eternal: So thou wilt grant us grace, with sincere hearts and fervent desires, to accept this great blessing at his hands. May we by lively faith partake of his body and blood, yea, of himself, true GOD and man, the only bread from heaven, which giveth life unto our souls. Suffer us no longer to live unto ourselves, according to a corrupt and sinful nature; but may He live in us, and lead us to the life that is holy, blessed, and unchangeable for ever. Thus make us true partakers of the new and everlasting testament, which is the covenant of grace. And thus assure us of thy willingness ever to be our gracious Father; not imputing unto us our sins, but that we may magnify thy name by our words and works, providing us as thy beloved children and heirs with all things necessary for our good. Fit us, O heavenly FATHER! so to celebrate at this time the blessed remembrance of thy beloved Son. Enable us profitably to contemplate his love, and show forth the benefits of his death: That receiving fresh increase of strength in thy faith and in all good works, we may with greater confidence call thee our FATHER, and evermore rejoice in thee: Through JESUS CHRIST, our Redeemer. Amen.[20]

It is, however, best understood as a communion invocation which asks that we might be made partakers of "the new and everlasting covenant, the covenant of grace."

Here again, Calvin is following the example of the Reformed Church of Strasbourg very closely. In neither liturgy is there anything which might be construed as a prayer of consecration. Nothing is said which might be interpreted as a formula of consecration. In the same way nothing is said which might be understood as the offering up of a eucharistic sacrifice. As we will see, John Knox

---
[20] Charles Washington Baird, *Eutaxia, or The Presbyterian Liturgies: Historical Sketches* (Grand Rapids, MI: Baker Book House, 1957), pp. 50–51.

and the English-speaking congregation in Geneva did develop a full-scale eucharistic prayer, but Calvin had not yet taken that step. His exegesis as well as his theology may have suggested that step, but he never took it.

What we do have in the communion service of the Church of Geneva is a rather full Post-communion Prayer of Thanksgiving comprising a Prayer of Dedication and a psalm of thanksgiving.[21] How are we to understand this? One thing is abundantly clear; the post-communion prayer is not the same thing as a eucharistic prayer. The prayer gives thanks for having received the benefits of the sacrament, not for God's mighty acts of creation and redemption. Apparently, receiving Christ was understood to entail the thanksgiving of the faithful. This thanksgiving includes prayers and hymns of thanksgiving, the witness to God's gracious acts of redemption, the living of the Christian life, and the rendering of Christian service to neighbors. Let us look first at this Prayer of Dedication:

> Heavenly Father! we give thee immortal praise and thanks, that upon us poor sinners thou hast conferred so great a benefit, as to bring us into the communion of thy Son JESUS CHRIST our Lord; whom having delivered up to death for us, thou hast given for our food and nourishment unto eternal life. Now, also, grant us grace, that we may never be unmindful of these things; but rather carrying them about engraven upon our hearts, may advance and grow in that faith which is effectual unto every good work. Thus, may the rest of our lives be ordered and followed out to thy glory and the edification of our neighbours: Through JESUS CHRIST our Lord; Who with thee, O FATHER! and the HOLY GHOST, liveth and reigneth in the unity of the Godhead, world without end. Amen.[22]

---

[21] Some writers have called the Prayer of Dedication the Post-Communion Thanksgiving. Gradually I have come to the opinion that it is better called the Prayer of Dedication.

[22] Baird, *The Presbyterian Liturgies*, p. 58.

The prayer begins by giving thanks for being united to Christ and having been blessed with all the benefits of being united with him. Then in the imagery of Jeremiah's vision of the new covenant, the prayer prays that this covenant be written on the tablets of our hearts and that thereby we might grow in both faith and works. It is in this way that God is truly praised and all peoples come to recognize the true glory of God.

Thanksgiving was further expressed in the singing of a psalm or hymn of thanksgiving. Among the psalms and hymns used at this point were Psalm 103, Psalm 138, and the Song of Simeon from the Gospel of Luke. The use of the Song of Simeon might be surprising at first glance, but it makes sense when one thinks about it. The Song of Simeon was the prayer of thanksgiving which Simeon sang when the infant Christ was presented in the Temple and the elderly priest recognized that the child which he beheld was the fulfillment of God's promises.

> Now let thy servant, LORD!
>   At length depart in peace;
> According to thy word,
>   My waiting soul release:
> For thou my longing eyes hast spared
>   To see thy saving grace declared.
>
> To see thy saving grace,
>   That soon dispensed abroad,
> The nations shall embrace,
>   And find their help in GOD:
> A light to lighten every land,
>   The glory of thy chosen band.[23]

It would have been particularly appropriate at the Christmas communion. One also notices that it specifically mentions the *seeing* of God's faithfulness to his people. Both Psalm 138 and Psalm 103 are thanksgiving psalms. In fact they are probably both votive

---
[23] Baird, *The Presbyterian Liturgies*, p. 48.

thanksgiving psalms. They recognize that God has heard the cry of his people, saved them when they were in need, and is now entitled to their devotion. God is faithful; he therefore deserves our faithfulness. Calvin had no doubt been inspired to use Psalm 138 by the use of a metrical version of this psalm in the communion liturgy of the German-speaking Church of Strasbourg. In fact Calvin himself wrote a metrical version of the psalm for the *French Evangelical Psalter*.

> Thanksgiving praise I will give to Thee,
> With all my heart Thee I'll magnify
> Before all princedoms and powers,
> In Thy temple I will Thee adore:
> I'll sing the magnitude of Thy name,
> For Thine own truth and Thy kindness.
> God, Thou hast exalted o'er all,
> By Thine own Word, Thy majesty.
> When with my voice I called on Thee,
> Straightway Thou gavest answer to me,
> Sustaining me by Thy vast might,
> My soul maintaining in Thy strength.
> Hallelujah, Hallelujah.
>
> All kings of earth praise to Thee will give,
> Unto Thy greatness they will bow down,
> Being instructed in Thy Word,
> Singing the dignity of Thy deeds:
> Heaven and earth as His own abode,
> He confined, to His great glory.
> High, lifted up our Lord in heaven
> Is seated, to rule and command.
> Yet nonetheless bends down His eyes,
> To gaze on the humble and poor:
> In judgment He views from afar
> Proud men and haughty with contempt.
> Hallelujah, Hallelujah.
>
> If by affliction sore I am crushed,
> To life and vigor revived, restored
> I'll be by Thy consolation.

> Thou on all my enemies wilt stretch
> Thy hand to shatter their raging wrath:
> >   Therein I shall possess safety.
> Forever in me will the Lord
> >   His wonderful kindness display.
> Thy mercy, O God, will persist,
> >   Surpassing the bounds of the earth.
> Thou ne'er wilt forsake or forget
> >   All works Thy hand has taken up.
> Hallelujah, Hallelujah.[24]

This thanksgiving, either as a liturgical prayer or a psalm, was only the beginning of something much greater. Far from being simply a postlude to the liturgical service, it was much more significantly a prelude to a life of Christian devotion and service. Calvin never wearied of reminding his congregation that the true thanksgiving is a life lived in the praise of God. In Calvin's *Short Treatise* of 1541 the Reformer tells us that the third use of the Supper is that it exhorts us to live a holy life and above all to maintain the bond of charity and fraternal love. For we have become members of the body of Jesus Christ, being incorporated into him and united to him as our head. We have good reason then to be conformed to his purity and innocence and especially that we share together the love and concord appropriate to the members of the same body.[25] The point is that the Supper empowers us and enlivens us for living the Christian life.

In the Easter communion sermon we looked at above, Calvin concluded by saying:

> That is how today we must make use of this Holy Sup-

---

[24] Ford Lewis Battles, trans. and ed., *The Piety of John Calvin* (Grand Rapids, MI: Baker Book House, 1978), pp. 163–165.

[25] "La troisiesme utilité gist en ce que nous y avons une vehemente exhortation à vivre sainctement et sur tout à garder charité et dilection fraternelle entre nous. Car puis que là nous sommes faictz membres de Iesus. Christ, estans incorporez en luy, et unis avec luy, comme à nostre chef, c' est bien raison premierement que nous soyons faictz conformes à sa pureté et innocence, et specialement que nous ayons ensemble telle charité et concorde comme doibvent avoir les membres d'un mesme corps." Calvin, *Opera selecta*, 1:510–511.

per which is prepared for us. That is, that it may lead us to the death and passion of our Lord Jesus Christ, and then to His resurrection, and that we may be so assured of life and salvation, as by the victory which He has obtained in rising from the dead righteousness is given to us, and the gate of paradise has been opened to us, so that we may boldly approach our God, and offer ourselves before Him, knowing that always He will receive us as His children.[26]

In this celebration of the Lord's Supper there is quite appropriately an emphasis on the resurrection of Christ and his victory over death and the grave. It is, therefore, that we are assured of resurrection and our entering through the gates of paradise. It is the promise of life everlasting that inspires the faith of those who take part in the service and by that faith are received into the house of the Father.

Thanksgiving is in the end the giving of ourselves to God in the living of the Christian life. To accept Christ is to give ourselves to him, and that is what these post-communion prayers signal. They lead us to that giving of ourselves which is thanksgiving. A true eucharistic prayer remembers God's mighty acts of creation and redemption by recounting them, but thanksgiving goes further. In true thanksgiving, we respond to God's gift of his Son by dedicating ourselves to him in living a Christian life.

In succeeding centuries Reformed churches would develop the eucharistic dimension of the service considerably. We find this development in the thanksgiving services which would be held on Sunday evenings or during the week following the celebration of the Supper. We also find it in the custom of collecting alms for the support of diaconal work. Even beyond these developments, we find that John Knox was able to provide the Reformed liturgy with a fully formed eucharistic prayer thanking God for his mighty and

---

[26] John Calvin, *Sermons on the Saving Work of Christ*, ed. and trans. Leroy Nixon (Grand Rapids, MI: Baker Book House, 1980), p. 196.

marvelous works of creation and redemption. This development, as we have seen, was already intimated in the liturgy of Geneva as it was celebrated in Calvin's time.

THE ESCHATOLOGICAL DIMENSION[27]

It was Calvin's custom to begin the communion service proper by calling the congregation to turn their minds to heavenly things as they approached the Lord's Table. This set the eschatological mood of the service. For Calvin the Lord's Supper always involved participation in a heavenly reality.[28] It was a foretaste of the life of the world to come. To use a modern term, Calvin saw in the sacrament of holy communion an element of realized eschatology. It was not only a remembrance of things past but an openness to the future. That was essential to the Hebrew concept of memorial. The Passover was both a remembrance of the deliverance of Israel in the past and a sign of the messianic deliverance yet to come.

We have already spoken of the Lord's Supper in terms of faith. The purpose of the Lord's Supper is to nourish faith. We have spoken of the Lord's Supper in terms of love, for the Supper is a revelation of the love of God and an exercise in expressing our love toward God as well as experiencing the love of the family of God one toward another. Now we must speak of the Lord's Supper in terms of hope. It is a sign and promise of our victory over death, our resurrection unto eternal life, and a foretaste of everlasting glory. We notice repeatedly that Calvin speaks of the sacrament as a sign and a seal of God's promises. With such an emphasis on God's promises, hope is bound to play a major role in Calvin's eucharistic theology.

The eschatological dimension of the Lord's Supper comes

---

[27] While part of a paper read at the Fourteenth Calvin Colloquium, this section was not read at the time because it was not then complete. See note 1 (p. 157).

[28] For a strong statement of this, see Calvin's commentary on 1 Cor. 11:24. Calvin, *Commentary on First Corinthians*, p. 247.

to prominent expression in the communion service as it was celebrated in Geneva during the time of Calvin's ministry there. We read in the *Genevan Psalter* of 1542 that the minister is to invite the congregation to approach the sacred table with an exhortation to repentance, to faith in God's love for us in Christ, and to hope in the life everlasting. This exhortation was to conclude with these words:

> And now, to this end, lift up your minds and hearts on high, where JESUS CHRIST abideth in the glory of his Father, whence we expect his coming at our redemption. Dwell not upon these earthly and corruptible elements, which we see present to our eyes, and feel with our hands, to seek him in them, as if he were inclosed in the Bread or in the Wine. For then only shall our souls be disposed to receive food and life from his substance, when they shall thus be lifted up above worldly things, even unto heaven, and enter into the kingdom of GOD, where he dwelleth. Let us be satisfied to have this Bread and this Wine for witnesses and signs; seeking spiritually the truth where GOD's word hath promised that we shall find it.[29]

Many have heard in this an echo of the *Sursum corda* of the Roman Mass. Certainly Calvin and his hearers would have recognized this echo from the old liturgy. The *Sursum corda* goes quite far back in the history of the liturgy, but for understanding the liturgy of Geneva it is probably more important to hear an echo of a very famous passage in a sermon of St. Augustine's concerning the meaning of these words, "Lift up your minds and hearts on high." Calvin was fond of citing this passage from Augustine and the rest of the passage makes it abundantly clear that Calvin has this well in mind. Calvin, to be sure, never used a responsive *Sursum corda* in his communion prayers. These so-called eucharistic dialogues would have sounded too much like the hocus pocus eucharistic prayers that were all too familiar to the Roman mass of years gone by.

The first thing that strikes us is that it is the risen and ascended

---

[29] Baird, *The Presbyterian Liturgies*, pp. 56–57.

5: Calvin on Communion
The Eucharistic and Eschatological Dimensions

Christ whom we encounter at a faithful celebration of the sacrament. It is not so much the Jesus of history who is remembered as it is the exalted Son of God at the right hand of the Father with whom the Christian here on earth has covenantal fellowship. To be sure this transcendent Jesus is the same Savior who was incarnate in the womb, suffered under Pontius Pilate, died on the cross, and rose from the grave.

One notices the strong reference to the Second Coming of Christ, "Lift up your hearts on high, where Jesus Christ abideth in the glory of his Father, whence we expect his coming at our redemption."[30] The church of today celebrates the eucharist in expectation. For Calvin, Christian hope is an aid to the Christian life as well as a Christian virtue. In the contemplation of the joys of heaven and the victory of the last day one gains strength to endure the trials of the present. There is great value for the Christian in lifting up his heart and mind on high. For, as Jesus put it, where our treasure is there our heart is as well.

The liturgy of Geneva calls us to "enter into the kingdom of God."[31] Here the element of realized eschatology is particularly strong. It is there, at the right hand of the Father in glory, that Christ dwells, and it is there where the Wedding Feast of the Lamb is celebrated. As time went on the Reformed Church developed this eschatological element very thoroughly. In the eighteenth century, it was common to preach on the Wedding Feast of the King's Son or on some text from the Song of Solomon at the celebration of communion. The singing of the twenty-third psalm at the Lord's Supper became a regular feature of the service and with the final line, "I shall dwell in the house of the Lord forever," the eschatological theme was strong and clear. To celebrate communion was to enter into the Kingdom of God, to celebrate the Wedding Feast of the Lamb.

---

[30] Baird, *The Presbyterian Liturgies*, pp. 56.

[31] Baird, *The Presbyterian Liturgies*, pp. 56–57.

In the *Short Treatise on the Lord's Supper* we read:

> In fact we ought to understand that we are not only called to possess the heavenly heritage at some time in the future but through hope we have already in a certain manner been introduced into possession of it; that not only are we promised life but we have already been transported into this heavenly life in our being rescued from death.[32]

This is, of course, one of the themes of the Gospel of John which is met throughout the Gospel. By faith we enter into eternal life even in this world. That life into which we enter even in this world is eternal and never ends. We pass from death to life. The promise of eternal life is one of the promises of the Gospel which is sealed in the Supper. To the eyes of faith the Supper is a sign of the heavenly banquet, and through faith, those who participate in the sacred meal receive a foretaste of the heavenly reality. The bread and wine of communion are a spiritual food which nourish us unto eternal life.

The eschatological dimension of the Lord's Supper is only occasionally alluded to in the *Institutes*. In the chapter on the Lord's Supper we find several short references in which the Reformer suggests that we should not think that being in the presence of Christ is only a matter of his being with us. It can just as well be a matter of our being with him and enjoying his heavenly presence.[33]

These passages in the *Institutes* are in a context which suggests that the sort of local presence which would attach Christ's presence to the bread does not take into account the fact of the ascension. Christ's ascension was to the end that we might follow

---

[32] "Car nous debvons entendre que non seullement il nous a appellez à posseder une foys son Heritage celeste: mais que par esperance il nous a desia aucunement introduictz en ceste possession: que non seullement il nous a promis la vie, mais nous a desia transferez en icelle, nous retirant de la mort." Calvin, *Opera selecta*, 1:504. (Translation by the author.)

[33] *Institutes* IV, xvii, 16, 18, and 31.

him. The heavenly presence is of a very different nature than the earthly presence. There is no necessity of the sacrament continuing or repeating the earthly presence. It is, however, of the essence of our salvation that in the Supper we are drawn to Christ in his heavenly presence. That is the ultimate goal of our salvation, that we enter into his heavenly glory. The presence that we experience here on earth is to draw us into the heavenly presence.

We experience the presence of Christ here on earth but it is not a local presence. It is an experience of his Word which when received by faith gives us life. This is what Calvin calls the spiritual presence. It is an experience of his grace which empowers us to live the life of the Kingdom. The presence of the ascended and glorified Christ, however, is of a very different nature from the presence of the Jesus whom the apostles saw with their eyes and touched with their hands. It is a presence which we experience by the power of the Holy Spirit. It is a saving presence. "Blessed are those who have not seen and yet believe" (John 20:29). It is a much more powerful presence, as Calvin often points out, because it is the presence of the Son of God at the right hand of the Father. To be at the right hand of the Father is to exercise the power of the Almighty. As Jesus explained to the disciples, it was necessary for the disciples that Jesus ascend to the Father that he might confer upon them the Holy Spirit. Jesus would be with them in a different and more important way once he had ascended.

It is that spiritual presence which Christians enjoy in this life. It is a presence which comes through the Holy Spirit. Surely that presence we enjoy at the Lord's Supper, but in addition we enjoy, as a foretaste, the heavenly presence, when at the Lord's Supper we are by the Holy Spirit lifted up to Christ who reigns in power at the right hand of the Father. "Behold, I stand at the door and knock; if any one hears my voice and opens the door, I will come in to him and eat with him, and he with me" (Rev. 3:20).

Calvin's perception of the eschatological dimension of the

Lord's Supper comes from his study of Scripture. As a theologian Calvin was especially sensitive to the transcendent. Anyone who puts so much stock in the eternal decrees of God and the working out of divine providence is bound to understand the sacrament in terms of the heavenly reality. We are not surprised therefore to find these comments on Matthew 26:29. The words of Jesus are well known, "I tell you I shall not drink again of this fruit of the vine until that day when I drink it new with you in my Father's kingdom." As Calvin understood it, these words are a promise of eternal life to the faithful. The Reformer paraphrases the promise:

> In other words, "Now indeed I hasten to my death, but from it I shall pass to blessed immortality, nor shall I live alone in a separate state in the Kingdom of God but I shall have you with me to share the same life."[34]

For Christians today, the remembrance of Christ's death is and will be to the end of the coming kingdom. For as often as they drink the cup and break the bread they show forth Christ's death until he comes. Calvin remarks:

> We can see how He leads the disciples by the hand to the cross, and thence raises them to the hope of resurrection. They had to be guided to Christ's death that they might use it as a ladder to ascend into heaven, so now, because Christ died and was received into heaven, by looking on the cross we should be led up to heaven, that His dying and life restored should hold together. As for Him promising them glory shared with Himself, this is clear from the words, *until the day when I drink it new with you*.[35]

This striking figure of the remembrance of the cross being a ladder to ascend to heaven is thoroughly Johannine. On the cross Christ was lifted up to heaven, and so for Christians our medita-

---

[34] Calvin, *A Harmony of the Gospels*, 3:137.

[35] Calvin, *A Harmony of the Gospels*, 3:137.

tion on the cross is not merely a remembrance of the past but a transition from this world to the world to come. It is a passage. The same had, of course, been true of Passover. One can hardly be surprised to find this eschatological dimension in the Lord's Supper as it is reported in the Gospels and one can hardly be surprised that Calvin discovered it in the Gospels.

In his commentary on 1 Corinthians 11:24, "This is my body broken for you. Do this in remembrance of me," Calvin makes the point that the Lord's Supper is a heavenly action. It is a heavenly banquet celebrated in the presence of Christ and yet Christ hardly needs to be dragged down from heaven for him to be present. It is by its very nature a heavenly banquet, "We must rise up to heaven . . . Let Him remain in His heavenly glory; and aspire to reach heaven yourself, that, from it, He may impart Himself to you."[36] Calvin's sense of the transcendent was always strong. Nowhere is it stronger than in his eucharistic theology. Yet it was a very different approach to the transcendent than the approach of the Middle Ages. It had more to do with eschatology than mysticism.

Another way one might explain it is to say that a strong belief in predestination is in the end a very deeply held mysticism. This, of course, with his strong Augustinian doctrine of grace was quite consistent. The mystery of the Lord's Supper revolves around the eschatology which senses in the divine word of promise the ultimate fulfillment. Faith mysteriously embraces things unseen, as we read in the Epistle to the Hebrews, and, from the certainty of God's future, gains strength for the present.

Surely what Calvin drew from these passages of Scripture is one of the most important elements of the earliest Christian understanding of the Supper. The Supper celebrated by the church here on earth is a foretaste of the heavenly banquet. If the Middle Ages had seen the mystery of the Eucharist in terms of a sort of continuation or propagation of the incarnation and

---

[36] Calvin, *Commentary on First Corinthians*, p. 247.

representation or even repetition of the sacrifice of the cross, Calvin saw that mystery in terms of a realized eschatology. In the Eucharist the faithful are joined to the incarnate Christ born in Bethlehem of Judea in the time of Herod the king, crucified and risen once and for all for our salvation. But we are also joined to that same Christ enthroned in glory and coming again. It is the mystery of maranatha. The Christ who has come is the Christ who is to come. The Second Coming, however, will not be a repetition of the first. It will be of a completely different order. It will bring with it the consummation of all the works of God, the unfolding of eternal destiny. It will usher in a new heaven and a new earth.

6

HOLY COMMUNION IN
THE REFORMED CHURCH OF ENGLAND

For the last half of the sixteenth century (1549–1603), the sacrament of Holy Communion was celebrated in the Church of England in a manner that was clearly Reformed, and yet it looked vaguely Catholic.[1] That, at least, was the intention. It was the working out of that typically English virtue of compromise. Elizabeth I reigned from 1558 to 1603.[2] She vigorously supported the Reformation because otherwise she did not have a legitimate claim to the throne. Elizabeth, like her father, Henry VIII, was a Machiavellian "prince." She was an Erastian, firmly believing in the right of Christian princes to direct everything in their realms, including the affairs

---

[1] For information on the English Reformation, see: Patrick Collinson, *The Elizabethan Puritan Movement* (Berkeley and Los Angeles: University of California Press, 1967); Horton Davies, *Worship and Theology in England: From Cranmer to Baxter and Fox, 1534–1690* (Grand Rapids, MI: Eerdmans, 1996); Norman L. Jones, *Faith by Statute: Parliament and the Settlement of Religion, 1559* (London: Royal Historical Society; and Atlantic Highlands, NJ: Humanities Press, 1982); Norman L. Jones, "Elizabethan Settlement," in *The Oxford Encyclopedia of the Reformation*, ed. Hans J. Hillerbrand, 4 vols. (New York: Oxford University Press, 1996), 2:36–38; Marshall Mason Knappen, *Tudor Puritanism: A Chapter in the History of Idealism* (Chicago and London: The University of Chicago Press, 1970); Hughes Oliphant Old, *The Reading and Preaching of the Scriptures in the Worship of the Christian Church*, vol. 4, *The Age of the Reformation* (Grand Rapids, MI: Eerdmans, 2002), pp. 134–157; Leo Frank Solt, *Church and State in Early Modern England, 1509–1640* (New York: Oxford University Press, 1990); and Bard Thompson, *Liturgies of the Western Church* (Philadelphia: Fortress Press, 1980), pp. 225–284.

[2] On Elizabeth I, see: Suzan Doran, *Elizabeth I and Religion: 1558–1603* (London and New York: Routledge, 1994); William Haller, *Elizabeth I and the Puritans* (New York: Cornell University Press, 1964); and Anne Lake Prescott, *Elizabeth and Mary Tudor* (Aldershot, UK: Ashgate Publishing Company, 2001).

of the Church.³ She and her advisors understood that if she wanted to be accepted as queen, the Church of England had to accept the Reformation and its worship had to be Reformed, although for the sake of compromise it needed at least to look something like Catholic worship. It needed to be celebrated in the same buildings and the ministers needed to be dressed in the same traditional vestments. It needed to look like a *reform* rather than a *revolution*.

It was, to be sure, really under the reign of Elizabeth's brother, Edward VI, that the actual liturgical changes were made,⁴ and it was in 1549 that the first *Book of Common Prayer* was promulgated.⁵ There was no question about it; this first prayer book was clearly Protestant, and yet there were many who figured it was not Protestant enough, and so in 1552 a second prayer book was published.

Edward VI was a precocious boy who had definite religious feelings. He believed very strongly in the reforms of Thomas Cranmer, Hugh Latimer, and Nicholas Ridley. He was favorably impressed with the preaching of John Hooper and had him, a well known disciple of the Zurich Reformation, appointed bishop of Gloucester.

Shortly thereafter Edward died and was succeeded by his half-sister Mary, a strong Catholic who was determined to restore Catholic worship. Mary had those who had developed this new Reformed worship burned at the stake. During Mary's reign, the Protestant forms of worship were put on hold. But then, five years later, Mary died as well and was succeeded by Edward's other half-sister, Elizabeth. Elizabeth, as I have already said, was Protestant and realized she had to support the reform of worship begun by her brother if she wanted to make good on her claim to the throne.

---

³ On Erastianism, see: J. Wayne Baker, "Erastianism," in *The Oxford Encyclopedia of the Reformation*, 2:59–60.

⁴ On the introduction of Protestantism by King Edward VI, see: Francis Aidan Gasquet, *Edward VI and the Book of Common Prayer* (London: J. Hodges, 1891); and Diarmaid MacCulloch, *Boy King: Edward VI and the Protestant Reformation* (New York: Palgrave, 2001).

⁵ See *The First and Second Prayer Books of Edward VI* (New York: E. P. Dutton, 1949).

So for forty-four years, Elizabeth maintained a form of worship that was clearly Reformed.

It would be a mistake to imagine that Elizabeth supported Protestantism only out of political realism. Elizabeth never let her personal feelings show, but she was the daughter of Anne Boleyn, a staunch Protestant. Anne's father, Thomas Boleyn, was even more thoroughly committed to reform. Elizabeth's mother died as a martyr to the cause of Protestantism, and one could well imagine that Elizabeth saw her support of Protestantism as her revenge for her mother's execution.[6]

Traditionally this form of worship maintained during the reign of Elizabeth has been called the Elizabethan Settlement. Elizabeth went back to the *Book of Common Prayer* as it was revised in 1552 shortly before the death of Edward VI. It was the more Protestant version, yet even at that a few nods were made to the old Catholic liturgical forms. The Elizabethan Settlement, as we have said, was consciously intended to at least *look* like a compromise. It was, however, heavily loaded toward Protestantism.[7]

Let us look at some of the particularly Reformed concerns of the communion service in the *Book of Common Prayer* as it was celebrated during the Tudor period.

KING EDWARD'S PRAYER BOOK[8]

First we notice the importance of a Prayer of Confession followed by an Assurance of Pardon.

---

[6] For a fresh look at the Boleyn family's role in England's Reformation, see: Joanna Denny, *Anne Boleyn: A New Life of England's Tragic Queen* (Philadelphia: Da Capo Press, 2006). The author uses previously unavailable original sources to paint a very different picture of the Boleyn family than is the current perception.

[7] For a fuller discussion of the Elizabethen Settlement, see Knappen, *Tudor Protestantism*, pp. 163-186. For a recent treatment of the English Reformation, see: Diarmid MacCulloch, *The Later Reformation in England, 1547-1603* (New York: Palgrave, 2001).

[8] See *The First and Second Prayer Books of Edward VI*; John E. Booty, "The Book of Common Prayer," in *The Oxford Encyclopedia of the Reformation*, 1:189–193; John E.

Almightie God, father of oure Lorde Jesus Christe, maker of all thynges, Judge of all men, we knowledge and bewayle oure manyfolde synnes and wyckednes, whiche we from tyme to tyme most grevously have committed, by thoughte, worde, and dede, agaynst thy devine Majestie: provoking most justely thy wrath and indignacion againste us: we doe earnestlye repente, and be hartely sory for these oure misdoynges: the remembraunce of them is grievouse unto us, the burthen of them is intollerable: have mercy upon us, have mercye upon us moste mercyfull father, for thy sonne oure LORDE Jesus Chrystes sake: forgeve us all that is past, & graunt that we maye ever hereafter, serve and please thee, in newnesse of lyfe, to the honour & glory of thy name: Through Jesus Christ our lord. Amen.

Then shall the Priest or the Bishop (being present) stand up, and turning himselfe to the people, saye thus.

Almightie God our heavenly father, who of his great mercy, hath promised forgeuenesse of synnes to al them, which with heartie repentaunce and true fayth turne unto hym: have mercy upon you, pardon and deliver you from all your synnes, confirme and strength you in all goodnesse, and bryng you to everlasting life: through Jesus Christ our Lord. Amen.[9]

This prayer was an important part of the public prayer in Geneva and it went back to the *Strasbourg Psalter*, as we have noted.[10] We find this prayer in both the 1549 *Book of Common Prayer* and the 1552 *Book of Common Prayer*. The use of the Ten Commandments in a sort of responsive litany found in the 1552 *Book of Common Prayer* looks very

---

Booty, *The Godly Kingdom of Tudor England: Great Books of the English Reformation* (Wilton, CT: Morehouse-Barlow Co., 1981); Frank Edward Brightman, *The English Rite: Being a Synopsis of the Sources and Revisions of the Book of Common Prayer*, 2 vols. (London: Rivingtons, 1915); Davies, *Worship and Theology in England*; and Joseph Ketley, ed. *The Two Liturgies, A.D. 1549 and A.D. 1552* (Cambridge: Printed at the University Press, 1844).

[9] Thompson, *Liturgies of the Western Church*, p. 278.

[10] Hughes Oliphant Old, *The Patristic Roots of Reformed Worship*, American edition (Black Mountain, NC: Worship Press, 2004), pp. 223–239.

6: Holy Communion in the Reformed Church of England

similar to the practice of both Geneva and Strasbourg.

We also notice the reappearance of the Pastoral Prayer or, as modern liturgiologists call it, the Prayer of the Faithful.

> Let us pray for the whole state of Christes Churche militant here in earth.
>
> Almightie and everliving God, which by thy holy Apostle haste taughte us to make prayers and supplicacions, and to geve thankes for all menne: we humbly beseche thee moste mercifully to accepte our almose [alms], and to receive these our prayers whiche we offre unto thy divine Majestie: beseching thee to inspire continuallye, the universal churche with the spirite of trueth, unitie and concorde: and graunte that al they that doe confesse thy holy name, maye agree in the trueth of thy holy word, and lyve in unitie and Godly love. We beeseche thee also to save and defende all Christian kynges, Princes, and governours, and speciallye thy servaunte, Edwarde our Kyng, that under hym we maye be Godlye and quietly governed: and graunte unto hys whole counsayle, and to al that be put in aucthoritie under hym, that they may truely and indifferentlye minister iustice, to the punishmente of wickednesse and vice, and to the mayntenaunce of Gods true religion and vertue. Geve grace (O heavenly father) to all Bisshops, pastoures and Curates, that they may both by theyr lyfe and doctryne set foorth thy true and lyvely worde, and rightly and duely administer thy holy Sacramentes: and to al thy people geve thy heavenly grace, and especially to thys congregacion here present, that with meke hearte & due reverence, they maye heare and receive thy holy worde, truely servynge thee in holynes and righteousness al the dayes of their lyfe. And we most humbly beseche thee of thy goodness (O Lord) to coumforte and succoure al them which in thys transitorye life be in trouble, sorowe, nede, sickenes, or any other adversitie: Graunt this O father, for Jesus Christes sake our onely mediatour and advocate. Amen.[11]

---

[11] Thompson, *Liturgies of the Western Church*, pp. 273–274.

This was a prayer going back to the famous Prayer of the Eighteen Benedictions so popular in the synagogue. We find traces of it in the New Testament. Many versions of it are found all through the literature of the ancient Church. The most elaborate version of it, however, is found in the *Apostolic Constitutions*. This prayer had strong patristic roots. The prayer had had an important place in the Reformed liturgy of Geneva in 1542, being adapted by Calvin from Bucer's Strasbourg liturgy.

The most obviously Reformed feature of the *Book of Common Prayer*, as it appeared in both the prayer books of Edward VI and the one used during the reign of Elizabeth I, was that it fully expected that the Sunday service featuring the celebration of the Lord's Supper was to include a sermon.[12] If the minister did not preach a sermon, he was expected to read one of the homilies provided by the English Reformers. These homilies were really rather exceptional works, provided by leading preachers during the reign of Edward VI. Today they are recognized for their literary value as well as their simple, thorough Christian teaching. Doctrinally these homilies were thoroughly Protestant. They clearly advocated the reforms of the sixteenth century Reformation. In actual fact they set the standard for the English pulpit for centuries to come. It took a few generations for the English Church to be able to produce the sort of regular preaching that the *Prayer Book* envisioned, but in time regular preaching did appear.

The *Book of Common Prayer* has clearly rejected any form of the veneration of the saints. The Scholastic doctrine of the eucharistic

---

[12] On the Book of Homilies, see: Terence R. Murphy, "Book of Homilies," in *The Oxford Encyclopedia of the Reformation*, 1:194–195. See also J. W. Blench, *Preaching in England in the Late Fifteenth and Sixteenth Centuries: A Study of English Sermons, 1450–c.1600* (New York: Barnes and Noble, 1964); John Griffiths, ed., *The Homilies: Appointed to be Read in Churches* (Hereford: Brynmill, 2006); and Mary Ellen Rickey and Thomas B. Stroup, eds., *Certaine Sermons or Homilies Appointed to be Read in Churches in the Time of Queen Elizabeth I, 1547–1571: A Facsimile Reproduction of the Edition of 1623 with an Introduction* (Gainesville, FL: Scholars' Facsimiles and Reprints, 1968).

6: HOLY COMMUNION IN THE REFORMED CHURCH OF ENGLAND

sacrifice, we notice, finds no place. There is no prayer of oblation, nor is there an elevation of the host. In its place there is an allusion to Romans 12:1–2, "We present unto thee ourselves, our souls, and our bodies to be a spiritual sacrifice." The same thought was found in the earlier editions of the *Strasbourg Psalter*, although it had been withdrawn by 1539. One does find quite clearly that the celebration of the Lord's Supper is to be understood as a memorial of Christ's atoning sacrifice, but, especially in the Words of Administration, it is phrased in a most ambiguous way so that one could understand the liturgy in terms of transubstantiation. This, of course, was the genius of the Elizabethan Settlement, or, at least, the way the moderate Reformers understood it.

Much could be said about the Eucharistic Prayer of the various Prayer Books during the reigns of Edward VI and Elizabeth I. We will have to leave the details of this to the specialists. Perhaps the best we can say is that it intended to be moderately Protestant. It intended to find a *via media* and yet both the Catholics on one hand and the Reformed on the other insisted that there was no *via media*. Luther argued this so dramatically at the Marburg Colloquy in 1529. There were Reformers, however, who were convinced that a *via media* was possible, especially those who had studied under Christian Humanism such as Melanchthon, Bucer, and, finally, Calvin. Well, one could argue this point.[13]

Surely one of the places where the most distinctly Reformed concerns carried the day, at least in the *Prayer Book* of 1552, was the matter of replacing the altars of Baal with the Lord's Table. Edward's *Second Prayer Book* literally says that the sacrament is to be celebrated on a Table in the body of the church covered with a fair white cloth. Nicholas Ridley, the Lord Bishop of London, one of the more scholarly bishops of his day, had done much to clean up

---

[13] A most helpful recent contribution to the discussion is Paul Rorem's study of the *Consensus Tigurinus*. Paul Rorem, *Calvin and Bullinger on the Lord's Supper* (Bramcote, England: Grove Books Limited, 1989).

the churches of his diocese. First of all, he rid the churches of any idolatrous statues, shrines, or pictures used in superstitious rites. But even more pressing for the theologian was the multitude of altars.[14] We noticed the same concern in Strasbourg.[15]

Another distinctly Reformed concern which comes out in the *First Prayer Book* of Edward VI is the objection to requiring the communicants to receive the bread and wine kneeling. This controversy over the so called "Black Rubric" really has a much more serious concern in it than the racy title of the affair by which it has ever since been known.[16] The medieval church had developed a liturgical rite for receiving the communion that obscured the sign of sharing a meal. The communicant was supposed to come up to the altar and kneel down so the celebrant could place the host in the mouth of the communicant. There was no question about it; this in no way looked like the sharing of a meal. This, as the Reformers understood it, was basic to the sign, the *signum* of the sacrament.

The "Black Rubric" is supposed to have been the work of John Knox. It did make its appearance in the second edition of the *Book of Common Prayer* in 1552, but eventually it was suppressed.[17]

The fact that the *Book of Common Prayer* provided a service of worship in English, the common tongue, was another obviously Protestant characteristic of it. It was not only in English, it was in very good English, and that surely contributed to the success of

---

[14] See: Eamon Duffy, *The Stripping of the Altars: Traditional Religion in England, 1400–1580* (New Haven: Yale University Press, 1992); Kenneth Fincham and Nicholas Tyacke, *Altars Restored: The Changing Face of English Religious Worship, 1547–c.1700* (Oxford: Oxford University Press, 2007); and Christopher Haigh, *The Plain Man's Pathways to Heaven: Kinds of Christianity in Post-Reformation England, 1570–1640* (Oxford: Oxford University Press, 2007).

[15] Ottomar Frederick Cypris, *Basic Principles: Translation and Commentary of Martin Bucer's "Grund und Ursach," 1524*, Th.D dissertation for Union Theological Seminary in the City of New York, 1971 (Ann Arbor: University Microfilms, 2003), pp. 196–207, hereinafter Bucer, *Basic Principles*.

[16] For more information on the Black Rubric, see: "Black Rubric," *Oxford Dictionary of the Christian Church*, ed. F. L. Cross (Oxford: Oxford University Press, 1974), p. 178.

[17] See "Knox, John," *Oxford Dictionary of the Christian Church*, p. 786.

English Protestantism in general and the prayer book in particular.

There was, however, a major problem with this prayer book; it was a religious rite completely at the service of the state. This incipient Erastianism became more and more pronounced.[18] As we will see, what started out as a Reformed rite became more and more an "Anglican" rite. This tendency to make worship Anglican is supposed to have first become explicit in the rift between John Knox and John Jewel in Frankfurt.[19] It was not until Richard Hooker's *Ecclesiastical Polity* that it became broadly accepted. With the Stuart dynasty, the divine right of kings became an article of faith. There were plenty of Protestants in England, however, who saw no value in exchanging papal authority for royal authority. They saw no reason the Church should allow the state to decide how it should worship.

THOMAS CRANMER

Thomas Cranmer (1489–1556) was a churchman who understood the ways of the world. He knew how to get things done for Christ, as some of my Southern California friends like to put it. Cranmer was a man who knew how to make a compromise with the world in which he lived and understood that the times have a way of changing and that one has to go along with the changing world. But in the end he was willing to stand for the truth and, finally and quite heroically, he did. He, too, was burned at the stake for the mystery of the eucharistic presence and a very confused sort of political piety.[20] From a distance the irony of it all is pathetic, and

---

[18] On Erastianism, see: Baker, "Erastianism;" and Neville J. Figgis, "Erastus and Erastianism," *Journal of Theological Studies* 2 (1901): 66–101.

[19] See: Gary W. Jenkins, *John Jewell and the English National Church: The Dilemmas of an Erastian Reformer* (Aldershot, UK: Ashgate Publishing Company, 2006); and Knappen, *Tudor Puritanism*, especially the chapter regarding Knox and the troubles at Frankfurt.

[20] For biographical material on Cranmer, see: Geoffrey W. Bromiley, *Thomas Cranmer, Theologian* (New York: Oxford University Press, 1956); Diarmaid MacCulloch, *Thomas Cranmer: A Life* (New Haven: Yale University Press, 1996); and Jasper Godwin Ridley, *Thomas Cranmer* (Oxford: The Clarendon Press, 1962).

yet he and the other English reformers were real people and were dealing with the truth as best they could.

In the early 1530s Thomas Cranmer was a student of canon law at Cambridge. He was a rather obscure figure until he devised a way to help King Henry VIII out of a jam. The king needed a divorce. His legitimate wife had not borne him a son and he needed an heir. The trouble was that this wife, Catherine of Aragon, had some pretty high connections, and the chance of getting an indulgence from the pope in his case was very slim. Thomas Cranmer came up with a brilliant argument to support Henry's case for an annulment. We don't need to go into all that royal intrigue once again. All we want to say is that Thomas Cranmer ended up being made Archbishop of Canterbury because he was a smart canon lawyer. He was not exactly a saint, nor was he really a theologian. There is a big difference between being a theologian and being a canon lawyer.[21]

There is no question, however, but that Thomas Cranmer was a disciple of the new learning and the sort of religious reforms that were advocated by the new learning. All the wrangling over the king's divorce and the authority of the Roman pope over the English Church had thoroughly convinced him that the Reformation was necessary. A Renaissance lawyer had to go through much the same kind of education that a Renaissance biblical scholar had to go through. The authenticity of source documents and text critical studies were just as important to a lawyer as they were to the biblical scholar. One can understand why the young canon lawyer could explain to Henry VIII why the Protestant Reformation might be seen as an ally to a Renaissance prince like Henry.

As the argument over the divorce got going, Henry sent Cranmer to Germany to see what support he might be able to find among the German Lutherans. There, among other things, he met and married the niece of one of the German theologians. Cranmer apparently found the German Lutherans quite compat-

---

[21] For a further discussion of Cranmer, see: Davies, *Worship and Theology in England*.

ible, or perhaps one might say Cranmer drank deeply of the German theological *zeitgeist*.

Put it any way you want, Cranmer was open to new ideas. The "new learning" school was weary of the old Scholastic theology—especially its understanding of worship. The core of that theology of worship, namely, the doctrine of transubstantiation, caught it from all sides in the intellectual circles of Germany. Cranmer came home from Germany increasingly sympathetic to the Reformation.

In 1532, Thomas Cranmer was appointed Archbishop of Canterbury. The church was so thoroughly dominated by the state in those days that the king, in effect, named the bishops, and the king, as any politician has a way of doing, would always name those whom he believed would be most compliant to the royal concerns.

There is a very important thing to be noted here. Cranmer understood the polemic against transubstantiation in terms of the Wycliffe controversy of the fourteenth century.[22] This is not surprising. They were both Englishmen, and viewed the elements in terms of Nominalist Scholasticism, whereas the Swiss Reformers viewed the Lord's Supper in terms of Christian Humanism and the new learning. They argued it in terms of biblical theology. The Swiss approached the Lord's Supper and baptism as signs of the covenant.

The English Reformers were much more thoroughly influenced by Nominalism and the *via moderna* than the Rhenish Reformers. Bullinger had studied the *via antiqua* in Cologne. Vermigli and Bucer were both *via antiqua* theologians.[23] The English were a couple generations behind the Rhenish Reformers in the study of Greek and Hebrew. As Horton Davies reports, Cranmer never discusses covenant, nor the Passover typology, nor even the

---

[22] For a brief discussion of the influence of Wycliffe on Cranmer, see: Old, *Reading and Preaching of the Scriptures in the Worship of the Christian Church*, 4:136.

[23] Bullinger, Bucer, and Vermigli were originally educated by the Dominicans in the *via antiqua*, that is, in classical Scholasticism. It was as they learned Greek and Hebrew and began to study the Scriptures in the original languages that they adopted the new learning and embraced the Reformation.

circumcision typology when it came to baptism.[24] The new biblical theology of the Christian Humanists is completely ignored.

A. Cranmer's Eucharistic Theology

According to Horton Davies, Thomas Cranmer's eucharistic doctrine is something of a mystery. It is hard to be sure whether what he says is his own personal belief or whether it is what he thinks the king wants. He really believed in the divine right of kings.[25]

We probably need to look at this a bit more realistically. More than one pastor has given long thought to whether his congregation will follow his leadership on a particular issue. A pastor would be foolish to advocate a program which shows little promise of being received. As one of my colleagues one time warned me, "You don't have to die on every hill." Cranmer actually was amazingly savvy in pushing the reforms he figured he could get through at any given time. But it is also the case that Cranmer's eucharistic theology went through considerable development. As late as 1538 he still seems to have supported the traditional doctrines of the late Middle Ages in regard to both transubstantiation and the eucharistic sacrifice.[26]

Returning from Germany in 1532 he was definitely inclined toward the positions being advocated by the Lutherans. Cranmer himself tells us that it was Nicholas Ridley, the Cambridge New Testament scholar, later Lord Bishop of London, who won him to a position very close to the position of the Reformers of Zurich. That, some have insisted, is where Thomas Cranmer finally ended up.[27] It is more likely the case that eventually he came much closer

---

[24] For a discussion of Cranmer's understanding of the sacraments, see: Davies, *Worship and Theology in England*, pp. 111–120.

[25] Davies, *Worship and Theology in England*, p. 111.

[26] *Encyclopedia Britannica*, 15th ed., says that he had abandoned these by 1538. Geoffrey R. Elton, et al., "Cranmer, Thomas," in *The New Encyclopedia Britannica*, 15th ed., 29 vols. (Chicago: Encyclopedia Britannica, Inc., 1994), 3:713–715.

[27] Among those who insist that was in the end Cranmer's position is Gregory Dix, *The Shape of the Liturgy* (London: Adam and Charles Black Ltd., 1975), pp. 640–699.

to the position reached by the pastors of Zurich and Geneva in the famous *Consensus Tigurinus*.

The *Consensus Tigurinus* was a document hammered together by Calvin, Bullinger, and the theologians of both Zurich and Geneva. Following in the tradition of the *Wittenburg Consensus* of 1535 it agreed that the sacraments were signs, but not empty signs. Furthermore the *Consensus Tigurinus* went so far as to agree that the sacraments were signs and seals. That is, they were effective signs. They helped bring about what they symbolized.

As we have said, Cranmer's eucharistic theology was thought out over against a Nominalist theology. Cranmer's theological education was Scholastic and it was *via moderna* Scholasticism, not *via antiqua*.[28]

Even more than that was the lingering influence of the eucharistic theology of John Wycliffe. Wycliffe had taught in Oxford in the thirteen hundreds, more than a hundred years before. Many of Zwingli's ideas were quite similar to the ideas of Wycliffe. But there were very definite differences. Zwingli was basically a Christian Humanist and he approached the doctrine of the Lord's Supper from the standpoint of Christian Humanism rather than Scholasticism. All one has to do is read Zwingli's *Treatise on the Lord's Supper* and it becomes evident that he is arguing from rhetoric not logic.[29] Zwingli, Oecolampadius, and Bullinger were concerned to know what the text said and what it meant by what it said. Cranmer listened to Zwingli, even more to Bullinger, and finally to Bucer, but he still saw the whole discussion in terms of the late medieval discussion, not the new approach to the study of

---

[28] For a discussion of *via antiqua* and *via moderna* Scholasticism on the early Reformation, see: Heiko A. Oberman, *The Harvest of Medieval Theology: Gabriel Biel and Late Medieval Nominalism*, rev. ed. (Grand Rapids, MI: Baker Book House, 2000); and Heiko A. Oberman, "*Via Antiqua* and *Via Moderna*: Late Medieval Prolegamena to Early Reformation Thought," *Journal of the History of Ideas* 48/1 (Jan-Mar 1987): 23-40.

[29] Geoffrey W. Bromiley, ed., *Zwingli and Bullinger*, Library of Christian Classics, vol. 24 (Philadelphia: The Westminster Press, 1953), pp. 176–238.

Scripture as the Christian Humanists understood it.

In his polemical writing on the subject of communion, Cranmer was much more concerned with attacking the medieval doctrines of transubstantiation and the eucharistic sacrifice than he was with advocating a positive doctrine of the sacrament. Horton Davies makes this especially clear in his study of Cranmer's work, *Defense of the True and Catholic Doctrine of the Sacrament of the Body and Blood of our Savior Christ*, published in 1550.[30] In this work Cranmer attacks the four principle errors of the medieval teaching: first, the doctrine of transubstantiation; second, the doctrine of corporal presence; third, concerning the *manducatio impiorum* (i.e., the teaching that non-Christians also partake of the body and blood of Christ just as surely as the devout); and fourth, the doctrine of the eucharistic sacrifice.[31]

One of the problems involved in this discussion is that the position Zwingli followed developed considerably between 1525, when he published his *Treatise on the Lord's Supper*, and 1550, when the more formative writings of Cranmer, such as his *Defense of the True and Catholic Faith of the Sacrament*, were published. As Horton Davies points out, the *Consensus Tigurinus* came out in 1549.[32] It was the same year the *Book of Common Prayer* came out.

B. Cranmer's Attempt at a Reformed Canon

Basic to Cranmer's effort to produce a liturgy for the celebration of the sacrament of communion was his attempt to produce a Reformed canon.[33] By that we mean a prayer of *thanksgiving* over the bread and wine that could be understood as a prayer of *consecration* that would in some sense be regarded as *blessing* the bread

---

[30] Davies, *Worship and Theology in England*, pp. 111–123.
[31] Davies, *Worship and Theology in England*, p. 113.
[32] Davies, *Worship and Theology in England*, p. 118.
[33] On Cranmer's communion service, see Brightman, *The English Rite*.

and wine.[34] The liturgiologist would probably want to call this the Eucharistic Prayer, one of the most traditional elements of worship in the biblical tradition. This Eucharistic Prayer was offered at a formal meal as an acknowledgment that the food about to be eaten is ultimately from the hand of God. Such a prayer renders thanks to God and thereby consecrates that food to the use of those about to partake of it. This is a basic principle of prayer, as we find in 1 Timothy 4:4, "For everything created by God is good, and nothing is to be rejected if it is received with thanksgiving."

At a formal meal such as the Passover meal this basic eucharistic prayer had become a series of prayers. There was a blessing over the wine at the beginning of the meal, then a blessing over the bread, and then another blessing over a second cup of wine at the end of the meal. This blessing over the second cup, the cup of blessing, was somewhat longer, including as it did a thanksgiving for sacred history. The *Didaché*, for instance, gives us three prayers of thanksgiving in the course of the meal.

Over the centuries this Eucharistic Prayer developed into a complicated formula which the celebrant was expected to recite word for word. The first examples we have of this prayer are fairly fluid, but as time went on the text became more and more set until the end of the sixth century when Gregory the Great regarded the canon as set. As Gregory and his contemporaries understood it, it was the reciting of this canon which consecrated the bread and wine. More and more this was regarded in ways that seem very close to magic. In the popular mind, this was what was understood as the "hocus-pocus" dimension of the mass, if we might be allowed a little of the leaven of levity.

It was from this most sacred core of the mass that the prayer of sacrifice had developed. It was in this canon that the bread and wine

---

[34] On the development of the canon, see: Joseph Andreas Jungmann, *The Mass of the Roman Rite: Its Origins and Development*, trans. Francis A. Brunner, 2 vols. (New York: Benziger, 1950–1955).

were offered up to God. It was through the necessary reciting of this text that the bread and wine were transubstantiated into the body and blood of Christ and then presented as a propitiatory sacrifice to God. It was in this prayer that the roots of this abuse were found.

At this point several of the continental Reformers such as Bucer and Calvin simply removed the canon and made no attempt to try to replace it with anything else. Cranmer, on the other hand, tried to re-write the canon, leaving out those prayers that were misleading, especially those that implied the sacrament was to be understood as a sacrifice.

The canon as we find it in the 1549 *Prayer Book* is as follows:[35]

> *Then the Prieste shall saye.*
> The Lorde be with you.
>
> *Aunswere.*
> And with thy spirite.
>
> *Priest.*
> Lift up your heartes.
>
> *Aunswere.*
> We lift them up unto the Lorde.
>
> *Priest.*
> Let us geve thankes to our Lorde God.
>
> *Aunswere.*
> It is mete and right so to do.
>
> *The Priest.*
> . . . It is very meete, righte, and our bounden duetie, that we shoulde at all tymes, and in all places, geve thankes to thee O Lorde, almightye everlastyng God, whiche arte one God, one Lorde, not one onely person, but three persones in one substaunce: For that which we beleve of the glory of the father, the same we beleve of the sonne, and of the holye ghoste, without anye dyfference, or inequalitie.[36]

---

[35] The text of the 1549 edition is in large part repeated verbatim in the 1552 edition.
[36] This "proper preface" is reserved for the Feast of Trinity. The 1549 *Book of Common Prayer* has a few different proper prefaces for different church holidays.

6: Holy Communion in The Reformed Church of England

...

After whiche preface shall folowe immediatly.

Therfore with Angels and Archangels, and with all the holy companye of heaven: we laude and magnify thy glorious name, evermore praisyng thee, and saying:

Holye, holye, holye, Lorde God of hostes: heaven and yearthe are full of thy glory: Osanna in the highest. Blessed is he that commeth in the name of the Lorde: Glory to thee O lorde in the highest.

This the Clerkes shal also syng.

...

O God heavenly father, which of thy tender mercie, dyddest geve thine only sonne Jesu Christ, to suffre death upon the crosse for our redempcion, who made there (by his one oblacion once offered) a full, perfect, and sufficient sacrifyce, oblacion, and satysfacyon, for the sinnes of the whole worlde, and did institute, and in his holy Gospell commaund us, to celebrate a perpetuall memory, of that his precious death, untyll his coming again: Heare us (O merciful father) we besech thee: and with thy holy spirite and worde, vouchsafe to blesse and sanctifie these thy gyftes, and creatures of bread and wyne, that they maie be unto us the bodye and bloude of thy moste derely beloved sonne Jesus Christe. Who in the same nyght that he was betrayed: tooke breade, and when he had blessed, and geven thankes: he brake it, and gave it to his disciples, saiyng: Take, eate, this is my bodye which is geven for you, do this in remembraunce of me.

Likewyse after supper he toke the cuppe, and when he had geuen thankes, he gaue it to them, saiyng: drynk ye all of this, for this is my bloude of the newe Testament, whyche is shed for you and for many, for remission of synnes: do this as oft as ye shall drinke it in remembraunce of me.

...

Let us praye.

> As our savior Christe hath commaunded and taught us, we are bolde to saye. Our father whyche art in heaven, halowed be thy name. Thy Kyngdome come. Thy wyll be doen in yearth, as it is in heauen. Geue us this daye our dayly breade. And forgeve us our trespaces, as wee forgeve them that trespasse agaynst us. And leade us not into temptacion.[37]

There is no question about it; from a Reformed point of view this is a great improvement over the Latin canon. It expresses many basic Protestant concerns. It is a far more thorough reform than a simple English translation of the Latin canon. On the other hand it encouraged halfway reforms of the worst sort. It allowed a magical understanding of the sacrament. It makes it too easy to imagine that by reciting a set formula, the bread and wine are magically transformed into the body and blood of Christ.

It has to be said in Cranmer's favor that he thought he was building on much more solid ground than he in fact had. He thought he had a copy of the eucharistic liturgy that was used in Rome at the time of Clement of Rome who was supposed to have been Bishop of Rome before the close of the first Christian century. I am told that the library of Lambeth Palace has a copy of the Clementine Liturgy which in actual fact dates to the end of the fourth century rather than the first.

Furthermore, the Clementine Liturgy was not at all what it claimed to be. Today scholars refer to it as the *Apostolic Constitutions*. It is a collection of liturgical materials from fourth century Antioch rather than first century Rome. Even more, it shows us that the Hellenistic mystery religions had by that time made major inroads into Christian worship. In no way should it be regarded as a witness to the worship of the Christian Church of the first century. To be sure there is much reported in the *Apostolic Constitutions* which would be helpful for today, but there is much that is misleading.

---

[37] Excerpted from Thompson, *Liturgies of the Western Church*, pp. 254–259.

6: Holy Communion in the Reformed Church of England

NICHOLAS RIDLEY

AND THE ALTARS OF BAAL

That the communicants should be gathered around a table to share the Lord's Supper was a major concern of the early English Reformation. Quite differently from the Lutheran Reformation in Germany, those influenced by the Swiss Reformation were concerned to emphasize the visual image of the congregation sharing a meal. Beside that, the English Reformers had noticed that the New Testament speaks very specifically of the sharing of the Lord's Supper at the Lord's Table (cf. 1 Cor. 10:16–17). It was Nicholas Ridley, the Protestant Bishop of London, who most conspicuously led the Church of England in this direction.

Nicholas Ridley, one of the best scholars among the English Reformers, was the son of an old Northumberland family.[38] His uncle, Richard Ridley, had a Cambridge doctorate and sponsored his nephew's studies at Pembroke Hall. Young Nicholas distinguished himself in Greek and the new biblical studies so popular among the Christian Humanists. He received his Master of Arts degree in 1526. Then he studied abroad, first in Paris and then in Louvain, returning to Cambridge in 1530. In 1537 he received the bachelor of divinity. More and more he identified himself with the supporters of the Reformation.

In 1537 Archbishop Cranmer appointed Ridley as his chaplain. In the manner of the day Ridley received one preferment after another. In 1540 he became Master of his college, Pembroke Hall,

---

[38] For biographical information on Ridley, see: David M. Loades, "Ridley, Nicholas," in *The Oxford Encyclopedia of the Reformation*, 3:431–432; David M. Loades, *The Oxford Martyrs* (Bangor, Gwynedd: Headstart History, 1992); Jasper Godwin Ridley, *Nicholas Ridley: A Biography* (London and New York: Longmans, Green, 1957); and "Ridley, Nicholas," in *The Encyclopedia Britannica*, 11th ed., 32 vols. (New York: Encyclopedia Britannica, Inc., 1911), 23:320. See also: Brian Douglas, "Nicholas Ridley, c. 1500–1555, Bishop of London," http://web.mac.com/brian.douglas/Anglican_Eucharistic_Theology/Blog/Entries/2006/5/28_Nicholas_Ridleyc1500_-_1555Bishop_of_London.html. Accessed June 17, 2009.

and in the following year chaplain to Henry VIII and Canon of Canterbury. He had obviously been recognized as one of the up-and-coming young men of the future. Positions like these came with handsome endowments. On the other hand, living on the cutting edge can be very dangerous. In 1542 Ridley was accused of heretical teaching and was examined by a royal commission. Not long after he was cleared of the charge. Still, a short time after that, he openly abandoned the doctrine of transubstantiation. It was about this time apparently that he convinced the archbishop, Thomas Cranmer, of the Reformed doctrine of the sacrament of Holy Communion. This was about the time Calvin was beginning to re-establish his position in Geneva and Bucer was leading the Rhenish Reformation to a more moderate position than Zwingli had at first set forth.

By 1547 Ridley was appointed bishop of Rochester, one of the most prestigious positions in the Church of England. At this point it is significant to note that Henry VIII was putting the leadership of the Church of England firmly in the hands of those who were promoting Reformed Protestantism, the Protestantism of the Swiss cities and of the German Rhineland. Liturgical reforms were developing fast in the 1540s and Ridley was one of the Archbishop's most trusted colleagues, especially as Cranmer began to work on the *Book of Common Prayer*, which finally appeared in 1549.

If Henry VIII had wavered from time to time in his support of the Reformation, his heir, Edward VI, was unhesitating in his support of the Reformation and the new form of worship. It was by the new king that the *Book of Common Prayer* was at last promulgated in 1549 and it was by him that the worship of the Church of England became clearly Reformed.

The very next year, 1550, Ridley was appointed Lord Bishop of London, a position of the highest authority. For the next four years Ridley had a tremendous influence on the worship of the Church of England, particularly in regard to ridding the Church from the idolatrous practices which had crept into the worship of the medieval Church.³⁹ Ridley was one of the first bishops to give unwavering support to the Reformed teaching on the sacrament of the Lord's Supper as well as a leading thinker in the question of the architectural setting of Reformed worship. Let us focus very briefly on Ridley's role in "stripping the altars."

As Bishop of London Ridley set out in a very orderly fashion to remove the statues and paintings of Christ, the Virgin Mary, the Apostles and saints, the martyrs, and the confessors that appeared in the churches of London. These were not iconoclastic riots of the sort that occurred in Germany under the influence of the Anabaptists. These were orderly removals carried out by those appointed by the appropriate authority—civil or ecclesiastical.

At the center of this cleansing of the Temple was the removal of all the altars in the church, whether the high altar or the many little altars in side chapels. This multitude of altars was replaced in each church by a single wooden table. This was a liturgical concern characteristic of the Rhenish Reformation from Zurich to Strasbourg.⁴⁰ Theologically this reform was well grounded. Even the Second Vatican Council in most recent times began to move in a similar direction.

Included in the volume of the collected works of Ridley is a short piece in which the venerable bishop put down his reasons for insisting that altars be removed from the churches and that they be replaced by wooden tables. The document is rather short and therefore we reproduce a number of quotations from it.⁴¹

The document is as remarkable as it is brief. It bears the title, "Reasons Why the Lord's Board Should Rather Be after the Form

---

³⁹ See: Duffy, *The Stripping of the Altars*; Fincham and Tyacke, *Altars Restored*; and Haigh, *The Plain Man's Pathways to Heaven*. See a review of the latter two books by Ian Green in *The English Historical Review*, 74/508:677–701.

⁴⁰ See Bucer, *Basic Principles*, p. 139–140, 149.

⁴¹ The following excerpts are taken from Nicholas Ridley, *The Works of Nicholas Ridley, D.D. Sometime Lord Bishop of London, Martyr, 1555*, ed. for the Parker Society by the Rev. Henry Christmas (Cambridge: Printed at the University Press, 1843), pp. 321–324.

of a Table, than of an Altar . . ."[42] These words serve as the title of the document but they are also a summary:

> (Certain reasons why the reverend father, Nicholas, bishop of London, amongst other his injunctions given in his late visitation, did exhort those churches in his diocese, where the altars, as then, did remain, to conform themselves to those other churches which had taken them down, and had set up, instead of the multitude of their altars, one decent table in every church. And that herein he did not only not any thing contrary unto the Book of Common Prayer, or to the king's majesty's proceedings, but that he was induced to do the same, partly moved by his office and duty, wherewith he is charged in the same book, and partly for the advancement and sincere setting forward of God's holy word, and the king's majesty's most godly proceedings). . . .[43]

Ridley makes very clear that what he is requiring the local churches in his diocese to do he is doing by virtue of his authority as a minister of the church, to be sure, but also under the authority of the state.

On a more popular front the Reformers were especially concerned to combat superstition:

> The form of a table shall more move the simple from the superstitious opinions of the popish mass, unto the right use of the Lord's Supper. For the use of an altar is to make sacrifice upon it; the use of a table is to serve for men to eat upon. Now, when we come unto the Lord's board, what do we come for? to sacrifice Christ again, and to crucify him again, or to feed upon him that was once only crucified and offered up for us![44] If we come to feed upon him, spiritually to eat his body, and spiritually to drink his blood (which is the true use

---

[42] "The Lord's Board" is the translation of 1 Cor. 10:21, as found in the Geneva Bible of 1580. Ridley, *Works*, p. 321.

[43] Ridley, *Works*, p. 321.

[44] All the Reformers from Luther to Zwingli agreed that the repetition of Christ's sacrifice was the greatest of all the abuses of the mass.

of the Lord's Supper), then no man can deny but the
form of a table is more meet for the Lord's board, than
the form of an altar. . . .[45]

One notices here that Ridley assumes the Reformed doctrine of the spiritual presence. This he probably picked up not so much from Calvin as from other Reformed pastors before him.

> The form of an altar was ordained for the sacrifices
> of the law. . . . But now both the law and the sacrifices
> thereof do cease: wherefore the form of the altar used
> in the altar ought to cease withal.
>
> . . .
>
> Christ did institute the sacrament of his body and
> blood at his last supper at a table, and not at an altar;
> as it appeareth manifestly by the three Evangelists.
> And St Paul calleth the coming to the holy commu-
> nion, the coming unto the Lord's Supper. And also it
> is not read that any of the apostles or the primitive
> church did ever use any altar in ministration of the
> holy communion . . .[46]

This subject will be vigorously debated for centuries to come. Indeed, even today it is vigorously contested, as the work of Duffy, Fincham, Tyacke and Haigh demonstrate.

MARTIN BUCER, *CENSURA*

Martin Bucer (1491–1551) is a Reformer who comes into the story at more than one point.[47] He first fits into the picture as an adolescent boy in Jakob Wimpfeling's Latin School at Sélestat. Sélestat

---

[45] Ridley, *Works*, p. 322.

[46] Ridley, *Works*, p. 323.

[47] For biographical material on Bucer, see: Hastings Eells, *Martin Bucer* (New Haven: Yale University Press, 1931); Martin Greschat, "Bucer, Martin," *Oxford Encyclopedia of the Reformation*, 1:221–224; Martin Greschat, *Martin Bucer: A Reformer and His Times* (Louisville: Westminster John Knox Press, 2004); Constantin Hopf, *Martin Bucer and the English Reformation* (Oxford: B. Blackwell, 1946); G. J. van de Poll, *Martin Bucer's Liturgical Ideas* (Assen: Van Gorcum, 1954); and David

is a storybook Alsacian town at the foot of the Voges Mountains. It is filled with flamboyant Gothic churches and chapels and is surrounded by vineyards. Bucer's father was the cobbler who had more children than he knew what to do with, so he turned young Martin over to the Dominicans who made a scholar of him, giving him one of the best educations the sixteenth century could provide. Jakob Wimpfeling, his teacher, was one of the great Christian Humanist scholars. He had broken away from Scholasticism, advocating a much more Augustinian theology.[48] Vigorously Wimpfeling pursued the Christian Humanist motto *ad fontes*, back to the sources. At an early age Martin knew his Latin and his Greek, and on the eve of the Reformation young Martin was a Dominican brother at the University of Heidelberg studying Hebrew. It was at this point when Luther arrived in the prestigious university town to lay out his demand for reform. This was one of the first statements Luther made of his position and Bucer quickly became one of Luther's first and most enthusiastic supporters. He was both Erasmian and Lutheran at the same time. So Bucer also figures at the Heidelberg Disputation, if not as a disputant, then at least as an enthusiastically applauding partisan.

Soon, however, we find that Bucer had been called to be preacher at Strasbourg. Strasbourg was a city that embraced the Reformation right from the beginning. There Bucer wrote out and published his *Basic Principles*, a work discussing the first attempts at developing a truly Reformed service of worship.[49] For the next twenty-four years Bucer exercised outstanding and creative leadership in developing

---

Wright, ed., *Martin Bucer: Reforming Church and Community* (Cambridge and New York: Cambridge University Press, 1994).

[48] This was the way the question was being discussed by the Alsacian Christian humanists such as Jakob Wimpfeling. See Hughes Oliphant Old, *The Patristic Roots of Reformed Worship*, American edition (Black Mountain, NC: Worship Press, 2004), p. 119, for a discussion of the issue.

[49] For a modern English translation of *Basic Principles*, see Cypris's translation.

6: Holy Communion in The Reformed Church of England

the liturgical and pastoral dimensions of Protestantism.[50] At Strasbourg he became pastor and protector to a whole host of Protestant refugees. One of the best known was John Calvin, who needed a safe house during the tumultuous days of the Reformation.

The time came, however, when Bucer himself had to flee Strasbourg. Charles V, the Holy Roman Emperor, had had sufficient military success that he was able to make things very uncomfortable for Bucer in Strasbourg, and yet in the providence of God Bucer was just the man Edward VI could use to help deepen the Reformation in England. So a new phase of Bucer's reforming career opened up in England where he was appointed Lady Margaret Professor of Theology at Cambridge University, one of the most distinguished academic posts in the kingdom of England.

Bucer arrived in England just at the time the Protestants of England had gotten the support of their young King Edward VI to begin a thorough reform of the worship life of England. Under Archbishop Thomas Cranmer, *The Book of Common Prayer* was published in 1549. It was to be the standard for public worship in the whole kingdom. Not surprisingly the Protestant Archbishop had himself directed much of the project, writing many of the prayers and selecting the scriptures to be read.

Quite naturally Cranmer asked Bucer to review his new *Prayer Book* and to suggest additions or omissions that might be made. Bucer honored the Archbishop's request. It is a rather lengthy document.[51] Bucer tended to meander at his writing desk, but this document, called today Bucer's *Censura*, is a most important

---

[50] Bucer has left us a large collection of theological works. See Martin Bucer, *Martin Bucers Deutsche Schriften*, ed. Robert Stupperich, 5 vols. (Gütersloh: Gütersloher Verlagshaus Gerd Mohn; Paris: Presses Universitaires de France, 1960).

[51] The original Latin edition can be found in: Martin Bucer, *Martini Buceri Opera Latina*, vol. 15, *De Regno Christi*, ed. François Wendel (Paris: Presses Universitaires de France; Gütersloh: C. Bertelsmann Verlag, 1955). Wendel gives a very fine introduction to Bucer in England in pp. ix-lxx.

source document for the history of worship.⁵²

Bucer was very much in accord with much Cranmer and his colleagues had done. It was indeed a thoroughly Reformed service of worship and it most obviously embodied many of the reforms Bucer had envisioned. There were, however, things that Bucer thought could be improved. Let us look at some of Bucer's proposed emendations as well as some of his commendations.

First, we should take Bucer's commendation quite seriously. Bucer recognized that the *Book of Common Prayer* contained much that he had himself written into the liturgical documents of Strasbourg. Right from the beginning of this document Bucer makes clear his concern that our worship be reformed according to Scripture. He would make his recommendations on the basis of their being "in accordance with the word of God."⁵³ This was a phrase used particularly by those Reformers who had been schooled by the Christian Humanists. This would be similar to a more Lutheran basis of *sola scriptura*, but not exactly the same.

The first subject Bucer takes up is the service of daily prayer, that is, morning prayer and evening prayer as they are observed each day of the week. As it happens, these daily prayer services became very popular in England for many years to come. Morning prayer even on Sundays became the most usually attended service. Bucer would more than likely have insisted on the celebration of the Lord's Supper on the Lord's Day but this subject is not broached. If I am correctly informed, it was only with the High Church movement in the nineteenth century that the communion service regained its priority.

Bucer is particularly positive about Cranmer's reform of the service of daily prayer. Bucer says, "In the presentation of the

---

⁵² For a modern edition, see: Martin Bucer, *On the Ceremonies of the Anglican Church: A Critical Examination*, found in Edward Charles Whitaker, ed., *Martin Bucer and the Book of Common Prayer*, Alcuin Club Collection, vol. 55 (Great Wakering: Mayhew-McCrimmon, 1974), pp.10–173. Hereinafter Bucer, *Censura*.

⁵³ Bucer, *Censura*, p. 12.

common daily prayers [Ep21f.] I find nothing set out in the book which is not taken from holy scripture, either word for word as the psalms and lessons, or in accordance with its meaning as the collects are."[54] We notice again that the standard is reformed according to Scripture, that is, in a manner "fully consistent with the word of God and the practice of the primitive churches."[55]

That Bucer should take special interest in Cranmer's morning and evening prayers is quite natural because Cranmer took over many of the reforms Bucer had advocated as early as 1524 in Strasbourg.[56] Among those matters in which Cranmer apparently followed Bucer was the reduction of the hours of prayer from seven to two. Bucer justifies this by the fact that the Law of Moses had specifically commanded morning sacrifices and evening sacrifices.[57] Cranmer had followed Bucer's system of reading through the whole Bible, both Old and New Testaments, in the course of the year using the *lectio continua*. He seems to have followed Bucer's prayer of confession, as well as the pastoral prayer.[58] Bucer's hearty approval of the daily prayer services was only natural, since much of it had been taken from the services Bucer had developed in Strasbourg.

One notices that Bucer is critical of the architectural arrangement of many of the English churches. They are awkward for the needs of the daily prayer services. Many of these churches had choir stalls built into them and by long tradition this was where the daily offices were said. What usually happened was that the ministers read the service in one part of the church while the people were

---

[54] Bucer, *Censura*, p. 14.

[55] Bucer, *Censura*, p. 14.

[56] See my study, "Daily Prayer in the Reformed Church of Strasbourg, 1523–1530," *Worship* 52/2 (March 1978): 121–138.

[57] Theologically, of course, Bucer and other theologians of the day had other arguments for abandoning the traditional seven hours of daily prayer. A very important attempt at revising the practice of daily prayer was begun by the Spanish Catholic reformer, Cardinal Quiñones.

[58] See, for example, a discussion of the Prayer of Confession in Strasbourg in Old, *Patristic Roots*, pp. 223–226.

relegated to another.[59] Bucer was not too clear about what could be done about the problem, but he at least shows he is aware of it.

The situation was somewhat similar regarding the question of clerical vestments.[60] Apparently Bucer found them unnecessary, but he was not ready to make a big fuss about it at that point.[61] The problem comes in when people begin to develop magical and superstitious attitudes toward what these vestments mean and what they can accomplish. Imaginative minds had invented all kinds of symbolic meanings for the stole, the alb, the chasuble, and all the rest. On the other hand the church would do well to have regard for the simplicity which Jesus maintained in his manner of life.

For Bucer one of the most pressing needs for reform was to understand communion as an act of fellowship with Christ. The covenantal dimension of the sacrament should teach us that, by sharing this meal with Christ, we are uniting with Christ. When we understand the covenantal nature of the sacrament, it is impossible for us simply to stand around and watch this sacred meal. Bucer was strongly opposed to celebrating the Supper when only a handful of the gathered congregation partook of the Sacrament. It amounts to holding back when we are so graciously invited.[62] On this point Cranmer probably had much the same feelings. In fact, he had probably gotten many of his ideas on this subject from Bucer to begin with. He needed no support on Bucer's part, but it was surely welcome just the same.

An important dimension of Christian worship for Bucer from his earliest writings on the subject was the diaconal dimension.

---

[59] Bucer, *Censura*, pp. 14–16.

[60] While I happily leave this question to specialists on such matters, what comes in question here is the wearing of first of all the stole, then the surplice for the service of prayer, and the chasuble for the eucharistic services. These were what was meant by the *vestments*. The black "preaching gown" was the normal attire for a scholar, whether he was teaching a class, delivering a lecture, or preaching a sermon. It was not considered a "liturgical vestment."

[61] Bucer, *Censura*, p. 18.

[62] Bucer, *Censura*, pp. 30–32.

Bucer did much to develop the diaconal ministry as a ministry to the poor, the suffering, and the stranger. Here we find Bucer still pushing this point.[63] As Bucer sees it, the service of worship should include a collection for the poor. Bucer had gone even further in Strasbourg. There one of his leading reforms was the ministry of the deacons. As Bucer understood it deacons were given the responsibility of overseeing the ministries of mercy. Rather than being understood as a step to the priesthood, it was understood as a distinct ministry.[64]

One of the most interesting reactions of Bucer is his disapproval of the multitude of gestures used in the celebration of communion. First there are the frequent signs of the cross, the beating of the breast, the genuflections, and the prostrations.[65] Today's liturgiologist finds it difficult to understand this annoyance with liturgical gestures. The problem was that, unlike in our day, the rites of witchcraft and the spells of magic were very much a part of sixteenth-century culture which was still permeated with amulets, charms, astrology, and fear of demonic powers. The numerous liturgical gestures made the sharing of the sacred meal seem like a magical rite. It confused the Christian sacrament with the ceremonies of the witch doctor. The sign of the cross seemed like a superstitious charm used to gain protection from evil spirits—like knocking on wood. The Renaissance was awakening from an age of magic and superstition and the students of Christian Humanism were looking for a faith that could leave all that behind.

Coming to the Order for Holy Communion found in the *Book of Common Prayer*, Bucer is most complimentary, "I thank God to the full extent of my power that he has enabled this to be drawn up with such purity and in such faithful conformity with the word of God, particularly considering the time at which it was done. For

---

[63] Bucer, *Censura*, pp. 36–38.

[64] Bucer, *Censura*, p. 38.

[65] Bucer, *Censura*, p. 42.

if we may assume that everything in it is performed and explained to the people of Christ with appropriate devotion, I see nothing in it with the exception of a very few words and signs, which is not derived from holy scripture."[66] As far as Bucer was concerned, one of the best things about the *Book of Common Prayer* was that it gave proper place to the reading and preaching of the Scriptures.[67] Bucer also approves of the homilies that Cranmer had provided in case the pastor of the church was not qualified to prepare his own sermons. Far too many parish priests and especially far too many curates did not have the education that the Christian Humanists demanded. Here Bucer and Cranmer are in full accord.[68]

Perhaps of greatest interest is Bucer's comments on Cranmer's attempt at a Protestant canon or better, a Eucharistic Prayer. As Bucer saw it the New Testament does not indicate that we are to offer a prayer of consecration at the communion service, but rather a prayer of thanksgiving for the bread and the wine. Even more, the prayer is to give thanks for that which the bread and the wine represent.[69] Bucer saw great importance in the prayer of thanksgiving that we offer at a meal.[70] He did not understand Cranmer's prayer of consecration as something the New Testament teaches us to do.[71] Instead he is concerned about the transforming of the human heart, rather than the transforming of bread and wine.[72] Bucer does not suggest what should replace this prayer of consecration. At least he does not suggest any text that ought to replace what Cranmer had written. On the other

---

[66] Bucer, *Censura*, p. 44.

[67] Bucer, *Censura*, p. 44.

[68] Bucer, *Censura*, p. 46.

[69] Bucer, *Censura*, p. 52–54.

[70] Bucer, *Censura*, p. 56.

[71] Bucer, *Censura*, p. 58.

[72] Ashley Null has provided us with a recent study on the subject of transformation. See: Ashley Null, *Thomas Cranmer's Doctrine of Repentance: Renewing the Power to Love* (Oxford and New York: Oxford University Press, 2000).

hand, he does suggest that the "prefaces" do give us a trace of the real Eucharistic Prayer as used in the ancient church.[73] There is a real point to this.[74] The prayer of thanksgiving at the heart of the communion service should give thanks for God's mighty acts of creation and redemption. It should be a recital of sacred history, like Psalms 78, 105, or 136. This was basic to the eucharistic prayers we find as late as the prayer in the *Apostolic Constitutions* or the Eucharistic prayer in the Liturgy of St. Basil. At this point, sad to say, Bucer goes no further.

Bucer gives his highest commendation for the Prayer of Humble Access. This prayer begins, "'We do not presume to come to this, etc.'"[75] There are several phrases here that make quite explicit what theologians have often called Bucer's "receptionist" theology. At one point the prayer speaks of "the true reception and eating and drinking of the body and blood of the Lord," and again, a bit further on, "'humbly beseeching thee that whosoever shall be partakers of this holy communion may worthily receive the most precious body and blood of thy Son Jesus Christ.'"[76] Then, still further on, "'Grant us therefore (gracious Lord) so to eat the flesh of thy Son Jesus Christ, and to drink his blood in these most holy mysteries, etc.'"[77]

The term "receptionist" hardly does justice to Bucer's teaching. What Bucer is talking about is union with Christ. Here we find Bucer's covenantal doctrine of the Lord's Supper. Here we are talking about *koinonia*, communion with Christ, the whole Christ, true God and true man.

---

[73] Bucer, *Censura*, p. 56.

[74] The "proper prefaces" of the Roman mass contained a large portion of the thanksgiving for God's mighty acts of creation and redemption. Cranmer had retained about half a dozen of these proper prefaces in his canon. Among them were the prefaces for Christmas, Easter, Ascension, and Whitsunday (Pentecost).

[75] Bucer, *Censura*, p. 64.

[76] Bucer, *Censura*, p. 64.

[77] Bucer, *Censura*, p. 64.

Bucer commends the *Prayer Book* for making it very clear that what we receive at communion is the whole Christ in both his divinity and his humanity.[78] Some had accused the Protestants of teaching a Nestorian view of the sacrament, but Bucer makes it very clear that this is not the direction Protestantism wants to go. "And so in this sacrament we receive not only bread and wine but at the same time his body and blood, and indeed not these only but with them the whole Christ, both God and man."[79] Also we receive a confirmation of our membership in the Church, the new covenant people of God, and the whole Spirit of Christ. He abides in us and we in Him.[80] Bucer develops this point at some length, assuring us that we receive the whole Christ, human and divine, by faith. We are saved by faith! He even supports this with a citation of Cyril of Alexandria. Here we must stick by the language of the *Prayer Book*, confirming the presence of the Lord with those who participate in the sacrament. He abides with us and dwells among us. He is near us and in us.[81]

The *Censura* turns now to the rite of baptism for the most part, but there are a few reactions to such things as the tolling of church bells and what feast days should be observed. Bucer's reactions are not terribly precise here. Then, he comes down on the evangelical feast days. One might call it the long list of evangelical feast days, however.[82] Some saints' days are admitted, such as those of St. Peter and St. Paul. So is Candlemas, but with a certain reserve. When Bucer was in Strasbourg the matter of feast days was discussed at length on several different occasions. One assumes he went along with the short list of evangelical feast days: Christmas, maybe Epiphany, Maundy Thursday and Good Friday, Easter,

---

[78] Bucer, *Censura*, p. 62.
[79] Bucer, *Censura*, p. 64.
[80] Bucer, *Censura*, p. 64.
[81] Bucer, *Censura*, p. 70.
[82] Bucer, *Censura*, pp. 140–142.

Ascension, and Pentecost. Cranmer had apparently allowed for a few others, but Bucer was not going to make an issue of it. That, at least, is the way we might interpret the vagueness and imprecision of the passage.

That the liturgical theology of Martin Bucer had a profound influence on the worship of the Church of England hardly needs to be argued. When it comes to worship, Bucer was one of the most creative of the Reformers. He had been well schooled by the Christian Humanism of Erasmus and Jacques Lefevre d'Étaples as well as the mystical passion of men like Jakob Wimpfeling. Bucer was above all an accomplished biblical scholar, having mastered both Greek and Hebrew, but he also had a wide knowledge of the Fathers of the ancient Church.[83] It was for this reason, of course, that he was so greatly respected by Cranmer and the Christian Humanist scholars of Cambridge.

Bucer was generously received in England, but age was catching up with him. His health began to fail him and he was beginning to find the winters hard to take. He died in exile, honored as he may have been. A few months after Bucer's death, his host, King Edward VI, died, and Mary Tudor came to the throne, determined to erase the influence of Protestantism. Bucer's body was exhumed and was burnt at the stake. It was a bizarre sort of posthumous martyrdom that won for Bucer an indelible place in the sacred history of England.

In the end Bucer realized that the sort of reform he envisioned demanded a new level of pastoral devotion. For too long Western Christendom had accepted poorly trained priests who had led indolent lives with little passion for the ministry they had been called to exercise. The politicians had gotten ministerial appointments tightly in their hands. The political control exercised over the ministry during the reign of Elizabeth I was especially tight.

---

[83] For further information on the patristic knowledge of Bucer, see: Old, *Patristic Roots*, pp. 119–130.

Erastianism was the primary weakness in the Reformed Church of England during the reigns of both the Tudors and the Stuarts.[84] In fact it was an even greater problem during the reigns of James I and Charles I. Bucer said this in his *Censura*, but he said it very politely and very gently. More importantly, during his twenty-five year pastorate in Strasbourg, he began to develop a church polity that made it possible for the church to stand on its own without the support of the state.

THE THIRTY-NINE ARTICLES

In an age of religious turmoil, the reign of Queen Elizabeth I was a time of peace and quiet.[85] It was not an age of great theologians or even great preachers. The classic English preachers were yet to come. John Donne and Richard Sibbes belong to a later generation. Thomas Cartwright and William Ames had to do their work in exile, George Herbert lived in obscurity and William Perkins died much too young. Any preacher who brought anything to the pulpit that did not conform to government policy on religious affairs was squelched. Be that as it may, for one long generation, forty-four years to be exact, the worship of the Church of England was Reformed, not in all particulars perhaps, but certainly in a good many. Some of these reforms were quite genuine, while others were only superficial. The reforms, however, were clearly Protestant. In regard to the sacrament of Holy Communion this is particularly evident from the famous Thirty-Nine Articles.[86]

---

[84] On the subject of Erastianism, see footnotes 3 and 18 above.

[85] For information on the Elizabethan Settlement, see: Winthrop S. Hudson, *The Cambridge Connection and the Elizabethan Settlement of 1559* (Durham, NC: Duke University Press, 1980); Jones, "Elizabethan Settlement," in *The Oxford Encyclopedia of the Reformation*, 2:36–38; Jones, *Faith by Statute: Parliament and the Settlement of Religion, 1559* ; and Solt, *Church and State in Early Modern England, 1509–1640*.

[86] On the Thirty-Nine Articles, see: Edward John Bicknell, *A Theological Introduction to the Thirty-Nine Articles of the Church of England* (London and New York: Longmans, 1955); William P. Hauggaard, *Elizabeth and the English Reformation: The Struggle for a Stable Settlement of Religion* (London: Cambridge University Press, 1968); Guy Fitch

6: Holy Communion in
The Reformed Church of England

Just as the *Book of Common Prayer* formulated the worship of the Reformed Church of England, so the Thirty-Nine Articles formulated its eucharistic theology. Let us look at a few prominent points of this document.

The Thirty-Nine Articles had evolved from an attempt to develop a statement or profession of faith for the English Church that made clear both its independence from the Roman Church and its adherence to historic Christianity. It clearly avowed Protestantism, but it understood its Protestantism as an English form of Christianity. This English form of Christianity was not to be understood as heresy or a schismatic sect and so the Thirty-Nine Articles was an attempt to demonstrate the essential orthodoxy of the Church of England.

The long reign of Queen Elizabeth wrote Protestantism on the English heart. Elizabeth reigned for forty-four years, as we have said, and during that time she established and maintained a distinct theological position and a characteristic form of worship. Today we call it the Elizabethan Settlement. Central to this settlement was, of course, the *Book of Common Prayer*. Elizabeth re-established the *Book of Common Prayer* as Edward VI had established it. What Edward had begun so well Elizabeth consistently promoted.

The *Prayer Book*, however, was not the only standard of the Elizabethan Settlement. It was early in the reign of Elizabeth that she promulgated the Thirty-Nine Articles. This document is a confession of faith drawn up by Convocation, the governing body of the Church of England. In actual fact it took a number of years to take shape, having begun to develop in the reign of Henry VIII, being revised in the reign of Edward VI, and taking final shape early in the reign of Elizabeth.

The Thirty-Nine Articles gives particular attention to the sacra-

---

Lytle, III, "Articles of Religion," in *The Oxford Encyclopedia of the Reformation*, 1:80–83; Oliver O'Donovan, *On the Thirty-Nine Articles: A Conversation with Tudor Christianity* (Exeter: Paternoster Press, 1986); and Kenneth Needham Ross, *The Thirty-nine Articles* (London: Nowbray; New York: Morehouse-Gorham, 1960).

ment of Holy Communion. In Article Twenty-five, "Of the Sacraments," we read, "Sacraments ordained of Christ be not only badges or tokens of Christian men's profession, but rather they be certain sure witnesses, and effectual signs of grace, and God's good will toward us, by the which he doth work invisibly in us, and doth not only quicken, but also strengthen and confirm our Faith in him."[87] This seems to be a rejection of Zwingli's earliest writings but it should probably also be regarded as an affirmation of the position reached by Bullinger and Calvin in the *Consensus Tigurinus*.

Article Twenty-five goes on to affirm another basic tenet of Reformed sacramental theology. "There are two Sacraments ordained of Christ our Lord in the Gospel, that is to say, Baptism, and the Supper of the Lord."[88] Penance, confirmation, marriage, ordination, and extreme unction are not sacraments because they have no sign ordained of God. This is the way Luther saw it early in the Reformation, and it remained the typical Protestant position even as Protestants continue to ordain ministers, perform marriages, offer prayers of repentance and assure the repentant of God's pardon.

Again we notice a distinctly Reformed concern in this article when we read, "The Sacraments are not ordained of Christ to be gazed upon, or to be carried about, but that we should duly use them. And in such only as worthily receive the same, they have a wholesome effect or operation . . ."[89] The Reformed criticism of some of the more popular eucharistic devotions here is very strong, but equally strong is the denial of the doctrine of the *manducatio impiorum* which was a characteristic Lutheran position. At this point the Articles are definitely more Reformed than Lutheran.

Article Twenty-eight, "Of the Lord's Supper," makes the

---

[87] *The Articles of Religion*, Article XXV, as found in *The Book of Common Prayer According to the Use of the Episcopal Church* (proposed) (The Church Hymnal Corporation and The Seabury Press, 1977), p. 872.

[88] Article XXV, *The Book of Common Prayer*, p. 872.

[89] Article XXV, *The Book of Common Prayer*, p. 872.

point that it is God who is operative in the sacrament. "The Supper of the Lord is not only a sign of the love that Christians ought to have among themselves one to another; but rather it is a Sacrament of our Redemption by Christ's death . . ."[90] This seems to be a conscious step away from an Anabaptist position.

Article Thirty is dedicated to insisting that the faithful be served both the bread and the wine whenever the sacrament is observed.

Article Thirty-one, "Of the One Oblation of Christ finished on the Cross," is likewise one of the theological affirmations shared by all of the Reformers—Luther, Zwingli, Calvin, and Cranmer. It was fully discussed in Luther's *Babylonian Captivity of the Church* and is repeatedly mentioned in all the foundational works of sixteenth-century Protestantism.

The Thirty-Nine Articles is a strongly Protestant confession of faith. Its statements on worship are clearly Reformed, although one would hesitate to claim that its confession as a whole is Zwinglian, Bucerian, or Calvinist. Elements of several Reformed theologians seem to be blended together. On the other hand, the document has a distinct character of its own. One thing, however, is clear; it is not a compromise between Protestantism and Catholicism. Here, at least, we have a clearly Protestant confession of faith.

JOHN JEWEL

John Jewel (1522–1571) defended Protestant worship and did much to win over England to the Reformed cause.[91] It was a defense that was both practical and scholarly, both courageous and pastoral.

John Jewel had only just begun to enter the theological discussion when it was suddenly cut short by the death of Edward VI and the accession of Mary Tudor, the daughter of Henry VIII

---

[90] Article XXVIII, *The Book of Common Prayer*, p. 873.

[91] For the significance of John Jewel and the reform of worship, see Jenkins, *John Jewell and the English National Church*.

and Catherine of Aragon. The new queen was a staunch Catholic, determined to avenge her mother. Only slowly, however, did it become evident to Jewel that it might be wise for him to go into exile.

At Oxford young Jewel had attached himself to a number of Christian Humanist scholars connected with Merton College. This group had particularly gathered around Peter Martyr Vermigli.[92] Vermigli was a first class patristic scholar who was particularly well versed in the works of the Greek Fathers. Cranmer had invited Vermigli to Oxford with the intention of introducing the torpid old university to first-class Reformed theology.[93] Vermigli had the distinction of being the most prominent Italian Reformer. He was a leading Dominican theologian who more and more became a supporter of Luther and finally had to flee Italy. Vermigli had a surprising influence on English Protestant theology, especially in regard to sacramental theology. Apparently much of this influence was mediated by Jewel. It was only natural, therefore, that Jewel headed first for Strasbourg where Vermigli had originally sought refuge after fleeing England. From Strasbourg Jewel went on to Frankfurt, where he took a major role in organizing a

---

[92] On the life of Peter Martyr Vermigli, see: Emidio Campi, ed., *Petrus Martyr Vermigli: Humanismus, Republicanismus, Reformation* (Geneva: Droz, 2002); Mariano di Gangi, *Peter Martyr Vermigli, 1499–1562: Renaissance Man, Reformation Master* (Lanham: University Press of America, 1993); Frank A. James, III, John Patrick Donnelly, and Joseph C. McLelland, eds., *The Peter Martyr Reader* (Kirksville, Mo.: Truman State University Press, 1999); Philip Murray Jourdan McNair, *Peter Martyr in Italy: An Anatomy of Apostasy* (Oxford: Clarendon, 1967); Peter Martyr Vermigli, *The Life, Early Letters and Eucharistic Writings of Peter Martyr*, intro. and ed. Joseph C. McLelland and Gervase E. Duffield (Appleford, UK: Sutton Courtenay Press, 1989).

[93] The influence of Vermigli is only recently being appreciated largely through the publication of his complete works: John Patrick Donnelly and Joseph C. McLelland, eds., *The Peter Martyr Library*, vols. 1–9 (Kirksville, MO: Thomas Jefferson University Press: Sixteenth Century Journal Publishers, 1994-). See also Torrance Kirby, Emidio Campi and Frank A. James, III, eds., *A Companion to Peter Martyr Vermigli* (Leiden and Boston: Brill, 2009); Salvatore Corda, *Veritas Sacramenti: A Study of Vermigli's Doctrine of the Lord's Supper* (Zurich: Theologischer Verlag, 1975); and Joseph C. McLelland, *The Visible Words of God: An Exposition of the Sacramental Theology of Peter Martyr Vermigli, A.D. 1500–1562* (Grand Rapids, MI: Eerdmans, 1957).

congregation of English exiles. It was there that a disagreement arose between Jewel and John Knox.[94] As it turned out, these disagreements foreshadowed differences of opinion that would play an important role in the Reformed churches of Great Britain for generations to come. At the center of these discussions was the question of just how English the Church of England wanted to become. Nationalism was a growing movement at the beginning of the sixteenth century.

Jewel's exile did not last long. In 1558 Elizabeth came to the throne. She was the daughter of Anne Boleyn, a staunch Protestant whose father had been an active supporter of the Reformation for some time. The only trouble was that Elizabeth had a strong attachment to the old ceremonial. On the other hand, Elizabeth firmly believed the Church of England owed no obedience to the Roman Church. Beside that, she regarded rather favorably the reforms of the Christian Humanists. One naturally asks why the reforms of Christian Humanism were more important than explicitly Lutheran approaches. The answer is probably that the reforms of Christian Humanism were more widely known and had been advocated for a good generation before Luther. Still, the bottom line was clear. Elizabeth had to embrace Protestantism in order to make good her claim to the throne. Whether Elizabeth was going to be able to draw the support she would need to remain on the throne was not at first clear. She held her cards close to her breast, giving few indications of what her religious feelings really might be.

A. John Jewel's "Challenge Sermon"

When Jewel arrived back in England he was an obvious choice for a major bishopric. Elizabeth appointed him bishop of Salisbury,

---

[94] For an introduction to the "Troubles at Frankfort," see: William Whittingham, *A Brief Discourse of the Troubles at Frankfort, 1554–1558 AD* (London: Eliot Stock, 1908). See also Jenkins, *John Jewell and the English National Church*, pp. 188–202.

one of the historic sees of England. For a young scholar, this was a prestigious post. And though he was a young scholar, he was also a capable and attentive pastor who nevertheless maintained an interest in the theological discussions of the age. His greatest work was his magisterial defense of the Protestant faith. Central to his theological concern was his defense of the Reformed doctrine of Holy Communion, which took its classic form in what has ever since been called Jewel's "Challenge Sermon."

First preached at Paul's Cross on November 26, 1559, John Jewel's "Challenge Sermon" is a fundamental statement of the Reformed Church of England. It was to the English Protestants in the reign of Elizabeth I something like the posting of the Ninety-Five Theses on the door of the Castle Church at Wittenberg. It was the salvo of the Elizabethan Settlement. It proclaimed a new liturgical order thoroughly attacking the Roman mass.[95]

When Elizabeth I ascended the throne it was not immediately clear whether she was going to be able to make good her claim to the throne, nor was it completely clear she would continue to support the worship ceremony of the *Book of Common Prayer* so courageously staked out by Edward VI. It was likely she would insist on some sort of Protestantism but some thought she, like her father Henry VIII, would prefer a merely political Protestantism. Henry wanted traditional Catholicism, but a Catholicism completely under his control. He wanted to dip his hand into its financial reserves and its property, choose its leaders, and generally make it subservient to his purposes, but theologically, Henry wanted the same old doctrine and the same old liturgy.

With this sermon it became clear that Elizabeth was going to support a thoroughly Protestant worship, but a worship that would make a few nods to Catholic sensitivities, notably in regard to vestments. Even more noticeably, it was becoming more and

---

[95] John Jewel, "Sermon preached at Paul's Cross," found in John Jewel, *The Works of John Jewel*, ed. John Ayre, The Parker Society edition (Cambridge: Printed at the University Press, 1845), pp. 1–25, hereinafter Jewel, "Challenge Sermon."

more clear that she was putting the leadership of the English Church into the hands of men who during the reign of Mary had taken refuge in Switzerland and the German Rhineland, Strasbourg, Frankfurt, Zurich, and Geneva.

John Jewel was one such leader. Inviting him to preach a sermon calling for the reform of the mass at Paul's Cross was a very effective announcement of the liturgical policy of the crown. It would be sort of like asking Billy Graham to preach at Riverside Church in New York or on the steps of the Capitol Building in Washington. Paul's Cross was a national pulpit in the heart of London. It was an outdoor pulpit which could handle a great crowd, but it was also a pulpit completely under the control of the establishment.

The sermon was made very dramatic by putting it in the form of a challenge. Jewel offered to admit defeat if anyone could prove him wrong on any of his points. In fact, if anyone could show that these abuses went back to the first five or six centuries of the church he would renounce his position. Jewel insisted none of these abuses were endorsed by Scripture or the practice of the ancient church.[96]

The sermon was first preached in late November of 1559, about a year after Elizabeth's accession. It was repeated at court the following Spring and then, two weeks later, it was repeated at Paul's Cross on the second Sunday before Easter, that is, right at the height of Lent, when good Catholics were busily preparing to make their annual communion.[97]

The sermon as it has come down to us was written up, as the preacher tells us, exactly as he had preached it.[98] It was a thorough criticism of the way the Roman mass had perverted the sacrament of Holy Communion. He takes as his text 1 Corinthians 11:23 and

---

[96] Jewel, "Challenge Sermon," pp. 20–21.

[97] The dates corresponding to the repetition of this sermon were March 17, 1560 at court, and then at Paul's Cross on March 31, 1560, the second Sunday before Easter. Jewel, "Challenge Sermon," p. 3n1.

[98] Jewel, "Challenge Sermon," p. 3.

following.⁹⁹ The point he wants to make is that just as the Corinthians had perverted the sacrament which Paul had delivered to them from the Lord, so the contemporary church had perverted the sacrament of the Lord's Supper delivered to them from the ancient church. This perversion, now called the mass, was a vast corruption made up of a whole host of novelties and inventions which the ancient church did not know.¹⁰⁰ The Apostle Paul denounced the abuses in the Corinthian church and demanded a reformation of its worship.¹⁰¹ We find the same thing with Jesus when he found the worship of the Jerusalem Temple so corrupted that it had become a den of thieves rather than a house of prayer. Then our Lord set about reforming the worship of that sacred place.¹⁰²

What we find the Apostle Paul doing in this passage is reforming the worship of the Corinthians by going back to the institution of Christ. He sets the original institutions found in Scripture before their eyes. Clearly for Jewel, the worship of the Church of England was to be reformed according to Scripture.¹⁰³ Let there be no doubt about it: John Jewel advocated a Reformed worship.

In this sermon our preacher left aside the more doctrinal abuses such as transubstantiation, the real presence, and the eucharistic sacrifice and focuses his attention on several very practical abuses, such as the celebration of the sacrament in a language unknown to the worshipers, communion under one kind, the superstitious prayers in the canon of the mass, the adoration of the host, and the celebration of private masses.¹⁰⁴ The body of the sermon then follows with the unfolding of Bishop Jewel's evidence that none of these five abuses was known in the first five or six centuries of the church. We need not look at any of these practices in detail. It will

---

⁹⁹ Jewel, "Challenge Sermon," p. 3.
¹⁰⁰ Jewel, "Challenge Sermon," pp. 3–5.
¹⁰¹ Jewel, "Challenge Sermon," p. 3–4.
¹⁰² Jewel, "Challenge Sermon," p. 4.
¹⁰³ Jewel, "Challenge Sermon," p. 4.
¹⁰⁴ Jewel, "Challenge Sermon," p. 8.

suffice to make a few comments.

One notices that the abuses attacked by Jewel are particularly abuses which compromise the kerygmatic nature of the sacrament.[105] The sacrament is supposed to proclaim, or show forth, the redemptive work of Christ in his death and resurrection. The sacrament is the Word made visible; it is message, not magic. How, then, can it be celebrated in a foreign tongue, a tongue unknown to the congregation? The Roman mass had become a work of magic in which bread and wine were turned into body and blood. The canon of the mass had become an incantation to secure the blessings of God rather than the sealing of the promises of the covenant. The use of Latin in the public worship of the Church of the late Middle Ages compromised the kerygmatic dimension of worship.[106]

We also notice that Jewel criticizes the mass because it compromises the covenantal nature of the sacrament. This is especially evident in the practice of the frequent observance of private masses, that is, the observance of the sacrament without the presence of a congregation. On a given day in any church in Western Europe at the end of the Middle Ages, a dozen or two masses could be celebrated by priests without a congregation to fulfill the terms of an endowment. The Reformers were especially critical of these votive masses because they so obviously neglected the criticism the Apostle Paul made of the Corinthian practice of eating the sacred meal before the poor of the congregation had been able to come. The Lord's Supper should be a communion, as was especially clear from the covenantal dimension of the sacrament. Withholding the cup from the people and reserving it to the clergy suggested the inferiority of the people and the superiority of the clergy rather than a communion of all. The English Reformers were especially fond of calling the sacrament "Holy Communion." Jewel used this

---

[105] Jewel, "Challenge Sermon," p. 8.
[106] Jewel, "Challenge Sermon," pp. 8–9.

reasoning to oppose communion in only one kind.[107] The practice compromised the covenantal nature of the sacrament.

Another abuse which Jewel finds particularly grievous is the adoration of the host.[108] Again we would like to point out that this was a concern especially important to the Christian Humanists. The reappearance of biblical Hebrew had had a great effect on the younger theologians of the day and had brought with it a growing sensitivity to the biblical abhorrence of idolatry in any form.

John Jewel has often been regarded as the leading polemicist of the Reformed Church of England. His comprehensive knowledge of the writings of the church Fathers made him specially effective in defining the English Protestant approach to the sacrament of Holy Communion. Of more than passing interest is the fact that he gave so much attention to supporting the liturgical reforms of the Elizabethan Settlement with evidence from the Fathers of the ancient church. His famous "Challenge Sermon" preeminently made the point that the ancient church had a purity in both its worship and its doctrine to which the Church of England at the end of the sixteenth century would do well to emulate. Acknowledging that throughout history there were times and places where things got out of line, he nevertheless argued that when this happens then the church needs to set about reforming these abuses. Jewel identified a specific list of abuses, as we have seen, and made the point that none of these abuses were the practice in the first five centuries of Christian history.

B. John Jewel and the Patristic Witness

There is no question about it: There were plenty of Protestants in the sixteenth century who had taken an interest in the worship of the ancient church. Many of the Reformers were students of the Christian Humanists and really did know quite a bit about the

---

[107] Jewel, "Challenge Sermon," p. 9.
[108] Jewel, "Challenge Sermon," p. 10.

worship of the early church. They had read a significant number of the basic documents that needed to have been read. The Reformers of the Upper Rhineland used as their motto, "Back to the Sources" (*ad fontes*), which meant returning to the Greek New Testament and the Hebrew Old Testament, but also to the Christian writers of antiquity. These were the doctors of the Latin Church, such as Augustine, Ambrose, Jerome, and Gregory the Great, and the Greek Fathers, such as Chrysostom, Gregory of Nazianzus, and Basil. It was in Basel and Strasbourg that the first generation of the Reformers were helping to publish the first printed editions of Augustine, Jerome, Chrysostom, and Gregory of Nazianzus. Erasmus sent Zwingli the first printed edition of the complete works of Jerome, and when he finished it he realized that the final authority could not be Jerome, as learned as he was, but rather the Scriptures themselves. One cannot help but notice that John Jewel had a very broad knowledge of the doctors of the ancient church, and that he was a student of Peter Martyr Vermigli, who had studied the church Fathers in Florence and Padua, two major centers of patristic studies. On the subject of the patristic roots of Reformed worship I have written at considerable length in another publication.[109]

Orthodox Protestantism has settled on *sola scriptura*, but it has always recognized a validity in *ad fontes*. We find it again on the title page of the *Genevan Psalter* of 1542, which reads, *Form of Prayers and Church Songs According to the Custom of the Ancient Church*. The Anabaptists, on the other hand, chose to follow the regulative principle, which they found in the writings of Tertullian. Tertullian was an important early Christian writer and the first edition of his complete works was published in Basel in 1522 by Zwingli's friend Beatus Rhenanus. Strangely enough, the Anabaptists quoted this principle against the Reformers, first of all in regard to the baptism of infants, second in regard to the singing of hymns

---

[109] See Old, *Patristric Roots*.

in worship, and finally against Lord's Day worship.[110]

One of the interesting points here is that Jewel had learned much from Vermigli while he was a student at Oxford. Archbishop Cranmer had given the Lady Margaret Chair of Theology at Cambridge to Bucer, and at the same time, he gave the Regius Chair at Oxford to Vermigli. For something like five years, the Italian patristic scholar gathered around himself a group of English students who all, in being thoroughly Protestant, were also enthusiastic about the new light being thrown on the church Fathers by Christian umanists.

The University of Padua had led the way in the study of patristic literature. With Erasmus in Basel and Jacques Lefèvre in Paris, patristic studies had taken different directions, but there was another approach in Italy. With the fall of Constantinople in 1453 a good number of Greek theologians had fled to Italy and helped the West recover quite a bit of ancient Christian thought. It was from the students of those refugees that Peter Martyr Vermigli learned about Cyril of Alexandria, Basil the Great, and John Chrysostom. No wonder John Jewel knew so much of the writings of the Greek Fathers. We know that when Vermigli left Italy he shipped his large library ahead of him. Possibly he had been able to do the same thing when he went to Oxford. Be that as it may, one can well imagine that the libraries of Oxford were well stocked when young John Jewel studied patristics under Peter Martyr Vermigli.[111] It was these resources, and this intellectual vitality, which fed the Reformation, both on the continent and in England.

---

[110] See Glen J. Clary, "Ulrich Zwingli and the Swiss Anabaptists: Sola Scriptura and the Reformation of Christian Worship," in *The Confessional Presbyterian*, vol. 6 (Rowlett, TX: Reformation Presbyterian Press, 1006), pp. 18–124.

[111] One should note that Vermigli's patristic library was not the same as Bucer's.

RICHARD HOOKER
AND THE BEGINNINGS OF ANGLICANISM

There might be those who would call Richard Hooker (1554–1600) the founder of Anglicanism. That, however, would be to say too much. Maybe it would be better to say that Hooker was the great apologist for Anglicanism, but that would not come near doing him justice, because it would overlook his originality and creativity. It was Hooker, really, who made a system of faith out of some very real political necessities. From a very different point of view, however, one might say Hooker laid the spiritual foundation stones of a great national church, a denomination that spread throughout the whole world.

Richard Hooker was born near Exeter during the short reign of Mary Tudor.[112] His family was hard pressed, although well connected. He attended the Latin school in Exeter. There, even as a young man, he established a reputation as an excellent student and through the patronage of John Jewel, Bishop of Salisbury, was given a scholarship to Corpus Christi College in Oxford.

In 1577 he became a fellow of Corpus Christi College and two years later found himself deputy professor of Hebrew. In 1585 he was assigned to a pulpit in Oxford. As it happened Walter Travers was assigned to the same pulpit, one preaching in the morning and the other in the evening. The preachers got into a controversy over church polity, Travers being a leading proponent

---

[112] For biographical material on Hooker the classic text will always be the biography by Izaak Walton, who gives us an idyllic portrait of the scholarly, country parson. Walton also gave us a similar picture of the poet George Herbert. Izaak Walton, *The Lives of Dr. John Donne, Sir Henry Wotton, Mr. Richard Hooker, Mr. George Herbert and Dr. Robert Sanderson* (London: Bell and Daldy, 1864). For further biographical material, see: Stanley Archer, *Richard Hooker* (Boston: Twayne, 1983); W. J. Torrance Kirby, *Richard Hooker, Reformer and Platonist* (Aldershot, UK and Burlington, VT: Ashgate Publications, 2005); W. J. Torrance Kirby, ed., *Richard Hooker and the English Reformation* (Dordrecht and Boston: Kluwer Academic Publishers, 2003); and Arthur Pollard, *Richard Hooker* (London: Published for the British Council and the National Book League by Longmans, Green, 1966).

of presbyterianism and Hooker countering him by defending episcopacy. Hooker did very well in these de facto debates and news of this soon came to the ears of the Archbishop of Canterbury, John Whitgift. The archbishop saw to it that, after finishing his studies, he was assigned to a quiet village church where he could spend his time doing research and writing.

The fruit of these quiet years in the parsonage of Bosecan, Wiltshire, was his multivolume *Treatise on the Laws of Ecclesiastical Polity*. Although some of it did not see the printing press until long after his death, the earlier volumes achieved publication in 1594 and 1597. What Hooker tried to do in these volumes was to create a systematic theology that would justify the Erastian approach to the polity and worship of the Elizabethan church. Essentially what Hooker wanted to do was justify the right of the Queen to call the shots. This, then, became the foundation of the Jacobean and Carolingian ecclesiastical polity of the seventeenth century. With Richard Hooker we begin to sense that an opposition to the Reformed approach to the Sacrament was developing, and this is our major concern.

As one contemporary scholar has put it, the key to understanding the eucharistic piety of Richard Hooker is a certain uneasiness which he had with the *Prayer Book* communion service. Apparently a good number of English Protestants felt a certain insufficiency with the *Prayer Book* service as well. They missed some of the features of the old Roman mass, and therefore, as one modern Anglican put it, "tentatively rehabilitated certain traditional features of sacramental theology and spirituality."[113]

The nationalism of the Church of England had been growing for several centuries. It had no trouble repudiating the Roman pope and the claims of Roman primacy. These proto-Anglicans found the new biblical studies of the Christian Humanists quite exciting. On a lot of issues they wanted to go along with good

---

[113] Christopher J. Cocksworth, *Evangelical Eucharistic Thought in the Church of England*, (Cambridge, UK: Cambridge University Press, 1993), p. 33.

Queen Bess and some of her reforms were clearly justified, but the pious habits of the old faith had a strong hold on their hearts.

Hooker's eucharistic theology is centered on the idea of "the real participation of Christ and of life in his body and blood by means of the sacrament."[114] According to Brian Douglas, "It is this motif of a union with Christ which pervades the whole of the *Polity* and which is central to Hooker's thinking on the Eucharist."[115]

What no one seemed to have noticed is that this is just exactly how the Reformers of the Upper Rhineland understood the covenantal dimension of their eucharistic theology by the time of the *Consensus Tigurinus*, drawn up and agreed on by Bullinger and Calvin, although perhaps not in the earliest writings of Zwingli in 1525. This is particularly strong in Bucer as we have shown above. Douglas, strangely enough, attributes this position not to Hooker's understanding of the biblical concept of covenant, but rather to his "realist" philosophical background: "It seems that Hooker is presenting a realist notion of the presence of Christ when he speaks of participation in the soul of the faithful communicant."[116]

Richard Hooker is a good example of what has often been called Protestant Scholasticism. From the twelfth century to the end of the Middle Ages, Scholasticism had gotten a strong grip on the intellectual life of western Europe. It was Scholasticism that founded the great universities. It was Scholasticism that hammered together the academic culture of society. Scholasticism was not quickly left behind. All the usual procedures for organizing the intellectual life of the day were assumed.

The new learning, on the other hand, was just as basic to the

---

[114] Hooker, *Of the Laws of Ecclesiastical Polity*, edn. Keble, 1865: II, 320, as quoted in Brian Douglas, "Richard Hooker, 1554–1600, Anglican Divine," http://web.mac.com/brian.douglas/Anglican_Eucharistic_Theology/Blog/Entries/2006/5/24_Richard-Hookerc._1554–1600Anglican-Divine.html. Accessed 3/25/2013.

[115] Douglas, "Richard Hooker."

[116] Douglas, "Richard Hooker."

Reformation. The Reformation was based on the new learning, especially on the learning of biblical Greek and Hebrew. Even more basic was the movement toward reading Scripture in the common tongue. Protestantism demanded learning a new language, actually several new languages. The old universities, on the other hand, were slow to move. They had to do their theology in Latin! Oxford, where Hooker had studied, was notorious for its torpitude. It was only natural that it should try to understand the Reformation in terms of the old learning instead of the new learning. Yet Protestant Scholasticism never quite worked. It was an ill-conceived attempt at trying to understand Scripture in terms of Greek philosophy. The whole point of Protestantism was to recover the biblical thought world and to distinguish it from the Neo-platonism of late antiquity.

We have already spoken of how the English Reformers tended to think out their eucharistic theology in terms of the Scholastic debates of the fourteenth century in which John Wycliffe took such an active part. Wycliffe, of course, had lived and taught in Oxford. He was a Nominalist through and through. The Rhenish Reformers, such as Zwingli, Bucer, and Oecolampadius, thought through the issues of eucharistic theology in terms of Christian Humanism, not Nominalism.

The interesting thing about Hooker is that he tried to think through Protestant eucharistic theology in terms of Realism. His argumentation is just as Scholastic as Cranmer's. It is just that he started off and built it up with Realism rather than Nominalism.

WILLIAM PERKINS:
Union with Christ and
Communion with the Brethren

The most popular English theologian during the reign of Queen Elizabeth I was William Perkins (1558–1602). Although he died in his mid-forties, his collected works take up three hefty volumes.[117] Frequently overlooked by those wishing to emphasize the High Church component of Anglicanism, Perkins has recently been rediscovered as historians have come to realize he was one of the most formative thinkers of his day. The work of Bryan Spinks is of special significance in this re-evaluation.[118]

It was in Warwickshire that the future theologian was born. His family is supposed to have had some means. The tradition is, however, that he lived a rather profligate life as a young man until he had a conversion experience and became a serious student.[119] His mastery of Greek was widely recognized. Perkins did his university studies at Christ College, Cambridge. He showed himself to be a dedicated student who had what we call today a photographic memory.

Perkins began his preaching career before he was twenty years old. What is unusual is that he began to exercise his vocation by preaching to the prisoners in the Cambridge jail where apparently he had remarkable success. In 1585 he was appointed rector of St. Andrews Church in Cambridge. Here he remained for eighteen years, building a solid reputation for his simple, unadorned sermons. Perkins became the paragon of Protestant plain style preaching. In fact his preaching manual, *The Art of Prophesying*, published in 1592 (English translation published in 1606) garnered a wide audience at the time, appearing in French, German, Dutch, Czech, and even Spanish. Today it is regarded as the clas-

---

[117] See: William Perkins, *The workes of that famous and worthy minister of Christ: in the universitie of Cambridge*, 3 vols. (London: Iohn Leggatt, 1612–1613); William Perkins, *The Works of William Perkins*, intro. and ed. Ian Breward, Courtenay Library of Reformation Classics, vol. 3 (Appleford, UK: Sutton Courtenay Press, 1970). On Perkins generally the biographical introduction is from Breward's anthology.

[118] For further information on William Perkins, see Bryan Spinks, *Two Faces of Elizabethan Anglican Theology: Sacraments and Salvation in the Thought of William Perkins and Richard Hooker* (Lanham, MD: Scarecrow Press, 1999).

[119] What little we know of Perkins comes from a biographical essay written in 1814 which seems to have been written with strong hagiographical motives.

sic Puritan guide to preaching.[120]

One of the remarkable characteristics of Perkins as a theologian is that he was well acquainted with the leading continental Reformed theologians of the second generation such as Theodore Beza, Girolamo Zanchi, Zacharius Ursinus, and particularly the French Huguenot philosopher Peter Ramus.[121]

At one point Perkins was cited before the Vice-Chancellor for having criticized the worship of the Church of England as it was then observed, which allowed the minister to receive the communion from his own hand rather than having him receive it from another. Even more Perkins had apparently criticized the practice of kneeling to receive the Communion. This had been a major Puritan criticism because it obscured the sign of the sharing of a meal. Thirdly Perkins is purported to have criticized the practice of requiring the communicants to receive the sacred food while facing toward Jerusalem. It is not known for sure whether he was found guilty or acquitted. The Elizabethan Settlement could get sticky about such things.

More generally Perkins was known for having clearly Puritan views but not getting involved in controversial disputes. At one point, however, Perkins did go out on a limb for his friend Francis Johnson, a strong proponent of presbyterian views on church polity. Archbishop Whitgift had Johnson thrown in prison because he had advocated his views in public. Apparently the archbishop decided it would be unwise to press the matter because Perkins was widely respected. While still a young man at the height of his career, Perkins suddenly died of kidney stones in 1602.

Perkins, as we have said, was widely read during his lifetime and was probably the most widely read English theologian abroad. He died very young but was particularly popular as a preacher

---

[120] On the preaching of Perkins, see my study in the *Reading and Preaching of the Scriptures in the Worship of the Christian Church*, 4:260–269.

[121] Cf. Donald K. McKim, *Ramism in William Perkins' Theology* (New York: Peter Lang, 1987).

in Cambridge, where so many of the ministers of the Church of England were trained. His *lectio continua* sermons on Galatians were especially popular.[122] Even more popular was his preaching manual, *The Art of Prophesying*. It had a great effect on English preaching, especially in Puritan circles.[123]

Bryan Spinks has done much to familiarize this other face of Anglicanism, as he puts it. Perkins is generally regarded as both a Calvinist and a Puritan. He was clearly one of those sixteenth-century theologians who was most creative in the shaping of Puritan worship. His insights on public prayer are particularly helpful. Indeed, he was what usually goes for a Calvinist in his theology; some would even insist that he was the arch-Calvinist. His popular work, *The Golden Chain*, won over many to the Calvinist point of view. Even so, Perkins was very much an Englishman, and both his Puritanism and his Calvinism had an English spin to it.

In addition to that, Perkins very carefully sought not to unsettle the Elizabethan Settlement. He steered clear of both the Vestiarian Controversy and the Admonitions Controversy. He was much more interested in matters of the heart than those questions of polity and liturgy which had so troubled the formal ecclesiastical institutions. The sort of things that troubled Jewel and Hooker just did not bother Perkins.

We notice with Perkins what we noticed with Thomas Cranmer. Perkins' doctrine of the Lord's Supper is largely thought out over against the presuppositions of Scholastic theology, particularly Nominalist Scholasticism. To be sure, the influence of the Swiss Reformers is strong. Perkins has been influenced by Zwingli but the Zwingli who influenced him is the Zwingli reinterpreted by Bullinger, especially as expressed in the *Consensus Tigurinus*. Perkins seems

---

[122] Apparently the series was published as a commentary. See: Old, *The Reading and Preaching of the Scriptures in the Worship of the Christian Church*, 4:260.

[123] This work is available in Perkins' complete works. A modern edition exists as William Perkins, *The Art of Prophesying*, rev. ed. (Edinburgh and Carlisle, PA: Banner of Truth Trust, 1996).

to understand the Rhenish Reformers on the subject of the covenantal dimension of the sacraments better than Cranmer and Jewel, though even Perkins' perspective could have been much more fully developed. We find some recognition of the pneumatic dimension, but Bucer does not seem to be as formative for Perkins as he might have been. What comes through most clearly is the background of Nominalist Scholasticism. Perkins' rejection of the doctrine of transubstantiation is clearly thought out against this background. For instance, transubstantiation is rejected because it is not according to Scripture, but when Perkins begins to argue the question he reaches back to the Scholasticism of the late Middle Ages.

As we have said, William Perkins was without doubt the most widely read English Reformed theologian during the reign of Queen Elizabeth I. His ideas on sacramental piety and eucharistic theology seem to be fairly representative of English Protestantism in his day.[124] This may not have been what the Queen or her archbishop, John Whitgift, wanted to hear, but for the more theologically sensitive Protestants of England, Perkins spoke the mind of the people. Perkins was the theologian of popular Protestantism. Eucharistic piety was at the center of religious reform in the sixteenth century. This may seem strange to theologians at the beginning of the twenty-first century, but when seen in terms of the Protestant concern to free itself from a magical, ceremonial approach to religion, it is readily understandable.

Let us notice four points in the eucharistic piety of William Perkins which seem to reflect the piety of English Protestantism at the end of the sixteenth century. In each case we are dealing with positions that are classically Protestant.

First, we find in the writings of Perkins a continuing emphasis on the sacrament as memorial. It needs to be pointed out, however, that Perkins understood "memorial" in the same sense in which the feast of Passover was a memorial. Here, of course, the

---

[124] Spinks, *Two Faces of Elizabethan Anglican Theology*, pp. 82–84.

understanding of Zwingli and the Rhenish Christian Humanists outstrips the eucharistic theology of John Wycliffe, with all of its Nominalist presuppositions. If the early Zwingli had not fully understood the covenantal nature of the Lord's Supper, he had at least begun to move in that direction, and his successor Henry Bullinger developed an elaborate covenantal theology to replace the Scholastic sacramental theology.[125] It was this more developed Zwinglianism that attracted Perkins and the English Reformers.

Second, we find that Perkins' sacramental theology emphasizes that the bread and wine are to be understood as spiritual food. Very important here once again is the typology. Here it is the type of the manna that fed Israel in the wilderness. The Bread of Life Discourse in the Gospel of John develops this theme at length. It is this idea of being fed at God's table which led so many Reformed churches to insist on celebrating the communion seated at a table. The Queen would have none of this, but apparently there were plenty of English Protestants who were in favor of the practice. In chapter 3 we spoke at length of Calvin's use of Old Testament wisdom theology as the background for his understanding of the Johannine saying about eating the flesh and drinking the blood of Christ. That the eating of Christ's flesh and the drinking of Christ's blood should give life to the body of Christ is an essential dimension of being united to Christ, of entering into the household of faith and sitting down at the table with the brethren. This is the promise proclaimed by the sign of sharing a meal.

Third, we notice that Perkins seems to have a preference for referring to the sacrament of the Lord's Supper as "communion."

---

[125] See: J. Wayne Baker, *Heinrich Bullinger and the Covenant: The Other Reformed Tradition* (Athens: Ohio University Press, 1980); Jack Cottrell, *Covenant and Baptism in the Theology of Huldreich Zwingli*, Th.D. dissertation (Princeton, NJ: Princeton Theological Seminary, 1971); and Charles S. McCoy and J. Wayne Baker, *Fountainhead of Federalism: Heinrich Bullinger and the Covenant Tradition* (Louisville: Westminster John Knox Press, 1991).

This obviously comes from 1 Corinthians 10:16 (KJV), "The cup of blessing which we bless, is it not the communion of the blood of Christ? The bread which we break, is it not the communion of the body of Christ?" The advantage of the word "communion" is that on one hand it can speak of union with Christ and on the other, communion with the brethren. Table fellowship was an important relationship in the ancient biblical world. The Reformers were slowly beginning to realize this was of the essence of this sacrament. As the Reformers moved away from seeing the sacrament as a magic spell that could bring blessing to life they began to see that the greatest blessing was to enter into the presence of God. Presence is a basic dimension of Reformed eucharistic theology. This Perkins understood quite well.

We need to remember that Perkins left us no major treatise on the sacrament of Holy Communion, nor did he leave us a series of catechetical sermons or even a series of preparatory sermons. Still, he expressed himself frequently on the subject of the sacrament of the Lord's Supper. Bryan Spinks is quite correct when he tells us that much of what Perkins writes is repetitive, making the same two points again and again.[126] First, he is strongly opposed to the doctrine of transubstantiation and second, to the sacrifice of the mass. Here Perkins followed Calvin, according to Spinks, in that they both very strongly objected to a corporeal presence. He, as Calvin, believed in some sort of presence. What Calvin meant by spiritual presence would probably have suited Perkins very well. The objection to transubstantiation was fairly standard for the time. With their eucharistic theology, the Scholastic doctors ended up undermining basic doctrines of the church. Besides that, the teaching of transubstantiation was a relative novelty. No one had ever heard of it until the twelfth century.

Much more interesting is Perkins' polemic against the sacrifice of the mass. Here his position is definitely more nuanced than

---

[126] Spinks, *Two Faces of Elizabethan Anglican Theology*, p. 82.

the usual Protestant polemic. He will allow that the communion service could be called a sacrifice of praise and thanksgiving. He insists that Malachi 1:11 speaks of a day when Christian worship will be celebrated over the whole of the earth.[127] It will not be in the form of the mass, but rather it will be the service of praise, prayer, and preaching—the continual sacrifice as we find it so often in Scripture. In this passage the word "sacrifice" is a metonym for the service of worship. Spinks points to the fact that much patristic literature speaks of the communion service "metonymically."[128] According to Perkins we can speak of the sacrament as a sacrifice because it is a memorial of a sacrifice.[129]

Fourth, we find that Perkins has a strong concern for protecting the Lord's Table from profanation by admitting unworthy and unrepentant persons. Jonathan Won has his finger on something very important when he says that preparation for communion becomes a focal point of sacramental piety.[130]

There is one thing more. We begin to see in the course of the history of doctrine that more and more the communion with Christ celebrated in the Lord's Supper came to be understood as union with Christ. In the seventeenth and eighteenth centuries this became

---

[127] Spinks, *Two Faces of Elizabethan Anglican Theology*, p. 84.

[128] Spinks, *Two Faces of Elizabethan Anglican Theology*, p. 89.

[129] Interestingly, Perkins offers a text from the *Apostolic Constitutions* to prove his point. He identifies the text as being from the *Clementine Liturgy* which was supposed to be the liturgy of Clement of Rome, Bishop of Rome before the end of the first century. It has been my contention for a long time that Thomas Cranmer in his attempt to write a Reformed canon had made the serious error of following the pattern of the *Apostolic Constitutions*, believing that it was a liturgy coming from the end of the first century. Here is evidence that the so-called *Clementine Liturgy* was indeed available to an English scholar in the sixteenth century. Spinks, *Two Faces of Elizabethan Anglican Theology*, p. 89.

[130] Jonathan Won. *Communion with Christ: An Exposition and Comparison of the Doctrine of Union and Communion with Christ in Calvin and the English Puritans*, Ph.D. dissertation (Philadelphia: Westminster Theological Seminary, 1989), p. 101. Further on this point, see E. Brooks Holifield, *The Covenant Sealed: The Development of Puritan Sacramental Theology in Old and New England, 1570–1720* (New Haven: Yale University Press, 1974).

so pronounced that it became a regular occurrence that ministers would preach on the Song of Solomon at their sacramental solemnities.[131] This tended to give the celebration a festive, mystical air.

---

[131] We notice this in Won's doctoral dissertation, *Communion with Christ*. See also the chapters in this volume on the English Puritans, eighteenth-century communion seasons, and the Great Awakening, particularly concerning Gilbert Tennent.

7

JOHN KNOX
AND THE SCOTTISH TRADITION

John Knox's insight into the ways of this world was often profound.[1] Not one of the Reformers was as perceptive as he in such matters. Unlike the English Reformers, John Knox never allowed the civil government to control the worship of the Church. For those who firmly believed in the divine right of kings, no one was so despised as John Knox, and consequently the Scottish Reformer was often painted as the most dangerous of fanatics.[2] Political savvy is one thing; devotional depth is quite another. John Knox was blessed with both. In actual fact, John Knox founded a distinct tradition of eucharistic piety which over the centuries has shown a very particular genius. It is that genius we will explore in the chapter ahead.[3]

JOHN KNOX'S LITURGY

The service for the Lord's Supper found in John Knox's *Book of Common Order* is all too often regarded as an unimaginative, even

---

[1] For biographical material on John Knox, see: Thomas M'Crie, *The Life of John Knox* (Glasgow: Free Presbyterian Publications, [1811] 1976); Rosalind K. Marshall, *John Knox* (Edinburgh: Berlinn, 2008); Hughes Oliphant Old, *The Reading and Preaching of the Scriptures in the Worship of the Christian Church*, vol. 5, *Moderatism, Pietism, and Awakening* (Grand Rapids, MI: Eerdmans, 2004), pp. 429-439.

[2] It was the pioneering biography of M'Crie that opened up a more positive appreciation of Knox. See M'Crie, *The Life of John Knox*.

[3] For two very different views of the life of John Knox see: Geddes MacGregor, *The Thundering Scot* (Philadelphia: The Westminster Press, 1957); and Dale W. Johnson and Richard G. Kyle, *John Knox: An Introduction to His Life and Works* (Eugene, OR: Wipf and Stock, 2009).

slavish, copy of the service in the *Genevan Psalter*.[4] Nothing could be further from the truth. It was a very creative recasting of the Genevan service, which by 1564, when it was adopted by the Scottish Parliament, had been in use in Geneva almost a full generation. The Genevan service had won considerable approval by the time John Knox adopted it. And, lest we forget, much of the material went back even further, having been originally composed by Martin Bucer, the Reformer of Strasbourg. Just as Calvin had adopted Bucer's prayers, so Knox had adopted Calvin's prayers. And, again, Knox, as Calvin before him, made a number of adaptations. As we set the Scottish service against the Genevan service we find it makes a number of improvements, subtle interpretations, and emphases. Others have suggested that the variations of the Scottish service are to be explained by another hand rather than that of Knox. Perhaps so, but be that as it may, the service we find in the *Book of Common Order* was the service Knox recommended. Besides that, they clearly show a real genius which Knox affirmed even if perhaps he might not have been the author.

The first thing we notice is that nothing is said about the Invocation, "Our help is in the name of the Lord who made heaven and earth." This invocation was popular with a number of the Reformers. It may have been used even if the *Anglo-Genevan Psalter* does not indicate it specifically. We might make the same observation about the singing of one or more psalms while the congregation gathered. The practical necessity of an introit psalm should be evident to anyone who has ever tried to settle a congregation sufficiently to enter into prayer with appropriate reverence.

---

[4] For the texts of these documents, see Bard Thompson, *Liturgies of the Western Church* (Philadelphia: Fortress Press, [1961] 1980); William D. Maxwell, *John Knox's Genevan Service Book* (Westminster: Faith Press, 1965), hereinafter Maxwell, *Anglo-Genevan Psalter*; and Charles W. Baird, *Eutaxia, or, The Presbyterian Liturgies: Historical Sketches* (Grand Rapids, MI: Baker Book House, 1957).

7: JOHN KNOX AND THE SCOTTISH TRADITION

A. Prayers of Lamentation, Confession, and Repentance

Whatever else may be the case, the *Anglo-Genevan Psalter*, as the record has come down to us begins with a prayer of confession and supplication much like the prayer in the *Genevan Psalter* and also, of course, much like the *Strasbourg Psalter* which went before it. Two versions of the prayer are given to us. Interestingly the second of these two prayers is much closer to the Genevan pattern than the first. It is specifically indicated as being a prayer of confession for more regular conditions and times.[5] The first prayer, on the other hand, is a prayer of confession very specifically appropriate to the congregation of English-speaking exiles worshiping in a foreign land. It is entitled, "A confession of our synnes, framed to our tyme, out of the 9. chap. of Daniel."[6] In other words, it is a prayer which laments the banishment of this congregation of Marian exiles from their native England. It is a prayer of lamentation for the spiritual condition of "our miserable contry of Englande."[7] While Knox was destined to be the Reformer of his native Scotland, he was at the time pastor of a congregation of English exiles. The prayer laments the turn of events. "For they which once were well instructed in the doctrine of thy gospel, are nowe gone backe frome the obedience of thy trueth, and are turned agayne to that most abhominable Idolatrie, from the which they were once called by the lyvely preachinge of thy worde." Incline your ears, O merciful Lord, "and open thyne eyes, to beholde the grevous plagues of our contrie, the continuall sorrowes of our afflicted bretherne, and our wofull banishment. And let our afflictions and juste ponishemente be an admonition and

---

[5] John Knox, *The Forme of Prayers and Ministration of the Sacraments* (Geneva, 1556). This study is taken from the edition of Bard Thompson, *Liturgies of the Western Church*, pp. 295–305, hereinafter to be referred to as: Knox, *Anglo-Genevan Psalter*. The second prayer begins on p. 297.

[6] Knox, *Anglo-Genevan Psalter*, p. 295.

[7] Knox, *Anglo-Genevan Psalter*, p. 296.

warninge to other nations." Here the prayer begins to follow the prayer from Daniel 9 very closely: "Wherfore o lord heare us, o lord forgive us, o lord consider and tary not over longe, but for thy deare sonne Jesus Christe sake, be mercifull unto us, and delyver us."[8]

One often paints John Knox as a firebrand, not ever imagining the depth of his insight into the life of prayer, but here we sense the more profound quality of the Scottish Reformer's spirituality. He understood the typology of prayer. He followed the spiritual model of the ancient biblical prophet.[9] Daniel, too, had been an exile in a strange land, and the prayer which he left is indeed a corporate prayer of confession. No prayer in Scripture could provide a better example for the confessions and lamentations of the Marian exiles in Geneva.

It was surely a significant reform of Christian worship when the sixteenth century Reformers began to recognize the importance of the ministry of leading in prayer. Leading the congregation in prayer is an important part of the Gospel ministry. Knox knew his Bible well enough to recognize how the prayer of Daniel could serve as a type for the prayers and lamentations of the Marian exiles in Geneva, but he also knew well other classical types of biblical prayer. The prayer of Elijah suggests much to us about how we should pray. The same is true of the prayers of Abraham and Moses and Hannah. The prayers of Jesus and the Apostles are also great paradigms for the prayer of the congregation. We can well imagine that Knox over the years used many of these prayer types in addition to Daniel. It would be in another generation that William Perkins would write in *The Art of Prophesying* of the two-fold prophetic ministry, presenting the Word of God to the people of God and presenting the prayers of the people of God to God. That the minister should give time and serious consideration to framing the prayers of the people, rather than simply reading them out of a prayer book, was obvi-

---

[8] Knox, *Anglo-Genevan Psalter*, p. 296.

[9] Knox, *Anglo-Genevan Psalter*, p. 295.

7: JOHN KNOX AND THE SCOTTISH TRADITION

ously a major consideration to John Knox.

There is much insight to be found in these prayers of lamentation and confession which were so important at the beginning of the services of worship held by the Reformers. When we come to worship there are often things we have to get out of the way. There are problems in our lives. There are situations in the community which obscure God's presence. These prayers of lamentation and supplication and repentance help us to get beyond the problems. They help us see the problems in their true perspective. The Reformers were particularly aware of this in regard to eucharistic worship. If we are to come together for the sacrament of Communion, we have to deal with the problems. When we think of the eucharistic prayers of the early Reformed churches, the Prayer of Confession should certainly be reckoned among them.

There is another thing we notice here, and that is the absence of an assurance of pardon. For the first prayer, the prayer based on Daniel 9, this can be explained by the fact that Knox is closely following the biblical pattern. At this point, Daniel's pleading, as we have noted, is especially eloquent. In the second prayer the assurance of pardon is worked into the text. We are assured, for instance, that for the sake of Christ all our sins are forgiven. Furthermore, the Holy Spirit assures our consciences that we are the beloved children of a most loving Father.[10] Apparently Knox and the English speaking Protestants of Geneva were beginning to think of the reformation of prayer as much as the reformation of preaching and the reformation of the sacraments. In the thirty years since their first attempt at recasting the liturgy they came to have an ever-growing appreciation of the various genres of public prayer. They found in Scripture a variety of examples of prayers of confession and supplication, prayers of thanksgiving, intercession, blessing and dedication. It was part of the minister's calling to open up to his people these various types and examples of prayer.

---

[10] Knox, *Anglo-Genevan Psalter*, p. 297.

Another genre of prayer we find in the *Anglo-Genevan Psalter* is the Prayer for Illumination. It is mentioned in passing, but it is mentioned. We are told that the people sing a psalm in a simple tune and that after that the minister prays for the assistance of the Holy Spirit.[11] Furthermore, the text makes quite explicit that the minister's prayer is supposed to be as the Holy Spirit leads him. As we have said, this is mentioned in passing at this point, but we find in a number of liturgical documents of the period something very similar. Here was the place where free, spontaneous prayer on the part of the minister was to take place on a regular basis.

The Prayer for Illumination leads to the sermon, about which nothing is said here in the rubrics. From other sources we know about the preaching of Knox, but, sad to say, we have few of his actual sermons.[12]

B. Pastoral Prayer

The prayer after the sermon is, however, given quite a bit of attention. This is one of the major components of the liturgy, the great prayer of intercession, or, as it is called in the text of the *Anglo-Genevan Psalter*, the Prayer for the Whole Estate of Christ's Church. The recovery of this comprehensive prayer of intercession for the leaders of the Church, the functionaries of the state, kings and governors, the spread of the Gospel, the relieving of the sick, the provision of orphans and widows, and the peace of the world had been a major feature of the ancient Church, but in the Middle Ages it had dropped out of the regular liturgy of the Western Church. The Reformation was quick to recover the prayer. It was an important liturgical reform in Strasbourg and a few years later it appeared in Cranmer's *Book of Common Prayer*.

Again, the prayer is recast in light of the situation of Knox's

---

[11] Knox, *Anglo-Genevan Psalter*, p. 297.

[12] See Old, *The Reading and Preaching of the Scriptures in the Worship of the Christian Church*, 5:429–439.

7: John Knox and the Scottish Tradition

congregation of English exiles. It asks for an increase in faith, continued obedience, and steadfastness against enemies.[13] God's support and nurture is sought for the faithful still in England and for the relieving of the persecuted wherever they might be. There is also a prayer for this city, its magistrates and council, that is, Geneva, into whose protection the exiles had been received. There is a prayer for any who are afflicted by any kind of cross or tribulation, whether war, sickness, or poverty. This long prayer, which goes back to the ancient Church and even to the synagogue, is concluded with the Lord's Prayer.[14]

This prayer of intercession, or Pastoral Prayer, as we usually call it, was particularly meaningful when it was at a communion service, for then it became a prayer for the ingathering of the people of God in the house of the Father. It prayed for the peace and unity of the children of God, the healing of the sick, and the feeding of the hungry.

After that, a psalm was sung and the Benediction was given. That, at least, was the way it happened on most Sundays. Communion, apparently, was celebrated once a month, but how the transition was made from the preaching service to the communion service is not completely clear. Perhaps after the singing of a psalm the Apostles' Creed was offered as a prayer for faith. The *Anglo-Genevan Psalter* gives us such a prayer:

> Almightie and ever lyvinge God, vouchsave we besech thee, to grant us perfite contynuance in thy lively faith, augmentinge the same in us dayly, tyll we growe to the full measure of our perfection in Christ, wherof we make our confession, sayinge. I beleuve in God &c.[15]

This was the arrangement in the *Genevan Psalter*, and generally Knox was careful to follow the Genevan pattern.

---

[13] Knox, *Anglo-Genevan Psalter*, p. 298–299.

[14] Knox, *Anglo-Genevan Psalter*, p. 299.

[15] Knox, *Anglo-Genevan Psalter*, p. 300.

C. Invitation

However the transition may have been made between the preaching service and the communion service, it is clear that the Invitation which follows was modeled after that of the *Genevan Psalter*. The minister rehearses the Words of Institution from 1 Corinthians 11, starting with

> I have . . . receyved of the lorde that which I have delivered unto you, to witt, that the lorde Jesus the same night he was betrayed toke breade, and when he had geven thankes, he brake it sayinge. Take ye, eate ye, this is my bodie, which is broken for you: doo you this in remebrance of me. Likewise after supper, he toke the cuppe, sayige. This cuppe is the newe testamet or covenat in my bloude; doo ye this so ofte as ye shall drinke therof, in remembrance of me. For so ofte as you shal eate this bread, and drinke of this cuppe, ye shall declare the lordes deathe untill his cominge. Therfore whosoever shall eate this bread, and drinke the cuppe of the lorde unworthely, he shalbe giltie of the bodye and bloud of the lord. Then see that everyma prove ad trye him selfe, ad so let hym eate of this bread ad drike of this cuppe, for whosoever eateth or drinketh unworthelye, he eateth and drinketh his owne damnation, for not havinge due regarde and consideration of the lordes bodye.[16]

This Invitation, or fencing of the table as it was so often called, was one of those elements of the Reformed communion service which was most obviously inspired by Scripture itself and most clearly commended by patristic example.[17] As we will see, Reformed churches began to emphasize the importance of examining our consciences before approaching the Lord's Table. They were obviously led in this direction by the admonition of the Apostle Paul, "Let a man examine himself, and so eat of the

---

[16] Knox, *Anglo-Genevan Psalter*, pp. 300–301.

[17] Hughes Oliphant Old, *The Patristic Roots of Reformed Worship* (Zurich: Theologische Verlag Zurich, 1975), pp. 271–282.

bread and drink of the cup" (1 Cor. 11:28). Each communicant is supposed to discover his or her own sin and heartily to repent of it. In these words the Apostle Paul "exhorteth all persons diligently to trye and examine the selves, before they presume to eate of that bread, ad drinke of that cuppe."[18] As much as this Invitation warns the careless to abstain from the sacrament, it is truly an invitation to receive this sacrament in faith and to approach the table in repentance, eagerly seeking its great benefits, "for then we spiritually eate the fleshe of Christ, and drinke his bloude . . . we be one with Christ, and Christ with us." If anyone is a blasphemer or a slanderer of God's Word, an adulterer, or consumed with envy, it would be better not to partake. "Judge therfore your selves bretherne, that ye be not judged of the lorde."[19]

While this is usually called a Communion Exhortation, or even the fencing of the table, or even worse the Dismissals, it is probably best called the Invitation. For many years I used the term Communion Exhortation, but finally I decided to use the term Invitation because it more adequately intimated the theological significance of what was going on. The point of this part of the service is to gather people in, not to cut them out.

This is an invitation to accept Christ, to have a lively and steadfast faith in Christ our Savior.[20] It is to appeal to Christ and the merits of his death and his salvation. It is an appeal to make a commitment to brotherly love and a godly life all the days of our lives. Here, once again, the covenantal dimension of the sacrament is underlined.

This Invitation, like its prototype in the *Genevan Psalter*, is aware that most of us in spite of our zeal for the things of God are constantly discouraged by our infirmities and failures. It is a very pastoral exhortation. "Let us consider then, that this sacrament is a singuler medicine for all poore sicke creatures, a com-

---

[18] Knox, *Anglo-Genevan Psalter*, p. 301.

[19] Knox, *Anglo-Genevan Psalter*, p. 301.

[20] Knox, *Anglo-Genevan Psalter*, p. 302.

fortable helpe to weake soules, and that our lord requireth no other worthines on our parte, but that we unfaynedly acknowlege our noghtines, and imperfection. Then to the end that we may be worthy partakers of his merites, ad moste comfortable benefits."[21] Let us not be overly concerned about these earthly elements of bread and wine which we see with our eyes and touch with our hands as though they themselves contain the bodily presence of Christ or as if these elements were changed into the substance of Christ's flesh and blood.[22] "For the onlye waye to dispose our soules to receive norishment, reliefe, and quikening of his substance, is to lift up our mindes by fayth above all thinges worldlye and sensible, and therby to entre into heaven, that we may finde and receive Christ, where he dwelleth undoutedlye verie God, and verie man, in the incomprehensible glorie of his father, to whome be all praise, honor, and glorye, now and ever. Amen."[23]

One thing is clear; Knox courts no ambiguity. He teaches neither a bodily presence of Christ at the Supper, nor a transformation of the bread and the wine into the body and blood of the Savior. He does, however, believe in a presence. The incarnate, crucified, risen, and ascended Christ who is at the right hand of the Father is present for us and for our salvation. What Knox has to say in this exhortation is essentially what Calvin had to say before him. The text is almost word for word the same.

D. SITTING AT THE TABLE

At this point the *Anglo-Genevan Psalter* provides a rubric telling us that, after the Invitation is given, the minister comes down from the pulpit and sits at the Table.[24] The rubric reads as follows: "The

---

[21] Knox, *Anglo-Genevan Psalter*, p. 302.

[22] Knox, *Anglo-Genevan Psalter*, p. 302.

[23] Knox, *Anglo-Genevan Psalter*, pp. 302–303.

[24] Special thanks are due to my student, Rev. Walter Taylor, for his insights on sitting at the table, which is the subject of his dissertation under my direction at Erskine Theological Seminary. See Walter L. Taylor, *As They Sat at Table: Presbyte-*

exhortation ended, the minister commeth doune from the pulpit, and sitteth at the Table, every man and woman likewise takinge their place as occasion best serveth . . ."[25] The text specifically speaks of a table, not an altar. Nevertheless the word "table" is capitalized and is often referred to as the Holy Table. The Table is obviously part of the sign. Every man and woman likewise takes his or her place as occasion best affords. Apparently this gathering around the Table, and even sitting at the Table, was regarded as a most symbolic act. It was seen as a sacramental act. It was one of those visual acts that was of the essence of the sacrament. Sitting around the Table or at the Table was part of the sign of sharing the meal. Going forward, standing in line, and receiving the bread and the wine from the hands of the clergy obscures the sign of sharing a meal almost as much as denying the cup to the laity, as was the custom in the late Middle Ages.

E. The Eucharistic Prayer

With the congregation gathered around the Table, the minister is to take the bread and give thanks. Again the point is made that the printed prayer of thanks is an example. It can be offered either in the words provided or to like effect.[26] We notice in the words, "He taketh the bread and giveth thanks," an echo of the biblical account of the Last Supper. From these words it should be clear that the pattern for the prayer is the prayer of thanksgiving which Jesus offered over the bread and wine at the Last Supper. Furthermore it would seem to indicate that the minister was expected to formulate the prayer in his own words, although the simple read-

---

rian *Communion Practices*, D.Min. dissertation (Due West, SC: Erskine Theological Seminary, 2012).

[25] Knox, *Anglo-Genevan Psalter*, p. 303.

[26] "The exhortation ended, the minister commeth doune from the pulpit, and sitteth at the Table, every man and woman in likewise takinge their place as occasion best serveth, then he taketh the bread and geveth thankes, either in these woordes followinge, or like in effect." Maxwell, *Anglo-Genevan Psalter*, p. 124.

ing of the prayer from the service book was apparently acceptable. The prayer found in the *Anglo-Genevan Psalter* goes as follows:

> O Father of mercye and God of all consolation, seinge all creatures do knowlege and confesse thee, as governer, and lorde, it becommeth us the workemanship of thyne own handes, at all tymes to reverence and magnifie thy godli maiestie, first that thou haste created us to thyne own Image and similitude: but chieflye that thou haste delivered us, from that everlasting death and damnation into the which Satan drewe mankinde by the meane of synne: from the bondage wherof (neither man nor angell was able to make us free) but thou (o lord) riche in mercie and infinite in goodnes, haste provided our redemption to stande in thy onely and welbeloved sone: whom of verie love thou didest give to be made man, lyke unto us in all thynges, (synne except) that in his bodye he myght receive the ponishmentes of our transgression, by his death to make satisfaction to thy justice, and by his resurrection to destroye hym that was auctor of death, and so to reduce and bring agayne life to the world, frome which the whole offspringe of Adame moste justly was exiled.
>
> O lord we acknowlege that no creature ys able to comprehende the length and breadthe, the depenes and height, of that thy most excellent love which moved thee to shewe mercie, where none was deserved: to promise and give life, where death had gotten victorie: but to receve us into thy grace, when we could do nothyng but rebell against thy justice.
>
> O lord the blynde dulnes of our corrupt nature will not suffer us sufficiently to waye these thy moste ample benefites: yet nevertheles at the commaundement of Jesus Christ our lorde, we present our selves to this his table (which he hath left to be used in remembrance of his death untyll his comming agayne) to declare and witnes before the world, that by hym alone we have receved libertie, and life: that by him alone, thou doest acknowlege us thy chyldren and heires: that by hym alone, we have entrance to the throne of thy grace:

> that by hym alone, we are possessed in our spirituall kingedome, to eate and drinke at his table: with whome we have our conversation presently in heaven, and by whome, our bodies shalbe reysed up agayne frome the dust, and shalbe placed with him in that endles joye, which thow (o father of mercye) hast prepared for thyne elect, before the foundation of the worlde was layde.
>
> And these moste inestimable benefites, we acknowlege and confesse to haue receaved by thy free mercie and grace, by thy onely beloved sonne Jesus Christ, for the which therfore we thy congregation moved by thy holy sprite render thee all thankes, prayse, and glorie for ever and ever.[27]

The prayer begins by invoking God as Father of mercy and God of all consolation. This is a marvelous invocation. It is the invocation found at the beginning of the prayer of thanksgiving which opens the Apostle Paul's Second Letter to the Corinthians. Invocations taken from Scripture are a common feature of the prayers found in the worship of Reformed churches of the Reformation period. This searching out of the biblical language of prayer was simply part of the attempt to recover the prayer life of Jesus and the Apostles. This invocation, on the other hand, is followed by a phrase very similar to the eucharistic prayer of the Roman mass, "It becommeth us the workemanship of thyne own handes, at all tymes to reverence and magnifie thy godli majestie."[28] This phrase, if nothing else, tips us off to the fact that whoever composed the prayer intended to provide a Protestant eucharistic prayer.

After this brief invocation the prayer mentions the subjects of thanksgiving specifically. Quite logically it is creation which is mentioned first, "First that thou haste created us to thyne own Image and similitude: . . ."[29] One cannot help but notice here that it is not

---

[27] Maxwell, *Anglo-Genevan Psalter*, pp. 124–126.

[28] The Roman mass reads, "Vere dignum et justum est, aequum et salutare, nos tibi semper et ubique gratias agere:. . .," Thompson, *Liturgies of the Western Church*, p. 68.

[29] Maxwell, *Anglo-Genevan Psalter*, p. 125.

creation in general which is remembered but rather the creation of salvation history. It is creation in God's image. It is our creation to the end that we might enter into communion with our Creator.

But if logically it is our creation which is mentioned first, the text goes on to mention that the principle subject of thanksgiving is our redemption, "But chieflye that thou haste delivered us, from that everlasting death and damnation into the which Satan drewe mankinde by the meane of synne: from the bondage wherof (neither man nor angell was able to make us free). . ."[30] This thanksgiving is thoroughly permeated with basic biblical concepts. It puts redemption in the center of its Gospel and it presents it as a history of redemption. It continues: ". . . But thou (o lord) riche in mercie and infinite in goodnes, haste provided our redemption to stande in thy onely and welbeloved sone: whom of verie love thou didst give to be made man. .."[31] The story of God's creation of the human race, that is, our creation, our fall, and God's provision for our redemption brings the prayer to the remembering of the incarnation of the Son of God, "whom of verie love thou didst give to be made man, lyke unto us in all thynges, (synne except). . ."[32] The story is continued, again in the briefest fashion, to speak of Christ's atoning sacrifice on the Cross, "to make satisfaction to thy justice."[33] The theology of Christ's redemptive work is as classic as it is brief. Finally the memorial of God's redemptive work in Christ is brought to a conclusion by speaking of the resurrection as the victorious destruction of the author of sin and death "and so to reduce and bring agayne life to the world, frome which the whole ofspringe of Adame moste iustly was exiled."[34] In the manner of the Hebrew Berakah the story of God's saving act is

---

[30] Maxwell, *Anglo-Genevan Psalter*, p. 125.

[31] Maxwell, *Anglo-Genevan Psalter*, p. 125.

[32] Maxwell, *Anglo-Genevan Psalter*, p. 125.

[33] Maxwell, *Anglo-Genevan Psalter*, p. 125.

[34] Maxwell, *Anglo-Genevan Psalter*, p. 125.

recounted. This is of the very essence of the biblical understanding of thanksgiving.

The prayer continues, developing another aspect of the biblical concept of thanksgiving. It glories in the mighty acts of God. Perhaps one might say that the prayer jubilates in the sacred story. Joyfully it meditates on the most excellent love of God which moved him to show mercy where none was deserved. The theological precision here is admirable. One makes clear that grace is the undeserved favor of God. God's favor toward us is caused by nothing else than his own love. Grace is based on God's goodness not our own. It is a complete marvel which rescued us, "when we could do nothyng but rebell against thy iustice."[35]

In wonder the prayer remembers that our Lord Jesus has commanded us to present ourselves to declare and witness before the world that by him alone we have received liberty and life. Here the prayer develops another aspect of the biblical concept of thanksgiving. Thanksgiving not only *remembers* the mighty acts of God for our salvation, it *witnesses* before the world God's covenant faithfulness. God fulfills his promises. This prayer declares and witnesses that by Christ alone we have been acknowledged children of God. By Christ alone we have entrance to the throne of grace. By Christ alone we are made heirs of his kingdom and welcomed to eat and drink at his table. The sense of being gathered about the heavenly table in the transcendent kingdom of God is very moving here. Surely here, at least, is part of the Reformed sense of the real presence. In the celebration of the sacrament we enter into the wedding feast of the Lamb, we take our place at the banquet table, and eat and drink with our risen Savior.

The prayer continues to meditate on the hope of heaven. It is with Christ in heaven that we will soon have our conversation as our bodies are raised up from the dust and we enter into eternal joy, "which thow (o father of mercye) hast prepared for thyne elect,

---

[35] Maxwell, *Anglo-Genevan Psalter*, p. 125.

before the foundation of the worlde was layde."³⁶ It is concluded by a majestic doxology:

> And these moste inestimable benefites, we acknowlege and confesse to have receaved by thy free mercie and grace, by thy onely beloved sonne Jesus Christ, for the which therfore we thy congregation moved by thy holy sprite render thee all thankes, prayse, and glorie for ever and ever.³⁷

The congregation, moved by the Spirit, gives thanks to the Father for the mercy and grace he has poured out upon us in the Son. The prayer is concluded in trinitarian terms. In this sense it is genuinely Christian prayer, understood in terms of the inner trinitarian conversation. It is prayer which is the work of the Holy Spirit in the body of Christ to the glory of the Father.

This is a great eucharistic prayer. One assumes it was written by John Knox but it could also have been written by one of the other Marian exiles. It certainly reflects a thoroughly Reformed understanding of the sacrament.

Perhaps the influence of Peter Martyr Vermigli is found in this prayer,³⁸ but most probably, it comes from John Knox. It is more than likely inspired by the biblical texts which tell us that Jesus gave thanks over the bread and wine. It was a fundamental principle of Reformed worship that the church in its worship was supposed to follow the example of Christ and his Apostles as we find it in Scripture. To offer a prayer of thanksgiving over the bread and wine is certainly indicated by the text of Scripture.³⁹ What is

---

[36] Maxwell, *Anglo-Genevan Psalter*, p. 126.

[37] Maxwell, *Anglo-Genevan Psalter*, p. 126.

[38] Over the years I have made several attempts to prove this hypothesis, but, alas, as yet I have not found the texts which would make the point.

[39] To reconstruct the example of Christ and the Apostles is rather complicated due to a few text critical problems of which any student of the Christian Humanists would have been well aware. Knox would have known how Erasmus interpreted this passage, and he might also have known how Nicholas of Lyra explained this

so beautiful about this prayer is that it not only follows the more explicit example of Scripture in giving a prayer of thanksgiving at this point, but that it has such a thorough understanding of the biblical concept of thanksgiving.

F. Prayer of Dedication

The Prayer of Dedication found in the *Anglo-Genevan Psalter* is a free translation of the prayer in the *Genevan Psalter* which itself is taken from the *Strasbourg Psalter*.

> Moste mercifull father, we render to thee all prayse thankes and glorie, for that thou hast vouchsafed to graunt unto us miserable synners so excellent a gifte and threasor, as to receave us into the felowship and company of thy deare sonne Jesus Christ our lorde, whome thou deliveredst to deathe for us, and haste give hym unto us, as a necessarie foode and norishment unto everlastynge life. And now we beseche the also (o heavenly father) to graunt us this request, that thou never suffer us to become so unkinde as to forget so worthy benefittes: but rather imprint and fasten them sure in our hartes, that we may growe and increase dayly more and more in true faithe, which continually ys excersised in all maner of goode workes, and so moche the rather o lord, cofirme us, in these perelous daies and rages of satan, that we may constantly stande and continewe in the confession of the same to the advancement of thy glorye, which art God over all things blessed for ever. So be it.[40]

The prayer invokes God as Father, rendering Him all praise, thanks and glory, for he has promised to us miserable sinners such an excellent gift and such a rich treasure as to receive us into the fellowship and company of his dear Son, Jesus Christ, our Lord.[41]

---

passage in light of the liturgical customs of the synagogue. Cf. Joachim Jeremias, *The Eucharistic Words of Jesus* (New York: Charles Scribner's Son, 1966).

[40] Knox, *Anglo-Genevan Psalter*, pp. 304–305.

[41] Knox, *Anglo-Genevan Psalter*, p. 304.

Here, again, we notice the strong covenantal dimension of the liturgy. It is essential to a covenantal understanding of the Lord's Supper that God has received us into the fellowship and company of his people so that he is our God and we are his people. The love of God is extolled for he has delivered up his only Son for our salvation as a necessary food and nourishment unto everlasting life. The prayer continues asking of God that the remembrance of his grace be printed on the tablets of our hearts. Here is an obvious Scriptural allusion to Jeremiah's prophecy of the New Covenant (Jer. 31:31–33), making even clearer the covenantal dimension of the sacrament. The sacrament which has just been received is the sign and seal of God's promise to nourish us in true faith, exercise us in good works, and confirm and strengthen us in our warfare with Satan, that we may constantly stand and continue in the confession of true religion and the advancement of the glory of God, who is blessed for ever.[42]

With this the congregation sang Psalm 103, one of the most profound of the canonical thanksgiving psalms. The minister pronounced the benediction, either the Aaronic Benediction or the Apostolic Benediction and then the people departed.[43]

The Prayer of Dedication which comes at the end of the communion service in the *Anglo-Genevan Psalter* is of the greatest possible theological significance. This was also true of its predecessors in the *Genevan Psalter* and the *Strasbourg Psalter*. It is implicit in the biblical concept of thanksgiving that true thanksgiving culminates in dedicating ourselves to God's service. Having received so excellent a gift as to be included in the bond of the covenant whereby God promises to be our God and we are received as his people, we in return dedicate ourselves to the service of God.

The communion service in the *Anglo-Genevan Psalter* makes a major step forward in the Reformed shaping of the communion service. The eucharistic dimension of the sacrament is markedly

---

[42] Knox, *Anglo-Genevan Psalter*, p. 305.

[43] Knox, *Anglo-Genevan Psalter*, p. 305.

7: John Knox and the Scottish Tradition

increased. This service can more truly than its predecessors in Strasbourg and Geneva be called the Eucharist. Not only have Knox and his congregation added a true Eucharistic Prayer, they have put it right at the center of the service. Why have they done this? Knox in his rubrics gives us a few hints.

As Knox saw it, we are bound to follow the example of Jesus when we celebrate his Supper. We first examine ourselves, according to St. Paul's rule. We prepare our minds that we may be worthy partakers of so high a mystery. Then taking bread, we give thanks, break, and distribute it, as Christ our Savior has taught us. Finally, the ministration ended, we give thanks again according to Christ's example. Without his word and warrant nothing is done in this sacred service.

Bard Thompson has called our attention to the similarity of Knox to Gregory Dix who wanted to reduce the Eucharist to a four action shape.[44] First, Christ took the bread, then he gave thanks, then he broke the bread, and finally he gave it to the disciples. Fifty years ago Gregory Dix, although a High Church Anglican, was regarded as the last word on liturgy. To be sure, John Knox gave us a six action shape rather than a four action shape. He found two acts Dix had not enumerated. The Apostle Paul tells us first to examine ourselves and then to take the bread, give thanks, break it, and distribute it. The Gospel of Matthew is particularly explicit about the prayer of thanksgiving which closed the service. Knox began with self-examination and concluded with what we have called the Prayer of Dedication. Even at that, there is a striking similarity here which Bard Thompson has rightly brought to our attention. There are certain acts which are essential to the service. Knox understood this long before Gregory Dix. If we are going to follow the example of Jesus we can hardly leave out the Eucharistic Prayer. To put it bluntly, the example of Jesus is a pretty strong argument.

---

[44] See Thompson, *Liturgies of the Western Church*, p. 292, in his introductory discussion of Knox's service. See also Gregory Dix, *The Shape of the Liturgy* (London: Adam and Charles Black Ltd., 1975).

In fact, one wonders why, in light of the text which recounts the institution of the Supper as we find it in the synoptic gospels and as it is reported by the Apostle Paul in 1 Corinthians 11, the earliest Reformers simply dropped in whole or in part what was called the canon or Eucharistic Prayer. What seemed to be on their minds, however, was that they wanted nothing that sounded like a formula of consecration or a prayer of oblation offering up the consecrated host as a sacrifice to God. In the *Anglo-Genevan Psalter* Knox makes a point of this.[45] It is for this reason that the Words of Institution are recited toward the beginning of the service as giving the warrant for our celebration of the sacrament rather than including them in the Eucharistic Prayer as a formula of consecration.

Going even further, Knox was no doubt familiar with the *Paraphrases* of Erasmus, which criticizes the usual translation of the account of the Last Supper. The Greek text of Matthew 26:26 does not tell us that Jesus blessed the bread in the sense that he consecrated it, but rather that he gave thanks over the bread and wine for God's mighty acts of creation and redemption. That this prayer of thanksgiving was an important part of the service Jesus celebrated ought to have come to Knox fairly easily, quite aside from other considerations. Certainly one could say that modern research supports Knox's insight.

There is another point to notice and that is that Knox offers two prayers of thanksgiving, the one over the bread at the beginning of the meal and the one over the cup when they had supped. "Finally, the administration ended, we give thanks again according to Christ's example."[46] The strong eucharistic dimension of Knox's liturgy is its most salient feature. The reason for this is quite simply that Knox was attempting to follow the example of Jesus as he found it in Scripture.

---

[45] Knox, *Anglo-Genevan Psalter*, p. 305.

[46] Knox, *Anglo-Genevan Psalter*, p. 305.

ROBERT BRUCE
The Mystery of the Lord's Supper, 1589

It was in the High Kirk of St. Giles, a full generation after John Knox had led the nation into the Reformation, that Robert Bruce, son of one of the ancient noble families of Scotland, preached these sermons on the Lord's Supper. [47] They belong to that genre of sermons, so popular in the Reformed pulpit, which are normally called preparatory sermons. They were called preparatory sermons because they were preached to prepare the congregation for the celebration of the sacrament of Holy Communion.

Robert Bruce came to his distinguished pulpit well prepared to address one of the sensitive issues of the day. For a good part of the sixteenth century much of Christendom had been embroiled in controversies over the sacrament of the Lord's Supper. Sir Alexander Bruce sent his son Robert to St. Salvator's College at the University of St. Andrews to study humanities. St. Andrews was at its zenith when young Robert was a student there. George Buchanan and Andrew Melville were teaching there and John Knox himself was frequently in the pulpit of the ancient Scottish university before he died in 1572 while Bruce was still a student. At first the study of the law occupied him, but then spending some time at Louvain, one of the centers of the Counter-Reformation, he became more and more interested in the study of theology. In fact, Robert Bellarmine was professor of theology at Louvain from 1569–1576 while Robert Bruce was a student of law. Could Bruce have attended Bellarmine's lectures? One wonders if their paths ever crossed outside of class, or if the young Scotsman ever discussed theology with Bellarmine's

---

[47] For biographical material on Robert Bruce, see: Iain H. Murray, *A Scottish Christian Heritage* (Edinburgh: The Banner of Truth Trust, 2006), pp. 37–72; Nigel M. de S. Cameron, ed., *Dictionary of Scottish Church History and Theology* (Edinburgh: T. & T. Clark; and Downers Grove, IL: InterVarsity, 1993); and Robert Bruce, *The Mystery of the Lord's Supper*, trans. and ed. Thomas F. Torrance (Richmond: John Knox Press, 1958).

students. One could hardly imagine that a young, adventurous Scot would not have been involved in long discussions of sacramental theology.[48] It was a hot issue in those days. Animated discussions in the taverns were a big part of the learning process. That is just the way sixteenth century universities worked. One always learned more from one's fellow students than from any professor on the faculty. It made no difference that Bruce was supposed to be studying law. In those days everyone discussed theology. That was what being a university student was all about.

When Bruce returned to Scotland he made rapid progress in his profession, and yet all the while he had inklings of a vocation to the pulpit. Finally he put away his law books, took up his Bible, and became one of the outstanding preachers of his generation. These sermons have for centuries been regarded as one of the classic statements of Reformed eucharistic theology.

Bruce had close connections to the Scottish royal court at Edinburgh. In the first place, through his mother, Janet Livingston, he was the double great grandson of the founder of the Stewart dynasty, James I. This made him a cousin of James VI, who reigned in Scotland from 1567–1623. Behind that, however, there was the fact that the Bruce family had royal roots which went back even further. They were Norman French, and back in the fourteenth century Robert de Bruce was able to make good his claim to being king of Scotland. While Robert Bruce, the Reformed theologian who claims our interest at the moment, was the second son of Sir Alexander Bruce, he did not inherit the principal estates of the Bruce family. His father, Alexander Bruce, nevertheless had endowed him with the barony of Kinnaird. It is therefore that our theologian was often called Robert Bruce of Kinnaird. He was popular at court, a young nobleman with wit and sincerity.

In addition to this, Bruce had become a popular preacher

---

[48] Eventually the King of Scotland and Robert Bellarmine would cross theological swords and Bellarmine would publish a major work in refutation of King James I of England and VI of Scotland.

7: John Knox and the Scottish Tradition

in Edinburgh once he began to study the Scriptures. At first his preaching was of an informal, voluntary nature. He had not sought formal ordination nor had he been received into the ministry. Nevertheless, since good preachers were in short supply in the late sixteenth century, the General Assembly of the Church of Scotland in 1587 appointed Bruce preacher of St. Giles, the principal pulpit in the Scottish capitol. It was one of those cases like that of Ambrose of Milan, where a devout Christian man, well known for his integrity in public affairs, was impressed into the ministry. During the threat of the invasion of the Spanish Armada, Bruce proved his value as a preacher. He taught the frightened people to put their faith in God, and indeed, in 1588, the Protestants of both England and Scotland were miraculously saved by a freak storm from an invasion by the hostile Spanish Armada of Philip II.

The new pastoral responsibility did not end Bruce's popularity at court. King James held him in high regard and in 1589 he was appointed privy councilor. Bruce became especially active at court when James left the kingdom to collect his bride, Anne of Denmark. James apparently enjoyed life at the Danish court and stayed there for some time, leaving Scottish affairs in the hands of the privy councilors. It was during this time that Bruce won the confidence of both king and people.

One should not assume that Bruce had come by his Protestantism naively. Janet Livingston, Bruce's mother, was a Roman Catholic, and, as we have said, Bruce had studied at Louvain during the days when Robert Bellarmine was making Louvain one of the centers of Counter-Reformation thought. Not only was Bellarmine a major Roman Catholic theologian, but he was also a Jesuit, the first Jesuit to be appointed to a major chair of theology. Robert Bruce, as these sermons show, was well acquainted with the discussion of eucharistic theology at a rather advanced level of the discussion.

The time would come when Robert Bruce would lose favor with the Scottish king. The king figured he had a right, a divine right, to a compliant clergy, something the Calvinist ministers of Scotland had no intention of granting him. Eventually the king banished Bruce from his pulpit in Edinburgh. At first he was put under house arrest at Kinnaird. People thronged to hear him, and so he was sent to Inverness, way up in the Highlands, where even then he developed an enthusiastic following. Finally he was allowed to live in his own home at Kinnaird where he died in 1631. All this, however, took place long after these sermons were preached. Banishment never stopped his preaching for long. Whenever a pulpit was opened to him the faithful flocked to hear him, recognizing him as a true confessor of the eternal gospel.

A. Meeting the Polemic of the Counter-Reformation

The interesting thing about Bruce's communion sermons is that they help clarify a Protestant understanding of the sacrament of the Lord's Supper in terms of the traditional Scholastic discussion. In the last analysis it is rather difficult to understand the Reformed position on the Lord's Supper in terms of Scholastic theology. We have spoken of this before, but we need to speak of it again. A Reformed approach demands a distinctly biblical theology, rather than a Scholastic theology. Bruce, however, helps to shed light on how Protestants understood the presence of Christ at the Supper in light of the Catholic discussion. In other words, Bruce gives us a Protestant response to a Catholic apologetic. He defends the Reformed teaching on the sacraments over against the Roman Catholic Scholastic teaching.

There are very definite strong points in Bruce's treatment. He is particularly helpful on the doctrine of the Holy Spirit and its relation to the sacrament. The pneumatic dimension of the Lord's Supper is amply treated while the eucharistic dimension and the eschatological dimension surface only occasionally. Our preacher has nothing to say about the doctrine of the eucharistic sacrifice, for example, even if the leading continental Reformers were all agreed that we are not to regard the sacrament as a sacrifice. This may be more than anything else a question of which sermons found their way to the printing press. Bruce more than likely followed the usual Protestant line of thought. What we have here seems to be a random collection of preparatory sermons rather than a more general treatise on the doctrine of the Lord's Supper. On the other hand Bruce is eloquent when it comes to the matter of sacramental piety.

Turning to the leading thoughts of Bruce's sermons, we note first of all that Bruce insists that in the sacrament of the Lord's Supper we have to deal with our union with Christ. He opens the first of his sermons with the following sentence: "There is nothing in this world, or out of this world, more to be wished by everyone of you than to be conjoined with Jesus Christ, and once for all made one with Him, the God of glory."[49] This is the sacrament of Communion and it is about communion that Bruce would speak. Bruce continues, "This heavenly and celestial conjunction is procured and brought about by two special means. It is brought about by means of the Word and preaching of the Gospel, and it is brought about by means of the Sacraments and their ministration."[50] Worship, whether it is a matter of the reading and preaching of Scripture, praise and prayer, or the celebration of the sacraments of baptism and the Lord's Supper is concerned with union or communion with God. The mystery of how this union comes about is the subject of these sermons.[51]

As Bruce regards it, fundamental to comprehending the sacrament is understanding the distinction between the sign offered by the sacrament and then the thing signified by that sign. This distinction goes far back into the history of Christian theology. Here we are at the heart of the Scholastic discussion. Already in Augus-

---

[49] Bruce, *The Mystery of the Lord's Supper*, p. 39.

[50] Bruce, *The Mystery of the Lord's Supper*, p. 39.

[51] Bruce, *The Mystery of the Lord's Supper*, p. 40.

tine we find the distinction made between the *res*, the "thing" signified, and the *signum*, the "sign" which points to it. Bruce invites his congregation into this century old discussion. While at the outset of the Reformation the Reformers had tried to move away from the traditional Scholastic categories in their attempts to understand the sacrament, here we find the same old terminology being reintroduced. Bruce would turn our attention to distinguishing the sign and the thing signified.[52]

Our Scottish theologian does not ignore the concern of the older Reformers to recover the biblical terminology. In fact he reminds us that the word "sacrament" itself is not a biblical term. It is a translation of the Greek word "mystery."[53] We would be better off, as Bruce sees it, if we would use the word "mystery" to speak of our union with Christ, that union which is begun here in this life and is continued in the life to come.[54] It is no doubt for this reason that the title, *The Mystery of the Lord's Supper*, has been given to this collection of sermons. On the other hand, the word "sign" is a biblical term. Bruce tells us that to use the word "sign" does preserve the biblical terminology. No doubt Bruce had in mind passages such as Romans 4:11 where the Apostle speaks of Abraham's circumcision "as a sign or seal of the righteousness which he had by faith." Perhaps he also has in mind the "signs" which Jesus performed in the Gospel of John or the prophetic signs of the Old Testament prophets. The word "sign" is a biblical term for Bruce, and his intention is to clarify its meaning.[55]

So, then, how are we to understand the sign that is given by the sacrament? The sacrament is the whole thing, both the sign and the thing signified. At this point Bruce gives us a definition of a sacrament as, "a holy sign and seal that is annexed to the

---

[52] Bruce, *The Mystery of the Lord's Supper*, p. 42.

[53] Bruce, *The Mystery of the Lord's Supper*, p. 40.

[54] Bruce, *The Mystery of the Lord's Supper*, p. 40.

[55] Bruce, *The Mystery of the Lord's Supper*, p. 40.

preached Word of God to seal up and confirm the truth contained in the same Word, ..."[56] The signs given by the prophets were perfect examples. Jeremiah confirmed his message with the breaking of a potter's vessel. Samuel confirmed his word concerning David by anointing him. Even clearer examples would be the signs of the covenant where God confirmed his promise by giving a sign. The rainbow given to Noah and circumcision given to Abraham were such signs. To make his point Bruce quotes Augustine, "'Let the Word come to the element and you shall have a Sacrament.'"[57] It is the Word and the sign together which makes the sacrament, but what Bruce wants to discuss here is the sign. He tells us, "I call the signs in the sacrament whatever I perceive and take up by my outward senses, by my eye especially."[58] In preaching we are concerned chiefly with what we hear, but in the sacraments we are concerned particularly with what we see.

There are two sorts of things which appear to us in the Lord's Supper; first there are the elements of bread and wine, and second there are the rites which we perform with these elements: the breaking of the bread and the distribution of it to the congregation, the pouring out of the wine, and the sharing of the cup. The communion rites of the Reformed churches have usually made a special point of the visual element of breaking the bread in the sight of the people, sitting about the table in some way, the pouring out of the cup, and the sharing of it by the whole congregation.[59] Bruce is careful to emphasize that these things are not vain ceremonies. These sacramental actions are the signs which Christ instituted.[60] Christ, just as the prophets before him, sealed the word that he preached by the giving of a sign, and that sign

---

[56] Bruce, *The Mystery of the Lord's Supper*, p. 41.

[57] Bruce, *The Mystery of the Lord's Supper*, p. 42.

[58] Bruce, *The Mystery of the Lord's Supper*, p. 43.

[59] Bruce, *The Mystery of the Lord's Supper*, p. 43.

[60] Bruce, *The Mystery of the Lord's Supper*, p. 43.

was the Supper. In fact, Jesus often concluded his teaching by the sign of sharing a meal. Bruce is careful to point out that the reason he calls these things signs is not that "they only signify something, as the bread signifies the Body of Christ, and the wine signifies the Blood of Christ; I do not call them something because they only represent something. I call them signs because they have the Body and the Blood of Christ conjoined with them."[61] This word "conjoined" is crucial to what Bruce is saying. The word "conjoined" may be a bit strange to our ears. What it means, however, is simply "united." The sign and the thing signified are united.

Bruce continues, "Indeed so truly is the body of Christ conjoined with the bread, and the Blood of Christ conjoined with the wine, that as soon as you receive the bread in your mouth (if you are a faithful man or woman) you receive the body of Christ in your soul, and that by faith. And as soon as you receive the wine in your mouth, you receive the Blood of Christ in your soul, and that by faith."[62] Up to this point, at least, what Bruce has to say sounds very much like Luther's consubstantiation. This is probably not, however, Bruce's intention. The point Bruce wants to make is that the bread and the wine are means to convey to us the grace of God. We read, "It is chiefly because of this function that they are instruments to deliver and exhibit the things that they signify."[63]

Early in the Reformation, the South German Reformers assured the Reformers of Wittenberg that while they believed the sacraments should be understood as signs, they did not believe they were empty signs. Referred to as the *Wittenberg Concord*, this agreement was an important step in the unfolding of Reformed eucharistic thought. Here Bruce makes the same affirmation, but goes a bit further by saying that in addition to being signs, they are signs which God has chosen to use as instruments. "The Sacrament exhibits

---

[61] Bruce, *The Mystery of the Lord's Supper*, p. 43–44.

[62] Bruce, *The Mystery of the Lord's Supper*, p. 44.

[63] Bruce, *The Mystery of the Lord's Supper*, p. 44.

and delivers the thing that it signifies to the soul and heart."[64] In this case a sacrament is different from a picture. A picture does not deliver the person of which it is an image. A sacrament, on the other hand, does deliver the grace which it signifies. The reason for this is that Christ has instituted the sacrament to this end, ". . . the Lord has appointed the Sacraments as hands to deliver and exhibit the things signified . . ."[65] The sacraments are instruments just as the Word is an instrument. "As the Word of the Gospel is a mighty and potent instrument for our everlasting salvation, so the Sacrament is a potent instrument appointed by God to deliver to us Christ Jesus for our everlasting salvation."[66] It is Christ himself who is delivered to us by the sacraments and it is Christ himself who established the means of this communion with himself. But not only was this means instituted by Christ, it is administered by the Holy Spirit.

It is Christ who comes to us in the sacrament, but he comes to us through his Holy Spirit.[67] Christ himself has appointed the Word and the sacraments as the instruments of this communion and he has given his Spirit as the minister of his presence. Only God himself, strictly speaking, can deliver Christ to us. "No one has power to deliver Christ but God the Father, or He Himself. No one has power to deliver the Mediator, but His own Spirit."[68] With this strong emphasis on the work of the Holy Spirit we recognize the distinct eucharistic theology of Calvin. Christ is spiritually present at the Supper in the sense that Christ is present through his Spirit. His presence is ministered through the Holy Spirit. We will have more to say about this further on.

Having spoken of the signs we now must turn to the thing signified. Bruce appeals to Irenaeus of Lyon to make his point that

---

[64] Bruce, *The Mystery of the Lord's Supper*, p. 44.

[65] Bruce, *The Mystery of the Lord's Supper*, p. 44.

[66] Bruce, *The Mystery of the Lord's Supper*, p. 44.

[67] Bruce, *The Mystery of the Lord's Supper*, p. 45.

[68] Bruce, *The Mystery of the Lord's Supper*, p. 45.

what is signified by the sign is "the whole Christ, with His whole gifts, benefits and graces, applied and given to my soul."[69] It is not enough, Bruce insists, to speak only of the benefits of Christ, the graces of Christ, or the virtues which flow out of Christ. One must go on to speak of "the very substance of Christ Himself, from which this virtue flows."[70] Bruce goes on then to say, "The substance with the virtues, gifts and graces that flow from the substance, is the thing signified here." As Bruce sees it, one cannot receive the benefits of Christ without receiving the substance of Christ. He goes on, making himself ever clearer, telling us that by substance he means "the whole Christ, God and Man, without separation of His natures, without distinction of His substance from His graces."[71] It is this which is signified by the sign in the sacraments. Here, again, Bruce is using the terminology of Scholasticism.

Bruce asks why it is that we must insist that it is the whole Christ who is the thing signified by the sacrament. He answers, "If no more is signified by the bread than the Flesh and Body of Christ alone, and no more is signified by the wine than the Blood of Christ alone, you cannot say that the Body of Christ is Christ; for it is but a piece of Christ. . . . Therefore, in order that the Sacrament may nourish you to life everlasting, you must get in it your whole Saviour, the whole Christ, God and Man, with all His graces and benefits, without separation of His substance from His graces, or of the one nature from the other."[72] That one should receive only Christ's flesh and blood at the Lord's Table would be of no profit at all to us. When we realize this, then it is clear that it is not by our mouths that we receive Christ, but by faith. "It is vain to think that we get God by

---

[69] Bruce, *The Mystery of the Lord's Supper*, p. 45. The interpretation of Irenaeus of Lyon was argued at length by the Counter-Reformation. The discussion was complicated by new discoveries of the words of Irenaeus. See Old, *The Patristic Roots of Reformed Worship*, pp. 171–172.

[70] Bruce, *The Mystery of the Lord's Supper*, p. 46.

[71] Bruce, *The Mystery of the Lord's Supper*, p. 46.

[72] Bruce, *The Mystery of the Lord's Supper*, pp. 46–47.

our mouth, but we get Him by faith. Since He is a Spirit, I eat Him by faith and belief in my soul, not by the teeth of my mouth–that would be folly."[73] When we understand that at the Lord's Supper we feed upon Christ by faith, then we understand how it is that it is the whole Christ that we feed upon.

Having spoken of first the sign and second the thing signified, Bruce now speaks of how the two come together and how the two are distinct. In other words, he returns to the question of our union with Christ. First is how the two are conjoined. It is not a matter of the two being joined by their occupying the same location. It is not as though they touch each other.[74] There have always been those for whom the doctrine of the real presence has been a problem because they insisted that they could not conceive of a presence beyond mere local presence. The whole concept of omnipresence transcends locality. God can be present without being tied to a particular locality, if God is indeed omnipresent. It is also true that the conjunction between the sign and the thing signified is not a visible conjunction. The one is perceived by the visible eye but not the other.[75] But to say that the conjunction between the sign and the thing signified is not a conjunction of locality or of visibility is to say what this conjunction is not; that is, to be sure, easier than saying what it is.

Bruce insists that this conjunction is a mystery. He reminds us that according to the Apostle Paul our union with Christ is a great mystery (Eph. 5:32). It is a mysterious, secret, and spiritual conjunction, but there is something that we can understand about it. There is a certain relationship between the sign and the thing signified which makes it possible for the thing signified to be signified by the sign. The bread and wine can speak to us of nourishment, just as in baptism the water can speak of the washing away of our sins. This conjunction is very much like the conjunction between the word that is

---

[73] Bruce, *The Mystery of the Lord's Supper*, p. 47.

[74] Bruce, *The Mystery of the Lord's Supper*, p. 51.

[75] Bruce, *The Mystery of the Lord's Supper*, p. 51.

spoken and the thing signified by the word. Here, of course, Bruce is following closely the thought of Augustine. We are hardly surprised then when Bruce says, "Recall, however, the conjunction between the simple word and the thing signified by the word. The same kind of conjunction exists between the Sacrament and the thing signified by the Sacrament, for the Sacrament is nothing else but a visible Word."[76] The term "visible Word" is, of course, the term coined by Augustine which so characterizes his eucharistic theology.

Bruce continues, "Why do I call it a visible Word? Because it conveys the signification of it by the eye to the mind."[77] In the outward sharing of the bread and the wine we are shown that God nourishes us unto eternal life. There is a semantic relationship between the sign and the thing signified. The bread and the wine quite naturally suggest the body and blood of Christ, particularly when the bread is broken and the wine poured out. The conjunction between signs and the thing signified is in the power of the sign to intimate the thing signified. This power comes from the institution of Christ on one hand and the inspiration of the Holy Spirit on the other.

But it is also true, as Bruce so clearly points out, that we must take care not to confuse the sign and the thing signified. "Beware lest you turn the one into the other, but keep each of them in its own integrity, without confusion or mixture of the one with the other."[78] One quickly recognizes the theological terminology of Chalcedon here. The Fathers of Chalcedon were concerned that in speaking of the two natures of Christ we should not confuse, confound, or mix the human nature and the divine nature.

Our theologian elaborates this by showing that the sign and the thing signified are not given by the same person. The sign is given to us by the minister while the thing signified is given to us by Christ

---

[76] Bruce, *The Mystery of the Lord's Supper*, p. 54.

[77] Bruce, *The Mystery of the Lord's Supper*, p. 54.

[78] Bruce, *The Mystery of the Lord's Supper*, p. 55.

7: JOHN KNOX AND THE SCOTTISH TRADITION

himself.[79] So it is with the way we receive Christ. The signs of bread and wine are eaten by our mouth just as any other food is eaten. The thing signified, however, is received by faith. It is by faith that we receive the bread of heaven. "There is no instrument, either hand or mouth, by which we may lay hold of Christ, but by faith alone."[80] Christ is both eaten and digested by faith. This is the *manducatio spiritualis* about which the Reformers spoke, but it is not to be confused with the eating of the signs of bread and wine. "Thus the sign and the thing signified are offered and given, not to one instrument, but to two, the one to the mouth of the body, the other to the mouth of the soul."[81] What Bruce is apparently getting at here is that by insisting on some sort of metamorphosis or conversion of the bread and wine into the body and blood of Christ there is a confusing of the sign and the thing signified. His argument is very sound.

B. THE WHOLE CHRIST

Another characteristic of Bruce's teaching on the sacrament is that we have to deal with the whole Christ, with his very substance, not merely with a part of him, namely with his flesh and blood. We have already said something about this, but there is more to say. The polemic of the Counter-Reformation had accused the Reformers of wanting communion with nothing more than a spiritual Christ, neglecting the incarnate Christ. That was not what the Reformers had in mind. It is with the whole person of Christ, who was born in Bethlehem, who ministered in Galilee, who was crucified and raised in Jerusalem, and who is now seated at the right hand of the Father in heaven, with whom we have fellowship. It is Christ who is the thing signified in the sacrament, the whole Christ, the substance of Christ, the real Christ. It is he and no other who nourishes us unto eternal life. "The Sacrament

---

[79] Bruce, *The Mystery of the Lord's Supper*, p. 60.

[80] Bruce, *The Mystery of the Lord's Supper*, p. 61.

[81] Bruce, *The Mystery of the Lord's Supper*, p. 61.

of the Supper . . . is nothing else than the image of our spiritual nutriment."[82] That which is signified in the sacrament of the Lord's Supper is none other than Christ, the bread of life, as we find it in the sixth chapter of the Gospel of John.

To make very clear what he means, Bruce goes on to speak of Christ as the substance signified by the Supper:

> In this Sacrament we have the fruits of Christ's death, of which I spoke; the virtue of His sacrifice, the virtue of His passion. I do not call these fruits and virtues alone the thing signified in the Sacrament of the Supper; the thing signified I call rather the substance, and the person out of whose substance this virtue and these fruits flow and proceed. I grant, and it is certainly true, that by the right use and participation of the Sacrament you partake of all these fruits, nevertheless the fruits themselves are not the first and the chief thing that you partake of in the Sacrament. You must first of all get something else. It is true that no man can partake of the substance of Christ without at the same time partaking also of the fruits that flow from His substance. Nevertheless, you must discern between the substance, and the fruits that flow from the substance.[83]

The first thing that we receive by participating in the sacrament is union with Christ. Being united to Christ, then, we are entitled to all the benefits of Christ's redemptive work. One must distinguish, however, between the substance of Christ and the fruit that flows from the substance. "In the Sacrament of the Supper, the fruits of the Sacrament are the growth of faith, and increase in holiness. The thing signified is the substance, that is, the Body and Blood of Christ is the substance, out of which this growth in faith and holiness proceeds."[84] Here we find Bruce bringing us back to a more covenantal understanding of the Supper. The Lord's Supper is

---

[82] Bruce, *The Mystery of the Lord's Supper*, p. 74.

[83] Bruce, *The Mystery of the Lord's Supper*, p. 74.

[84] Bruce, *The Mystery of the Lord's Supper*, p. 75.

7: John Knox and the Scottish Tradition

truly *communion*—fellowship with Christ and participation in the covenant community.

All of this may seem like quite a bit of theology for a preparatory service. We need to remember, however, that these sermons were preached at the High Kirk of St. Giles, the church attended by many of the leading figures of the kingdom. The people in this congregation were the people whom the Jesuits had in their sights. These were the people the Counter-Reformation polemic was trying so desperately to convince. Irenaeus of Lyon and Augustine were major figures in the Catholic argumentation, especially Irenaeus.

Let us turn now to another subject which Bruce treats particularly well. He asks the question, "What power has the bread in the Sacrament to be a sign, more than the bread used in common houses? Where does that power come from?"[85] To this he answers, "This bread has a power given to it by Christ and His institution, by which it is appointed to signify His Body, to represent His Body and to deliver His Body."[86] When the minister performs the sacred rites with the bread and the wine and when he sets them apart by prayer to this sacred use, then, "they are holy things."[87] They are holy when they are applied to this sacred use. No longer are they used for the ordinary purpose of feeding the body, but the sacred purpose of feeding the soul. As long as the sacred service continues, the bread remains holy, but when it is concluded, then the bread and the wine revert to common use.

Then Bruce goes on to make a very important point. It is not only the bread and wine which are signs, but the sacred actions as well. The breaking of the bread, the pouring out of the wine, and the sharing of the sacred meal are all part of the sacramental sign. The breaking of the bread and the pouring out of the wine

---

[85] Bruce, *The Mystery of the Lord's Supper*, p. 77.
[86] Bruce, *The Mystery of the Lord's Supper*, p. 77.
[87] Bruce, *The Mystery of the Lord's Supper*, p. 77.

signify the sacrificial death of Christ for us. They are essential ceremonies and should not be omitted. In the same way the giving of the bread and wine to us and the eating of the bread and drinking of the wine show us that the death of Christ is for our salvation. "The pouring out of the wine, therefore, tells you that he died for you, that His blood was shed for you, so that this is an essential ceremony which must not be omitted."[88]

Having spoken of the sacramental actions, Bruce now moves on to explaining the sacramental words, "Take, eat, this is my body" (Matt. 26:28). These words tell us, Bruce says, that "the soul eats the Body of Christ and drinks the Blood of Christ."[89] What is meant by this? "When we speak about eating the Body and drinking the Blood of Christ, these expressions are sacramental." Properly speaking, eating and drinking are the actions of the body only, ". . . but here they are ascribed to the soul by a translation, by a figurative manner of speaking."[90] What is properly said of the body is ascribed to the soul. This can be done because there is a resemblance between the eating of the soul and the eating of the body. Very simply put, the eating of the soul is the application of Christ to the soul. It is believing that Christ has shed his blood for me and has paid the ransom for my redemption.[91] Bruce then asks why this is called eating. It is called eating because it is our way of acquiring nourishment. The Reformers had spoken of it as the *manducatio spiritualis*. Learning how to do this is spiritual wisdom at its most profound. The eating of Christ's body and the drinking of Christ's blood is to experience the healing presence of Christ. This presence is what makes us spiritually alive. It is a quickening, vivifying presence.

> As the soul quickens the body, so He quickens the soul, not with an earthly or temporal life, but with the

---

[88] Bruce, *The Mystery of the Lord's Supper*, p. 78.

[89] Bruce, *The Mystery of the Lord's Supper*, p. 89.

[90] Bruce, *The Mystery of the Lord's Supper*, p. 89.

[91] Bruce, *The Mystery of the Lord's Supper*, p. 90.

life which He lives in heaven. He makes you live the same life which the angels live in heaven. He makes you move, not with worldly motion, but with heavenly, spiritual and celestial motions. Again, He inspires in you not outward senses, but heavenly senses. He works within you a spiritual feeling, that in your own heart and conscience you may find the effect of His Word. Thus by the conjunction of Christ with my soul, I get a thousand times a greater benefit than the body does by the soul, for the body by the presence of the soul gets only an earthly and temporal life, subject to continual misery, but by the presence of Christ in my soul, I see a blessed life, I feel a blessed life, and that life daily increases in me more and more.[92]

C. The Work of the Holy Spirit

The most obvious place where we find the influence of the earlier Reformed eucharistic faith in the teaching of Robert Bruce is in his strong pneumatic emphasis. It is the doctrine of the Holy Spirit which is the key to the Reformed tradition of worship. All the way through these sermons there are important statements on the ministry of the Holy Spirit in regard to the sacraments.[93]

At the end of the second sermon in a passage about how in the Lord's Supper we are joined to Christ, Bruce says, "So the Spirit of God conjoins the Body of Christ with my soul."[94] This union with Christ is impossible apart from the work of the Spirit. Alluding to John 3:5 Bruce reminds us that what is born of the flesh is flesh, and must remain flesh, unless the Holy Spirit himself makes it spiritual. It is, therefore, that we must be born again of the Spirit.[95] This is what we find so clearly in the Gospel of John:

> This secret conjunction, then, is brought about by faith and by the Holy Spirit. By faith we lay hold upon the

---

[92] Bruce, *The Mystery of the Lord's Supper*, pp. 90–91.
[93] See, for example, Bruce, *The Mystery of the Lord's Supper*, pp. 173f.
[94] Bruce, *The Mystery of the Lord's Supper*, p. 96.
[95] Bruce, *The Mystery of the Lord's Supper*, p. 95.

> Body and Blood of Christ, and though we are as far distant as heaven and earth are, the Spirit serves as a ladder to conjoin us with Christ, like the ladder of Jacob, which reached from the ground to the heavens. So the Spirit of God conjoins the Body of Christ with my soul.[96]

In the third sermon there is another passage on the ministry of the Holy Spirit in bringing about the union:

> Therefore yearn no more for a carnal delivery, and do not think further of any carnal reception of Christ. You must not think that God gives the Flesh of Christ to the mouth of your body, or that by the mouth of your body you receive the Flesh of Christ. You must understand this principle of the Scriptures of God: our souls cannot be joined or united with the Flesh of Christ, nor can the Flesh of Christ be joined to your souls, except by a spiritual bond—not by a carnal bond or alliance of blood, nor by the contact of His Flesh with our flesh. He is conjoined with us by a spiritual bond, that is, by the power and virtue of the Holy Spirit, and therefore the Apostle says in I Corinthians 12:13, that by means of His Holy Spirit all we who are faithful men and women are baptised into the one Body of Christ, that is we are conjoined and bound together with one Christ by means of one Spirit, not by a carnal bond or by any gross conjunction, but only the bond of the Holy Spirit.[97]

It has often been claimed that the concern of Reformed eucharistic theology to emphasize Christ's "spiritual presence" at the Lord's Supper ends up giving a "spiritualist" interpretation of the sacrament. Nothing could be further from the truth. The whole point of the Reformed teaching is that Christ is present through the working of his Holy Spirit. It is the Holy Spirit working in our hearts for our redemption and for our sanctification that unites us to Christ. Through the work of the Holy Spirit the presence of Christ is a transforming presence. It is through this transforming

---

[96] Bruce, *The Mystery of the Lord's Supper*, pp. 95–96.

[97] Bruce, *The Mystery of the Lord's Supper*, p. 102.

7: John Knox and the Scottish Tradition

presence of the Holy Spirit that Christ's presence is manifested.

In the fifth sermon we find another significant passage on the work of the Holy Spirit. Bruce tells us:

> Everything depends, then, upon the operation of the Holy Spirit; the whole regeneration of mankind, the renewing of the heart and of the conscience, depend on the power of the Holy Spirit; and therefore it behoves us carefully to employ our labours in calling upon God for His Holy Spirit. It is by this means and no other that the Holy Spirit begets faith in us, and nourishes and augments what He has already begotten.[98]

It was only natural that the invocation of the Holy Spirit would eventually become an important part of the prayers offered at the communion service. The *epiclesis*, or invocation of the Holy Spirit, has a long history, a subject we have treated elsewhere at length.

At one point Bruce addresses himself specifically to the question of the Communion Invocation. The point is made that in the communion service after the Words of Institution have been recited, ". . . we use an invocation, and in this invocation we use a thanksgiving. Thus the elements are not made holy by the will of God only, but by the use of prayer and thanksgiving. These three are the only means and ways by which these things are sanctified."[99] Bruce sketches in his exegesis, which we have suggested was also behind the communion prayers of John Knox. Essentially he shows that the words "bless" and "give thanks" are used interchangeably by the evangelists and even by the Apostle Paul in their respective versions of the institution of the Supper. By invoking God's name over the bread and wine and giving thanks for his manifold blessings, we sanctify the elements to our use as we have it in 1 Tim. 4:4–5. We bless the cup and the loaf in the sense that we give thanks to God for his blessings.[100]

---

[98] Bruce, *The Mystery of the Lord's Supper*, p. 174.

[99] Bruce, *The Mystery of the Lord's Supper*, p. 116.

[100] Bruce, *The Mystery of the Lord's Supper*, p. 117.

When the New Testament speaks of blessing the bread or blessing the cup there is, to be sure, a sense in which the elements are consecrated for a sacred purpose, but it does not mean that Jesus in his prayer transubstantiated the bread and the wine. If anything is transformed, converted, or changed, it is the congregation.

D. Real Presence

In the end it is quite clear that Bruce has a well-defined doctrine of the real presence. As we have already indicated, he clearly teaches that Christ is spiritually present in the sense that Christ is present through his Holy Spirit. Christ is present redemptively. Through the sanctifying presence of the Holy Spirit, Christ is manifest in the covenant community.

There is another sense in which Christ is present. Bruce asks what it means to say that something is present, and he answers: "Things are said to be present as they are perceived by any outward or inward sense, and as they are perceived by any of the senses."[101] Bruce goes on to elaborate this. For example, if it is perceived by the outward sight of our eyes, by outward hearing, by outward feeling of the hands, it is outwardly present. On the other hand, if anything is perceived by the inward eye or the inward feeling of the soul then we can say that something is spiritually present.[102] Bruce now takes another step forward:

> It is not distance of place that makes a thing absent, or nearness of place that makes a thing present, but it is only the perception of anything by any of your senses that makes a thing present, and it is the absence of perception that makes a thing absent. Even if the thing itself were never so far distant, if you perceive it by your outward sense, it is present to you.[103]

---

[101] Bruce, *The Mystery of the Lord's Supper*, p. 134.

[102] Bruce, *The Mystery of the Lord's Supper*, p. 134.

[103] Bruce, *The Mystery of the Lord's Supper*, p. 134.

7: John Knox and the Scottish Tradition

With this Bruce gives us an example. We here are about as far distant from the sun as we can imagine, almost as far distant in place as heaven and earth. Yet this distance does not prevent me from being conscious of the presence of the sun. Why is this? It is because ". . . I perceive the sun by my eye and my other senses. I feel it and perceive it by its heat, by its light, and by its brightness."[104] This figure or illustration has been used again and again. I don't know who used it first, but it makes the point that, if we have senses to perceive it, be it ever so far away to us, it is present. "The distance of place, then, does not make a thing absent from you if you have senses to perceive it."[105] So, then, how is the body of Christ present? He is present to the inward senses even if he is not present to the outward senses. Christ is present to those who are blessed with the gift of faith. Through the working of the Holy Spirit, our faith perceives the presence of Christ at his table.

There is one other thing to be noticed here. If we consider the purpose for which Christ instituted the sacrament, it should be clear to us that Christ was not concerned to ennoble the physical element of bread and wine but rather to transform people's hearts:

> . . . that the institution of Christ is not concerned with the elements in altering their nature, indeed it is appointed to alter us, to change us, and to make us more and more spiritual, and to sanctify the elements to our use. But the special end is this: to make us holy, and more and more to grow [us] up in a sure faith in Christ . . .[106]

That, of course, is why the doctrine of the Holy Spirit is so important to the eucharistic teaching of the Reformed churches. The Supper is given to us that we might be nourished to holiness.

---

[104] Bruce, *The Mystery of the Lord's Supper*, p. 134.

[105] Bruce, *The Mystery of the Lord's Supper*, p. 134.

[106] Bruce, *The Mystery of the Lord's Supper*, p. 137.

It is through our participation in the fellowship of Christ that this comes about. The presence of Christ is in the end redemptive, gloriously so.

E. THE CALL FOR REPENTANCE AND RESTORATION IN THE COVENANT COMMUNITY

Increasingly Reformed piety began to emphasize the importance of preparation to receive the sacrament of the Lord's Supper. By the end of the sixteenth century, the Scottish preparatory sermon had almost become a distinct homiletical genre. This speaks to the genius of the eucharistic piety of the Scottish Church. Five of these preparatory sermons have come down to us from Robert Bruce. The first takes up the theme of sacraments in general while the next two have to do with the Lord's Supper in particular. These, of course, are the traditional *loci* of Scholastic theology. These are doctrinal sermons, not expository sermons. They have as their goal teaching the traditional doctrine of the church regarding the sacraments and, in particular, eucharistic doctrine. In so doing the preacher was expected to prepare the congregation to receive the sacrament the following Lord's Day. These sermons were no doubt preached on a weekday the week before the observance of the sacrament. Sermons four and five are particularly intended as preparation for the Lord's Supper. They could have been preached on a Sunday evening.

What we see developing here is noteworthy. If Calvin prepared his congregation for Easter communion by preaching on the passion narrative in the Gospels, Bruce prepared his congregation first by lecturing on eucharistic doctrine and by instructing his congregation on the devotional exercises appropriate for approaching the celebration of the sacrament.

Sermon four gives particular attention to the discipline of the examination of the conscience, a discipline which became highly developed in both Reformation and Counter-Reformation circles.

7: JOHN KNOX AND THE SCOTTISH TRADITION

First Bruce tells us what is meant by the conscience. The conscience is a certain feeling in our hearts resembling the righteous judgment of God, following upon a deed done by us and flowing from a knowledge in the mind, a feeling accompanied by a motion in the heart, of fear or joy or trembling or rejoicing.[107] For Bruce it is important to remember that a conscience must be informed before it can function properly. "Therefore knowledge must ever go before feeling."[108] There is a surprising amount of introspection here. Clearly Bruce is very interested in religious experience. No matter how corrupted by sin a man might be, he always has a spark of conscience which will not let him rest until he finds his peace with God.[109]

At considerable length Bruce goes into the reasons why we must examine our consciences.[110] First we should try our conscience because this is where our Lord takes up his residence in us. Our consciences then must be swept clean and kept in order. Besides that, we should maintain a good conscience because God is Lord of the conscience. However, one of the chief reasons we should keep our consciences clear is that our health and welfare depends on it.[111] Much of Bruce's argumentation here sounds like Scholastic moral theology, and it has real value, to be sure, but it has a distinctly Scholastic air. Bruce makes the point that the first step to maintaining a good conscience is to keep a steadfast persuasion of the mercy of God in Christ Jesus, "When you lie down, and when you rise up, examine your relation with God, and see whether you may look for mercy at His hand or not."[112]

The final sermon in the series focuses on encouraging the repentant to take heart and receive the sacrament to their spiritual nourishment. It is a call to repentance and an assurance of God's

---

[107] Bruce, *The Mystery of the Lord's Supper*, pp. 140f.
[108] Bruce, *The Mystery of the Lord's Supper*, p. 142.
[109] Bruce, *The Mystery of the Lord's Supper*, p. 146.
[110] Bruce, *The Mystery of the Lord's Supper*, p. 147.
[111] Bruce, *The Mystery of the Lord's Supper*, p. 148.
[112] Bruce, *The Mystery of the Lord's Supper*, p. 149.

grace. Not even Schleiermacher could have been more interested in religious experience. Bruce addresses himself to Christians in need of repentance and restoration to the fellowship of the covenant community. This is evangelistic preaching not addressed to those who have never heard but to those who have heard again and again. It is addressed to those who have made a decision for Christ, often repeatedly, but they need to be confirmed and nourished in their faith. Here we see a true unfolding of a specifically Protestant sacramental piety. It is an elaboration of the Prayers of Confession and Assurance of Pardon that we found in the earliest psalters of Strasbourg, Zurich, and Geneva.

SAMUEL RUTHERFORD

Samuel Rutherford (1600–1661) is a Christian thinker of broad interest.[113] One of the architects of Presbyterian polity, he was a father of the Westminster Assembly. He was a Scot who resisted the Anglicanization of the Church of Scotland, insisting on pure Reformed theology and Presbyterian order. Imprisoned for his resistance to the program of Charles I and his Archbishop of Canterbury, William Laud, he produced a series of letters from prison which today are regarded as being among the classics of mystical literature.

Samuel Rutherford was born at Nizlet near Roxburgh, not far from Edinburgh, in the year 1600. He was sent off to the University of Edinburgh at a rather young age and graduated with a Master of Arts degree in 1621. By 1623 he was appointed professor of humanities, teaching Latin in the tradition of the Renaissance. Under the guidance of Andrew Ramsay he began reading theology and in 1627 he became pastor at Anwoth in Galloway in the far southwest of Scotland. It was a period of great tension in the

---

[113] For biographical material on Rutherford, see: John Coffey, *Politics, Religion and the British Revolutions: The Mind of Samuel Rutherford* (Cambridge: Cambridge University Press, 1997); Marcus L. Loane, *Makers of Puritan History* (Edinburgh: Banner of Truth, 2009), 45–85; and S. Isbell, "Rutherford, Samuel," in Cameron, *Dictionary of Scottish Church History and Theology*, pp. 735–36.

7: John Knox and the Scottish Tradition

religious life of Scotland. Charles I was trying to force episcopalianism on the Scottish Church and many in Scotland were resisting it firmly. Rutherford's resistance was sufficiently blatant that in 1630 he was cited to appear before the Court of High Commission in Edinburgh for nonconformity. In 1636 his attack on Arminianism, *Exercitationes Apoligeticae Pro Divina Gratia* was published in Amsterdam.[114] This angered Archbishop Laud, who had made the establishment of Arminianism a major plank in his program for state control of religion. Rutherford was removed from his pulpit and banished to Aberdeen. While in Aberdeen, however, he was far from silent. In Aberdeen a widely publicized debate was held between Dr. Robert Baron and Rutherford. The main point of issue was Arminianism. Rutherford's triumph was clear cut.

The tide was soon to turn. Rutherford's imprisonment in Aberdeen lasted less than two years. In 1638, the National Covenant was signed, and the Covenanters re-established Reformed theology and presbyterian polity in the Church of Scotland. Rutherford was restored to his former church at Anwoth and as minister of that church attended the General Assembly held in Glasgow. The General Assembly appointed him professor of divinity at St. Mary's College in St. Andrews. There he taught for a number of years, preaching as well in the town pulpit side by side with Robert Blair, surely one of the outstanding preachers of that generation.

In 1643 Rutherford was sent as one of the Scottish commissioners to the meeting of the Westminster Assembly held in London. With the conclusion of the Assembly, Rutherford returned to St. Andrew's where he became rector of St. Mary's College. For the next dozen years he taught in that prestigious institution and did much to solidify the traditions of Scottish Presbyterianism.

The peace of the Scottish Church did not last for long, however. In 1660 Charles II was able to reclaim his throne and once

---

[114] An English version of this work was published as: Samuel Rutherford, *A Free Disputation Against Pretended Liberty of Conscience* (London: Printed by R. I. for Andrew Crook, 1649).

more the religious traditions of Scotland were threatened by the English. In 1661 Rutherford was charged with treason, but happily he died before he could be brought to trial. The Restoration monarchists had good reason to hunt Rutherford down. He had been one of the most effective opponents of monarchism. His *Lex Rex* had wounded the monarchists's cause substantially.

Lex Rex is undeniably Rutherford's most famous work.[115] Being one of the seminal works on constitutional law, it is widely read even today by political theorists. Rutherford also contributed a weighty volume defending the Reformed doctrines of grace, election, and the sovereignty of God.[116] On the other hand his highly mystical letters occupy themselves with the opposite end of Christian experience. They are written in the tradition of Bernard of Clairvaux's sermons on the Song of Solomon, and the metaphysical poets.[117] This is not at all surprising in the middle of the seventeenth century. In England the metaphysical poets were very popular. They had a tremendous influence on the pulpit, as Horton Davies has shown.[118]

The *Communion Sermons* to which we now want to turn our attention are quite different from Rutherford's other works.[119] They were for the most part taken down by an interested listener. The manuscript survived several centuries of neglect before someone saw to its publication. These sermons are in no sense a series,

---

[115] Samuel Rutherford, *Lex Rex, or, The Law and the Prince*, reprint (Harrisonburg, VA: Sprinkle Publications, 1982).

[116] For an eighteenth-century edition, see: Samuel Rutherford, *Christ Dying and Drawing Sinners to Himselfe* (Edinburgh: Printed by T. Lumisden and J. Robertson for James Weir, 1727).

[117] Several editions of Rutherford's letters exist. Perhaps the classic edition is that by Andrew A. Bonar: Samuel Rutherford, *Letters of the Rev. Samuel Rutherford, With a Sketch of His Life*, ed. Rev. Andrew A. Bonar (New York: Robert Carter & Brothers, 1851).

[118] Horton Davies, *Like Angels from a Cloud: The English Metaphysical Preachers, 1588–1645* (San Marino: Huntington Library, 1986).

[119] This study is based on Samuel Rutherford, *Fourteen Communion Sermons*, preface and notes by Andrew A. Bonar (Edinburgh: J. A. Dixon, 1986), hereinafter, Rutherford, *Communion Sermons*.

but rather random sermons preached at various communion seasons starting in 1630 and continuing as late as 1645. There is one "communion address" delivered at the Scots Church in London during the Westminster Assembly. According to Andrew Bonar, who republished the sermons in 1876, the first printed edition appeared in Glasgow. It contained only nine sermons. The publisher claimed these sermons had been taken from an old manuscript.[120] Andrew Bonar, well known for his interest in the Protestant understanding of piety, was able to add several more communion sermons in his second enlarged edition of 1877.[121]

One of the most attractive features of these sermons is a certain racy Scot's diction. Whoever took these sermons down was a good enough stenographer that it comes through quite clearly. For the modern reader there will be words and phrases not readily understandable. But, then, there are brilliant expressions, marvelous illustrations, and fresh insights into Scripture that keep one reading.

These sermons are best understood when seen in the context of a communion season, as this tradition of eucharistic piety was beginning to unfold. The preparatory sermon had one liturgical function, the action sermon another, and the thanksgiving sermon still another.

A. Communion with the Christ to Come

The first sermon in the collection is a thanksgiving sermon. It comes first in all probability because it was the first sermon recorded. The sermon, however, is not dated, although we are told that it was preached at Kirkcudbright in Galloway, a parish not far from Rutherford's own parish. To fully understand the sermon we would have to have heard the other sermons preached by the other preachers who had been invited to preach this particular

---

[120] For greater detail, see the preface to Bonar's edition reprinted in 1986.
[121] Samuel Rutherford, *Fourteen Communion Sermons*, 2nd ed. (Glasgow: Charles Glass, 1877).

communion season. There would have been at least two preparatory sermons, probably by another neighboring minister. Then there would have been the action sermon, preached in all probability by the minister of the parish. Rutherford's sermon would have come as the conclusion to the season.

The remarkable thing about the sermon is its vivid portrayal of the final triumph of Christ. The sermon takes as its text Revelation 19:11–14, "And I saw heaven opened, and behold a white horse; and he that sat upon him was called Faithful and True, and in righteousness he doth judge and make war . . ."[122] Our preacher begins by telling his congregation that except when God opens up for us the heavenly dimension, Christ is seen as nothing more than a poor itinerant preacher traveling along on foot, persecuted and banished, fallen on hard times.[123] This is too often the problem with the celebration of the Lord's Supper, be it in Gothic chapels or Evangelical revival tents. We show forth the Lord's death and leave out his glory.

We have no idea, of course, what the other preachers had said in their preparatory sermons or what the pastor might have said in his action sermon, but we can be well assured that the theme of the Suffering Servant and the atoning sacrifice of Christ was at the center of the celebration. The mystery, however, is that behind all this is the eschatological dimension. This dimension had become increasingly important since the beginning of the Reformation.[124] It taught the faithful to understand their participation in the Lord's Supper as a foretaste of the wedding feast of the Lamb. It brought to the celebration many sermons on texts from Revelation, the Song of Solomon, and the parallels of the wedding feast, as we shall see

---

[122] Rutherford, *Communion Sermons*, p. 7.

[123] Rutherford, *Communion Sermons*, p. 8.

[124] Eucharistic sermons based on the Song of Solomon typology can be found in such diverse corners of the Protestant world as Utrecht in the Netherlands and Cambridge in New England. See my study of the eucharistic sermons of Jodocus van Lodenstein in Hughes Oliphant Old, *The Reading and Preaching of the Scriptures in the Worship of the Christian Church*, vol. 4, *The Age of the Reformation* (Grand Rapids, MI: Eerdmans, 2002), pp. 461–467.

in this selection of Rutherford's communion sermons.

Our preacher devotes quite a bit of time to drawing out the imagery of Christ's triumphant rejoicing in heaven with his elect attending him all robed in gold and white.[125] He uses in particular Song of Solomon 3:10; Colossians 1:15–17, and Revelation 3:14. The reality behind the Lord's Supper is the heavenly feast acclaiming the Lamb who has conquered. As John puts it in Revelation, "After this I beheld, and, lo, a great multitude, which no man could number, of all nations, and kindreds, and people, and tongues, stood before the throne, and before the Lamb, clothed with white robes, and palms in their hands; And cried with a loud voice, saying, Salvation to our God which sitteth upon the throne, and unto the Lamb" (Rev. 7:9–10).[126]

The point of all this in a thanksgiving sermon is that, having received the sacred bread and wine, the promise of participation in that glorious day has been sealed to us. Believe the promises that have been given to you![127] That is the gospel Rutherford preaches.

B. Communion with the Smitten Christ

Next we want to look at the following two sermons in our collection, Sermon II and Sermon III. The two sermons are preached on the same text but to two different congregations. They say much the same thing, and they both appear to be preparatory sermons. Sermon II was preached at Rutherford's own church at Anwoth in Galloway, and Sermon III at Kirkmabreck, a nearby congregation.

The text for these sermons is Zechariah 13:7–9:

> Awake, O sword, against my shepherd, and against the man that is my fellow, saith the Lord of hosts: smite the shepherd, and the sheep shall be scattered; and I

---

[125] Rutherford, *Communion Sermons*, pp. 8–9.

[126] Rutherford, *Communion Sermons*, p. 9.

[127] Rutherford, *Communion Sermons*, p. 12.

will turn mine hand upon the little ones . . .[128]

What is interesting here is that if the first sermon speaks of communion with the Christ to come, the triumphant Christ, these two sermons speak of the presence of the smitten Christ.

The text Rutherford has chosen is admittedly difficult. One can sense that the preacher is himself struggling with it. Apparently, however, the text has spoken to him in the midst of the struggle the Scottish Church was going through at the time. Charles I, even if he was of Scottish line and lineage, was determined to rule the Church of Scotland even as he ruled the Church of England. The Scots, however, were stoutly resisting their king, even if he was a Stuart. In the early 1630s church leaders who refused to submit to government control were experiencing real persecution. The leaders of the state smote the shepherds of the church and indeed the sheep were scattered.

There is nothing new about this, of course. "The world is aye picking quarrels with Christ and His followers. 'Let us break their bands asunder, and cast away their cords from us (Psalm ii: 3).'"[129] The refusal of the world to accept divine authority is the basic problem. Christ has divine authority—full divine authority. He is the image of the invisible God, the first born of all creation. He is the exact character of his person (Col. 1:15). "Hence learn, that Christ in nature is even the brightness of God's glory."[130] Christ is the express image of his person (Heb. 1:3). Rutherford leans heavily on his congregation to make the point that the incarnate Christ is both true man and true God, having all the authority of God himself. "As all men honour the Father, so should they honour the Son."[131] Rutherford puts great emphasis on the full divinity of Christ, making the point that it is in the end God himself

---

[128] Rutherford, *Communion Sermons*, pp. 27 and 46.

[129] Rutherford, *Communion Sermons*, p. 29.

[130] Rutherford, *Communion Sermons*, p. 34.

[131] Rutherford, *Communion Sermons*, p. 34.

7: JOHN KNOX AND THE SCOTTISH TRADITION

with whom we have to deal in this sacred celebration. The Word became flesh that we might become companions of God.[132] This is what communion is all about. We come to the Lord's Table to enter into fellowship with God himself. It is fellowship with Christ that you are being offered. "Take Him, take Him, then, with God's blessing. God gave you Him with good will, take ye Him with heart and good will then."[133] So this seventeenth-century Scottish minister gives the invitation to trust Christ as Lord and Savior.

But to preach on this text at the celebration of communion is to make it clear that this is the Lord and Savior who has been smitten by an unbelieving world. The smitten shepherd preached by Zechariah is, as Rutherford understands the text, nothing less than the Suffering Servant of Isaiah 53 and with this, he elaborates the doctrine of the vicarious atonement at length.

The text itself makes the point that when the Shepherd is stricken, the sheep are scattered. The unbelieving world smites the sheep no less than the shepherd:

> Faith, as it were, goes through fire and water to heaven. . . . It is because the elect are truly united to Christ that they are persecuted by the world. It is not because God has given us up that we are experiencing persecution, but rather because we are truly united to Christ. Some of you are troubled not only by persecution itself but by the way persecution has betrayed you into doubt. You find yourself doubting the resurrection, doubting heaven itself. Have no fear: This is only part of the trials and tribulations which come when the Shepherd is stricken. Christ suffered for our salvation and he came through triumphantly. The same shall be true for us.[134]

Then Rutherford gives us a real gem, a gem that can only be appreciated by those of us who have spent a winter in Scotland,

---

[132] Rutherford, *Communion Sermons*, p. 35.

[133] Rutherford, *Communion Sermons*, p. 35.

[134] Rutherford, *Communion Sermons*, p. 37.

"True faith is an herb that grows best in winter weather."[135]

As Rutherford saw it, it is the refiner's fire that the elect must go through.[136] Lose not your faith, he exhorts his congregation. Sermon III is even more pastoral at this point. Our preacher takes up the problem of assurance. Many true Christians do not yet have assurance, but they will be saved if they have faith.[137] Though you have sinned, and even though you have sinned much, do not give up your faith. Here, again, our preacher leans on his congregation to come to the Lord's Table and renew the covenant vows. "Call on God by prayer, and ye shall obtain mercy. Thus the fire at last brings out mercy: and prayer in the fire is one of those sweet smells that God's spices cast forth. In the fire, the smoke of prayer, sighing and groaning that comes forth, goes up to heaven."[138] Sermon III is much more explicit about coming to the Table to renew the covenant. Quoting Jeremiah 1:4–5, "Come, and let us join ourselves to the Lord in a perpetual covenant, that shall not be forgotten."[139]

Coming to the close of his sermon Rutherford urges his congregation to approach the Table. This, to be sure, is a major liturgical function of the preparatory sermon. "Christ seeks you in the sacrament, seek ye Him again, and though the devil should say the contrary, there shall be a meeting."[140] As we shall see again and again, the imagery of the Song of Solomon surfaces as we return to the subject of the love of God. The love of God awaits all those who would approach the Holy Table. "Let His love get a meeting; . . . seek ye Him through all troubles."[141] The invitation to the wedding feast of the Lamb has been made. The preacher urges his congregation to accept that priceless invitation.

---

[135] Rutherford, *Communion Sermons*, p. 37.

[136] Rutherford, *Communion Sermons*, pp. 42 and 43.

[137] Rutherford, *Communion Sermons*, p. 54.

[138] Rutherford, *Communion Sermons*, p. 44.

[139] Rutherford, *Communion Sermons*, p. 58.

[140] Rutherford, *Communion Sermons*, p. 45.

[141] Rutherford, *Communion Sermons*, p. 45.

C. The Lord's Supper and the Parable of the Great Feast

Again we are dealing with a preparatory sermon preached in a nearby parish, that of Kirkmabreck, in the year 1634.[142] Like most of Rutherford's sermons, it is the old style of expository sermon, taking four, five, or six verses and commenting on them as he goes along. There is no more introduction other than a certain amount of dividing up the text. In this he is much more like Calvin than some of the seventeenth century Reformed preachers such as Manton or Goodwin, who rarely preached on much more than one verse at a time.

The choice of the parable of the great feast for a preparatory service hardly needs an explanation for a Reformed theologian. If the parable is preached in the context of a preparatory service several things are immediately implied. As we find the parable in the Gospel of Luke, and indeed it is on the Lukan version that the preacher has chosen to preach, it is not the wedding feast of the king's son, but simply a feast. Preached at a preparatory service, however, it cannot help but have a very special meaning. The gracious invitation to come to the feast tells us of the invitation to come to the Lord's Supper and there to accept Christ as Savior. As the parable of Jesus tells it, when the time for the feast approached, none of the invited guests had appeared, so the host sent out his servants to invite the poor, the maimed, and the blind. "Remember that it is even now Supper-time, while the word is preached, and the Sacrament of the Lord's body and blood offered; and blessed are they who come to the Supper."[143] Nothing could be more evangelical, nothing simpler, nothing more profound.

There is, however, a dimension to the Lord's Supper which Rutherford brings into this sermon which we find especially significant, and that is the Wisdom dimension. Rutherford very quickly

---

[142] Rutherford, *Communion Sermons*, pp. 60–88.

[143] Rutherford, *Communion Sermons*, p. 65.

brings in that wonderful passage from Proverbs 9 which tells of Wisdom giving a great feast and sending out her maids to invite the simple to come to her feast and become wise:

> Wisdom has built her house,
> > she has set up her seven pillars.
> She has slaughtered her beasts, she has mixed her wine,
> > she has also set her table.
> She has sent out her maids to call
> > from the highest places in the town,
> "Whoever is simple, let him turn in here!"
> > To him who is without sense she says,
> "Come, eat of my bread
> > and drink of the wine I have mixed.
> Leave simpleness, and live,
> > and walk in the way of insight."
> (Proverbs 9:1–6)

The parallels between this passage from Proverbs and the parable of Jesus are hard to dismiss. This is even more the case when one looks at the version found in Matthew, as Rutherford himself points out.[144] To find a reference to the sacrament of the Eucharist may seem farfetched to today's New Testament scholar, but for a theologian of the seventeenth century it was eminently obvious.

The Wisdom typology is of the greatest possible importance for a Reformed eucharistic theology. It is in terms of the Wisdom typology that we understand how it is that we eat the body of Christ and drink his blood. At this point in his sermon Rutherford digresses into a passionate rhapsody on the feast Wisdom has prepared:

> [Christ] has dressed the whole Supper Himself, covered the table, and there is no more for us to do, but sit down and eat. If we look to this dressed Supper, Christ dressed it all Himself, in the furnace of God's wrath, and the bread that we here eat is His flesh, which He gave for the life of the world. John vi. 51, The wine

---

[144] Rutherford, *Communion Sermons*, p. 66.

7: John Knox and the Scottish Tradition

which is mingled and drawn is His blood.[145]

We have noticed elsewhere that Reformed theologians are quite willing to follow the sixth chapter of the Gospel of John and speak of eating Christ's flesh and drinking his blood because the passage from the Gospel of John is speaking in terms of the Wisdom theology. This rhapsody goes on for several pages where Rutherford uses all his poetic imagination. We quote but another few lines because they make especially clear the central focus of the sacrament, namely, communion, or, in more precise terms, covenant fellowship:

> Jesus craves no more for all His pains, but only that His friends come to the banquet and eat and be merry; and if ye will come, Christ will pay all the reckoning. When the Israelites were fed with manna, they behoved to go out of the camp, and gather it themselves; but we furnish nothing of this Supper. God be thanked, Christ bears all the expense. Alas! alas! that the unhappy world will not eat heartily, since Christ pays for all.[146]

All the way back to the Jewish synagogue and the Wisdom teachers of Israel, God's people have understood the holy Wisdom of God to be a feast of unspeakable delight and transcendent joy. All of this in its fullness Samuel Rutherford claimed for his parishioners off in a remote corner of Scotland. What a treasure was found hidden in the fields of those simple crofters.

D. The Lord's Supper and the Presence of the Risen Christ

Passing over a few sermons, something we do with regret, we come to Sermon VIII, which has to do with Mary Magdalene's encounter with the risen Christ.[147] The sermon was preached in the evening following a communion service at Anwoth in the year

---

[145] Rutherford, *Communion Sermons*, p. 67.

[146] Rutherford, *Communion Sermons*, p. 67.

[147] Rutherford, *Communion Sermons*, pp. 165–199.

1634. Apparently, it was a thanksgiving sermon.

Sticking close to his text, Rutherford recounts the story, making comments as he goes. Again we point out that Rutherford is an expository preacher of the old style. Mary comes to the empty tomb of Jesus and finds the body of Jesus is not there. Mary Magdalene had a great love for Jesus because he had changed her life. Finding his body had been removed, she feared it had been desecrated and she broke into tears. The attending angels ask her, "Why weepest thou?" Our commentator meditates on the question of the angels. Should not Mary and the other disciples as well have rejoiced that Jesus had gone to prepare a place for them?[148]

> Some think He feeds not His people in His absence: nay, but let me say it, God indeed not only feeds his people with a sense of presence but also with absence. . . . "Why weepest thou?" Christ is risen. He is not here. That is no cause for weeping. It is rather a cause for rejoicing. Christ is risen! The promises made to the fathers have been fulfilled. As the Apostle Paul put it, "He was delivered for our offenses, and was raised again for our justification (Rom. iv. 25).[149]

Mary was anxiously seeking the corporeal presence of a dead body not yet having realized that the presence of a living Savior was even more important. Christ was not there in a grave outside Jerusalem. Rather, he was present as a risen Savior although Mary had not recognized him.

Rutherford is concerned with a much more profound sense of presence.[150] Finally Jesus spoke to Mary, but even then she did not at first recognize him. So it is with faith; the first sparks need to be blown upon before we have a real fire. Then Jesus calls her by name and she recognized the Savior who on this earth had changed her life. She recognized the old Jesus, the historical Jesus

---

[148] Rutherford, *Communion Sermons*, p. 176.

[149] Rutherford, *Communion Sermons*, p. 177.

[150] Rutherford, *Communion Sermons*, p. 182.

as we might put it today. She reached out to hold him and Jesus told her not to cling to him. As Rutherford understands this, it was a challenge to Mary to let go of the earthly Jesus and to follow after a heavenly Jesus who was even then going on before her. Jesus sent Mary to the disciples to tell them that even then he was ascending to the Father. It was with the risen, ascended Jesus that they would henceforth have communion.

This is a long sermon, and it is filled with marvelous insights. It is an expository sermon and Rutherford's ideas open up as he goes through the text phrase by phrase. Commenting on the question Jesus puts to Mary, "Whom do you seek?" Rutherford puts the same question to his congregation. What is it we would seek at this sacred Supper? Is it that we seek comfort, some sort of relief, some sort of supporter, or is it Christ whom we seek? Is it not Christ for himself that we seek? Again, using the imagery of the Song of Solomon he would have us recognize, "So must ye seek Christ for Himself, and not Christ for comfort. For, I say, Joy and Comfort is but the bridegroom's jewels; but the bridegroom himself is better."[151] Be he the crucified Christ or be he the risen Christ, it is Christ Jesus with whom we would have fellowship in this sacrament.

Rutherford makes quite a bit here of the words of Jesus concerning his ascension. Jesus would have Mary Magdalene and the disciples recognize that the resurrection means much more than that Jesus had returned to them. It is not as though Jesus in his crucifixion and death left his friends and followers and then three days later came back. It is rather that in his death and resurrection he was ascending to the Father. He is ascending that he might prepare a place for them as he had promised (John 14:1–3). "And therefore, He forbids them to dream of a Christ ever bodily present with them on the earth. And therefore they that would have Christ must follow His trodden path, and trace him all the way to

---

[151] Rutherford, *Communion Sermons*, p. 193.

heaven, and they shall find Him there."¹⁵²

What Rutherford has done here is to raise the question of the real presence to a very different level. In the last chapter of the Gospel of Matthew Jesus very pointedly brought up the question of presence, "Lo I am with you always." In Matthew the promise is made in relation to the continual presence of Christ to the sacrament of baptism. As he understands his text, the presence is a transcendent presence. It is a presence of the risen and ascended Christ. If Christ is ascended into heaven we must go after him. The Lord's ascension should lift us up to heaven by giving us a taste of heavenly food. It should make us realize that our treasure is in heaven and when we do that then our hearts will be there also (Matt. 6:21). Rutherford exhorts his congregation, "If ye be risen with Christ, seek the things that are above, where Christ sitteth at the right hand of the Father. For except we sunder with Christ, we must be where He is, and He is now up in heaven. He is now up in glory . . ."¹⁵³

Concluding his sermon, Rutherford appeals to his people who have come from the Lord's Table, who have been given Christ's flesh and blood in the sacrament of his Supper, to lift their thoughts from this vain world and all the transitory concerns here below "and let us set our hearts and affections on things heavenly and divine, trusting in the Lord through the whole of our wilderness journey, and inquiring for Him all the way to the very ports and gates of heaven."¹⁵⁴

E. The Lord's Supper and the Wedding Feast of the Lamb

Typology was a favorite theme of seventeenth and eighteenth-century Reformed eucharistic preaching. The Reformed pulpit produced a great many sermons based on the idea that the sacrament

---

[152] Rutherford, *Communion Sermons*, p. 196.

[153] Rutherford, *Communion Sermons*, p. 197.

[154] Rutherford, *Communion Sermons*, p. 199.

of the Lord's Supper was a foretaste of the wedding feast of the Lamb. This wedding feast typology may be an embarrassment to modern scholars, but to Reformed preachers of the seventeenth and eighteenth centuries, it was a delight.

It was a few years ago that Iain Mclean brought to my attention a communion sermon of the Dutch Pietist, Jodocus van Lodenstein (1620–1677).[155] My first impression was that the sermon was rather obscure, but then I began to put some pieces together. It was about that time that I had occasion to study some sermons of Gilbert Tennent and discovered that he, too, had preached a communion sermon that had used a considerable amount of material from the Song of Solomon. There is another interesting connection. Richard Sibbes (1577–1635), the superb English Puritan preacher, left us a whole series of expository sermons preached on the Song of Solomon, starting where Bernard of Clairvaux left off. To Richard Sibbes must be added America's first preacher-theologian, Thomas Shepard, who produced a whole volume of sermons on the parable of the wise and foolish virgins.

Seventeenth-century writers generally appreciated the Solomonic typology, as anyone reading the metaphysical poets is well aware. As for Samuel Rutherford, he was especially fond of it. In his widely admired letters from prison, Rutherford's mysticism had a strong Solomonic coloring to it. A good portion of the sermons in this collection make frequent use of the wedding feast typology. Even more, several sermons actually choose texts from the Song of Solomon. Sermon IX takes as its text Song of Solomon 5:1–3a:

> I come to my garden, my sister, my bride,
> > I gather my myrrh with my spice,
> > I eat my honeycomb with my honey,
> > I drink my wine with my milk.
> Eat, O friends, and drink:

---

[155] Iain S. Maclean, "The First Pietist: An Introduction and Translation of a Communion Sermon by Jodocus van Lodenstein," in *Calvin Studies VI*, ed. John Leith (Davidson, NC: Calvin Colloquium, 1992), pp. 15–34.

> drink deeply, O lovers!
>
> I slept, but my heart was awake.
> Hark! my beloved is knocking.
> "Open to me, my sister, my love,
>   my dove, my perfect one;
> for my head is wet with dew,
>   my locks with the drops of the night."
>
> I had put off my garment,
>   how could I put it on?

The sermon treats the hesitation we have to commit ourselves to Christ fully. We come to the Lord's Table but have our hesitations and our reservations. Rutherford has a strong covenantal understanding of the sacrament. To participate in the sacred meal is an act of commitment. It is an act of commitment first on the part of Christ, the Bridegroom, but it must also be an act of commitment on the part of God's people.

Sermon X takes Revelation 21:4–7 as its text. The larger context of these verses is the final consummation of the Kingdom of God and the appearance of Christ triumphant over all his foes. This, Rutherford tells us, is the most joyful of all occasions, when the bride is at last united to the Bridegroom. "If ever there was a blythe meeting betwixt two, it must be betwixt the Bridegroom and the bride in the marriage-day."[156] In this preparatory sermon all who have a thirst for the presence of God are encouraged to come to the Table. Our preacher encourages his congregation not to hold back. If they have a hunger for true faith, if they have a thirst for the love of God, then they are welcome at the holy Table.[157] There were, no doubt, many in Rutherford's congregation who at one time or another sensed God's presence, but somehow they had lost that sense. They imagined that they were disqualified from participation in the Supper. Rutherford assured

---

[156] Rutherford, *Communion Sermons*, pp. 224–25. The entire Sermon X comprises pp. 223–247.

[157] Rutherford, *Communion Sermons*, p. 137.

them that they were especially welcome to the Table. That is just what we find in the Song of Solomon 3:8. The beloved is seeking her lover and is discouraged because she cannot find him. "Let me now tell you weak ones who are Christ's companions, and who it is shall drink with Him, and get their hearts and heads full of the water of life—even the tender Christians who are aye seeking."[158] It is those who hunger and thirst who shall be filled.

For Rutherford, presence is an essential element of true communion. One gets the feeling that it is an almost mystical experience. God is, of course, always present, even if we are unaware of it. But sometimes we are very much aware of it and this is a blessing of the greatest sort. Rutherford was especially aware of the presence of Christ in his times of tribulation and imprisonment. There is something very Pauline about this. Paul was especially conscious of being united to Christ in his suffering. Apparently, on the other hand, there were also times when Rutherford could invite his congregation to come to the Lord's Supper that they might have a foretaste of the joyful wedding feast of the Lamb. In the Sacred Supper we are united to Christ both in his suffering and in his glory.

Sermon XI again picks up a text from the Song of Solomon.[159] The sermon is identified as having been preached at a communion in Anwoth in 1630. Apparently a number of sermons on the Song of Solomon were preached by Rutherford at that particular communion season, as is clear at several points in the text. Only a few of these have been preserved.[160] Here we have an exposition of Song of Solomon 2:14–17:

> "O my dove, in the clefts of the rock,
>   in the covert of the cliff,
> let me see your face,
>   let me hear your voice,
> for your voice is sweet,

---

[158] Rutherford, *Communion Sermons*, p. 238.
[159] Rutherford, *Communion Sermons*, pp. 248–77.
[160] Rutherford, *Communion Sermons*, p. 315.

> and your face is comely.
> Catch us the foxes,
> the little foxes,
> that spoil the vineyards,
> for our vineyards are in blossom."
> My beloved is mine and I am his,
> he pastures his flock among the lilies.
> Until the day breathes
> and the shadows flee,
> turn, my beloved, be like a gazelle,
> or a young stag upon rugged mountains.

The sermon begins by opening up the metaphor of the dove. Consequently the sermon has the title, "Christ and the Dove." The dove, following the Christian interpretation, represents the Church. Here Rutherford specifically tells us that he is following the interpretation of Bernard of Clairvaux.[161] The dove is an appropriate figure for the Church because of its innocence and humility.

This is a beautiful passage, but for our concerns we press on to another even more beautiful. Commenting on the line, "My beloved is mine and I am his," Rutherford tells us that just as in a marriage husband and wife are united in a covenant in which they share all things with each other, so God's people as members of the Church share all things together. Rutherford, Christian Humanist that he was, is opening up the Greek word *koinonia*. There is a sharing between Christ and the Church, God's people. There is a communion between Christ and the Christian. This is at the heart of what the sacrament is all about, the covenantal sharing, "My beloved is mine and I am his."[162]

Our preacher unfolds this in the following points. There is a sharing of nature between us and Christ.[163] Christ has taken on our flesh and we have received his Spirit. The doctrine of the incarnation is fundamental to Rutherford's eucharistic doctrine.

---
[161] Rutherford, *Communion Sermons*, p. 351.
[162] Rutherford, *Communion Sermons*, p. 263.
[163] Rutherford, *Communion Sermons*, p. 264.

7: John Knox and the Scottish Tradition

In Christ we share the divine nature. In Christ God has taken on human nature. Second, Christ belongs to us and we belong to Christ because between us there is true community. "We got all His good, and He gets all our ill, that's a good coss [exchange] for us. He took our curses, we took His blessings; He our shame, we His glory; He our sins, we His righteousness: He is the Kirk's, and the Kirk is Christ's."[164] In preparation for the Lord's Supper we should turn over our sins that Christ might crucify them for us. Give him your anger; he will give you his zeal. Give him your folly, and he will give you his wisdom.

Third, there is a community of gifts and graces between Christ and the Christian. The gifts of God are given to us by the hand of Christ. We receive them because we are in Christ. He is a fountain of blessings full and overflowing. Even more, the blessings we receive are a pledge of even greater blessings. Christ is for us the source of all spiritual gifts, that out of his fullness we might all receive grace upon grace.[165] The ultimate spiritual gift is eternal life. In the resurrection of Christ we have the pledge that we, too, shall receive eternal life.

Fourth, there is a community of suffering between us and Christ.[166] We have already noticed that this is a theme very dear to Rutherford. We found it developed especially in his two sermons on Zechariah. We also find it frequently in his letters from prison. He has himself experienced this mysticism of Christ's sufferings. No doubt Rutherford learned this approach from the Apostle Paul. But if we suffer in Christ we also share in Christ's glory. Here is the fifth point. There is a communion of glory.[167] Those who have been crucified with Christ will also be raised with Christ. We are heirs and joint heirs with Christ. As Jesus promised to his disciples,

---

[164] Rutherford, *Communion Sermons*, p. 265.

[165] Rutherford, *Communion Sermons*, p. 266.

[166] Rutherford, *Communion Sermons*, p. 266.

[167] Rutherford, *Communion Sermons*, p. 268.

as the Father had appointed for him a kingdom, so Christ will appoint a kingdom for us, that we might eat and drink at his table in his kingdom sitting on thrones (Luke 22:29). It would be hard to overlook the importance of the wedding feast typology for Rutherford's eucharistic theology.

We skip over Sermon XII, which seems to be notes on a sermon Rutherford preached in London about ten years after the others. It does not particularly address the concerns of our study. Sermon XIII, however, very much speaks to our concerns.[168] The text is taken from Revelation 19:7–14. It was preached at Kirkcudbright in 1634. The title of the sermon, "The Lamb's Marriage," is indeed of special interest. If nothing else, the title once more indicates that it was fairly common in those days to understand the Lord's Supper in terms of the wedding feast of the Lamb. Sermon XIII is a typical preparatory sermon, that is, it is a sermon that exhorts the congregation to prepare for the celebration of the sacrament. Just as the bride of the Lamb prepared herself for this glorious feast, so each Christian should prepare himself to enter the presence of Christ, the Bridegroom.

Sermon XIV, the last sermon in the collection, appears to have been taken down by another hand. The language has been modernized and the basic ideas seem blunted; especially the more theological insights seem a bit hazy. The stenographer seems to have been primarily interested in a moralistic interpretation of these sermons, otherwise quite foreign to Rutherford's thought. The sermon is of interest, however, because it confirms what we have already found, namely, that the wedding feast typology was very important to Rutherford's eucharistic theology. The sermon chooses a text once again from the Song of Solomon, namely, Song of Solomon 2:8–12.[169]

> The voice of my beloved!
> Behold, he comes,

---

[168] Rutherford, *Communion Sermons*, pp. 291–314.

[169] Rutherford, *Communion Sermons*, pp. 315–362.

leaping upon the mountains,
   bounding over the hills.
My beloved is like a gazelle,
   of a young stag.
Behold, there he stands
   behind our wall,
gazing in at the windows,
   looking through the lattice.
My beloved speaks and says to me:
"Arise, my love, my fair one,
   and come away;
for lo, the winter is past,
   the rain is over and gone.
The flowers appear on the earth,
   the time of singing has come,
and the voice of the turtledove
   is heard in our land.

Typical of the seventeenth century, Rutherford was a preacher who was a sort of mystical poet. We have already mentioned the study of Horton Davies, *Like Angels from a Cloud*. Perhaps even more to the point was the great Puritan poet, John Milton (1608–1674). Rutherford, as Milton, had a keen sense of the realities of a transcendent world. Perhaps preachers like Rutherford should be called meta-historical preachers rather than metaphysical poets. They had a keen sense of the reality that was over and beyond the world in which they lived. To such preachers it is only natural to understand the Lord's Supper in terms of the wedding feast of the Lamb.

To share in the Lord's Supper is, to be sure, to share in Christ's incarnation. It is to be united to Him in both his human nature and his divine nature. It is also, most assuredly, to share in Christ's suffering. It is to claim the atonement Jesus achieved on the cross and the victory he won through his resurrection. To participate in the Lord's Supper is to share in the Passover Lamb and to pass out of Egypt and taste of the manna in the wilderness. It is to cite that line from the Passover liturgy, "This is what the Lord did for me when he brought me out of Egypt." It is to take one's place at the Lord's Table in the Upper Room, both on the night in which he was betrayed and on the evening of the first day of the week when Christ appeared to his own. Even more, to participate in the Lord's Supper is to lift up our hearts and minds to the ascended Christ who abides in the glory of the Father, and there to rejoice in the wedding feast of the Lamb.

8
URSINUS, BULLINGER,
AND THE SECOND GENERATION

Toward the end of the sixteenth century, Reformed theology went through a vigorous development.[1] Calvin had brought Reformed theology a long way. He produced a systematic theology offering a full menu of theological thought from the formal Trinitarian and Christological doctrines to the more practical issues of polity and worship. It is not, however, as though Reformed theology was, with the work of Zwingli, Bucer, and Calvin, finally finished. Not at all! Reformed theology had a good way to go yet.

One of the theological giants of this second generation was Zacharias Ursinus.[2] Ursinus was a native of Breslau (modern day Wroclaw, Poland) in Silesia. Apparently, he came from an honorable but humble family, and he had won a reputation as a hardworking and devout student. The family name was Baer which, in the custom of the day, was Latinized as Ursinus. (*Ursus* is the Latin word for "bear.") The City Council of Breslau, desiring to

---

[1] At this point, it would surely be most appropriate to acknowledge the help of my assistant Rev. Glen Clary, who has done much to help me overcome my failing eyesight.

[2] For recent studies on Ursinus, see: Lyle D. Bierma, ed., *An Introduction to the Heidelberg Catechism: Sources, History, and Theology* (Grand Rapids, MI: Baker Academic, 2005); Jon D. Payne and Sebastian Heck, eds., *A Faith Worth Teaching: The Heidelberg Catechism's Enduring Message* (Grand Rapids, MI: Reformation Heritage Books, 2013); Derk Visser ed., *Controversy and Conciliation: The Reformation and the Palatinate 1559–1583* (Allison Park, PA: Pickwick Publications, 1986); Derk Visser, *Zacharias Ursinus: The Reluctant Reformer, His Life and Times* (New York: United Church Press, 1983). See also John Williamson Nevin's "Introduction" in *The Commentary of Dr. Zacharias Ursinus on the Heidelberg Catechism*, fourth American edition (Cincinnati: Elm Street Printing Company, 1888), pp. vii-xxiii.

provide a more cultivated religious instruction for the youth of the city, awarded their most capable young scholar a fellowship to study at the University of Wittenberg with the understanding that he would in time return home and enrich his native town with the latest theological teachings being offered in Germany.

URSINUS AND
THE *HEIDELBERG CATECHISM*

In 1557, when Zacharias Ursinus arrived in Wittenberg to learn the fundamentals of the Protestant Reformation, Protestantism was entering its second generation. Luther had died in 1546. Bucer had died in 1551. Cranmer had died in 1556. Of the first generation of Reformers, Zwingli had been the first to die, and Calvin, who died in 1564, was the last.

Ursinus studied in Wittenberg some seven years off and on. He became the student of Melanchthon as much as the student of Luther.[3] The two men, that is, Ursinus and Melanchthon, became close friends. At one point, the University had to close down because of the plague, and for several months, Melanchthon and Ursinus shared the same lodgings as they waited out the pestilence. Ursinus and his famous teacher finally returned to Wittenberg, and Ursinus apparently finished up his degree. Finally, the City Council of Breslau called him home and gave him the job of organizing a theological academy for their town.

Before too long, there were complaints that the new theol-

---

[3] For information on Melanchthon, see: Karin Maag, ed., *Melanchthon in Europe: His Work and Influence Beyond Wittenberg* (Grand Rapids, MI: Baker Books, 1999); Clyde L. Manschreck, *Melanchthon: The Quiet Reformer* (New York: Abingdon Press, 1958); Ernest Gordon Rupp, "Philip Melanchthon and Martin Bucer," in *A History of Christian Doctrine*, ed. Hubert Cunliffe-Jones (London: T&T Clark, 2006), pp. 373–383; Heinz Scheible, "Philipp Melanchthon" in *Oxford Encyclopedia of the Reformation*, ed. Hans J. Hillerbrand, 4 vols. (New York: Oxford University Press, 1996), 3:41–45; John R. Schneider, "Philipp Melanchthon" in *Dictionary of Major Biblical Interpreters*, ed. Donald K. McKim (Downers Grove, IL: InterVarsity Press, 2007), pp. 716–721; and Robert Stupperich, *Melanchthon* (Philadelphia: Westminster Press, 1965).

ogy professor was not a strict Lutheran. These Gnesio-Lutherans were beginning to organize all over Germany.[4] In Breslau, their chief complaint was that Ursinus was under the influence of the Christian Humanists. The Gnesio-Lutherans were not happy with the teaching of Philipp Melanchthon, but Luther's support of Melanchthon was too solid for these strict Lutherans, who had to content themselves with attacking figures such as Ursinus.[5]

The great contribution of Ursinus was the *Heidelberg Catechism*.[6] It first appeared in 1562, although its magisterial commentary came out in succeeding editions as late as 1591.[7] The *Heidelberg Catechism* is widely used even down to this day in German-speaking Reformed Churches as well as in the Netherlands.

Ursinus was by nature an irenic man and he did not want to become involved in the controversy that was developing. He therefore asked the city council to give him a study leave. The study leave being granted, Ursinus headed off to Zurich with the intention of studying Hebrew under Peter Martyr Vermigli. Vermigli had been called to Oxford by Thomas Cranmer, but when Mary Tudor came to the English throne, he fled to Zurich. Ursinus's action, of course, annoyed the Gnesio-Lutherans. For them, it was proof that Ursinus had gone over to the "Sacramentarians," as they were calling the Swiss.

Ursinus is purported to have studied with several Reformed

---

[4] For a more thorough discussion of Gnesio-Lutheranism, see James Arne Nestingen, "Gnesio-Lutherans," in *Oxford Encyclopedia of the Reformation*, 2:177–180.

[5] Among the better known Gnesio-Lutherans should be numbered Matthias Flacius Illyricus, Joachim Westphal, and Tilemann Heshusius.

[6] For the text of the *Heidelberg Catechism*, see *The Constitution of the Presbyterian Church: Part I, The Book of Confession*s (Louisville: The Office of the General Assembly, 2004), pp. 27–50. For a critical edition of the text, see *The Heidelberg Catechism, 1563–1963: 400*[th] *Anniversary Edition* (New York: United Church Press, 1962). For a recent study of the *Heidelberg Catechism*, see Lyle D. Bierma, et al., *An Introduction to the Heidelberg Catechism: Sources, History, and Theology* (Grand Rapids, MI: Baker Academic, 2005).

[7] See Nevin, "Introduction," *Commentary of Dr. Zacharias Ursinus on the Heidelberg Catechism*, p. xix.

theologians in the Rhineland, but it is not too clear exactly with whom and how long. One thing is clear; the theologian whom Ursinus found most helpful was John Calvin. Calvin was in Geneva at the time. Apparently, Ursinus had crossed over into France and eventually settled in Geneva. More and more, Ursinus found himself supporting Calvin's eucharistic theology. The influence of Calvin was growing in the late 1550s. As it happened, one of the supporters Calvin had found in the question of sacramental theology was the elector of the Palatinate, Frederick III, known as Frederick the Pious. Frederick was one of the kingpins of the German nobility. There were seven electors in the Holy Roman Empire, and it was these electors who had the responsibility of choosing the emperor. As it happened, Frederick was a serious Christian, completely committed to the Reformation and very distinctly inclined toward a Christian Humanist interpretation of the Reformation.

The Palatinate was a rich province in the heart of the Rhineland. It was comprised of holdings on both sides of the Rhine, Heidelberg being its principal city. The University of Heidelberg made the area a center of learning and culture. Frederick had the intention of establishing a series of schools in his principality that would support Reformed Protestantism, and so he appointed Ursinus as professor of systematic theology at Heidelberg. This was a major appointment, making Ursinus one of the high-ranking theologians of Germany. The position was not too stable, however. Frederick himself had succession problems, and yet, much of his reform continued, especially Ursinus's *magnum opus*, the famous *Heidelberg Catechism* and its commentary.

The *Heidelberg Catechism* appeared in 1562, but some of the commentary came out a few years later. What is of particular interest here is the strength of the *Heidelberg Catechism*. There is no question about it, the *Catechism* was promulgated by a very important prince, but it was not merely its political legitimacy that established it as an authoritative resource. It was its spiritual maturity and its theological depth that gave it such wide recognition over the centuries from Rotterdam at the mouth of the Rhine to the German-speaking communities in the Mississippi Valley during the nineteenth century.

Ursinus was not what might be called a charismatic leader. Luther was the charismatic leader. Rather, Ursinus was the devoted scholar. He was a writer, and the most important aspect of his ministry was the writing of his commentary which he provided for the *Heidelberg Catechism*. Let us look at some of its most characteristic teachings.

The first thing we notice is that the *Heidelberg Catechism* draws directly from the central teaching of the Reformation as Martin Luther had preached it. Question 65 asks, "Since then we are made partakers of Christ and all his benefits by faith only, whence does this faith proceed?" Clearly the *Heidelberg Catechism* assumes the teaching of Luther and the leaders of the Protestant Reformation. Ursinus clearly intends for this catechism to be a statement of classical Protestantism. Ursinus recognizes that if we are going to understand ourselves as being justified by faith rather than being saved by going through a series of rites and ceremonies one has to be very clear as to how one understands the place of those rites and ceremonies that are clearly an essential element in the Christian life. It is very clear from the New Testament that Christians are to be baptized at the beginning of the Christian life, and they are to join together in the celebration of Holy Communion on a regular basis.

The *Heidelberg Catechism* makes it very clear that it is by faith and by faith alone that we are made partakers of Christ. That means that it is by faith that we are joined to Christ, that we are saved, counted as members of the church and citizens of the kingdom of God. "We are made partakers of Christ and all his benefits by faith only."[8] To be sure, this salvation is the gift of God. It is the Holy Spirit who works this saving faith in our hearts. God does this by the preaching of the gospel, and he confirms it by the sacraments.

---

[8] *Heidelberg Catechism*, Q. 65.

The *Heidelberg Catechism* definitely picks up on the *Wittenberg Concord* of 1536, one of the more successful attempts at reconciling the Wittenberg Reformers and the Swiss Reformers. Question 66 defines the sacraments as "visible signs and seals, appointed of God for this end."[9] The *Wittenberg Concord* agreed that the sacraments are indeed signs, but they are not empty signs. This clearly takes a fundamental move away from the more radical position Zwingli had at first taken. The Swiss had agreed that the sacraments are indeed signs, but they are not to be regarded as empty signs. Following the Apostle Paul's explanation of circumcision, the sacraments are signs of God's grace. The sacraments seal to us the promise of the Gospel. Something happens in the celebration of the sacrament of Communion. It is not merely that something is said. God puts in our hands that which the gospel promises.

Particularly characteristic of the *Heidelberg Catechism* is the teaching that it is God who saves us. We are not saved by our own efforts and wisdom. By grace, we are saved through faith, and even that is not of ourselves. "The Holy Ghost teaches us in the gospel, and assures us by the sacraments, that the whole of our salvation depends upon that one sacrifice of Christ which he offered for us on the cross."[10] We notice here, as we will notice repeatedly in regard to the *Heidelberg Catechism*, the role of the Holy Spirit is especially important in Reformed eucharistic theology.

Another characteristic feature of the *Heidelberg Catechism* is that it takes special care to understand that the sacrament of Holy Communion is to be celebrated in remembrance of Christ. "Christ has commanded me and all believers, to eat of this broken bread, and to drink of this cup, in remembrance of him . . ."[11] The key to understanding the position of the Swiss Reformers is

---

[9] *Heidelberg Catechism*, Q. 66.

[10] *Heidelberg Catechism*, Q. 67.

[11] *Heidelberg Catechism*, Q. 75.

the depth of their understanding of what Scripture means by this word "remembrance." Zwingli, Oecolampadius, and Bullinger understood the Eucharist to be a memorial similar to that found in the Passover story in Exodus. The observance of Passover was an act of memorial as we find it in the New Testament where Jesus tells his disciples we are to "do this in remembrance of me." That word *anamnesis* is a very rich word in the biblical vocabulary. Neither Ursinus in the *Heidelberg Catechism* nor Bullinger in the *Second Helvetic Confession* will let us neglect it.[12]

One of the best statements in the *Heidelberg Catechism* is found in Question 76 where Ursinus poses the question, "What is it then to eat the crucified body, and drink the shed blood of Christ?" The answer tells us that it is not only to embrace with believing heart all the sufferings of our Lord Jesus Christ, but also to be united to his sacred body. What Ursinus is talking about is saving faith which by partaking participates in the highest expression of worship. We are talking about union with Christ here, and once more we find Ursinus making a point of the agency of the Holy Spirit, for it is the Holy Spirit, the Spirit of the Father and of the Son, who dwells both in Christ and in us.

The sacrament of Holy Communion, as we find it discussed in the *Heidelberg Catechism*, is concerned with our union with Christ. As Christians, we are one with Christ. We are flesh of his flesh and bone of his bone. We are by this fact one with each other. We are members of the one body of Christ who is both in heaven and within us.[13]

The *Heidelberg Catechism* is very straightforward. Question 78 asks, "Do then the bread and wine become the very body and blood of Christ?" The answer is very plain and simple:

> Not at all: . . . the bread in the Lord's supper is not changed into the very body of Christ; though agree-

---

[12] *Heidelberg Catechism*, Q. 75.

[13] *Heidelberg Catechism*, Q. 76.

ably to the nature and properties of sacraments, it is called the body of Christ Jesus.[14]

Ursinus is very much aware that the very essence of a sacrament is that one is speaking in terms of metonymy. This is, of course, only natural for the Christian Humanists. They were careful students of rhetoric. The Reformers of Zurich were especially aware of how the ancient world had used rhetoric. They had carefully studied the Christian rhetoric of Augustine.

In his exposition of the *Heidelberg Catechism*, Ursinus takes up at length Augustine's *De Doctrina Christiana*, which tells us so much about how the sacraments are visible words. The champion orator of the Latin Church had had a tremendous influence on how the Reformation understood its use of word and sacrament. The same was true in regard to what they understood about the meaning of the word "sacrament." It was in 1521 that Beatus Rhenanus had discovered a whole collection of the writings of Tertullian. Tertullian, like Augustine, was one of the classic rhetoricians of the ancient church. Writing around the year 200, Tertullian is the first Christian writer to give us a sizable collection of literature in the Latin language. In fact, sometimes he is called the father of Christian Latin.

By the beginning of the Middle Ages, Christian theologians had forgotten what the word "sacrament" really meant. The newly discovered manuscripts of Tertullian contained several passages which helped the Swiss Reformers recover the meaning of the word. This made quite a splash in theological circles. In fact, the Gnesio-Lutherans began to call the Swiss Reformed "Sacramentarians." In his exposition of the *Heidelberg Catechism*, Ursinus goes into considerable detail unrolling the meaning of the term. For the *Heidelberg Catechism*, the whole idea of the sacraments being an oath of allegiance to God and a divine promise to his people is particularly strong.

---

[14] *Heidelberg Catechism*, Q. 78.

BULLINGER AND
THE *SECOND HELVETIC CONFESSION*

Another of the more remarkable leaders of the second generation was Heinrich Bullinger, Zwingli's successor.[15] Zwingli died in 1531 at the Battle of Kappel. There were those who figured that this battle would finish off Protestantism in Switzerland. Finding a capable leader for the Church of Zurich was urgent. It had to be done quickly. It was difficult because it could easily happen that Zwingli's successor would become a target for assassination. It was therefore only a few weeks later that the city council of Zurich decided on Bullinger.

The battle of Kappel was a rather disgraceful chapter in Swiss military history. Zwingli's body was desecrated, and the Reformed minister of Kappel decided it might be wise to flee from Kappel with his family. That minister, of course, was none other than Heinrich Bullinger. The Bullinger family understandably fled to Zurich, where Bullinger took office as Antistace in 1531 and continued in office until 1575. For forty years he directed the tremendously influential church of Zurich.

The life story of Heinrich Bullinger is of particular interest because it gives us a strong sense of the blood, sweat, and tears of the Reformation. Heinrich Bullinger was the fifth son of a Catholic priest. His father was parish priest in Bremgarten, a small city about half way between Zurich and Basel. His mother was the daughter

---

[15] For biographical material on Bullinger, see: J. Wayne Baker, *Heinrich Bullinger and the Covenant: The Other Reformed Tradition* (Athens: Ohio University Press, 1980); Fritz Busser, "Bullinger and 1566," in *Controversy and Conciliation*, pp. 21–31; George Ella, "Henry Bullinger: Shepherd of the Churches," in *The Decades of Henry Bullinger*, ed. Thomas Harding (Grand Rapids, MI: Reformation Heritage Books, 2004); Bruce Gordon and Emidio Campi, eds., *Architect of the Reformation: An Introduction to Heinrich Bullinger* (Grand Rapids, MI: Baker Academic, 2004); and Robert C. Walton, "Heinrich Bullinger," in *Shapers of Religious Traditions in Germany, Switzerland, and Poland, 1560–1600*, ed. Jill Raitt (New Haven: Yale University Press, 1981), pp. 69–87.

of the mayor of Bremgarten. She was born into the upper levels of small town society. This sort of thing was standard in late medieval Switzerland. Most Swiss Catholic pastors were, in effect, married. They would have a wife who lived in the parsonage, took care of the house, cooked the meals and bore the priest's children. Now, true, the priest had to pay a penalty for this indiscretion. One year, the bishop of Constance received over two thousand remunerations for the birth of these clerical children. But once the tax had been paid, everyone was quite relaxed about it.

Heinrich's father recognized he had a son of considerable gifts and saw to it that he received the best possible education. Heinrich's older brother was a student at Emmerich and so young Heinrich, too, was sent off to begin his studies at Emmerich, a sort of prep school for the University of Cologne. It was in 1519 that Heinrich Bullinger began his studies at Cologne, which at the time was the most prestigious theological faculty in Germany. At Cologne the purest *via antiqua* Scholasticism was taught. Both Albertus Magnus and Thomas Aquinas had taught at Cologne. Bullinger got his bachelor of arts degree in 1520 and his master of arts degree in 1522. It was in those years that the Protestant Reformation first sounded its trumpet. Young Heinrich was caught up in all the excitement. By the time he returned home in 1522, he was a committed Protestant.

In 1523, young Bullinger got a job lecturing on the New Testament at the Cistercian monastery in Kappel. In the next three years, he published a series of commentaries on various books of the Old and New Testaments. He was obviously an avid scholar. He had high hopes of making his mark as a biblical scholar. By 1526, he had introduced to the Church of Kappel the celebration of the Reformed Eucharist in German. It was not until 1523, however, that Bullinger met Zwingli. It was at the disputations with the Anabaptists that the two finally came together. Bullinger was hardly a clone of Zwingli. The two men had been educated in very different ways. Bullinger was given a first class education as understood by the late medieval Schoolmen, whereas Zwingli's education was much more the education of Christian Humanism.

The theological literature produced by Bullinger was rather amazing.[16] A forty year pastorate is something of a surprising accomplishment even today, but in the sixteenth century, it was extraordinary. Bullinger maintained a broad correspondence. I think at one time something like five thousand of his letters had been collected and published. Then, there was his four volume systematic theology, the *Decades*, which in its day was even more popular than Calvin's *Institutes*.[17] His commentary on the Revelation of John had the honor of being presented to every parish church in England by Queen Elizabeth.

The *Second Helvetic Confession* belongs to a distinct type of theological literature. It is a sort of theological position paper.[18] One notices that it is much like the *Sentences* of Peter Lombard. That is, it is textbook theology through and through. The *Sentences* of Peter Lombard would have been familiar to any theology student at the University of Cologne. And that, of course, is just where Heinrich Bullinger studied.

A. THE *SECOND HELVETIC CONFESSION* ON THE SACRAMENTS

The *Second Helvetic Confession*, following the example of Peter Lombard, included a collection of position statements of theological teachings based on the traditional formulation of Christian theology roughly based on the Creed. Here, of course, we are inter-

---

[16] For a study of Bullinger's theology in general, see Ernst Koch, *Die Theologie der Confessio Helvetica Posterior* (Neukirchen-Vluyn: Neukirchener Verlag des Erziehungsvereins GmbH, 1968).

[17] See Thomas Harding, ed., *The Decades of Henry Bullinger* (Grand Rapids, MI: Reformation Heritage Books, 2004).

[18] See my paper entitled "Bullinger and the Scholastic Works on Baptism: A Study in the History of Christian Worship," in *Heinrich Bullinger: 1504–1575, Gesammelte Aufsätze zum 400. Todestag* (Zurich: Theologischer Verlag Zürich, 1975), pp. 191–207.

ested in only two chapters of the *Confession*—the chapter on the Sacraments in general and, then, the chapter on the Lord's Supper.

These affirmations or sentences seem to follow in a traditional order, but they follow that order in a very loose fashion. They only treat the topics that they find of special interest. The topics are very loosely connected. What these sentences do, however, is present a number of position statements very briefly to give us a profile of how the Swiss churches felt about a number of the theological issues of the day. Let us look at some of these affirmations.[19]

1. AFFIRMATION 169

> From the beginning, God added to the preaching of his Word in his Church sacraments or sacramental signs. For thus does all Holy Scripture clearly testify. Sacraments are mystical symbols, or holy rites . . . instituted by God himself, consisting of his Word, of signs and of things signified, whereby in the Church he keeps in mind and from time to time recalls the great benefits he has shown to men; whereby also he seals his promises . . . .[20]

It is here, of course, that the *Second Helvetic Confession* goes beyond the simple memorialism that the Swiss pastors seemed at first to affirm. The point is that the sacraments not only signify the promises of God, they *seal* these promises as well.

In the sacraments, God "offers to our sight those things which he inwardly performs for us and so strengthens and increases our faith through the working of God's Spirit in our hearts." At this point, Bullinger makes very clear the importance of the doctrine of the Holy Spirit to Reformed sacramental theology.

One more thing needs to be pointed out about this affirmation.

---

[19] For the text of the *Second Helvetic Confession*, see *The Constitution of the Presbyterian Church: Part I, Book of Confessions*, pp. 51–116. The Affirmation numbers are taken from this edition of the *Second Helvetic Confession*.

[20] *Second Helvetic Confession*, Affirmation 169.

In the sacraments, God distinguishes us from all other people and religions, "and consecrates us and binds us wholly to himself . . ."[21]

2. Affirmation 170

An important feature of the sacramental theology of the Reformed Church in Switzerland was the importance the Swiss gave to the continuity between the Old Testament and the New Testament. It all had to do with the rediscovery of biblical Hebrew, so important to Christian Humanism. The understanding of the sacraments among the Swiss was clearly developed from what the Old Testament taught the Reformers about the sacraments of circumcision and Passover, the principle sacraments of the Old Testament.[22]

3. Affirmation 171

The *Second Helvetic Confession* presents what had now become the traditional Protestant teaching on the number of the sacraments. One does recognize the necessity of ordination and marriage, to be sure. One recognizes that repentance is an essential element in prayer, but these things are not to be considered sacraments as are baptism and the Lord's Supper.[23]

4. Affirmation 172

> The author of all sacraments is not any man, but God alone. Men cannot institute sacraments. For they pertain to the worship of God, and it is not for man to appoint and prescribe a worship of God, but to accept and preserve the one he has received from God. Besides, the symbols have God's promises annexed to them, which require faith.[24]

Following Luther and the other Reformers as well, Bullinger gets

---

[21] *Second Helvetic Confession*, Affirmation 169.

[22] *Second Helvetic Confession*, Affirmation 170.

[23] *Second Helvetic Confession*, Affirmation 171.

[24] *Second Helvetic Confession*, Affirmation 172.

back to faith—faith in God's Word and promises. Now faith rests only upon the Word of God; and the Word of God is like papers or letters, and the sacraments are like seals which only God appends to the letters.[25]

Understanding the sacraments as signs and seals of the gracious promises of God opened up in the reading and preaching of the Gospel was a fundamental teaching of the Swiss Reformed Church. Particularly important for the Swiss in this matter was Romans 4:11 which tells us that circumcision is a sign and a seal of the Old Covenant.

5. Affirmation 173

Christ still works in the sacraments, "so he continually works in the Church in which they are rightly carried out; so that the faithful, when they receive them from the ministers, know that God works in his own ordinance."[26] One has often noticed that Bullinger has a very strong doctrine of the church and the ministry. This comes to play here where Bullinger reminds us that the validity as well as the effectiveness of the sacraments ultimately falls on God himself.

6. Affirmation 175

One notices in this affirmation that Bullinger is thinking out his eucharistic theology in the language of Scholasticism, in which he was trained at the University of Cologne. As Bullinger saw it, the substance of the sacraments is Christ the Savior. It is this which God promises in the sacraments of both the Old and New Testaments. "The principle thing which God promises in all sacraments and to which all the godly in all ages direct their attention . . . is Christ the Savior."[27] With this, Bullinger reminds us of a whole wealth of sacramental typology. Bullinger was particularly well

---

[25] *Second Helvetic Confession*, Affirmation 172.
[26] *Second Helvetic Confession*, Affirmation 173.
[27] *Second Helvetic Confession*, Affirmation 175.

informed on this subject as we find in many of his writings.

7. Affirmation 178

A sacrament, as Bullinger understands it, consists of three parts: the Word, the sign and the thing signified. "For the Word of God makes them sacraments which before they were not."[28] Here again, we are dealing with the terminology of Scholastic theology. What Bullinger wants to talk about is the consecration of the elements of Holy Communion.

> In the Lord's Supper, the outward sign is bread and wine, taken from things commonly used for meat and drink; but the thing signified is the body of Christ which was given, and his blood which was shed for us.[29]

As Bullinger understands it, the bread and wine are always bread and wine, but when the Word is preached and the divine name is invoked, they are set aside to a sacred use and thereby become something special. When in the service of worship we repeat the Words of Institution, these signs are consecrated. "For Christ's first institution and consecration of the sacraments remains always effectual in the Church of God."[30]

8. Affirmation 180

Bullinger very specifically tells us that the sacraments are mystical signs of sacred things. They are sacramentally joined together and united by a mystical signification. This was the intention of him who instituted the sacraments. When joined together in this way, they are not common but rather holy.

> . . . he who commanded the bread to be eaten and the wine to be drunk in the supper did not want the faithful to receive only bread and wine without any mystery

---

[28] *Second Helvetic Confession*, Affirmation 178.
[29] *Second Helvetic Confession*, Affirmation 178.
[30] *Second Helvetic Confession*, Affirmation 178.

as they eat bread in their homes; but that they should spiritually partake of the things signified . . .[31]

Bullinger is well aware that in the Greek Church the sacraments are called mysteries. What is meant by mystical signs is, quite simply then, sacramental signs.

B. THE *SECOND HELVETIC CONFESSION* ON THE LORD'S SUPPER

Having finished talking about the nature of sacraments in general, Bullinger presses on to discuss the two Protestant sacraments specifically. Skipping his chapter on Baptism, we will concern ourselves with his thoughts on the Lord's Supper.

1. AFFIRMATION 193

Bullinger opens up the subject by discussing several names that the Church uses to speak of this sacrament. It can be spoken of as the Lord's Supper or as the Lord's Table, or it can simply be called the Eucharist.[32]

2. AFFIRMATION 195

What comes next is of particular interest for this confession of faith of the Swiss Reformed Church. It has to do with the Lord's Supper as a memorial.[33] As Bullinger puts it,

> By this sacred rite the Lord wishes to keep in fresh remembrance that greatest benefit which he showed to mortal men, namely, that by having given his body and shed his blood he has pardoned all our sins, and redeemed us from eternal death and the power of the devil . . .[34]

---

[31] *Second Helvetic Confession*, Affirmation 180.
[32] *Second Helvetic Confession*, Affirmation 193.
[33] *Second Helvetic Confession*, Affirmation 195.
[34] *Second Helvetic Confession*, Affirmation 195.

All this is made most clear by the words of Jesus himself when at the Last Supper he said, "Do this in remembrance of me." While it has to be admitted that early in the Reformation there were those, especially among the Swiss Reformers, who tried to understand these words by what is usually called a straightforward memorialism, in a short length of time it became clear to the Swiss Reformers that there was more to these words of Jesus. The word "remember" has a very rich meaning, especially in the Old Testament. Bullinger had led the Swiss theologians to a more comprehensive view as we find in the *Zurich Consensus* of 1549.

3. Affirmation 198

Bullinger's more mature position tells us that we must be aware of the spiritual eating of Christ's body. This does not mean that the food is changed into spirit. Reformed Protestantism is not interested in a spiritualistic understanding of the sacraments. They teach rather that the bread and the wine are spiritually communicated. They are not communicated in a corporeal but in a spiritual way. That is, they are communicated by the Holy Spirit at work in our hearts. They are applied to us in such a way ". . . that Christ lives in us and we live in him." What Bullinger is getting at is that in sharing in the sacrament of Holy Communion we have union with Christ. Here, of course, is the essence of Reformed Eucharistic theology. The whole point of the sacrament is union with Christ.[35]

> For even as bodily food and drink not only refresh and strengthen our bodies, but also keeps them alive, so the flesh of Christ delivered for us, and his blood shed for us, not only refresh and strengthen our souls, but also preserve them alive, not in so far as they are corporeally eaten and drunken, but in so far as they are communicated unto us spiritually by the Spirit of God. . . .[36]

---

[35] *Second Helvetic Confession*, Affirmation 198.
[36] *Second Helvetic Confession*, Affirmation 198.

Here, Bullinger makes generous use of passages from the Gospel of John. To be sure, Bullinger is following the lead of Zwingli.

4. Affirmation 200

Again, Bullinger returns to that bedrock of the Protestant religion—Christ is received by faith.

> As we must by eating receive food with our bodies in order that it may work in us, and prove its efficacy in us . . . so it is necessary that we receive Christ by faith, that he may become ours, and he may live in us and we in him . . .[37]

At this point, Bullinger refers to a number of passages from the Bread of Life Discourse in the Gospel of John.

5. Affirmation 201

From all this, it should be clear, as Bullinger puts it, that by spiritual food we do not mean some imaginary food but the very body of the Lord given to us. It is received spiritually by faith.[38]

6. Affirmation 203

Bullinger is quite clear about the meaning of spiritual eating, but it is important to understand what he has to say about sacramental eating. The spiritual eating in the Gospel of John is a matter of the reading and preaching of the Word, but Bullinger, having spoken of this, wants to go beyond this to speak of the sacramental eating of the sacred Supper. By coming to the Table of the Lord, one ". . . outwardly receives the visible sacrament of the body and blood of the Lord. To be sure, when the believer [first] believed, he first received the life-giving food, and still enjoys it."[39] When he now receives the sacrament, he does not receive a mere invention,

---

[37] *Second Helvetic Confession*, Affirmation 200.

[38] *Second Helvetic Confession*, Affirmation 201.

[39] *Second Helvetic Confession*, Affirmation 203.

for he witnesses before the Church, of whose body he is a member. Something really happens in the celebration of the sacrament. Assurance is "given to those who receive the sacrament that the body of the Lord was given and his blood shed, not only for men in general, but particularly for every faithful communicant, to whom it is food and drink unto eternal life."[40]

Of the essence of the Lord's Supper is that it is a promise and an assurance that God through his Spirit working in our hearts gives us progress in the things of the Spirit. Our faith is kindled, and we grow more and more. "He who outwardly receives the sacrament by true faith, not only receives the sign, but also, as we said, enjoys the thing itself."[41] This is the memorial we have been commanded to make before all nations and all peoples. When we do this, we can be well assured that the body and blood of the Lord was given, not only for men in general, but particularly for every faithful communicant, to whom it is food and drink unto eternal life.[42]

7. AFFIRMATION 205

It is in regard to the presence of Christ at the Supper that Bullinger is especially interested. First of all, Bullinger looks at several positions that were important in his day: the position of Catholic Scholasticism, the position of the strict Lutherans and, finally, the position of the Anabaptists. Coming to the position of the Swiss Reformers, Bullinger states,

> The body of Christ is in heaven at the right hand of the Father; and therefore our hearts are to be lifted up on high, and not to be fixed on the bread . . . . Yet the Lord is not absent from his Church when she celebrates the Supper.[43]

---

[40] *Second Helvetic Confession*, Affirmation 203.
[41] *Second Helvetic Confession*, Affirmation 203.
[42] *Second Helvetic Confession*, Affirmation 203.
[43] *Second Helvetic Confession*, Affirmation 205.

With this, Bullinger repeats the comparison so often used by Reformed theologians. It is like the presence of the sun which is absent from us in the heavens and yet effectually present among us.

> How much more is the Sun of Righteousness, Christ, although in his body he is absent from us in heaven, present with us, not corporeally, but spiritually, by his vivifying operation, and as he himself explained at his Last Supper that he would be present with us (John, chs. 14, 15, and 16). Whence it follows that we do not have the Supper without Christ, and yet at the same time have . . . a mystical Supper, as it was universally called by antiquity.[44]

There is no question about it: Bullinger had a very strong doctrine of the presence of Christ at the Supper. This is the point John Williamson Nevin got from the *Second Helvetic Confession*.[45] Right here, we find the mystical presence about which he so prophetically wrote.[46]

---

[44] *Second Helvetic Confession*, Affirmation 205.

[45] See Nevin, in *The Commentary of Dr. Zacharias Ursinus on the Heidelberg Catechism*.

[46] See chapter 20, pp. 753–769 in this volume.

9
THE ROOTS OF ENGLISH PURITANISM

The spiritual wealth of the Puritans is only now beginning to be calculated. Our parents too hastily threw out the devotional literature of the Puritans, blaming it for the feelings of guilt and "repression" that so tormented them. A younger generation, however, has begun to suspect that they have lost something of far greater value than they had been told. They have begun to retrieve some precious treasures from the attic. To be sure not everything that was thrown out was of real value. One cannot always distinguish the junk from the real family heirlooms, but sifting through it has its rewards. All it needs is a little dusting and polishing.[1]

---

[1] For some of the more recent work on the piety of the Puritans see the following: Joel R. Beeke and Mark Jones, eds., *A Puritan Theology: Doctrine for Life* (Grand Rapids, MI: Reformation Heritage Books, 2012); Joel R. Beeke and Randall J. Pederson, *Meet the Puritans* (Grand Rapids, MI: Reformation Heritage Books, 2006); J. I. Packer, *A Quest for Godliness: The Puritan Vision for the Christian Life* (Wheaton, IL: Crossway, 1990); William S. Barker, *Puritan Profiles, Fifty-four Puritans: Personalities Drawn Together by the Westminster Assembly* (Fearn, UK: Christian Focus Publications, 1996); Patrick Collinson, *The Elizabethan Puritan Movement* (Berkeley: University of California Press, 1967); Patrick Collinson, *English Puritanism* (London: Historical Association Pamphlet, 1983); John S. Coolidge, *The Pauline Renaissance in England: Puritanism and the Bible* (Oxford: Clarendon, 1970); Gerald Robertson Cragg, *Puritanism in the Period of the Great Persecution, 1660–1688* (Cambridge, UK: Cambridge University Press, 1957); Horton Davies, *Worship and Theology in England*, 5 vols. (Princeton, NJ: Princeton University Press, 1961–1975); Everett H. Emerson, *English Puritanism from John Hooper to John Milton* (Durham, NC: Duke University Press, 1968); Michael George Finlayson, *Historians, Puritanism, and the English Revolution* (Toronto and Buffalo: University of Toronto Press, 1983); William Haller, *The Rise of Puritanism; or, the Way to the New Jerusalem as Set Forth in Pulpit and Press from Thomas Cartwright to John Lilburne and John Milton, 1570–1643* (New York: Columbia University Press, 1947); Paul Helm, *Calvin and the Calvinists* (Carlisle, PA.: Banner of Truth Trust, 1982); E. Brooks Holifield, *The Covenant Sealed*:

The chapter ahead of us will take up the story of the eucharistic piety of the English Puritans beginning with the Admonition Controversy in the early 1570s. It was not until the reign of the Stuarts that Puritan literature started to compose a distinct school of thought. We will consider the *Sacramental Meditations* of Edward Reynolds, written in the 1630s. Then in chapter 10, we will move on to the Westminster Assembly of the mid-1640s and its *Directory of Worship*. In 1662 Charles II was restored to the throne and Puritanism was politically defeated, although Richard Baxter published his *Reformed Liturgy* in 1662 as a sort of swan song. Finally we will look at the *Sacramental Discourses* of John Owen, one of the treasures of Puritan devotional literature.

One thing needs to be made quite clear; there was not a single Puritan way of serving the sacrament. This is made especially clear by the *Westminster Directory for Worship*. It does not take very long to discover that the *Westminster Directory* did not simply translate the *Genevan Psalter* into English. Jeremiah Burroughs saw things about as differently from Richard Baxter as one could possibly imagine. Generally speaking the Congregationalists and the Presbyterians saw worship as differently as they saw polity. This will become obvious as we proceed.

The subject of these two chapters has been particularly difficult because of the sheer mass of material available. Many ministers published devotional booklets designed to help people prepare

---

The Development of the Puritan Sacramental Theology in Old and New England 1570–1720 (New Haven, CT: Yale University Press, 1974); Marshall M. Knappen, *Tudor Puritanism: A Chapter in the History of Idealism* (Chicago and London: University of Chicago Press, 1970); William M. Lamont, *Puritanism to Nonconformity*, 2 vols. (New York: Harper, 1848–49); Robert S. Paul, *Assembly of the Lord: Politics and Religion in the Westminster Assembly and the "Grand Debate"* (Edinburgh: T. & T. Clark, 1985); Leonard J. Trinterud, ed., *Elizabethan Puritanism* (New York: Oxford University Press, 1971); Owen C. Watkins, *The Puritan Experience* (New York: Schocken Books, 1972); George Yule, *Puritans in Politics: The Religious Legislation of the Long Parliament 1640–1647* (Appleford, UK: Sutton Courtenay Press, 1981); David Zaret, *The Heavenly Contract: Ideology and Organization in Pre-Revolutionary Puritanism* (Chicago: University of Chicago Press, 1985).

9: The Roots of English Puritanism

to receive the sacrament. It was a popular genre of literature. We have studied only one example of this sort of devotional literature, but hundreds were available. It was also true that controversy over eucharistic doctrine had a special fascination for Puritan theologians. Hundreds of treatises on the mystery of God's presence in the sacrament were published. Some of these were controversial literature of questionable value, but there were masterpieces as well.

Another difficulty with writing these chapters is the question of deciding who is to be regarded as a Puritan and who is not. It would be a mistake to treat only the Nonconformists as the true Puritans. If that were taken as the measuring stick, many of the early Puritans would not make the cut. One didn't have to be a Separatist to be a true Puritan. We have selected only a short list, but we have tried to offer a variety of types and examples.

ADMONITION, 1570

In 1572 two young Cambridge scholars, John Field and Thomas Wilcox, published a series of protests demanding the further reform of the Church of England.[2] Originally this admonition was published anonymously. Later Field and Wilcox confessed to being responsible for the document and were imprisoned for it. Queen Elizabeth was adamant that she was going to rule the church and that, as temporal authority of all that took place in her land, she had final authority on all matters, including the church's government and worship. The Admonition had argued that the government and the worship of the church were supposed to be according to Scripture. That is, the first Admonition argued for a proto-presbyterian position. It was the first expression in England

---

[2] "Admonition to the Parliament," found in *Puritan Manifestos*, ed. W. H. Frere and C. L. Douglas (London: SPCK, 1954) Hereinafter "Admonition." See also Peter Lake, "Admonition Controversy," *Oxford Encyclopedia of the Reformation*, ed. Hans J. Hillerbrand, 4 vols. (New York and Oxford: Oxford University Press, 1996), p. 1:7; and Donald J. McGinn, *The Admonition Controversy* (New Brunswick, NJ: Rutgers University Press, 1949).

of a *divinely ordained* presbyterianism. The Admonition became something of a scandal and was widely discussed. Not long after the first Admonition a second admonition appeared written by the distinguished Cambridge professor, Thomas Cartwright.[3] Cartwright was the Lady Margaret Professor of Divinity, one of the most distinguished chairs of divinity in the English-speaking world.[4] Cartwright had studied under Theodore Beza in Geneva and had presented many Reformed teachings on church polity in a series of expository lectures on the Acts of the Apostles. Cartwright had essentially taught that the church should govern itself; it should not be under the control of the State. John Whitgift, who was the Master of Trinity College in Cambridge, was a thorough supporter of the Queen's views on the divine right of the Christian prince and sounded the alarm with his rebuttal to the Admonition.[5] Whitgift won considerable favor at court and was eventually given the archbishopric of Canterbury. Thomas Cartwright, however, ended up losing his job at Cambridge and eventually had to spend most of the rest of his life in exile.

The Admonition's strongest objection was to ministers who

---

[3] See A. F. Scott Pearson, *Thomas Cartwright and Elizabethan Puritanism, 1535–1603* (Cambridge, UK: The University Press, 1925).

[4] For more information on Cartwright see: Peter Lake, "Cartwright, Thomas," *Oxford Encyclopedia of the Reformation*, 1:269–70; Peter Lake, *Moderate Puritans and the Elizabethan Church* (Cambridge and New York: Cambridge University Press, 1982); Peter Lake, *Anglicans and Puritans? Presbyterianism and English Conformist Thought from Whitgift to Hooker* (London: Allen & Unwin, 1988); and Albert Peel and Leland H. Carlson, *Cartwrightiana*, Elizabethan Nonconformist Texts 1 (London: George Allen and Unwin, Ltd., 1951).

[5] For more information on John Whitgift and Erastianism, see John Whitgift, *The Works of John Whitgift: containing The defence of the answer to the admonition, against the reply of Thomas Cartwright* (1851), 3 vols., reprint (New York: Johnson Reprints, 1968); J. Wayne Baker, "Erastianism," *Oxford Encyclopedia of the Reformation*, 2:59–60; Powel M. Dawley, *John Whitgift and the Reformation* (New York: Charles Scribner, 1954); Peter Lake, "Whitgift, John," *Oxford Encyclopedia of the Reformation*, 4:270–71; Harry C. Porter, *Reformation and Reaction in Tudor Cambridge* (Cambridge, UK: University Press, 1958); and John Strype, *The Life and Acts of John Whitgift*, 3 vols. (Oxford: Clarendon Press, 1822).

either could not or would not preach. The system of benefices had been recognized as an abuse for some time.[6] It was common for ministers to be appointed to pulpits and to receive the income from the endowment but then to farm out the actual responsibilities of the position to a vicar who might or might not have a theological education but who could recite the mass and repeat the benedictions and perform the ceremonies. The Admonition complains about the vicars reading little snippets of the Epistles and Gospels but not getting around to preaching the passages they read.[7] Objecting to the lectionary as "fragments" of holy Scripture was a major complaint of sixteenth-century Protestantism, especially where the influence of Christian Humanism was strong. The Admonition continued the objection to the pompous vestments which had been used by priests in the Middle Ages.[8] Especially mentioned were the surplice and the cope which the Puritans found to be in contrast to the simplicity of the ancient church.[9] The stole, although not specifically mentioned in this text, was a particular annoyance because many believed it to have magical powers. During the reign of Edward VI, the Vestiarian Controversy had broken out among the most hard-line supporters of the Reformation, but it was by no means a major concern. Elizabeth had insisted on conformity in this matter only in order to make it clear that she was calling the shots. This demand came to have great symbolic importance.

Another major concern of the Admonition was the requirement that the communicants receive the bread and the wine kneeling. The Puritans were more inclined to receive the sacred meal

---

[6] An account of the history of benefices can be found at "Benefices," *Encyclopedia Britannica*, 11th ed., 32 vols. (Chicago: Encyclopedia Britannica, 1910), 3:725–26.

[7] The Puritans advocated using the *lectio continua* instead. For a discussion of this see Hughes Oliphant Old, *The Reading and Preaching of the Scriptures in the Worship of the Christian Church*, vol. 4, *The Age of the Reformation* (Grand Rapids, MI: Eerdmans, 2002), pp. 134–157.

[8] On the Puritan objection to vestments see Patrick Collinson, "Vestiarian Controversy," *Oxford Encyclopedia of the Reformation*, 1:231–232.

[9] "Admonition," p. 14.

either standing or seated. The Admonition argues for both standing as the Jews received the Passover or seated as at the Last Supper.[10] The objection was that kneeling before the bread and wine was an open invitation to idolatry. Too many of the eucharistic devotions of the Middle Ages assumed that in looking at the consecrated host one caught sight of the deity. However that might have been, kneeling before the bread and the wine certainly obscured the visual sign of the believers sharing a meal in the house of the Father.

Not all Puritans would have fussed over the Introit, the *Gloria in excelsis*, and the reciting of the Nicene Creed. It sounds like the Admonition objected to both singing in church and playing the organ, but more probably this was a concern of only the most radical Puritans. The Admonition mentions singing and piping but does not dwell on the subject.[11]

The Admonition is not a profound document. Its value is that it was politically effective. It was blunt and it dealt with practical issues. It made clear above all that basic to this reformation of the church is that the church must be governed by the elders, the teachers and the pastors of the church. State control would not be accepted. Neither the Tudors nor the Stuarts would go along with this. As far as they could see only episcopalianism in the church could be consistent with the monarchy. Presbyterianism, therefore, could not possibly be allowed. As King James I put it: "No bishop, no king."

EDWARD REYNOLDS

Edwards Reynolds (1599–1676), the bishop of Norwich, was a moderate Puritan.[12] He was a strong supporter of evangelical Protestantism and, from a theological standpoint, he was clearly Reformed.

[10] "Admonition," p. 14.
[11] "Admonition," p. 14.
[12] For biographical material on Reynolds, see: Barker, *Puritan Profiles*, pp. 179–185; and the biographical sketch by Alexander Chalmers in Edward Reynolds, *The Whole Works of the Right Rev. Edward Reynolds, D.D.*, 6 vols. (London: Printed for B. Holdsworth in St. Paul's Church-yard, 1826), 1: xvii–lxxiv.

9: THE ROOTS OF ENGLISH PURITANISM

Reynolds has always been especially beloved for his *Meditations on the Holy Sacrament of the Lord's Last Supper.*[13] It is one of the classics of a specifically Puritan piety. Purportedly, these meditations were written as a devotional exercise while young Reynolds was yet a student at Oxford. Some time later a friend made arrangements to have them published. This was all quite unknown to Reynolds. The manuscript in the meantime was lost and Reynolds had to rewrite his meditations. They were finally published in 1639.[14] However the meditations may have found their way to the publisher, they show great depth and maturity. This series of twenty meditations is a work of devout scholarship. Reynolds knows both the church Fathers and the doctors of the medieval church. He quotes from the Continental Reformers such as Beza, as well as the Lutherans and Catholics. He even brings us some of the insights of Richard Hooker.

Presumably the meditations in the form they have come down to us were written while Reynolds was minister at Braunston in Northamptonshire during his ten year pastorate there. These meditations are pastoral rather than academic. They were supposed to guide the meditations of the faithful as they attended the celebration of Communion. Here we have a document that tells us much about the sacramental piety of an English Puritan during the reign of Charles I and his High Church Archbishop William Laud.

Edward Reynolds was born the son of a customs official at Portsmouth. There he attended a particularly fine Latin school and from there he went on to Oxford, where he studied at Merton College. He received his bachelor's degree in 1618, and was awarded

---

[13] This work first appeared in 1639. A more widely accessible edition of this work is found in his complete works under the title, *Meditations on the Holy Sacrament of the Lord's Last Supper*, Reynolds, *Works*, 3:5–163. A modern reprint exists: Edward Reynolds, *The Whole Works of the Right Rev. Edward Reynolds, D.D.*, vol. 3, photolithographic reprint of the 1826 edition (Morgan, PA: Soli Deo Gloria Publications, 1999), pp. 5–163. Page numbers will be referenced from this reprint, although they seem to be identical to the 1826 edition, and the work will be cited as Reynolds, *Meditations*.

[14] See the biographical sketch by Chalmers in Reynolds, *Works*, 1:lxx.

a doctor of divinity degree in 1648. Apparently he did quite a bit of preaching in Oxford because in 1624 he was called to the chaplaincy of Lincoln's Inn, London's famous law school. This was a most distinguished pulpit, having been filled at one time by John Donne, one of England's greatest preachers. From his years at Lincoln's Inn we have several collections of his sermons, namely his sermons on Ecclesiastes, his sermons on First John, and a collection of sermons on several chapters from the Pauline Epistles.[15]

Edward Reynolds could hold his own with the literate preachers of the day. His elegant prose, typology, and brilliant biblical metaphors all contributed to his wide reputation. Even more importantly he had a reputation for being a peacemaker. He was a man of irenic spirit. It was not at all surprising, then, that in 1643 he was called to be a member of the Westminster Assembly. By conviction, Edward Reynolds was a Presbyterian. The sort of moderate Puritanism he advocated probably represents the way most Englishmen thought about it in the 1630s. They were not at all sympathetic with the High Church tendencies of the House of Stuart.

As things developed, Edward Reynolds was one of the most influential of the fathers of the Assembly. He was almost always in attendance and took an active role in several subcommittees. He was largely responsible for the moderate, ecumenical spirit, particularly, of the *Confession of Faith*. In the end, he mistakenly assumed the integrity of Charles II and agreed to accept a bishopric in the established Church.

A. The Covenantal Dimension

As one of the more moderate Puritans, Reynolds is of special interest to us. There were, of course, many like him. They remained within the Church of England and yet they read with interest the devotional and theological writings so abundantly published at the time. These moderate Puritans followed the more Protestant

---

[15] These sermons are included in Reynolds, *Works*, vol. 1.

preachers, both those who had conformed and those who had not conformed. It was to such people that Reynolds directed his devotional classic, *Meditations on the Holy Sacrament*.

Reynolds had a strongly covenantal understanding of the sacrament. Right from the beginning he tells us that sacraments are signs and seals of the covenant (cf. Romans 4:11). They confirm to us the promises of God.[16] Here is the teaching we find from the very beginning of the Reformation. Ever since the early sixteenth century this teaching had been elaborated, showing how the rainbow had been a sign of the covenant given to Noah and circumcision a sign of the covenant given to Abraham. Many more examples were added in the century and a half that Protestants had tried to understand the sacraments. There is nothing new or unique here. As Reynolds somewhat elaborately puts it: ". . . So is the sacrament a visible seal, and earnest to the sense: . . . ratifying and confirming the infallible expectation of that future reward, which as well the senses as the soul shall, in God's presence, really enjoy . . ."[17] Reynolds points out that even in the Garden of Eden, there were sacraments. There we find truth veiled in divinely given signs and pictures. They are types of truths yet to be revealed. This connection between typology and sacraments is very strong in the piety of the Reformed faith. God was not communicated even to Adam without the veil of a sacrament. Moses himself did not see God except in a cloud, and even in the New Testament we read that we see now only through a glass darkly.[18]

B. Divine Origin of the Sacrament of Communion

Another typically Reformed emphasis that we find underlined by Reynolds is that the sacraments are of divine institution. They derive both their value and being from the Author who inspired

---

[16] Reynolds, *Meditations*, p. 6.

[17] Reynolds, *Meditations*, p. 7.

[18] Reynolds, *Meditations*, p. 8.

them.[19] One wonders why such simple things, the water of baptism and the bread and wine of communion, should be used for such a noble end. Sounding remarkably like Tertullian, Reynolds points out the simplicity of the Christian sacraments.[20] One might ask if it would not be more appropriate to provide more glorious ceremonies to serve as signs of the covenant. To argue this way would be highly irreverent! Reynolds, true to the Puritan cause, found the elegant ceremonialism of the medieval church superstitious and pretentious. The Puritans liked to call it "will-worship," a literal translation of the Greek term in Colossians 2:23. We must worship as an act of obedience to God's Word rather than as a work of our own creativity.[21] Typically Puritan, Reynolds insists, "Horrible then, and more than heathenish, is the impiety of those, who mixing human inventions and ceremonies of their own unto the substance of these sacred mysteries, and imposing them as divine duties with a necessity of absolute obedience,—do, by that means, wrench Christ's own divine prerogative out of his own hands..."[22] It is God himself who has given us these signs and seals of his holy covenants and it is God himself who determines their form and nature. The bread and wine of communion, like the water of baptism, are appropriate because they are specified by God's Word.

C. Scholastic Terminology

Reynolds may have ended up with a thoroughly Reformed theology of the sacraments, but he often thinks it out in Scholastic terminology. Notice how his chapter on the matter of the Lord's Supper discusses the problem. It all sounds very Platonic. Bread and wine are

---

[19] Reynolds, *Meditations*, p. 13.

[20] See Tertullian, *De baptismo liber: Homily on Baptism*, ed., comm. and trans. Ernest Evans (London: SPCK, 1964).

[21] Reynolds, *Meditations*, pp. 15–16.

[22] Reynolds, *Meditations*, p. 16.

9: The Roots of English Puritanism

the matter of the sacrament while the Word of Christ is the form.[23] He discusses the question in the traditional terms. He tells us that the matter of this sacrament is bread and wine. Disappointingly the terminology does not quite fit. What is meant by "form" is rather uncertain. Protestants are very foolish when they try to explain their eucharistic theology in the terms of Scholasticism. They would do much better to stick with biblical terminology.[24]

Reynolds observes that the use of bread and wine is particularly appropriate as a type or sign of Christ's passion:

> Pictures ought to resemble their originals; and the sacrament, we know, is the picture or type of him who was a man of sorrow; and this picture was drawn, when the day of God's fierce wrath was upon him: and can we expect from it any satisfaction or pleasure to the senses? This body was naked on the cross; it were incongruous to have the sacrament of it pompous on the table. As it was the will of the Father, which Christ both glorifies and admires, to reveal unto babes what he hath hidden from the wise; so is it here his wisdom to communicate, by the meanest instruments, what he hath denied unto the choicest delicates, to feed his Daniels rather with pulse, than with all the dainties on the king's table.[25]

Reynolds' eloquent rhetoric we have quoted once more. One can well believe he was a powerful preacher. Here, however, his profound insight into the nature of the sacrament is what really interests us. Rhetoric is not our principle concern. Even at that we have

---

[23] Reynolds, *Meditations*, pp. 24f.

[24] Scholasticism can mean a method of theological inquiry or it can mean the discussion of theology carried on in Western Europe during the Middle Ages. The center of the discussion is Peter Lombard's *Sentences*. In the sixteenth century in the days of the Protestant Reformation, there were several approaches to using the Scholastic method, among them the *via moderna* and the *via antiqua*, but generally the Rhenish Reformation was interested in getting beyond the Scholastic approach. See Werner Kaegi, *Erasmus ehedem und heute, 1469-1969* (Basel: Helbing and Lichtenhahn, 1969). I was a student working on my dissertation when this book came out. The subject was hotly contested.

[25] Reynolds, *Meditations*, pp. 24–25.

to give one more quotation:

> And if we observe it, divine miracles take ever the poorest and meanest subjects to manifest themselves on. If he want an army to protect his church, flies, and frogs, and caterpillars, and lamps, and pitchers, &c. shall be the strongest soldiers and weapons he useth; the lame and the blind, the dumb, and the dead, water, and clay, these are materials for his power.—Even where thou seest the instruments of God weakest, there expect and admire the more abundant manifestation of his greatness and wisdom: undervalue not the bread and wine in this holy Sacrament, which do better resemble the benefits of Christ crucified, than any other the choicest delicates.[26]

That bread and wine are appropriate signs and seals of the covenant is, to be sure, often expounded in Reformed churches at either a preparatory service before the actual celebration or at the actual eucharistic celebration. One assumes this was a theme often preached by this Puritan bishop of the Church of England. Bread is a sign of God's strengthening us and wine is a sign of God's comforting us. The bread and the wine are furthermore appropriate signs or sacraments of the unity of the Church, for just as the grains grown over the hillsides are joined together into one loaf of bread, so Christians sharing this sacred meal are made one body.[27] This was a popular simile in the literature of the ancient church, as Reynolds obviously knew.

Even at that, in the popular piety of the Reformed Church one makes even more a point of the sacramental acts of Holy Communion. This presumably is what the Scholastic theologians meant by the *form* of the sacrament. First we find that Christ took the bread and wine and blessed it. He gave thanks for it and so consecrated it. He set it apart to a sacred use. That, according to

---

[26] Reynolds, *Meditations*, p. 25. Note the use of the word "delicates."

[27] Reynolds, *Meditations*, p. 31.

9: The Roots of English Puritanism

Reynolds, is why the Apostle Paul calls it a cup of blessing.[28] Right here Reynolds makes an important theological point. It is a point of biblical theology rather than Scholastic theology. Biblical theology makes the point that it is the prayer of thanksgiving which consecrates the gifts of God to our use, our enjoyment, and, yes, even to our need (1 Tim. 4:1–4). This is why the sacrament is often called the Eucharist.[29] It is because the prayer of thanksgiving is at its center. It is its key. It is with this prayer of thanksgiving that our humanity is set apart, anointed, and consecrated to the purpose for which God created it.[30] It is in giving thanks for the creation of sun and moon and stars, for the creation of Adam and Eve and the election of Israel, for the promise of a Savior and the fulfillment of the promise, for the incarnation of Christ, for Christ's sacrifice on the cross and his victory over the grave, and finally for the pouring out of the Holy Spirit and the establishing of the Church, that the grace of God is bestowed upon us. This prayer consecrates God's mighty acts of creation and redemption to our salvation. In giving thanks, we accept the gift and we dedicate ourselves to the perpetual recognition of the debt of service and obedience we owe to God for his inestimable gifts of grace.

If the first act of the sacrament is the giving of thanks over the bread and wine, the second act is the breaking of the bread and the pouring of the wine.[31] This, of course, brings us nearer to the cross. These acts remind us very particularly of the breaking of Christ's body and the pouring out of his blood. Here we notice again the figurative or symbolic nature of the sacrament. The breaking of the bread and the pouring of the wine cannot help but remind us of the crucifixion, the wounding of his body, and the suffering of his soul.

---

[28] Reynolds, *Meditations*, p. 32.
[29] Reynolds, *Meditations*, p. 32.
[30] Reynolds, *Meditations*, p. 33.
[31] Reynolds, *Meditations*, p. 33.

Reynolds goes on to give us a third action of the sacrament, namely, the delivering of the sacrament to those who participate in the service.[32] Here Reynolds emphasizes that as Jesus at the Last Supper delivered these signs to his disciples, so Jesus himself today in our observance of the sacrament reaches out to us, offering to each one of us the blessings of God.

Finally there is a fourth action, and that is the actual eating of the bread and the drinking of the wine.[33] This actual eating and drinking is essential because in this act we receive Christ and all the benefits of his saving work. After we have taken these elements from the hand of Christ we eat the bread he has given us and drink the wine he has poured out for us to signify that we receive Christ. It is in so receiving Christ that we confess to both men and angels that we are members of the household of faith and children of God. It is in this way that we are engrafted into the true vine that our life comes from the crucified and risen Christ. It is here that we enter into the mystical unity between Christ and his Church.

D. Mystical Union with Christ

Reynolds speaks at length on the subject of our mystical union with Christ.[34] What Reynolds has to say is of particular interest and therefore we will again quote him at length.

> We eat and drink the sacrament of Christ crucified, to signify that real and near incorporation of the faithful into Christ their head: for the end of eating is the assimilation of our nourishment, and the turning of it into our own nature and substance: whatsoever cannot be assimilated, is ejected: and thus is it between us and Christ.[35]

---

[32] Reynolds, *Meditations*, p. 34.

[33] Reynolds, *Meditations*, p. 37.

[34] Reynolds, *Meditations*, pp. 42–48.

[35] Reynolds, *Meditations*, p. 42.

9: THE ROOTS OF ENGLISH PURITANISM

For some reason this aspect of Reformed eucharistic theology is often regarded as confusing, but Reynolds actually is quite clear. He goes on to say:

> Whence it cometh that we so often read of the inhabitation of Christ in his church; of his more peculiar presence with, and in, his people; of our spiritual ingrafture into him by faith; of those more near and approaching relations of brotherhood and coinheritance between Christ and us; that mutual interest, fellowship, and society, which we have to each other; with infinite other expressions of that divine and expressless mixture, whereby the faithful are, not only by a consociation of affections and confederacy of wills, but by a real, though mystical, union.[36]

All of this, of course, Reynolds is very carefully bringing out of the New Testament, especially the epistles of the Apostle Paul. As Reynolds sees it, this mystical unity between Christ and his Church is expressly signified by eating and drinking, that is, by sharing a meal. In the sharing of this meal God signs over to us all the blessings and all the promises of the covenant. It is here that Reynolds begins to open up the subject of our union with Christ, or, to use a more theological term, our incorporation with Christ.

While it is true that all mankind may be said to be in Christ in as much as in the mystery of his incarnation he took on himself our human nature, there is beyond this a special union between the elect and Christ which comes about through sharing our faith and devotion to the one truth of the Gospel.[37] Beside this there is a more special union of Christ with the faithful in the resemblance of a building, or again, in the limbs and members of a body. These biblical figures of the church all make the point that Christ

---

[36] Reynolds, *Meditations*, p. 42.
[37] Reynolds, *Meditations*, pp. 45–46.

is the original and wellspring of all spiritual life.[38] The Christian is joined to Christ in that Christ is the source of a new life. This is the mystery of godliness. There is a continual transfusion of the life of Christ into the believer. It is here that the work of the Holy Spirit is most clearly discernable. Purity, holiness, self-control, gentleness, and reverence are the fruit of the Holy Spirit working within us.[39] Reynolds sums up this point by saying that "We eat and drink the Sacrament of Christ's passion, that thereby we may express that more close and sensible pleasure, which the faithful enjoy in receiving of him."[40]

For Reynolds the sacrament of Holy Communion is indeed a sacrament. It is a visible sign and it is in this that something might be learned from its celebration, that we might come to know something that might not otherwise be understood. The good bishop begins his meditation on the real presence with the following:

> Having thus far spoken of the nature and quality of this holy sacrament, it follows in order to treat of the ends or effects thereof, on which depends its necessity, and our comfort. Our sacraments are nothing else but evangelical types or shadows of some more perfect substance.[41]

This phrase, "evangelical types," cannot help but capture our attention. It means the types we find in the New Testament, or the types or figures we find in the Gospel. Reynolds goes on to unpack this phrase:

> For as the legal sacrifices were the shadows of Christ expected, and wrapped up in a cloud of predictions, and in the loins of his predecessors; so this new mystical sacrifice of the gospel is a shadow of Christ, risen indeed, but yet hidden from us under the cloud of those heavens, which shall contain him until the dis-

---

[38] Reynolds, *Meditations*, p. 46.

[39] Reynolds, *Meditations*, p. 47.

[40] Reynolds, *Meditations*, p. 48.

[41] Reynolds, *Meditations*, p. 64.

9: The Roots of English Puritanism

solution of all things. For the whole heavens are but as one great cloud, which intercepts the lustre of that sun of righteousness, who enlighteneth every one that cometh into the world.[42]

E. The Real Presence

Inevitably, of course, Reynolds gets around to the subject of the real presence. He has to get around to this subject because he recognizes the importance of the ecumenical discussion. Much more naturally, however, Reynolds begins his meditations by discussing the covenantal dimension of the sacrament. The sacrament of Holy Communion is the sign and seal of the covenant of grace.

Scholastic theology, however, wants to emphasize the doctrine of the real presence and therefore we read in Chapter XIII, "So then, in this Sacrament we do most willingly acknowledge a real, true, and perfect presence of Christ,—not in, with, or under the elements, considered absolutely in themselves, but with that relative habitude and respect, which they have unto the immediate use, whereunto they are consecrated."[43] While Reynolds understands that Christ is truly present in the observance of the sacrament, he does not believe in anything like the doctrine of transubstantiation. Again we read:

> Nor yet so do we acknowledge any such carnal trans-elementation of the materials in this Sacrament, as if the body or blood of Christ were, by the virtue of consecration, and, by way of a local substitution, in the place of the bread and wine,–but are truly and really by them, though in nature different, conveyed into the souls of those, who by faith receive him.[44]

Reynolds gives quite some time to distinguishing several ways

---

[42] Reynolds, *Meditations*, p. 64.
[43] Reynolds, *Meditations*, p. 68.
[44] Reynolds, *Meditations*, p. 68.

in which we can understand presence. What he finally comes down to is that "we come to a fourth presence of Christ, which is by energy and power. Thus, 'Where two or three be gathered together in his name, Christ is in the midst of them' by the powerful working of his holy Spirit; even as the sun is present to the earth, inasmuch as, by its influence and benignity, it heateth and quickeneth it."[45] The example given here is the presence of the sun which while still in heaven is seen and felt to be present on the earth. This is the classical figure for the Reformed understanding. Unfortunately it is sometimes called the dynamistic view, but this term does not do justice to the concept. The point is made much better by the text of Matthew 28, where the promise is given to those who are baptized that God remains forever with those who are baptized. "Lo, I am with you always" (Matthew 28:20). Furthermore, while this view is often dismissed as "spiritualist," the point, as my doctor father, Jean-Jacques von Allmen used to say, is that God is present at the celebration of the Supper through the work of the Holy Spirit. Reynolds makes this point at considerable length. "The principle of life in a Christian, is the very same, from whence Christ himself, according to his created graces, receiveth life; and that is the Spirit of Christ, a quickening Spirit, and a strengthening Spirit."[46]

In a particularly important chapter, Reynolds directs our attention to what is meant by remembering Christ in the celebration of the sacrament. That we should do this is made particularly clear by the words of Jesus, "Do this in remembrance of me." As Reynolds understands it, this means we are to remember Christ in faith. We are to remember him by receiving him as Savior.[47] Neither an historical memory nor a festival solemnity is sufficient. Here Reynolds is at his best. Again we must quote him. "It is not therefore

---

[45] Reynolds, *Meditations*, p. 72.

[46] Reynolds, *Meditations*, p. 76.

[47] Reynolds, *Meditations*, pp. 104f.

9: THE ROOTS OF ENGLISH PURITANISM

logical, historical, or speculative remembrance of Christ, but an experimental and believing remembrance of him, which we are to use in the receiving of these sacred mysteries, which are not a bare type and resemblance, but a seal also, confirming and exhibiting his death unto each believing soul."[48] Remembering Christ's death is to recount the story of his passion. It is a review and reflection of the story of our salvation and in doing this we adore the Savior who has suffered all this for us. If in our observance of the sacrament we remember Christ in this way, then the sacrament has been properly observed. We recount the history of salvation as our history; we own it and confess that this is the source of our life, the blessing of our existence. So it is that "we must remember the death of Christ with a remembrance of thankfulness."[49]

Finally we must remember the death of Christ as an act of prayer in which we recount the sacrifice of Christ for our redemption. As Reynolds puts it, "We must remember the death of Christ with prayer unto God: for as by faith we apply to ourselves, so by prayer we represent unto God the Father that his death, as the merit and means of reconciliation with him."[50] The point is that this remembering is the ultimate worship, the confession that Christ is our worth, our ultimate Lord.

The last three chapters of Reynolds' work are devoted to the subject of what is traditionally called worthy reception of the sacrament. This will become particularly important as Puritanism developed, but even more during the age of Pietism. At the end of chapter eighteen Reynolds tells us that it is necessary before participating in the communion service to prepare oneself by some "previous devotions."[51] English Puritanism produced an abundant crop of devotional guides for just exactly this sort of devotional reading. In

---

[48] Reynolds, *Meditations*, p. 107.
[49] Reynolds, *Meditations*, p. 107.
[50] Reynolds, *Meditations*, p. 110.
[51] Reynolds, *Meditations*, p. 132.

fact, the publication of this work in 1639 probably was intended to fill just such a need. Reynolds suggests several biblical types for these devotional preparations for receiving the sacraments. It is, Reynolds suggests, like our Savior washing his disciples' feet before instituting the sacrament. Then he provides us with a great text, namely, Psalm 24: "Lift up your heads, O ye gates; and be ye lifted up, ye everlasting doors; and the King of glory shall come in" (Psalm 24:7, KJV).[52]

Reynolds insists on one primary qualification for the worthy reception of the sacrament. That requirement is faith. Nothing is said about articles of faith to which one must subscribe or moral disciplines that must be maintained. Reynolds points out that what is required is a living, vital faith. Baptism is, of course, objectively required, but that is not the concern of Reynolds. Like Puritans generally, Reynolds' primary concern is what is going on in the heart.[53]

F. THE OPERATIONS OF THE HOLY SPIRIT

Not at all surprisingly, therefore, we find that Reynolds gives us a long discussion of the operations of the Holy Spirit. One might say Reynolds gives us a rhapsody on the theme of the operations of the Holy Spirit.[54] The pneumatic dimension of eucharistic theology is very important to Reformed piety.[55] We have already spoken of it briefly, but for Reynolds we notice the following points. First, the Holy Spirit is a spirit of liberty and a spirit of prayer. The Spirit frees us from fear, the fear that we have by nature, the fear that makes us run from God when he calls us to himself. The Holy Spirit is a witness who leads us into all truth. It is because of this that Jesus himself calls the Holy Spirit the

---

[52] Reynolds, *Meditations*, p. 132.

[53] Reynolds, *Meditations*, p. 133.

[54] This rhapsody on the operations of the Holy Spirit looks suspiciously like a list of points and sub-points of a sermon or, better, a series of sermons on the doctrine of the Holy Spirit.

[55] Reynolds, *Meditations*, pp. 137f.

9: THE ROOTS OF ENGLISH PURITANISM

Spirit of Truth (John 14:17). It is the Holy Spirit who convinces us of the truth of God's Word. Then, again, it can be said that the Spirit of God is a seal ratifying to us the covenantal promises. Or, again, the Spirit fashions our hearts into conformity with Christ. He renews in us the image of God.[56]

A figure Scripture often uses for the operations of the Holy Spirit is ointment. Ointment has the quality of penetration. The ointment of the Spirit teaches the faithful all things. It opens their eyes to see the wonders of God's law and the beauty of his grace. Ointment refreshes and heals so that the Holy Spirit is called the Comforter. In the levitical law anointing with oil was a rite used in the consecrating of men to the priesthood. It is in this sense, then, that Christ is said to have been anointed by the Father to the redemption of the world. In the same way Christians are anointed to be a royal priesthood, a holy nation, a people set at liberty (cf. 1 Peter 2:9). Still another figure for the operations of the Holy Spirit is fire (Hebrews 1:9). Fire is a good figure for the work of the Holy Spirit because fire is always active. It never stands still. It is ever doing something.[57] Furthermore, fire always burns up, moves in an upward direction, and spreads wider and higher. So it is the nature of the Spirit of God to ascend. Fire inflames with a heavenly tendency. Fire consumes; it purifies. It is the same way with the Spirit; it transforms all things with its holy activity and cleansing power.

It is the doctrine of the Holy Spirit that preserves us from what might be called sacramental magic. A big point had been made of this at the Council of Basel in the middle of the fifteenth century. The Church in its long history has all too often approached the sacraments as though they were magical rites that needed only to be performed to obtain the blessing of God. What Edward Reynolds would teach us is the importance of transcending the mere observance of rites and discovering the work of the Spirit in the

---

[56] Reynolds, *Meditations*, p. 138.
[57] Reynolds, *Meditations*, p. 139.

reading and preaching of Scripture, the ministry of praise and prayer, and participation in the sacraments.

The sacrament of Holy Communion in the end is a work of the Holy Spirit in our hearts. We should approach the sacrament in a spirit of meditation and prayer. We should participate in the sacrament of Holy Communion meditating on what we are doing and what God is doing for us in this sacrament, so that when we depart from the worshiping assembly we can dedicate ourselves to the service of God and the fellowship and support of our neighbor.[58]

JEREMIAH BURROUGHS

Something of a hardliner, Jeremiah Burroughs (1599–1646) was the staunchest of the staunch Puritans. Greatly admired, to be sure, pious and learned, he was a Congregationalist who would brook no state interference in the affairs of the Church.[59] He was, in fact, an Independent as the British use the term, or, as we Americans use the term, he was a Separatist who under the Stuart dynasty preferred to go into exile in the Netherlands rather than obey the dictates of the "High Church" Anglican bishops. For several years he was pastor of the English congregation in Rotterdam. Only after the Puritan ascendency began to materialize did he finally return to London where he became preacher at two of London's most prominent churches, Cripplegate and Stephany. Burroughs did have the classical theological education for the ministry of the Reformed Church of England at the beginning of the seventeenth century. He had a degree from Emmanuel College, Cambridge. Today he is regarded as one of the most copious fountains of English Protestantism.

---

[58] Reynolds, *Meditations*, p. 140.

[59] For biographical information on Burroughs, see: Phillip Simpson, *A Life of Gospel Peace: A Biography of Jeremiah Burroughs* (Grand Rapids, MI: Reformation Heritage Books, 2011); Barker, *Puritan Profiles*, pp. 80–84.

9: THE ROOTS OF ENGLISH PURITANISM

A. Worship as Sanctifying God's Name

Burroughs has left us a number of literary treasures. He is particularly well known for several series of sermons.[60] His sermons on the Beatitudes are especially prized.[61] He also produced a commentary on Hosea.[62] What is of particular interest to us, however, is his treatise on the nature of worship. Significant is the full title of the work, *Gospel Worship, or, the Right Manner of Sanctifying the Name of God*.[63] The work is unfolded into three parts: sanctifying the name of God in the ministry of the Word, sanctifying the name of God in observing the Lord's Supper, and sanctifying God's name in the exercising of prayer.

Gospel Worship is a series of sermons based on the text of Leviticus 10:3, "I will be sanctified in them that come nigh me, and before all the people I will be glorified." We will begin with Sermon XI, where the discussion of the Lord's Supper begins. Quite appropriately to the introduction of this sermon, Burroughs tells us that the ancient church defined the Lord's Supper as a sacrament. This, Burroughs tells us, we learn from Tertullian. We notice immediately that Burroughs goes back to Tertullian's use of the Latin word *sacramentum*.[64] This is of tremendous importance to our understanding of the unfolding of Reformed sacramental theology, as I have pointed out at several points in my research.

One needs to see the works of Tertullian in context, of course, but the rediscovery of many of his works just at this time gave them special significance. Many of the works of Tertul-

---

[60] One particular volume of sermons is Jeremiah Burroughs, *The Rare Jewel of Christian Contentment*, reprint (London: Banner of Truth Trust, 1964).

[61] Jeremiah Burroughs, *The Saints' Happiness*, reprint (Beaver Falls, PA: Soli Deo Gloria Publications, 1989).

[62] Jeremiah Burroughs, *An Exposition of the Prophecy of Hosea*, reprint (Beaver Falls, PA: Soli Deo Gloria Publications, 1989).

[63] Jeremiah Burroughs, *Gospel Worship, or, the Right Manner of Sanctifying the Name of God*, ed. Don Kistler (Ligonier, PA: Soli Deo Gloria Publications, 1990).

[64] Sermon XI is contained in Burroughs, *Gospel Worship*, pp. 282–309.

lian had been lost during the Middle Ages. In 1521, right at the beginning of the Reformation, a disciple of Erasmus, Beatus Rhenanus, had rediscovered most of Tertullian's lost works and had published them in Basel. Tertullian, who lived at the end of the second century, was the first Christian to write extensively in Latin. Naturally his works were an important source for a lot of new information on the subject of the worship of the ancient church. It was Tertullian apparently who coined the Latin word *sacramentum* and applied it to baptism and the Lord's Supper. These ordinances, Burroughs tells us, were properly to be called "sacraments." A "sacrament" is an oath made by soldiers when they enter the armed services. It is an oath of allegiance to the emperor. Tertullian's explanation of the meaning of the sacraments had a strong influence on early Reformed sacramental theology. This might seem a bit farfetched if it were not that Konrad Pellikan, one of the early Reformed pastors of Zurich, had written the preface to the new edition of Tertullian. The Reformers of Zurich had enthusiastically received the newly rediscovered writings of Tertullian. They knew them well.[65]

Burroughs, being on top of this discussion, tells us that from the very word *sacramentum* we understand that when we come to the Lord's Supper we come to seal a covenant with God. We come to make an oath, a solemn promise, before God. When we properly understand this then the sacred service is nothing less than a holy communion with the God and Father of our Lord Jesus Christ.[66] To receive the bread and wine of the Lord's Supper is to enter into fellowship with God and with one another in the household of faith, as we have it in 1 Corinthians 10:16 (KJV): "The cup of blessing which we bless, is it not the communion of the blood of Christ? The bread which we break, is it not the communion of the body of Christ?"

[65] For further discussion of the influence of Tertullian on the Protestant Reformers, see Hughes Oliphant Old, *The Patristic Roots of Reformed Worship*, American edition (Black Mountain, NC: Worship Press, 2004), pp. 109 and 286–287.

[66] Burroughs, *Gospel Worship*, p. 283.

9: The Roots of English Puritanism

One thing ought to be clear from the beginning, and that is the basically covenantal eucharistic theology of Jeremiah Burroughs.

B. Fencing the Table

Most of us feel a certain amount of embarrassment when we get to the subject of church discipline and its relation to the observance of the Lord's Supper. Our culture tends to look rather skeptically at any kind of discipline. We take great pride in our inclusiveness. This was not the way things were in the seventeenth century. Then, the church had an appreciation for the need of church discipline. This was the case all across the board from the Jesuits to the English Separatists.

As the Puritans saw it, the problem was that, once the authority of the Roman Pope had been denied, the State had developed a tendency to insist that all authority ultimately resided with it. The Stuart dynasty firmly believed in the divine right of kings. That the English Church might have its own authority was unacceptable to both James I and Charles I. This was what the Puritan revolution was all about. When it gets down to the question of eucharistic discipline the real problem is the danger that Protestantism simply become a civil religion, a series of customs and ceremonies that bind a nation together. The Puritans understood that Christianity had to be a way of life, a system of values, and a living faith in the God of Abraham, Isaac, and Jacob, the God and Father of our Lord Jesus Christ, rather than a series of rites for making it through the passages of life. If Burroughs largely devotes his first sermon on the Lord's Supper to this subject of eucharistic discipline, this is surely the reason. The English Puritans were concerned that Protestant Christianity not simply devolve into a civil religion.

The fencing of the table goes far back in the history of the liturgy. Basically it is on the one hand an invitation to the faithful to approach the holy table, and on the other a warning to those who are not at peace with God to abstain from the sacrament. Sometimes this fencing of the table included a whole catalogue of sins which were thought to prevent worthy communion. Sometimes this fencing is put very delicately, and sometimes it is rather blunt. What it amounts to is the excommunicating of members of the church who are for one reason or another to be considered scandalous. Divorced Roman Catholics today can get quite sensitive about this, but then the same is true about politicians who approve of abortion. Mainline Congregationalists and Presbyterians today would not dare to warn members of the congregation to refrain from approaching the table, no matter what might be the problem. That would be a sin against inclusiveness.

Burroughs is, of course, aware of the role of the dismissals in the liturgies of the ancient church.[67] After the reading of the Scriptures and the preaching of the sermon, the deacon would cry out, "Holy things to the Holy," or, in other words, holy blessings for a holy people.[68] The Reformation liturgies generally preserved the dismissals but we also notice that they usually balanced the dismissals with an invitation, encouraging those of true faith, repentant of their sins, to come to the holy table and receive the eucharistic bread and wine. The problem, of course, was that sometimes this fencing of the table got much more attention than the encouragement to participate. That is certainly the case with this sermon.

The body of the sermon is made up of five requirements for the true worship of God. Starting with the third commandment, "Thou shalt not take the name of the Lord thy God in vain," Burroughs gives us five principles.[69] First we should notice that those who would sanctify God's name must themselves be holy.[70] Here we find in the clearest possible terms one of the primary principles of Separatism as it developed among the English Puritans of the seventeenth cen-

---

[67] See Hughes Oliphant Old, *The Patristic Roots of Reformed Worship* (Black Mountain, NC: Worship Press, 2004) pp. 271–282.

[68] Burroughs, *Gospel Worship*, p. 293.

[69] Burroughs, *Gospel Worship*, p. 292.

[70] Burroughs, *Gospel Worship*, p. 293.

9: THE ROOTS OF ENGLISH PURITANISM

tury. Incidentally, this was the difference between the Puritans who founded the Plymouth Plantation in 1620 and the Puritans who founded Massachusetts Bay a few years later. Our preacher brings up the distinction between a converting ordinance and a nourishing ordinance. The preaching of the Word is a converting ordinance. It is performed among any that care to listen, but the Lord's Supper is only to be observed, according to the Separatists, among those who have previously been converted. The covenant must already have been made before the seal can be set upon it.[71]

This argumentation will become quite prominent in the eighteenth century. Both John Wesley and Jonathan Edwards will become interested in the issue, as we will see later on. Here, however, Burroughs argues that only logically can a child take nourishment if that child first has life. Let no dead soul come to this ordinance! Only those who are genuinely converted should participate. Otherwise God's name is taken in vain.[72] Here, of course, is the whole point of Burroughs' liturgical theology. Worship must above all glorify God's name, as we find it in the text, "I will be sanctified in them that come nigh me . . ." (Lev. 10:3, KJV).

Burroughs returns to that key text, "Let a man examine himself and so come to the Supper" (cf. 1 Cor. 11:28). We are to prepare for the Supper by examining ourselves in regard to our godliness. We are to examine the work of God in our souls. What graces has the Holy Spirit poured out on us? How is it we have been brought into the covenant? Only those who discover indications of God's work in their hearts should come to receive the Supper.[73] Yet another requirement for the worthy reception of the Supper is that there be communion not only with God but with his saints as well.[74] Apparently it is not only a matter of holy individu-

---

[71] Burroughs, *Gospel Worship*, p. 294.

[72] Burroughs, *Gospel Worship*, p. 295.

[73] Burroughs, *Gospel Worship*, p. 296.

[74] Burroughs, *Gospel Worship*, p. 297.

als but a holy assembly. Here is the big idea, and for the rest of his sermon Burroughs develops it thoroughly.

The next sermon comes down very hard on what is required for worthy participation in the Lord's Supper.[75] At the head of the list Burroughs puts the importance of fully understanding what one is doing when one participates in the Supper.[76] One must have a solid knowledge of a covenantal theology of the sacrament. One must realize that one has come to this holy table to renew the covenant. One must participate by beholding in visual representation the mystery upon which angels long to look. This mystery is set out before us that it might be sealed and we join the communion of the saints.[77] This is all standard Reformed teaching on the nature of the sacrament.

C. Worship as Meditation on the Cross

There is one thing here that is a typically seventeenth-century development. As we read on we become more and more aware that, as Burroughs understands it, a major part of the celebration of the Supper is the meditation of the recipient. It is, above all, a meditation on the passion of Christ.[78] We are to picture Christ being on the Cross.[79] Some of us may figure Burroughs has gone too far here. He seems almost like Ignatius Loyola. It is nevertheless in this meditating that one moves from beholding the cross to closing with Christ. It is in this meditating on the cross that we set our "Amen" to the promise of the gospel. Burroughs opens this up, showing how in the eucharistic meditation we should become aware of the gravity of our sin, the pain and suffering it laid on Jesus in his passion, and the redemptive glory of his sacrifice. This devotional meditation should

---

[75] For Sermon XII, see Burroughs, *Gospel Worship*, pp. 310–339.
[76] Burroughs, *Gospel Worship*, p. 313.
[77] Burroughs, *Gospel Worship*, p. 314.
[78] Burroughs, *Gospel Worship*, p. 315.
[79] Burroughs, *Gospel Worship*, p. 317.

9: THE ROOTS OF ENGLISH PURITANISM 353

bring us both to repentance and to thanksgiving that Christ's death in the end brings us to salvation. It must be said that Burroughs does allow for both joy and thanksgiving in his eucharistic meditation, but in the end this meditation puts the emphasis on repentance. The heavy weight of the meditation is on the passion. This is penitential worship through and through.

One more major point Burroughs makes is that the observance of the Lord's Supper is of divine institution and therefore we are to observe it as it was instituted, departing neither to the right nor to the left.[80] We should be careful not to introduce ceremonies of human invention. Particularly objectionable is the custom of having the minister hand first the bread and then the wine to each communicant. It would be better for the communicants to pass it to each other. The minister should serve the first communicant and he or she should pass it to the next communicant so that each communicant is both served and serves.[81]

The "High Church" expected the communicants to come forward to the altar and receive the bread and wine kneeling. The Puritans, like the Scottish Presbyterians, sat around the table to receive the sacred meal. Burroughs makes the point that in the heavenly banquet we will sit down with Abraham and judge the nations. As Burroughs sees it, there is real spiritual significance in this table gesture. It makes visible the eucharistic typology of sharing a meal in the house of the Father.[82]

---

[80] Burroughs, *Gospel Worship*, p. 340.

[81] Burroughs, *Gospel Worship*, p. 345.

[82] Burroughs, *Gospel Worship*, p. 342.

10
THE PURITANS AT WESTMINSTER

The *Westminster Directory for the Publique Worship of God* was received by Parliament on January 3, 1645, just a little more than a century after the *Genevan Psalter* of 1542. It reflects the vigorous discussion Protestants in the English-speaking world carried on in their efforts to reform Christian worship according to the Word of God.[1] The *Westminster Directory* was a compromise document. Stephen Marshall headed the committee which drafted it. Marshall was a convinced

---

[1] Among the many versions of the *Westminster Directory* which have been published over the years are the following: *A Directory for the Publique Worship of God, Throughout the Three Kingdoms of England, Scotland, and Ireland* (London: Printed for Evan Tyler, Alexander Fifield, Ralph Smith, and John Field, 1644); *The Confessions of Faith, Catechisms, Directories, Form of Church-Government, Discipline, etc., of Public Authority in the Church of Scotland* (Glasgow: Printed by Robert and Thomas Duncan for the Church of Scotland, 1771); *The Directory for the Publick Worship of God* (New York: Reprinted for Robert Lenox Kennedy, 1880); *A New Directory for the Public Worship of God: Found on the Book of Common Order, 1560–64, and the Westminster Directory, 1643–45* (Edinburgh: Printed for the Free Church of Scotland by MacNiven and Wallace, 1898); *The Directory for the Worship of God*, found in *The Constitution of the Presbyterian Church in the United States of America* (Philadelphia: Published for the General Assembly by the Board of Christian Education of the Presbyterian Church in the U.S.A., 1955), pp. 335–355; *The Directory for the Publick Worship of God*, found in *Westminster Confession of Faith* (Inverness, UK: Printed by John C. Eccles for the Publications Committee of the Free Presbyterian Church of Scotland, 1976); and *The Westminster Directory: Being a Directory for the Publique Worship of God in the Three Kingdomes*, intro. Ian Breward (Bramcote: Grove Books, 1980). Among recent works on the subject are John L. Carson and David W. Hall, eds., *To Glorify and Enjoy God: A Commemoration of the 350th Anniversary of the Westminster Assembly* (Edinburgh and Carlisle, PA.: The Banner of Truth Trust, 1994); and Richard A. Muller and Rowland S. Ward, *Scripture and Worship: Biblical Interpretation and the Directory for Public Worship* (Phillipsburg, NJ: Presbyterian & Reformed Publishing, 2007). Quotations will be from the 1976 edition published by the Free Church of Scotland and cited as *Westminster Directory*.

355

Presbyterian but he was determined to keep the Congregationalists in the discussion. Marshall had a strong sense not only of the theological appropriateness, but also of the political necessity of keeping the Protestant witness together.[2] When he submitted the first draft to the Assembly he admitted that a consensus had been achieved only with much patience. Although Marshall, one of the staunchest Presbyterians, had been chairman of the committee, Thomas Goodwin, one of the most articulate of the Congregationalists, balanced Marshall and the Presbyterians more than adequately.

The *Westminster Directory* was anything but a clone of the *Genevan Psalter*. The continental Reformation certainly had a tremendous influence: many of the deepest insights of the *Genevan Psalter* were taken up by the *Westminster Directory*, but others show little trace. The reform of worship had taken a very different route in the British Isles than it had in the Upper Rhineland. The Puritans had other roots, and they were concerned with other problems. To be very clear, the *Westminster Directory* has its own insights and its own genius.[3]

Not the least of these insights is the recognition of the importance of the freedom and spontaneity of public worship. The Westminster divines were determined at all costs to rise above "canned" liturgical prayers. They had no interest in producing a literary masterpiece that could be read again and again to the point of boredom. The Westminster divines had a vision of prayer that welled up from a pastoral heart—prayer brooded over by the Holy Spirit. They saw prayer as a sort of pastoral rhapsody like the High Priestly Prayer of Jesus. This was the real point of the Puritan objection to the *Book of Common Prayer*. The Puritans wanted more than memorized prayers. They wanted ministers who were men of prayer, who knew how to lead in prayer, and who could

---

[2] William S. Barker, *Puritan Profiles, Fifty-four Puritans: Personalities Drawn Together by the Westminster Assembly* (Fearn, UK: Christian Focus Publications, 1996), pp. 120–127.

[3] Even Strasbourg, Zurich, and Geneva were not at all carbon copies of each other, and if variety existed even within the continental Reformation, we should not be surprised to find that the English Reformation also had its own unique qualities.

10: THE WESTMINSTER PURITANS

formulate prayers for the occasion. They wanted ministers who by their examples taught their people to pray.

When it comes specifically to the celebration of the Lord's Supper, the Puritans had a vision of the sacrament as the communion of a Christian congregation with God, the God and Father of our Lord Jesus Christ. It was a communion in the household of faith, a wedding feast given by the King for his Son. Another one of the visions which guided the *Westminster Directory* was its high sense of the sanctification of the Lord's Day. For the seventeenth-century Puritan the celebration of the Lord's Supper was bathed in the peace and calm of the Christian Sabbath. It is on the day of resurrection that the Christian congregation comes together to celebrate the mighty acts of God which have won our redemption. The whole service must be seen in this light.

A. Frequency of Celebration

When we look at the specific directions for the celebration of the sacrament of Holy Communion, the first thing we find is a discussion of the frequency with which the Supper is to be celebrated. The question is not decided by the *Directory* other than to say it should be celebrated frequently. It is left to the pastor and those in charge of the pastoral care of the congregation to decide exactly how often. Apparently there was considerable diversity in English Protestant congregations in the middle of the sixteenth century. As is well known, Calvin had advocated that the sacrament be celebrated each Lord's Day. On the other hand, neither he nor any of the Reformers wanted to celebrate the sacrament without the participation of the congregation. For centuries the congregation had come to church Sunday by Sunday to watch the celebration, but not to partake. One could hardly expect the congregation suddenly to present itself every Lord's Day to receive the Lord's Supper when for centuries the Supper had been received but once a year at Easter. In some areas, Protestant churches celebrated the sacrament more frequently than others.

For one reason or another, there was considerable popular resistance to the weekly celebration. The moral and spiritual intensity required for weekly communion was more than the average congregation could support. Perfunctory celebrations were an offense to the Puritans. The dilemma was simply that if the Puritans insisted on a frequent celebration, the celebrations would become more routine. If they wanted a more intense celebration they would have to be less frequent. This would allow for preparatory services with special preaching to help communicants prepare for the sacrament as well as to allow the elders to exercise true sacramental discipline.

Confronted with a choice between weekly celebrations that lacked intensity and more disciplined and intense celebrations observed less frequently, the Puritans chose the latter. The sacredness of the sacrament was a fundamental assumption. The Puritans, of course, were not the first Christians to be confronted with this problem. Already at the end of the fourth century both John Chrysostom and Augustine had been confronted with the problem of Christians who came to the sacred service but did not receive communion. Sometimes it was because of an overly scrupulous concern that they not receive the sacrament unworthily; sometimes it was simply that they had settled for a lukewarm Christian life and a partial commitment and were afraid to come too close to God lest they fall under his judgment.

B. Preparation for the Sacrament

The *Westminster Directory* makes a point of the pastoral preparation of the congregation for the observance of the Lord's Supper. We read that if the communion is not celebrated frequently the congregation should be notified on the Lord's Day beforehand and either at that time, or at some time during the week before the observance, there should be some teaching about the appropriate

10: THE WESTMINSTER PURITANS

preparation for the participation of the sacrament. Many of us will remember the preparatory services which until recent times were such a regular feature of Reformed devotional life. We have spoken at some length of how these preparatory services were developed in Geneva during Calvin's pastorate there. In Scotland they were observed with impressive solemnity. Later on in this study, we will give attention to a work by John Willison which discusses this preparation for the Supper at length.

According to the Puritans, nothing should be avoided quite so carefully as allowing the ignorant or the scandalous to take part in the service. Nothing could harm them more than to allow them to participate. Young people before their first communion were expected to recite the catechism. The Westminster Assembly provided its *Shorter Catechism* for this purpose. The scandalous were to be reconciled to the church before being admitted to the Lord's Table. The Assembly carefully worked out the procedure for this in the *Book of Discipline*. The great reverence the Puritans had for the sacrament of the Lord's Supper is manifested by the care with which they tried to avoid casual participation. Fundamental to the Puritan understanding of this communion was that it was a whole-hearted, whole life, commitment to God, to his people, and to the ways of the Christian life. That was what the covenant was all about.

C. Sunday Celebration

The actual celebration of the Supper was supposed to follow the usual Sunday morning sermon with its prayers and psalms. It began with an exhortation or invitation. While the ignorant and the scandalous were warned not to participate, the repentant were invited, and even warmly encouraged, to participate. By way of inviting the congregation to participate, the minister is first of all to remind the congregation of the ". . . inestimable benefit we have by this sacrament . . ." and of ". . . the great necessity of having our comforts and strength renewed thereby in this our pilgrimage and warfare: how necessary it is that we come unto it with knowledge, faith, repentance, love, and with hungering and thirsting souls after Christ and his benefits: how great the danger to eat and drink unworthily."[4] While in these remarks he is to warn those who would participate casually not to approach the table, he is on the other hand to ". . . encourage all that labour under the sense of the burden of their sins, and fear wrath, and desire to reach out unto a greater progress in grace than yet they can attain unto, to come to the Lord's table; assuring them, . . . of . . . refreshing, and strength to their weak and wearied souls."[5]

D. Arrangement of and at the Table

The next thing we find in the *Westminster Directory for Worship* is a statement of how the table and the seating about it is to be arranged. This was of high importance to the thoroughgoing and serious Protestants of the period. The celebration of the Lord's Supper was to look like a meal. It was not to look like the sacrifice of the mass as it was performed at the high altar of a medieval cathedral. The text actually reads that the table is to be so placed, "that the communicants may orderly sit about it, or at it."[6] The practice of lining up to receive the bread and wine from the hand of the minister or the practice of kneeling at the altar rail hardly conveyed the idea of the family of God sharing a meal together. In some places a large table was specially set up at which the communicants could sit. This was particularly the usage in Scotland. It was also a common practice in the Netherlands. In other places the practice was to arrange the pews around three sides of the communion table so that the congregation was gathered "about the table." This was the way the seating was set up, Sunday by Sunday, whether communion was to be celebrated or not. On

---

[4] *Westminster Directory*, p. 384.

[5] *Westminster Directory*, p. 385.

[6] *Westminster Directory*, p. 385.

communion Sundays, then, the congregation remained in place. With the assistance of the elders and the deacons, the communicants served each other. In this way the visual impression of the people sharing a meal together was clearly emphasized. Visual elements such as this had always been important in the Reformed celebration of the sacrament. Seeing the congregation gathered together about the table was fundamental to the sacramental sign.[7]

The rubrics tell us that, before the service, the table is to be "decently covered" and that the bread and wine are to be in "comely and convenient vessels." This we take to mean that the communion vessels are to be attractive and appropriate. In the Netherlands, particularly, one took care to use the finest table linens, while in England churches often had beautiful silver plate for the communion vessels. Furthermore we read that the bread is to be "so prepared, that, 'being broken' by the minister 'and given' it may be distributed amongst the communicants; the wine also in large cups."[8] In the Scottish *Book of Common Order*, the rubrics had been very clear that the bread was to be broken, and the wine was to be poured out in the sight of the people. For the Scottish service this is obviously one of the visual elements of the sacramental sign. Less concerned about breaking the bread and pouring the wine, the *Westminster Directory* emphasizes that the communicants are to pass the elements one to another. Remembering that the Gospel of Luke specifically reports that Jesus told his disciples to take the cup and divide it among themselves (Luke 22:17), the fathers of the Westminster Assembly taught that the members of the congregation are to serve each other. The sacred food was not, as it were, to be passed out by the hands of the clergy alone. This sharing one with another is one of the major visual elements of the sacrament.

---

[7] See the most recent study of this subject by my student Walter Taylor in his doctoral dissertation at Erskine Theological Seminary: Walter L. Taylor, *As They Sat at Table: Presbyterian Communion Practices*, D. Min dissertation (Due West, SC: Erskine Theological Seminary, 2012).

[8] *Westminster Directory*, p. 385.

We will see this very clearly again with Matthew Henry, then again with John Willison, and finally in America with Timothy Dwight.

E. Liturgical Elements

According to the *Westminster Directory for Worship*, the bread and the wine are to be "set apart and sanctified to this holy use, by the word of institution and prayer."[9] The Words of Institution are to be read from either one of the gospels or from 1 Corinthians. The minister may make commentary on the reading if he finds it appropriate. With this the minister offers the prayer of thanksgiving or blessing over the bread and wine. This, properly speaking, is the Eucharistic Prayer. It is, above all, a prayer of thanksgiving for all the blessings we have received from the hand of God. It is a thanksgiving especially ". . . for that great benefit of our redemption, the love of God the Father, the sufferings and merits of the Lord Jesus Christ the Son of God, by which we are delivered; and for all means of grace, the word and sacraments; and for this sacrament in particular, by which Christ, and all his benefits, are applied and sealed up unto us. . . ."[10]

It was expected, of course, that the minister in his prayer would enlarge at length on this thanksgiving for God's mighty acts of creation and then of redemption. This was the *anamnesis*. This prayer is not only to give thanks, but also "to profess that there is no other name under heaven by which we can be saved, but the name of Jesus Christ, by whom alone we receive liberty and life, have access to the throne of grace, are admitted to eat and drink at his own table, and are sealed up by his Spirit to an assurance of happiness and everlasting life."[11] According to the Apostle Paul, whenever we celebrate the Lord's Supper, we proclaim the Lord's death until he comes. In this sacred supper we give thanks to God, thereby wit-

---

[9] *Westminster Directory*, p. 385.

[10] *Westminster Directory*, p. 385.

[11] *Westminster Directory*, p. 385.

nessing before the world our source of liberty and life. We proclaim God's saving mercy to us. We take to ourselves, before the congregation, the body offered up for our salvation and the cup poured out that we might have life. Again, the visual element of being "admitted to eat and drink at his own table" is underlined.

This prayer has first of all the eucharistic dimension; it is a prayer of thanksgiving. Second it has the kerygmatic dimension; it proclaims the Lord's death until he comes. It is a witness to the congregation of God's people as well as to the world. But finally the prayer has another dimension, the epicletic dimension. It prays that through the working of the Holy Spirit in our hearts we might be one with Christ and he one with us. The prayer tip-toes through the theological issues which had been discussed, especially in England, since the beginning of the Reformation.[12]

Returning to the prayer before us, we notice that God, the Father of all mercies, is called upon:

> . . . to vouchsafe his gracious presence, and the effectual working of his Spirit in us; and so to sanctify these elements both of bread and wine, and to bless his own ordinance, that we may receive by faith the body and blood of Jesus Christ, crucified for us, and so to feed upon him, that he may be one with us, and we one with him; that he may live in us, and we in him, and to him who hath loved us, and given himself for us.[13]

As we have said, the English church had for several generations tried to find a middle way to understand the doctrine of Christ's presence in the sacrament of communion. What the *Westminster Directory for Worship* attempted here is to find a statement that could satisfy moderates on both sides of the discussion. It is likely that the Fathers of the Westminster Assembly agreed that the commu-

---

[12] In fact, when talking of English theology, we really have to go all the way back to John Wycliffe, who as early as the fourteenth century began to challenge the eucharistic theology of late medieval Scholasticism.

[13] *Westminster Directory*, p. 385.

nion service of the *Book of Common Prayer* gave too much room for a superstitious understanding of the Supper. On the other hand, they wanted to make clear that Christ is indeed present. The divine presence is affirmed, although nothing is said about how that presence is understood. The prayer asks that the Holy Spirit sanctify the bread and wine and the congregation. It also asks that we receive the body and blood of Christ, although in what sense we are to receive it is left unsaid. Finally there is a statement of the covenantal dimension of the sacrament. We are to pray that we be united to Christ and that he be united to us. One could very easily complain about the inadequacies of this statement, but simplicity and moderation are its greatest value. It leaves many theological issues open, while humbly receiving the mystery of our union with Christ.

Having concluded the eucharistic prayer, the minister "is to take the bread in his hand," break it, and give it to the communicants, saying, "According to the holy institution, command, and example of our blessed Savior Jesus Christ, I take this bread, and having given thanks, break it, and give it unto you; . . . *Take ye, eat ye; this is the body of Christ which is broken for you: do this in remembrance of him*."[14] Following the same procedure the minister is to take the cup, and giving it to the congregation he is to say, "*This cup is the new testament in the blood of Christ, which is shed for the remission of the sins of many: drink ye all of it.*"[15]

After all had received communion, the minister may have given a short exhortation urging the congregation to live a life worthy of the grace they had received. This was then followed by a prayer of dedication asking the assistance of the Holy Spirit that the communicants would be strengthened to live a good Christian life. Finally a collection was taken for the poor. Strangely enough nothing is said about the concluding psalmody or hymnody. From other sources we know that was the usual practice, and, of course,

---

[14] *Westminster Directory*, pp. 385–86.

[15] *Westminster Directory*, p. 386.

10: THE WESTMINSTER PURITANS 365

the whole service would be concluded with a benediction. The deacons' collection, at the close of the service, honors this rubric even down to our own time. That the sacrament of the Lord's Supper was to have a diaconal dimension was a significant feature of Puritan eucharistic piety.

RICHARD BAXTER'S
REFORMED LITURGY, 1661

Deeply devout and truly original, Richard Baxter was one of the most creative theological thinkers of the seventeenth century.[16] Yet, systematic theology was not really his strong point. One might say he was a theologian of the heart. He was a man of prayer and piety and he had a way with words. In fact he left us some two hundred written works, a good portion of which were devotional works. He was an outstanding preacher; at least, that was the reputation he had. Few of his sermons, however, have survived. His most beloved work, one of the devotional classics of Puritanism,

---

[16] Among the many works by and about Richard Baxter are the following: Richard Baxter, *The Autobiography of Richard Baxter* (London and Toronto: J. M. Dent & Sons, Ltd., 1925); Richard Baxter, *A Christian Directory: or, A Summ of Practical Theologie* (London: Printed by Robert White, for Nevill Simmons, 1673); Richard Baxter, *The English Nonconformity, as Under King Charles II, and King James II* (London: Printed by Tho. Parkhurst, 1690); Richard Baxter, *The Practical Works of Richard Baxter*, 4 vols. (Ligonier, PA: Soli Deo Gloria Publications, 1990–91), hereinafter, Baxter, *Works*; J. William Black, *Reformation Pastors: Richard Baxter and the Ideal of the Reformed Pastor* (Carlisle [England]: Paternoster Press, 2004); Edmund Calamy, *An Abridgement of Mr. Baxter's History of His Life and Times* (London: Printed for J. Lawrence, etc., 1713); John Hamilton Davies, *The Life of Richard Baxter of Kidderminster* (London: W. Kent, 1887); Nigel Knowles, *Richard Baxter of Kidderminster* (Bewdley: Star and Garter, 2000); Charles F. Kemp, *A Pastoral Triumph: The Story of Richard Baxter and His Ministry at Kidderminster* (New York: Macmillan Co., 1948); Irvonwy Morgan, *The Nonconformity of Richard Baxter* (London: Epworth Press,[1946]); Geoffrey Fillingham Nuttall, *Richard Baxter* (Stanford: Stanford University Press, 1965); William Orme, *The Life and Times of the Rev. Richard Baxter*, 2 vols. (Boston: Crocker & Brewster; and New York: J. Leavitt, 1831); Frederick J. Powicke, *The Life of the Reverend Richard Baxter: 1615–1691* (Boston: Houghton Mifflin Co., 1824); and John Tulloch, *English Puritanism and its Leaders: Cromwell, Milton, Baxter, Bunyan* (Edinburgh: Blackwood, 1861).

is *The Saints' Everlasting Rest*.[17] Another perennially popular work of his, *The Reformed Pastor*, is a manual of pastoral care.[18] Baxter, so typical of Puritanism, was an experiential theologian. It was religious experience that interested him. Theologically he is supposed to have been a bit soft, especially when it came to the question of Arminianism. But this is probably to be explained by the fact that his priority was not systematic theology but rather questions of piety and religious experience.[19]

For our purposes, his work *The Reformed Liturgy* is of the greatest possible interest.[20] Put together in the course of a few days in 1661, it was an attempt to produce a document that would express something of how the Puritans thought worship ought to go. The Puritan cause was politically defeated in 1661. Cromwell's commonwealth had failed, and the Stuart monarchy had been restored. To be sure, Baxter, like so many of the moderate Puritans, had never countenanced the measures of Cromwell. Moderate Puritans like Baxter had opposed the execution of Charles I and even supported the restoration of Charles II. Baxter was one of many Puritans who had hoped that after Cromwell's commonwealth a more moderate form of Puritanism could be worked out. Charles II, recognizing the importance of moderate Puritan support, made a few symbolic

---

[17] There are many editions of this work, such as: Richard Baxter, *The Saints' Everlasting Rest* (Evansville, IN: Sovereign Grace Book Club, 1950); and Richard Baxter, *The Saints' Everlasting Rest*, ed. and introduced John T. Wilkinson (Vancouver: Regent College Publications, 2004). This work is also contained in volume 3 of Baxter, *Works*.

[18] This volume has many editions, among which are: Richard Baxter, *The Reformed Pastor*, ed. Hugh Martin (London: SCM Press, 1956); Richard Baxter, *The Reformed Pastor* (Edinburgh and Carlisle, PA: Banner of Truth, 1974); and Baxter, *Works*, volume 4.

[19] This aspect of Baxter's theology is discussed in Carter Lindberg, ed., *The Pietist Theologians: An Introduction to Theology in the Seventeenth and Eighteenth Centuries* (Malden, MA: Blackwell Publications, 2005).

[20] Baxter's *The Reformed Liturgy* is part of Richard Baxter, *A Christian Directory*, as contained in Baxter, *Works*, 1:923–948. The work will be cited as Baxter, *Reformed Liturgy*.

gestures in that direction although he had no intention of satisfying even the least of the Puritans' demands.

The Savoy Conference of 1661 was one of these symbolic gestures.[21] It met at the warrant of the king. Included in the conference were twelve Anglican bishops and twelve Presbyterian ministers. The *Book of Common Prayer* was discussed from the fifteenth of April to the twenty-fourth of July. The bishops had little interest in making any accommodations to the Presbyterians and as a result the Presbyterians who persisted in their views were required to leave the Church of England. At one point in the conference, Richard Baxter was asked to draw up a liturgy that Presbyterians would find acceptable. This he did very quickly in the course of a few days. *The Reformed Liturgy* is what he produced.

The Presbyterians did not really want a Presbyterian *Book of Common Prayer*, which was apparently what the bishops wanted Baxter to produce. Both they and the Congregationalists wanted a directory for public worship. What they really wanted was something like the *Westminster Directory* almost twenty years before. If they had to make it look like the *Book of Common Prayer* to satisfy the king and his bishops then Baxter's *Reformed Liturgy* could serve the purpose. Sad to say, Baxter's proposals were never seriously discussed. The bishops had only one thing in mind, the submission of the Presbyterians and the total defeat of Puritanism of all sorts.

What Baxter's *Reformed Liturgy* really tells us is how a moderate Puritan conducted worship. This is especially true of the prayers. These prayers give us an insight into how the Puritan pastor prayed. Not all Puritan pastors had the magnificent language Baxter was able to formulate, but using the language well was the heart of a good education in that age and ministers worked very hard at learning how to speak spontaneously and do it with both clarity and beauty. Above all they gave the most careful attention to leading in prayer.

---

[21] For a recent discussion of the Savoy Conference of 1661, see Colin Buchanan, ed., *The Savoy Conference Revisited: The Proceedings Taken from the Grand Debate of 1661 and the Works of Richard Baxter* (Cambridge, UK: Grove Books, Ltd., 2002).

Richard Baxter lived when baroque culture was at its height. John Milton was his contemporary. From the standpoint of literary style his work was intricate, learned, and convoluted perhaps, but it was rich and full of meaning. To appreciate Baxter's accomplishment we need to realize that he did not have the advantage of a formal university education. He was not a product of either Oxford or Cambridge. Besides that, he never studied abroad. He did, however, read prodigiously. Rather surprisingly he read widely among the Schoolmen of the Middle Ages. Apparently it was the Nominalists who most interested him. The continental Reformers seem to have had little direct influence on him. He was from beginning to end an English theologian.

Turning to the communion service which we find in the *Reformed Liturgy* we notice that it follows rather closely what the *Westminster Directory* had outlined. Baxter leaves considerable latitude in some of the matters which were vigorously discussed. Whether one was to bless the bread and wine with separate prayers or whether they might be blessed at the same time in a single prayer was left open. In the same way, the Words of Institution might follow the epiclesis or they might precede it. Even the question of receiving the bread and the wine kneeling or standing or sitting is left open. What attracts us most about this eucharistic liturgy is not the rubrics but the prayers. They tell us much about the eucharistic piety of the Puritans. Compared to the prayers of the sixteenth century they are much more devotional. That is, they express a devotional intensity which we do not find in the more objective prayers of the Reformers, or, for that matter, the patristic prayers. Baxter's communion prayers have a strong epicletic dimension. What we mean by this is that they are prayers of supplication, prayers in which we express our need and call on God to supply that need. Let us look at several of Baxter's prayers in particular.

10: THE WESTMINSTER PURITANS

A. Collect for Pardon

First we notice a short collect which Baxter provides after the bread and the wine have been consecrated by prayer and the Words of Institution have been read:

> Most merciful Saviour, as thou hast loved us to the death, and suffered for our sins, the just for the unjust, and hast instituted this holy sacrament to be used in remembrance of thee till thy coming; we beseech thee, by thine intercession with the Father, through the sacrifice of thy body and blood, give us the pardon of our sins, and thy quickening Spirit, without which the flesh will profit us nothing. Reconcile us to the Father; nourish us as thy members to everlasting life. Amen.[22]

That this prayer is addressed to the Savior, rather than to the Father, immediately claims our attention. This is not the usual practice in public prayer, but one often finds prayers addressed to Christ in private devotional life. The point of the prayer is supplication. It cries out for the pardoning of our sins. It asks of Christ that through his intercession he reconcile us with the Father. One might call this a para-liturgical prayer. It is not really part of the liturgy so much as auxiliary to the liturgy. It is a private prayer rather than a corporate prayer. It is a personal prayer rather than a corporate prayer. Prayers of this sort were typical of late medieval Nominalism.

B. Epiclesis

The next prayer is one of the most elaborate expressions of the epicletic dimension of worship that has come down to us. This prayer is addressed to the Holy Spirit:

> Most Holy Spirit, proceeding from the Father and the Son, by whom Christ was conceived, by whom the prophets and apostles were inspired, and the ministers of Christ are qualified and called, that

---

[22] Baxter, *Reformed Liturgy*, p. 932.

dwellest and workest in all the members of Christ, whom thou sanctifiest to the image and for the service of their Head, and comfortest them that they may show forth his praise; illuminate us, that by faith we may see him that is here represented to us. Soften our hearts, and humble us for our sins. Sanctify and quicken us, that we may relish the spiritual food, and feed on it to our nourishment and growth in grace. Shed abroad the love of God upon our hearts, and draw them out in love to him. Fill us with thankfulness and holy joy, and with love to one another: comfort us by witnessing that we are the children of God. Confirm us for new obedience. Be the earnest of our inheritance, and seal us up to everlasting life. Amen.[23]

The prayer expresses a keen awareness of the role of the Holy Spirit in our redemption. We find not only the epicletic dimension of worship but the pneumatic dimension as well. With a marvellous baroque prolixity, the prayer remembers that it is the Holy Spirit who proceeds from the Father and the Son, pointedly adopting the filioque clause. It then remembers that it was by the Holy Spirit that Christ was conceived. The prayer is clearly following the lead of the Nicene-Constantinopolitan Creed, as it goes on to celebrate the Holy Spirit as the one who inspired the prophets and the Apostles, and even, striking a note important to Calvin, inspires, qualifies, and calls the ministers of Christ. The prayer goes on to remember that it is the Holy Spirit who dwells in all the members of Christ, continually working for their sanctification. One might almost say that the prayer contains an outline of the Reformed doctrine of the Holy Spirit.

The actual supplication or petition of this prayer asks that the Holy Spirit illuminate us that we might see Christ as he is here represented to us. It is a rather subjective petition, asking that the Spirit might "soften our hearts, and humble us for our

---

[23] Baxter, *Reformed Liturgy*, pp. 932–933.

sins."[24] What the Spirit is asked to do in our hearts is to sanctify and quicken us: "Shed abroad the love of God in our hearts, and draw them out in love to him."[25] It is the Holy Spirit who is the bond of love between the Father and the Son, as Baxter must surely have learned from his Schoolmen. It is only natural, then, that he should pray to the Spirit to draw us together to God and to one another in the same bond of love. This prayer is a masterpiece, an epitome of theological doctrine on its knees.

C. Prayer of Consecration

Of particular interest is the Prayer of Consecration which begins the communion service proper:

> Almighty God, thou art the Creator and the Lord of all things. Thou art the Sovereign Majesty whom we have offended; thou art our most loving and merciful Father, who hast given thy Son to reconcile us to thyself, who hath ratified the new testament and the covenant of grace with his most precious blood; and hath instituted this holy sacrament to be celebrated in remembrance of him till his coming. Sanctify these thy creatures of bread and wine, which according to thy institution and command, we set apart to this holy use, that they may be sacramentally the body and blood of thy Son Jesus Christ. Amen.[26]

The prayer remembers, that is, celebrates before God, his love in giving his Son to reconcile us to himself by establishing the covenant of grace. It furthermore remembers that it was to this end that Christ instituted this sacrament. This sacrament celebrates God's mighty acts of creation and redemption as we find them in Christ.

The prayer then asks God to sanctify the bread and wine which he has created, that, "according to thy institution and com-

---

[24] Baxter, *Reformed Liturgy*, p. 932.

[25] Baxter, *Reformed Liturgy*, pp. 932–933.

[26] Baxter, *Reformed Liturgy*, p. 932.

mand we set apart to this holy use . . ." The understanding of consecration which we find here is very different from the understanding of consecration the Schoolmen had developed. There is no ontological change here. The bread and wine are simply set aside from a common to a sacred use.[27] Sacramentally they are to be the body and blood of Christ. We take this to mean that they are to serve as signs of the body and blood of Christ, but there is no ontological change in the bread and wine. From beginning to end they remain bread and wine. One imagines that Baxter, unlike Calvin, thought of this in Nominalist terms. Baxter still thought in terms of ontology although, from a Nominalist standpoint, there was precious little ontology left.

One of the most characteristic features of Baxter's *Reformed Liturgy* is its approach to the eucharistic dimension of the sacrament. Following both the *Westminster Directory* and Calvin there is no long prayer of thanksgiving over the bread and wine before they are distributed. Knox, on the other hand, had realized the value of this, and, as we have said, he may have gotten this from Peter Martyr Vermigli.[28] This long prayer of thanksgiving over the bread and wine had been the practice in the patristic age, as we find it in the Liturgy of St. Basil and the liturgy of the *Apostolic Constitutions*. What we find in Baxter and in Calvin is that the Prayer of Thanksgiving appears in the liturgy after communion. Though this differed from patristic tradition and the habit of centuries, the Reformers were actually following even more ancient traditions than the patristic age. For instance, the thanksgiving for the history of salvation was apparently offered with the cup of blessing at the close of the meal in the Passover Seder. We find an indication in 1 Corinthians 10:16 that

---

[27] That the bread and wine should be set aside from a common to a sacred use was used by a number of Reformed theologians. Its origin does not seem to be known. I had suspected that it came from Vermigli. My student Walter Taylor suggests John Laski. See Taylor's doctoral dissertation, *As They Sat at Table*.

[28] Again, more recent research by Walter Taylor suggests that this, too, shows the influence of John Laski.

10: The Westminster Puritans

this practice was continued in the New Testament church. This was also clearly the procedure in the eucharistic prayers of the *Didaché*.

D. Eucharistic Prayer

Let us turn to what Richard Baxter has left us for a eucharistic prayer. There is something even more interesting about how Baxter handled the eucharistic dimension of the sacrament. The prayer goes as follows:

> Most glorious God, how wonderful is thy power and wisdom, thy holiness and justice, thy love and mercy in this work of our redemption, by the incarnation, life, death, resurrection, intercession, and dominion of thy Son! No power or wisdom in heaven or earth could have delivered us but thine. The angels desire to pry into this mystery, the heavenly host do celebrate it with praises, saying, Glory be to God in the highest; on earth peace, good-will towards men. The whole creation shall proclaim thy praises. Blessing, honour, glory, and power be unto him that sitteth upon the throne, and unto the Lamb for ever and ever. Worthy is the Lamb that was slain, to receive power, and honour, and glory; for he hath redeemed us to God by his blood, and made us kings and priests unto our God. Where sin abounded, grace hath abounded much more. And hast thou indeed forgiven us so great a debt, by so precious a ransom? Wilt thou indeed give us to reign with Christ in glory, and see thy face, and love thee, and be beloved of thee for ever? Yea, Lord, thou hast forgiven us, and thou wilt glorify us, for thou art faithful that hast promised. With the blood of thy Son, with the sacrament, and with thy Spirit, thou hast sealed up to us these precious promises. And shall we not love thee, that hast thus loved us? Shall we not love thy servants, and forgive our neighbours their little debt? After all this shall we again forsake thee, and deal falsely in thy covenant? God forbid! O set our affections on the things above, where Christ sitteth at thy right hand. Let us no more mind earthly things, but let our conversation be in heaven, from whence we expect

> our Saviour to come and change us into the likeness of his glory. Teach us to do thy will, O God, and to follow him, who is the author of eternal salvation to all them that do obey him. Order our steps by thy word, and let not any iniquity have dominion over us. Let us not henceforth live unto ourselves, but unto him who died for us and rose again. Let us have no fellowship with the unfruitful works of darkness, but reprove them. And let our light so shine before men, that they may glorify thee. In simplicity, and godly sincerity, and not in fleshly wisdom, let us have our conversation in the world. Oh that our ways were so directed that we might keep thy statutes! Though Satan will be desirous again to sift us, and seek as a roaring lion to devour, strengthen us to stand against his wiles, and shortly bruise him under our feet. Accept us, O Lord, who resign ourselves unto thee, as thine own; and with our thanks and praise, present ourselves a living sacrifice to be acceptable through Christ, useful for thine honour: being made free from sin, and become thy servants, let us have our fruit unto holiness, and the end everlasting life, through Jesus Christ our Lord and Saviour. Amen.[29]

This is the major prayer of the service. It is twice or even three times as long as the *epiclesis*. Baxter begins with invoking God as "Most glorious God," then reciting his attributes, "how wonderful is thy power and wisdom, thy holiness and justice, thy love and mercy."

This ample invocation is followed by an *anamnesis* which celebrates the incarnation, the life, death, resurrection, and the heavenly intercession and dominion of Christ. The major stages of Christ's redemptive ministry are explicitly recounted. Each of these stages of our redemption may be mentioned in this *anamnesis*, but only in the briefest way possible. What we have here is far from a hymnic recounting of the history of salvation. In fact, this should be the touchstone of the prayer. It is to this that the broken bread and poured out wine have first reference. This is the mystery into which angels long to look. With this *anamnesis*, then, the minister para-

---

[29] Baxter, *Reformed Liturgy*, p. 933.

10: THE WESTMINSTER PURITANS

phrases the angelic song from the Gospel of Luke, "Glory to God in the highest!" It is because of this that in the last day all creation will sing together, "Blessing, honor, power, glory and praise be unto him who sitteth upon the throne, and unto the Lamb forever and ever." Again we notice the eschatological dimension as the prayer continues to meditate on the praises offered to the Lamb of God who presides over the consummation of the last day. The eschatological dimension of the prayer comes through very clearly as Baxter rejoices in the faithfulness of Christ who in the last day will bring us into his kingdom. "Yea, Lord, thou hast forgiven us and thou wilt glorify us, for thou art faithful that have promised." Christ's faithfulness to his promises is at the heart of a covenantal theology of worship and here, once more, this theme is clearly heard.

The prayer once more rises to a contemplation of heavenly things. It is heaven where Christ sits at the right hand of eternal majesty. "Let our conversation be in heaven, from whence we expect our Saviour to come and change us into the likeness of his glory." It is to the risen Savior that Baxter's prayer now turns. "Let us not henceforth live to ourselves, but unto him who died for us and rose again." Then, paraphrasing the famous lines at the beginning of Romans 12, Baxter prays that we might present ourselves a living sacrifice to Christ, that in all things we might live for him. The beautiful thing about this prayer is the way it moves from thanksgiving to dedication. This is, to be sure, implicit in the biblical understanding of thanksgiving. The Hebrew word *yadah* means to give thanks, to confess, and to witness, all at the same time. It means to give a sacrifice of thanksgiving by recounting the story of how God has saved us from our sorrow, how God has brought us from death to life, and so we witness to this by confessing our obligation to him who has given us new life, and that new life we pledge to his service.

There are, to be sure, many good things to be said about this prayer, and some of these we have mentioned, but there is one thing missing. We do not hear a hymnic recounting of God's mighty acts of redemption. We hear much more about what we are going to do in dedicating ourselves to God's service. The prayer focuses on our dedication rather than God's grace. It is not primarily a eucharistic prayer but rather a prayer of dedication. In the end, what we have here is a distinctly Nominalist piety. It is not the objective mighty acts of God that interest Baxter so much as the subjective experience of the heart that Baxter is finally concerned with. One misses the hymnic recounting of the mighty acts of God that we found in the eucharistic prayer of John Knox or that we found in Basil of Caesarea or in the *Apostolic Constitutions*. What we have here, however, does express at least some of the eucharistic dimension of the sacrament.

The psalmody which Baxter suggests for the celebration of the sacrament gives us another important expression of the eucharistic dimension. This is especially the case with Psalm 116, which is clearly a votive thanksgiving psalm. Especially with the following lines the full biblical understanding of thanksgiving is developed:

> What shall I render unto the Lord
>   for all his benefits toward me?
> I will take the cup of salvation,
>   and call upon the name of the Lord.
> I will pay my vows unto the Lord
>   now in the presence of all his people.
> Precious in the sight of the Lord
>   is the death of his saints.
> O Lord, truly I am thy servant;
> I am thy servant, and the son of thine handmaid:
>   thou hast loosed my bonds.
> I will offer to thee the sacrifice of thanksgiving,
>   and will call upon the name of the Lord.
> I will pay my vows unto the Lord now
>   in the presence of all his people,
> In the courts of the Lord's house,
>   in the midst of thee, O Jerusalem.
> Praise ye the Lord.
> (Psalm 116:12–19, KJV)

The same thing is obviously true for Psalm 103, which is so often sung at the close of the Reformed communion service. Psalm 100 is mentioned, although its appropriateness might not be obvious. The reason for its use, however, is found in the psalm title, which indicates that it is a psalm to be sung to accompany the sacrifice of thanksgiving. That such psalms were appointed to conclude the service made very clear the eucharistic dimension of the sacrament.

Richard Baxter may not have been a systematic theologian nor even a classical Reformed theologian, but he was certainly a very pastoral one.

THOMAS DOOLITTLE'S
A Treatise Concerning the Lord's Supper

Puritan eucharistic piety in the century between the *Genevan Psalter* and the *Westminster Directory* developed some distinctive features. There was quite a bit of variety in this development. Thomas Doolittle (1630–1707) gives us only one example of how these disciplines developed.[30] Doolittle was neither particularly perceptive nor particularly profound. He was just one of many seventeenth century writers of devotional guides of the period whose work was particularly popular. Doolittle's *Treatise Concerning the Lord's Supper* is reported to have gone through more than twenty editions before the author died in 1707.

Doolittle grew up in Kidderminster, where Richard Baxter was pastor at the time.[31] Doolittle started out working for a county lawyer, but Baxter encouraged him to become a minister shortly after his conversion. After studies at Pembroke Hall, Cambridge,

---

[30] Thomas Doolittle, *A Treatise Concerning the Lord's Supper*, ed. Don Kistler (Morgantown, PA: Soli Deo Gloria Publications, 1998), hereinafter Doolittle, *Lord's Supper*.

[31] For biographical background on Doolittle, see: "Doolittle, Thomas," in the *Oxford Dictionary of National Biography*, ed. H. C. G. Matthew and Brian Harrison, 60 vols. (Oxford and New York: Oxford University Press, 2004), 16:561; "Thomas Doolitle (1630–1707)" www.monergism.com/directory/link_category/ Puritans/Misc-Puritans/Thomas-Doolitle/. Accessed April 7, 2011.

where he earned both a Bachelor of Arts and a master's degree, Doolittle received presbyterian ordination. He was called to a prominent Church of England congregation in London, and was one of those ministers who was expelled from the Church of England in 1662 when Charles II ascended the throne and insisted on strict conformity to the Anglican *Prayer Book*. After being ejected from his church, he established a school that soon became very popular. In fact, the school had more students than it could handle. Among its more well-known students was Matthew Henry.

Right from the first chapter of this devotional book, Doolittle makes his primary concerns clear. First, Doolittle wants to impress upon Christians the importance of participating in the Lord's Supper regularly, and then he wants to encourage diligent preparation for the observance.[32] It is almost startling that a work with the title *A Treatise Concerning the Lord's Supper* should settle down so quickly to these two questions. One might even say that the work is misnamed. It should have been named *A Treatise on the Proper Preparation for Receiving the Lord's Supper*. In fact, Doolittle specifically says that he intends to skip over subjects such as the nature, use, and ends of the sacrament so that he might concentrate on the preparation for receiving the sacrament.[33]

A. Frequency of Celebration

The treatise begins with an overall look at 1 Corinthians 11, where the Apostle Paul admonishes the Corinthians on the proper celebration of the sacrament. In the course of a few pages, Doolittle expounds the text, pointing out that what we are to do is "in remembrance of me."[34] It all seems very perfunctory and abbreviated. While the modern reader might have a hard time with Doolittle's legalistic approach to proving that regular receiving of the

---

[32] Doolittle, *Lord's Supper*, p. 5.

[33] Doolittle, *Lord's Supper*, p. 6.

[34] Doolittle, *Lord's Supper*, p. 11.

10: THE WESTMINSTER PURITANS

Lord's Supper is required of the faithful Christian, there are nevertheless several helpful pages here. Just as the annual observance of Passover was obligatory for serious Jews, so the observance of the Lord's Supper is obligatory for Christians.[35] There is also a beautiful passage showing the value of remembering God's mighty acts of creation and providence. Doolittle's insights here are based on several of the thanksgiving psalms, notably Psalms 103, 104, 105, and 106.[36] The Puritans did know their Old Testaments and this gave them good insights when it came to eucharistic theology.

It is easy to conclude that the proper frequency for celebrating the sacrament was vigorously debated, among both Puritans and Anglicans. There were those who argued that like Passover it should be celebrated once a year. Most Protestants agreed that daily celebrations constituted an abuse. More realistic ministers figured that while weekly observance was ideal, few of their people would present themselves for a weekly celebration. The more usual practice for Puritans would be quarterly, maybe monthly for the most devout. There were plenty of good Catholics, it must be remembered, who considered the annual Easter obligation sufficient while Protestants who observed it only once a year made it a high holy day. When it was celebrated but once a year it was celebrated with great solemnity. Preparatory services and thanksgiving services were held each day for a week. Frequency was no indication of the seriousness with which it was celebrated. The trouble, of course, was that Scripture is not at all clear how often Jesus intended it to be celebrated. The text simply says, "Do this as often as you do it in remembrance of me." The argument from the usage of the early church seems to favor the celebration of the sacrament each Lord's Day, but by late antiquity daily celebration was widespread.

Doolittle contented himself with the ambiguity of the discussion, arguing simply that it should be observed frequently. That, at

---

[35] Doolittle, *Lord's Supper*, pp. 11–13.

[36] Doolittle, *Lord's Supper*, p. 14.

least, he could draw out of Scripture. Nevertheless he based his argument on common sense. We need to be reminded of God's love frequently because our memories are short-lived. Celebrating the sacrament nourishes our thankfulness toward God. Our faith will be supported by regularly enjoying the intimate presence of our Savior in the observance of the holy feast.[37]

B. Preparation for the Lord's Supper

The main theme of Doolittle's work, however, is the preparation required for worthy participation. By the end of the sixteenth century we hear of special preparatory services held in connection with the celebration of the Lord's Supper pretty much throughout the Reformed churches from the Scottish Highlands to the Swiss Alps. However, what we have here in Doolittle's work is not a series of sermons for a preparatory service, but much more a collection of devotional guides to be read at home in order to assure the conscientious Christian that he or she is prepared to receive the sacrament. This is something to be read while the believer sits by the fire at home the evening before a Communion Sunday. Perhaps it might be a guide to the conversation at the dinner table during family prayers.[38]

This is a book of "directions" for disposing our hearts to partake of the Supper.[39] First we should search our hearts, inquiring as to our relationship with God. We should investigate our souls. We should examine our consciences to discover any sin hiding in our lives. Thinking of the Passover typology, we should search through the whole house to discover any morsel of the leaven of sin that might have gone unnoticed. Then we should solemnly turn our minds to the great themes of God's grace which would serve to kindle our hearts to prayer and praise. We should betake

---

[37] Doolittle, *Lord's Supper*, p. 32.
[38] Doolittle, *Lord's Supper*, p. 78.
[39] Doolittle, *Lord's Supper*, p. 61.

ourselves to prayer in order to worthily partake of the sacrament. If possible we should then converse with other Christian friends that our devotion and religious affections might be quickened. Sad to say, much of this material seems to delight in rigorism. Doolittle seems to search out sins of the most obscure nature so that one might mortify these sins.[40]

The Puritans, of course, have long had a reputation for being killjoys. Their spirituality is all too often starkly serious. As one of my professors in college put it, they were obsessed by the possibility that someone, somewhere, might actually be enjoying life. The caricature behind this jibe has kept us from discovering the spiritual riches of a great age in our spiritual history. Still, one has to admit that rigorism was characteristic of the age, be it Protestant or Catholic. It was groans and tears through and through. What we really have here, however, is an expression of the piety of late medieval Nominalism. This is the piety of Thomas à Kempis, the Brethren of the Common Life, and John Tauler.[41] It is not, however, the piety of the Continental Reformers such as Martin Luther, Ulrich Zwingli, Martin Bucer, John Calvin and the Christian Humanists. The classical Reformers developed a much more objective approach to the Christian life. The sixteenth-century Reformers were not Pietists. Pietism came much later in the Reformed Church, beginning to be found in the seventeenth century, especially among the Puritans, but more typically in the eighteenth century.

C. Preoccupation with Worthiness

Maybe my reading of Doolittle is insensitive. Maybe I am too much under the influence of a soft culture, but I have to be honest here. Pietism may be found up in my attic, but I am not the least bit inter-

---

[40] Doolittle, *Lord's Supper*, pp. 63–64.

[41] See Hughes Oliphant Old, *The Reading and Preaching of the Scriptures in the Worship of the Christian Church*, vol. 3, *The Medieval Church* (Grand Rapids, MI: Eerdmans, 1999), pp. 491f. See as well, Hughes Oliphant Old, *The Shaping of the Reformed Baptismal Rite in the Sixteenth Century* (Grand Rapids, MI: Eerdmans, 1992).

ested in dusting it off and bringing it downstairs. Doolittle would have us come to the Lord's Table filled with expressions of guilt and lamentation.[42] The prayers and meditations with which he would fill our thoughts are meditations on the value and power of the blood of Christ. They are a little like Mel Gibson's film *The Passion of the Christ*. Instead of the simple recounting of the Gospel story of Christ's passion it is all covered over with thick brush strokes in garish colors. Puritanism often developed into Pietism, as we find it here. Here, sad to say, Pietism seems to have overcome Puritanism.

Typical of late medieval Pietism is Doolittle's long chapter meditating on the blood of Christ. He comes up with twenty properties or virtues of the blood of Christ.[43] The blood is precious both absolutely and comparatively, as Doolittle sees it. When we come to the Lord's Table we should look at Christ's blood as being sufficient to pay the price of our ransom.[44] Not only should we look at Christ's blood as ransoming blood but as pacifying, reconciling blood. It is cleansing, purifying blood.[45] The blood of Christ is comforting blood. It cools our distempers and it cools the heat of God's wrath. When we come to the Lord's Table we should behold the wine as the sign of the quickening blood that flowed from his pierced side.[46] This is a long meditation on the blood of Christ. The prolixity of this meditation on the blood of Christ for some of us would seem to our generation to lack taste. My personal feelings on it mirror how I feel about the *Spiritual Exercises* of Ignatius of Loyola. Maybe it is just the mark of the seventeenth century. What is amazing about this devotional guide is that it completely ignores the preaching of the minister as well as the corporate prayer of the congregation. It replaces prayer

---

[42] Doolittle, *Lord's Supper*, pp. 92–99.
[43] Doolittle, *Lord's Supper*, pp. 80f.
[44] Doolittle, *Lord's Supper*, p. 81.
[45] Doolittle, *Lord's Supper*, p. 83.
[46] Doolittle, *Lord's Supper*, p. 86.

with meditation and the preaching of the Word with the private thoughts of the worshiper. Even more striking is the way Doolittle makes the Eucharist into a penitential rite. It is a service of worship that cries out for salvation rather than a service primarily rejoicing in the mighty acts of God.

Doolittle seems constantly preoccupied with whether our worship is acceptable. The text which seems to dominate Doolittle's thought is 1 Corinthians 11:28, "Let a man examine himself, and so eat of the bread and drink of the cup." In all honesty, Doolittle probably recognized the danger of his preoccupation.[47] Still, the overall problem remains. The Lord's Supper as Doolittle presents it is more supplication than eucharist. Here is a real contradiction between the classical Reformed eucharistic piety and much of the eucharistic piety of the late seventeenth and early eighteenth century.

Sad to say, Doolittle continues on his moralistic way with his remarks about the devotions and meditations that should follow the receiving of the sacrament. Again it is clear that Doolittle is not talking about the thanksgiving service that was usually held on Sunday evening or Monday morning. He is talking about devotions exercised on the walk home from church or before retiring Sunday evening at night.[48] With perhaps a play on words Doolittle speaks of what is appropriate walking, and by it he means appropriate conversation while walking home. Of course, there is the more basic meaning of how the believer lives after participating in the sacrament.[49] The tone of all this is distinctly moralistic and, to use the word used in the seventeenth century, "painful." What was meant, of course, was that the Christian should take great pains to be very exact in his or her religious duties. Sometimes, however, those who were too meticulous in these matters came off as "painful" to have around.

---

[47] Doolittle, *Lord's Supper*, pp. 98–100.

[48] Doolittle, *Lord's Supper*, p. 117.

[49] Doolittle, *Lord's Supper*, p. 120.

The one unmistakable impression Doolittle's devotional guide leaves us with is that the sacrament has become primarily a penitential rite. It is with disappointment that I have to admit this, but it is obvious from reading over the text. Doolittle always gets back to the same verse, "Let one examine oneself." The observance of the sacrament as Doolittle presents it should call us to examine our hearts, to discover our sins, and to meditate on the broken body and poured out blood of Christ, which cleanses us from our sin. For this Puritan, at least, one gets the impression that the sacrament has become a matter of remembering our sins rather than bearing witness to the redemptive work of Christ.

JOHN OWEN'S
Sacramental Discourses (1669–1682)

John Owen (1616–1683) was a consistent Congregationalist, one of the bulwarks of the left wing of the Puritan movement. He was an important advisor of Cromwell's during the period of his ascendancy and a prolific theological author. Will Barker considers him the leading theologian of Puritanism, while J. I. Packer tells us that he was both consciously and consistently close to the center of seventeenth-century Reformed thinking.[50]

John Owen was born in Oxfordshire where his father, Henry, was a minister.[51] At times he was a parson and at times a school master. We know little about his early years. The Owen family was of Welsh origin and one of his uncles was a man of consider-

---

[50] Quoted by Barker, *Puritan Profiles*, p. 295.

[51] For further biographical material on Owen see: Sinclair B. Ferguson, Graham S. Harrison, Michael A. G. Haykin, Robert W. Oliver, and Carl R. Trueman, *John Owen: The Man and His Theology* (Phillipsburg, PA: Presbyterian and Reformed Publishing Co., and Darlington, UK: Evangelical Press, 2002); John Owen, *The Correspondence of John Owen (1616–1683): With an Account of his Life and Work*, ed. Peter Toon (Cambridge, UK: James Clarke, 1970); Jon D. Payne, *John Owen on the Lord's Supper* (Edinburgh and Carlisle, PA: Banner of Truth Trust, 2004), pp. 1–17; and Peter Toon, *God's Statesman: The Life and Work of John Owen* (Exeter, UK: Paternoster Press, 1971).

able property. His uncle, however, was a staunch Royalist and as his nephew more and more found himself supporting the Puritan movement, the uncle was offended and disinherited him. At more than one point in his life, however, John Owen found himself in possession of private means. This apparently made it possible for him to support his extensive literary productivity.

Owen's education began with his attending a grammar school in Oxford. He completed his preliminary courses very quickly. In fact, he was something of a prodigy. Shortly afterward he matriculated at Queens College, receiving his Bachelor of Arts in 1632 and his Master of Arts in 1635. In 1637, already ordained in the Church of England, he became chaplain and tutor to Sir Robert Dormer. Sometime after that we hear of his being appointed to a similar position with John, Lord Lovelace, in Berkshire. Due to the increasing severity of Archbishop Laud toward those of Puritan leaning, Owen went to London and apparently there continued his theological studies, publishing his *Display of Arminianism* in 1642. Finally he became pastor of St. Peter's Coggeshall, in 1646. Owen was an especially gifted preacher, drawing large crowds of people. In spite of his obscurity during these years, he was able to publish his masterpiece, *The Death of Death in the Death of Christ*.[52] This classic of Reformed theology expounds the high Calvinistic doctrine of the atonement with both profundity and majesty. This was only the first of many theological treatises that Owen would eventually produce. His treatise on the Holy Spirit is also highly regarded.

Owen began to gain a reputation as a theologian and preacher who supported the Puritans. He had achieved such a significant renown that he was chosen to preach before Parliament on the day following the execution of Charles I in 1649. This, of course, marked Owen as being in a very different camp from more moderate Puritans such as Thomas Manton. By this

---

[52] John Owen, *The Death of Death in the Death of Christ: A Treatise of the Redemption* (Philadelphia: Green and M'Laughlin, 1827).

time Cromwell had reached the height of his power and he found in John Owen a man on whom he could rely to advise him on ecclesiastical policy. Cromwell appointed Owen as his chaplain during his campaign in Ireland. Returning to England he relied on Owen in his attempt to reorganize Oxford University, appointing him Dean of Christ Church in 1651 and then Vice-Chancellor of the University the following year. For the next five years he preached at St. Mary's University Church, Oxford every other week, alternating with Thomas Goodwin. Owen, however, was hardly Cromwell's "yes man." When Cromwell began to act too much like the king he had deposed, Owen opposed him and Cromwell let his displeasure be known. But then, Cromwell's days were numbered. A year later, Owen was among the ministers who attended to him on his deathbed. The Commonwealth soon came apart and Owen returned to his estate at Stadhampton outside of Oxford where he continued to write until his death in 1683.

During his twenty-five years of retirement Owen was regarded as an elder statesman of the Puritan movement. The repression of Puritan preaching relaxed from time to time and he would preach in London where he helped organize an Independent congregation. While never imprisoned himself, he was able to support several Puritans who had been. Apparently he was able to gather a Nonconformist congregation from time to time while living on his estate at Stadhampton in Oxfordshire. His works have been republished in sixteen volumes.[53]

The *Sacramental Discourses* were preached for the most part in the 1670s, while Owen found himself in his enforced retirement. This series of twenty-five sermons were taken down by Sir John Hartopp, but they were not published until 1760. They were pre-

---

[53] John Owen, *The Works of John Owen*, ed. William H. Goold, 16 vols. (Edinburgh: Banner of Truth Trust, 1965–1968). The *Sacramental Discourses* can be found in volume 9, pp. 515–622. Hereinafter Owen, *Sacramental Discourses*.

served in the private library of the Hartopp family.[54] The sermons include dates, but they do not indicate where they were preached. The fact that the sermons were preserved by the Hartopp family indicates that they were preached in London.[55] The sermons as they have come down to us are rather short. Obviously the stenographer condensed the sermon as he heard it from the pulpit. However, as the stenographer has preserved them, they do give us another view of Owen's preaching which is much more immediate. Owen's long commentary on the Epistle to the Hebrews no doubt preserves in much more detailed form his sermons from his five year tenure at St. Mary's Church in Oxford. The sermons on Hebrews are thoroughly worked over and were originally published in seven volumes.[56] What the stenographer has taken down records Owen's fascinating style. To read these sermons is like reading Tertullian or, for a more modern example, Martin Heidegger. There are numerous interesting and freshly-coined words.

These discourses give us as fresh and profound an insight into Reformed eucharistic piety as has come down to us.[57] Here we find a Protestant theologian of mature insight taking the classic biblical texts and asking what these texts really mean. This is not systematic theology. Rather, it is biblical theology. There is no attempt to treat

---

[54] On the manuscript tradition of these discourses, see Payne, *John Owen on the Lord's Supper*, p. 51–53.

[55] For further information on the Hartopp family, see Payne, *John Owen on the Lord's Supper*, pp. 52–53.

[56] A modern edition of the seven volume exposition of the Epistle to the Hebrews is: John Owen, *An Exposition of the Epistle to the Hebrews*, ed. W. H. Goold, 7 vols. (Edinburgh and Carlisle, PA: Banner of Truth Trust, 1991).

[57] Scholarly interest in the sacramental theology of Owen up to this point has been meager at best. Some exceptions, however, may be found in Payne, *John Owen on the Lord's Supper*; Kelly M. Kapic, *Communion With God: The Divine and the Human in the Theology of John Owen* (Grand Rapids, MI: Baker Academic, 2007), pp. 207–234; John Williamson Nevin, *The Mystical Presence*, reprint, ed. Augustine Thompson (Eugene, OR: Wipf and Stock, 2000); and Stephen Mayor, "The Teaching of John Owen Concerning the Lord's Supper," *Scottish Journal of Theology* 18 (1965): 170–181.

the whole subject from beginning to end. This is not book theology; this is pastoral preaching. Let us look at some of the more memorable insights we find in these "sacramental discourses."[58]

A. The Supper as Memorial of the Gospel

One of the most obvious features of Owen's *Sacramental Discourses* is a very profound doctrine of the eucharistic memorial. This is bound to develop when the basic biblical concept of memorial is studied. Scripture says quite a bit about the importance of maintaining a memorial of God's mighty acts of salvation. Owen is well aware of the importance of maintaining the Sabbath memorial as we find it in the fourth commandment, "Remember the Sabbath Day to keep it holy." Then there was the Passover memorial (Exodus 12:14) which remembered the deliverance from Egypt. These memorials, however, were festal assemblies. They were far more than recalling the history of creation and redemption, although they were at least that. They were a sacred exercising, a devout experiencing of the truth behind the story. In an even more profound way the celebration of the Lord's Supper is the exercising of ourselves in the truth of the Gospel. The memorial is to share a meal in the house of the Father and at the same time it is the opening up of the essence of reality, that God is our God and we are his people. We come to the Lord's Supper to remember how God has delivered us from our sin. "God would have us remember and call to mind the state whereinto we are brought—which is a state of righteousness; that we may bless him for that which in this world will issue in our righteousness, and in the world to come, eternal glory."[59] When we celebrate the Lord's Supper we celebrate the love of God in Christ Jesus, particularly in the sacrificial death of Christ.

---

[58] The phrase "sacramental discourses" is meant to be taken in a technical sense. The pastor was to make these invitations immediately before the celebration of the sacrament. These are not preparatory sermons for a communion season.

[59] Owen, *Sacramental Discourses*, p. 523.

The third discourse goes into this at some length, making the point that when we celebrate the sacred meal we show forth the Lord's death until he comes.[60] The sacred meal celebrates the paternal love of the Father in the household of faith but it celebrates even more specifically the redemptive, obedient, sacrificial love of the Son. Owen speaks at great length of how the sacrament reveals to us the faith of Christ, the obedience of Christ, and the work of Christ.[61] Here it is, as Owen sees it, that the ultimate love of God is revealed. Christ had faith in a vision of how he would deliver the elect from sin and death and hell itself and so bring the children of the Father to glory and seat them at the banquet table of the Father.[62] Frequently Owen makes the point that, in the sacrament, God reveals ultimate reality. "You see, then, the end of this ordinance of the Lord's supper, is to stir us up to call over the obedience of Christ, both as to his love in it, as to his readiness for it, submission to the will of God in it, and patience under it."[63] The eucharistic memorial, as Owen understands it, is the Gospel in capsule.

In Discourse Six we once again hear of the nature of the eucharistic memorial and how the observance of the sacrament is a proclamation of the essentials of the Gospel. When we come to the Lord's Table we should meditate on ". . . *the infinite wisdom and the infinite love of God, that found out this way of glorifying his holiness and justice*, and dealing with sin according to its demerit. 'God so loved the world,' John iii. 16, 'that he gave his only begotten Son'. And, 'Herein is love,' –love indeed! I John iv. 10, 'that God sent his Son to be the propitiation of our sins.'"[64] The celebration of the Lord's Supper makes clear the wisdom of God's love.

If the celebration of the Supper reveals the love of the Father,

---

[60] Owen, *Sacramental Discourses*, pp. 529–530.

[61] Owen, *Sacramental Discourses*, p. 530.

[62] Owen, *Sacramental Discourses*, p. 530.

[63] Owen, *Sacramental Discourses*, p. 536.

[64] Owen, *Sacramental Discourses*, p. 559.

it reveals as well the love of the Son. "Let the *infinite love of Jesus Christ himself* be also at such a season had in remembrance. Gal. ii. 20, 'Who loved me, and gave himself for me.'"[65] We find again and again in these discourses that for John Owen, as for Calvin before him, the basic sign of the sacrament is the sharing of the meal in the house of the heavenly Father, where the bread that is shared and the wine that is poured out is the memorial of the well-beloved Son. In this end, God gives us of himself and nourishes us of his very own life even to that day that knows no end. Owen's theology is strongly trinitarian. We will notice this again and again as we read these discourses. Owen displays this in the relation between the Father and the Son as well as in the emphasis he puts on the work of the Holy Spirit in the sacrament.

In Discourse Twenty-two, which Owen delivered in 1676, we have another strong sermon on the nature of the eucharistic memorial and its role in Puritan piety. The sermon begins:

> We are met here to remember the death of Christ, in the way and by the means that he himself hath appointed; and in remembering *the death of Christ* we are principally to remember *the love of Christ* 'who loved us, and washed us from our sins in his own blood' [Rev. 1:6].[66]

What is particularly interesting in this discourse is what he says about the source of our love to Christ as being the love of the Father for the Son. Taking as his text Matthew 3:17, "This is my beloved Son," the words heard from heaven at the baptism of Jesus, Owen wants to focus our attention on the love of the Father for the Son. First Owen brings a number of texts from Scripture such as Proverbs 8:30 and several passages from the Gospel of John to make his point. Then he begins to explain from systematic theology what is meant by the *opera ad intra*, that is, the relation of the persons of the Trinity one to another. The inner-trinitarian conversation may

---

[65] Owen, *Sacramental Discourses*, p. 560.

[66] Owen, *Sacramental Discourses*, p. 612.

sound like rather obscure theology but it helps us understand some very important things, and here is one of them. We need to understand that it is the eternal and unchangeable love of the Father for the Son and the Son for the Father that is the foundation of all love, wherever we find it, binding together creation.[67]

B. The Supper as Invitation

For one of his sacramental discourses Owen takes as his text 1 Corinthians 11:26, "As often as ye eat this bread, and drink this cup, ye do shew the Lord's death till he come." The word translated "shew" here is a rather unusual word in the biblical vocabulary. It could be translated in different ways: to declare, to represent, to show forth, or to hold forth.[68] The point is that Christ should be "shown forth" or "exhibited" in such a way that he is offered to the faithful. Christ should be held forth as our Savior. The promises of the Gospel should be held forth so that they might be accepted.

Owen is particularly eloquent when he speaks of how the promises of the Gospel are to be made not only generally to the Church as a whole, but particularly as well. The promises of the Gospel are to be offered to each person in the congregation. These promises are tendered to the congregation in the preaching of the Word. At the heart of the communion service is the invitation to accept Christ.[69] In the eucharistic memorial should be a representation of Christ and the promises of the Gospel. They should be held out and exhibited. The promises should be tendered even as the sacramental elements are distributed.

> The very elements of the ordinance are a great representation of the proposal of Christ to a believing soul. God holds out Christ as willing to be received, with an

---

[67] Owen, *Sacramental Discourses*, p. 614.

[68] Owen, *Sacramental Discourses*, p. 538.

[69] Owen, *Sacramental Discourses*, p. 540.

invitation. So we show forth the Lord's death.[70]

Owen often speaks of the celebration of the Lord's Supper as "tendering" the gospel or "tendering" Christ. Owen even says at times that in the sacrament Christ himself tenders to us the Gospel. Today the word is a bit archaic except perhaps when we talk of tending sheep. In tending sheep the shepherd sees to it that sheep are guided to good pasture and otherwise cared for. We also speak of bartenders, those who deliver the drinks that have been ordered. We also speak of "tenders," the small boats in a harbor which care for the great men-of-war, delivering supplies to them and helping to maneuver them into position. So it is that Owen speaks of the Lord's Supper as tendering Christ or tendering the gospel. In the parable of the king's feast, Jesus tells of a king who gave a feast, and when all was in readiness, he sent out his servants to tender the invitation. As Owen saw it, the sacrament tenders the great invitation to the soul.[71]

In Discourse Ten Owen speaks of the Supper as exhibiting Christ. The eucharistic presence is to the end of exhibiting Christ that he might be received. "If Christ be present with us by way of *exhibition*, we ought to be present by way of *admission*. It will not advantage you or me that Christ tenders himself unto us, unless *we receive him*."[72] It is the responsibility of the ministers to tender the gospel to the faithful, but it is the responsibility of the congregation to receive the gospel. Owen speaks as a minister of the gospel to his congregation. "If in the name of Christ we make a tender of him unto you, and he be not actually received, there is but half the work done."[73] One notices again in these various Puritan works on the Lord's Supper that the celebration is not merely something done by the minister, but something done by the min-

---

[70] Owen, *Sacramental Discourses*, p. 541.

[71] Owen, *Sacramental Discourses*, p. 541.

[72] Owen, *Sacramental Discourses*, p. 575.

[73] Owen, *Sacramental Discourses*, p. 575.

ister and the congregation together. Owen exhorts his congregation to receive Christ. "Let Christ be received into your hearts by faith and love, upon this particular tender that he assuredly makes in this ordinance of himself unto you; for, as I said, he hath not invited you unto an empty, painted feast or table."[74] It is at the Lord's Table that the invitation to receive Christ as Lord and Savior is both made and accepted.

C. THE SUPPER AS PROFESSION OF FAITH

One of the chief ends of the sacrament of the Lord's Supper is that when we participate in it we make a profession of faith.[75] Already in the second of these sacramental discourses we have a brief enumeration of the purposes of this sacrament. Owen says, "The very nature of the ordinance itself gives us a peculiar communion; and there are four things that attend the nature of this ordinance that are peculiar:—It is commemorative, professional, eucharistical, and federal."[76] Although we may find the language archaic, it might easily, with certain adjustments, serve as a preview of Owen's eucharistic theology. In the course of this sacramental discourse he opens up these four terms. What we want to concentrate on here is the "professional" dimension of the Supper. Owen says that the right celebration of the Supper involves the making of a very definite profession of faith.[77] It is in the actual eating of the bread and drinking of the cup that the profession of faith is made. It is not enough simply to remember the saving work of Christ. It must be shown forth as well. What Owen seems to have in mind here is that, in actually participating in the service by eating the bread and drinking the wine, one makes clear that the sacrifice of Christ is the source of both our faith and our life.

---

[74] Owen, *Sacramental Discourses*, p. 575.
[75] See Payne, *John Owen on the Lord's Supper*, p. 69–71.
[76] Owen, *Sacramental Discourses*, p. 527
[77] Owen, *Sacramental Discourses*, p. 527.

By "professional," Owen means a particular dimension of the Lord's Supper. Elsewhere, we have referred to this same dimension in different terms—as the "kerygmatic" or "evangelistic" dimension of the Supper. Owen seems to have this same dimension in mind when he uses the term "professional." The point is that by participating in the Sacrament we witness to our faith in the redemptive power of Christ's atoning sacrifice, his death, and his victory over the grave. We confess that this is the source of our life, and every time we receive this broken bread and this poured out wine we make clear to ourselves, to each other, and to the world that Christ is our Savior.

In this particular text Owen makes clear that as well as the "professional" dimension of the Supper, there is the "eucharistic" dimension of this witness. He is quite explicit about this.

> It is peculiarly *eucharistical*. There is a peculiar thanksgiving that ought to attend this ordinance. It is called "The cup of blessing," or "The cup of thanksgiving;" –the word εὐλογία is used promiscuously for "blessing" and "thanksgiving." It is called "The cup of blessing," because of the institution, and prayer for the blessing of God upon it; and it is called "The cup of thanksgiving," because we do in a peculiar manner give thanks to God for Christ, and for his love in him.[78]

We spoke about this in regard to the different dimensions of Calvin's eucharistic theology. John Knox, as we noted, is even clearer.

In the third discourse, Owen takes up the text from Romans 10:10, "With the heart man believeth unto righteousness, and with the mouth confession is made unto salvation."[79] In this text we have the two immediate ends of the Supper. The one has to do with our faith and the other our profession. The first is the commemoration of the death of Christ. It remembers, or, to use Owen's word, "calls over" the death of Christ. This commemo-

---

[78] Owen, *Sacramental Discourses*, p. 527–528.

[79] As quoted in Owen, *Sacramental Discourses*, p. 529.

10: THE WESTMINSTER PURITANS

ration, this believing in our hearts, is to the end of our spiritual nourishment, while the confession with our lips is for the edification of others, both other Christians and those as yet outside the household of faith. What we find clearly in Romans 10:10 is that for us as Christians there should be both the inward believing of the heart and the outward confession of the mouth, that is, the public witness.[80]

D. THE SUPPER AS COVENANT

Those who are dedicated to understanding the Lord's Supper biblically can hardly avoid covenantal theology. As the Apostle Paul reports, Jesus took the cup and, offering it to the disciples, said, "This cup is the new covenant in my blood; all of you drink of it" (cf. 1 Corinthians 11:25). As we have already pointed out, very early in the Reformation a number of the Reformers began to develop a distinctly covenantal theology both in regard to baptism and the Lord's Supper. We find this very obviously in the second of Owen's discourses. We have already quoted from this discourse Owen's dictum: "The very nature of the ordinance itself gives us a peculiar communion; and there are four things that attend the nature of this ordinance that are peculiar:—It is commemorative, professional, eucharistical, and federal."[81] Here the word "federal" is an obvious and significant synonym of the word "covenantal." Here, again, we want to make special note of this.

A bit further on in this same discourse, Owen opens up this term "federal." There it is quite obvious that what he has in mind is what we have fairly consistently been calling the "covenantal" dimension of the Sacrament.

> It is a *federal* ordinance, wherein God confirms the covenant unto us, and wherein he calls us to make a recognition of the covenant unto God. The covenant

---

[80] Owen, *Sacramental Discourses*, pp. 529–530.
[81] Owen, *Sacramental Discourses*, p. 527.

> is once made; but we know that we stand in need that it should be often transacted in our souls,—that God should often testify his covenant unto us, and that we should often actually renew our covenant engagements unto him.[82]

All this, of course, Owen found in his careful exegesis of the basic text, "This cup is the New Testament in my blood." He also finds it in the text which he has chosen for his sermon, namely, 1 Corinthians 10:16, "The cup of blessing which we bless, is it not the communion of the blood of Christ? The bread which we break, is it not the communion of the body of Christ?" In the celebration of the covenant meal we are made partakers of the covenant community. We are joined to Christ and to each other. It is fundamental covenant theology that

> God never fails nor breaks his promises; so that he hath no need to renew them, but testify them anew: we break and fail in ours; so that we have need actually to renew them. And that is it which we are called unto in this ordinance; which is the ordinance of the great seal of the covenant in the blood of Christ.[83]

Here Owen makes quite clear why Reformed churches so often like to speak of the Supper as the sign and the seal of the covenant.

Reformed churches have generally made much of the rich biblical imagery used in regard to the sacraments which is found so generously already in the New Testament and on into the age of the church Fathers. The Passover typology was thought of as especially significant for understanding the Lord's Supper. Discourse Sixteen is filled with insights from typology, especially the typology found in the Gospel of John.[84] Much of what we read concerning the observance of the Supper has to do with the ful-

---

[82] Owen, *Sacramental Discourses*, p. 528.

[83] Owen, *Sacramental Discourses*, p. 528.

[84] Owen, *Sacramental Discourses*, p. 594.

filling of the types. We find a good number of meals in the Old Testament which confirmed one covenant or another. Owen mentions the covenant between Isaac and Abimelech and the covenant between Jacob and Laban. In each case they sealed the covenant by sharing a meal. The feast was a meal on the sacrifice that had been made. Feasts such as these sealed the covenant that had been made. Owen then concludes by saying, "Christ by his sacrifice has ratified the covenant between God and us."[85] Typology was very important to John Owen. We remember that he published a rather long commentary on the Epistle to the Hebrews, a book of the Bible that revels in typology. So much of the New Testament teaching on the sacraments is based on typology. A biblical approach to the sacraments must deal with the sacramental typology. For Owen, it is very clear that the Lord's Supper is the fulfillment of the covenant meals of the Old Testament.

E. THE SUPPER AS COMMUNION

The Reformed churches have always had a preference for the word "communion" when it comes to the sacrament of the Lord's Supper. The word serves us well because it speaks of the intimate fellowship between Christians and God as well as the union between Christians one with another. We find Owen using this word to get across this point in the second of his sacramental discourses.

The text of this sermon very obviously supports this approach, "The cup of blessing which we bless, is it not the communion of the blood of Christ? The bread which we break, is it not the communion of the body of Christ?" (1 Cor. 10:16).[86] The word translated here as "communion" is the Greek, *koinonia*. Sometimes it is translated "fellowship" or "participation." It is a uniquely Christian word. It speaks of an intimate union at the same time as a sacred relationship, and, of course, this is just the sense the English word "com-

---

[85] Owen, *Sacramental Discourses*, p. 596.
[86] As quoted in Owen, *Sacramental Discourses*, p. 523.

munion" implies today. In this text from 1 Corinthians 10:16, the Apostle Paul very simply teaches us that the sacrament of the Lord's Supper is a service of holy communion, communion with God and communion with our fellow Christians. The discourse begins with this most perceptive line, "There is, in the ordinance of the Lord's supper, an especial and peculiar communion with Christ, in his body and blood . . . One reason why we so little value the ordinance, and profit so little by it, may be, because we understand so little of the nature of that special communion with Christ . . ."[87] The question Owen wants to put his finger on is the question of the eucharistic presence. To Owen the presence of God is experienced in communion. It is a very real experience of God. It demands that we take our shoes from off our feet and bow our foreheads to the dust.

The great value of this collection of the *Sacramental Discourses* of John Owen is that he so beautifully elaborates the nature of the sacrament. As several Reformed theologians before him, Owen spoke of a number of dimensions of eucharistic piety and theology. In Discourse Two, as a sort of prelude, we have an enumeration of these dimensions. For this study we have focused on several emphases of Owen's thought, but there are others that could have been chosen. These are of special interest. Owen mentions the commemorative dimension. Surely the Supper is a memorial, and, as Owen understood it, this is indeed a very rich and deep dimension of the Supper. There is also a kerygmatic dimension to the Supper and Owen is especially eloquent when he speaks of the kerygmatic or evangelistic nature of the Supper. The sacrament is an invitation to receive Christ, an invitation made as often as we celebrate it. Even further, by participating in the sacrament we make a public profession of faith. There is a eucharistic dimension to this "peculiar communion" we have with Christ and one another.[88] Finally we would point out that, for Owen, the word

---

[87] Owen, *Sacramental Discourses*, p. 523.

[88] Owen, *Sacramental Discourses*, p. 528.

communion sums up all these dimensions. He believed in a real presence, the presence of the Christ whose passion and resurrection is remembered. Christ is present to be received by faith. He is present that we might unite in him and exercise the new life of the New Covenant. This is the great truth that Christians have tried to understand generation after generation.

Turning to the fifth discourse, we find another thought on the Lord's Supper as communion. It is when we begin to speak of the sacrament as communion with God that we need to think about the presence of God. As Owen sees it, the presence of God in our worship should be preeminent. Owen says, "We are to consider God in Christ as *the immediate object of that worship which in every ordinance we do perform.*"[89] We do not always sense his presence. Owen reminds us of the story of Jacob spending the night at Bethel and having a dream in which God spoke to him. When he awoke from his dream he said, "Surely the Lord is in this place and I knew it not" (Gen. 28:16, KJV). Owen comments that it is always this way when we worship. God is there even if we do not sense it. This is true generally about the presence of God, but then we must go on to speak of the gracious presence of God in this sacrament.[90] This presence we find in all the ordinances established by God—the preaching of the Word, prayer in the name of Jesus, baptism and the Lord's Supper. It is true in the coming together of the Church in the name of Jesus, and it is true when we share with those in need. That which has divine institution is blessed by the divine presence.[91]

In Discourse Seven Owen again takes up the subject. He first of all wants to make clear that it is a mystery, involving great wisdom and faith. In the Supper there is a genuine exhibition of Christ. Here, again, we have a word that has a much stronger meaning in Owen's seventeenth century English than it does in

---

[89] Owen, *Sacramental Discourses*, p. 548.

[90] Owen, *Sacramental Discourses*, p. 549.

[91] Owen, *Sacramental Discourses*, p. 550.

our parlance. "Exhibition," meant for Owen holding something out to be received. To say that he exhibited means that he is shown to be received. He is held forth to be believed.[92] It is he, Jesus himself, who makes the offer, "Take eat; this is my body broken for you." Here we are confronted by Jesus himself. He invites us to be united to him through participation in the feast. He offers us incorporation into his body. This incorporation, moreover, is a union with the broken body, with the blood poured out in sacrifice. It is an invitation to become one with the Savior, that he might be our Savior.[93] Incorporation is the ultimate presence.

Finally what Owen would teach is that holy communion is nothing less than union with Christ. It is when our faith discovers Jesus as our Savior by virtue of his perfect sacrifice and glorious resurrection that the celebration of this sacrament becomes worship. It is when we remember Christ as the Lamb of God who has taken away the sin of the world that Jesus is glorified.[94] Our pastor/theologian makes his appeal:

> Brethren, can we receive Christ thus? Are we willing to receive him thus? If so, we may go away and be no more sorrowful. If we come short herein, we come short of that faith which is required of us in this ordinance. Pray let us endeavour to consider how Jesus Christ doth hereby make a tender of himself unto us,—as one that hath actually taken away all our sins, and all our iniquities, that none of them shall ever be laid unto our charge; and to receive him as such, is to give glory unto him.[95]

So it is that we come to Christ in this celebration of the Lord's Supper. We come placing our faith in Christ, submitting to his authority,

---

[92] Owen, *Sacramental Discourses*, p. 564. See also Payne, *John Owen On the Lord's Supper*, pp. 38–44.
[93] Owen, *Sacramental Discourses*, p. 564.
[94] Owen, *Sacramental Discourses*, pp. 564–565.
[95] Owen, *Sacramental Discourses*, p. 565.

10: The Westminster Puritans

and believing his promises, that he is indeed with us and within us. "That he will be present with us and give himself unto us."[96] In this the covenant is renewed. God is our God and we are his people.

Owen would sum up his message in these words: "And lastly, in one word, faith is so to receive him as to enable us to sit down at God's table as those that are the Lord's friends,—as those that are invited to feast upon the sacrifice."[97] This is the fulfillment of the Lord's Passover.[98] Once again we notice the prominence of these two types, the feast in the house of the Father and the Passover. These two types are fundamental to Owen's Reformed eucharistic piety.

There are several other of these discourses that speak of the Lord's Supper in terms of the eucharistic presence or in terms simply of communion, but we must go on to the last of these discourses, Discourse Twenty-five. This discourse was delivered some years after most of the other sacramental discourses. Owen sets out to speak of the peculiar communion we have with Christ in this ordinance. Here we are very much aware that we are reading a document written in the seventeenth century. We use the word "peculiar" quite differently today. In current usage we might speak of the "unique" communion that Christians have in the Lord's Supper. There is something about the Lord's Supper which is peculiar in the old sense of the word, but in our day we might more appropriately speak of the Lord's Supper providing us with a "special" communion with Christ. It gives us a special participation in Christ. This is the affirmation of the whole Christian church and has been all down through the ages.[99]

Referring to the sixth chapter of the Gospel of John, Owen reminds us of the text, "It is the Spirit that quickeneth; the flesh

---

[96] Owen, *Sacramental Discourses*, p. 565.

[97] Owen, *Sacramental Discourses*, p. 566.

[98] Owen, *Sacramental Discourses*, p. 566.

[99] Owen, *Sacramental Discourses*, p. 620.

profiteth nothing: the words that I speak unto you, they are spirit and they are life.'"[100] Our theologian comments: "'It is a spiritual communication,' saith he, 'of myself unto you; but it is as intimate, and gives as real an incorporation, as if you did eat my flesh and drink my blood.'"[101] Owen goes on, giving us four points in which the Lord's Supper is distinct or unique. The first thing he wants to mention is that, in the celebration of the Lord's Supper, ". . . faith hath a peculiar respect to the *sole authority of Christ* in the institution of this ordinance."[102] That we should receive Jesus by eating bread and drinking wine only makes sense if we do it because Jesus so instituted it. The light of nature certainly does not suggest it. Here we honor Christ in his kingly office. We do this because Christ commanded it. Secondly, there is a uniqueness to the Supper in that it speaks so clearly of the love of Christ. Christ's love toward us is manifested by his passion, the body broken and the wine poured out. Here, then, we give glory to Christ in his priestly office. Thirdly, in the celebration of the Lord's Supper faith lays hold of the invitation of Christ to the souls of believers, not to the words only but to the sharing of the sacred meal. The faithful recognize what they really are. One receives the sacraments, both the eucharistic words and the eucharistic acts, from Christ himself as indeed what they really are, what they signify. They are participation in the mighty acts of God for our salvation. By the institution of Christ there is a sacramental union between the bread and the wine and what they stand for. Here we glorify Christ for his prophetic office.[103] Finally there is a mysteriousness to the observance of the Lord's Supper. This many of us have regularly experienced. We have experienced this receiving of Christ. We know it is real. How many of us have experienced this reality? How many of us

---

[100] John 6:63, as quoted in Owen, *Sacramental Discourses*, p. 620.

[101] Owen, *Sacramental Discourses*, p. 620.

[102] Owen, *Sacramental Discourses*, p. 621.

[103] Owen, *Sacramental Discourses*, p. 621.

have known "a mysterious reception and incorporation of him,—receiving him to dwell in them, warming, cherishing, comforting, and strengthening their hearts"?[104]

We wish Owen had written a formal theological treatise on the Lord's Supper. It would more than likely be a masterpiece. What we have can only be regarded as extracts from his thought which happily found their way into the pulpit and which someone had the wisdom to get down on paper. Even if it is a collection of fragments, it does show us a number of important dimensions of the Puritan eucharistic piety.

---

[104] Owen, *Sacramental Discourses*, p. 622.

11

THE AGE OF PROTESTANT ORTHODOXY

By the middle of the seventeenth century, Protestantism was no longer new and exciting. In certain areas of northern Europe it was indeed quite traditional. It was in some areas strongly supported by the civil government, and outward conformity to the official religion of the state often led to an outward pro-forma faith. On the other hand, the Protestant Orthodoxy of the seventeenth century was often well thought out and profoundly held. Sometimes it was the faith of a persecuted minority which had paid dearly for its doctrine, its form of prayers, and its moral discipline. Both among the Lutheran and the Reformed in Germany, the age of Protestant Orthodoxy produced great theology, brilliant preaching, and inspiring hymnody. We find this depth of devotion especially in the Netherlands. In a moment we will focus on that most pious land, although first we will study a particularly rich collection of eucharistic sermons preached by the French Huguenot preacher Jean Daillé.

JEAN DAILLÉ
AND THE HUGUENOT TRADITION

Jean Daillé (1594–1670) has left us a large number of communion sermons. In fact, he may have left us more sermons than any other French Protestant preacher of the seventeenth century.[1] When it comes to the sacrament of Holy Communion we are faced with an

---

[1] See my treatment of Jean Daillé in Hughes Oliphant Old, *The Reading and Preaching of the Scriptures in the Worship of the Christian Church*, vol. 4, *The Age of the Reformation* (Grand Rapids, MI: Eerdmans, 2002), pp. 414–441.

embarrassment of riches. In the first place, we have several sermons in his series of sermons on 1 Corinthians 10 on the sacrament as union with Christ and communion with the brethren.[2] Then there is a collection of nineteen sermons on the sacrament of the Lord's Supper as we find it in 1 Corinthians 11.[3] Finally, we have several sermons on the sacrament in volume III of his series of sermons on the Huguenot catechism.[4] Compared to other preachers this really makes a large collection. These sermons are not, however, organized into a treatise. Daillé was a preacher rather than a writer and yet these sermons contain a real depth of insight and an admirable balance between practical piety and theological reflection.

A. Outside the Gates of Paris

Paris had been the capitol city of Scholasticism. It was there that Peter Lombard compiled his *Sentences*. It was in Paris that Thomas Aquinas worked out his synthesis of high medieval Scholasticism. The whole thing, of course, found artistic expression in the gothic arches, flying buttresses, and pinnacles of Notre Dame Cathedral. For centuries, the theological faculty of Paris was the final word on orthodox Christian doctrine. There were all kinds of schools in that clearing house of medieval theology. There was St. Victor for the Augustinians and San Jacques for the Franciscans and Dominicans. The Carmelites had their school, too.

The first glimmers of Protestantism had appeared in Paris rather early in the sixteenth century. One can still find the old monastery of Saint-Germain-des-Prés right in the middle of the

---

[2] Jean Daillé, *XXI sermons de Iean Daillé, sur le X. Chapitre de la I Epitre de S. Paul aux Corinthiens: prononcez à Charenton, l'an 1664, 1665, 1666* (Genève: Iean Ant. & Samuel de Tournes, 1668). Hereinafter Daillé, *I Corinthians 10*.

[3] Jean Daillé, *Exposition de l'institution de la S. Cene: rapportée par Saint Paul en sa I. Epitre aux Corinthiens: en xix sermons* (Genève: Iean Ant. & Samuel de Tournes, 1664). Hereinafter Daillé, *Exposition de l'institution de la S. Cene*.

[4] Jean Daillé, *Sermons sur le Catéchisme des Eglises Reformées* (Genève: Pour le Societé de Libraires, 1701). Hereinafter, Daillé, *Catechetical Sermons*.

Latin Quarter. It was there that the Christian Humanist scholars Étienne Briçonnet, Gérard Roussel, and Guillaume Farel gathered around the venerable Jacques Lefèvre d'Étaples and began to take a new, fresh view of Holy Scripture. Then came the sad stories—the massacre of St. Bartholomew's Eve, the wars of religion, and the attempt to suppress the Reformation. With the Edict of Nantes, Protestants were banished from the theological capitol of the western church. They were allowed to worship, however, as long as they worshiped *extra muros*, that is, outside the walls of Paris.

The Huguenots, as the Protestants of France were called in those days, built their meeting house at Charenton, up river from the city. During Jean Daillé's pastorate, the *extra muros* congregation at Charenton had half a dozen preachers. In fact, a vigorous preaching ministry was maintained at Charenton, even if it was officially banished from the city itself. Let us look at several themes that we find in these sermons that seem particularly important to Daillé's eucharistic preaching.[5]

B. THE SACRAMENT AS AGAPÉ

We usually turn to 1 Corinthians 11:17–34 first when we want to understand the Lord's Supper. The passage recounts the story of the institution of the sacred rite as the apostle received it from the Lord himself. That, at least, is the way the text puts it. Even more, the account the apostle gives us is in a particular context, namely, an abuse which had falsified the sacrament. Daillé explains the situation.[6] Some of the more prosperous members of the church had turned the sacrament into a feast in the fashion of that day. In the Greek-speaking world, it was a custom to invite a congenial group of friends to a symposium at which one would have a discussion of

---

[5] I must express my appreciation to Hannah Chase Old, my daughter, for providing me with digests of these sermons from the archives of Princeton Theological Seminary.

[6] Daillé, *Exposition de l'institution de la S. Cene*, pp. 79f.

some philosophical subject. These feasts were more than simple dinner parties. A major activity of the evening was supposed to be serious intellectual discussion. They offered both good food and good conversation. These were occasions of both entertainment and fellowship as well as a sort of intellectual exercise. Those who had the leisure would come early and bring expensive and luxurious foods and perhaps choice wine, but when the members of the church who had to work for a living arrived not much food was left. Some were filled while others went home hungry.[7]

In the second and third centuries, as Daillé understood it, the actual feasting that in earlier days was a natural part of the occasion began to be left out. This was regrettable because there were important charitable aspects to the sacrament when it was properly observed, such as when the prosperous shared their prosperity with the poor. When in the course of time the love feast disappeared, the sense of community that is the actual love feast began to disappear as well. In Augustine's time most people did not participate in the meal except on Maundy Thursday and then they only took a bite of bread and a sip of wine. The abuse of the Corinthians was that when the poor came to the service they did not feel loved at all. One can imagine how they felt when they arrived only to find that there was little or nothing left for them. How degrading that must have been.[8] Needless to say, this left nobody in the proper frame of mind to celebrate the Lord's Supper properly.[9]

One might say that the Lord's Supper is the ultimate love feast. The love signified here is the love among the brethren as well as the love of God for us. It shows us that we feast on the lamb of God who was slain on our behalf. Above that, as Daillé sees it, this whole feast, is a feast of thanksgiving to God for what he has done and a sharing

---

[7] Daillé, *Exposition de l'institution de la S. Cene*, p. 85.

[8] Daillé, *Exposition de l'institution de la S. Cene*, p. 99.

[9] Daillé is probably right in assuming that Corinthian Christians had let the Greek symposium influence their communion celebrations far too much.

of the love of the family of God with one another. For Daillé the sacrament of Holy Communion is both love feast shared by believers and Eucharist, that is, a feast of thanksgiving to God for his mighty works of creation and redemption. The two go naturally together.

We should, on the one hand, guard against eating and drinking in excess and on the other insisting on requiring that the communicant receive the sacrament fasting as was the custom with the Roman mass at the beginning of the sixteenth century. The Apostle Paul warned against excess in the feasting in his letter to the Corinthians. The exaggerated asceticism that too often was practiced in the Middle Ages deforms the worship of the church just as much as excessive feasting. We should keep in mind that the purpose of the sacrament is to feed the soul and that can be done if we worship in spirit and truth. It can be done if we remember that our whole purpose in worship is to honor him who washed his disciples' feet.[10] While on one hand our celebrations should keep in mind the needs of the brethren, and while it should clearly be a love feast, promoting the fellowship of the brethren, reverence, and awe must be the prevailing mood of the service.

C. The Sacrament as Commemoration

Any series of sermons on the Lord's Supper as we find it in First Corinthians will have to deal with 1 Corinthians 11:24, "This do in remembrance of Me."[11] What is remarkable here is that Daillé has such a profound understanding of that key word, "remembrance," and what it means particularly in the Scriptures of the Old and New Testament. He understands the word to mean celebrate or commemorate. For Daillé it is not only a recalling to mind but a commemoration.[12] In the observance of the sacrament we commemorate first of all the risen Christ. Then we commemorate

---

[10] Daillé, *Exposition de l'institution de la S. Cene*, p. 109.

[11] Daillé, *Exposition de l'institution de la S. Cene*, pp. 284f.

[12] Daillé, *Exposition de l'institution de la S. Cene*, p. 287.

his passion and especially his atoning sacrifice. In fact the commemoration of Christ's atoning sacrifice is especially important to Daillé. For Daillé the uniqueness of Christ's sacrifice is a major theological concern. Our Huguenot theologian then insists that at the celebration of Communion we are to remember all that Christ did. We are to commemorate both creation and providence, even the judgments of history, but also we are to form our prayers so that the whole story of redemption is commemorated.

Daillé makes it very clear that he has come to understand the meaning of remembrance from the feast of Passover. The text of Exodus specifically directs that Passover is to be kept as a day of remembrance (Exod. 12:14). At the feast of Passover, the father of the family was to narrate the history of salvation. He is to tell once again the story of how the Israelites were enslaved in Egypt and how God delivered them from that slavery. He is to celebrate how God opened up the sea so that the Israelites passed through it as on dry land, how God led them through the wilderness, and then brought them into the promised land. Even so the Christian minister at the celebration of the Lord's Supper is to recount once more the story of Christ foretold by the prophets, born in Bethlehem of Judea, brought up in the fear of the Lord, and yet, in truth, the incarnate son of God. Once more we are to remember Christ's ministry of preaching and teaching, his mighty works of healing, calming the fevered, opening the eyes of the blind, and providing for the hungry. Once more the Christian minister must remember how Christ went to the cross, how he was betrayed, and how he was scourged for our transgression. Then, above all, we are to remember his resurrection, his ascension into heaven and his sitting down at the right hand of the Father. Clearly for Daillé the celebration of the Lord's Supper is the fulfillment of the Passover.

Our Huguenot theologian has a remarkably strong doctrine of the Holy Spirit and a profound appreciation of the Spirit's function in the observance of the sacrament. This is, to be sure, a recurring theme of Reformed eucharistic theology. From John 14:26 Daillé learned that it is the Holy Spirit who brings to our minds all that Christ did and said. At one place our preacher tells us that the Lord gives us these memories by his Holy Spirit. We read his Word and learn what he has done, and the Spirit reminds us of these things for our encouragement.[13]

Another important point we find in this sermon is that we as Christians have a life-long duty to praise God for what he has done. Here, of course we come to the eucharistic dimension of the sacrament. It is a theme which appears and reappears in these sermons. Recounting the mighty acts of God is of the essence of the biblical concept of worship. Day and night our praises should go out to him. This strengthens our love for God but it also strengthens the faith and devotion of the worshiping congregation.[14]

D. THE SACRAMENT AS SIGN AND SEAL OF THE COVENANT

Sermon number 9 in Daillé's series of sermons on 1 Corinthians 11 is for the most part a long Christian interpretation of the Feast of Passover. The sermon contains much interesting material but we have frequently made the point that for Reformed theologians, the Christian interpretation of Passover is a major interest.

Toward the end of the sermon, Daillé takes up the subject of the sacrament as sign and seal of the covenant. To be sure Jesus himself gave a strong covenantal dimension to the sacrament when he administered the cup with the words, "This cup is the New Covenant in my blood." Daillé now proceeds to discuss what this covenant is: It is the relationship which Christ has offered to have with us, if we receive him by faith. It is a relationship of peace, joy, grace, perseverance, sanctification, and glorification.[15] This is followed by an intense discussion of a number of Old Testament passages on

---

[13] Daillé, *Exposition de l'institution de la S. Cene*, p. 300.

[14] Daillé, *Exposition de l'institution de la S. Cene*, p. 319.

[15] Daillé, *Exposition de l'institution de la S. Cene*, p. 325.

the covenant relation between God and his people. Special attention is given to the relation of the Old Covenant to the New Covenant.

Daillé asks what it means when Jesus said, "This cup is the New Covenant in my blood." It means that the covenant was ratified, satisfied, and paid for by the shedding of Christ's blood. In the Old Covenant sin was paid for through sacrifice. However, insists Daillé, the blood of Christ is much more precious, and it is ultimately necessary because the justice of God demands a perfect sacrifice to fulfill the demands of the old Law. Here Daillé carefully follows the thinking of the Epistle to the Hebrews. Daillé continues asking what role this communion cup has. It is a sign of the covenant which was granted to us. It is a symbol of our communion with God. When the cup is passed to us it is a sign that we are in the good graces of God. It is like being knighted by the king. It means we are in favor at court.

E. The Sacrament as Communion

It is in a completely different work that we find a most generous treatment on the subject of the Lord's Supper as communion. Daillé's *lectio continua* sermons on the Apostle Paul's First Epistle to the Corinthians has several sermons on chapter ten of that epistle where we find some rich passages on the sacrament.[16] For a Reformed eucharistic theology these verses are especially important.

> The cup of blessing which we bless, is it not a participation in the blood of Christ? The bread which we break, is it not a participation in the body of Christ? Because there is one bread, we who are many are one body, for we all partake of the one bread. (1 Corinthians 10:16–17)

Three sermons are given to opening up these verses. The first takes up a number of practical subjects. In regard to some of these, Daillé is willing to admit they are practices which might be classed as *adiaphora*. Daillé is not a hard liner.

---

[16] Daillé, *I Corinthians 10*, pp. 520f.

11: THE AGE OF PROTESTANT ORTHODOXY

What concerns our Huguenot theologian is that the sacrament is supposed to bless Christians with spiritual nourishment. The sacred meal should look like a meal. It should be a meal for Christians regardless of how strong or how feeble their faith might be. Celebrations of the mass in which only the priest consecrates for himself a wafer and cup of wine mixed with water are a noteworthy abuse. The priest may be blessed but the people are ignored. Even more the ceremony of the adoration of the host and the benediction of the sacrament are even worse. The latter, as Daillé sees it, is most objectionable.

Daillé inveighs against the Roman vestments because they encourage pride of office, but much more he turns his scorn against the little wafers that are used instead of real bread. The text of 1 Corinthians 10 makes a point of having one loaf of bread and breaking it into pieces. Daillé sees real significance in the sacramental action here and he obviously has gotten it from this passage in 1 Corinthians.[17]

It is really in the following sermons that Daillé takes up the heart of the matter. To participate in the sacrament of Communion is to have union with Christ and communion with the brethren. By participation in the sacrament we become members of the mystical body of Christ. Daillé reminds us of the words of the Gospel of John that if we do not have the Son, we do not have life, for he is the sole medium for our salvation. This comes about through union or communion with Christ. It is of this that the sacraments are signs and seals. The apostle could not be more clear. Paul goes on to stress that this communion is not only with Christ but with each other as the Body of Christ. The key to what the apostle is saying is the word communion or, as it is in the Greek, *koinonia*.[18] Here Daillé goes into the philology of the Greek word at length. The sermon comes to a marvelous conclusion telling us

---

[17] Daillé, *I Corinthians 10*, p. 520.
[18] Daillé, *I Corinthians 10*, p. 529.

that to worship truly is to worship him in spirit and in truth, not in pomp and ceremony. What could be better than being a people in communion with Christ, enlivened by his Spirit governed by his providence and crowned with his glory?[19]

Devoting another sermon to the same subject Daillé looks once more at the text.[20] The sermon is begun with a statement of the unity of the Church—rather surprising for the seventeenth century. It is almost prophetic of the social ideology of the end of the eighteenth century when France had its revolution. Then the motto was *liberté, egalité, fraternité*. A century before that terrible revolution, Daillé put it much more pastorally. We are all equal as members of the body of Christ. No Christian is superior to another. Likewise we have different gifts as the Lord gives them to us but none is more important than another. We are rather all the children of God through our union with Christ, and brothers and sisters in Christ through adoption. Daillé's main theme is quite simple. The eucharist is the sacrament of union with Christ and with one another. It is of the greatest importance, however, to notice the pneumatic dimension of Daillé's understanding. Daillé goes on to tell us that it is the gift of the Holy Spirit which binds us to Christ and to one another.

F. THE UNIQUENESS OF CHRIST'S SACRIFICE[21]

Let us look at another group of sermons on the sacrament of the Lord's Supper by Jean Daillé. These sermons are found in a series of catechetical sermons preached shortly before Daillé's death in 1670.[22] Daillé makes several points in these catechetical sermons that we find of particular interest. He makes these with the candor appropriate to a series of catechetical sermons. They are, in

---

[19] Daillé, *I Corinthians 10*, p. 559.

[20] Daillé, *I Corinthians 10*, p. 562f.

[21] Appreciation is due to Rev. Glen Clary, one of my graduate students, for providing me with digests of these sermons on the Huguenot catechism on which this section is based.

[22] See Daillé, *Catechetical Sermons*.

11: THE AGE OF PROTESTANT ORTHODOXY

fact, points that have become part and parcel of classic Reformed eucharistic theology.

The first of these points might be summarized as follows: The Reformed Church bears witness to the unique priesthood of Christ and celebrates the sacrament of Holy Communion as its eucharistic memorial. Daillé follows closely the teaching of the Epistle to the Hebrews, depending very heavily on its typology to make his point. As the priesthood of Melchizedek is eternal, so is the priesthood of Christ.[23] For the New Testament church there is but one high priest and but one sacrifice. The one sacrifice on the cross was perfect and sufficient to atone for the sins of the whole world.[24] In Old Testament times, there were indeed many sacrifices to be made and there was a priesthood founded to offer these sacrifices, but we find nothing of this sort in the New Testament. Christ alone is the high priest ordained to offer himself as the pure and perfect offering.[25]

To be sure, as a metaphor we find in the New Testament that all Christians have a priestly service to perform. We are supposed to offer ourselves unto God as a spiritual service in praise and prayer, in giving alms to the poor and performing works of mercy. We find this in Romans 12:1–2, 1 Peter 2:5, and Hebrews 13:15–16.[26] These passages, however, are clearly metaphorical. Daillé, following the traditional Protestant polemic, reminds us of the teaching of the Epistle to the Hebrews. There in chapters nine and ten, we are specifically taught that Christ offered on the cross one perfect sacrifice that never needs to be repeated, because it was the perfect and complete propitiatory sacrifice.[27] This complete, unique sacrifice of Christ is a primary emphasis of the Epistle to the Hebrews. It is the text of Scripture to which Protestantism has

---

[23] Daillé, *Catechetical Sermons*, p. 537.

[24] Daillé, *Catechetical Sermons*, p. 539.

[25] Daillé, *Catechetical Sermons*, p. 542.

[26] Daillé, *Catechetical Sermons*, pp. 544f.

[27] Daillé, *Catechetical Sermons*, p. 556.

always returned. It is a hymn to the uniqueness of the sacrifice of Christ. In this sacrament we are united to our Lord Jesus Christ's sacrifice on the cross for us. Just as baptism and the preaching of the Word bring us into communion with Christ, so does the Holy Supper.[28] Daillé sums up his teaching on the sacrament of the Lord's Supper by saying that communion is the purpose and end of all evangelical religious services. These services are the way we are united to Christ. Being in him, then, we receive both the salvation of our souls and eternal life.[29]

G. THE NATURE OF THE REAL PRESENCE

Jean Daillé continues his series of catechetical sermons on the sacrament of the Lord's Supper by treating the subject of the real presence.[30] First of all our preacher wishes to make perfectly clear that the Reformed faith teaches that Christ is indeed present at the Holy Supper. But it must also be made clear that Christ is present in the same way that he is present at baptism, when we preach the word, or unite in prayer. Did not Christ promise to those who are baptized that he would be with them always? It is the same way with all other legitimate acts of our religion. It is not a matter of the omnipresence of the divine nature, but rather that our Lord is specifically present when we come to him, his hands filled with spiritual gifts and gracious acts.[31] Moreover, Daillé teaches that Christ is present through his Holy Spirit. Through the illumination of his Spirit, he truly communicates his body and his blood to those who receive the sacrament as it was instituted. In this way believers receive the virtue of Christ's atoning passion and enjoy all the benefits of his broken body and poured out blood offered up on the cross.

At this point our Huguenot theologian gets to a discussion of

---

[28] Daillé, *Catechetical Sermons*, p. 565.

[29] Daillé, *Catechetical Sermons*, p. 567.

[30] Daillé, *Catechetical Sermons*, p. 573.

[31] Daillé, *Catechetical Sermons*, p. 573.

11: THE AGE OF PROTESTANT ORTHODOXY

substance and accidents. Rather rapidly Daillé goes over the different positions of the different schools of Scholastic philosophy. Daillé could have learned all of this in any university in Europe. Like many scholars of this day he was thoroughly bored with the well-worn formulas of Scholasticism.[32] Interestingly enough, the arguments of the various schools of philosophy are passed over rather quickly. Daillé wants to make his point from Scripture.

By the time Jean Daillé preached these sermons, these same arguments had been batted around for several generations. One of these traditional arguments was that if the bread is understood as the body of Christ in a literalistic way, then how are we going to explain what happens to the body of Christ when it is chewed, swallowed, and digested? One hesitates to go further, but again Daillé wants to get back to Scripture. When the church has allowed itself to be instructed by Scripture, it has recognized that the bread and wine are signs and figures. If, on the other hand, they are the real thing, that is, human flesh and blood, instead of bread and wine, then they are no longer signs, and the Supper is no longer a sacrament.[33]

H. Preparation for Receiving the Sacrament

Not surprisingly, these catechetical sermons give particular attention to the exercises of piety. They are interested not only in eucharistic theology, but in eucharistic piety. The piety of the seventeenth century was strongly introspective. Meditation played a major part in the worship of the seventeenth century, whether it was in the *Spiritual Exercises* of Ignatius of Loyola or the sacramental meditations of Samuel Rutherford. The sixteenth century, on the other hand, the century of Luther and Calvin, had tended to be much more objective in its worship.

Daillé begins his sermon on the meditation appropriate to preparing to receive the Communion by a typological interpreta-

---

[32] Daillé, *Catechetical Sermons*, p. 577.

[33] Daillé, *Catechetical Sermons*, p. 578.

tion of the levitical ceremonial.³⁴ As we find it in Leviticus 22 any beast to be offered on the altar must first be inspected by the priest to assure the offering of sacrifices without blemish. So it is with us as Christians. When we offer up ourselves as a sacrifice to God we must inspect our lives in an attempt to root out any love of sin or harboring of vanity, that we might in truth present ourselves a continual oblation to the Father. This is indeed the priestly service of the New Testament.³⁵ It is in forsaking sin that we perform the substance of our religion. In so doing we celebrate the Supper as our Lord instituted it. Here Daillé gives us an impassioned description of the spiritual worship of the priesthood of all believers. This is what we have in the Prayer of Dedication that comes at the end of the Reformed communion service. It is in forsaking sin that we truly worship God. It is in such sacred devotion accompanied by praises, humble thanksgiving, and expressions of appreciation that we present to God the calves of our lips.³⁶ One realizes as one reads this sermon that we have here a certain vestigial trace of what had been in the Middle Ages the sacrament of penance. Here the confessional has been replaced by self-examination.

The seventeenth century saw the beginning of the preparatory service, a liturgical development that came to its fullest development in eighteenth-century Scotland. It had not yet become an important development among the Protestants in France. However, the penitential dimension was certainly an important dimension to Protestant piety. We saw this in the Prayers of Confession and Supplication found in the *Genevan Psalter*. The Assurance of Pardon made this even more explicit.

It often happens that ministers preach in such a way that preparation for the sacrament is so emphasized that some in the congregation who have been careless in their preparation are

---

[34] Daillé, *Catechetical Sermons*, p. 607.

[35] Daillé, *Catechetical Sermons*, p. 608.

[36] Daillé, *Catechetical Sermons*, p. 609.

therefore hesitant to actually receive the sacred food. Daillé feels it is important to warn against this abuse.[37] Our preacher makes it very clear that Christians are obligated to receive the sacrament frequently.[38] The Christian, to be sure, must renounce sin, passions, and fleshly desires. The Christian must leave behind the animosities and impurities of the flesh rather than deprive himself or herself of communion with the Lord.[39]

I. The Frequency of Communion

One way of coming to an understanding of this problem of the frequency of our participation in the Supper is to contrast it with the sacrament of baptism.[40] One of the reasons for this is that baptism introduces us to the church. The Supper, on the other hand, nourishes us in the faith.[41] Quite simply, then, it belongs to the symbolism of the sacred meal that it must be often repeated. One remembers that Calvin's *Short Treatise on the Lord's Supper* begins the discussion by pointing out this distinction. The *Genevan Psalter* reminds us that in baptism we are received into the household of faith. It is once and for all. Then, in the Supper, we are fed and nourished, and this is continual.[42] This continuity belongs to the essential nature of the sign.

Furthermore, very interestingly, Daillé links this with a discussion of the doctrine of the perseverance of the saints.[43] What Daillé seems to have in mind is that there is a paradox in the teaching of the Reformed church. Baptism is seen as the once and for all nature of the Christian life while Communion points to the con-

---

[37] Daillé, *Catechetical Sermons*, p. 633.
[38] Daillé, *Catechetical Sermons*, p. 635.
[39] Daillé, *Catechetical Sermons*, p. 635.
[40] Daillé, *Catechetical Sermons*, p. 635.
[41] Daillé, *Catechetical Sermons*, p. 637.
[42] Daillé, *Catechetical Sermons*, p. 638.
[43] Daillé, *Catechetical Sermons*, p. 639.

stant renewal of the work of God in our hearts. Again, Daillé comes up with a beautiful typological interpretation of the Old Testament. He sees in the story of Joshua and the children of Israel crossing the Jordan River a type of baptism. Joshua crossed from the hunger of the wilderness to the fat of the Promised Land. Once in the Promised Land he and all the people of God continually drank from the river of his delights, the sacred feast of Holy Communion.[44]

THE NETHERLANDS
IN ITS GOLDEN AGE[45]

Those who lived in the Dutch Republic during the age of Frans Hals, Jan Vermeer, and Rembrandt van Rijn were indeed blessed. It was one of the bright clear days of human civilization. The United Provinces had won their independence from their Spanish overlords. In religious matters, the Reformation had been widely accepted and was beginning to shape the character of the people. A very distinct Protestant culture was developing. For the most part it was a middle class culture. Dutch artisans were producing wares of high quality. Textiles, lace work, metal work, ceramics, scientific instruments, and lenses were being manufactured and marketed throughout the land. The ship building industry prospered and Dutch merchants were trading their goods for exotic wares from as far away as the islands of Japan, Brazil, Curaçao, and, lest we forget, the port of New Amsterdam. The Netherlands was open to the world. For its day, it was a tolerant society. It was a prosperous, hard-working land. Creative people found it a good place to live and work. In fact, our own Pilgrim Fathers found refuge in the Netherlands when they were driven out of their native England. For the French philosopher René Descartes it was an intellectual haven. The

---
[44] Daillé, *Catechetical Sermons*, p. 641.
[45] This section is largely taken from Old, *The Reading and Preaching of the Scriptures in the Worship of the Christian Church*, pp. 4:449–473.

11: THE AGE OF PROTESTANT ORTHODOXY

Dutch Republic was a good place to be, as we see it painted by the seventeenth-century Dutch Masters.

The Netherlands was a good place to preach as well.[46] The Dutch have always loved solid preaching.[47] What a pity it is locked away in leather bound volumes only Dutchmen can read! Dutch preaching is rather inaccessible, because apparently few Dutch preachers committed their sermons to writing.[48] Traditionally Dutch preaching is divided into several schools. It was recognized that in addition to the usual preaching of the Dutch Reformed Church there was Lutheran preaching, Mennonite preaching, Walloon preaching, and Remonstrant preaching. In the port cities and in several cities in the north there was Lutheran preaching with the usual Lutheran pattern of lectionary preaching. Apparently there were several very prominent Mennonite preachers. One remembers Rembrandt's portrait of the Mennonite preacher, Cornelius Anslo. It was in reference to this famous preacher that the jest was made that not even Rembrandt could paint his magnificent voice.

---

[46] For the context of seventeenth-century Dutch preaching in general, see the following: Heinrich Heppe, *Geschichte des Pietismus und der Mystik in der reformirten Kirche, namentlich der Niederlande* (Leiden: E. J. Brill, 1879); Albrecht Ritschl, *Geschichte des Pietismus in der reformirten Kirche* (Bonn: A. Marcus, 1880), reprinted in Albrecht Ritschl, *Geschichte des Pietismus*, 3 vols. (Berlin: de Gruyter, 1966) ; and F. Ernest Stoeffler, *The Rise of Evangelical Pietism* (Leiden: E. J. Brill, 1965).

[47] On the history of Dutch preaching, see the following: Izak Boot, *De Allegorische Uitlegging van het Hooglied, voornamelijk in Nederland* (Woerden: Zuiderduijn, 1971); T. Brienen, K. Exalto, et al., *De Nadere Reformatie. Beschrijving van haar voornaamste vertegenwoordigers* ('S-Gravenhage: Uitgeverij Boekencentrum B. V., 1986); T. Brienen, *De Predeking van de Nadere Reformatie. Een Onderzoek nnar het gebruik van het klassifikatiemethode binnen de predeking van de Nadere Reformatie* (Amsterdam: Uitgeverij Ton Bolland, 1974); T. Brienen, K. Exalto, et al., *Theologische Aspecten van de Nadere Reformatie* (Zoetermeer: Uitgewerij Boekencentrum, 1993); Jan Hartog, *Geschiedenis van de Predikkunde in de Protestantsche Kerk van Nederland* (Utrecht: Kemink & Zoon, 1887); and Klaas Runia, *Het hoge Woord en de Lage Landen: hoe er door de Eeuwen heen in Nederland gepreekt is* (Kampen: J. H. Kok, 1985).

[48] Appreciation is hereby expressed to the Reverend Dr. Iain Stewart Maclean, who, in addition to supplying me with a translation of sermons by Teellinck and van Lodenstein, has supplied me with generous amounts of information on seventeenth-century Dutch preaching.

The Walloon preachers were those Protestants who preached in French to French-speaking congregations. Jacques Saurin, a French Huguenot who preached to a French-speaking congregation in the Hague, would be the best known example, but another prominent Walloon preacher was Jean d'Outrein (1662–1722).

More important were the Remonstrant preachers. The Remonstrance was a group of Dutch ministers who, influenced by Jacobus Arminius, opposed the teachings of the Synod of Dort (1618–19). The Remonstrance challenged what it perceived to be the Calvinist doctrines of predestination, human depravity, and irresistible grace. It opposed Calvinism not only in regard to these theological issues but also it opposed the Calvinist insistence on the independence of the church from state control. Hugo Grotius was a strong supporter of the Remonstrance. The Remonstrance was very important intellectually, but it did not win a popular following. It was civic religion at its most obvious.

In addition to these schools there was the usual preaching of the Dutch Reformed Church. Traditionally that preaching took one of two directions. Either it followed in the direction of Gisbertus Voetius (1589–1676) or in the direction of Johannes Cocceius (1603–1669). Another very important figure for the history of Dutch preaching was Willem Teellinck.

A. Willem Teellinck

The main stream of Dutch Protestant preaching as it developed in the seventeenth century owes much to Willem Teellinck (1579–1629). He was one of the first to emphasize the concerns of piety which became so important in Dutch preaching for the following century. Some scholars would bestow on him the title of founder of Dutch Pietism, but there are others who would confer the title on Wilhemus à Brakel and still others on Jodocus van Lodenstein. We make no attempt to arbitrate this dispute.

Bringing together the typical strands of Dutch spirituality

which for generations had been brewing in that most devout land, Willem Teellinck preached a very serious Christian piety.[49] He has often been regarded as a Protestant Thomas à Kempis. He was intent on deepening the theological insights of the Protestant Reformation so that they bore their fruit in the Christian life. One might say that Teellinck was not so much concerned with theological Protestantism as he was with devotional Protestantism.

Teellinck had received the blessings of a thoroughly cosmopolitan education. As a young man he had studied law at the University of St. Andrews in Scotland and then had gone to France where he studied at the University of Poitiers. From Poitiers he went to England where he was attracted by William Perkins and the early Puritans. Moving in these circles he underwent a conversion experience and dedicated his life to the service of the gospel. Then, returning to the Netherlands he took up theological studies, being a student of both Gomarus, the famous proponent of orthodox Calvinism, and Arminius, Calvin's equally famous detractor. In 1606 Teellinck was called to be minister at Hamstede en Berg and finally in 1613 he was called to Middelburg, a major city in Zeeland in the far southwest of the Netherlands.

Teellinck wrote a considerable amount of material. Particularly important was his work on conversion, *Noodwendigh vertoogh aengaende den tegenwoordigen bedroefden staet van God's volck (Necessary Protest Against the Present Sorrowful State of God's People)*, published in 1627. This work was so highly valued at the time that Voetius, the champion of Dutch Orthodoxy, made it required reading for his students. In 1620 he published a book on simplicity of dress, a concern generally shared by Protestants at the time as any admirer of Dutch seventeenth century portraits will recognize. The lavish styles promoted by the French court were offensive to the Protestants of the day. Protestant plain style had wide repercussions. Yet another typical

---

[49] For further information on Teellinck, see W. J. M. Engelberts, *Willem Teellinck* (Amsterdam, 1898).

concern of seventeenth century Protestantism was the observance of the Sabbath. Teellinck wrote on this subject as well. His work, *De rustijd, ofte tractaet van d'onderhoudinge des christelijcken rustsdachs (Concerning the Time of Rest, or, a Tractate on the Keeping of the Christian Days of Rest)*, develops the role of the Christian observance of the fourth commandment in the Christian life. Still another theme which Teellinck developed was the missionary imperative. The Dutch East India Company and the Dutch West India Company were coming into increasing contact with people to whom the gospel had not yet been taken and Teellinck pressed the demands of the Great Commission both in his writing and his preaching. Toward the end of his life he wrote several other devotional guides which had a wide circulation in the Netherlands. Particularly to be noticed were his *Het Nieuwe Jerusalem (The New Jerusalem)* and his *Sleuetel der devotie (Key of Devotion)*. One really needs to spread all of this out in order to appreciate Dutch Protestantism. This is especially the case with the sacramental piety of the Dutch Church.

Dutch Protestantism gave a high priority to the solemn observance of the Lord's Supper. The celebration of the Lord's Supper, as simply and directly as it was done, was a high point of the devotional life. This is very clear from a collection of four sermons preached by Teellinck in preparation for communion. *The Spiritual Adornment of Christ's Wedding Guests, Or, the Practice of the Holy Supper*, was published in Middelburg in 1620.[50] In these sermons our preacher directs his congregation in the devotional participation in the sacrament. In the first sermon of the series our preacher takes the imagery of the parable of the guests invited to the wedding feasts as a figure for our spiritual approach to the sacrament. The parable, of course, makes a point of the fact that one of the guests was thrown out of the feast

---

[50] Willem Teellinck, *Het Geestelyk Cierat van Christi Brutlofts-Kinderen, ofte de Oractijke des Heylighen Avondtmaels Daer inne* (Middelburg, 1620). The following study is based on a twentieth-century edition, Willem Teellinck, *Het Geestelyk Cierat van Christi Brutlofts-Kinderen, ofte de Oractijke des Heylighen Avondtmaels Daer inne*, 20th ed. (Franeker: T. Wever, 1969). Hereinafter referred to as Teellinck, *Preparatory Sermons*.

because he had not come suitably dressed. We learn from this that we should not approach the Holy Supper carelessly prepared. In the second sermon Teellinck speaks at length of the preparation which should be made in one's prayer closet during the week before a celebration of the sacrament. More and more as the seventeenth century unfolded this devotional preparation for the sacrament became a central feature of Protestant spirituality.

The point of the preparation Teellinck envisions would hardly be possible if one observed (or, better, partook of) the sacrament weekly. It makes sense if the sacrament is celebrated once or twice a year. Today weekly celebrations would tend to work against preparatory services. The same would be true in the opposite direction. The observance of preparatory services would tend to work against weekly celebrations.

The third sermon treats the devotional exercises which are appropriate for the communicant during the actual celebration of the sacrament. For Teellinck the presence of Christ at this feast is the key to the spiritual appreciation of the sacrament. Christ is surely present, seated with us at the table.[51] He may indeed be present in a different manner than he was at the Last Supper in the Upper Room, but he is, to be sure, present. It is he who presides at the meal. It is because the congregation senses the presence of Christ at the celebration of the sacrament that so many hundreds of people in the church sit in solemn silence. All in turn come to the table, seat themselves, and then return to their places without making a sound. Is any other meal eaten with such reverence and solemnity?[52] The vivid picture Teellinck draws of a celebration of communion in a seventeenth century Dutch Reformed Church is moving. One cannot help but be reminded of the many paintings the Dutch Masters painted of their majestic churches, all white-washed inside, filled with light and resounding with the thoughtful teaching of the Word.

---

[51] Teellinck, *Preparatory Sermons*, p. 98.

[52] Teellinck, *Preparatory Sermons*, p. 98.

The poetry of these paintings tells us so much about the interiority of the worship which took place in them.

If my readers will allow me a few words of admiration for one of my personal delights, I would like to say something about this interiority of the Dutch Masters as a witness to the depth of Dutch Reformed worship. It has a lot to do with what Reformed theologians have to say about the spiritual presence of Christ at the celebration of Holy Communion. While it has to be admitted that not even Rembrandt could paint a spiritual presence, it also has to be admitted that Rembrandt captured in expression, demeanor, and carriage a sense of the spiritual depth that the truly devout often have. This is what makes a Rembrandt a Rembrandt, and one also has to say this is what makes a Frans Hals a Frans Hals. These wonderful portraits have a sense of presence, whether a Rembrandt patriarch, a Hals fisherboy, or a Vermeer housewife.

Teellinck's description of a typical Dutch Reformed communion service must have been a regular experience of his congregation. This vivid word picture is used to introduce a favorite text for the Protestant communion service, "Behold, I stand at the door and knock; if any one hears my voice and opens the door, I will come in to him and eat with him, and he with me" (Rev. 3:20).[53] This text was commonly used to bring out the eschatological dimension of the celebration of the sacrament of Holy Communion. The sacrament was regarded as a foretaste of the heavenly banquet, the wedding feast of the Lamb. In this text one discovers that in the Lord's Supper it is both true that Christ is present in our celebration of the sacrament here on earth and that we by means of this sacrament enter into the heavenly celebration of the wedding feast of the bridegroom before the throne of God.

When I first came to study Teellinck somehow I overlooked the fact that his ministry took place at the same time our Puritan forefathers were founding New England and Thomas Shepard was

---

[53] Teellinck, *Preparatory Sermons*, p. 99.

11: THE AGE OF PROTESTANT ORTHODOXY

preaching his great series of sermons on the wedding feast to the pastors of Massachusetts Bay. It is this vivid sense of Christ's presence at the Supper which inspires us to be careful to conduct ourselves appropriately. The sermon suggests several things which would define an appropriate demeanor at the celebration of the Lord's Supper. First we should have a deep sense of awe before the divine majesty.[54] To make his point Teellinck marshals a series of rhetorical questions based on Old Testament texts. Solomon teaches us to conduct ourselves wisely when we sit down at the feasts of the rulers of this world. How much more should we be careful of our deportment at this banquet in the presence of God? (Prov. 23:1). Isaiah tells us that even the angels approach the divine presence with covered faces. Should we not show our most profound deference at the celebration of this holy sacrament? (Isa. 6:2).[55] Even Moses teaches us that God will be glorified in all those who approach him. How much more should the Christian approach God in holiness? (Lev. 10:3). The Gospels tell us that the woman who secretly touched the hem of Christ's robe fell down before Jesus with fear and trembling when he spoke to her. So should we approach this sacred table with deep reverence, not to touch his garment, but to be fed with his flesh and blood that we be refreshed to eternal life (Mark 5:33).[56]

It is because Christ is truly present at this sacred meal that we must partake of the feast in awe and wonder. Here at this feast we are seated next to him. We must open the eyes of faith, and observe the presence of the Lord Christ.[57] It is with us as it was with the patriarch Jacob who in his flight to Haran came to Bethel and there was given a dream in which the Lord appeared to him. On awakening from that dream, Jacob spoke with wonderment and deep reverence. He exclaimed that certainly the Lord was in that place, and

---

[54] Teellinck, *Preparatory Sermons*, p. 100.

[55] Teellinck, *Preparatory Sermons*, p. 101.

[56] Teellinck, *Preparatory Sermons*, p. 101.

[57] Teellinck, *Preparatory Sermons*, p. 102.

he did not know it. Jacob was afraid and said: How fearful is this place! Is this not the house of God and the door to heaven? (Genesis 18:16ff.).[58] So when we approach the Lord's Supper let us regard everything with the eyes of faith and be filled with awe and wonder, for indeed we are entering through the gates of heaven itself.

The second point Teellinck makes in this sermon is that we must approach the table with meekness and humility.[59] The previous sermon had spoken at length of the self-examination and confession of sin that was appropriate before coming to the Supper. It is in the consciousness of all this that we sit at the table. But even more, we should sit at this table with a sense of thanksgiving. Thanksgiving is a key concept for Teellinck's eucharistic doctrine. It should be a heartfelt thanksgiving which should fill us as we sit at the table of the Lord. It should be a thanksgiving which recognizes the friendliness and openness of God toward us. As we remember the story of Christ's passion and resurrection, our hearts should overflow with thanksgiving.[60] It is all this which makes us hunger and thirst for this sacred food and drink.[61]

Next we should think of the all-sufficiency of the Lord Jesus Christ whose benefits are offered us in this supper.[62] He can forgive all our sins and heal all our wounds, for his blood is powerful. It is able to cleanse us from all our sin. Our preacher goes through some of the key passages of the New Testament which speak of the power of Christ's redemptive sacrifice (Romans 3:24–25; 1 Peter 2:24; and Hebrews 9:14) to assure his congregation of the sufficiency of Christ's sacrifice to save us from all our sins and deliver us from our tribulations.

Our preacher has much to say on the nature of the Lord's

---

[58] Teellinck, *Preparatory Sermons*, p. 103.

[59] Teellinck, *Preparatory Sermons*, p. 103.

[60] Teellinck, *Preparatory Sermons*, pp. 111–117.

[61] Teellinck, *Preparatory Sermons*, pp. 118–123.

[62] Teellinck, *Preparatory Sermons*, p. 133.

Supper as a sign of the covenant. For Teellinck there is no suggestion that these signs are "mere signs" or "empty signs." They were instituted by Christ to seal his covenant promises.[63] With this our preacher goes on to speak of the assurance we can have that the promises of God, set forth in these signs, will at last be fulfilled. This assurance which comes so richly to those who devote themselves to seeking it is the source of an amazing joy.[64]

Finally Teellinck comes to the subject of fellowship with other Christians who participate with us in the sacrament. The Supper is not only communion with God; it is communion with fellow Christians as well. "Cast now your eyes upon those who are seated with you; . . . look at them with eyes full of Christ-like love."[65] At the Supper the Christian should meditate on the wonder of God's redemption of these our brothers and sisters. We should think to ourselves that they are dear and valuable, beloved and pleasant. What a glorious and attractive people true Christians are!

For Protestant piety, the meditation, inspired by the celebration of the Lord's Supper, was a fundamental spiritual discipline. The liturgical service itself was simple and that simplicity enhanced its solemnity. In fact, as seventeenth century Protestants understood it, the high solemnity demanded the utmost simplicity. The meditation required from the communicant was essential to a true celebration. It was all part of the interiority demanded by Protestant worship. The preparatory sermons, which by this time were becoming such an important part of Protestant sacramental piety, led the communicant in this meditation.

B. Jodocus van Lodenstein

While Teellinck opened the seventeenth century, Jodocus van Lodenstein (1620–1677) lived during the middle of those golden

---

[63] Teellinck, *Preparatory Sermons*, p. 134.

[64] Teellinck, *Preparatory Sermons*, p. 143.

[65] Teellinck, *Preparatory Sermons*, p. 144.

years of the Dutch Republic.[66] His ministry took place when that glorious age was in full bloom. He was born in Delft and studied at Franeker. At Franeker he studied under Johannes Cocceius and lived in his house for two years as well. After two shorter pastorates in Zoetemeer and Sluis, van Lodenstein began his twenty-four year pastorate in Utrecht. There he was the younger colleague of Gisbertus Voetius.

Van Lodenstein is chiefly remembered as one of the leading spirits of the movement to deepen the Reformation, the so-called *Nadere Reformatie*. This movement was characteristic of seventeenth-century Dutch Protestantism. It was not some marginal splinter group; it was the central thrust of the most devout members of the Dutch Protestant Church. It was similar to Puritanism in England. It pressed for a deepening of the Reformation, but it never resulted in a schism. As van Lodenstein understood it, the Reformation only began the reform that needed to be made. The Reformation was too concerned with correct doctrine and too quickly lost sight of the practical applications of their doctrines. Van Lodenstein's criticisms of the Reformation were not at all theological. He and the *Nadere Reformatie* were quite firm in their insistence that the theological insights of the Reformers were all quite sound. This was especially the case with the strong doctrine of grace taught by Luther and Calvin. At this point van Lodenstein appeals to Teellinck's *Noodwendig Vertoog*, making the point that external reform requires a corresponding internal reform.

Sometimes the *Nadere Reformatie* is explained as Puritanism in the Netherlands, but this does not get to the truth of the matter. The *Nadere Reformatie* was never marginalized the way English Puritanism was. There was nothing schismatic about van Loden-

---

[66] For further information on van Lodenstein, see: J. Proost, "Jodocus van Lodensteyn," *Academic Proeschrift* (Amsterdam,1880); M. Goebel and S. D. van Been, "Lodenstein, Jodocus van," in *Realencyklopädie für protestantische Theologie und Kirche*, 11:572–574, ed. J. J. Herzog, 24 vols. (Leipzig: J. C. Hinrichs, 1896–1913); and Marinus Johannes Antoinie de Vrijer, *Lodenstein (Uren met Lodenstein)* (Baarn, 1947).

stein. He was on friendly terms with his colleagues. Cocceius had been his teacher and continued throughout his ministry to exercise a strong influence on him. In Utrecht, Voetius, as pastor of St. Catherine Church, was a colleague of van Lodenstein and apparently the two got along quite well. This concern to deepen the Reformation was the common concern of seventeenth century Protestantism. This was true of English Puritanism, German Pietism, and the Dutch *Nadere Reformatie*.

There were certainly those who criticized van Lodenstein. Some opposed his mysticism, others opposed his asceticism. To some this seemed to return to medieval spirituality. We regret that we have not been able to study a Dutch preacher who opposed the *Nadere Reformatie*. If we had been able to find some less intense preachers perhaps van Lodenstein might appear as a marginal figure, but we have not found them.[67] It is Teellinck and van Lodenstein whose sermons have come down to us. Even more, this deepening of piety seems to be characteristic of seventeenth-century Protestantism as a whole.

Again, it is a series of preparatory sermons which enables us to get a look at this major emphasis of the preaching of orthodox Protestantism in the seventeenth century.[68] The series originally contained at least four sermons, only three of which have come down to us.[69] The series at one time included a preparatory ser-

---

[67] Perhaps a less intense form of Dutch Protestantism might be found in the preachers of the Remonstrance. Indeed, the Remonstrance is much closer to Anglicanism and the preachers of the Remonstrance were Erastian and Arminian as well.

[68] It was several years ago that Iain Maclean, at that time a graduate student at Harvard Divinity School, read a paper at the Calvin Colloquium at Davidson College on these preparatory sermons. Immediately the importance of these sermons for the history of Christian worship became evident to me. Very graciously, Dr. Maclean has provided me with an English translation of the complete series of these sermons.

[69] The three sermons available to this study are found in a collection of van Lodenstein's sermons: Jodocus van Lodenstein, *Geestelyke Opweker voor het Onverloochende, Doode en Geestelose Christendom* (Amsterdam: Andr. Douci, 1732).

mon based on Song of Solomon 2:4, "He led me to his wine cellar, and love is his banner over me." This earlier sermon is mentioned in the last of the published sermons but is not found in the standard collection of van Lodenstein's sermons. There is a sermon based on Song of Solomon 5:3, "I had taken off my garment; how could I put it on again?" and another based on Song of Solomon 5:8, "I adjure you, you daughters of Jerusalem, that if you find my beloved that you tell him that I am sick with love." These two sermons are clearly preparatory sermons preached before the communion service. The sermon for the actual communion service does not seem to be included.[70] Finally, there is a thanksgiving sermon which was preached at a service following the actual communion service. This was preached on the text of Song of Solomon 1:4, "The King brought me into His Inner-Room."[71] Series of eucharistic sermons, such as these, played an important role in the piety of Protestantism in the seventeenth century as is clear from the number of series of such sermons which were published.[72]

For twentieth-century tastes, a series of sermons on the Song of Solomon may seem a bit subjective. Serious exegesis on this text

---

[70] This seems to be the convention for a series of preparatory sermons. Apparently the tradition was that the preparatory sermons as well as the thanksgiving sermon were preached by a guest preacher, specially invited to preach for the communion season, whereas the actual communion sermon would be preached by the pastor.

[71] It is this final sermon which Prof. Maclean published in *Calvin Studies VI*: Iain S. Maclean, "The First Pietist: an Introduction and Translation of a Communion Sermon by Jodocus van Lodenstein," found in *Calvin Studies VI*, ed. John Leith (Davidson, NC: Calvin Colloquium, 1992), pp. 15–34. References to the sermon on Song of Solomon 5:3 as well as references to the sermon on Song of Solomon 5:8 will appear as *Eucharistic Sermons* 2 and 3 respectively, followed by the page number of the Amsterdam edition, translations of which Prof. Maclean has provided me. References to the sermon which Professor Maclean published in *Calvin Studies VI* are given under the title, *Eucharistic Sermons* 4, followed by the page number in *Calvin Studies VI*.

[72] These sermons of van Lodenstein's were among the first sermons that helped me get a more developed picture of this special genre of preparatory sermons. I began to detect a very similar genre in seventeenth and eighteenth-century Scottish communion seasons. This idea will develop in chapters yet to come.

11: THE AGE OF PROTESTANT ORTHODOXY

seems so difficult for the contemporary preacher, but seventeenth-century preachers did not look at it that way. They figured that the key to the interpretation of the Song of Solomon is given to us in the parables of the wedding feast and the wise and foolish virgins, the story of the marriage at Cana, and the vision of the wedding feast of the Lamb in the Revelation of John. As seventeenth-century preachers understood it, the ancient church's exegesis of Song of Solomon was well grounded. Calvin had defended the traditional Christian interpretation, and orthodox Protestantism continued in train.

A number of remarkable features appear in these sermons which help us to understand this concern to deepen the Reformation. To begin with, these preparatory sermons show us the tremendous importance which the celebration of the Lord's Supper occupied in Protestant piety. All too many have imagined that the frequency with which the sacrament was celebrated is the index to its evaluation—those churches which celebrate the sacrament daily treasuring it most dearly, those celebrating it but quarterly valuing it least. Nothing could be more misleading. One need only read the preparatory sermons of the English Puritan John Owen or the American Presbyterian Gilbert Tennent to realize that the celebration of the Lord's Supper was the high feast of the Christian life. These preparatory sermons of van Lodenstein show us the same thing. They are symptomatic of the deepening of the devotional life which was being experienced throughout Protestantism during the seventeenth century.

One notices in these sermons an intensified sense of the presence of Christ. Christ is understood to preside at this feast. Granted, he is present in a different way than he was present at the Last Supper, but he is present nevertheless.[73] This presence is, to be sure, not so much a matter of his body being on the plate or his blood in the cup, but rather his being present as the bride-

---

[73] Van Lodenstein, *Eucharistic Sermons*, 4:23.

groom at the wedding feast.[74] The presence of Christ is intensified because it is a transcendent presence. One notices how often the seventeenth-century Protestant communion sermons were on texts from the Song of Solomon, Revelation, or Jesus' parable of the wedding feast. The reason would appear to be that this imagery well expressed a sense of the transcendent presence of Christ in the celebration of the sacrament.

A particularly important text for van Lodenstein was Revelation 3:20, "Behold, I stand at the door and knock; if any one hears my voice and opens the door, I will come in and eat with him and he with me."[75] This had been an important text for Teellinck as well. Just as it did for Teellinck, this text evokes the imagery of the Supper both in terms of Christ's presence at our Supper here on earth and our presence at his Supper in heaven. There is both our eating with him and his eating with us.[76] As we have already pointed out, this text from Revelation evokes as well the eschatological dimension of the Supper. The Lord's Supper is a foretaste of the wedding feast of the Lamb to be celebrated at the consummation of existence. Such an emphasis had long been characteristic of the Reformed understanding of the Supper. We find it already in Calvin's interpretation of the *Sursum corda* which concluded the Communion Exhortation found in the eucharistic liturgy of the *Genevan Psalter* of 1542. Calvin exhorts his congregation not to dwell upon these earthly and corruptible elements which we see present with our eyes and feel with our hands, but

---

[74] No doubt van Lodenstein could also have preached on the sacrament in terms of the Passover imagery. At the Supper we feast upon the Lamb of God, offered up as a sacrifice to atone for our sins. Christ is present at the Supper both as the Lamb who was sacrificed and as the High Priest who once and for all made the sacrifice and who now, as often as we keep the feast, presides over it. The sermons before us emphasize the wedding feast imagery rather than the Passover imagery, but the two are by no means incompatible with each other. Calvin's preparatory sermons which we studied above are more inclined toward the Passover imagery.

[75] Van Lodenstein, *Eucharistic Sermons*, 2:266.

[76] Van Lodenstein, *Eucharistic Sermons*, 4:19.

to lift up our hearts and minds on high, where Jesus Christ abides in the glory of his Father whence we expect his coming at our redemption. To come to the Lord's Supper is to enter into the heavenly reality while still living in this life.[77]

Again van Lodenstein follows the lead of Teellinck in his interpretation of Jacob's dream at Bethel.[78] Jacob saw heaven open up before him with a staircase leading up to the divine presence. On it were angels ascending and descending, and Jacob awoke saying, "'How awesome is this place! This is nothing else but the house of God, and this is the gate of heaven'" (Gen. 28:17). These words are, for van Lodenstein, a confession of Christ's presence in the celebration of the Supper. It is not through the outward senses that one becomes aware of this presence. It is rather a deeper, spiritual realization. "'Surely the LORD is in this place; and I did not know it'" (Gen. 28:16).[79]

For van Lodenstein the celebration of the Lord's Supper is an experience of communion. The text chosen for the final sermon, "The king hath brought me into his chambers," naturally suggests communion with Christ.[80] The New Testament word *koinonia* is the word most aptly used here, and our preacher, who obviously has given himself to a careful study of the original languages, is fully aware of this.[81] *Koinonia* is an important word for his understanding of the sacrament. Our preacher does a beautiful piece of exegesis to show that the king mentioned in the text is none other than Jesus, the royal bridegroom. He supports this with texts from Daniel, Zechariah, and the Psalms. In each case they are

---

[77] Interestingly enough, we find this same eucharistic theme in a Pentecost sermon by the German Lutheran pastor Heinrich Müller, who preached at just about this time in Rostock.

[78] Van Lodenstein, *Eucharistic Sermons*, 4:26.

[79] Van Lodenstein, *Eucharistic Sermons*, 4:26.

[80] Van Lodenstein, *Eucharistic Sermons*, 4:21.

[81] Van Lodenstein, *Eucharistic Sermons*, 4:22.

among the classic messianic texts of the Old Testament.[82] Then van Lodenstein turns his attention to the chamber and again gives us a beautiful piece of exegesis.

For those who knew their Bibles well, as so many every day Dutchmen did, the exciting thing about these sermons was the wealth of parallel passages which were brought out to elucidate the text. To explain the inner room, several passages are brought out from the Old Testament, but even more interesting are the two references from the gospel. Jesus at one point tells us that when we pray we are to go into our inner-room or closet. Then in the Gospel of John we read that in our Father's house are many rooms.[83] These are for the Christian what the Holy of Holies was in the Temple. By this inner-room our preacher understands the tender love of Christ and the inner communion of the soul with her Lord.[84] What a magnificent unfolding of the biblical imagery van Lodenstein has laid before us!

It is in the sermon on the text of the Song of Solomon 5:8, "I adjure you, you daughters of Jerusalem," that our preacher brings out the idea that in the Lord's Supper there is communion with fellow Christians. The *koinonia* goes in two directions. It is fellowship with Christ and it is fellowship with the congregation. Again we notice the resourcefulness of his exegesis in showing that the daughters of Jerusalem are fellow Christians. In her plight the bride, who is estranged from the bridegroom, cries out to the daughters of Jerusalem to ask their help.[85] This is what the church is all about, according to our preacher. The daughters of Jerusalem are the true professors of the faith, who have God as their Father and the church as their Mother. Quite naturally they exercise love

---

[82] Van Lodenstein, *Eucharistic Sermons*, 4:20.

[83] Van Lodenstein, *Eucharistic Sermons*, 4:21.

[84] Van Lodenstein, *Eucharistic Sermons*, 4:21.

[85] Van Lodenstein, *Eucharistic Sermons*, 3:234.

11: The Age of Protestant Orthodoxy

toward one another as best they can.[86] It is particularly the duty of Christians to comfort and exhort one another, as we find in 1 Thessalonians 2:11 and 4:18.[87] This is elaborated at some length, finally making the point that there is nothing the Lord blesses so abundantly as our sharing our blessings one with another.[88] This is why the Prayer of Intercession is so important in public worship. Nehemiah is a good example of a godly man who exercised a ministry of intercessory prayer. So should all of us as Christians exercise a ministry in easing the burdens of one another.[89]

Perhaps one of the most striking features of this series of sermons is its strong sense of the primacy of grace. There is nothing here of the Pelagianism which was so common in late medieval pietism. There may be similarities to Thomas à Kempis in the emphasis on piety, but the strong Reformed doctrine of grace is most evident. Van Lodenstein's Protestantism is a completely orthodox Protestantism. This comes out particularly in the sermon on Song of Solomon 5:3, "I had taken off my garment; how could I put it on again?" As van Lodenstein interprets this passage, these words speak of the Bride of Christ having lost her first love.[90] This is often the case with Christians that they lose their first love and become worldly, as was the case with the church of Ephesus. We read about this in Revelation.[91] The sermon develops this theme at length, speaking of the spiritual condition of worldly Christians who have lost their initial devotion. Apparently this was the way our preacher regarded many in his congregation; they were Christians who had lost their first love. Even at that van Lodenstein insists on both the irresistible nature of grace and the perseverance of the saints. Christ remains steadfast in his eternal

---

[86] Van Lodenstein, *Eucharistic Sermons*, 3:235.

[87] Van Lodenstein, *Eucharistic Sermons*, 3:235.

[88] Van Lodenstein, *Eucharistic Sermons*, 3 :237.

[89] Van Lodenstein, *Eucharistic Sermons*, 3:239.

[90] Van Lodenstein, *Eucharistic Sermons*, 2:207.

[91] Van Lodenstein, *Eucharistic Sermons*, 2:214.

love, van Lodenstein insists. He does not change his goodness nor does he revoke his covenant of peace. He still remains the sworn comforter of his bride.[92] Here is the orthodoxy of the Synod of Dort in all its mysterious beauty.

These sermons make it very clear that the concern to deepen the piety of the faithful was in no way at the expense of Reformed orthodoxy. It is not as though orthodoxy and pietism were in some sort of Hegelian dialectic. They were quite complimentary. We notice here an enrichment of classical Protestantism. In the seventeenth century the sacramental life, the prayer life, and the moral life intensified. The intensity of devotion in the celebration of the Lord's Supper is most obvious from these sermons. These sermons were well received. According to Professor Maclean, over thirty editions were published.

What got these sermons across was not magnificent oratory. These sermons were Protestant plain style from beginning to end. From time to time one finds a metaphor, a few simple exempla, but for the most part the beauty of these sermons is their exegesis. They offer a rich supply of parallel passages and biblical examples. There is such wisdom in the applications, such insight into the human condition. Rather, what got these sermons across was their interiority. That is not quite the same thing as subjectivity. These sermons have a tremendous sense of interiority in that they bring us into the inner-room, just as the sacrament itself does. What we find in these seventeenth-century Dutch sermons is the same thing we find in the seventeenth-century Dutch paintings. The Dutch Masters had a marvelous ability to intimate the interiority of human existence. All one has to do is look at the interiors of seventeenth century Dutch homes as they were painted by Pieter de Hooch, Gerard Terborch, and Jan Vermeer. They tell us much about life and what it meant to these people. One looks at an interior of de Hooch and one marvels at the eloquence of their sim-

---

[92] Van Lodenstein, *Eucharistic Sermons*, 2:222.

plicity and order. Or, again, one looks at an interior by Vermeer and one senses the quiet of the room. Perhaps it is a woman reading a letter or doing a simple household task. Perhaps it is a man contemplating the vanities of life. It all had to do with the mystery of the inner-room, that Holy of Holies, the Song of Songs. That is what Protestantism is all about. It is not about baroque power and authority but interiority, the secret communion with God. That is what justification by faith is all about and that is what sanctification by faith is all about as well.

These sermons speak to us of communion, union with Christ, and union one with another. And what they tell us about communion is its interiority. That, in the end, is what Rembrandt was all about. Applied to theology, that is what piety is all about as well.

12

MATTHEW HENRY

Matthew Henry (1662–1714) was one of those who staked out the main road of English-speaking Protestantism as it entered the eighteenth century.[1] Born the son of a minister of the Church of England who was deprived of his pulpit in the great ejection, Henry was educated by his father in the best traditions of Puritan scholarship.[2] Today we would say he was home schooled. His father taught him the Latin, Greek, and Hebrew which classical Protestantism considered essential to a theological education. The Anglican Settlement denied a university education to the Puritans, but, informal as it may have been, Matthew Henry's education was superb! He knew all the classics very well, but, even more, he had the good sense to put it all together. His father had studied at Westminster School in London and Christ Church College in Oxford, but above all he knew the disciplines of holiness, and it was in these that he educated his son.

---

[1] For biographical material on Matthew Henry, see: Allan Harman, *Matthew Henry: His Life and Influence* (Fearn, UK: Christian Focus Publications, 2012); Hughes Oliphant Old, "Henry, Matthew," *Dictionary of Major Biblical Interpreters*, ed. Donald McKim (Downers Grove, IL and Nottingham, UK: InterVarsity Press, 2007), pp. 520–524. See also J. B. Williams, *Memoirs of the Life, Character and Writings of the Rev. Matthew Henry* (London, 1828; reprinted with Henry's biography of his father [Edinburgh: Banner of Truth Trust, 1974]).

[2] For a particularly helpful study of Phillip Henry's contribution to Reformed piety, see Matthew Henry, *An Account of the Life and Death of Mr. Philip Henry* (London: Printed for Tho. Parkhurst and John Lawrence, 1698). There were several later editions of this work. Among them was Matthew Henry, *Life and Times of the Rev. Phillip Henry, M. A., Father of the Commentator* (New York: R. Carter, 1849). See also Williams, *Memoirs*, above, for a more recent reprint.

One way of looking at Matthew Henry is as one of the reliable spokesmen of the Old School. He speaks for classical Protestantism. He is the voice of moderation, the voice to which Moderatism aspired, but rarely attained. He rises above the usual schools and parties of his day, being much too big to be put in any cubby hole. This implies that the Old School had a surprising vitality. But, then, that is often the way it is.

Matthew Henry was a pastoral theologian. As the phrase is used today, he was a "master of the spiritual life."[3] It was in 1687 that Henry was called to be pastor of the Presbyterian church in Chester, a prosperous city in the west of England. In the last decade of the seventeenth century he served not only his own congregation but many of the Congregational and Baptist churches of the area that were beginning to organize under the toleration of the reign of William and Mary. Henry was greatly respected for being both fervent and broad-minded, both deeply spiritual and thoroughly orthodox.

A COMMUNICANT'S COMPANION, 1704

Henry's *A Communicant's Companion*, published in 1704, is best described as a devotional book, and yet it is a work of real theological depth.[4] With an amazing clarity and brevity, it displays

---

[3] Among his many works having to do with the Christian life are: Matthew Henry, *A Church in the House: or, Family Religion* (New York: American Tract Society, [1824?]); Matthew Henry, *The Communicant's Companion: or Instructions and Helps for the Right Receiving of the Lord's Supper* (Morris-town, NJ: Printed by Henry P. Russell, 1809); Matthew Henry, *An Exposition of All the Books of the Old and New Testaments*, six volumes (Edinburgh: Printed by and for Colin Macfarquhar, 1772) and frequently reprinted; Matthew Henry, *An Exposition of the Shorter Catechism* (Edinburgh: J. Lowe, 1857); Matthew Henry, *Matthew Henry's Commentary on the Whole Bible* (Peabody, MA: Hendrickson Publishing Co., 1991); and Matthew Henry, *A Method for Prayer* (Philadelphia: Towar, J. & D.M. Hogan, and Thomas Kite, 1831), reprint ed. J. Ligon Duncan III (Greenville, SC: Reformed Academic Press, 1994).

[4] The edition of the *Communicant's Companion* used for this study is found in volume 1 of Matthew Henry, *The Complete Works of the Rev. Matthew Henry . . .(His Commentary Excepted)*, 2 vols., reprint of the 1855 edition (Grand Rapids, MI: Baker Book House, 1979), hereinafter Henry, *Companion*.

the eucharistic piety of classical Protestantism at the beginning of the eighteenth century. The insights of the sixteenth century had now had time to develop into established devotional practices. The theological affirmations of Luther, Zwingli, and Calvin had matured into a well-established discipline of Christian faith. Henry's *A Communicant's Companion* makes this very clear.

A. The Names of The Lord's Supper

The work begins with two different attempts to tell what the sacrament of Holy Communion is and why we celebrate it. One easily imagines that each of these chapters was originally preached at a preparatory service as a sermon to help his congregation prepare for a solemn celebration of the sacrament. Let us look at each of these chapters in turn.

1. "Sacrament"

The first chapter is devoted to explaining the meaning of the sacrament by discussing the names by which it is most often called. First of all we call it the "sacrament."[5] We call it the sacrament, Henry explains, because it is a sign. Recalling the well-worn definition of Augustine, Henry says that communion ". . . is a sign, an outward and visible sign of an inward and invisible grace . . ."[6] Here is one of the most obvious patristic roots of Protestant sacramental theology. Henry goes on to explain this definition by saying that God has designed the sacrament to be "a parable for the eye."[7] We live in a physical world and we deal with this world by sense perception. God has accommodated himself to our capacities by giving us this sacrament. Alluding to John 3:12 Henry says, that in this sacrament "Christ tells us earthly things, that thereby we may come to be more familiarly acquainted, and more warmly

---

[5] Henry, *Companion*, p. 285.

[6] Henry, *Companion*, p. 285.

[7] Henry, *Companion*, p. 285.

affected, with spiritual and heavenly things."[8] It is "because we find it hard to look above the things that are seen, we are directed in a sacrament to look through them, to those things not seen."[9]

At this point Henry is very careful to distinguish between the visible representation of Christ's saving work in the sacrament and the paintings of the passion of Christ which were so popular in Catholic devotion. It is through preaching and the sacraments that Christ is portrayed as crucified among you, as we find it in Galatians 3:1. To go beyond this is of no advantage nor is it honoring to God. God in his infinite wisdom saw that it is sufficient to institute this sacrament to excite our devotion. We should leave it at that.

But then we also call the Lord's Supper a sacrament because it is an oath. To be sure Henry is familiar with Tertullian's explanation of the word "sacrament." As we will see again and again Tertullian's explanation of the word *sacramentum* was fundamental to the Protestant understanding of sacramental theology. He speaks of the military oath taken by soldiers entering the Roman army. They took an oath of allegiance to their commander. This was called a *sacramentum*. So it is when we celebrate the Lord's Supper, we solemnly bind ourselves to our Lord. "It is a freeman's oath, by which we enter ourselves members of Christ's mystical body, and oblige to observe the laws, and seek the good, of that Jerusalem which is from above . . ."[10] Here, of course, the covenantal dimension of the Lord's Supper comes through very clearly, and Henry is well aware that this dimension of eucharistic theology goes far back in the history of the Church.

2. "The Lord's Supper"

The second name we have given this sacrament is the "Lord's Supper." This term is used by the Apostle Paul in 1 Corinthians 11:20.

---

[8] Henry, *Companion*, p. 285.

[9] Henry, *Companion*, p. 285.

[10] Henry, *Companion*, p. 285.

Henry makes the point that in those days supper was the principal meal of the day.[11] There is no reason why it should only be celebrated in the evening. Such matters can be decided according to the good order of the Church, but the evening meal was a more relaxed and festive meal at the time, because it came after the day's work had been finished. Today, the word "supper" might imply a more casual meal, but that is not the way we should understand it; this supper is a festive evening meal. Even more, it is the Lord's Supper. It is the Lord who has invited us and the Lord who has provided it. "The ordaining of this sacrament was an act of his dominion . . . In receiving this sacrament, we own his dominion, and acknowledge him as our Lord."[12] The substance of this supper is the grace of Christ. He is the Bread of Life upon which we feed as we find it in the Gospel of John (John 6:35), and he is our Beloved and our friend with whom we feast as we find it in the Song of Solomon (Song of Solomon 5:16). Again, as we find it in the Revelation, it is the Lord's Supper because he sups with us and we with him (Rev. 3:20).

3. "Communion"

The third name which we use to designate the sacrament of the Lord's Supper is "communion." The Greek word behind communion which Henry has in mind is apparently *koinonia*, for he alludes to I John 1:3, "Our fellowship is with the Father and with his Son Jesus Christ." It is at the celebration of the Lord's Supper that this fellowship or communion is particularly manifested. "He here manifests himself to us, and gives out to us his graces and comforts: we here set ourselves before him, and tender him the grateful return of love and duty."[13] Communion is a personal relationship above all but it is a personal relationship which is manifested in sharing. God pours out for us his spiritual goods and we devote our lives to his ser-

---

[11] Henry, *Companion*, p. 286.

[12] Henry, *Companion*, p. 286.

[13] Henry, *Companion*, p. 287.

vice. Henry with his gift for saying things succinctly puts it this way, "A kind of correspondence between Christ and our souls is kept up in this ordinance; . . . Christ by his word and Spirit abides in us; we, by faith and love, abide in him."[14] Henry uses the word "correspondence," which to us suggests an exchange of letters, but for Henry it meant, perhaps, less narrowly—keeping in contact.

Henry makes clear just what this personal relationship is. It is the sharing of bread and wine, and entailed in that is the sharing of material goods, food, clothing, housing, and all the material things of life, but it is far more than that. It is mutual commitment. It is a sharing of lives. It is a sharing of thoughts and beliefs and commitment. "Here, therefore, where Christ seals his Word, and offers our faith, and have our love inflamed, there is communion between us and Christ."[15] The sacrament exercises our faith, to be sure. It is the experiencing of faith and in this sense, it exercises it.

Henry is not talking about conjuring up before our minds a picture of Christ's passion, a form of devotion dear to Baroque piety. In the end, communion is a covenantal relationship. Again he puts this very well, "This communion supposes union; this fellowship supposes friendship; for 'can two walk together except they be agreed?' Amos iii.3. We must therefore in the bond of an everlasting covenant, joint ourselves to the Lord, and entwine interests with him, and then pursuant thereto, concern him in all the concerns of our happiness, and concern ourselves in all the concerns of his glory; and this is communion."[16] The allusion to the text from Amos, "can two walk together except they be agreed?" is helpful because it brings out the dimension of friendship. It suggests that there is a profound friendship in the sharing of the Word, in being agreed in the Gospel. The real heart of what Henry is saying here, however, is in the covenantal dimension of communion. The word "com-

---

[14] Henry, *Companion*, p. 287.

[15] Henry, *Companion*, p. 287.

[16] Henry, *Companion*, p. 287.

munion," just as the word "sacrament," underlines this covenantal dimension of the sacrament.

For the Christian who approaches the celebration of the Lord's Supper the communion must go in two directions. The communion must have a heavenly direction which experiences communion with the Father, and with his Son, Jesus Christ, and an earthly direction which experiences communion with our brothers and sisters in Christ. Henry calls on the text from the Apostle Paul, "for we all partake of the one bread" (1 Cor. 10:16–17). Just as the communion service begins with one loaf of bread which is divided up and shared by the whole congregation, so participation in the service is a demonstration of our unity. We all feed from one loaf. In the same way we all drink from one cup. As we find it in another Pauline text, 1 Corinthians 12:13, we are all made to drink of one Spirit. Henry goes on to say that as Christians, although we are various, coming from different places and belonging to different social classes and societies, and having different attainments and ways of looking at things, nevertheless we are incorporated "in one and the same covenant, and stamped with one and the same image, partakers of the same new and divine nature, and entitled to one and the same inheritance."[17] Quite clearly for Henry, the unity of the communion both in regard to our unity with Christ and in regard to the Church is a covenantal unity.

4. "Eucharist"

The fourth name which we sometimes use for the sacrament of the Lord's Supper is the "Eucharist." This name we have taken over from the Greek Church. The word "eucharist" means thanksgiving. We read in 1 Corinthians 11:24 that when Christ instituted the sacrament he took the bread and the wine and gave thanks over them. This thanksgiving which Christ offered over the bread and wine is seen as the fulfillment of the worship of Melchizedek who brought

---

[17] Henry, *Companion*, p. 287.

out bread and wine and set them before Abraham and blessed the Most High God (Genesis 14:18–20). As Henry interpreted it, when Christ celebrated the Supper in the Upper Room, he was fully aware of the sacrifice which he had been appointed to make. He understood the suffering that he must go through, and yet he was confident of the victory over sin and death that he would achieve and so even in that dark hour he gave thanks to the Father.[18]

When we participate in this Supper we, too, must give thanks. Henry calls the supper "an ordinance of thanksgiving appointed for the joyful celebrating of the Redeemer's praises."[19] Henry follows the lead of Luther, Calvin, and the Protestant Reformers of the sixteenth century in insisting that Christ's sacrifice on the cross was unique. It was sufficient to win the salvation of all people in all ages. It therefore never needs repeating. It was the full and perfect sacrifice of atonement and yet it is appropriate that every day in our praise and prayer we offer a sacrifice of thanksgiving. This is the sacrifice of which the prophet Hosea spoke, "the fruit of our lips, giving thanks to his name" (Hosea 13:15). In the same way, the Jews used to close the Passover meal with a prayer of thanksgiving over the cup of blessing. It was the intention of Jesus that in the celebration of this Supper his disciples should observe a perpetual thanksgiving until the day when we should enter into his glory.[20]

Here we may very well have an explanation of why in so many of the Reformed eucharistic liturgies there was no eucharistic prayer over the bread and wine before they were distributed to the congregation, but rather a prayer of thanksgiving *after* the bread and wine had been received. These liturgies had been put together by people who knew enough about the Passover Seder to realize that thanksgiving was said over the cup of blessing *after* the meal had been eaten. This is, to be sure, very strong support for

---

[18] Henry, *Companion*, p. 288.

[19] Henry, *Companion*, p. 288.

[20] Henry, *Companion*, p. 288.

the practice taught by the *Westminster Directory*, and this was without doubt the practice followed by Henry. One thing is clear: Henry at least knew this practice was consistent with the Passover Seder.

5. "Feast"

Finally Henry suggests a fifth name for the sacrament of the Lord's Supper. It is a "feast." The text which suggests this name to him is 1 Corinthians 5:7–8, "Christ our passover is sacrificed for us: therefore let us keep the feast, . . ." (KJV). Henry admits that this word does not exclusively speak of the sacrament and yet so often the feasts spoken of in the Bible have implications for the Lord's Supper. Sometimes they are types of the Lord's Supper or perhaps, even better, foretastes of the Lord's Supper. At considerable length Henry looks at these feasts, drawing out the implication found in them for the meaning of the sacrament. Here Henry is at his best as he explores the rich imagery of the Bible.

The first point Henry makes is that the sacrament of the Lord's Supper is a royal feast.[21] As the feast of Ahasuerus it is designed "not only to show his good will to those whom he feasted, but to 'show the riches of his glorious kingdom, and the honor of his excellent majesty'" (Esther 1:3–5).[22] In the Lord's Supper the unsearchable riches of Christ are displayed before us. The royal imagery naturally leads to the imagery of the Wisdom theology of the book of Proverbs. This is the feast which Wisdom herself, as a queen, has prepared. "Wisdom hath killed her beasts and mingled her wine" (Prov. 9:1–2, KJV). Henry's commentaries on the Wisdom books of the Old Testament have always been highly prized. We are hardly surprised, therefore, that he recognizes here the Wisdom dimension of the sacrament. A royal feast, Henry assures us, serves the richest and most noble dishes, far beyond the fare to which we are accustomed. The Lord's Supper is like the wedding feast which the king

---

[21] Henry, *Companion*, p. 288.

[22] Henry, *Companion*, p. 288.

gave for his son in the parable of Jesus. The wedding feast is also a favorite image of the Wisdom school as we find it in the Song of Solomon. The uniqueness of this feast is underlined by this imagery. It is the most important feast possible, this wedding feast of the king's son. It is a feast for which we must carefully prepare ourselves, dressing in suitable clothing (Matt. 22:11). In the seventeenth and eighteenth centuries, as our research is making ever clearer, the sermon preached at a communion service often used the imagery of the royal wedding feast so popular in the Wisdom literature.

Indeed this feast is not only a royal feast but a wedding feast. We therefore are to celebrate it with great joy. It is a wedding feast in that the church as the bride of Christ is joined in an eternal covenant to the heavenly Bridegroom (Eph. 5:31–32). At this feast "the espousals of believing souls are here solemnized. It is a foretaste of the wedding feast of the Lamb."[23]

This feast is also a memorial feast. It is like the Passover of which we read, "This day shall be unto you for a memorial" (Exod. 12:14). As Henry understands it, the Exodus was a mighty act of redemption so great that it was never to be forgotten, and therefore the Passover was to be celebrated every year by the Jews as a solemn memorial. As great an act of deliverance as the Passover was, it was, however, a foreshadowing of the even greater act of redemption, the redemption accomplished by Christ in his passion and resurrection. It was therefore that Christ instituted the Supper as a solemn memorial of his redemptive work to succeed and fulfill the ancient feast of the Jews. Jesus said to his disciples, "This do in remembrance of me" (1 Cor. 11:24). The memorial of the old Passover was taken up into the passover of Christ.

The sacrament of the Lord's Supper is also a feast of dedication. Here Henry speaks of several feasts of dedication in the Old Testament. He mentions the feast given by Solomon at the dedication of the Temple, the feast which celebrated the bringing

---

[23] Henry, *Companion*, p. 289.

of the ark into Jerusalem, and the feast which was held when the Temple was rebuilt after the exile. Henry comments, "In the ordinance of the Lord's Supper we dedicate ourselves to God as living temples, 'temples of the Holy Ghost,' separated from everything that is common and profane, and entirely devoted to the service and honor of God in Christ."[24]

Furthermore the Lord's Supper is "a feast upon a sacrifice."[25] Very briefly Henry explains how the sacrifices of the Old Testament were followed by a feast in which the sacrificial animals were roasted and eaten by the worshipers. The theological implications of this are important. The Lord's Supper is such a feast. Christ was offered as the sacrifice once for all but the feast is for us repeatedly to enjoy in the sacrament. As we find it in 1 Corinthians 5:7–8 (KJV), "Christ our passover has been sacrificed, . . . therefore let us keep the feast."

Finally it is a feast upon a covenant.[26] Henry recalls the covenant meals about which we read in Genesis to show that feasts were celebrated to solemnize the making of covenants. He makes the point that these feasts were covenanting rites. They were a token or expression of peace between those who shared the meal. "In the Lord's Supper we are admitted to feast with God, in token of reconciliation between us and him in Christ."[27]

B. The Nature of the Lord's Supper

Having explained the meaning of the Lord's Supper by means of the names that we use to speak of the sacrament, Henry now tries another approach. He considers it according to its nature. Four things come into view: the Lord's Supper is a commemorative ordinance, a confessing ordinance, a communicating ordinance,

---

[24] Henry, *Companion*, p. 289.

[25] Henry, *Companion*, p. 289.

[26] Henry, *Companion*, p. 290.

[27] Henry, *Companion*, p. 290.

and a covenanting ordinance. We can imagine that this chapter was once a four-point sermon.

1. A COMMEMORATIVE ORDINANCE

Henry first considers the Lord's Supper as a commemorative ordinance. The text from which he makes this point is, "Do this in remembrance of me" (Luke 22:19). As Henry sees it, this text tells us that the sacrament is to be observed as a sacred memorial to Christ. Furthermore it is the memorial which Christ himself instituted for the remembrance of his atoning sacrifice.[28] Henry, being well grounded in the biblical languages, was aware of what a rich meaning "remembrance" has in both Hebrew and Greek. The Hebrew word *zakar* is used in several crucial theological texts, such as the institution of the Passover in Exodus 12 and the fourth commandment.

There have been those who have been very critical of this commemorative understanding of the Lord's Supper. The charge is made that thinking of the sacrament as a memorial of the death of Christ makes for an inevitably morose service of worship. Not only that, to understand the sacrament as a memorial implies not the presence of Christ but his absence. Whatever grounds this criticism may have, the text, not only of the Gospel of Luke but of First Corinthians 11:25 as well, makes it very clear that it was indeed Jesus himself who taught us to "Do this in remembrance of me." Apparently Jesus intended the Supper to be his memorial.

If Henry speaks of the Supper as a commemoration of one who is absent, he nevertheless makes it clear that Christ is away on our business. Jesus has gone to prepare a place for us, as He said (cf. John 14:2). Even more he is now at the right hand of the Father to intercede for us. Henry underlines the transcendent presence of Christ by bringing in an eschatological theme. Our commemoration is not only of him who offered himself for our redemption but who comes again to establish his kingdom.

---

[28] Henry, *Companion*, p. 290.

12: Matthew Henry

Henry says nothing of the commemoration of Christ's incarnation at the Supper. This we find a bit troubling. He does not even speak of the Supper as a commemoration of his resurrection. One often finds this in the devotional literature of the Church. One finds it in a large spread of authors regardless of denomination or century. No doubt it goes with the centrality of the broken bread and the poured out wine. No doubt it also has to do with the fact that the Gospels repeat the story of the institution of the sacrament in the context of the passion narrative. Even when the Apostle Paul recounts the story he begins it by saying, ". . . The same night in which he was betrayed . . ." Finally, it hardly needs to be pointed out that the Apostle Paul teaches ". . . For as often as ye eat this bread and drink this cup, ye do shew the Lord's death till he comes" (1 Cor. 11:23–26, KJV). That the sacrament is in remembrance of Christ's sacrifice is written deeply into the tradition. No doubt the incarnation and the resurrection are implied both by Scripture and by the tradition of Christian piety, and surely Henry would agree to this. Even further, one can point out that the Lord's Supper is normally celebrated on the Lord's Day, especially in Reformed churches, and this should make clear that it is also a memorial of his resurrection. This concept, however, is not nearly as obvious as the memorial of his passion.

The incarnation and resurrection are, to be sure, implicit in the memorial. We find this point made quite explicitly when Henry begins to speak of the sacrament as a "confessing" or "witnessing" ordinance. What is crucial to understand here is that the commemoration is fundamental to a covenantal approach to worship. As we find it already in the fourth commandment, the Sabbath, the day of worship, is a day of remembering. "Remember the Sabbath day to keep it holy." At worship the congregation came together to remember the mighty acts of salvation. This remembering was a celebrating, rejoicing, and recounting of the holy history.

2. A Confessing Ordinance

Let us turn now to Henry's thoughts on the sacrament of the Lord's Supper as a confessing ordinance. Here Henry addresses the kerygmatic dimension of the sacrament. As he puts it, "The Lord's Supper is a solemnity by which we constantly avow the Christian name, and declare ourselves not ashamed of the banner of the cross under which we were listed, but resolve to continue as Christ's faithful servants and soldiers to our live's end, according to our baptismal vow."[29] The text which Henry has specially in mind is 1 Corinthians 11:26, "For as often as ye eat this bread, and drink this cup, ye do shew the Lord's death till he come" (KJV). This showing forth of the Lord's death is nothing less than the confession of faith which is made unto salvation. It is the profession of faith that makes us a Christian. When we partake of the Lord's Supper, according to Henry, "We profess our value and esteem for Christ crucified."[30] We have every reason to put a high value on the cross, for it has borne to us the richest and ripest fruits. The suffering of the cross has been crowned with the resurrection. The victory of the Christ has won us the most sublime triumphs and therefore we confess it has become our crown of glory.

Here, to be sure, we are dealing with the Lord's Supper as "worth-ship." The English word "worship" makes the point that what we are doing when we gather together to preach the Word, celebrate the sacraments, and proclaim the praises of God is to bear witness to God's worth. The English word "worship" emphasizes the kerygmatic dimension of what we are doing. The celebration of the sacrament is worship because it is a witness to God's mighty acts of salvation.

When we participate in the Lord's Supper we confess Christ not only to be our glory, but our Lord, the Lord to whom we owe both homage and service. It is to Christ that we have called out in

---

[29] Henry, *Companion*, p. 292.
[30] Henry, *Companion*, p. 292.

our time of need. He has heard our cry and come to our aid and therefore we owe him our homage. Because he has been faithful in the past we cry out to him in our constantly recurring need. "By this solemn rite, we deliberately and of choice put ourselves under the protection of his righteousness, and the influence of his grace, and the conduct and operation of his Holy Spirit."[31] That we cry out to him in need is a confession of our confidence and reliance on him as Lord and God. Henry has tapped into that biblical insight of covenantal theology, that having received the grace of God we are obligated to witness to the goodness of God who has poured out this grace upon us. To recount with adoration the story of God's mighty acts of salvation is at the same time thanksgiving and witness.

Henry puts this very well: "When we receive the Lord's Supper: we confess that Jesus Christ is Lord, and own ourselves to be his subjects, and put ourselves under his government: we confess that he is a skillful physician, and own ourselves to be his patients . . . we confess that he is a faithful advocate, and own ourselves to be his clients . . ."[32]

3. A Communicating Ordinance

The third point Henry wants to make is that the Lord's Supper is a communicating ordinance. He draws this point from 1 Corinthians 10:16, "The cup of blessing which we bless is the communion of the blood of Christ; the bread which we break is the communion of the body of Christ." Henry is fully aware that the Greek behind this word communion is *koinonia* and so he paraphrases the text of the King James Version by saying the cup of blessing which we pray to God to bless, which we bless God with and for, and in which we hope and expect that God will bless us, is the communion of the blood of Christ and the bread which we break is the

---

[31] Henry, *Companion*, p. 293.

[32] Henry, *Companion*, p. 293.

communion of the body of Christ. The point Henry makes is that, in our participation in the Supper, the Lord gives out blessings to us. He portions out to us a rich share of his blessing. "By the body and blood of Christ, which this ordinance is the communion of, we are to understand all those precious benefits and privileges, which were purchased for us by the death of Christ and which are assured to us on the Gospel terms in the everlasting covenant."[33] As Henry sees it, what we receive at the Lord's Supper is not "his real body and blood . . . but his merit and righteousness for our justification, his Spirit and grace for our sanctification."[34] In short it is his grace that we receive. The phrase, "his real body and blood" as it was understood by Scholastic theology is a rather slippery term. Henry wants to avoid it by a more straightforward language.

We see no attempt here on Henry's part to accommodate himself to Catholic sacramental theology as it was discussed in the seventeenth century. Henry makes no attempt to enter into the ecumenical discussion. In this he differs from Calvin who was never quite willing to leave the old terminology behind. This reflects the fact that Henry is thinking out the significance of the sacrament in a very different intellectual environment. Still, he is very clear that the Lord's Supper is more than a simple remembrance. By participating in the Supper one makes a profession of faith and one receives the grace of God and all the blessings that flow from it. Something is communicated; something is given us by God himself, and something is received by us. That something is grace, the rich blessing of God. Even more, to participate in the Lord's Supper is to enter into a covenantal relationship with God and with the people of God. It is to share in the life of the disciples of Christ and to devote ourselves to the service of the God and Father of our Lord Jesus Christ. Even beyond that, this service is bearing witness to the redemptive and sanctifying glory of the crucified and risen Christ.

---

[33] Henry, *Companion*, p. 294.

[34] Henry, *Companion*, p. 294.

4. A Covenanting Ordinance

This brings us to Henry's fourth point. The sacrament of the Lord's Supper is a covenanting ordinance.[35] Here Henry takes off from Luke 22:20, "This cup is the new covenant." He comments that the sacrament not only pertains to the new covenant, it contains it. It has the whole new covenant in it. It is the sum and substance of it. To take part in the sacrament is to enter into the covenant. It is to receive from Christ the covenantal promises and to make to him and to his people the covenantal vows. Alluding to Hebrews 6:17 and 18, Henry tells us that our Lord Jesus Christ, in order, "more abundantly to show to the heirs of his promise the immutability of his counsel, has confirmed it by an oath,—by a sacrament which is his oath to us, as well as ours to him."[36]

As Henry understood it, the covenant is a mutual agreement. The tenor of this covenant is, "Believe in the Lord Jesus Christ and thou shalt be saved" (Acts 16:31). Our part of the agreement is to believe in Christ; God's part is to save us. "Salvation is the great promise of the Covenant; believing in Christ is the great condition of the Covenant."[37] Here is the real foundation of an evangelical understanding of the Lord's Supper.

The Old Testament type Henry used to explain this aspect of the sacrament is particularly interesting. Henry is directed to this type by the Words of Institution which tell us that the cup is the seal of the new covenant (cf. Matt. 26:28 and 1 Cor. 11:25). Just as the Passover meal is one of the canonical types of the Lord's Supper, so is the story of the sealing of the covenant in the twenty-fourth chapter of Exodus. Jesus himself made the typological connection between the Supper and the sealing of the covenant at the foot of Mount Sinai when he said, "This cup is the new covenant in my blood" (1 Cor. 11:25), an obvious allusion to the text of Exodus 24.

---

[35] Henry, *Companion*, p. 295.

[36] Henry, *Companion*, p. 296.

[37] Henry, *Companion*, p. 296.

Henry points to the fact that Moses read the Book of the Covenant to the people. The people gave their consent to it, "All that the Lord has said we will do, and will be obedient" (Exod. 24:7, KJV). Here we have the covenant vows. This covenant was then sealed by the sprinkling of the blood of the covenant sacrifice on both the altar and the people. At this point Moses said, "Behold the blood of the covenant" (Exod. 24:8, KJV), just as Jesus said when he took the cup, "This cup is the new covenant in my blood." It was clearly Jesus who drew the typological connection. The Sinai typology is just as much a part of the sacrament of the Lord's Supper as the Passover typology. To explain further the typological significance, Henry calls on Hebrews 9:12–20, where we read of another typology, the ceremonial typology so powerfully elaborated by the Epistle to the Hebrews. Christ, Henry explains, having made the perfect sacrifice, which never needs to be repeated, entered once for all into the holy place to intercede for us. Just as according to the Law of Moses the people were sprinkled with the blood of the covenant sacrifice (cf. Heb. 9:19), so in this sacrament the people partake in the blood of the new covenant.[38]

Henry goes on to make the point that in the sacrament the covenant is sealed. He distinguishes between an inward sealing and an outward sealing. The outward seal is the sacrament but the inward seal is the Holy Spirit. "A bargain is a bargain," Henry insists, "though it be not sealed, but the sealing is the ratification and perfection of it. The internal seal of the covenant, as administered to true believers, is 'the spirit of promise,'. . . whereby we are sealed to the day of redemption. . . . But the external seals of the covenant, as administered in the visible church, are the sacraments" (cf. Eph. 1:13 and 4:30).[39] The sacraments are given to us to make our covenant with God especially solemn. Moreover, the covenant is of the most solemn sort. It establishes that God is

---

[38] Henry, *Companion*, p. 296.

[39] Henry, *Companion*, p. 296.

our God and that we are his people. It is this sacred bond that the sacrament of the Lord's Supper seals.[40]

Matthew Henry was one of the great biblical scholars of the church. His six volume commentary on the whole of the Bible ranks him with the leading expositors of all time. Quite consistent, then, we discover him trying to understand the eucharistic mystery not in terms of Scholastic theology but rather in terms of biblical theology.

C. Henry's Eucharistic Piety

Having devoted two chapters of *A Communicant's Companion* to eucharistic doctrine, Henry now turns to eucharistic piety. By "eucharistic piety" we mean the devotional practices Christians use to celebrate the sacrament of the Lord's Supper. By the beginning of the eighteenth century, Reformed churches had developed a whole series of such devotional practices to help celebrants both prepare for the Lord's Supper and apply it afterward. One finds this particularly in Scotland, but the same thing could be found in Congregational churches in England and America, as well as in continental Reformed churches. A celebration of the Lord's Supper usually began with several preparatory services and concluded with a thanksgiving service.

1. Proclaiming the Feast

One of the functions of these preparatory services was to proclaim the feast. Henry treats this at some length in the third chapter of *A Communicant's Companion*. Here the kerygmatic dimension of the sacrament comes through very clearly. It is the job of ministers to go out and invite all manner of people to come in to the great feast.[41] As in the parable of Jesus, the preachers are the heralds who proclaim the feast which the king provides (cf. Luke 14:17) .

---

[40] Henry, *Companion*, p. 297.

[41] Henry, *Companion*, p. 297.

The invitation to the table has often had generous liturgical development in Reformed worship. Early in the sixteenth century the communion services of Strasbourg, Basel, and Zurich provided an exhortation for the minister to use to invite people to come to the table. Calvin's invitation is still used in some churches as a fairly regular feature of the celebration of the sacrament. In the revivalist tradition, every sermon is concluded with an "invitation" which may or may not have any sacramental implication. The invitation, no matter how one construes it, has a definite place in Protestant worship.

Strikingly, Henry develops this kerygmatic theme with a reference to biblical Wisdom theology.[42] As Henry sees it, the preacher is to call us to come to Christ. He has already alluded to the famous passage Proverbs 9:1–6:

> Wisdom has built her house,
>   she has set up her seven pillars.
> She has slaughtered her beasts, she has mixed her wine,
>   she has also set her table.
> She has sent out her maids to call
>   from the highest places in the town,
> "Whoever is simple, let him turn in here!"
>   To him who is without sense she says,
> "Come, eat of my bread
>   and drink of the wine I have mixed.
> Leave simpleness, and live,
>   and walk in the way of insight."

Like the passover typology, the Sinai typology, the wedding feast typology, and the Father's house typology, the Wisdom typology was very important for Henry's understanding of the sacrament. It speaks of the divine Wisdom as a lady who has prepared a great feast and has invited every passerby to leave foolishness and enter into a seven-pillared house and feast on divine truth.[43] "In Wisdom's name I am to tell thee, that notwithstanding all thy former

---

[42] Henry, *Companion*, p. 299.

[43] Henry, *Companion*, p. 297.

follies, thou art welcome to her house, welcome to her table; freely welcome to eat of her bread, and drink of the wine which she has mingled.'. . . Be wise for thy self, wise for thy own soul."[44] As Henry sees it, there is something evangelistic about the invitation to the Lord's Supper; it is the call to accept Christ. This, of course, is all quite consistent with the *Westminster Directory*. Part of the proper celebration of the Lord's Supper is the giving of a public and solemn invitation to participate in the sacrament.

Henry further develops the kerygmatic dimension of the sacrament with another aspect of the Wisdom theme. In this case it is the parable of the wise and foolish virgins which provides Henry with his imagery. It is the job of the preacher to announce to the virgins, both the wise and the foolish, that the Bridegroom comes.[45] As minister of Word and sacrament, the preacher is to prepare the congregation to receive Christ when he presents himself at the banquet which he has prepared for us.

2. Self-Examination

A good part of Henry's *A Communicant's Companion* is devoted to preparations for the celebration of the sacrament. Chapters III through VII are devoted to this subject. Chapter IV, which no doubt was originally a sermon Henry had preached at a preparatory service, is devoted to the subject of self-examination. The obvious text for his deliberations is from 1 Corinthians 11:28 (KJV), "But let a man examine himself, and so let him eat of that bread and drink of that cup." Henry comments, "Now the duty most expressly required by our preparation for the ordinance of the Lord's Supper is that of self-examination."[46] This examination might take the form of a meditation on the commandments or perhaps the Beatitudes. It might take the form of a meditation of

---

[44] Henry, *Companion*, p. 299.

[45] Henry, *Companion*, p. 302.

[46] Henry, *Companion*, p. 309.

the gospel. The penitential psalms might be used for this purpose. The genius of the preparatory service would be in suggesting passages of Scripture appropriate to guiding our self-examination.

3. Renewing Our Covenant

Aside from self-examination, another part of our preparation for the Supper is renewing our covenant with God. Henry urges those who approach the Lord's Table to renew their familiarity with the basic terms of the covenant and then once more to give their assent to it. Particularly indicative of the way Henry understands this is that he speaks of this in terms of the twenty-fourth chapter of Exodus. Again we see the importance of the Sinai typology. It is in this passage that we learn of how God established his covenant with Israel—making himself the God of Israel and Israel the people of God. The passage tells how Moses read to the people the Book of the Covenant and how Israel made a vow to keep the covenant and the laws of the covenant as they had been read to them. It was then that the people were sprinkled with the blood of the covenant and the elders of Israel went up on the mountain and ate and drank and beheld God.[47]

Apparently there were a number of devotional books popular at the time which went quite directly into the matter of renewing the covenant. It was a popular theme of the devotional life. Henry mentions works by Baxter and Allen.[48] One is aware that John Wesley was sufficiently introduced to this devotional theme to have developed a covenant renewal service for use on New Year's Eve.

---

[47] Henry, *Companion*, p. 328.

[48] See Richard Baxter, "The Order of Celebrating the Sacrament of the Body and Blood of Christ," in *The Reformed Liturgy*, contained in Richard Baxter, *A Christian Directory*, reprint (Ligonier, PA: Soli Deo Gloria Publications, 1990), pp. 930–934. See also Thomas Allen, *The Call of Christ unto Thirsty Sinners to Come to Him and Drink of the Waters of Life*, 4th ed. (Boston: Printed by J. Allen for Eleazar Phillips, 1710).

4. Meditation and Prayer

The sixth chapter takes up the subject of preparing for the celebration of the Lord's Supper with meditation and prayer. One of Henry's great contributions to the development of the Protestant devotional life was his elaboration of our understanding of meditation. He obviously does not mean the sort of thing that was popular among the Spanish mystics, nor the sort of thing that we find in the religious exercises of Ignatius of Loyola. He gives us a classic definition: "Meditation and prayers are the daily exercise and delight of a devout and pious soul. In meditation we converse with ourselves; in prayer we converse with God."[49]

A few lines further on he tells us, "Meditation is thought engaged and thought inflamed."[50] Here we find nothing of what the Maharishi understands by meditation. There is no emptying of the mind. There is no hint of the sort of mystical trance like what we find in some of the late medieval Christian saints. Meditation as Matthew Henry understands it is much closer to what we find in Gregory the Great and the Fathers of the patristic era. It is thinking over the truths of the Gospel; it is thinking about what one has read in the Scriptures or heard in the sermon.

Henry suggests eight subjects upon which the Christian might meditate in preparation for receiving the sacrament of the Lord's Supper. To us, at the beginning of the third millenium, the first of these may seem a bit gloomy, but for the beginning of the eighteenth century, Henry's meditations are amazingly upbeat. First he suggests that we "set ourselves to think of the sinfulness and misery of man's fallen state."[51] As we find again and again in the Psalms, lamentation is a constantly recurring concern of our prayer. To try to escape these meditations about our sins, our frustrations, and our disappointments would be unrealistic. This

---

[49] Henry, *Companion*, p. 330.

[50] Henry, *Companion*, p. 330.

[51] Henry, *Companion*, p. 331.

is part of the epicletic dimension of our worship. As we find in Psalm 23, the Lord prepares a table before us in the midst of our enemies. How often we come to the Lord's Table in tears.

Our meditations can also be very abstract and theological. Henry goes on to tell us that we should meditate on the divine attributes, on the love and mercy of God, on the justice and holiness of God, and on the power and wisdom of God. "Let us set ourselves to think of the glory of the divine attributes shining forth in the work of our redemption and salvation."[52] More concretely, he also teaches us to meditate on the person of Jesus, the humility of his birth, his patient obedience to his Father, and his works of kindness and mercy. To be sure, we are to meditate on the cross of Christ, his passion, and the victory of his resurrection.[53] Here we find again the eucharistic dimension of the Lord's Supper. Here we find again the dimension of *anamnesis*, the dimension of remembering the history of salvation.

From these thoughts our meditation should go on from the history of God's mighty acts of salvation in his incarnate Son here on earth to a meditation on the transcendent Christ. We should meditate on "the present glories of the exalted Redeemer."[54] Among transcendent glories we should meditate on the unsearchable riches of the new covenant made with us in Jesus Christ and sealed to us in this sacrament. We are to meditate on the communion of the saints.[55] We should keep in mind our communion with those who are seated with us at the table as well as with those who have gone before and now enjoy the life of the Church triumphant. The Lord's Supper is a foretaste of the wedding feast of the Lamb and therefore it should evoke from us meditations on the joys of heaven. Again the eschatological dimension of the Lord's Supper comes into focus.

---

[52] Henry, *Companion*, p. 332.
[53] Henry, *Companion*, p. 333.
[54] Henry, *Companion*, p. 334.
[55] Henry, *Companion*, p. 335.

12: Matthew Henry

5. The Affecting Sights

In chapter VIII Henry addresses himself to "the affecting sights" which one encounters in the sacrament of the Lord's Supper. This is a particularly interesting portion of Henry's work because it takes up a theme which Reformed theologians have always insisted on, namely, that there is a visual aspect of the sacrament, and that visual aspect is of the essence of the sacrament. Reformed theologians have always repeated the dictum of Augustine that the sacraments are the Word made visible. This visual aspect, however, is very different from the whole idea of the liturgy being an icon of eternal reality as this idea developed, especially in the Eastern Church.

It is not crucifixes or altar pieces that we see when we come to the celebration of the Lord's Supper. Just before the Reformation the faithful would go to mass and see a passion play in which the drama of Christ's passion was unfolded in liturgical symbol and gesture. The altar was equipped with altar pieces on which were painted the central stages of the history of redemption. One saw in works of art the incarnation, the passion, and the resurrection. But that is not at all what the faithful saw at a Reformed celebration of the Lord's Supper. What the faithful saw in a Reformed celebration was the breaking of the bread, sharing it one with another, the pouring out of the cup, and passing the cup around. Each worshiper was supposed to see the congregation around the table, each serving one another the gifts of God. It was a group of brothers and sisters in Christ sharing a meal—that is, the visual sign. As Henry put it, "Here is his body broken, his blood shed, his soul poured out unto death; all his sufferings, with all their aggravations, are pictured here in such a manner as the Divine Wisdom saw fit, by an instituted ordinance, represented to us, and set before us."[56] These are the fundamental sights we come to see in the sacrament as Christ instituted it: the breaking of the bread and sharing of the cup around the Lord's Table. Other sights are

[56] Henry, *Companion*, p. 348.

distracting, as much as they might be aesthetically pleasing.

There is another sense, however, in which at the Lord's Supper we see the sights of our redemption. Henry reminds us of the story of the burning bush. He comments that Moses turned aside to see that great sight. What he beheld was a great mystery and from out of the bush God spoke to him. There was obviously more to this than simple sight. It was the same way when John the Baptist saw Jesus coming to him and said, "Behold the Lamb of God who takes away the sin of the world." Much more was involved than simple seeing. It is the same way with the call which John the Divine heard when he was called to witness the Lamb in his heavenly glory in Revelation 6:1–7. As Henry understands it, the same call is given to us "when in this sacrament there is a door opened in heaven, and we are bidden to 'come up hither'" (Rev. 4:1).

The Bible speaks about seeing that which is by nature invisible at several important junctures. That tremendously important passage for the biblical concept of worship, Exodus 24, after it has spoken of Moses reading to the congregation of Israel and sprinkling the blood of the covenant first on the altar and then on the people, tells us that Moses and Aaron, Nadab and Abihu, and the seventy elders of Israel went upon the mountain and beheld God and ate and drank. That somehow this profound beholding of God takes place at the Lord's Supper is written deeply in Protestant piety. As a witness to this we have Horatio Bonar's famous communion hymn, "Here, O my Lord, I see thee face to face. . . . Here would I touch and handle things unseen."

Here traditional Protestant piety comes very close to the piety of Eastern Orthodoxy. Here we are very close and yet distinctly different. What it all means is that in the sacrament we realize that which is beyond the grasp of sense perception. This is the sacred truth which Western pietism so wisely held on to in the face of the myopic teachings of the Enlightenment. There is a reality beyond that which we can see and touch, and yet with the eyes of faith we can, nevertheless, see it, and even hold it in our hands. Concerning communion Henry says, "In this ordinance is showed us the Lamb as it had been slain. . . . This is the sight, the great sight, we are here to see; the bush burning, and yet not consumed, for the Lord is in it, his people's God and Savior."[57]

One notices here that this kind of seeing has to do with the Lamb who takes away the sin of the world, the Lamb that was slain and lives forevermore. It is the Lamb that is seen. We do not have to do with the same sight which Mary Magdalene saw in the garden. That was natural sight. Here the heart of what we are seeing is the broken body, the poured out wine. Here we are showing forth the Lord's death until he comes. Here we have to do with the seeing of the transcendent God as the Lamb. This kind of seeing is, if we are allowed to use the word, supernatural.

6. The Benefits of the Sacrament

Let us turn our attention now to chapter IX, a chapter on the benefits we receive from the sacrament. Here Henry passes on much traditional material, material which has figured prominently in the teaching of the Church all down through the centuries. The beautiful thing about what Henry gives us is his rich development of the biblical imagery. Henry carries through the biblical language with such mastery that our understanding of the sacrament is greatly enlarged.

The first point Henry makes is that when we come to the Lord's Supper we must be more than spectators. For many centuries the sacrament had been watched, as though it were a passion play. Most of the congregation watched the drama of the mass but did not receive the bread and wine. It was as though the liturgy alone could teach us something visually. The allegorical interpretations of the mass which had become so popular with Dionysius the Areopagite emphasized looking at the liturgy as though it were

---

[57] Henry, *Companion*, p. 348.

an icon. With the Reformation the emphasis changed. Protestantism taught that we come to the sacrament to share in the feast, rather than to look at it.[58] Again Henry alludes to Proverbs 9:1–6. Wisdom's invitation is, "Come, eat of my bread, and drink of the wine which I have mingled" (v. 5, KJV).[59]

At the top of the list Henry puts the forgiveness of sins. This is the fundamental benefit of the sacrament. The very fact that we are received at the table, handed the bread, and offered the cup demonstrates to us that we have been forgiven of our sins and accepted into communion with God. This is more than a picture; it is an act. To be sure this is one of the sights which we see, this acceptance into the table fellowship, but it is something more than that which is watched from afar; it is something into which we enter and see close at hand. It is something we see happening to us. "Christ and his benefits are here not only set before us, but offered to us; not only offered to us but settled upon us, . . . so that a believer who sincerely consents to the covenant, receives some of the present benefits of it in and by this ordinance."[60] For Henry the experience of being received at the table, eating the bread and drinking the wine, is a foretaste of the heavenly banquet. It is here on earth both an experience of communion with God and an expectation of communion with him in glory.[61] By participating in the sacrament, we experience the forgiveness of our sin.[62]

In the same way we experience our adoption as sons and daughters into the household of faith:

> The covenant of grace not only frees us from the doom of criminals, but advances us to the dignity of children: Christ redeemed us from the curse of the law, in order to do this, that "we might receive the adop-

---

[58] Henry, *Companion*, p. 355.
[59] Henry, *Companion*, p. 356.
[60] Henry, *Companion*, p. 356.
[61] Henry, *Companion*, p. 356.
[62] Henry, *Companion*, p. 356.

> tion of sons," Gal. iv. 5. The children's bread given us in this ordinance, is as it were livery and seisin, to assure us of our adoption . . .[63]

The fact that we are being fed in this sacred meal is clear from this visible Word. With the eyes of faith we understand that this is the house of the Father and that we have been received into this house and are being fed at his table. If in Christ we take the God and Father of our Lord Jesus Christ to be our God and Father, then, "God here seals us the grant both of the privileges of adoption, and the Spirit of adoption."[64]

Like the passover typology, the wedding feast typology of the Song of Solomon, or the harvest feast parables, the figure of the house of the Father is a distinct eucharistic imagery. This image is expressed in John 14, "In my Father's house . . ." We find it again in Ephesians, "the household of faith . . ." Henry sees in the basic sacramental action not only a promise of adoption but also a sign of God's providential care. "Providence shall be thy protector, and the disposer of all thy affairs for the best; so that whatever happens, thou mayest be sure it will be made to work for thy good, though as yet thou canst not see how or which way."[65] While the visible sign speaks to us of God's regular provision for us in the things of this world, to the eyes of faith it speaks far richer blessing in terms of the life of the world to come.[66]

A most precious benefit of the sacrament is spiritual peace. In receiving the sacrament with faith and sincerity we are assured that we have peace with God. Peace is proclaimed to us because we have found rest in the house of the Father. "Come, my soul, and take possession of this Canaan, by faith enter into this rest."[67]

---

[63] Henry, *Companion*, p. 357.

[64] Henry, *Companion*, p. 358.

[65] Henry, *Companion*, p. 358.

[66] Henry, *Companion*, p. 359.

[67] Henry, *Companion*, p. 360.

From this Henry goes on to speak of the spiritual nourishment which is one of the benefits of the sacrament. The sacred meal is most obviously a sign of our being spiritually fed. We see the bread and wine not outwardly but inwardly; in a way we cannot see, God supplies us with spiritual food that we might grow in grace. Henry says, "We have as much need of the influences of the spirit to furnish us for our duties, as we have of the merit of Christ to atone for our sins, and as much need of divine grace to carry on the work as to begin it."[68] The spiritual nourishment signified and promised by the sacrament is the sort of nourishment we need to live the Christian life, to continue on our pilgrimage, and, at last, to enter the land of promise.

It is clear throughout this chapter that there is a strong relation between what the sacrament signifies and the primary benefits to be received from the sacraments. Once again Henry takes up the visual aspect of the sacrament.[69] The signs point to the benefits. The broken bread and the poured out wine seal to us the forgiveness of sin. The table fellowship assures us of the peace that passes understanding. The fact that we are fed with bread and wine is a foretaste of our spiritual nourishment. That we find our place about the table together with our brothers and sisters in Christ proves to us our welcome in the household of faith. As Henry understood it, staunch Protestant that he was, the true evangelical communion service should be celebrated in such a way that it looked like a meal. It should be celebrated around a table with bread and wine that look like real bread and wine. We should be seated about the table in such a way that it looks like we are sharing a meal. Lining up and going down the center isle and kneeling at the altar rail before an elaborate altar quickly dissipates the picture of a meal. It was not "biblicistic literalism" which led the Puritans to replace the altar with a communion table. It was rather a concern to be faithful to the

---

[68] Henry, *Companion*, p. 361.

[69] Henry, *Companion*, p. 364.

basic signs implicit in the sacrament. If the evangelical Lord's Supper is served to a seated congregation, it is to preserve the imagery of the Supper. Ideally that seating should be arranged around the table, even if it is only the seats of the elders that complete the circle. The point is that the communion should look like a meal, that what is signified might in fact be seen.

There is much more to be learned from Henry's *A Communicant's Companion*. It is a true devotional classic, worthy of reading and re-reading.

13

COMMUNION SEASONS
IN EIGHTEENTH-CENTURY SCOTLAND

The seventeenth century, the age of Protestant Scholasticism, had been an age of deepening piety just as much as it had been an age of flowering orthodoxy. To be sure, there was a real difference between the fresh insights of the sixteenth century Reformation and the established orthodoxy of the seventeenth century.

One often gets the impression that the age of Protestant Orthodoxy was sort of stuffy, and yet, it was clearly a stream both deep and wide. But it is difficult to characterize the eighteenth century. Could one call it classical Protestant piety or simply Old School piety? One thing is clear. There are some very fine representatives of this Old School Reformed piety first in Matthew Henry, about whom we have just spoken, and in John Willison, the pastor of South Church in Dundee, Scotland. The two are quite different. Matthew Henry was clearly the heir of English Puritanism while Willison inherited Scottish Presbyterianism. Both represent distinct developments in Reformed piety.

In the next chapter, we will study some of the communion sermons of the Erskine brothers, Willison's contemporaries, as well as the communion sermons of Robert Walker, pastor of St. Giles in Edinburgh, to show that Willison was far from being an isolated case, but rather the superb example of a widespread tradition.

It was in fact a number of years ago when I was studying seventeenth and eighteenth-century Scottish preaching that I began to notice that the sermons preached for the Scottish communion seasons formed a very special genre of sermon. At the time I resolved to come back and study Scottish sacramental preaching for what it can tell us about Reformed communion piety. So here we are once again studying the communion sermons of five Scottish eighteenth century preachers to see what they can tell us about the sacrament of Holy Communion and how it fits into the Christian life.

One thing that is of particular interest about the eucharistic piety of the Scots is that it is not simply a Celtic manifestation of Pietism such as we have in Spener, Francke, Zinzendorf, or the Wesleys. It reaches back to the eucharistic piety of John Knox and even further to Calvin, Bucer, and Zwingli. One sees the influences of Pietism here and there but the influence of the sixteenth century is much stronger. In fact, what we find here in Willison, especially, is a maturing of Reformed eucharistic piety. We found much the same thing in Matthew Henry, of course, but Willison's maturity has its own stamp on it. It is so distinctly a churchly piety. It assumes a devout and well-informed congregation. The preacher's grasp of Scripture is astounding. For me, at least, the discovery of the communion piety of eighteenth century Scotland has been a revelation.

JOHN WILLISON[1]

As no one else, John Willison (1680–1750) represents the historic tradition of Scottish Presbyterian piety. From no other writer do we get such a clear picture of Scottish Presbyterian worship. Here is Old School Presbyterianism at its best.[2] During the first half of the eighteenth century he produced several manuals of devotion which were widely read in Scotland, England, Ireland, and America. His *Treatise concerning the Sanctification of the Lord's Day* appeared

---

[1] For biographical information on Willison, see John R. McIntosh, "Willison, John," in *Dictionary of Scottish Church History and Theology*, ed. Nigel M. de S. Cameron (Edinburgh: T. & T. Clark, 1993), pp. 873–874. See also John Willison, *A Sacramental Catechism*, ed. Don Kistler (Morgan, PA: Soli Deo Gloria Publications, 2000), p. v.

[2] By Old School Presbyterian here we mean Presbyterianism unaffected by the Great Awakening or any of the forms of revivalism of the eighteenth or nineteenth century as they developed in America or the British Isles.

in 1712.³ This was followed in 1716 by *A Sacramental Directory, or Treatise concerning the Sanctification of a Communion Sabbath*.⁴ This was several times enlarged and republished. True to the spirit of the eighteenth century these works speak of Christian worship in terms of the inclination of the heart. They are not so much works on liturgical rites as they are works on liturgical piety. That, of course, was what interested the eighteenth century. In 1737, at the height of that sad controversy in which Moderatism tried to suppress the Covenanter spirit, Willison published *The Afflicted Man's Companion* as well as his very influential *Example of Plain Catechising*.⁵ While the two works are very different in purpose, they both nourished the religious aspirations of the people in a day when ecclesiastical politics seemed to be quenching the Spirit.

In 1742 Willison published a series of twelve sermons, *The Balm of Gilead*, which addressed the spiritual maladies of the nation and prayed for a revival.⁶ One thing of particular interest to Americans about these sermons is that Willison had obviously read Jonathan Edwards' *A Faithful Narrative*, telling of the spiritual awakening in the Connecticut Valley. Willison greets this news with enthusiasm. Only a few months after the appearance of Willison's work, the famous Cambuslang Revival began. *The Balm of Gilead* is a series of prophetic sermons in the truest sense of the word. They offer a vision of the awakening that was to come, not only in America and the British Isles, but even on the continent of Europe. Inspired by the ministry of the French Huguenot prophets in the mountains of Southern France, he spoke with amazing clairvoyance of the

---

³ For a text of *Treatise concerning the Sanctification of the Lord's Day*, see John Willison, *The Practical Works of the Rev. John Willison*, ed. W. M. Hetherington (Glasgow, Edinburgh, and London: Blackie and Son, [1830]), pp. 1–126. Hereinafter, Willison, *Works*.

⁴ See John Willison, *A Sacramental Directory*, in Willison, *Works*, pp. 127–241.

⁵ For *The Afflicted Man's Companion*, see Willison, *Works*, pp. 728–823. For *Example of Plain Catechising*, see Willison, *Works*, pp. 513–727.

⁶ See John Willison, *The Balm of Gilead*, in Willison, *Works*, pp. 391–441.

French Revolution which would begin in 1789. As Willison saw it, both revolution and revival were on their way. For those who would not repent, there was judgment, but for those who would, there was joy everlasting.

Willison died a very happy man. His long pastorate in Dundee had produced a large and flourishing congregation. The time of refreshment for which he had prayed was showing signs of its coming. It would be easy to see in Willison a forerunner of Pietism, or even to claim him as a Scottish version of eighteenth-century Pietism. Such an evaluation, however, would really miss the mark. There are two important respects in which he differed from the pietism of Spener, Francke, and Zinzendorf; Wesley and Whitefield. First, he addressed himself to the church rather than to the faithful few within the church. He was concerned for the *ecclesia* not the *ecclesia in ecclesiola*. Second, the piety which he encouraged was in the closest relation to the regular worship of the church. At the center of the sanctification of the Lord's Day is the coming together of the church for public worship. The celebration of communion is the high feast of the Christian life. It is there that the covenant vows are made and renewed; it is in publically participating in the body and blood of Christ that the profession of faith is made. The subjective devotion and the objective celebration are kept closely together.

But if Willison was not really a Pietist, nor even a forerunner of Pietism, he was certainly an ally of Pietism. He saw it coming and greeted it with enthusiasm. Like Jonathan Edwards, Benjamin Colman, and perhaps, when all is said and done, Gilbert Tennent, Willison was one who had always known a deep personal piety and was therefore one of the first to recognize the spiritual integrity of the Pietists, whatever hesitations he may have had about certain aspects of the movement.

Let us focus in on some of Willison's works dealing most specifically with what we might call eucharistic piety.

A. *Five Sacramental Sermons*, 1722

In 1722 Willison published *Five Sacramental Sermons*, a series of sermons preached at a typical Scottish communion season.[7] There were three preparatory sermons preached during the week before the celebration and two thanksgiving sermons, one preached on the Sunday afternoon following the sacrament, and the other on the Monday following. The preparatory services and thanksgiving services were an important part of the Scottish communion celebration. Together they formed what was called a communion season. Frequently neighboring ministers were asked to assist in these seasons, preaching one or more of the sermons. The sermon preached at the actual celebration, called the "action sermon," is not included in this series of five sermons. Just why there was not an action sermon included in the *Five Sacramental Sermons* we cannot say for certain. Perhaps Willison had been invited to preach at the preparatory and thanksgiving services in another congregation and the host pastor would himself have preached the "action sermon." Afterwards the host might have urged the publication of his guest's sermons, but out of modesty refrained from publishing his own. We have a particularly fine action sermon from Willison which was published elsewhere. We will study it in addition to the preparatory and thanksgiving sermons in order to get a full picture of how Scottish eucharistic preaching was handled in the eighteenth century.

The first of the three preparatory sermons is devoted to the subject of Christ's presence with his people. The matter of Christ's presence is one of the classic themes of sacramental meditation. The text is taken from Jeremiah 14:8, "O Hope of Israel, the Saviour thereof in time of trouble; why shouldest thou be as a stranger in the land, and as a way-faring man, that turneth aside to tarry for a night?"[8] The fourteenth chapter of Jeremiah is a great passage on

---

[7] John Willison, *Five Sacramental Sermons*, found in Willison, *Works*, pp. 309–349.
[8] As quoted in Willison, *Works*, p. 309.

spiritual drought. After commenting on the meaning of the text as it is found in the book of Jeremiah, and speaking of why God's presence was withdrawn from Israel in the days when Jeremiah was sent to preach, Willison draws the following point, "That as it sometimes pleaseth God to withdraw himself, and behave as a stranger to his church and people; so there is nothing in the world that will be such matter of exercise and trouble to the serious seekers of God, as such a dispensation."[9] With great sensitivity Willison paints in somber tones the sufferings of spiritual drought. He does it in such a way that one understands that it is not only a problem for the people as a whole, but a problem which we all face personally from time to time.

> When the Lord denies access to his people in duty, and breaks off his wonted correspondence with them: they come to God's ordinary meeting-places with his people, ordinances both public and private, but he is not there; they seek him, but still they miss him, so as they are put to cry with that holy man, Job xxiii. 3, "O that I knew where I might find him." O that I knew the place, the duty, the sermon, the sacrament, where I might find him; there I would go and seek him; I try prayer (saith the poor soul), but that brings me not to him; . . .[10]

Then Willison begins to explore why God sometimes withdraws his presence. His biblical illustrations are superb. When God's people "turn earthly-minded and prefer the delights of sense to precious Christ, then he withdraws, Isa. lvii. 17. They that have a strong relish for the flesh-pots of Egypt, are not fit to taste the hidden manna. When the Gadarenes came that length as to prefer their swine to Christ's presence, he turned his back, and departed from their coasts, Mat. viii. 28."[11]

Another biblical figure for God's presence is taken from the Song of Solomon. One notices here how important the Song of Solomon

---

[9] Willison, *Works*, p. 310.
[10] Willison, *Works*, p. 311.
[11] Willison, *Works*, p. 311.

and the nuptial imagery of both the Old and New Testaments is in Willison's sacramental sermons. It appears here as a sort of hint of things to come. In fact nuptial imagery surfaces again and again in the sacramental sermons of the Puritans in both England and New England during the seventeenth and eighteenth centuries. In treating the question of how the Christian is to deal with these seasons of spiritual drought, Willison tells us that we should lay hold of all the appointed means of finding God's presence. Like the spouse in the Song of Solomon who sought her beloved all about the city (Song of Solomon 3:2), "In all duties and ordinances, both private and public, our souls should follow hard after him, and pursue him closely, as it were, from one ordinance to another."[12] Our preacher tells us we are to seek God's presence in prayer by pleading with him as Jeremiah does in this text, and as he did in fact in his whole ministry. Jeremiah pleaded the glory of God's name and the helplessness of his people. He pleaded his former mercies and the sufficiency of his power. But what is particularly interesting here is that Willison tells us Jeremiah, "pleads the outward symbols and pledges of his presence . . . his temple, his ark, and oracles."[13]

The outward forms of worship are obviously quite real for Willison. We find no radical subjectivism here. There is no suggestion that the objective forms of worship and subjective experience of piety are opposed to each other or are in some sort of dialectical relationship. If the objective and subjective are divided, God's people can never be satisfied. "If God be not in the ordinances, nothing can please them, not the most powerful sermons, though an angel were to preach them; nor the most lively communions, though a glorified apostle should come and dispense them. The absence of God is such a great want to them, that nothing in heaven or earth can fill up, but himself."[14] Yet these outward

---

[12] Willison, *Works*, p. 312.

[13] Willison, *Works*, p. 313.

[14] Willison, *Works*, p. 313.

forms of worship can be and often are the means of experiencing God's presence. That is what is to be expected in worship. It is that the congregation may indeed experience God's presence in the regular celebration of worship that Willison preaches this sermon. There is no beauty in worship if Christ is absent, but if he is present then there is beauty. "It is his presence that puts a lustre on ordinances, and makes them shine, so as to confirm the friends of the gospel, . . . It is his presence that puts life in communions, and life in communicants, and causes them to prefer a day in 'God's courts to a thousand elsewhere.'"[15]

We notice very specifically that this is called a fast day sermon.[16] We assume that those who intended to receive the sacrament would have fasted from early morning and would continue to fast for the other preparatory sermons, although these preparatory sermons do not insist on the length or the severity of the fasting. One thing is clear; there is a very definite penitential dimension to the prayers offered in the celebration of the Lord's Supper. As we shall see, however, it is magnificently overcome by the joy of the wedding feast.

The second preparatory sermon takes up the subject of "the happiness of being in covenant with God." The text is Psalm 144:15, "Happy is that people whose God is the Lord."[17] Our preacher dwells at length on the meaning of this verse in the context of the psalm in which it is found and then draws out the point he wants to make. To be in covenant with God and to have God as our God is the greatest happiness we can have. In developing this theme our preacher spends some time distinguishing between an outward participation in the covenant and an inward participation in the covenant. "All members of a visible church are federally in covenant with God by their profession of Christ, and being baptized in his name."[18] But

---

[15] Willison, *Works*, p. 315.
[16] Willison, *Works*, p. 309.
[17] Willison, *Works*, p. 316.
[18] Willison, *Works*, p. 318.

just as in ancient Israel there were many who belonged to the covenant people outwardly but not inwardly, so among Christians those who do not seek earnestly to make this an inward reality miss the blessings of the covenant relationship. For us to come into the bond of the covenant of grace is a matter of faith. It is by faith in Christ that we inwardly participate in the covenant. Genuinely to enter into the covenant relationship is to be thoroughly convinced of our sin and our inability to achieve our salvation by our own work; it is to accept Christ as our righteousness, our only Mediator, Surety, and Peacemaker. It is to choose God, Father, Son, and Holy Spirit, as our God; it is to give ourselves to Christ and walk with him in newness of life as becomes his covenant people. It is the inward apprehension of faith which makes the covenant relation our greatest happiness. Willison concludes his sermon by appealing to his congregation to go home and in their secret prayers to renew their covenant vows and then return to the communion service and make their vows before men and angels. As Willison envisions it, the objective formal act of public worship, if his congregation heeds his word, will be supported by an inner devotion that will make it a great source of blessing. He obviously expects the outward forms to be filled with inward reality. There is no suggestion that only the inner experience is important.

The third preparatory sermon urges the congregation to take advantage of the season of grace that is offered to them. Now is the acceptable time. The text is taken from Hebrews 3:7–8: "Wherefore, as the Holy Ghost saith, To-day if ye will hear his voice, harden not your hearts as in the day of Provocation."[19] In the preparatory sermons there is definitely a place for the minister to plead with his listeners to accept the invitation to make the vows of faith and be received into the fellowship of the church. Here is the prototype of what a century later will be called the American frontier revival.

In good eighteenth-century style Willison begins his sermon by analyzing his text and formulating the doctrine found in it. The

---

[19] Willison, *Works*, p. 324.

point which he wants to bring to the attention of his congregation is "that all who sit under the gospel should be careful to improve the seasons of grace, and opportunities of hearing Christ's voice, which God alone allows them."[20] The lingo is obviously from another day, but the point is clear enough. This invitation is offered by none other than the Holy Spirit. This invitation is from Christ himself. Here the Spirit of Christ strives with us, and to resist the striving of the Holy Spirit is the unforgivable sin.

Scripture speaks of these seasons of grace as "'an acceptable time and day of salvation.' II. Cor. vi. 2."[21] These times should be carefully managed, lest they be lost, for indeed they can be lost, and, being lost, they may never again present themselves. This is an old theme in Christian preaching. Evangelists in every age have developed it from Gregory of Nazianzus to George Truett. Any time there is true gospel preaching, it is an acceptable time, but when we sense that there is an inward working of the Spirit on the conscience taking place in the external dispensation of the word and sacraments, we can be assured that we have such a season of grace.[22] When we feel this striving of the Holy Spirit with our hearts we realize that a great door is being opened in both the preaching of the minister and the soul of the congregation.

For Willison the epiclesis is an important part of the communion service. It is in the conviction which the Holy Spirit works in our hearts that we come to feel the need we have of the bread of life and the cup of salvation. In our prayers we should give thanks for this conviction "and entreat that these sparks, kindled by the breath of God, may not be smothered, but blown up into a flame."[23] For a Reformed theology of worship the epiclesis has always played a major role. This is true for preaching and baptism, but especially

---

[20] Willison, *Works*, p. 325.

[21] Willison, *Works*, p. 326.

[22] Willison, *Works*, p. 327.

[23] Willison, *Works*, p. 329.

for communion. The preparatory service gives special attention to the need for the Church, corporately and individually, to cry out to God to satisfy our spiritual hunger and thirst with the sacred table that has been set before us. Having heard these three preparatory sermons the congregation would then arrive at the church Sunday morning ready to participate in the celebration of the actual sacrament. It was a service of the greatest possible solemnity.

When Willison preached at the communion service he must have had a tremendous sense of being carried into the highest of heavenly realities. As it has often been said, the Reformed understanding of the Lord's Supper is not so much in terms of the incarnation of Christ as it is in terms of the ascension of Christ. The text for the one action sermon which we have from Willison is taken from the Song of Solomon, "He brought me to the banqueting house, and his banner over me was love."[24] One might be tempted to imagine that the choice of a text from the Song of Solomon was some sort of eccentric quirk in the piety of one isolated Scottish minister if it were not that we have a number of Dutch Reformed, Presbyterian, and Congregational communion sermons from the seventeenth and eighteenth centuries which draw heavily on the nuptial imagery to celebrate the mutual relationship of love between Christ and his church. Obviously the choice of a text like this makes it very clear that the Lord's Supper is not merely a memorial of Christ's death; it is even more a celebration of the wedding feast of the Lamb. The Protestant communion services of that day were not as funereal as some have imagined.

Introducing the sermon Willison outlines the Christian interpretation of the Song of Solomon. The whole book celebrates the communion between Christ and his church. It is Christ who is the Bridegroom. Given the Christian interpretation, our text tells us that Christ brings his bride into the wedding feast. He brings her under a banner, and that banner is love. "Love is the banner that

---

[24] The action sermon is contained in Willison, *Works*, pp. 303–309.

Christ lifts up and displays this day to engage you to come to him, and enlist yourselves under his banner. Love is that which leads to the banqueting-house."[25] The first point this dour Scotsman wants to make is the richness of the banquet which has been prepared by Christ. Almost as a fanfare Willison brings to our attention a series of biblical images for spiritual food: the feast of the Lady Sophia, the fountain of life and the wells of salvation, the hidden manna, the bread of angels, and the grapes of Canaan. Letting his imagination have its play he suggests seven dishes which are served at this spiritual feast. Here on this banquet table is pardon of sin sealed to the believer. Here we have the rare dish of peace and friendship with God. Yet another dish is our adoption as heirs and joint heirs with Christ. Then there is peace of conscience, comforting and strengthening graces, Christ's presence and the sight of his countenance. Finally there is that most delectable of dishes, the pouring out of the Holy Spirit.

> Thus I have shown you some of the rich provision and noble entertainment prepared in this banquet before you: yea, you see it is not only rich provision, but there are choice rarities here, . . . plenty and variety, . . . food to nourish, strengthen, delight, and refresh the soul. Here is food suitable to all the faculties, light to the mind, peace to the conscience, satisfaction to the will, and food for all the affections. Here love may satisfy itself in clasping the Desire of all nations. Delight may here bathe itself in the rivers of pleasure.[26]

The whole sermon is a lyrical proclamation of the love of Christ, and an expression of holy delight in the presence of God. It is only when one has understood this typology that one understands the Reformed eucharistic theology. Here is the key!

We will return to look at this action sermon in more detail further along, but let us first look at the two thanksgiving services.

---

[25] Willison, *Works*, p. 303.
[26] Willison, *Works*, p. 305.

The communion held on Sunday morning was followed by a thanksgiving service on Sunday afternoon and a second thanksgiving service on Monday. For the first of these thanksgiving services Willison chose the text, "Wherefore thou art no more a servant, but a son: and if a son, then an heir of God through Christ."[27] The sermon is a meditation on the benefits of our redemption. It stresses the filial nature of the new covenant. In the new covenant we are adopted as sons of God. Although only our Lord Jesus Christ is the son of God by eternal generation, all believers are sons by grace and adoption. At considerable length Willison draws out the imagery of the spiritual inheritance which the Christian has in Christ. Then Willison, in a particularly apt metaphor, goes on to speak of the Holy Spirit as the executor of the will. It is the Holy Spirit who invests believers in the bequeathed inheritance "by renewing their souls, working faith in them, and disposing them to close with the Redeemer; planting all gracious habits in them, and thereby giving them the earnest and first fruits of the inheritance."[28] It is by this work of the Holy Spirit that we become heirs not only by adoption but by redemption as well. By the gracious work of the Holy Spirit dwelling within us we become godly by nature. He gives us power actually to become children of God in that we more and more come to share the divine nature.

A careful theologian will want to inquire very carefully into what Willison means by sharing the divine nature. He does not appear to mean what some theologians have called "theosis."[29] It means rather, holiness. To share God's nature is to bear his image. It is to be holy. It is to have the character of God's children. It is to choose

---

[27] Galatians 4:7 as quoted in Willison, *Works*, p. 333.

[28] Willison, *Works*, p. 337.

[29] On the subject of *theosis* in Reformed theology, see Bruce L. McCormack, "Union with Christ in Calvin's Theology: Grounds for a Divinization Theory?" in *Tributes to John Calvin: A Celebration of His Quincentenary*, ed. David W. Hall, The Calvin 500 Series (Phillipsburg, NJ: Presbyterian and Reformed Publishing, 2010), pp. 504–529.

God as your Father and dedicate yourself to him in the eternal covenant. It is to receive Christ as mediator by a true and lively faith.

Within the idea of thanksgiving is the idea that, having received God's gracious gift of redemption, Christians must give themselves to God in Christian service, in living according to God's will, and in deeds of love toward their neighbors. This is the subject of the second thanksgiving service. The sermon takes as its text Isaiah 40:29, "He giveth power to the faint; and to them that have no might, he increaseth strength." The title is, "The fainting believer strengthened for his work."[30] The overall theme is to encourage the communicants to live the Christian life by assuring them of God's support. It is only by God's strength that we can do God's work, Willison tells us. Then as was often the case in sermons of this period, our preacher gives a set of "directions" for receiving such strength. The point, so essential to Reformed theology, that the Christian life is lived in thanksgiving for our salvation, is clearly made.

In this final sermon of the series, Willison particularly emphasized the theme of the sacrament as manna in the wilderness. Certainly one of the spiritual delights in the observance of the Lord's Supper is in discovering that in our trials we have been strengthened by this divinely given meal. "O communicants, examine if you have got any spiritual strength at this solemn feast. Many a weak believer has found it a strengthening meal to their fainting souls."[31] Not only is the sacrament of the Lord's Supper the Christian Passover and the marriage feast of the Lamb, but it is also manna in the wilderness. These three typological figures of the eucharist were very popular in the eighteenth century, especially in Reformed circles.

It is with a great deal of sensitivity that Willison develops this type of the sacrament. He tells us that in the new covenant God brings those who have been freed from the spiritual bondage of an old Egypt through the Red Sea. He does not simply leave that

---

[30] Willison, *Works*, p. 342.

[31] Willison, *Works*, p. 347.

new Christian to fend for himself alone. Far more, a fresh supply of nourishment is provided day after day as we go through the wilderness on the way to the promised land. The sermon is concluded with the assurance that in feeding on this bread and wine we can receive them as a sign that God will henceforth provide us with a seasonable supply of strength from God, that we will be helped, "safe through the wilderness, without fainting or failing."[32]

The eucharistic preaching of John Willison is evangelistic. In Scotland it was at the communion seasons that the minister proclaimed the most central and essential matters of the gospel. This was because of the strong covenantal dimension of Reformed theology. It was in receiving the sacred bread and wine that the Christian accepted Christ and promised to live and die in his service. Scottish evangelistic preaching, following the practice of John Calvin's preparatory services during Holy Week in Geneva, was understood in terms of the celebration of the Lord's Supper. It was preparatory to the Lord's Supper, preparing the members of the covenant community to make the vows of faith at the covenant meal.

B. Action Sermon

Let us go back to the action sermon Willison published in 1722. We have already looked at this sermon in terms of its place in the typical Scottish communion season. Now we want to look at it because of some particularly rich insights it gives us into Willison's eucharistic theology.[33] The sermon has come down to us in the collected works of Willison. No title is given to the sermon; however, our attention is immediately caught by the text:[34]

> He brought me to the banqueting house,

---

[32] Willison, *Works*, p. 348.

[33] The following study of the eucharistic theology of Willison was given at a meeting of the Evangelical Ministerial Association in Lafayette, Indiana, in 1975.

[34] Willison, *Works*, pp. 303–309.

and his banner over me was love.
(Song of Solomon 2:4)[35]

To contemporary audiences, perhaps this seems a bit obscure. Song of Solomon is rarely preached on today. Over the years, however, I have discovered that a good number of important Reformed preachers have chosen texts from the Song of Solomon for their eucharistic sermons. The earliest one I have found is by the late sixteenth-century Dutch preacher Jodocus van Lodenstein.[36] I have even discovered a eucharistic sermon by Gilbert Tennent that draws on the amorous hymns of Solomon.[37] The Song of Solomon was, at one time at least, a favorite passage of Scripture to direct the meditation, the praise, and the thanksgiving of the congregation at the celebration of the Lord's Supper.

Today we are much more accustomed to thinking of the Lord's Supper in terms of the Passover typology, and indeed the Passover feast is perhaps the primary type for understanding the Christian sacrament. Surely the manna which fed God's people in the wilderness is another important type of the Lord's Supper. The abundant meal in the house of the Father is a type. Abraham particularly is a type of the household of faith. This is a type found frequently in the parables of Jesus. The Solomonic typology, or perhaps one should call it the Wisdom typology, is also clearly to be found in the New Testament as a type of the sacrament. One need only to mention the parables of Jesus on the wedding feast in the synoptic gospels, the references to the wedding feast of the Lamb in the Revelation, and particularly the story of the

---

[35] Willison, *Works*, p. 303.

[36] For a discussion of the eucharistic sermons of Jodocus van Lodenstein, see Hughes Oliphant Old, *The Reading and Preaching of the Scriptures in the Worship of the Christian Church*, vol. 4, *The Age of the Reformation* (Grand Rapids, MI: Eerdmans, 2002), pp. 461–467. See also pp. 430–439 of this volume.

[37] Hughes Oliphant Old, "Gilbert Tennent and the Preaching of Piety in Colonial America: Newly Discovered Tennent Manuscripts in Speer Library," *Princeton Seminary Bulletin* 10/2 (1989): 132–137.

wedding feast at Cana. There Jesus turned the water into wine, revealing himself to be the true Bridegroom of Israel. Whatever today's New Testament scholars might want to add to the story, the typological development is clear.

One of the beauties of taking a text from the Song of Solomon for the central sermon of a communion season is that it casts a joyful glow over the whole celebration. It becomes an *agapé*, a love feast. Too often the Lord's Supper is treated as a memorial feast like those the ancient Greeks and Romans shared at the tomb of a departed relative or friend. Some might mistakenly read certain New Testament texts in this way, yet both the Passover typology and the Wisdom typology lead in another direction. The wedding feast of the Lamb is a triumphant feast celebrating the resurrection, Christ's victory over the powers of death and hell, and his victory over sin and Satan.

From the very beginning the Reformed churches preferred the Lord's Day for celebrations of the Lord's Supper. We find this especially in Strasbourg. By reserving the Lord's Supper to the Lord's Day they emphasized that Christ not only died for us, but also rose for us. It is with the risen Christ that we share this meal.

It has long been my belief that Christian piety has all too frequently overemphasized the memorial of Christ's redemptive sacrifice in its celebration of the Lord's Supper and left to a distant second place the memorial of Christ's resurrection.[38] Sometimes there is a memorial of the incarnation and sometimes there is an intimation of the Second Coming, but the resurrection is frequently left in the background. Again and again the cross becomes the crucifix in Christian devotion, whether in Catholic, Orthodox, or Protestant communities. For Reformed churches the balance is, at least to some extent, restored by its rich development of the

---

[38] This is not to deny the insights of such Princeton theologians as J. W. Alexander and B. B. Warfield, who insisted on the sacrament as a sign of the propitiatory nature of Christ's sacrifice over against the tendency of liberal Protestantism to interpret the sacrament as a Sunday School picnic. See chapter 19.

observance of the Lord's Day, the Christian Sabbath, the weekly celebration of the resurrection.

Very closely related to the Bridegroom typology of the Song of Solomon is the Wisdom typology of the Lady Sophia, as some people have called it. Willison, whose sermons are always bountifully enriched by references to parallel texts, speaks specifically of this brilliant biblical image. Willison understood the feast that Wisdom prepared (Prov. 9:1–6) as a type of the Lord's Supper.[39]

This close connection between the Wisdom theology of the Old Testament and the eucharistic theology of Reformed churches has already been noted.[40] It is particularly noticeable in discussion of the manna and the meaning ascribed to the manna in the sixth chapter of the Gospel of John.[41] Willison understands the Lord's Supper as a sign of spiritual food, just as the sign of the manna in the wilderness was a sign of spiritual food. Here, of course, we recognize that Willison was following close on the heels of Calvin as we find it in his *Short Treatise on the Lord's Supper*.[42] Simply suggesting that the wedding feast of King Solomon spoken of in the Song of Solomon is a type of the sacrament of Holy Communion opens up an important dimension of eucharistic theology. Several details of his exposition deserve, however, special attention.

First, Willison tells us that the whole of the book of Solomon "is an allegorical description of the mysterious union and communion betwixt Christ and his Church."[43] Furthermore we should notice that it is Christ and no other who brings his spouse into this banqueting house. But for Christ we would have no right of entry into this feast. We should notice particularly the freeness of the grace of Christ here. He gives us both strength and preparation of soul.

---

[39] Willison, *Works*, p. 303.
[40] Cf. Old, *Reading and Preaching*, volume 4.
[41] Willison, *Works*, p. 304.
[42] See the discussion in chapter 2.
[43] Willison, *Works*, p. 303.

Of special import is the manner in which the spouse is to be brought into the banqueting house. She is to be brought in under a banner, standard, or ensign. We are dealing with a military term here. Banners are used in battle to gather the troops around their commander. Battle flags make clear to the troops the direction the commander is going. The different commanders can be distinguished by their banners or their colors. The banner that Christ lifts high above his own is love. Our preacher formulates his interpretation, "Love is the banner that Christ lifts up and displays this day to engage you to come to him, and enlist yourselves under his banner. Love is that which leads to the banqueting-house, and furnishes provision and entertainment for us there."[44]

Let us look now at several theological themes which Willison develops in this sermon. First of all, we consider the theme of covenant which we so often notice in the sermons of Reformed ministers. Quite naturally these figures from the Song of Solomon lead our preacher to develop a distinctly covenantal understanding of the sacraments. He puts it quite explicitly, ". . . in this sacrament a covenant of peace and friendship is sealed and confirmed."[45] The concept of covenant had played an important role in the religious history of Scotland. In the previous century the leaders of the Church of Scotland had signed the National Covenant which united Scotland in its support of a Reformed theology and a presbyterian polity. Ever after those leaders were called Covenanters. To be regarded as a Covenanter was to be considered a most loyal supporter of the Reformed cause. To enter into the covenant you are not only made a friend of God you are made a member of God's family as well. You are made sons of God and heirs. By means of sharing in this sacrament you are made eligible to all rights and privileges which come to you from your Father in heaven. You are given peace of conscience which is one of the most precious lega-

---

[44] Willison, *Works*, p. 303.
[45] Willison, *Works*, p. 304.

cies we can receive. It is here at this sacrament. Here the testament is sealed. As we find it in the fourteenth chapter of the Gospel of John, "Peace I leave with you; my peace I give to you" (John 14:27).

Another theme which Willison addresses in this sermon is presence: "Here is Christ's gracious presence, and a sight of his countenance."[46] Just what Willison means by this is opened up by a reference to Psalm 16, "In thy presence is fullness of joy." It is here at the Lord's Table that Willison finds the presence of Christ, "It is here Christ meets with his people, here he walks with them, . . . and holds communion with them. . . . Here they see the King in his beauty, here the saints have beheld the beauty of the Lord, Psal. xxvii. 4."[47] What we have here is a vivid experience of the presence of Christ, the sort of experience about which mystics speak, the sort of experience David Brainerd had in the woods of Pennsylvania as he pursued his mission to the Indian tribes of the Susquehanna Valley. It was the sort of experience the Scottish hymnist Horatio Bonar spoke of in his Communion hymn, "Here, O my Lord, I see thee face to face." The celebration of communion is a high point in the Christian life because it is a vivid experience of communion with God. Our preacher cries out, "O let it be our errand this day to meet with Christ, and see his blessed face."[48] Let us seek to see the face of Christ, our preacher urges his congregation, as the Bride sought to see the Bridegroom. It was her transporting experience as we find it in the Song of Solomon, "Saw ye him whom my soul loveth?"[49]

Willison finds a number of passages from the Song of Solomon to help him develop his sermon. For Willison, presence has a number of dimensions. We need to speak of the divine presence, to be sure, but we need to speak of the presence of both the

---

[46] Willison, *Works*, p. 305.
[47] Willison, *Works*, p. 305.
[48] Willison, *Works*, p. 305.
[49] Song of Solomon 3:3 as quoted in Willison, *Works*, p. 305.

bridegroom and the bride. Quoting the Song of Solomon 5:1 our preacher invites the congregation to partake of the feast, "Eat, O friends, drink, yea, drink abundantly, O beloved."[50] God's ministers are stewards of the feast and it is their job to see that all the children of God receive their appointed share, but it is the master of the feast, Christ himself, who has commanded the blessing.[51]

An important feature of this feast is the fellowship of so many. There is the fellowship with the Bridegroom, that is, Christ, but there is also the fellowship with the King, that is, the Father. "The King sits at this table," the Song of Solomon reminds us (Song of Solomon 1:12). The King is none other than the King of Glory. Christ himself is there present, "for in this feast we have fellowship with the Father and the Son, through the Holy Spirit."[52] But going even further we have fellowship at this table with all the saints above, with those who have gone before us and entered into their eternal destiny. If Belshazzar made a feast for a thousand of his lords, here we have a feast for many thousand more. If Ahasuerus held a feast for all his princes and all his servants which lasted for a hundred and eighty days, here we have a feast which lasts for eternity.[53]

Surely another major theme of Willison's eucharistic theology is redemption. The sacrament is a sign and seal of our redemption in Christ. We notice here with particular interest that Willison relates this theme of the Song of Solomon typology very closely to the theme of the Passover typology. Communion is to be a solemn memorial of Christ's love to sinners and his atoning death for them, just as the Passover was a memorial of God's gracious act of redemption in bringing Israel out of slavery in Egypt. The Song of Solomon typology and the Passover typology go hand in hand, but there is a big difference between them. The Passover

---

[50] Song of Solomon 5:1 as quoted in Willison, *Works*, p. 305.
[51] Willison, *Works*, p. 306.
[52] Willison, *Works*, p. 306.
[53] Willison, *Works*, p. 306.

typology shows us how Christ fulfilled the sacrificial system of the Old Testament in his passion and his death. The typology of the Song of Solomon, however, is a memorial of things to come. It is an anamnesis, to be more exact, of things to come. It is a foretaste of the wedding feast of the Lamb. We will hear more of this further on because this eschatological dimension of the sacrament has long been an important dimension of Reformed sacramental theology, as is obvious from Calvin's communion invitation in the *Genevan Psalter* of 1542.

Finally we must notice that the eschatological theme of Willison's sermon goes hand in hand with the covenantal theme. Willison tells us that one of the purposes of celebrating the sacrament is to "ratify and confirm the covenant between God and us."[54] It was quite common, he tells his congregation, that in the ancient Orient covenants and contracts were ratified by the sharing of a meal. He makes his point by telling of the ratification of the covenant between Isaac and Abimelech (Gen. 26:28–30). To use Willison's term, it was a "federal rite" which united Laban and Jacob in Genesis 31:46. So also it was the meal which sealed the agreement of the Israelites and the Gibeonites in Joshua 9:14 and the covenant between David and Abner in 2 Samuel 3:20. "Consider then, this is a covenanting feast, here a solemn bargain between God and us is sealed and ratified."[55] We agree to believe in Christ and he agrees to save us from our sins. God promises to be our God and we promise to be his people. God promises to us the benefits of the covenant and we promise to fulfill the duties of the children of God.

Once again the covenant theme directs our preacher to the future. In the covenant, God promises us his providential care in life, but, even more, in the life to come God will in his time call you to

---

[54] Willison, *Works*, p. 306.

[55] Willison, *Works*, p. 306.

enter into "the marriage supper of the Lamb above."[56] But in the meantime this sacrament weans us from the vain comforts and pleasures of this world and makes us long for that glorious feast above. "This is a foretaste of it, and should stir up a hunger for it; for this feast is the first fruits of heaven."[57] It is about this feast we read in the beginning of the Revelation. "Behold, I stand at the door, and knock: if any man hear my voice, and open the door, I will come in to him, and will sup with him, and he with me" (Rev. 3:20, KJV).[58] For a Reformed understanding of the Lord's Supper it is equally true that by faith in Christ's atoning death and resurrection Christ enters into our celebration of the sacred feast and that he opens to us a place at the marriage supper of the Lamb as well. It is therefore that we approach this table with holy awe and reverence.[59]

C. *A Sacramental Catechism*, 1720

A much more detailed presentation of Willison's eucharistic theology and above all his eucharistic piety is found in his *A Sacramental Catechism* of 1720.[60] Characteristic of eighteenth-century Protestantism is an overwhelming concern for piety. There was nothing new about this piety. We have found it especially in Matthew Henry, who like Isaac dug so deeply the wells which his father had dug before him. Willison has dug deeply into the eucharistic faith and practice of the Reformation in which he was brought up. He made explicit what had since the days of John Knox been thoroughly implicit.

Willison's *A Sacramental Catechism* is a devotional guide to prepare young people for their first communion. The first section of this catechism bears the title, "A Familiar Instructor for Young

---

[56] Willison, *Works*, p. 307.
[57] Willison, *Works*, p. 307.
[58] Willison, *Works*, p. 308.
[59] Willison, *Works*, p. 308.
[60] *A Sacramental Catechism* is found in Willison, *Works*, pp. 442–543. Material for this section was also taken from the modern edition edited by Don Kistler, cited as Willison, *A Sacramental Catechism*. See note 1 of this chapter (p. 474).

Communicants."[61] Yet, it is clearly directed to more mature Christians as well. One gets the impression that what started out as a guide for a communicants' class for young people soon became a devotional guide for adult communicants as well.

Let us look at several dimensions of Willison's eucharistic faith and worship.

1. COVENANTAL DIMENSION

Right from the beginning this work makes a strong point of the covenantal dimension of the sacrament of the Lord's Supper. The first question proposed in this catechism is:

> Q. For what end hath the Lord appointed sacraments in his church?
>
> A. To be visible signs and seals of his gracious covenant with man, in order to represent and apply Christ and his benefits to his covenanted people; to strengthen their faith in his promises, and solemnly to engage them to his service.[62]

The Lord's Supper is defined as a sign and a seal of the covenant. The purpose of the Lord's Supper is to receive the blessings of the covenant, to make the covenant promises and be joined to the covenant people to the end that God be our God and we be his people.

As we have been pointing out all along, the Reformed churches from the very beginning of the Reformation developed a covenantal theology to explain their approach to the sacraments. By the beginning of the eighteenth century this covenantal theology had undergone an elaborate development. A variety of different covenants had been distinguished. There was the covenant made with Adam, the covenant made with Noah, the covenant made with Abraham, the covenant made with Christ and so forth. Willison gives quite a bit of attention to explaining what a covenant is and what the terms

---

[61] Willison, *A Sacramental Catechism*, pp. 1–40.

[62] Willison, *Works*, pp. 446–47. See also Willison, *A Sacramental Catechism*, p. 1.

of the various covenants are. At the same time he makes very clear the essential unity of all the covenants. They all point to the one eternal covenant. Very early in his catechism Willison distinguished between the covenant of works and the covenant of grace.

In Scotland covenantal theology had been of great importance. In time it became one of the fundamental concepts of the national self-consciousness. We really do not want to get covenantal eucharistic theology mixed up with the national self-consciousness any more than it already has been, but we do need to mention it because it helps explain something of the passion of the discussion. As the Stuart monarchy tried to force Scotland to accept the English religious establishment, the Scots insisted on their own religious traditions. The Church of Scotland had no intention of submitting to the sort of government control the Church of England had accepted. The basis of this religious independence was formulated in what came to be called the National Covenant. Representatives from all over Scotland came together in Greyfriars churchyard in Edinburgh and swore to defend the Protestant faith and Presbyterian church order. From that point on, the devout of Scotland were known as Scottish Covenanters. The word "covenant" had special meaning in Scotland. Scotland was a land held together by a covenant just as ancient Israel was a people held together by a covenant. To enter into the covenant was to dedicate one's self to its support.

A covenantal theology of the sacrament of the Lord's Supper is to understand that when we participate in this meal we partake of all the promises of God's grace, the forgiveness of sin, peace with God in this life, and the hope of eternal glory. Through this sacrament, communion with the living God is opened up to us as well as fellowship with his people. Having these promises signed and sealed to us we pledge our faith to Christ as Lord and Savior and engage ourselves to live in his service.[63]

Vows are very important to the covenantal dimension of the

---

[63] Willison, *A Sacramental Catechism*, p. 12.

sacrament. Further on in his catechism Willison takes up this subject, asking:

> Q. Are not vows and prayers requisite at the Lord's table?
>
> A. Yes; for here we are to profess our sorrow for sin, and thankfulness for God's favours, and join ourselves to the Lord in an everlasting covenant; and it certainly becomes all true penitents, thankful souls, and honest covenanters, to make vows; and these vows are nothing worth without prayers to God joined therewith, for strength to keep them. And these vows and prayers seem to be most seasonable after our receiving of the elements, and our exerting of the direct acts of communicating. Job xxxiv. 31, 32; Gen. xxviii. 20; John i. 16; Nehemiah x. 29.[64]

Then Willison goes on to make this even more explicit:

> Q. What is the nature of these vows, which we ought to come under, at this juncture?
>
> A. A religious vow is a serious oath of dedicating ourselves to the Lord's use and service; or, it is a solemn engagement and promise unto the Lord, whereby we bind and oblige ourselves to be the Lord's dutiful children and servants, Num. xxx. 2; 1 Chron. xv. 12–15.[65]

At this point, at least, Willison seems to have in mind the vows of faith implied in the reciting of the Creed at the beginning of the communion service proper. The Creed is, of course, the baptismal creed. Even more, Willison is talking about the vows one makes at the thanksgiving service to continue in the service of Christ through the rest of one's life. Very particularly, Willison seems to have in mind the prayer of dedication which follows the receiving of the bread and wine.

---

[64] Willison, *Works*, p. 522.
[65] Willison, *Works*, p. 522. See also Willison, *A Sacramental Catechism*, p. 261.

2. Sacramental Dimension

Another important dimension of Willison's eucharistic theology is the sacramental dimension.

With the recovery of the works of Tertullian early in the sixteenth century, theologians discovered the original meaning of the word "sacrament." We have spoken of this several times before. What needs to be pointed out here is that Willison, like many of his contemporaries, was fully aware of the original meaning of the word "sacrament." Willison's catechism proposes the question:

> Q. What is the proper significance of the word sacrament?
>
> A. It is not a scriptural word, more than the word Trinity is: yet seeing the thing signified is there, and the word is very significant, it may be lawfully used. Anciently the word sacrament was a military word, in use among the Romans, and signified the "solemn oath which soldiers took, to be true to their general"; afterwards, it was used by ecclesiastical writers, to signify any holy mystery, and particularly the sealing ordinances of baptism and the Lord's supper; and indeed it is very applicable to them, seeing, by receiving these seals, we solemnly engage ourselves to be the Lord's, and swear to stand by him as faithful soldiers, fighting under his banner against all his enemies.[66]

As we have noted elsewhere, the North African theologians from the time of Tertullian to the time of Augustine were especially fond of the word when they wanted to speak of "the sealing ordinances of baptism and the Lord's supper." The word "sacrament" itself underlines that participation in the Lord's Supper is a solemn engagement to be the Lord's. In this sacrament we "swear to stand by him as faithful soldiers, fighting under his banner against all his enemies."

Willison's catechism stands very close to the Westminster Standards. Often it quotes or closely paraphrases both the *Larger Catechism*

---

[66] Willison, *Works*, p. 456. See also Willison, *A Sacramental Catechism*, p. 34.

and the *Shorter Catechism*. We read, for instance, that a sacrament is "a holy ordinance instituted by Christ in his church, and annexed as a seal to the covenant of grace; wherein, by outward and sensible signs, Christ, and the benefits of his mediation are represented, sealed, and applied to those that are within the covenant."[67]

If the Lord's Supper is a sacrament in the true sense of the word, then it is understood particularly as a sign of one's loyalty to Christ and his church, and it becomes a visible way of distinguishing between "those that belong to the church and the rest of the world."[68] Much is implied about the meaning of the Lord's Supper through the proper use of the word "sacrament."

Willison's catechism goes on to point out that a sacrament has two parts, ". . . the one external and earthly; and the other spiritual and heavenly."[69] On the one hand there is the outward, sensible sign and on the other there is the spiritual blessing represented, conveyed, sealed, and applied by that sign. The catechism asks:

Q. What is a sensible sign?

A. That which is obvious to the outward senses of hearing, seeing, tasting, smelling, or hearing [feeling]. And such are both the sacramental elements and sacramental actions.[70]

Here we should underline that the sensible part of the sacrament is thought of both in terms of the sacramental elements, that is, the bread and wine, and the sacramental actions, that is, the

---

[67] Willison, *Works*, p. 456. The *Shorter Catechism* reads, "A sacrament is a holy ordinance instituted by Christ; wherein, by sensible signs, Christ, and the benefits of the new covenant, are represented, sealed, and applied to believers." As quoted from *The Confession of Faith: The Larger and Shorter Catechisms* (Edinburgh: The Free Church of Scotland, 1976), p. 313. This quotation is also contained in Willison, *A Sacramental Catechism*, p. 34.

[68] Willison, *Works*, p. 457. See also Willison, *A Sacramental Catechism*, p. 34.

[69] Willison, *Works*, p. 457; Willison, *A Sacramental Catechism*, p. 35.

[70] Willison, *Works*, p. 457. Kistler is surely correcting a typographical error when he substitutes "feeling" for the second "hearing." Willison, *A Sacramental Catechism*, p. 35.

breaking of the bread, the pouring of the wine, the sharing of the meal around a table, the giving of the bread and wine, and then actually eating and drinking it with one another.

The catechism goes on to ask about that which is signified:

Q. What things do sacraments signify and seal?

A. 1. As they are signs, they signify and represent the grace and good-will of God in Christ to his covenanted people. 2. As they are seals, they ratify and confirm his people's right to all the blessings and promises of the covenant, and likewise their engagements to new obedience.[71]

Two things should be recognized here. In the first place sacraments not only signify, they seal as well. Here, again, this is implicit in the word "sacrament" as it was understood in the ancient Latin church. A sacrament was an engagement. It not only signified one's enlistment in military service; it sealed the relationship as well. The second matter to be recognized is what it is exactly which is conferred by the sacrament. It is, "the grace and good-will of God in Christ."

The blessing of God's grace is, of course, not something which can be seen. It is of incalculable value to us but it is hard for us to lay hold of because our human nature finds it hard to have dealings with. Such great blessings are beyond the reach of our material existence and it is therefore that God communicates it to us by visible signs. Words are hard enough for us to understand. We need signs to support the words. Willison says, "Sacraments are, as it were, a visible gospel; the offers of free love and benefits of Christ's purchase are thereby exposed to the eye, as the word doth sound them in the ear."[72]

If Willison follows the ancient church by explaining the Lord's Supper in terms of the pledge of allegiance, or sacrament of a soldier on enlisting in military service, he also wants to explain

---

[71] Willison, *Works*, p. 457. See also Willison, *A Sacramental Catechism*, pp. 35–36.

[72] Willison, *Works*, p. 457. Cf. Willison, *A Sacramental Catechism*, p. 37.

the Lord's Supper in terms of signs of the covenant found in the worship of ancient Israel. As circumcision was a "sign or seal of the righteousness that comes by faith" (Rom. 4:11), and Passover was to be a sign and a memorial for Israel (Exod. 11:13–14 and 13:9), so baptism and the Lord's Supper were to be a sign and seal, a memorial observance of God's mighty acts of redemption to the church. The Old Testament had its sacraments—circumcision and Passover, and the New Testament had its sacraments as well—baptism and the Lord's Supper.[73]

As Willison understood it, the sacraments of the Old and New Testaments had the same substance, "for they both represent and exhibit Jesus Christ, and the same spiritual benefits and mercies through him, Rom. iv. 11; 1 Cor. x. 1."[74] What seems to be the point here is that the *res* of the sacrament is the grace of God as it is found in Christ. Then, Willison's catechism goes on to ask:

Q. Is there no difference between them?

A. Yes, in several respects: 1. The old sacraments represented Christ as to come; but the new, as already come. 2. The old represented Christ more darkly; but the new more clearly and plainly. 3. The old were only to endure till Christ's coming in the flesh; but the new, until Christ's coming in glory. 4. Their outward signs differ much from each other.[75]

The sacraments of the Old Testament point to Christ. Especially in the case of the Passover they intimate Christ, his atoning sacrifice, and our final communion with him.[76]

If we are to discuss the patristic roots of Reformed worship, the rediscovery of a number of the works of Tertullian was a definite case in point. In the sixteenth century the Reformers of the

---

[73] Willison, *A Sacramental Catechism*, p. 38.

[74] Willison, *Works*, p. 457. See also Willison, *A Sacramental Catechism*, p. 38.

[75] Willison, *Works*, pp. 457–58. Cf. Willison, *A Sacramental Catechism*, p. 38.

[76] Willison, *A Sacramental Catechism*, p. 39.

Swiss city-states such as Zurich, Schaffhausen, Bern, and Basel were often called sacramentarians because of their new interpretation of the word "sacrament." Interestingly enough, the first edition of the complete works of Tertullian appeared in Basel in 1522. Reformed eucharistic theology has always taken the sacramental dimension of the Lord's Supper very seriously.

3. THE COMMUNION DIMENSION

Another dimension of Willison's eucharistic theology is the dimension of communion. A bit further on, Willison, turning his attention more specifically to the Lord's Supper, gives us the following definition:

Q. What is the Lord's Supper?

A. The Lord's supper is a sacrament of the New Testament; wherein, by giving and receiving bread and wine, according to Christ's appointment, his death is showed forth: and the worthy receivers are, not after a corporal or carnal manner, but by faith, made partakers of his body and blood, with all his benefits, to their spiritual nourishment and growth in grace; to the confirming of their union and communion with Christ, renewing of their covenant with God, and their thankfulness to him; and their mutual love to, and fellowship one with another, as members of the same mystical body, Matt. xxvi. 26–28; 2 Cor. xi. 23–26; 1 Cor. x. 16, 17.[77]

Here Willison is building on the *Shorter Catechism*.[78] The use of the word "sacrament" is clearly affirmed. It may not be a bibli-

---

[77] Willison, *Works*, p. 466. In the modern edition, the words in italics are quoted from the *Shorter Catechism*. Willison, *A Sacramental Catechism*, p. 68.

[78] The *Shorter Catechism* reads as follows: Q. 96. *What is the Lord's supper?* A. The Lord's supper is a sacrament, wherein, by giving and receiving bread and wine, according to Christ's appointment, his death is shewed forth; and the worthy receivers are, not after a corporal and carnal manner, but by faith, made partakers of his body and blood, with all his benefits, to their spiritual nourishment, and growth in grace." *The Confession of Faith: The Larger and Shorter Catechisms* (Edinburgh: The Free Church of Scotland, 1976), p. 314.

cal word, but it certainly conveys a biblical truth. It makes clear the covenantal dimension of the Lord's Supper. A few pages later Willison asks why the Lord's Supper is called the sacrament. He answers, "It is called so, by way of eminency: and because here we take a most solemn oath of fidelity to our Redeemer."[79] Yet, ultimately for Willison the Lord's Supper is best understood in terms of the feast of the Passover, the sign and seal of the Old Testament. It is this typology which speaks most clearly to Willison, which, no doubt, is the reason he expands on the traditional phrase of Westminster to include that the Lord's Supper is a sacrament of the New Testament.

He includes yet another elaboration of the traditional phrase of Westminster. Willison tells us, "to the confirming of their union and communion with Christ, . . . and their mutual love to, and fellowship one with another . . ."[80] It is obviously the Greek word *koinonia* which is behind this phrase. To be sure, this is a very big theological word in the New Testament. What is interesting here is that Willison uses a whole cluster of words to translate it into English. In relation to God it has to do with our union with him or communion with him. Even more specifically it has to do with our covenantal union with God. Surely this is the point Willison is making when he says that the goal of the sacrament is to confirm our "union or communion with Christ, renewing . . . [our] covenant with God."[81] The union we enter into with God by means of the sacrament has been understood in very different ways. There are those who would understand it as ingesting some sort of substance. No doubt those who look at it this way can perceive this in varying degrees of sophistication. For Willison it is quite clear that

---

[79] Willison, *Works*, p. 467. Kistler substitutes the word "distinction" for "eminence." Willison, *A Sacramental Catechism*, p. 71.

[80] Willison, *Works*, p. 466. Cf. Willison, *A Sacramental Catechism*, p. 68. The allusion is to the *Larger Catechism*, Q. 168. See *The Confession of Faith: The Larger and Shorter Catechisms*, p. 258.

[81] Willison, *Works*, p. 466.

at the Lord's Supper we are joined to Christ in a communion, a fellowship, a covenantal bond.

But *koinonia*, the *koinonia* we experience in the Lord's Supper, has to do not only with our relation to God. It has to do with our relationship with other Christians, too. As Willison puts it here, it has to do with our "mutual love to, and fellowship one with another, as members of the same mystical body."[82]

In another place Willison has another question to this point:

Q. Why is it called the communion?

A. Because in the right partaking of this ordinance, we have communion and fellowship with Christ, share with him in the benefits of his death and purchase, and also have communion one with another.[83]

Here clearly the union with Christ is understood as fellowship. We have fellowship with God just as we have fellowship with God's people. It is a very special type of social union. It is the sort of union spoken of by the covenant. God is our God and we are his people. We are not absorbed into God. Our humanity is neither destroyed nor eliminated. Our personality is not violated. We do, however, come into communion with God in a profound way. God is our God and we are his people. Our union with God is a *koinonia*, a covenant fellowship.

There is another term here, and that is the "mystical body." In his definition of the Lord's Supper Willison tells us that our "fellowship one with another . . . [is as that of] . . . members of the same mystical body."[84] Here, again, we are dealing with a very traditional theological term. The mystical body of Christ is a term which speaks of the church. The term implies a transcendent reality, a reality yet to come, a heavenly reality which is known by faith. The mystical body of Christ is Holy Communion at its most profound. It

---

[82] Willison, *Works*, p. 466. Cf. Willison, *A Sacramental Catechism*, p. 68.

[83] Willison, *Works*, p. 467. Cf. Willison, *A Sacramental Catechism*, pp. 71–72.

[84] Willison, *Works*, p. 466; Willison, *A Sacramental Catechism*, p. 68.

4. THE SACRAMENT AS SIGN

Traditional sacramental theology had spoken extensively of *signum* and *res*, the sign and that which is signified. Augustine in his *De doctrina christiana* had set the terms of the discussion, but behind these Latin words there are some even more profound biblical concepts. The Gospel of John uses the word "sign" (*sêmeion*) in a most significant way, and even behind that is the concept of "sign" in the Hebrew Scriptures. About all this we have spoken elsewhere.[85] Scottish sacramental theology, however, gives the discussion some fresh insights.

Willison opens up the discussion by posing this question:

Q. What parts does the Lord's supper consist of?

A. Of two parts: 1. The outward, sensible signs. 2. The spiritual and heavenly things thereby signified.[86]

First, we want to notice that Willison takes up the traditional terms even if he does not use the Latin words *res* and *signum*. *Signum* is obviously translated by "sign" and *res* is translated by "things," as in "heavenly things thereby signified."[87] What is fresh in the discussion is the answer to the next question:

Q. What are the sensible signs made use of in this sacrament?

A. They are of three sorts; 1. Sacramental elements. 2. Sacramental actions. 3. Sacramental words.[88]

The sacramental elements are obviously important, but for centuries they had monopolized the discussion. The sacramental words

---

[85] See page 75 of this volume.

[86] Willison, *Works*, p. 467. See also Willison, *A Sacramental Catechism*, p. 73.

[87] Willison, *Works*, p. 467; Willison, *A Sacramental Catechism*, p. 73.

[88] Willison, *Works*, p. 467.

were discussed as well, but the sacramental actions were all but ignored. That bread and wine were signs was often discussed, but the breaking of the bread, the pouring of the cup, the sharing of the meal, and the serving of one another rarely entered into the picture.

One often spoke of the bread as the sign of Christ's body or of the wine as the sign of Christ's blood. Even further, one frequently spoke of the breaking of the bread and the pouring out of the wine as the sign of Christ's atoning sacrifice. This could be developed at some length, even to the point of turning the celebration of the mass into a passion play. The Roman mass during the Middle Ages was regarded by some as a sacred drama.[89] Following this further, one might have thought of the miracle of transubstantiation as the basic sign, the point being that by the grace of God we are transformed into the likeness of God. This is not the way Willison looks at it. The pastor of Dundee finds the basic sign to be the sharing of a meal.

There is something very sound about Willison's teaching regarding the sacramental action. His catechism asks the following:

Q. What are the outward sacramental actions in the Lord's supper?

A. They are twofold, some on the part of the administrator; and some on the part of the receivers.[90]

Q. What are the actions on the administrator's part?

A. They are four; as may be seen in Christ's example: 1. He took bread. 2. He blessed the bread and wine. 3. He broke the bread. 4. He gave both of them to His disciples.[91]

The first thing that one cannot help but notice is how much Willison anticipates Gregory Dix, the Anglican Benedictine monk whose

---

[89] Cf. Adolf Frantz, *Die Messe im deutschen Mittelalter, Beiträge zur Geschichte der liturgie und des religiösen Volkslebens* (Darmstadt: Wissenschaftliche Buchgesellschaft, 1963).

[90] I have amended the text which read "two-old." The antique edition I have in my library reads "twofold." Willison, *Works*, p. 469.

[91] Willison, *Works*, p. 469. Willison, *A Sacramental Catechism*, p. 78.

book, *The Shape of the Liturgy*, was so influential in the liturgical renewal movement of the last generation.[92] Dix makes much of the four-action shape of the liturgy. No doubt it would have embarrassed Dix to no end if he had discovered that a Scottish Presbyterian had so completely scooped him. Amazingly, not only did Willison anticipate Dix in the basic idea that the actions are fundamental to the sign, but we also find that the four actions are very similar. There is one important difference, however. Willison is interested not only in the actions of the minister of the sacrament but in the actions of the communicants as well. Dix, on the other hand, seems interested only in the actions of the celebrant. For Dix the important thing is that the celebrant, following the example of Christ, performs the sign.

One notices that the minister of the sacrament is called the "administrator" of the sacrament rather than the "celebrant." The way Willison puts it, however, tends in the direction of understanding the whole church as the celebrant. The action of the congregation is as important to the performing of the sign as the action of the minister. But before we get into that subject, let us look at the four actions of the minister.

> Q. What is signified by the minister's taking of bread?
>
> A. It signifies God the Father's choosing and taking Christ among men, to be a surety and sacrifice for lost sinners, and his laying upon him, as such, all the sins of the elect, John iii. 16; Isa. liii. 6; 2 Cor. v. 21.[93]

In other words, it signifies the Father's election of the Son. From all eternity the Father destined the Son to be the perfect sacrifice who would atone for the sin of the world.[94]

> Q. What is signified by the blessing of the bread and wine?

---

[92] Gregory Dix, *The Shape of the Liturgy* (London: Adam and Charles Black Ltd., 1975). See also the section on William Perkins in chapter 6, pp. 230–237.

[93] Willison, *Works*, p. 469. See also Willison, *A Sacramental Catechism*, p. 78.

[94] Cf. Frantz, *Die Messe im deutschen Mittelalter*.

A. It signifies these things:

    1. The consecrating and setting apart of the bread and wine, from a common to an holy and sacramental use; and that by solemn prayer for a blessing from heaven upon them.

    2. This blessing being also expressed by the giving of thanks, it signifies a solemn thanksgiving to God for his astonishing grace and mercy to lost sinners in giving them a Saviour and surety: and also for his giving them this blessed ordinance for conveying and sealing Christ's glorious purchase to them.

    3. This blessing being of the same import as consecrating or sanctifying, it signifies God's sending his Son into the world, sanctified, blessed, and furnished with all gifts and graces needful for the discharge of his mediatory offices, and for answering of his people's exigencies.[95]

Three answers are given. The first concerns the offering of a prayer of epiclesis, "consecrating and setting apart of the bread and wine, from a common to an holy and sacramental use." The words are almost identical to the *Westminster Directory for Worship*.[96] Beyond that they can probably be traced to Bullinger or even more to Peter Martyr Vermigli.[97] This prayer is indeed part of the sign. Apparently Willison thought of it in terms of epiclesis. We cry out to God in our hunger and thirst for righteousness, for God is our help and our salvation. We consecrate the bread and wine "by a solemn prayer for a blessing from heaven." When God's people cry out to him in time of need, then God's glory is served. He is revealed as a saving God to whom his people have always turned when they were hard pressed.

---

[95] Willison, *Works*, p. 469. Cf. Willison, *A Sacramental Catechism*, pp. 78–79.

[96] The *Westminster Directory* says in part, "The minister is to begin the action with sanctifying and blessing the elements of bread and wine set before him . . . having first, in a few words, shewed that those elements, otherwise common, are now set apart and sanctified to this holy use . . ." From *The Directory for the Publick Worship of God*, in *The Confession of Faith: The Larger and Shorter Catechisms*, p. 385.

[97] The source of this phrase is of considerable interest to me, but a satisfactory answer has eluded me for years.

This prayer is also a prayer of thanksgiving, solemnly acknowledging God's grace and mercy in sending us Jesus Christ as our Savior. The prayer of thanksgiving over the bread and wine is one of the most basic religious rites of human devotion. It acknowledges all the good gifts of creation. This rite signifies that man at his most blessed is a receiver of the gifts of God. It says something about our nature. We are creatures of need and in having our needs fulfilled we flourish. The prayer of thanksgiving over the bread and wine is part of the sign because it signifies our dependence on God's blessing. It testifies to God's goodness in blessing us. Going further, it makes the source of our blessing very clear. It recognizes that God is the Father, the all-providing Father of his people. This prayer of thanksgiving is a witness to the paternal blessings of God.

It is also true that this prayer consecrates God's gifts to our use and us to his service, as table prayers so often say. The principle is set down in 1 Tim. 4:4–5, "For everything created by God is good, and nothing is to be rejected if it is received with thanksgiving; for then it is consecrated by the word of God and prayer." This prayer of thanksgiving witnesses to the consecrating and sanctifying power of prayer. By giving thanks for God's mighty acts of redemption in the incarnation and atoning sacrifice of Christ, we consecrate them to our use, just as giving thanks for our daily bread consecrates it for our bodily nourishment. In this prayer we appropriate for our own salvation God's redemptive work in Christ for ourselves. We make what God did in Christ effective in ourselves. By giving thanks for it, what God did in history he now does in us through the work of his Holy Spirit. It is not that it is repeated in us but rather that it bears fruit in us.

We should particularly notice here that Willison speaks of God's redemptive work in terms of the incarnation of Christ. As Willison puts it, this prayer "signifies God's sending his Son into the world, sanctified, blessed, and furnished with all gifts and graces needful for the discharge of his mediatory offices, and for answering of his people's exigencies."[98] In other words, this prayer should give thanks for the whole of God's redemptive work in Christ. This includes his birth according to the promises of the prophets, his healing ministry, his sacrifice on the cross, the resurrection, ascension, and pouring out of his Spirit starting at Pentecost, and his continued presence even to the celebration of "this blessed ordinance." In short the prayer of blessing over the bread and wine signifies Christ's redemptive work by recounting it.

We have often noticed how in the worship of the Old Testament a hymnic recounting of salvation history is a central act of worship. We notice this with the Passover Haggadah, where the father recounts to his son the Exodus from Egypt. We find the same thing in Deuteronomy 26, where the worshiper presents a basket of the fruits of the land and recounts the sacred history:

> "A wandering Aramean was my father; and he went down into Egypt and sojourned there, few in number; and there he became a nation, great, mighty, and populous. And the Egyptians treated us harshly, and afflicted us, and laid upon us hard bondage. Then we cried to the LORD the God of our fathers, and the LORD heard our voice, and saw our affliction, our toil, and our oppression; and the LORD brought us out of Egypt with a mighty hand and an outstretched arm, with great terror, with signs and wonders; and he brought us into this place and gave us this land, a land flowing with milk and honey. And behold, now I bring the first of the fruit of the ground, which thou, O LORD, have given me." (Deuteronomy 26:5–10)

Several of the thanksgiving hymns among the Psalms (e.g., 78, 105, and 136) exemplify this as well.

Willison continues on to the third action—the breaking of the bread.

---

[98] Willison, *Works*, p. 469. Cf. Willison, *A Sacramental Catechism*, p. 79.

Q. What is signified by the breaking of the bread in this sacrament?

A. It signifies the breaking and wounding of Christ's body, and the bruising of his soul for elect sinners, in order to satisfy God's justice, pacify divine wrath, and purchase salvation for them. And that now the whole work of man's redemption is completed by Christ's death, John xix. 30, which is here represented by these elements and signs.[99]

This point is fairly obvious, of course, and Willison does not go into it at any length. A similar point is made about the pouring of the wine a bit further on.[100] John Knox in his *Book of Common Order* early in the Scottish Reformation tells us the breaking of the bread and pouring out of the wine were to be done in the full sight of the people. This was obviously insisted upon because it was thought of as being central to the visible sign.

The fourth sacramental action is the giving out of the bread and wine. It signifies God's gracious gift of his Son to all who put their faith in him. Christ and all the benefits of his work of salvation are offered to us to be received by faith. "For as truly as bread and wine are put into their hands, and given them to be their own, . . . so truly are Christ and all the benefits of the covenant made over, given, and sealed to them . . ."[101] The point of the sign is the sharing of a meal. We are invited to the wedding feast of the King's Son. We enter into the feast, sit at the banquet table, and enjoy the rich feast the Bridegroom has provided. This is the visible sign. This is what faith perceives when we come to the Lord's Table, simple as it may be spread either in ancient Jerusalem, early eighteenth century Dundee, Scotland, or a modern American inner-city church.

One detail stands out here. Willison emphasizes that the minister is not supposed to give the bread and the wine into the mouth

---

[99] Willison, *Works*, p. 469. Cf. Willison, *A Sacramental Catechism*, p. 79.

[100] Willison, *A Sacramental Catechism*, p. 81.

[101] Willison, *Works*, p. 469. Cf. Willison, *A Sacramental Catechism*, p. 80.

of each individual communicant. Rather, the elements are to be passed from one communicant to another as is usually done when a group of people share a meal together.[102] Here, of course, a Presbyterian, Dutch Reformed, or French Huguenot communion service differs considerably from an Anglican or Catholic service. Essential to a Reformed celebration of the sacrament is that it look like a meal.

Next Willison takes up the sacramental action of the communicants. It is here, of course, where Willison shows a particularly important aspect of Reformed liturgical tradition.

> Q. What are the outward sacramental actions on the part of the communicant?
>
> A. They are these, 1. Their taking the bread and the cup into their hands. 2. Their eating the bread, and drinking the wine. 3. Their dividing the elements among themselves and giving to one another. 4. Their doing all this sitting in a feasting posture.[103]

Reaching out to receive the bread and the cup has, to be sure, the significance of accepting the offer of the Gospel. It is the visible sign of our accepting Christ. In fact Willison speaks of this as reaching out the hand of faith.[104] It is because of this aspect of the sacramental sign that the Lord's Supper played such an important role in an evangelistic understanding of the Supper. To participate in the Supper is to accept the offer of the Gospel.

As one would expect, there is a discussion of communion in both kinds and an insistence on receiving both elements.[105] Here

---

[102] Willison, *A Sacramental Catechism*, p. 81.

[103] Willison, *Works*, p. 470. See also Willison, *A Sacramental Catechism*, p. 82.

[104] Willison, *A Sacramental Catechism*, p. 82.

[105] People often ask whether it is permissible to take the bread and abstain from the wine. I see no reason why this cannot be done, if it is done for a specific reason. For instance, those having gluten allergies might wish to abstain from the bread, or those resisting alcoholism might wish to abstain from the wine. It is another matter, however, when the cup is denied to the laity because of an exaggerated doctrine of the real presence or a hierarchical doctrine of the ministry.

again the importance of following the example of Christ and the apostles is maintained.

Coming back to his subject Willison makes a big point of the congregation sharing the bread and the wine with one another. The Gospel of Luke reports that Jesus handed the cup to the disciples and told them to take it and divide it among themselves (Luke 22:17). This mutual serving of each other and sharing a meal was essential to the sign. In doing this they "testify their mutual Christian love and union among themselves, and their communion and fellowship with one another, 1 Cor. x. 16–17."[106]

Before ending this section of his catechism Willison returns again to the subject of sitting at the Lord's Table. As is well known, in the early eighteenth century it was the practice of Reformed churches to set up a long table in the church for the celebration of communion. Those who wished to participate would come forward and sit at this table. It might take three or four sittings to serve the whole congregation. In Zurich and among some of the English Puritans the practice was to serve the congregation in their pews. In some cases the pews were arranged around three sides of the communion table so that the visual impression was given that the whole congregation was gathered around the table. In a few instances the participants would stand around the table, passing the bread and the cup around the circle, but no matter how it might be worked out, the important thing was to preserve the visual image of sharing a meal.

Here Willison discusses at considerable length the custom of sitting at the table. The question is asked:

Q. What should be the bodily posture of the communicants in time of receiving?

A. It ought to be a feasting-posture, or such a table-posture as is ordinary at feasts in the place of the world where we live; and that is sitting. And this we have

---

[106] Willison, *Works*, p. 471. Cf. Willison, *A Sacramental Catechism*, p. 85.

> authorised by the example of Christ and his apostles at the first institution, Matt. xxvi. 20, 26; Luke xxii. 14; John xiv. 31. . . . This also is proper to signify that holy familiarity which Christ allows his people with himself at this ordinance; for it is a blessed love-feast wherein he treats his people as his friends and intimates.[107]

One will inevitably want to ask why it was that the disciples of Jesus sat to eat the Passover when the text of Exodus carefully stipulates that the Israelites were to eat the feast standing. The rabbis of later times explained that once the Israelites had entered the Promised Land they changed to a sitting position because they were now at home in their own land. This may well have been how Jesus and his disciples would have understood their sitting or reclining at the table during the celebration of Passover in the Upper Room.

5. Meditation

Still another aspect of the communion celebration as it was observed by Willison is the meditation of the communicants.

A major feature of Willison's approach to the Lord's Supper is that just as the sacramental action of the congregation is given as much attention as the sacramental action of the minister, so the meditation of the communicants is as important as the minister's reciting of the liturgical texts and the preaching. We find a tendency in this direction in Calvin; in fact, we find that this has been essential to the celebration of the Lord's Supper down through the history of the Church. In the Middle Ages a whole host of eucharistic devotions were developed for the congregation. Meditation played an important role in the piety of the Wisdom school, as we have pointed out elsewhere. As we find it in the first psalm, the delight of the godly is in meditating on the Law of the Lord day and night. The same was true for meditating on the sacraments, before their celebration, in the course of their celebration, and after their celebration.

The center of this meditation was, to be sure, the meditation

---

[107] Willison, *Works*, p. 471. Cf. Willison, *A Sacramental Catechism*, p. 85.

of the congregation in the course of the service, but the meditation in preparation for the service was given great importance as well. A good number of preparatory services occurred in the week before the actual celebration of the Supper itself. At the very least there was a preparatory sermon the Lord's Day before the celebration. By the beginning of the eighteenth century a typical communion season would allow for a whole week of preparatory services. Then it would be followed by a thanksgiving service on Sunday afternoon and perhaps another on Monday. All these services were supposed to stimulate devotional meditation. In addition one was expected to do much meditation in private. Or, to use the terminology of the day, this meditation was to take place in the prayer closet. This devotional meditation was often guided by devotional manuals such as Willison's *A Sacramental Catechism*. A faithful celebration of the Lord's Supper gave as much attention to the meditation of the congregation as it did the preaching of the preacher.

As Willison presents it, the meditation of those who approached the Lord's Table should include two things: first, our self-examination to bring us to a proper evaluation of our need, that is, our hunger and thirst for the gifts of God, and second, a contemplation, or evaluation, of the gifts of God, his covenant promises, and the riches of his grace. Willison's catechism asks:

Q. What are the parts of preparation required of us in order to our approach to God's table?

A. There are generally two, but very comprehensive, viz. self-examination and exciting of the graces.[108]

A good number of pages are given to explaining what is meant by self-examination.[109] Only further on does our catechist turn to the question of exciting the graces.[110] Self-examination is a major con-

---

[108] Willison, *Works*, p. 483. For a more modern version, see Willison, *A Sacramental Catechism*, pp. 126–127.

[109] Willison, *A Sacramental Catechism*, pp. 162–229.

[110] Willison, *A Sacramental Catechism*, pp. 230–248.

cern of the work before us. The importance of self-examination is obviously due to the fact that the Apostle Paul expressly directs us to examine ourselves before participating in the communion, "Let a man examine himself, and so eat of the bread and drink of the cup" (1 Cor. 11:28). In fact, the apostle makes a very strong point of it.[111] Those who do not prepare themselves with such spiritual discipline are guilty of profaning the Lord's body. No wonder Willison puts such an emphasis on this self-examination.

Looking more closely at sacramental self-examination, we find it treats a number of subjects. The catechism asks:

Q. What are the things about which we ought to examine ourselves, before we approach to the Lord's table?

A. Concerning these five things: 1. Our state and condition. 2. Our sins and shortcomings. 3. Our wants and necessities. 4. Our ends and designs. 5. Our graces and qualifications.[112]

We are occasionally troubled by the subjectivity of these exercises. Sometimes we get the impression that it is in the meditation with which we approach the sacrament that we find the focus of the observance. In other words, we sense the pietistic influence in these observances. Typical of the early eighteenth century, Willison focuses on the inner experience of the communicant.

As communicants we are supposed to meditate on our state and condition, that is, our standing in relation to the covenant. Do we belong to the covenant people of God? This is an important matter to consider, "because . . . we can never be at too much pains to make it sure."[113] Our preacher would have us probe our conscience to discover if our Christian commitment might have cooled or become formal or perfunctory. He brings out examples of how God's people have from time to time found it necessary

---

[111] Willison, *A Sacramental Catechism*, p. 125.

[112] Willison, *Works*, p. 483. Cf. Willison, *A Sacramental Catechism*, p. 128.

[113] Willison, *Works*, p. 486; Willison, *A Sacramental Catechism*, p. 138.

to renew the covenant and freshen the devotion of the covenant people. To be sure, the covenant is the eternal covenant, but, still, it is appropriate from time to time to renew it.[114]

This affirming of the covenant or, to use the archaic phrase Willison seems to prefer, "closing with Christ," is nothing else than the conversion experience so basic to the Pietists who were Willison's contemporaries in Germany and the Netherlands. Willison in one place makes this quite explicit. He asks:

> Q. What are the marks of those who are truly God's covenanted people?
>
> A. They are a willing people, a humble and self-denying people: they are an holy people, zealous for good works; they are a thankful and God-exalting people. Jesus Christ the Mediator and Surety of the covenant is very precious to them. The free grace of the covenant is the matter of their wonder and admiration. They are inclined to perform covenant-duties, and that in a covenant way, relying on covenant-strength, from a principle of love and gratitude to their covenanted God, and with an eye to glorify his name, Psal. cx. 3; cxv. 1; Ezek. xvi. 62, 63; Tit. ii. 14; Isa. lv.1; xiv. 24; lvi. 4–6.
>
> Q. Are not those who are truly in covenant with God, acquainted with the new birth and a work of regeneration?
>
> A. Yes; for these two, being in covenant with God by faith in Jesus Christ, and being renewed or born again, are inseparably connected, Ezek. xxxvi. 26–28; 1 Cor. v. 17.[115]

One wonders how a Scottish pastor might have gotten wind of this Pietist teaching, but then very little work has been done on Willison. Perhaps what Willison has done here is interpret the traditional Scottish Reformed eucharistic doctrine and practice in

---

[114] Willison, *Works*, pp. 486–87.

[115] Willison, *Works*, pp. 489–90. Cf. Willison, *A Sacramental Catechism*, pp. 148–149.

terms of the Pietist conversion experience. On the other hand, I am more and more inclined to think that in Willison we have a piety that antedates Pietism.

Having given much time to the meditation appropriate in preparation for the sacrament Willison now turns to the meditation appropriate to the actual celebration of the sacrament.[116] Now it is finally clear that it is in the actual sharing of the meal that we experience the grace of the sacrament. To be sure the meditation which accompanies the participation is important. It is obviously even more important than the meditation which prepares for the sacrament. When we come to sit at the Lord's Table our meditation focuses in on God's mighty acts of redemption. First, there is the sending of his Son into the world to win us back to himself.[117] Second, we should meditate on Christ's atoning sacrifice.[118] Third, there is Christ's victory over sin, the power of evil, and death.[119] Finally, there is "the riches and glory of the heavenly feast."[120] This, of course, corresponds to the subject matter of the Eucharistic Prayer.

The meditation of the communicants at the Lord's Table is aided by both the eucharistic words and the eucharistic acts. We meditate on the bread and wine, on the breaking of the bread and the pouring of the wine. We meditate on the bread and wine being offered to us by the ministers, on its being shared with us by our neighbors and our sharing it with them. We listen to the promises of the Gospel, "This is my body, which is broken for you: this do in remembrance of me . . . This cup is the new testament in my blood: this do ye, as oft as ye drink it, in remembrance of me . . ." (1 Cor. 11:24–25, KJV). We believe these signs and these words, and receive

---

[116] Willison, *A Sacramental Catechism*, p. 249.
[117] Willison, *A Sacramental Catechism*, p. 253.
[118] Willison, *A Sacramental Catechism*, p. 252.
[119] Willison, *A Sacramental Catechism*, p. 253.
[120] Willison, *A Sacramental Catechism*, p. 252.

them by faith. But, to put it even more explicitly, we embrace Christ; we eat the bread and the wine. To use Willison's favorite expression, we close with Christ. In the end it is eminently clear—communion is more than meditation; it is the sealing of a covenant.

Making the vows of the covenant has always played a major role in a Reformed celebration of the Lord's Supper. This is particularly evident in the communion rite of Geneva at the time of Calvin where the reciting of the Apostles' Creed figures so prominently. The way Willison put it is:

> 2. On the believers' part; communicating lies mainly in their receiving the seal of God's covenant with them, and the seal of all his gracious promises to them in Christ; and particularly in laying hold and applying of Christ for pardon of sin, for cleansing from sin, and for strength to do every commanded duty, all which is promised in this covenant. So that the work of communicating doth not (as some are ready to think) lie principally in our meditating upon Christ's love and sufferings, engaging and covenanting to be the Lord's, making vows against sin, or putting up of prayers and requests to God. All these, indeed, ought necessarily to attend our communicating, but they are not the direct and principal acts of it. The nature whereof, as is said, consists mainly in our cordial receiving of Christ and his purchased benefits, as they are tendered in the covenant of grace, and sealed and applied in this sacrament: and in our believing that Christ's broken body and shed blood, here represented, with all his merits and graces, are as truly applied to us for curing and saving our souls, and become ours by faith; as the consecrated bread and wine enter into our bodies, and become ours by feeding thereon. And these acts are to be accompanied with the lively exercise of all the sacramental graces, particularly faith, repentance, desire, love, and joy.[121]

Here Willison makes it very clear that the heart of the sacrament is not meditating on Christ and his benefits, but rather receiving

---

[121] Willison, *Works*, p. 520. Cf. Willison, *A Sacramental Catechism*, p. 256.

Christ as he is offered to us in the covenant of grace. The Supper is not merely a memorial. That is the case for Willison as it was for the earliest Swiss Reformers. That is what the whole discussion of the covenant was all about.

Particularly we want to mark how faith figures in this. Our catechism asks:

> Q. How is faith to be exercised in partaking of the Lord's Supper?
>
> A. Faith being as the eye of the soul, to discern Christ; as the hand of the soul, to receive him; and as the mouth of the soul, to feed on him in this ordinance, should be most actively employed and diligently exercised in our partaking . . .[122]

Much of the experiential dimension of the Lord's Supper comes from the metaphor alluded to in the phrase that faith is "the mouth of the soul, to feed on him." This is, to be sure, analogous to the metaphor that faith is the hand of the soul to receive him as well as faith being "the eye of the soul, to discern Christ." Willison has obviously tapped into the typical eighteenth-century concern that our religion be experiential.

There is one more thing to be said. Just as faith is essential to the sacrament, so is hope. One notices that hope figures prominently in the celebration of the sacrament. Those who come to the Lord's Table come hungering and thirsting for righteousness. They come as the deer panting for streams of refreshing water. For such there is a "holy joy to be exercised in partaking." They rejoice in the coming of the kingdom.[123] As we notice in so many of the eucharistic sermons preached in the eighteenth century, the imagery of the Song of Solomon was vigorously elaborated at the celebration of communion. One understood the sacrament as a foretaste and a promise of the wedding feast of the Lamb.

---

[122] Willison, *Works*, p. 520. Cf. Willison, *A Sacramental Catechism*, pp. 256–257.
[123] Willison, *A Sacramental Catechism*, p. 258.

6. Thanksgiving

Reformed theologians when they discuss the Lord's Supper usually note that in the ancient church the sacrament of the Lord's Supper was frequently called the Eucharist or the feast of thanksgiving. In fact, when Zwingli published his communion service in 1525 he used the term "thanksgiving" as a sort of synonym. Eucharist is simply the Greek word for thanksgiving. The theme of thanksgiving appears at several points in Willison's catechism. We find prayers of thanksgiving as follows: the thanksgiving over the bread and wine; the thanksgiving at the end of the meal; the thanksgiving service on Sunday evening; and thanksgiving in our prayer closet.

We have already spoken of the prayer of thanksgiving over the bread and wine. This is the Eucharistic Prayer, properly called, the central prayer of the whole service. We have already spoken of this prayer at length.[124] We wish Willison had left us an example of one of his eucharistic prayers. Sad to say one has not come to my attention. Presumably the Eucharistic Prayer of John Knox was the model for Willison's prayer, a description of which Willison included in his catechism.[125] According to this description it is a prayer of thanksgiving for God's mighty acts of creation and redemption.

Here, however, we are dealing with a short prayer of thanksgiving and dedication at the end of the service. While still sitting at the table, and having shared the sacred meal, before we rise from the table we should give thanks to God. Our catechist asks:

Q. Are not vows and prayers requisite at the Lord's table?

A. Yes; for here we are to profess our sorrow for sin, and thankfulness for God's favours, and join ourselves to the Lord in an everlasting covenant; and it certainly becomes all true penitents, thankful souls, and honest covenanters, to make vows; and those vows are nothing worth without prayers to God joined therewith, for strength to

---

[124] See chapters 1 and 7.

[125] Willison, *A Sacramental Catechism*, pp. 78–79.

> keep them. And those vows and prayers seem to be most seasonable after our receiving of the elements, and our exerting of the direct acts of communicating, Job xxxiv. 31, 32; Gen. xxviii. 20; John i. 16; Neh. x. 29.[126]

It is clear that Willison is thinking in terms of the theology of the covenant. Having cried out to God for help in our troubles and God having answered our prayers, we are obligated to give thanks to God by dedicating ourselves to his service. This is an essential to understanding worship in covenantal terms. Having received God's grace we owe God thanks and this thanks is expressed in service to God, the observance of God's commandments, and the witness of public worship that it is this God who has saved us in our time of need. It is this dedication to God's service which is the substance of the thanksgiving we should offer after having received communion. Our catechist asks:

> Q. What is the nature of these vows, which we ought to come under, at this juncture?
>
> A. A religious vow is a serious oath of dedicating ourselves to the Lord's use and service; or, it is a solemn engagement and promise unto the Lord, whereby we bind and oblige ourselves to be the Lord's dutiful children and servants, Num. xxx. 2; 1 Chron. xv. 12–15.[127]

This, of course, is just exactly the sort of prayer which we find in Calvin's *Genevan Psalter* of 1542 as well as in the *Book of Common Order* which Knox prepared for the Church of Scotland. The point of this prayer is that the thanksgiving we owe to God is the dedication of our lives to the service of God. We find this in so many of the votive thanksgiving psalms in the book of Psalms, such as Psalms 116 and 138, so often sung at the conclusion of the communion service.

There is more, however, and that concerns the thanksgiving which takes place after the actual communion service. Willison's

---

[126] Willison, *Works*, p. 522. See also Willison, *A Sacramental Catechism*, p. 261.

[127] Willison, *Works*, p. 522. Cf. Willison, *A Sacramental Catechism*, p. 261.

chapter, "Concerning the Duties Required after Partaking,"[128] has to do with the subject of the thanksgiving services traditionally held on the afternoon or evening of a Communion Sunday or the Monday following, but it also treats the meditation which should occupy the faithful communicant "when we go to our retiring places."[129] This quaint phrase apparently intends to recommend once again the importance of private meditation in the prayer closet as an essential component of a reverent observance of the sacrament.

What is interesting about the chapter is not so much what it says about the thanksgiving service as what it shows us about the mystical quality of Willison's piety. When Willison talks about the awe and wonder of the experience of communion one realizes that here is a pastor who knows the depths and heights of religious experience. Like Matthew Henry and David Brainerd, the son-in-law of Jonathan Edwards, the observance of the sacrament of the Lord's Supper for John Willison was to enter into the Holy of Holies. Willison asks:

Q. How do we know if the Lord hath dealt bountifully with us in this ordinance?

A. The Lord deals bountifully with his people in this ordinance, when he visits them with his gracious presence, draws nigh to them by his Spirit's operations, and vouchsafes to hold communion with them.[130]

There is no question about it; there was a strong strain of mysticism in Protestant eucharistic piety in the seventeenth and eighteenth centuries. Christ was understood to be present through his Holy Spirit.

A Reformed understanding of the Lord's Supper always gives

---

[128] Willison, *A Sacramental Catechism*, p. 265–320. This corresponds with a section entitled, "The Duties Requisite after Partaking," in Willison, *Works*, pp. 523–525.

[129] Willison, *A Sacramental Catechism*, p. 265.

[130] Willison, *Works*, p. 530. Kistler substitutes the word "promises" for "vouchsafes." Willison, *A Sacramental Catechism*, pp. 291–292.

special attention to the work of the Holy Spirit. It is through his Spirit that Christ is present in the sacrament. The Holy Spirit dwells in the Christian, and that is a continuing reality of the Christian life whether we are aware of it or not, but it is also true that there are moments in public worship when God's presence is made particularly clear.[131]

7. PNEUMATIC DIMENSION

The doctrine of the Holy Spirit is essential to any Reformed theology of the sacraments. It is here, toward the end of his catechism, that Willison takes up in more detail the pneumatic dimension of his eucharistic theology. He tells us, "Though God is always near to his people, in respect of his Spirit's inhabitation; yet not always in respect of his sensible operation. Though Christ still dwells in the heart by his Spirit, yet he doth not always act alike in the soul, but only according to his good pleasure."[132] This distinction between the indwelling presence of the Holy Spirit and the operation of the Spirit is important. Again Willison poses a question:

Q. How is it that God draws nigh to his people by his gracious presence, and holds communion with them by the special operations of his Spirit?

A. He draws nigh and communicates himself to his people, by his spiritual influences: 1. Of light. 2. Of life. 3. Of strength. 4. Of comfort.[133]

Willison goes on to elaborate how God in the sacrament draws nigh to his people through his divine light. Here we are dealing with Willison's thought at its most mystical. Here we are talking about communion as an experience of divine illumination. He gives Christians "gracious and satisfying discoveries of God, and Christ, and spiritual

---

[131] Willison, *A Sacramental Catechism*, p. 292.

[132] Willison, *Works*, p. 531. Cf. Willison, *A Sacramental Catechism*, p. 292.

[133] Willison, *Works*, p. 531. Cf. Willison, *A Sacramental Catechism*, p. 293.

objects."[134] He gives them a view of God's glory as he gave it to Moses on Mount Sinai. When God made "his goodness and mercy pass before them, proclaiming his name in their hearing, 'The Lord, the Lord God, merciful and gracious, long-suffering, and abundant in goodness' & etc. Exod. xxxiv. 6, 7."[135] Surely this is about as close to a biblical description of mystical experience as we find in Scripture. It is this sort of experiential piety that Willison teaches us to expect in the observance of the sacrament.

Willison has much the same thing to say about the profound mystical experience of Isaiah when in the year that King Uzziah died he went to the Temple and saw the Lord high and lifted up and his glory filled the Temple. There God showed Isaiah his infinite holiness and purity. Isaiah was filled with holy fear and reverence (Isa. 6:5). It is this sort of experience that at times God bestows upon us in the celebration of the sacrament.

To be sure, for the Christian there is still a greater glory to be revealed in the celebration of the Lord's Supper, for there God "lets us see all the divine fullness dwelling in a crucified Redeemer."[136] It is in the cross that God's greatest glory is revealed. It is there we find his justice and his mercy joined together. In the sacrament God lets us see the beauty of holiness.[137] Holiness is indeed the beauty of God and when we perceive this beauty in the celebration of the Supper then we hunger and thirst even more to reflect that holiness.

There is yet more to the illumination of the Holy Spirit. "When he gives a soul-ravishing discovery of the things that are unseen in the other world, the glory of heaven, and the unexpressible happiness of the saints who dwell there; so as to make us long for the finishing of our pilgrimage, that we may depart and be with Christ."[138]

---

[134] Willison, *Works*, p. 531. Cf. Willison, *A Sacramental Catechism*, p. 293.

[135] Willison, *Works*, p. 531. Cf. Willison, *A Sacramental Catechism*, p. 293.

[136] Willison, *Works*, p. 531; Willison, *A Sacramental Catechism*, p. 294.

[137] Willison, *Works*, p. 531. Kistler attributes this teaching to Philippians 1:23. Willison, *A Sacramental Catechism*, p. 295.

[138] Willison, *A Sacramental Catechism*, p. 296.

It is very important to notice here that all this happens in the regular worship of the church. It is not something found in some group apart, some *ecclesiola in ecclesia*; it is not something which is achieved only in the privacy of one's prayer closet but rather in the public worship of the church. "These, and such like discoveries, the Lord oftentimes makes by his Spirit to his people in this ordinance; by opening their understandings to see divine things in another way than ever they saw before."[139]

Illumination is not only the operation of the Holy Spirit. Our catechist continues by asking:

Q. How is it that the Lord draws nigh and communicates himself to his people in the sacrament by the influences of life?

A. By sending his quickening Spirit to put life in their graces, and to draw them forth to a lively exercise.[140]

It is the Holy Spirit who actuates the faith of Christians. He enables them to go out to Christ and lay their burdens upon him, to lean on him for their salvation. It is the Holy Spirit who quickens our repentance, and melts our hearts in tears and godly sorrow for our sin. It is the Holy Spirit who "kindles love in the heart, and makes it burn, while he talks to them, and opens to them the scriptures."[141] It is the Holy Spirit who quickens our prayers. So it is that God draws nigh to us through the operations of the Holy Spirit.[142]

Willison takes up another aspect of the operation of the Holy Spirit by telling us that at times the Holy Spirit strengthens our weak faith, our staggering hope, and our fainting love. It is the operation of the Holy Spirit to anoint God's people with power from on high as Jesus promised his disciples at the time of his ascension. The Holy Spirit works when and where and how he

---

[139] Willison, *Works*, p. 531. Cf. Willison, *A Sacramental Catechism*, p. 296.

[140] Willison, *Works*, p. 531. See also Willison, *A Sacramental Catechism*, p. 296.

[141] Willison, *Works*, p. 531. Cf. Willison, *A Sacramental Catechism*, p. 296.

[142] Willison, *A Sacramental Catechism*, p. 297.

pleases. It is not as though the Holy Spirit were some sort of power under the control of the clergy or affected by the reciting of some sort of liturgical formula. The Spirit is sovereign and free. The Holy Spirit works in infinite wisdom, according to the counsel of God's will. It is the Holy Spirit who gives us the power to resist temptation and to overcome the assaults of Satan. Again it is the Holy Spirit who anoints us with power when he heartens us patiently to bear the cross and all those afflictions and burdens that the Lord thinks fit to lay upon us.[143]

Finally, the pastor of Dundee speaks of the operation of comfort. To use the more abstract theological vocabulary, he intends to speak of the Holy Spirit as Paraclete. As we find in the Gospel of John (John 14:26), Willison tells us that the Holy Spirit comforts God's people "in the sacrament, by intimating to them the pardon of their sins, and a free discharge of all their debts, graciously whispering by his Spirit into the ear of the soul such a word as that which Christ spoke to the man sick of the palsy, 'Son, be of good cheer, thy sins be forgiven thee,' Matt. ix. 2."[144] The Holy Spirit comforts God's people by hearing and answering their prayers.[145] Willison has much to say on real beauty. God in his holiness is the ultimate beauty. This holy beauty is the beauty hid from our eyes by the wings of the seraphim. The time will come when the veil will be taken away and we will behold his beauty and reflect his holiness.

We notice particularly his lines on the breathing of God's Spirit on his people:

> A. 7. He comforts them, by letting out upon their souls the sensible breathings and influences of his Spirit, that are like the dew to the withered grass, the rain to the dry ground, or the south wind to the spices. And those enlarge their hearts, put an edge upon their faith

---

[143] Willison, *Works*, p. 531; Willison, *A Sacramental Catechism*, p. 298.

[144] Willison, *Works*, p. 531. See also Willison, *A Sacramental Catechism*, p. 298.

[145] Willison, *A Sacramental Catechism*, p. 299.

and love, and make them cheerful in every duty, Psal. lxxii. 6; cxix. 32; Hos. xiv. 5; Cant. iv. 16.[146]

Again, the imagery of the Song of Solomon comes quite naturally when Willison tells us, "He sometimes comforts them, by bringing them into his banqueting-house, and setting them under the banner of his love. He sheds abroad his love in their hearts, and gives them peace and joy in believing."[147] As we have seen, this was a favorite text for Reformed communion sermons in the eighteenth century. In fact, it was quite common to interpret the Lord's Supper in terms of the imagery of the Song of Solomon, the wedding feast of the king's son, and the marriage supper of the Lamb.[148]

The eucharistic writings of John Willison have a wonderful mystical imagination. They show a deep sacramental piety. Unlike much of the pietism of the early eighteenth century in England or on the continent it is a piety which is at home in the church. It is not over against the church or gathered out of the church but a fruition of life in the church. For our age this sacramental piety is much too introspective, much too grave. The penitential dimension we find excessive. But, then, Willison is hardly unique in this. We find this repeatedly among the most profound and pious souls of Christendom. One sometimes wonders if the problem is not so much that their spiritual lamentations are excessive as that our age is hardened to this natural dimension of life. The power of positive thinking may be more a weakness than a power. Be that as it may, the more melancholy meditations are balanced by the hope of eternal life. For Willison the Lord's Supper is clearly a foretaste of the wedding feast of the Lamb.

---

[146] Willison, *Works*, p. 533. Cf. Willison, *A Sacramental Catechism*, p. 299.

[147] Willison, *Works*, p. 533. See also Willison, *A Sacramental Catechism*, p. 299.

[148] For more discussion on this subject, see chapter 16 on the Great Awakening, pp. 611–617.

14

THE ERSKINE BROTHERS
AND THE COVENANTER TRADITION

By the beginning of the eighteenth century Pietism was having a strong effect on European Christianity, whether it was the Jansenists in Catholic France, the Wesleys in England, Spener and Francke in Lutheran Germany, or Ebenezer and Ralph Erskine in Scotland.[1] Pietism at its most basic is a concern to deepen the piety of the individual Christian. It is concerned not so much with the teaching of Christian doctrine as with the development of the Christian life. It was only natural, then, that Pietism would give special attention to the celebration of the sacrament of Holy Communion.

Indeed the Erskine brothers gave elaborate attention to the celebration of the sacrament. Often their celebrations would last until late at night. The communion seasons in Presbyterian Scotland would take a week of preparatory services and would then be followed by several thanksgiving services. Ralph Erskine reports that at one service it took thirty-eight seatings to distribute the bread and

---

[1] On Pietism generally, see: Martin Brecht, Klaus Deppermann, Ulrich Gäbler, and Hartmut Lehmann, *Geschichte des Pietismus*, 2 vols. (Göttingen: Vandenhoeck & Ruprecht, 1995); Dale W. Brown, *Understanding Pietism* (Grand Rapids, MI: Eerdmans, 1978); Heinrich Heppe, *Geschichte des Pietismus und der Mystik in der reformierten Kirche* (Leiden: Brill, 1879); John Charles Hoffman, "Pietism," in *New Catholic Encyclopedia*, 17 vols. (Washington, DC: Catholic University of America Press, 1968), 11:355; Ronald A. Knox, *Enthusiasm: A Chapter in the History of Religion* (London: Oxford University Press, 1950); Albrecht Ritschl, *Die Geschichte des Pietismus*, 3 vols. (Bonn: A. Marcus, 1880–86); M. Schmidt, "Pietismus," in *Die Religion in Geschichte und Gegenwart*, 3rd ed., 6 vols. (Tübingen: J. C. B. Mohr [Paul Siebeck], 1957–65), 5:370–81; and F. Ernest Stoeffler, *Continental Pietism and Early American Christianity* (Grand Rapids, MI: Eerdmans, 1976).

the wine to the assembled crowd.² Ralph Erskine left us several complete communion series, as well as numerous individual sermons.³

Communion seasons as they were observed by the Erskines were the devotional high point of the year. They would go on for hours as one table after another would be served while psalms were sung, passages of Scripture read, and pastoral admonitions delivered. The devout might walk miles to attend a communion season if a renowned preacher such as one or the other of the Erskines were among the pastors participating. We have chosen to look more carefully at the communion services of the Erskine brothers because they were especially diligent in their observance of the sacrament.⁴ The Covenanter spirit lived on in these celebrations in a way that heightened the intensity of the celebration.

The Covenanter spirit is certainly understood when we realize that the father of Ebenezer and Ralph Erskine, Henry Erskine, had been ejected from his church in 1662 as a young pastor when Charles II came to the throne.⁵ Henry Erskine was one of those ministers who kept on preaching when the occasion presented itself. Inevitably he was arrested and imprisoned, and it was not until 1690 that he was restored to the pastorate. For the last six years of his life—he died in 1696—he was pastor of the parish

---

[2] See the introduction by Joel R. Beeke, "Ebenezer and Ralph Erskine: Their Lives and Their Preaching," in Ebenezer Erskine, *The Beauties of Ebenezer Erskine*, selected by Samuel McMillan (Grand Rapids, MI: Reformation Heritage Books; and Fearn, UK: Christian Focus Publications, 2001), p. vi.

[3] For a sampling of Ralph Erskine's sermons, see Ralph Erskine, *The Works of Ralph Erskine*, 8 vols. (Glasgow: Free Presbyterian Publications, 1991).

[4] I admit that I am also especially interested in the Erskines because, for the last several years, I have been teaching at Erskine Theological Seminary. It is of even more interest to me that the family of my wife, the McCaw family, proudly traces its roots to the earliest Associate Reformed Presbyterian settlements in South Carolina.

[5] For information on Henry Erskine, see the article on his son Ebenezer: "Erskine, Ebenezer," *The Encyclopedia Britannica*, 11th ed., 32 vols. (New York: Encyclopedia Britannica, 1910), 9:754–755; and Donald Fraser, *The Life and Diary of the Reverend Ebenezer Erskine, of Stirling: Father of the Secession Church, to Which is Prefixed a Memoir of His Father, the Rev. Henry Erskine, of Chirnside* (Edinburgh: W. Oliphant, 1831).

church of Chirnside in Berwickshire. It was Henry Erskine's two sons, Ebenezer and Ralph Erskine, however, who left us with a large collection of eucharistic sermons. These sermons are among the treasures of Reformed devotional literature. We turn first to Ebenezer and then to his brother Ralph.

EBENEZER ERSKINE

Ebenezer Erskine (1680–1754) was born in June, 1680.[6] He grew up knowing that his father was from time to time imprisoned for having the courage to preach and realizing full well that he might also be imprisoned for his faithfulness. Indeed, while Ebenezer was growing up, his father was several times imprisoned for preaching the Gospel. Nevertheless, Ebenezer did have the opportunity to study at the University of Edinburgh, graduating with the Master of Philosophy degree in 1697, a year after his father's death. In 1703 he was licensed by the Presbytery of Kirkaldy and was ordained to the pastorate of Portmoak, Kinross-shire. At first he had real doubts and hesitations. It was not until 1708 that he reached real assurance of salvation and was able to exercise his pulpit ministry with confidence.

In 1731 Ebenezer Erskine was called to Stirling to serve the West Congregation of Stirling, and he remained there for twenty-eight years. It was while he was in Stirling between 1717 and 1723 that he became involved in the Marrow Controversy.[7] The Marrow Controversy might best be described as a doctrinal dispute which later resulted in the split between moderatism and what would later be called evangelicalism, and Ebenezer Erskine sup-

[6] For biographical material on Ebenezer Erskine, see: "Erskine, Ebenezer," *The Encyclopedia Britannica*, 11th ed., 9:754–755; E. Erskine, *The Beauties of Ebenezer Erskine*; Fraser, *The Life and Diary of the Reverend Ebenezer Erskine of Stirling*; John Ker, *The Erskines: Ebenezer and Ralph* (Edinburgh: James Gemmell, 1881); Alexander R. MacEwen, *The Erskines* (Edinburgh and London: Oliphant, Anderson & Ferrier, 1900); and Jean L. Watson, *Life of Ebenezer Erskine* (Edinburgh: James Gemmell, 1881).

[7] For information on Erskine's ministry in Stirling, see: Kenneth B. Scott, *Ebenezer Erskine: the Secession of 1733, and the Churches of Stirling* (Stirling, UK: Viewfield Church, 1983); and the introduction in E. Erskine, *The Beauties of Ebenezer Erskine*.

ported the Marrow Men vigorously.[8]

From the standpoint of the church historian, the most notable thing about Ebenezer Erskine, however, was that he was one of the founders of the Secession.[9] Ebenezer Erskine took an active part in a number of the controversies of the day. Nevertheless he was much better known as a spiritual director and preacher. He drew large crowds as a preacher. When he preached at a communion season thousands would come from all the neighboring parishes. Many of Ebenezer Erskine's sermons have been published.[10] Let us look at several of his communion sermons.[11]

A. A Sermon on the Beauty of Holiness

The first sermon to which we will turn was preached at Erskine's church at Portsmoak in 1714.[12] The sermon significantly is based on a text from the third chapter of Revelation (cf. Rev. 3:1–6). We

---

[8] For further information on the Marrow Controversy, see Philip G. Ryken, *Thomas Boston as Preacher of the Fourfold State* (Carlisle, England: Published for Rutherford House by Paternoster Press, 1999); William VanDoodewaard, *The Marrow Controversy and the Seceder Tradition* (Grand Rapids, MI: Reformation Heritage Books, 2011).

[9] The modern successor of the Seceders is the Associate Reformed Presbyterian Church. See Joseph H. Hall, "General Synod of the Associate Reformed Presbyterian Church," in *Dictionary of Christianity in America* (Downers Grove, IL: InterVarsity Press, 1990), p. 479. For a more complete history of the Secession Church, see John M'Kerrow, *History of the Secession Church* (Edinburgh: Oliphant, 1839).

[10] On the preaching of Ebenezer Erskine, see: Ebenezer Erskine, *The Whole Works of the Late Rev. Mr. Ebenezer Erskine: Consisting of Sermons and Discourses on the Most Important and Interesting Subjects in Three Volumes* (London: William Baynes, 1799); Ebenezer Erskine, *The Rainbow of the Covenant Surrounding the Throne of Grace, Being the Substance of Some Sermons, Preached at the Sacrament of Muckart, June 23, 1728* (Belfast: James Magee, 1780); Ebenezer Erskine, *Sermons Upon the Most Important and Interesting Subjects* (Philadelphia: John M'Culloch, 1792). For a modern edition of his works, see Ebenezer Erskine, *The Works of Ebenezer Erskine* (Glasgow: Free Presbyterian Publications, 2001). For an analysis of Erskine's preaching, see William John Bovard, *The Preaching of Ebenezer Erskine: His Contributions to the Evangelical Pulpit of Today* (Pittsburgh: n.s., 1961).

[11] Special thanks is given to my daughter, Hannah Chase Old, for preparing digests of the sermons of Ebenezer and Ralph Erskine.

[12] E. Erskine, *Whole Works*, 1:5–32.

14: The Erskine Brothers and The Covenanter Tradition (1680–1754)

have noticed several times that preaching from a text from Revelation at a celebration of communion seems to be characteristic of Reformed eucharistic piety.

First, Erskine notes how there were few in Sardis who were true professors. Most of the other Sardisian church members were much more complacent and worldly. Those true professors got the reward of walking with Christ. There is a careful discussion of what the term "white garments" meant: everything from the priests in the Temple wearing white to the adornment of Roman royalty in white at special events.[13]

Erskine expounds on the little remnant of the visible church, which walks in godliness and will share with Christ in the joys of heaven. The remnant are given to Christ by the Father, and it is these for whom our Lord died to save them from their sins. They are justified and sanctified in holiness. Each of them, through the power of the Holy Spirit, will become more and more able to obey the Lord and his commands. Likewise, their sins are cleansed by him.[14] Their holiness of life is what marks them as Christians. They are much beloved by their Lord. Everyone in this elect group will someday be drawn to Christ through the work of God in the world, and none of them will escape from his love. They are small in number in comparison to the population of the earth, and don't even include the whole of the visible church, for there are many who think they are Christians but lack the "credentials" of faith. Nonetheless, the remnant perseveres through the worst of storms, and the Lord always has his remnant on the earth doing his work.[15]

Here we recognize a typical pietist theme, the church within the church. That this sort of teaching would eventually end up in schism is not at all surprising. For some of us this tendency towards schism is a most regrettable and painful aspect of Pietism. On the

---

[13] E. Erskine, *Whole Works*, 1:6–7.

[14] E. Erskine, *Whole Works*, 1:8.

[15] E. Erskine, *Whole Works*, 1:9.

other hand, sometimes a schism seems to be the only option. Erskine continues: Jesus assigns a high value to the remnant, regardless of what the world thinks. It will be gathered into his barns while the chaff is burned. Erskine reminds us that as his children, we are the desire of God's heart, his loved ones, his treasure. We are united with Christ.[16]

With an ardor and beauty rivaling that of Jonathan Edwards, Erskine spends considerable time on the beauty of the love between Christ and the invisible church, and how he takes such care of us. Jesus refers to us as his love, his dove, and the apple of his eye. He would give up everything else just to have us as his beloved children, and therefore he treats us to the best of his providence. Because we are united to Christ, we are beneficiaries with him of all his goodness, all his inheritance. The Lord values our prayers, and even our tears are kept by him. Our death is precious, for through it we come home to him. This love for us is deep, irrevocable, and covenantal. In fact, the giving of the Holy Spirit is itself a token of our preciousness to God, for the Spirit is a deposit towards the glorious inheritance which awaits us. While we live here on earth, the Holy Spirit also gives us his fruits, so we may have peace, and joy, and love.[17] There is a real beauty to holiness. To appreciate it, however, requires a definite spiritual maturity. It requires growth in grace. This is of the essence of sanctification.

B. Communion as Union with Christ

For Ebenezer Erskine, as indeed for his brother Ralph, the ultimate meaning of the sacrament of Holy Communion is our union with Christ. That is, when we partake of the sacrament we are united to Christ in such a way that we participate both in the death of Christ and the resurrection of Christ.

---

[16] E. Erskine, *Whole Works*, 1:10.

[17] E. Erskine, *Whole Works*, 1:12.

Continuing with his exposition, Erskine asks, What is the import of the white robes (cf. Rev. 3:5)? White robes represent the righteousness of Christ which covers us. It is the uniform of the people of God. The meaning of the clean robes is that they have not been defiled by sin. Although it is necessary to walk the dirty streets, we do not have to let our garments drag in the mud. The point is, we don't become worldly although we are surrounded by the worldly. Erskine expounds on this thought a little, and includes in the components of this holiness that believers should not compromise on doctrine, nor should they exchange the truth of the gospel for anything, great or small. Rather, believers should strive for holiness of life all their days.[18]

So, what of the promise of consolation given in the passage? First of all, we see the promise of life after death. That the soul "walks" with Christ indicates that it is lively rather than sleeping. The soul is in the presence of Christ, and is in perfect agreement with him so that there is no longer any concern about displeasing him. The communion between Christ and the believer, which is experienced even here and now, will become complete in the next life. Better yet, this communion will be enjoyed in his presence rather than enjoyed from the distance between earth and heaven.[19]

Holiness is more than just living a good life. To think otherwise is to make the same mistake that the Pharisees made. Those who fail to wash their garments in the blood of the Lamb, and therefore persist in sin, will not enter heaven but will go to the lake of fire. Conversely, there is considerable comfort to be had by those who truly belong to Christ. Death has no sting, for as it approaches the believer knows he will soon be in the sweet presence of the Lord. One must contrast this to the fear which comes over the unbeliever, which will be justified when he or she discov-

---

[18] E. Erskine, *Whole Works*, 1:13–14.
[19] E. Erskine, *Whole Works*, 1:14–19.

ers the depths of eternal misery. We must take care to be sure we truly belong to Christ, especially in such times as these.[20]

Those who belong to Christ should bemoan the abuses of the day. Erskine mentions the current political situation, full of false swearing as well as the breaking of national covenants.[21] How, then, should we examine ourselves to be sure we are part of the remnant? Erskine lists several areas for examination. First of all, the very name of Jesus is sweet to his own, and they think fondly of him. Believers know that the earth is not their home, and they long to be with their Lord. They speak highly of Christ because they love him. The people of faith pray to Christ, seeking his wonderful face. They mourn not only about their own sins, but also the sins of others. Finally, the remnant love holiness and faithfulness to Jesus so much that they will risk displeasing all the powers of this world to follow Christ.[22]

After this long discussion of areas for examination in faithfulness, Erskine lists warnings which must also be considered. Our preacher first mentions that the world seeks to destroy us on every side. This attempt at destruction varies in focus from heresy to cheap grace to the temptation of hypocrisy. Sometimes, when these efforts fail, the world will persecute the true followers of Christ. Worse, we have the devil seeking to devour us. And, lest we think that external forces are required to get us to defile our garments, the conditions of our own hearts tempt us also.[23]

Some people say that just because we are elect, and therefore our salvation is a sure thing, we can sin all we want. This, too, is dangerous, for it causes us to lie to God and to subvert his purposes. We were not saved to sin with impunity, but to be set free from the power of sin. At baptism, we promise to live holy lives before the face of God, and at the Lord's Supper these vows are

---

[20] E. Erskine, *Whole Works*, 1:20–22.

[21] Note that Bonnie Prince Charlie is referred to as a "popish pretender," so it is unlikely that Erskine was a Jacobite. E. Erskine, *Whole Works*, 1:22.

[22] E. Erskine, *Whole Works*, 1:23–25.

[23] E. Erskine, *Whole Works*, 1:25–26.

reiterated. If we defile our garments, we lose our good reputation. This will prevent us from carrying out an effective ministry, or of having an effective witness to others, and, even though God will not ultimately damn one of his wayward children, we do risk punishment from the Lord in this life. We also would cast reproach on the gospel of Christ, and hurt the little ones of God.[24]

Erskine then asks the congregation, what are the advantages of living a holy life? He answers by saying that we experience a deeper sense of the presence of God. We have the satisfaction of seeing others grow in their faith because of our examples. We have a more effective ministry, and when we meet our maker, we will hear him say "well done." This is worth far more than anything that this world can offer us. Erskine closes with what amounts to a summary of what has been said before, as well as a reminder that all our good deeds which we do on account of Christ are enabled by his grace.[25]

C. Communion as Delight in the Divine Presence

We turn now to another sermon. This sermon is based on the Song of Solomon 7:5, "The king is held in the galleries."[26] An Old Testament scholar will have all kinds of problems with this text. The translation our preacher uses is a long way from the way it is translated in more recent versions. The RSV reads, "The King is held in her tresses." However we would translate it today, our preacher does seem to have gotten the general gist of the passage, namely, that the people of God delight in the presence of their Lord. To celebrate the sacrament of Holy Communion is to enter into the divine presence and to be refreshed and nourished by that presence.

The senior Erskine brother explains the context of the verse, in which the lover praises his beloved bride. Then he gets to the text itself. The galleries, he says, are the gospel. And our Lord is

---

[24] E. Erskine, *Whole Works*, 1:26–29.

[25] E. Erskine, *Whole Works*, 1:30–32.

[26] E. Erskine, *Whole Works*, 1:76f.

constrained to stay with us, his beloved bride. The bride responds appropriately, holding him in her arms and enjoying his presence.[27]

The focus first falls on Christ as our king. He is the royal seed of David, the priest Melchizedek, the Lion of Judah, the Son of God. As king, Jesus is in charge of meting out justice for wrongdoing and avenging the oppressed, as well as comforting those who do his will. A long section follows, which goes through the excellencies of Christ one by one, especially as regards his kingship. Our king is immortal, having conquered death and hell, and will sit on his throne forever, clothed in his eternal power and glory. Though he is invisible to our eyes for now, we may see him through the eyes of faith and will one day delight in looking upon him with our eyes. His subjects delight in him, and he in them. Nothing escapes his sovereign rule, in this world or the next, and even hell must submit to his power. The point is that we should be honored to be his children, his beloved bride in whom he takes delight.[28]

Erskine then explains that the galleries in which the king lingers are the means of grace. The tools of our relationship with him are prayer, sacraments, meditation, and preaching. They are places where a king goes to be with a friend or a loved one. Jesus takes us into his galleries, has fellowship with us, shows us what is in his loving heart, and walks with us. It is there that we feast on the richness of his glory and love, and are taken up in his love to rejoice in his presence.[29]

There is no question here but that the subject of this sermon is presence. The question of presence in the celebration of Christian worship is, however, much broader than merely the eucharistic presence. There is the matter of baptismal presence. Jesus promised when he instituted the sacrament of baptism that he would be with us always. But it is also true that Christ is with us through the Word,

---

[27] E. Erskine, *Whole Works*, 1:76–79.

[28] E. Erskine, *Whole Works*, 1:79–81.

[29] E. Erskine, *Whole Works*, 1:82.

by reading it and meditating on it, and especially through hearing it preached. This is the emphasis our preacher wants to make here. The kerygmatic and the eucharistic presence go hand in hand.

What, then, does it mean for us to hold Christ in the galleries? It is to thirst after him. It is to enjoy his presence and not want to let him go, no matter the consequences. When his presence is our delight, then we know we belong to him, for if we have not been brought into those galleries by him we would have no desire for them. A true Christian never tires of the presence of the Lord, but seeks him out continually. For the follower of Jesus, holding Christ in the galleries describes an act of the will to never let go of Christ. It means continual prayer to Christ that he might stay with us, and expresses the exercise of our love towards him at all times.[30] Again, we could speak at length about experiencing the presence of Christ in prayer. Even when two or three are gathered together to pray in the name of Jesus, he has promised to be in their midst.

Christ, likewise, must want to stay in the galleries. That Christ is so inclined can be seen from three things. First of all, the Lord has promised his covenant faithfulness to us, and by this covenant he is bound to us forever. This is his pledge to never leave us or destroy us. Second, he is bound to us by love, both the love of a parent and the love of a husband. He is no more likely to leave us than a mother is to reject her child. This leads us to the third reason he will never leave, and that is his marriage with us. Because he has married us, he has made a commitment never to leave us but to remain always with us.[31]

Erskine now turns to the application of this teaching. He makes the point that as the people of God we know that we belong to Christ when our delight is in the things of God. Our desire more than all else is to spend time in fellowship with him. We can use this doctrine as a means of examination to determine

---

[30] E. Erskine, *Whole Works*, 1:83–85.

[31] E. Erskine, *Whole Works*, 1:85–86.

whether or not we belong to him. What did we hear, see, and taste in these galleries? We should hear the Lord say that he loves us and delights in us. From this we can know that we truly belong to Christ. Erskine asserts that any profession of faith by a person who has not experienced these things is wishful thinking.[32] This is rather hardline Pietism. Apparently the older Erskine brother insisted that to be a real Christian one had to have a conversion experience. We will have to leave that question to others.

Returning to Erskine's sermon we find that he exhorts three different kinds of people in the congregation: those who have not met the Lord in the galleries, those that have, and those that have searched for it and not been rewarded. To the first group he underlines their wickedness of heart, and reminds them that if they took Communion they did so unworthily. These, then, are warned about the fires of hell which await them should they not repent of their sins. To the second, Erskine gives a reminder that they need to take their love out of the public galleries of the church and into the private ones of prayer and meditation. They are not to let go of Christ for any reason, but are to seek out his continual presence. This is important because his presence in the galleries is a foretaste of heaven when they will be with him forever. God strengthens his people. He directs their work. His presence is a token of his personal relationship with his people. When they do not feel his presence it can resemble a sort of hell on earth. Erskine asks, how do we keep him with us? By being diligent in entertaining him. We must continue to make our souls a welcome place for his presence by avoiding sin and delighting in him as we look lovingly at him. We should open our hearts to his work, by telling him what our struggles are and what pains we bear, and then laying everything at his feet.[33]

To the third group, that is, those who long to be with Christ in the galleries, Erskine offers encouragement. This situation, he says,

---

[32] E. Erskine, *Whole Works*, 1:86–89.

[33] E. Erskine, *Whole Works*, 1:90–94.

14: The Erskine Brothers and the Covenanter Tradition (1680–1754)

is not unusual. At times the king seems to be absent to our consciousness, but is he really absent, or are we just going through a spiritual dry period? It could be that Jesus is there with us, but we fail to see it. Or, it could be that our Lord is teaching us, or rebuking us for some sin in our lives. He sometimes does chastise us, and for that reason his spending time with us is not always sweetness. It could also be that we are blaming ourselves for not feeling his presence, and this is not necessarily good. But if we long to see him again, he will surely come and our joy will be great in that day. What, then, should we do? We should not let ourselves get depressed in his absence. Wait on the Lord and renew your strength. Be patient, but seek him out at every opportunity until we finally find the one whom our soul loves.[34]

D. Communion as Embracing Christ

Let us look at a third sermon of Ebenezer Erskine. This sermon would appear to be an action sermon, that is, a sermon preached immediately before the sharing of the sacred meal. The title is "Christ in the Believer's Arms."[35] It was preached on Psalm 73 and Luke 2 at a communion service in May, 1724.

This sermon is about Simeon, the priest in the Temple when Jesus was brought in to the holy place by Mary and Joseph. Luke tells us that the Holy Spirit rested on Simeon and when Simeon took Christ into his arms, he immediately blessed the Lord. This was because Simeon took him in the arms of faith. This, to be sure, is the privilege of all believers even today.[36] Erskine meditates on how wonderful it is to take hold of Christ, so that the thought of dying to be with him consumes our thoughts.[37] Then he discusses what it is to take hold of Christ. First of all, we must take that which is offered to us which is presented so enticingly that we

---

[34] E. Erskine, *Whole Works*, 1:94–96.

[35] E. Erskine, *Whole Works*, 1:180f.

[36] E. Erskine, *Whole Works*, 1:180.

[37] E. Erskine, *Whole Works*, 1:181–182.

would be fools not to accept it. Unfortunately those who reject the gift are miserable through all eternity. Erskine then asks: what does it mean to take what is offered? He answers his question with the following suggestions. We must know our sins, that we deserve death. We must have an intimate knowledge of Christ which only special revelation and the work of the Holy Spirit can give. Then we must assent to what is required. The final step is taking Jesus as our Lord and wishing nothing more than to live for him.[38]

What is involved, then, in this taking? We must receive him, and his love, into our hearts so that he is our possession. Next, we need to recognize him as the surety securing our salvation. Then we should take refuge in him who has the power to forgive sins. We need to rest in that forgiveness and humble ourselves to accept his righteousness as cover for all our iniquity. The soul comes to rest upon Christ for salvation and cleansing. It asks that God take that which he has graciously offered and prepared for us. We open our hearts to him, and allow him to envelope us in his loving arms. By this we receive the inheritance which we buy without cost. Finally, we must trust him to stay with us, to forgive us, and to bring us home to heaven.[39]

The soul, when grabbing hold of Christ, does so with all it has. We as Christians want to be found in him who loves us and who will never let us go. We don't just trust that he won't let us go; we cling to him with all our might. We forever seek to know him better, and we lean on him for strength. We are willing to give up whatever we have just to be with our loving savior. This grip of faith is so strong that we want to be full of Christ and never let him go. In fact, we never loosen our grip on him, but become one with our Lord for all eternity, caught up in his love and power such that nothing in the universe can separate us. This grip of love is so strong that we can go through the valley of death with him, and still be comforted in his presence. We can be persecuted and not feel abandoned, belea-

---

[38] E. Erskine, *Whole Works*, 1:182–184.

[39] E. Erskine, *Whole Works*, 1:184–186.

guered but not crushed by the darkness, for Christ will hold us in his love. Moreover, the arms of faith know that we may wait for the Lord to visit in his time, or to fulfill his purposes, but know that one day he will do as he has promised us. We feed on Christ, taking our spiritual strength and power from him. While doing this, we become more obedient to Christ, and allow him to form us for his service. We fight in his army, knowing that we are "more than conquerors through him who loves us." Most importantly, it is by this arm of faith that we are saved.[40] This arm of faith grabs hold of Christ as he is offered in the gospel. This offer to us is free, without any demand of holiness to prove our fitness to approach him. By faith we come to Jesus admitting we have nothing to offer him, but reaching out to take what he offers without cost. To do otherwise is to try and pay a price which God does not accept.[41]

By faith we also embrace the whole of Christ, as prophet, priest, and king. First we accept him as our priest, then learn to follow him as our prophet and king. We come to his mercy. Then we must learn to accept his teaching and leadership. This separates true believers from hypocrites, who are only interested in escaping hell but who are not interested in changing lives. We do not accept Christ in an unemotional way. Rather, we feel the cordial, warm affections of a Father who wants so much to make us his children, and we respond with a warm love for him as well. Then the Lord becomes our delight, the one for whom we will do whatever is required. Of course, this offer of salvation must be applied by faith to our individual souls. Just believing God is merciful is not sufficient if we do not take this mercy and love to ourselves, and rest upon it.[42]

When our souls get hold of Christ, we will, like Simeon, break out in songs of praise to our king. We will bless him who has given us such love and boundless grace. Our hearts will be full of grati-

---

[40] E. Erskine, *Whole Works*, 1:186–190.

[41] E. Erskine, *Whole Works*, 1:191–193.

[42] E. Erskine, *Whole Works*, 1:193–196.

tude that the Lord no longer sits in judgment against us, but that he has shown us his mercy, even though our sins are offensive to him. We will rejoice that God has given us the righteousness of Christ to cover our sins, and that he has adopted us as his beloved children, giving us a permanent place in his everlasting kingdom. Because of this we praise him, that we may approach his throne with boldness as his children.[43] There is no doubt in faith, for faith is certain of what God has promised to do, and lays hold of the riches God has given us in Christ. Our faith is strengthened by the assurance of the love of God, which fills us with thanks and praise.[44]

There are several ways this doctrine applies. Faith is a special grace, without which even the most copious following of the Law would be offensive to almighty God. Therefore it is necessary for salvation. To have faith is a joyous privilege, for it brings us close to God in a way even David longed for. God uses faith to comfort us, both when we think of our sins and as we encounter the trials of life. It is when we take our eyes off of Christ that we begin to founder. We must keep our eyes on faith, looking at how our faith sustains us. We must meditate on the joys of heaven which we will experience when we go to live with him forever.[45]

Likewise, Erskine gives us a primer whereby we can judge our faith in times of trial. We never have saving faith unless the Lord embraces us first and draws us to him. This love also causes us to "divorce" our old master the Law along with its onerous demands. This is difficult, because the Law promises life, and because it is much harder to convince a servant of the Law that they are destined for hell than someone who is involved in rampant sin. Once the other loves leave, however, we come to desire nothing besides the one who loves us unconditionally. Those who have laid hold of Christ find that they love him, and that

---

[43] E. Erskine, *Whole Works*, 1:196–198.

[44] E. Erskine, *Whole Works*, 1:199–200.

[45] E. Erskine, *Whole Works*, 1:201–202.

this love works in their hearts for their sanctification even as their desires become only for him.[46]

Erskine continues the sermon with a plea to those who do not yet have saving faith. They are reminded that they are already condemned to die for their sins, and told they should consider the excellency of our Lord. The Savior is mighty to save, losing none of the sheep given to him. He heals the soul in the name of the Father who sent him. His willingness to catch us in his arms is demonstrated by his obedient work on the cross, which purchased our peace. By taking him into our arms, we become beneficiaries of the many benefits of grace, from salvation to sanctification.[47]

Concerned that some of his listeners will reject his plea, our preacher treats several objections to receiving the gospel. The first objection is that if the gifts of God are so wonderful, how can anyone hope to obtain them? This person, Erskine explains, wants to keep the right to alter the gift proffered by the Lord. Erskine counters such an argument by saying that it is absolutely necessary for salvation that the soul embrace Christ; in fact this was the purpose of Christ's coming to earth. The revelation of his mission on earth, as well as the clear call of the Gospel, should be enough to convince us. There is no need to bring anything but ourselves, whatever our circumstances, for God does not want our gifts but only for us to give ourselves to him. Indeed, God commands us to embrace Christ or face damnation, while at the same time promising to accept all who call on his name. We need not be concerned that he will reject us because of our position in life, our residence, or our deeds. There is room in the covenant for all who will by faith sign their names to it, like drowning men who grab at a rope cast to save them. Erskine challenges us to consider the warm welcome which the saints of old received, and contrasts this to the

---

[46] E. Erskine, *Whole Works*, 1:202–203.
[47] E. Erskine, *Whole Works*, 1:203–205.

upbraiding which Satan will no doubt give to those who go to hell with him having rejected the invitation.

The second objection of the doubter is that since Christ is in heaven, we can't possibly reach him. Yet this argument also does not apply, because Christ has come down to us. By his Spirit he is with us. Erskine likens it to our receiving a bank check from someone in America, knowing that we will surely get the money as promised. Erskine then asserts that we cannot be so defiled by other loves that the Lord will not take us back. This is contrary to the opinion of others. Remarkably, he insists that even if we have a reduced capacity we only have to reach out to Christ with whatever we have, believing that Christ will accept us, and we will pass from death to life. Then Erskine attacks the notion that we cannot embrace Christ because we do not know if we are elect or not. This is a trick of the devil, Erskine says, because the will of God is hidden from us until we are ready to learn it. Since the gospel is presented to us, we are to reach for Christ to lay hold of him, and when we lay hold of Christ by faith, we immediately know that we are, in fact, elect. Before that, we cannot know. That is why we must reach for him with all our might. Those who fail to believe are likewise cut off for that unbelief, and are not of the elect.[48]

Finally, Erskine exhorts the members of two groups in the congregation. The first group is made up of those who believe and joyously take Christ into their arms, while the second is made up of those who come to church and yet experience a certain emptiness within themselves. They therefore are disappointed. Nevertheless, Erskine challenges us all to embrace Christ as Simeon did. We are to rejoice in Christ our savior. We are to draw near to him. We are to entreat him with our love, and to learn of him so that we are continually transformed by his redeeming love. To help us hold onto Christ, Erskine offers us the advice that we should guard our hearts. Guarding the heart should keep us from doing

---

[48] E. Erskine, *Whole Works*, 1:206–212.

anything which would grieve the Spirit and cause him to withdraw the sense of his presence from us. Erskine exhorts his congregation to keep the fire of love burning on the altar of their hearts. It is this which pleases God.[49]

To the second group, Erskine speaks words of comfort. If you are feeling emptiness, it is nothing other than a period of spiritual dryness. That you desire to get Christ back in your arms indicates you belong to him. Remember that even Christ had such an experience while on earth, so he knows your pain. Jesus never shuts out the believer, but returns to him and enfolds the believer in his arms once more. Meanwhile, you should lay hold of his promises and treasure the memories of his presence. Continue to lay claim to the covenant promise of his love and favor, for after the weeping come songs of gladness when your loved one reappears.[50] Surely this sermon makes very clear how Scottish piety understood the sacrament of Holy Communion as embracing Christ.

RALPH ERSKINE

Ralph Erskine (1680–1725) was born five years after his brother.[51] He, too, grew up taught to admire the costly service of his father. He, too, studied at the University of Edinburgh. While on vacation he would often visit his brother at Portmoak. The two were great supporters of the other. In 1711 Ralph was ordained to the second post in Dunfermline and a few years later to the first post. As we would put it today, he was made senior pastor. There he remained until his death in 1752. While Ralph did not take significant leadership in the church politics of his day as his brother did, he was more popu-

---

[49] E. Erskine, *Whole Works*, 1:212.

[50] E. Erskine, *Whole Works*, 1:213–214.

[51] For information on the life of Ralph Erskine, see: "Erskine, Ralph," in *The Encyclopedia Britannica*, 11th ed., 9:755–756; E. Erskine, *The Beauties of Ebenezer Erskine*; Ker, *The Erskines: Ebenezer and Ralph*; MacEwen, *The Erskines*; and Ralph Erskine, *The Life and Practical Works of the Reverend Ralph Erskine* (Xenia, OH: Board of the Calvinistic Book Concern, 1844).

lar as a preacher. He also published more than his brother did.[52] We notice two separate sets of communion sermons and many pieces for the communion services published separately.

We will look at two thanksgiving sermons from Ralph Erskine which we find in *Select Sermons of Ralph Erskine*.[53] The sermons are of interest to us first because they are good examples of the typical thanksgiving sermon preached after the observance of a Scottish communion season. A thanksgiving sermon might have been preached at the evening service following the communion that had been celebrated in the morning, or it could have been preached on the Monday after the celebration of the sacrament. The second of the sermons we will look at is a double-barreled sermon, that is, a sermon preached over two sessions. It was probably one sermon begun at the morning service and completed at the evening service. The second session of the thanksgiving sermon might have been left to Monday. Be that as it may, the thanksgiving services were an essential part of the celebration.

A. Mounting Up on Eagles' Wings

The first of these two sermons has the title, "The Mounting Christian, or, the Eagle-Winged Believer."[54] This sermon is obviously based on Isaiah 40:31 (KJV): "But they that wait upon the

---

[52] A sampling of the works of Ralph Erskine include: Ralph Erskine, *Sermons and Other Practical Writings: To Which Is Prefixed a Short Account of the Author's Life and Writings* (Glasgow: Robert Urie, 1765); Ebenezer and Ralph Erskine, *A Collection of Sermons from Various Important Subjects and on Divers Occasions* (London: Edward Dilly, 1757); and Ralph Erskine, *The Sermons and Other Practical Works: Consisting of About One Hundred and Fifty Sermons, Besides His Poetical Pieces* (Glasgow: Printed by J. Bryce, 1777–1778); Ralph Erskine, *Gospel Sonnets, or Spiritual Songs: To Which Is Prefixed an Account of the Author's Life and Writings* (Pittsburg: Luke Loomis & Co., 1831). For a modern edition of Ralph Erskine's work, see R. Erskine, *The Works of Ralph Erskine*.

[53] Ralph Erskine, *Select Sermons of Ralph Erskine*, vol. 1 (London: Houlston and Wright, 1863). The editor of this volume is unknown, and its contents are distributed in other published works.

[54] R. Erskine, *Select Sermons*, pp. 3–27.

14: THE ERSKINE BROTHERS AND
THE COVENANTER TRADITION (1680–1754)

LORD shall renew their strength; they shall mount up with wings as eagles; they shall run, and not be weary; and they shall walk, and not faint." It was preached in June of 1735, probably at an evening service.[55] What interests us especially about these sermons is that they show the role the observance of Holy Communion played in Scottish piety.

Erskine's thesis is that the Christian should always fly to Jesus wherever he is and in whatever circumstances. As we do so, we are taken up on wings like eagles. Our search for him must be relentless.[56] In the context of this verse, Isaiah was correcting Israel for her failures: for failing to trust in God for salvation, failing to believe in God's omnipotence in all things, and failing to look to God for the strength he would surely supply. Rather, Israel trusted in the sufficiency of its own strength. To answer those weaknesses, Isaiah gives answers the strong Christian would be wise to follow. A Christian must wait upon the Lord. In waiting we will get strength from God so that the strong Christian can handle the trials of his or her life. The strong Christian will never tire of doing God's work, but will always have strength through the power of God, for God's true servants will be filled with his grace.[57]

This passage speaks in very pictorial language by comparing Christians to eagles. This is because the use of such imagery helps us to remember the truth, and, by the connection to creatures, remember the Creator. Erskine expounds on the wings of the eagle, which are the gracious works of the Holy Spirit in our lives. The first wing is that of faith; the second is love.[58] These wings bind us to Christ with such power nothing can overcome them, and they allow us to soar to heaven. Now, we do not mount up to heaven with theoretical knowledge, which even devils have,

---

[55] Appreciation is expressed to my daughter Hannah Chase Old who provided the following digests of these sermons.

[56] R. Erskine, *Select Sermons*, p. 4.

[57] R. Erskine, *Select Sermons*, p. 5.

[58] R. Erskine, *Select Sermons*, p. 8.

nor do we seek to know the secrets of election and reprobation, although if we belong to Christ our election is sure. We also do not mount up in spiritual pride, nor in transient times of affection, but in humility of spirit. By meditating on the things of God, we rise up, seeking to serve the Lord in all we do and looking for his face wherever he may be found. Daily the true Christian seeks to become more sanctified, to deepen his or her piety before the Lord and to share his heart. We seek to have fellowship with other Christians, and to walk as becomes our calling.[59]

The believer does rise up continually through the Christian life. This rising begins at conversion when we find ourselves to be the children of God, and we continue without interruption to wake up in the arms of Christ. Daily when the Spirit sends his breath of influence upon us, we experience growth. Likewise, when we come to the Lord's Table, we seek nothing less than the heart of Christ, which beats out love for us, and we hold him in our arms forever. In death, too, we rise up, for though our bodies are left on this earth, our souls will rise to the presence of those who are with Christ already. And this will become complete finally at the last judgment, when we will again have our bodies in the kingdom of our Lord.[60]

This rising of the soul is natural to the believer, who has been set free and seeks to rise higher and higher into the grace of God. Nothing will stand in the way of this rising of soul, for the strength and determination overcomes everything else. The rise is gradual, for there is much to learn, and it continues on a daily basis as we seek to know God better. We do this because of our new nature, which has come from heaven and wants to return there. The sight of this heavenly reality makes us seek it more even on earth, for there is our safety, affection, and treasure. Furthermore, as we come to the Lord's Table, and partake of his goodness,

---

[59] R. Erskine, *Select Sermons*, pp. 10–12.

[60] R. Erskine, *Select Sermons*, pp. 13–14.

our strength for this flight is renewed.[61] Here, again, we have the theme of covenant renewal. Holy Communion is above all a feast of covenant renewal.

There are several means of application for this principle. For one thing, it is a regrettable fact that many Christians have their minds too much on the world, and do not therefore rise up as they should. Also, one must try and discern whether or not we are rising up to God, for it distinguishes us from those who are not Christians. The Lord sets us free from the cage of our sin, and makes us able to rise to heaven. We daily seek to be nourished by the Word, even feeding on the Lord, and refuse to touch anything which is unworthy of our noble hearts. Continually we seek to avoid those things which are not pleasing to God, our own conceits, and sinful tendencies, and develop a great hatred for the serpent who clipped Adam's wings. An eagle Christian sees the Son, and what he has to offer, so that the clouds of doubt and fear give way to a clear view of him. This view is precious to us, and when we climb to the heights of communion with Christ, the things of the Earth seem very small to us such that we may not want to come down off the mountain.[62]

B. THE BETHEL EXPERIENCE

Let us turn our attention to a second sermon from Ralph Erskine. The title is, "A promising God, a Performing God." It is based on the story of the promise God gave to Jacob at Bethel. (Cf. Genesis 28:10–22). It was preached in October of 1733.[63]

The younger Erskine says the basic meaning of the text is that if we hear God saying something to us, we can be sure he will fulfill what he has promised. The context of the verse described how Jacob had run from Esau and had spent the night with his stone pillow while dreaming of the stairway to heaven. It was during

---

[61] R. Erskine, *Select Sermons*, pp. 15–17.

[62] R. Erskine, *Select Sermons*, pp. 17–20.

[63] R. Erskine, *Select Sermons*, pp. 28–48.

this dream that Jacob received an important message spoken from heaven by our great Mediator. God told Jacob how, although he fled the wrath of his brother, the Lord would be with him, guiding and protecting him the whole way. In addition, God promised Jacob to bring him back to his family and to be by his side. This promise was important in two ways: first, it confirmed what God intended to do in Jacob's life, and, second, it provided a source of strength for Jacob during the long years in which he waited for those promises to be fulfilled. As this applies to the believer, we must say that we can be sure God will never leave us and never stop working in us until his purposes are fulfilled. This assurance can be counted upon, no matter how long we might have to wait. That this is true we can see in several areas. First we see how the Lord sustains Jacob through very dark days and protects him in his return home. Then this promise continued to be fulfilled in the settling of Canaan by Israel many years later.[64]

Likewise there are applications of this principle to the Christian life. Those of us who are brought into a relationship with Christ have at some point had a meeting with the Lord in our spirits in which God gave us some promises or comforts. These are what Erskine calls "Bethel moments." One part of a "Bethel moment" or "Bethel experience" is that God manifests his glory to us in Christ, and this can be at any point in our lives. The other part is that God opens his heart to us, showing us how much he loves us, or giving us some gospel promise we are supposed to hold on to. These visits may not be immediately obvious to our spirits until we reflect on them, but we will come to know God was speaking to us. This will fill us with reverence, awe, and holy fear even as we are filled with rejoicing in his Spirit. Such visits can take place any time or anywhere, and they transform that moment into the very heaven of God's presence. When the moment has passed, we are renewed in our devotion

---

[64] R. Erskine, *Select Sermons*, pp. 28–32.

to the Lord, and from that communion we find the strength to follow him better.[65]

Such "Bethel moments" are often ushered in by struggles which press in on us, those dark nights of the soul in which we all but give up. Then God speaks to us, drawing us close. This presence or fellowship with God comes to us like daybreak after a long night, filling us with joy. Here one is surprised to discover that Ralph Erskine is using some of the terminology of the classic mystics of the past, such as Gregory of Nyssa, Teresa of Ávila and Thomas à Kempis. Yet, often this moment is strengthening us for an even darker night ahead, such as Jacob's mistreatment at the hand of Laban. We should therefore not be surprised if afterwards God seems to hide his face from us for a time.

Erskine then goes on to meditate on how life may be difficult after these experiences of the Lord's love. It may be that we will have a time in which God seems to hide from us, or perhaps a time of sore trial. Perhaps we will forget what we learned at Bethel until God reminds our hearts of it, and sometimes we even feel that God must be angry with us, but we never are outside of his care. Poverty and persecution sometimes follow, but we are always reminded of the covenant love of God. Our faith may fail, and a dark night of the soul follow from which there is no rest. Reflecting on his own battle with the church judicatory, the younger Erskine adds that dark times may include being denounced by one's brethren, and even being excommunicated. However, through it all God is faithful, and will never abandon those whom he loves.[66]

Understanding that there may be dark times, how do we understand the promise that God will never leave until he fulfills his purposes? First of all, his kind words to our hearts announce who is speaking to us. He speaks to each of us individually, drawing us by his love to our Bethel where he addresses all our heart's desires,

---

[65] R. Erskine, *Select Sermons*, pp. 32–35.
[66] R. Erskine, *Select Sermons*, pp. 35–41.

concerns, and needs. We are left with no doubt to whom we belong. From this, we see that God will be faithful to do what he has promised, and will even work miracles if necessary. God's work is so marvelous that it will be remembered fondly and we will see his glory in it. The work of God likewise comes at the proper time. It may be when we are having trials of faith, or when we are oppressed by others. Perhaps God's word will be fulfilled in resisting temptation. Whatever the situation we find ourselves in, we cannot forget that victory which will be achieved in our deaths, when we go to be with the Lord, and in the last judgment, when God will condemn the wicked and raise the righteous to life. Of this last part we already have a foretaste, through our union with Christ and our enjoyment of his benefits in this life. The fruits of the Spirit and the spiritual intimacy we already have with Christ and his people are a small part of what we have to look forward to in the hereafter.[67]

Ralph Erskine's sermon, "Bethel moments," makes very clear how he understands the sacrament. The Lord's Supper is our union with Christ and our fellowship with his people. To hear him preach about Bethel and Jacob's experience there reminds one of the journal of David Brainerd out on the frontier of New Jersey only ten years later. In other words, these two mystics were contemporaries.

This sermon, as we have said, comes in two parts. Our preacher begins the second half of his sermon with a question.[68] Why is it important that God will not leave without accomplishing his purposes? Various kinds of the Lord's leaving are possible, which we see through the Bible, such as spiritual famine or our being unable to experience the ministry of the Spirit in our lives. Yet these withdrawals are never complete. God hides his face, allows trials of faith, and withholds visible answers to prayer. But his lovingkindness, his grace, and the covenant love of our Father will never leave us, even if we are unaware of his presence for a time. The person he saves

---

[67] R. Erskine, *Select Sermons*, pp. 41–48.

[68] R. Erskine, *Select Sermons*, pp. 49–70.

he never leaves, and the sense of his love and presence returns after awhile. Even in the darkest pit of Christian experience, God is always there, holding us up and keeping us from despair, never withdrawing his love, goodness and presence from our souls.[69]

Likewise, we must understand the conditional "until." Because God's promising means it is already in process, we can be assured that he is continually working on whatever he has promised us, so that even if the interval between the beginning and the ending is long, we know he is keeping that promise. Accordingly, we may not see the progress God is making towards the fulfillment of his promise, but like Joseph we must have faith that God is working those purposes out even in the face of difficulty.[70] The Reformed doctrine of the real presence is closely related to the doctrine of providence. This is even more clearly seen in the work of John Flavel, *The Mystery of Providence*.

As believers, we have several assurances that God will do as he promised at Bethel. First, we may rest in the unchangeableness of God, that he will *always* love those upon whom he has sent his love. The foreknowledge and faithfulness of God mean that no matter what befalls us, no matter how much we hurt him, he will never turn away. Because God is almighty, nothing can snatch us away from his power and love, and experience shows us of his faithfulness throughout our lives. Whenever we find ourselves thinking God will never return to us, there he is waiting. God will never leave us, because he made an everlasting covenant with us, and because this was the agreement between the Father and the Son, that the Father would give to Christ those for whom he died. Finally, it is the will of God to do what he has promised, and whatever God wills, he will surely do.[71]

The younger Erskine now applies the lessons of this discussion

---

[69] R. Erskine, *Select Sermons*, pp. 49–52.

[70] R. Erskine, *Select Sermons*, pp. 52–53.

[71] R. Erskine, *Select Sermons*, pp. 53–56.

to the Christian life. One often sees Christians who, by all accounts, are in miserable life circumstances. Yet these are the most happy, for they know they have God on their side. Conversely, the most miserable people of all are those who, though they may have an easy life, are without Christ. Saving faith overcomes all the obstacles that life puts up for it. In fact, when a struggling Christian has nothing else, he still has the promise of faith. True Christians are a blessing to their churches and nations, because the presence of God goes with them. If all the Christians were to leave a place, that place would be destroyed by the absence of God. Likewise, the safety of Christians is their relationship with God. This safety does not extend, however, to a particular church or denomination. God can and does abandon such bodies to destruction if they cease to be faithful, but true believers he will never leave. Our preacher at this point begins to lament the situation in the Church of Scotland, which at that time was in turmoil over patronage and oaths to civil authority. Erskine claims that the actions of the Church of Scotland were against Scripture and threatened the very freedoms that the Reformers fought so hard to win.[72]

Everyone should likewise examine their own hearts, to see if they have had a "Bethel moment" with God, because all who have been born of the Spirit have had such a meeting and those who have never had such a meeting are, like Esau, children of divine wrath. To this latter group, Erskine gives a warning. Just as believers are assured of their blessed state in Christ, so are unbelievers assured of divine wrath, for God has sworn an oath never to let such enter into his rest. Erskine challenges them to make today the day in which they cry out to God for salvation, begging to see his face. If not, then the times they heard the gospel preached but refused to believe will become another reason for God to judge them on that great day. To the believers, Erskine gives encouragement. We should always seek to be joyful in the Lord, rejoicing

---

[72] R. Erskine, *Whole Works*, pp. 57–61.

in his promises to us. If we are going through a dry period, not feeling the presence of God in our lives for a time, we should take heart. God is always present with us, and there are always tokens of his presence and affection. Those tokens include the fact that we hate our sinful backsliding, or that we long to feel the presence of the Lord. In brief, if we are satisfied with anything less than his pleasure and love then we know he has not left us. In such times, we should look to the Son, and let the Spirit remind us of what he has told us at Bethel. We belong to Christ, and he will bring us home to him. Meanwhile, we ought to let our lives show that we belong to Christ, that we will be good witnesses of his all our days. As our lives remain lives of faith, the word of God is fulfilled that he will not leave us without accomplishing his purposes.[73]

There is no question about it; this sermon shows strong Pietist influences. Perhaps one needs to go beyond this and say that the sermon shows a mystical approach to the celebration of the Sacrament. This is shown by the opening words of the sermon, which are best understood as referring to a mystical experience. Our preacher is speaking of a mystical flight into the very presence of God. Those who approached the Sacrament that they have just shared in true faith have mounted up on eagles' wings to taste of the wedding feast of the Lamb. While it would seem to be quite clear that the Erskines had a mystical understanding of the sacrament of Holy Communion, it is just as clear that their Pietism moved in a rigorist direction.

C. Communion as Tasting the Wedding Feast of the Lamb

Let us look at another sermon from Ralph Erskine. Once again we have a sermon on a text from the Revelation of John. This text speaks of "The Lamb in the midst of the throne" (Revelation 8:17).[74]

The Lamb in the midst of the throne feeds his people. Some

---

[73] R. Erskine, *Select Sermons*, pp. 62–70.
[74] R. Erskine, *Select Sermons*, pp. 119–142.

argue this is meant to be only in the future, others in the present. But we must properly understand this passage as referring to both the present and future feeding of the people of God. It also teaches us about how Christians who endure suffering for the Lord are filled with joy now on earth, but someday will have their reward fully in heaven.[75] Even now we rejoice in being washed with the blood of Christ, in our position as the children of God. We joyfully serve our precious Lord, and enjoy our fellowship with both him and each other. Peace with God is ours, and the freedom in knowing that we will lack nothing. With joy we receive the comfort of the Holy Spirit even in the worst of situations, and this joy will be completed in heaven.[76]

By the phrase, "Lamb which is in the midst of the throne," we can gather two things about Jesus: first, that he is humble, and, second, that he is exalted in power and authority.[77] How does Jesus come to be called a lamb? Because of his meek, gentle character, and because he was the perfect lamb who made the ultimate sacrifice for sin. Jesus is also called a lamb because he came down from heaven, took our form, was humiliated on the cross, and now is exalted above the heavens. It is this triumphant lamb on the throne of which the text at hand speaks.[78] The seven horns and seven eyes with which Christ is pictured point to the perfect power and wisdom of God, which dwell in him both in his divinity and his humanity. The throne on which Jesus sits is nothing less than the throne of God. Only, for believers, this throne is one of grace, and the One who sits on that throne shows all the glory of God. God's throne is one of holiness and justice, which are satisfied and fulfilled in Christ for our salvation. Thus, Christ's sitting on the throne shows for us how we are assured of his grace because

---

[75] R. Erskine, *Select Sermons*, p. 119.

[76] R. Erskine, *Select Sermons*, pp. 120–122.

[77] R. Erskine, *Select Sermons*, p. 122.

[78] R. Erskine, *Select Sermons*, p. 123.

of the justice satisfied in him. The throne of Christ declares the power, glory, and authority of our risen Lord. It reveals how all good things come from him who has triumphed over evil. Believers share in these things also, as members of his kingdom.[79]

The throne belongs to Christ by virtue of his role in the history of salvation. It was promised to him when Jesus agreed to come down and redeem man from his sins; it is a part of his seeing the results of his work and being satisfied in them. Here is the glorification of the god-man. Our Lord has earned the throne by the defeat and utter destruction of his and our enemies. Indeed, the throne is his reward for his suffering and dying for our sins. The dignity of his person, and his exaltation above all kings and rulers, is demonstrated by Jesus sitting on the throne. And because he is mediator, he is seated in the center of the throne, showing his perfect administration and even the accessibility of the throne to every believer. We can thus approach the throne of grace from whatever direction we wish, whether boldly from the front, or crawling with the timid uncertainty of our unworthiness from the back. Along with these things, Jesus is the center of every good thing, every sweet delight that comes in the Christian life. He is our joy, our portion, our happiness.[80]

Likewise, this Lamb is the one who feeds us: He is both the food, and the feeder.[81] He feeds us with his kindness, tenderness and love. Through his power and love he compels us to open our hearts to the food which he offers to us, though we take it willingly. We are offered, then, spiritual food which comprises all the richness that is Christ. We receive from him his wisdom, love, strength, and holiness. By his wisdom, Christ gives us all the food we need, no more and no less. Our souls are satisfied in him.[82] We eat joyfully and freely of the righteousness and goodness of Christ, not

---

[79] R. Erskine, *Select Sermons*, pp. 124–126.
[80] R. Erskine, *Select Sermons*, pp. 126–130.
[81] R. Erskine, *Select Sermons*, p. 131.
[82] R. Erskine, *Select Sermons*, p. 133.

relying on ourselves for salvation. This heavenly food is not something that lasts for a while and then disappears. Rather, it is the food that springs up to eternal life, for the Lamb is forever feeding us, praying and providing for our every spiritual need.[83]

How, then, do we apply these things? First, we must recognize Christ as the paschal Lamb. In his glorification, the shame of the cross was swept away, and now the cross has become our rallying cry in every situation.[84] We as believers can rejoice, because our head and husband is in control of all things. Likewise, we know that the enemies of God are afraid of Christ, the Lamb of God, because they never stop plotting against him. Yet we are forever secure because our lamb is also a lion who has defeated our enemies and will not permit them to prevail against us.[85] This should lead us to honor and praise our Lord, who is in the midst of the throne and makes that throne a haven for us. The wicked look on that throne and tremble, but we look upon it and rejoice. In addition, because of Christ's place on the throne, we can be assured of the work of the Holy Spirit in our lives. We can know that we will be included in the resurrection on the last day. By this we can rejoice in our salvation, acknowledging Jesus' place on the throne of grace as we seek to fly to that throne. In short, if the Lord is our all, and sin is not allowed to have a stronghold, then we can see quite clearly that we belong to him.[86]

Unbelievers are challenged to come to know the lamb in the midst of the throne. In so doing, all the terrors which accompany the throne of God will vanish into his mercy. The new believer will begin to observe that peace which comes from knowing that God is in charge of all things. In coming, sinners become part of the marriage supper of the Lamb, having been divorced from the Devil and

---

[83] R. Erskine, *Select Sermons*, p. 134.

[84] R. Erskine, *Select Sermons*, p. 134.

[85] R. Erskine, *Select Sermons*, p. 136.

[86] R. Erskine, *Select Sermons*, p. 138.

14: THE ERSKINE BROTHERS AND THE COVENANTER TRADITION (1680–1754)

married to Christ. Our marriage to Christ reveals to us that Jesus is loving and lovely, blessed and bountiful, beloved, and generous to us as a husband should be. He offers us an eternal relationship, for he has paid the price of our redemption. Erskine warns us that it is a grievous blasphemy not to accept the gift of our Lord, for he draws all who will come to him in faith, and this by the eternal decree of the Father. For those groaning under sin and wishing to be led to the Lamb on the throne, take comfort, for you are being drawn to him already. You have only to be introduced to the Lord and live.[87]

This is really a very long sermon. It is in effect an invitation to come to Christ and be assured of one's salvation. It is further evidence of how Reformed piety has understood the sacrament of the Lord's Supper in terms of the parable of the wedding feast. Yes, the paschal image is there, too, and so is the type of the manna in the wilderness as well as a few others. Above all, however, we are reminded that to approach the Lord's Table is to appear before the throne of grace and to be received into the glories of heaven. It is to take one's place at the wedding feast of the Lamb.

ROBERT WALKER

The sermons of Robert Walker (1716–1784) were commended to me by a portrait of my great-great grandfather, Robert Chambers. I mentioned this on the first page of the introduction to my volumes on the history of preaching. It is a book of Walker's sermons that my lace-collared ancestor holds in his hand in that portrait. The edition he owned was no doubt that edition which was published in Trenton, New Jersey, in 1820. I always figured that Robert Chambers, in identifying this book in his hand, was letting his descendants know what he understood the true preaching of the gospel should be.[88]

---

[87] R. Erskine, *Select Sermons*, p. 142.
[88] This section on Walker was previously published in Hughes Oliphant Old, *The Reading and Preaching of the Scriptures in the Worship of the Christian Church*, vol. 5, *Mod-*

Robert Walker was born in Edinburgh, Scotland in 1716, the son of one of Edinburgh's ministers.[89] It was the Canongate Church of which Robert's father was minister. Today the ancient building is still standing on the Royal Mile down close to Holyrood Palace. Young Robert would have been given all the cultural and educational advantages of the city of Edinburgh, which in the eighteenth century was the Athens of the North, the Weimar of Great Britain. Eighteenth-century Edinburgh was the city of David Hume, the philosopher, Adam Smith, the economist, and Robert Burns, the poet. The Enlightenment was at high tide in the Scottish capitol. This was the age in which Edinburgh was a center of mathematics, medicine, science, and the literary arts. It was at the University of Edinburgh that Robert Walker was privileged to study. To study there in the eighteenth century was to have studied at one of Europe's centers of learning.

After completing his university training, the young theologian was sent out to the southwest of Scotland to preach under the guidance of the local pastors. This was the way things were done in Scotland at the time. Internship was an important part of theological education. It amounted to a sort of ministerial apprenticeship. In 1737 Walker was licensed to preach by the Presbytery of Kirkcudbright. A year later he was ordained minister of Straiton by the Presbytery of Ayr. Eight years after that he was called to the second charge at South Leith, a suburb of Edinburgh. Finally he was called to be one of the ministers of Edinburgh itself. There he exercised a collegiate ministry at the High Church, at the other end of the Royal Mile from where his father had served. Here Walker was a colleague of the Reverend Hugh Blair, the famous preacher of Moderatism. One gets the impression that the two

---

eratism, Pietism, and Awakening (Grand Rapids, MI: Eerdmans, 2004). It has been altered from the original. The biographical material is taken from pp. 464-465.

[89] For further biographical information on Robert Walker, see also: John Macleod, *Scottish Theology in Relation to Church History Since the Reformation* (Edinburgh and Carlisle, PA: Banner of Truth Trust, 1974), pp. 207-208.

preachers were thought of as balancing each other. We remember that the famous German preacher Friedrich Schleiermacher had given careful attention to studying the homiletical art of Hugh Blair. Blair's ministry was to the liberal literati; Walker's to those of more orthodox temper. For almost thirty years he served in that pulpit made sacred by the memory of John Knox.

While Hugh Blair has come down in history as the superb rhetorician, Robert Walker has come down in history because of a painting of him by one of Scotland's more famous painters, who painted the highly respected dominie ice-skating on a frozen pond.[90] It is a droll painting, showing another side of the distinguished parson's ministry.

One of the most attractive features of Scottish Protestantism is the way it joins evangelism to the celebration of the Lord's Supper.[91] In this regard Robert Walker is especially interesting because he is one of the early leaders of Scottish evangelicalism. Among the Scottish evangelical preachers such as Thomas Chalmers and Thomas Guthrie it is Walker who has left us the most notable communion sermons. Repeatedly we find that the most powerful presentations of the gospel are made in the context of the observance of the sacrament of communion. In the worship of the Reformed churches it was at the celebration of the Supper that one made and renewed the covenant vows of faith which brought one into communion with Christ and his church. Formally it was through communion that one joined the church, but more subjectively, participation in the sacrament was indeed communion, that is, communion with God. Evangelism, then, at its most profound, was the invitation to come and sit at the Lord's Table and receive Christ by sharing in the sacred feast. This is no doubt the reason that so many of the best examples of Scottish evangelistic preach-

---

[90] Sir Henry Raeburn, *The Reverend Robert Walker Skating on Duddingston Loch*, c. 1794.

[91] This section is largely contained in Old, *Reading and Preaching*, 5:471–476.

ing are to be found in communion sermons. The Church of Scotland may have celebrated the Supper but once or twice a year, but those celebrations were the spiritual focal points of their worship.

Like the collection of sacred orations which has come down to us from Gregory of Nazianzus, the collection of Robert Walker's sermons is a selection of the best examples of his preaching art.[92] With Walker's colleague, Hugh Blair, teaching rhetoric at the University of Edinburgh, the interest in the art of oratory was strong in eighteenth-century Scotland. Cultivated Christians liked to read sermons for their literary excellence as well as their devotional value. Sad to say, both in regard to Walker and in regard to Nazianzus, the historical context of the individual sermons has been lost. There is no recognizable series of *lectio continua* sermons or catechetical sermons from Walker. Each sermon in this collection stands pretty much on its own. One exception is a group of five sermons which the editor tells us were preached at the celebration of the Lord's Supper. The editor does not indicate whether they were preached in the course of a single communion season or whether they were preached at different communion services as part of the celebration. However that may be, they are magnificent examples of evangelistic preaching filled with gospel and grace. Let us look, then, at one of these communion sermons.

The text of the first of these communion sermons is drawn from the Gospel of Matthew, "Come unto me, all ye that labour, and are heavy laden, and I will give you rest" (Matthew 11:28). The text is particularly appropriate for a communion service. As is often the case with Walker, the introduction is brief, "It was prophesied of our Lord long before his manifestation in the flesh, that he should 'proclaim liberty to the captives, and the opening

---

[92] The text of the sermons which will be studied is taken from Robert Walker, *Sermons on Practical Subjects, Late one of the Ministers of the High Church of Edinburgh; to which is prefixed a character of the Author by Hugh Blair, D. D.*, 5th ed., 3 vols. (Edinburgh: E. Elliot and G. Robinson, 1785). The sermons on the Lord's Supper are contained in volume 1.

of the prison to them that are bound:' And lo! here he doth it in the kindest and most endearing manner, offering *rest*, or spiritual relief, to every *labouring and heavy laden* sinner.—*Come unto me all ye that labour, and are heavy laden, and I will give you rest.* [Matt. 11:28]."[93]

This is a remarkably short introduction but it is significant nevertheless. It interprets one of the classic texts on evangelism, namely, Isaiah 61:1–3 (KJV):

> The spirit of the Lord GOD is upon me; because the LORD hath anointed me to preach good tidings unto the meek; he hath sent me to bind up the brokenhearted, to proclaim liberty to the captives, and the opening of the prison to them that are bound; To proclaim the acceptable year of the LORD, and the day of vengeance of our God; to comfort all that mourn; To appoint unto them that mourn in Zion, to give unto them beauty for ashes, the oil of joy for mourning, the garment of praise for the spirit of heaviness; that they might be called trees of righteousness, the planting of the LORD, that he might be glorified.

Jesus himself had appealed to this same text when he preached in the synagogue in Nazareth. As Luke reports it, Jesus used this text to explain his preaching ministry. It has been used this way ever since. It makes clear that, for Jesus, his whole preaching ministry was evangelistic. The Father had sent him and the Holy Spirit had anointed him to preach the gospel. To preach the gospel was to bring the good news of God's grace to the spiritually poor, the weighed down, the mourning and lamenting children of God, who were troubled by the reversals, the hardships, and the inequities of life. That was what preaching was for Jesus and that was what preaching was for Robert Walker.

The division of the text is simple and clear. First, Walker tells us who these people are to whom this promise is given.[94] Second,

---

[93] Walker, *Sermons*, 1:186. Italics in original.
[94] Walker, *Sermons*, 1:187.

he explains the invitation itself and shows what is involved in coming to Christ. Finally, he illustrates the gracious promise of our Lord to grant us rest.[95]

Walker begins to make his first point. Again we notice his clean, sober prose:

> I begin with the character of those to whom the invitation is addressed. They are such, you see, as *labour and are heavy laden*; that is, who feel the unsupportable load of guilt, and the galling fetters of corrupt affections, and earnestly long to be delivered from both; for these were the persons whom our Saviour always regarded as the peculiar objects of his attention and care.—By our fatal apostacy, we forfeited at once our innocence and our happiness; we became doubly miserable, liable to the justice of God, and slaves to Satan and our own corruptions. But few, comparatively speaking, are sensible of this misery! The bulk of mankind are so hot in the pursuit of perishing trifles, that they can find no leisure seriously to examine their spiritual condition. These indeed have a load upon them, of weight more than sufficient to sink them into perdition; but they are not *heavy laden* in the sense of my text. Our Savior plainly speaks to those who feel their burden, and are groaning under it; otherwise the promise of rest, or deliverance, could be no inducement to bring them to him.[96]

There are two reasons why this call is addressed to them. First, because our Lord knew well that none else would respond to it.[97] Such is the pride of our hearts that each of us would wish to be a savior to himself and to purchase heaven by his own personal merit.[98] Walker makes his point by quoting Romans 10:3, "Being ignorant of God's righteousness, they went about to establish their own righteousness, and did not submit themselves unto the righ-

---

[95] Walker, *Sermons*, 1:187.

[96] Walker, *Sermons*, 1:187–188.

[97] Walker, *Sermons*, 1:188.

[98] Walker, *Sermons*, 1:188.

14: THE ERSKINE BROTHERS AND
THE COVENANTER TRADITION (1680–1754)

teousness of God."[99] The soul that is enlightened by the Spirit of God is humble and looks to God for salvation. "It was therefore with peculiar significancy, that our Lord introduced his sermon upon the mount by adjudging the kingdom of heaven to the 'poor in spirit,' placing humility in the front of all the other graces, as being the entrance into a religious temper, the beginning of the divine life, the first step of the soul in its return to God."[100]

The second point Walker wants to make is that the laboring and heavy laden are particularly distinguished because otherwise they might despair of any hope of salvation. They would exclude themselves because they imagined they would be considered unworthy of God's mercy. The teaching of Jesus in this matter is very clear. God is merciful, ". . . he 'who will not break the bruised reed, nor quench the smoking flax,' doth kindly encourage them by this special address."[101] This saying of Jesus taken from Matthew 12:20 is a classic text on God's patience and mercy toward the slow in heart. The bruised reed that cannot stand straight as well as the dimly burning wick God will patiently set in order, just as the shepherd gently carries the exhausted lamb. This invitation is extended not just to the swift and the strong, but to the slow and the weak as well.

The promise found in this text is made to those who are troubled about being alienated from God. The very thing which to themselves appeared the greatest obstacle in the way of mercy, might become the means of assuring them that they are the very persons for whom mercy is prepared.[102] Another beautiful passage follows which needs to be quoted in its entirety:

> Let this then encourage every weary selfcondemning sinner: The greater your guilt appears in your own eye, the greater ground you have to expect relief if you apply for it. Mercy looks for nothing but an affecting

---

[99] Walker, *Sermons*, 1:188.

[100] Walker, *Sermons*, 1:189.

[101] Walker, *Sermons*, 1:190.

[102] Walker, *Sermons*, 1:190.

sense of the need of mercy. Say not, If my burden were of a lesser weight, I might hope to be delivered from it; for no burden is too heavy for Omnipotence: he who is "mighty to save," can easily remove the most oppressive load; "his blood cleanseth from all sin," and "by him all who believe, are justified from all things."— This great physician did not come to heal some slight distempers, but to cure those inveterate plagues, which none beside himself was able to cure.[103]

In the second point of his sermon, Walker explains what it means to come to Christ. For this point, he draws from the *Westminster Shorter Catechism*, which his congregation, of course, would have known quite well. The catechism explains it in terms of the three offices of Christ: Christ as prophet, Christ as priest, and Christ as king. Because Christ has been given to us as a prophet we need to have our minds enlightened by Christ's teaching. Because Christ is our king we need to submit our wills to his rule. Finally, because Christ is our priest we need to accept his sacrifice for our atonement.[104] The priestly office of Christ is especially emphasized. One notices this here because this emphasis shows how stoutly Walker insisted on those elements of the Christian faith which the Enlightenment tended to ignore. While the Enlightenment emphasized the prophetic, or teaching, office of Christ as well as his kingly office—the moral and ethical dimensions of the Christian faith—it tended to ignore the priestly, or "cultic," aspects of the Christian faith. Not so with Walker. Here, as so often in these sermons, the cultic dimensions of Christian faith are given full treatment. This is especially the case because here we have to do with the sermons preached at a communion service. While Walker would never have thought of the communion as a sacrifice, he did understand it as the commemoration of Christ's sacrifice. The adoration of that sacrifice was at the heart of the celebration.

---

[103] Walker, *Sermons*, 1:190–191.

[104] Walker, *Sermons*, 1:196.

14: THE ERSKINE BROTHERS AND THE COVENANTER TRADITION (1680–1754)

The third point our preacher makes is that, to those who come to Christ, Christ gives rest. Come unto me and I will give you rest is the promise we have from Christ.[105]

> There can be no doubt that the *rest* here spoken of, must be, at least, of equal extent with the *burthen*, and include a deliverance from every cause of trouble to the soul. But this subject is an ocean without bottom or shore; we cannot measure the length or breadth of it, neither can its depth be fathomed; for "the riches of Christ are unsearchable"; and surely no tongue can express what the mind itself is unable to comprehend. Nevertheless I shall attempt to say a few things which may be of use to help forward your comfort and joy, till eternity shall unfold the whole to your view.[106]

Our preacher builds his point with a series of rhetorical questions. Does the guilt of sin and the curse of the Law lie heavily upon your soul? "Behold, the Lamb of God, who takes away the sin of the world!" (John 1:29). In the sacrifice of Christ there is an infinite merit that can never be exhausted.[107] Do you feel a law in your members warring against the law of your mind? Are you harassed with temptation and weighed down with the preoccupations of the flesh, that you cry out with the Apostle Paul, O wretched man, who shall deliver me?[108]

These rhetorical questions all urge the evangelistic invitation. Do you fear he might forsake you? Christ is the Good Shepherd who carries the lambs in his bosom, and therefore they cannot perish, because none is strong enough to pluck them out of his hand. "The believer is not left to stand by himself; he who is the author is likewise the finisher of his people's faith. Omnipotence is their guardian; and they are 'kept,' not by their own strength, but 'by

---

[105] Walker, *Sermons*, 1:198.
[106] Walker, *Sermons*, 1:198.
[107] Walker, *Sermons*, 1:199.
[108] Walker, *Sermons*, 1:200. Cf. Rom. 7:23–24.

the power of God, through faith unto salvation.'"[109] While this part of the sermon is built on a series of rhetorical questions it is filled with brilliant scriptural allusions. Not every congregation would be able to follow this. Preaching at this level demands a biblically literate congregation, and Scotland had such congregations in the eighteenth century! Walker's final point is summed up by these words:

> Such, my brethren, is that rest which Christ will finally bestow upon his people. They shall "enter into the joy of their Lord." All their burthens shall drop with their natural bodies; none of them can pass beyond the grave. Then faith and hope shall become sight and enjoyment; then love grown perfect shall cast out fear; and nothing shall remain of all their former trials, but the grateful remembrance of that friendly hand which supported them, and hath at length crowned their "light and momentary afflictions," with a "far more exceeding and eternal weight of glory."[110]

Walker tends to conclude his sermons with very practical applications. By "practical" he means that for the life of faith the sermons are spiritually and devotionally practical. That, of course, is why these sermons were so eagerly followed by his congregation. The practical application in this case is to invite the congregation to receive the sacrament. The remainder of the sermon is an invitation to receive Christ in the communion service. Our preacher figures that all who have heard his sermon up to this point should be ready to receive Christ at the Lord's Table. Our preacher draws out the invitation at some length, emphasizing that it is truly made to all. Jesus himself when he preached in the Temple of Jerusalem stood up on the last day of the feast and cried, "'If *any man* thirst, let him come to me, and drink.' [John 7:37]"[111] Jesus said the same thing to the degenerate Church of

---

[109] Walker, *Sermons*, 1:201. Cf. 1 Pet. 1:5.

[110] Walker, *Sermons*, 1:203.

[111] Walker, *Sermons*, 1:206.

the Laodiceans, "'Behold, I stand at the door, and knock: If *any man* will hear my voice, and open the door, I will come in to him, and sup with him, and he with me.' [Rev. 3:20]"[112] With this passage of Scripture particularly, the invitation to the Lord's Supper is clearly made to all.

At this point our preacher becomes very specific in his invitation, "Come now and receive the new testament in Christ's blood:—For confirming your faith, and increasing your joy, he hath instituted this visible pledge of his love, this external seal of his gracious covenant."[113] The covenantal dimension of Reformed eucharistic doctrine comes strongly to the fore. To come to the table is to come and take with one's own hand the promise of rest which Christ himself has given. Our preacher urges his congregation to come to the Lord's Table and find in this sacrament, ". . . something of that *rest* . . . which he is always ready to dispense to those who feel their need of it, and who know its worth."[114]

Again and again, we find the genius of the Scottish communion service was on the one hand its covenantal theology, and on the other its evangelistic proclamation.

ANDREW THOMSON

The Enlightenment had been an inhibiting force in the Church of Scotland toward the end of the eighteenth century. Andrew Thomson (1779–1831) was a minister, however, who courageously threw this "enlightenment" off. One might say he reasserted the religious values of religion.[115]

Andrew Thomson deserves to be considered one of Scotland's

---

[112] Walker, *Sermons*, 1:206.

[113] Walker, *Sermons*, 1:211–212.

[114] Walker, *Sermons*, 1:212.

[115] Much of this material has already been published in my volumes on the history of preaching. Here we put it in a different context. See the section on Thomson: Old, *Reading and Preaching*, 5:497–512.

major liturgical reformers.[116] He is remembered for his work in the restoration of catechetical instruction, for his work on the Psalter, and for the recovery of systematic expository preaching. These were, of course, all very important features of Scottish Presbyterian worship. It was not that any of these things had completely lapsed by 1800. It was more that during the ascendancy of Moderatism, roughly the last half of the eighteenth century, they had not been cultivated. The Enlightenment wanted to have nothing to do with catechisms. Ministers no longer devoted themselves to the task of catechetical preaching as they once had, and parents began to neglect teaching the catechism at home. During the age of George Frederick Handel, the Scottish Psalter seemed terribly old-fashioned in more cultivated circles. For the common people, the hymns of the Methodists were much more attractive. The Scots were not yet ready to give up their psalms but they were ready to try some new tunes and Andrew Thomson apparently provided some music for this purpose. For us, Thomson's most important liturgical reform was the recovery of classical Reformed expository preaching. As we find it in the memoir which precedes a posthumous volume of his sacramental sermons, he was one of the chief causes of "the revival of taste for the faithful preaching of the Gospel." It was a good number of years ago after discovering a volume of Thomson's *Sacramental Exhortations* in the stacks of Speer Library that I began to realize the importance of these collections of sacramental sermons for the eucharistic piety of the Reformed churches.

Andrew Thomson was a son of the manse. Eventually his father,

---

[116] For biographical material on Thomson, see: William Garden Blaikie, *The Preachers of Scotland* (Edinburgh: T. & T. Clark, 1888), pp. 272–276; David C. Lachman, "Andrew Mitchell Thomson," in *Dictionary of Scottish Church History and Theology*, ed. Nigel M. de S. Cameron (Edinburgh: T. & T. Clark, 1993), pp. 819–820; and the memoir introducing the volume Andrew Thomson, *Sermons and Sacramental Exhortations by the Late Andrew Thomson, D. D., Minister of St. George's Church Edinburgh* (Edinburgh: Printed for William Whyte & Co., William Collins and M. Ogle, Glasgow; J. Dewar, Perth; and Longman, & Co., London, 1831). Hereinafter referred to as Thomson, *Sacramental Exhortations*.

Dr. John Thomson, had become one of the most respected of Edinburgh's pastors, but when young Andrew was born his father had just begun his ministry in the village of Sanquhar in Dumfriesshire. By the time young Andrew was ready for the university his father had been called to a church in Edinburgh. Naturally he did his theological studies in Edinburgh as his father had before him. In 1802 he was licensed by the Presbytery of Kelso and a few months later ordained to the Church of Sprouston. Eventually he was called to be the first pastor of St. George's Church in Edinburgh. St. George's had just been built on the park at the end of George Street, in a newly built and rather stately quarter of Edinburgh. Even today it is an area of the city marked by its handsome Regency buildings. When Andrew Thomson was pastor of St. George's Church, it was the very fashionable big new church in "the new town," that is, the newest, most fashionable section of town. He served a congregation of the city's most progressive and enlightened citizens.

It was not until Thomson was established at St. George's that he began to make considerable departures from Moderatism. His departures were in two directions. He had a sincere love for the doctrinal and liturgical traditions of classical Protestantism, and at the same time he had a number of passionate social concerns. This was typical of the younger "evangelicals" of the day such as John Newton and William Wilberforce. Thomson stood very strongly for the abolition of slavery in the British colonies. The issue at the time was the use of slave labor in Jamaica and the West Indies. The plantation owners had argued that they could not make these tropical islands productive without the use of slave labor and that therefore they should be granted an exception to the usual laws, or at the least, as the discussion of the subject went in those days, they ought to be given a delay in the enforcement of abolition in order to make the necessary adjustments to ensure continuous production in the islands. The large sugar plantations of the West Indies were extremely profitable at the time and the use of slave labor in the colonies was hotly debated. Andrew Thomson was one who demanded the immediate abolition of slavery. To say the least, he was hardly the delight of Edinburgh's Tories.

Andrew Thomson's revival of expository preaching is of particular interest because it recovered a number of significant features of systematic preaching which had eroded over the years. He preached the *lectio continua* more rapidly than had become the practice in earlier generations. Under the Puritans, one rarely got through more than a verse or two per sermon, and except for shorter books such as the General Epistles, ministers tended more and more to preach through chapters rather than whole books. This made the *lectio continua* move very slowly, and, as we have had occasion to remark elsewhere, only too often led to the ultimate abandonment of the practice. Thomson reversed this process and began to go through the various books of the Bible at six to twelve verses per sermon. In 1816 two volumes of his sermons were published, *Lectures, Expository and Practical, on Select Portions of Scripture*.[117] The two volumes contain only twenty-five sermons and are obviously intended to give a sampling of Thomson's preaching.[118] What appears to be the case is that the sermons came from a *lectio continua* series on the Gospel of Luke, another on the Acts of the Apostles, and a third on the Sermon on the Mount. Thomson was a pastor who had a concern for the restoration of the most historic forms of Christian worship. The reforms he made in the pulpit help us put in context the reforms he led in the observance of communion.

---

[117] Andrew Thomson, *Lectures, Expository and Practical, on Select Portions of Scripture*, 2 vols. (Edinburgh: Printed for William Blackwood, Edinburgh; and T. Cadell and W. Davies, London, 1816). Hereinafter referred to as Thomson, *Lectures*.

[118] There is no introduction to this collection of sermons and no indication why these particular sermons were chosen, or why they were arranged as they are. No dates are given to indicate when the sermons were preached. While the six sermons in Acts are in order, as are the eight sermons on Luke chapters seven, thirteen, and fourteen, the six sermons on Matthew's version of the Sermon on the Mount are scattered throughout the two volumes. I can find no explanation for this arrangement.

14: THE ERSKINE BROTHERS AND THE COVENANTER TRADITION (1680-1754)

As we have seen several times now, by long tradition in the Church of Scotland the preaching which accompanied the celebration of the Lord's Supper had a particularly evangelistic function. This tradition had hardly been erased during the ascendancy of Moderatism. It was at communion that young people first made the covenant vows. Having learned the catechism they were admitted to the Lord's Table. They professed their faith implicitly in receiving the bread and wine of communion. For older members of the congregation each new celebration of the sacrament was an occasion for the renewing of the same covenant vows, the same confession of faith. Covenantal theology was fundamental to the celebration of the Supper. It was appropriate, therefore, that the preaching which preceded the giving of the bread and wine call the people to faith.

Several of Andrew Thomson's communion sermons have been preserved in a posthumous volume, *Sermons and Sacramental Exhortations by the Late Andrew Thomson, D. D., Minister of St. George's Church Edinburgh*. The second sermon in the collection is a particularly fine example of a Scottish communion sermon. The sermon is given the title, "Human and Divine Love Contrasted." The text is Romans 5:7–8, "For scarcely for a righteous man will one die; yet peradventure for a good man some would even dare to die. But God commendeth his love toward us, in that, while we were yet sinners, Christ died for us."[119] The sermon is an exposition of this text in the formal sense of expository preaching, and yet it is a textual and thematic sermon in that the text is apparently chosen for its suitability to the occasion.[120] It is one of those classic texts which sums up the heart of the Christian message and is, therefore, from the Scottish point of view, at least, particularly appropriate for the celebration of communion.

---

[119] As quoted in Thomson, *Sacramental Exhortations*, p. 32.

[120] A prominent Edinburgh preacher would often have been asked to preach at a communion season in a country church. A communion season would often feature three or four guest preachers, so a prominent preacher would doubtless have several "communion sermons" in his barrel.

The sermon begins with a short introduction setting forth the theme of the sermon. "God's love to men, in its various relations, and in its various expressions, is the great and prevalent theme of the gospel. The gospel, indeed, is altogether a manifestation of that love, . . . It is not only asserted that God loves us, but one principal object of whatever the sacred writers have been prompted to say, appears to be that of magnifying the divine attribute, ..."[121] It is about that divine attribute, the love of God, that Thomson preached.[122]

This is the very heart of the gospel, and Thomson preached it to inspire faith in the hearts of his people. Thomson goes on to introduce his subject by making the point that there are all kinds of figures and analogies given in Scripture for God's love but as we study them we find that God's love surpasses any attempt to express it by analogy. It is this which is made so clear by our text. The love of God is without parallel.[123]

The sermon is divided into two parts. First our preacher sets out to speak of the love of God toward our fellow creatures.[124] He tells us that the instances of human beings sacrificing their lives for another are rare. The Apostle grants that there might well be some, but he does not seem to have any in mind. This is clear from the indefinite words we find in the text, "*Scarcely* for a righteous man will one die; yet *peradventure* . . ." (The italics are Thomson's.) Even if one finds examples occasionally, one must allow that there is in these acts a frequent mixture of desire for glory or other forms of self-interest. To develop his point Thomson suggests a series of hypothetical situations which might inspire one to sacrifice one's life for another. Even with these appealing and appropriate possibilities one cannot be sure that even the most highly motivated and altruistic of people would be willing to sacrifice their lives. Even when a

---

[121] Thomson, *Sacramental Exhortations*, p. 32.

[122] We will notice very similar sentiments in several of the communion sermons J. W. Alexander preached a few years later in New York. See chapter 19, pp. 718f.

[123] Thomson, *Sacramental Exhortations*, p. 33.

[124] Thomson, *Sacramental Exhortations*, p. 34.

very strong bond of friendship or family is involved, the giving of one's life for another is seldom to be observed. Even Jesus himself made this point, "Greater love hath no man than this, that a man lay down his life for his friends."[125] As Thomson puts it, "This is the utmost limit to which human affection can go."[126]

Our preacher makes a magnificent transition. "Now, in all the examples to which we have referred, the sacrifice is made in consideration of motives that arise from worth exhibited, or benefits conferred, or obligations of some kind or other imposed, by them on whose account it has been demanded."[127] One might well imagine that one could give one's life for a good man, or for a man from whom one had received much good, but could one give one's life for one who had been unfriendly and ungrateful? Could one die for someone who had been "iniquitous, malevolent, and hostile; . . . guilty of atrocious crimes committed against the comfort, the reputation, the honour, of one who had lavished upon him every token of kind regard, who had treated him with the confidence of a friend, with the affection of a brother, with the tenderness of a parent . . ."?[128]

The tragic tone of Thomson's language is gripping. Even reading it today we are mesmerized. ". . . And supposing that for all his demerit, he had been condemned to die, and under his sentence of condemnation, cherished as bitter an enmity, and expressed as determined a vengeance, against his benefactor as he had ever done before—would that benefactor, or would any of the children of men, consent to occupy his room, and suffer his judicial fate, in order to send him back again to the life, and the liberty, and the enjoyment, which he had so justly forfeited?"[129] This long rhetorical question

---

[125] John 15:13, as quoted in Thomson, *Sacramental Exhortations*, p. 39.

[126] Thomson, *Sacramental Exhortations*, p. 39.

[127] Thomson, *Sacramental Exhortations*, p. 40.

[128] Thomson, *Sacramental Exhortations*, p. 40.

[129] Thomson, *Sacramental Exhortations*, p. 41.

finally demands its answer, "Ah! no: that is a height of love, which humanity has never reached, and of which humanity is utterly incapable. Philosophy may conjecture it as possible, and poetry may give it a place in her fictitious delineations. But we observe not the seeds or elements of it in the moral constitution of man."[130]

This brings Thomson to his second point. "But that which man in all his love to his brethren has never felt, or offered, or accomplished, has been realized and manifested in the love which he has experienced from the holy God. 'God commendeth his love toward us, in that, while we were yet sinners, Christ died for us.'"[131] This second point is developed in two respects. First, Christ died for us, and second, he died for us while we were yet sinners.

In developing the idea that it was Christ who died for us, Thomson wants to make it clear that the death of Christ demonstrated the love of God. Christ's death demonstrates God's love because Christ is God. With this our preacher brings out a whole series of passages from Scripture to support his point. Our preacher then takes up the doctrine of the Trinity and holds forth on that subject at length to show that Christ's sacrifice of himself was an expression of the love of the Father as much as the love of the Son. This is characteristic of Scottish preaching, which never flinches at either long deliberations on the precise meaning of the text nor on involved discussions of fine points of theology.

The sermon comes to its climax with a marvelous passage:

> But there are resources in the eternal mind, which are equally beyond our reach and our comprehension. There is a power, and a magnitude, and a richness in the love of God towards those upon whom it is set, to which the love of the creature cannot even approximate, of which the imagination of the creature could not have formed any previous idea, and which, even to the experience of the creature, presents a subject of inscrutable

---

[130] Thomson, *Sacramental Exhortations*, pp. 40–41.

[131] Thomson, *Sacramental Exhortations*, pp. 41–42.

mystery—a theme of wondering gratitude and praise.[132]

Human love, on the other hand, is something quite different.

> Man may love, man should love, man must love his fellows; but he never did, and never can love them like God. His is a love that throws man's into the distance and the shade. Had he only loved us as man loves, there would have been no salvation—no heaven—no felicity for us—no glad tidings to cheer our hearts;—no promised land on which to fix our anticipations—no table of commemoration and of communion spread for us in the wilderness, to refresh us amidst the toils, and the languishings, and the sorrows of our pilgrimage thither.[133]

For Thomson the mystery of God's love is beyond human understanding.

> But behold! God is love itself; and his love, in all its workings, and in all its influences, and in all its effects, can stoop to no parallel with the best and most ardent of human affections. Guilt, which forbids and represses man's love, awakens, and kindles, and secures God's. Death for the guilty is too wide a gulf for man's love to pass over. God's love to the guilty is infinitely "stronger than death," and spurns at all such limits, and smiles at the agonies and the ignominies of a cross, that it may have its perfect work.[134]

As Thomson presents the love of God, it is surprising—incredibly surprising. Certainly it is beyond the limits of reason alone. It is beyond anything eighteenth-century rationalism would allow. "God, in the exercise of his love towards our sinful and miserable race, is concerned, where man would be unmoved, indifferent, and cold. God is full of pity, where man would frown with stern

---

[132] Thomson, *Sacramental Exhortations*, p. 44.

[133] Thomson, *Sacramental Exhortations*, p. 44.

[134] Thomson, *Sacramental Exhortations*, p. 45.

and relentless aversion. God forgives, where man would condemn and punish. God saves, where man would destroy. 'While we were yet sinners, Christ died for us.'"[135] Having made his essential point, Thomson relates the sermon to the celebration of communion which follows. Such a great love of God should be remembered, celebrated, and proclaimed at every possible opportunity. Such love obligates us to devote ourselves to God's service. It demands that we pledge our allegiance to Christ and that we follow his example in all our ways, that we forsake the ways of this world. It is this, Thomson tells his congregation, which we are to do at this sacred table. "In the good providence of God, that opportunity is now before us. . . . Let us sit down at a communion table with hearts overflowing with love to Him who first loved us, and who loved us in the midst of our unworthiness, and who loved us even to the death. Let us exercise a vigorous and a lively faith in the merit of that great atonement, . . ."[136] What we need to notice here is the centrality of this hymnic expression of the saving love of Christ. It sets the whole tone of the communion celebration.

It is with love, with faith, and with hope that we approach the Lord's Table. Hope for the future is just as important as remembering the past. "And having experienced the love of God in giving Christ to the death for us, let us rest upon the promise, that this divine Saviour will come again—that he, whom we commemorate as having once suffered for our transgressions, will appear hereafter, and ere long, to give us complete and eternal redemption, and that, having rescued us from the dishonours of the grave, and clothed us with the robe of immortality, and introduced us into the incorruptible inheritance of his Father's kingdom, . . ." Christ will receive us in his heavenly glory.[137] In the end God will transform us into the image of his Son, ". . . and will tune our hearts

---

[135] Thomson, *Sacramental Exhortations*, pp. 47–48.

[136] Thomson, *Sacramental Exhortations*, p. 47–48.

[137] Thomson, *Sacramental Exhortations*, pp. 51–52.

for pouring forth the rapturous strains of that high anthem, 'Unto him that loved us, and washed us from sins in his own blood, and hath made us kings and priests unto God even his Father; to him be glory and dominion for ever and ever. Amen.'"[138]

Here we see something of the greatest possible importance. We see evangelistic preaching which is integrally related to the sacrament of the Lord's Supper. The call to faith is an invitation to the Lord's Table. Perhaps it is appropriate here to explain that it was in reading this volume of communion sermons by Andrew Thomson that I first began to realize that the key to understanding the sacramental piety of the Reformed faith is the communion season.

What we find in the eighteenth-century Scottish communion season is an increasingly profound sense of God's presence. We find the same thing in the prayer life of David Brainerd. It is not in communion alone that we experience the divine presence, as we are assured in the conclusion of the Gospel of Matthew. The baptized are assured, "Lo, I am with you always." In the same way we are assured that whenever two or three of us are gathered in the name of Jesus and offer up our prayers in his name, he is present among us. He hears our prayers and graciously grants our request. So it is whenever the church proclaims the gospel. We are aware of the kerygmatic presence of our Savior. Whenever the church teaches all that Jesus has commanded, he is indeed with us. Here one might speak of the catechetical presence. As the mystics all the way through the history of the church have continually taught, the presence of the Savior is manifold.

---

[138] Thomson, *Sacramental Exhortations*, pp. 51–52.

15

DUTCH PIETISM

The place of Holy Communion in the worship of Dutch pietism is legendary.[1] This was especially the case in the late seventeenth century and on into the beginning of the eighteenth century. Two documents available in English give us a good picture of this eucharistic piety. First we will want to look at Wilhelm à Brakel's *The Christian's Reasonable Service*.[2] Following that we will look at Peter Immens' *The Pious Communicant*.[3] We will conclude the chapter with a brief look at the ministry of Theodorus Jacobus Frelinghuysen, who brought the teaching of Dutch pietism to America, where it became one of the sources of the Great Awakening.[4]

Recently there has been a revival of interest in Dutch pietism. It has become increasingly clear that what the Dutch have always

---

[1] For more information on Dutch pietism, see: F. Ernest Stoeffler, *Continental Pietism and Early American Christianity* (Grand Rapids, MI: Eerdmans, 1976); James R. Tanis, *Dutch Calvinistic Pietism in the Middle Colonies: A Study in the Life and Theology of Theodorus Jacobus Frelinghuysen* (The Hague: Martinus Nijhoff, 1967); Arie de Reuver, *Sweet Communion: Trajectories of Spirituality from the Middle Ages through the Further Reformation*, trans. James A. DeJong (Grand Rapids, MI: Baker Academic, 2007); and Bartel Elshout, *Pastoral and Practical Theology of Wilhelm à Brakel* (Grand Rapids, MI: Reformation Heritage Books, 1997).

[2] Wilhelmus à Brakel, *The Christian's Reasonable Service*, trans. Bartel Elshout, 4 vols. (Grand Rapids, MI: Reformation Heritage Books, 1992).

[3] Peter Immens, *The Pious Communicant Encouraged, and Directed in What Manner He May Approach the Holy Supper of the Lord, Acceptably to God and Profitably to Himself, in a Series of Lectures*, trans. John Bassett (New York: Isaac Collins and Son, 1801). Hereinafter, Immens, *The Pious Communicant*.

[4] Theodorus Jacobus Frelinghuysen, *Forerunner of the Great Awakening: Sermons of Theodorus Jacobus Frelinghuysen (1691–1747)*, ed. Joel Beeke, The Historical Series of the Reformed Church in America, no. 36 (Grand Rapids, MI: Eerdmans, 2000).

called the *Nadere Reformatie* was part of a widespread awakening of Christian piety.[5] There was Catholic pietism, particularly represented by Jansenism in France. Then in Germany there was the pietism of Spener and Francke, and, of special interest to us, there was the pietism of the American Great Awakening. It took different forms in Protestantism and in Catholicism, but the similarities are obvious.

There is considerable difference in opinion as to how to translate *Nadere Reformatie*. Some call it simply the Second Reformation, while others call it the Latter-Day Reform or the Deeper Reform. One thing is clear: This *Nadere Reformatie* was significantly spread by both Englishmen and Scots. A large amount of Dutch pietism went back to the English Puritans and the Scottish Covenanters. According to Joel Beeke, at one point in the seventeenth century tens of thousands of refugee Puritans had taken up residence in the Netherlands. They were served by over three hundred and fifty ministers. With the approval of the Dutch government a special English speaking classis was organized.[6] The number of English theological books translated into Dutch was amazing. In the first twenty years of the seventeenth century, one hundred and fourteen editions of English theological works were produced in the Netherlands, and one English theologian who was especially popular was William Perkins.[7]

While it would be left to the Scots to develop the Reformed communion season to its most elaborate form, Dutch Calvinism had shown a very definite tendency to move in that same direction.

---

[5] For further information on the *Nadere Reformatie*, see Joel R. Beeke, "The Dutch Second Reformation," in à Brakel, *The Christian's Reasonable Service*, 1: lxxxv-cxi.

[6] See Joel R. Beeke, *The Quest for Full Assurance: The Legacy of Calvin and His Successors* (Edinburgh and Carlisle, PA: Banner of Truth Trust, 1999), p. 289.

[7] Beeke, *Quest for Full Assurance*, p. 290.

WILHELM À BRAKEL

The son of a Dutch Reformed pastor, Wilhelm à Brakel (1635–1711) was born in Leeuwarden in the year 1635.[8] Greatly beloved as one of the founders of Dutch pietism, à Brakel was by birth Frisian, although he served in Rotterdam for twenty-eight years. It was in Rotterdam that he died in 1711. His ministry there was almost patriarchal. In the Netherlands, even today, he is referred to as Father à Brakel.

À Brakel's theological education began at Franeker in the northernmost part of the Netherlands. It was completed in Utrecht under the famous orthodox Calvinist theologian, Gisbertus Voetius. Starting out his pastorate at the early age of twenty-four he served several village churches in Friesland until he was finally called to Rotterdam. There he moved in the world of Witsius, Coccius, and van Lodenstein. For a period à Brakel came under the influence of the French Jansenist Jean de Labadie. Labadie had passed through several theological persuasions from Jesuit to Calvinist. He influenced many of the early pietists, the German pietist Philipp Spener being the most noteworthy example.

The great theological tome of Father à Brakel is usually regarded as a classic of spiritual theology. That is, it treats systematically the devotional life. Its title, *A Christian's Reasonable Service*, is an obvious play on Romans 12:1 (KJV), "I beseech you therefore, brethren, by the mercies of God, that ye present your bodies a living sacrifice, holy, acceptable unto God, which is your reasonable service." This four volume work sums up Dutch pietism as it was practiced in that golden age of the Dutch Republic depicted so magnificently by Frans Hals, Rembrandt, and Vermeer. This

---

[8] For biographical information, see the extensive introduction by W. Fieret in à Brakel, *A Christian's Reasonable Service*, 1: xxxi-lxxxi. Appreciation is given to Rev. Kevin Cauley, one of my students at Erskine Theological Seminary, for calling my attention to Father à Brakel. It is his paper which is the basis of this study.

work was the devotional guide of the *Nadere Reformatie*.⁹ Originally published in the year 1700 it went through twenty editions in the eighteenth century alone.

Dutch pietism had deep roots in late medieval mysticism, in the literate piety of the *Devotio moderna*, and in the ministry of the Brethren of the Common Life. Thomas à Kempis and John Tauler had had their influence. Erasmus himself had come out of a strong Dutch pietist background. Dutch pietism is a major school of Christian spirituality.

Of particular interest is à Brakel's understanding of the pastoral office. As à Brakel sees it, the first responsibility of the Reformed pastor is to lead the congregation in prayer. Preaching comes second, followed by catechizing and pastoral visitation. Important to this pastoral visitation is the encouragement of family prayer and preparation to receive communion. One notices here a similarity to the writings of William Perkins, but especially to the classic of Richard Baxter, *The Reformed Pastor*. Pietism in effect demanded a pastoral revolution. Closely related to this was à Brakel's insistence on the independence of the church. He would have nothing to do with Erastianism. No interference in the calling of ministers on the part of the state was to be allowed. The Classis of Rotterdam and the City Council of Rotterdam locked horns on this several times.

Eucharistic devotion is a central concern in the piety of Father à Brakel.[10] Very briefly, however, we might note the following points. À Brakel saw the sacrament as a visible sign and seal of the covenant of grace which was instituted by God to display Christ's suffering and death to believers and to assure them that they are partakers of Christ and all his merits. This is fairly standard Reformed sacramental theology. What interests us about this experiential theologian is not his theology of the sacrament so much as the devotional preparations he recommends for Chris-

---

⁹ On Dutch pietism in general, see de Reuver, *Sweet Communion*.

[10] This discussion is taken from à Brakel, *The Christian's Reasonable Service*.

15: Dutch Pietism

tians to make before receiving the sacrament.

First of all we notice that Father à Brakel recommends spending a day in prayer and fasting before receiving the sacrament. This day of prayer and fasting should be regarded as a day of preparation. It should be a day devoted to clothing oneself in festal wedding garments as Jesus himself teaches us in his parable (cf. Matthew 22:1–14). This, to be sure, is understood metaphorically. One would dress very simply in actual fact. This special day should be a day set aside for gathering God's people around their Father's table. It should be a day of invitation and a day of evangelism. Pietism saw great value in what might be called spiritual stimulation, that is, in cultivating the religious emotions. We should turn our thoughts to appreciating the beauty of the Lord's house and the joy of Christian fellowship.

À Brakel gives us six suggestions for preparing ourselves to receive the sacrament. These are means for devotionally adorning ourselves. First he suggests meditating on the history of redemption. Second we should put ourselves in a spiritual frame of mind by prayer. Third, we should renew our covenant with God by surrendering ourselves to God's will. Fourth, we should resolve to live a more holy life. Fifth, we should concentrate on developing a high esteem of the Church. Finally we should increase our love for God's people. This would particularly include removing any specific barriers to harmony in the congregation.

When it comes to the actual celebration of the sacrament on the Lord's Day, the communicant should take care to meditate on devout themes while walking to church. Arriving in time to be properly composed in one's seat well before the sermon is important. The actual service proceeds slowly so that there is time to meditate. This is especially the case when sitting down at the table. The participant should meditate on the meaning of the broken bread and the poured out wine and the fact that it is offered to us for our nourishment. For Rhenish spirituality, both before the Reformation and after, the meditation of the communicant is essential to the service.

Finally, à Brakel comes to speak of reflection. Perhaps the most significant thing here is what he has to say about those occasional experiences when we become aware that God is very near, when we realize that heaven is open to us and that in truth we are seated at the wedding feast of the Lamb. This is the full experience of communion. Here we find what Ralph Erskine later called the "Bethel Experience." God is truly with us and we recognize that he is indeed present. In this we experience what is really true even if we do not always recognize it. It is thereby that we are assured that we are members of the household of faith, the elect of God. More and more we will find that what Reformed piety has come to understand by the "spiritual" presence is a sort of mystical presence. Communion is, in the end, union with Christ. It is communion with God himself in the person of his Son.

Short and to the point, this is what the saintly spiritual master of Rotterdam had to say, but in actuality, he wrote this out in the most long and involved form. Brevity was not one of à Brakel's virtues. Yet, his works are still read and published today, three hundred years later.

PETER IMMENS

Peter Immens (1664–1720) was born in Oirschot, the son of a Reformed pastor.[11] He was one of four boys in the family who became Reformed pastors. His father, Robert Immens, was also a Reformed pastor of strong pietist leanings. The story goes that the discipline of the household was so strict that children were not allowed to speak unless they were spoken to.

---

[11] For biographical information on Immens, see the article by H. Florijn, "Immens, Petrus," in *Biografisch Lexicon voor de Geschiedenis van het Gereformeerd Protestantisme*, vol. 5, ed. C. Houtman e.a. (Kampen: Kok, 2001), pp. 275–276. Appreciation is given to Prof. Arnold Huijgen of the Theological University of Apeldoorn, The Netherlands, for providing me with this article. Appreciation is also expressed to Agnes Taylor for translating the article from Dutch to English.

Immens pursued his studies at the University of Utrecht, the theological faculty where Reformed orthodoxy was taught with the greatest vigor. After his studies he was called to an assistantship in the town of his birth, Oirschot. In the usual way he filled several other positions until, in 1698, he was appointed director of the Latin school and pastor of the church in Middelburg, in the far southwest of The Netherlands on the shores of the English Channel.[12]

Peter Immens is particularly well known as one who gave special attention to eucharistic piety. Coming toward the end of the movement he summed up the ideas of many who had gone before him, his father particularly. His book, *The Pious Communicant*, is a collection of eighteen lectures designed to help congregants prepare to take part in the sacrament of communion.[13] While we cannot study this work with the thoroughness it deserves, we do want to make several observations about the devotional disciplines taught by this famous guide.

A. A Day of Preparation

First of all, we notice that Immens strongly advocates setting aside a day of prayer and fasting.[14] We have already called attention to this in regard to Wilhelm à Brakel. He does not, however, make this a requirement, but we get the impression that on Monday, prior to a communion Sabbath, Immens' church in Zeeland held a special preparatory service as we find it in Scotland a generation or two later. He recognizes not everyone has the leisure to spend a whole day in prayer and meditation. Perhaps there are some of his readers,

---

[12] Among the works of Immens which have been translated into English is Peter Immens, *True and False Assurance* (Grand Rapids, MI: Free Reformed Church, 19–).

[13] The original Dutch volume had many editions, among them Petrus Immens, *De godvruchtige avondmaalganger* (Groningen: R. Boerma, 1900). We will be studying from the English translation. See Immens, *The Pious Communicant*. It has come to our attention that the English translation was released in ebook form by Forgotten Books in 2012.

[14] Immens, *The Pious Communicant*, pp. 130f.

however, who had the opportunity to devote themselves to this kind of spiritual discipline. For those who can devote themselves to such spiritual labors a bountiful spiritual harvest is to be awaited.

Immens's typology is particularly interesting. Immens reminds us of the parable of the wedding feast so frequently alluded to in the Reformed communion celebrations (cf. Matthew 22:1–14). The Christian, like those invited to the wedding feast in the parable of Jesus, should dress himself in the most suitable festal robes. The most suitable robe of all is self-examination. This should be followed by purifying oneself from every spot or wrinkle. To be sure this was all thought out quite moralistically, but that was the nature of pietism.

When we consider that we are about to approach this most intimate communion with God what could be more appropriate than to confess our backslidings and offenses?[15] The whole purpose of observing this holy ordinance is to meet the Eternal, "for in the sacrament of the Supper, God appears as the God of the covenant, who will hold the most intimate fellowship with his people."[16] We notice this phrase "intimate fellowship." This is the key to the whole thing. When we consider that Christ himself, the host of this feast, is present, we realize that our true spiritual state is known to him. He searches our hearts whether they are arrayed with the true wedding garment. Surely the realization that Jesus is present should excite us to the most scrupulous adornment. Long before Jesus told this parable, however, the book of Job exhorted the devout to prepare their hearts by stretching out their hands to him and devoting themselves to prayer (Job 11:13). The prayer of Job was a type of penitential preparation. Even more specifically, the Apostle Paul tells us, "Examine yourselves, whether ye be in the faith; prove your own selves" (2 Cor. 13:5, KJV). It is for this reason that the Apostle teaches us, "Let a man examine himself, and so let him eat of that bread, and drink of that cup" (1 Cor. 11:28, KJV). It would appear

---

[15] Immens, *The Pious Communicant*, p. 131.

[16] Immens, *The Pious Communicant*, p. 131.

15: Dutch Pietism

that it was precisely because the Dutch pietists had such a strong sense of Christ's presence at the Supper that they began to develop such a disciplined approach to preparation for the celebration.

As this lecture goes on, the subject is addressed more specifically as to how we should set aside a particular day for penitential preparation, that is, for prayer and fasting. Immens outlines how such a day might go.[17] It should begin with family prayers. This is, to be sure, social prayer, but this social prayer should be followed by closet prayer. That is, each person should retire to his or her prayer closet and spend time reading and meditating on Scripture. There is even mention of singing psalms, hymns, and spiritual songs. What is of particular interest here is what Immens says about renewing our covenant with God. This is apparently what makes a day of prayer and fasting before a sacramental occasion unique. It is above all a time for going over the covenant each Christian has made with God. The believer is to give himself over to God, to claim God as God, one's own personal God, and to promise to live as a child of God. Each believer renews the promise of faithful discipleship made when joining the church and claims Christ as Lord and Savior. This covenant renewal is the primary subject of our prayer on such a day. It is a solemn surrender of the soul to him who brought it into existence.[18]

It should be noted that Dutch pietism, like English Puritanism, produced many devotional guides for those who would rightly observe Holy Communion. Immens called the attention of his readers to this abundance and recommended that they supply themselves with a few such books and read them again and again.[19]

When we come to the Lord's Table it is in wonderment that we are not only invited to enter into covenant with God, but that God himself puts into our hands the signs and seals, and, with

---

[17] Immens, *The Pious Communicant*, pp. 141f.

[18] Immens, *The Pious Communicant*, p. 146.

[19] Immens, *The Pious Communicant*, p. 147.

an oath, swears to be our God.[20] As Peter Immens understood it, Holy Communion is a very deep personal experience. In this sacrament, "God may perhaps meet with you . . . and speak peace to your souls."[21] When this happens it results in a transforming joy. We simply know that God has spoken to us. It can also be that our prayers and meditations are cold and lifeless and bring us neither a sense of reality or vitality. God is still there, Immens assures us, and he is faithful to us nevertheless.[22] The value of the sacrament does not depend on our feelings but rather on God's promise. God fulfills his promises to us. He is honored when we remember these promises and hunger and thirst for their fulfillment. By carefully preparing for the celebration of Holy Communion we make it very clear that the chief desire of our souls is to have fellowship with God, and it is to this end that we approach the holy Table.

B. The Invitation

The second feature of the Reformed communion service Immens developed is the Invitation. Somewhat perversely, it is often called "fencing the Table." Some liturgiologists call it the Dismissals. This term is most appropriate for the classical liturgies of the fourth and fifth centuries when it was the practice to ask those who had not yet been baptized to leave the church before the communion service began. The catechumen were asked to leave but the faithful were asked to remain and to approach the holy Table. As time went on fewer and fewer unbaptized people were in the congregation and the problem became getting the faithful to gather around the Table and receive the bread and wine. As the sacrament was more and more turned into a ceremonial spectacle the congregation came to watch the liturgy rather than share the sacred meal.

This was the situation the Reformers faced at the beginning of

---

[20] Immens, *The Pious Communicant*, p. 151.

[21] Immens, *The Pious Communicant*, p. 152.

[22] Immens, *The Pious Communicant*, p. 154.

15: Dutch Pietism

the sixteenth century. What we find in the *Genevan Psalter* of 1542 is that the minister made a special point of inviting the congregation to approach the Lord's Table and receive the bread and wine. This took the form of a pastoral admonition based on the Words of Institution as they are found either in the Gospels or in 1 Corinthians 11. This pastoral admonition, however, not only invites the congregation to approach the Table, it also warns those who have not received the faith as well as those who have rejected the Christian way of life not to approach the sacrament. It is quite clear from Immens' Lecture XIII that by the middle of the seventeenth century in The Netherlands, the Invitation had become a set liturgical text that the minister was expected to read from the book.[23]

The Form of Administration, as Immens calls it, is a highly regarded liturgical text, and he goes into considerable detail on what the pious communicant is supposed to learn from it.[24] He is supposed to be reminded of the biblical warrant of the sacrament. It is Christ himself who commanded us to observe this sacrament. Furthermore we are to observe it so that we might "experience the virtue of Jesus' blood which cleanseth from all sin."[25] This phrase, "experience the virtue of Jesus' blood," is a very precise theological expression. It not only makes clear the nature of Christ's presence, but also it makes clear that the Christ who is present is the Lamb of God who takes away the sin of the world. Christ is present as Savior!

It is, to be sure, in this Form of Administration that we find the infamous fencing of the table, that is, the warning against unworthy participation. The minister at this point is supposed to warn all those who harbor sin in their lives to refrain from participation until such a time as they repent. On the other hand, the pious communicant is supposed to be assured that if we confess our sins

---

[23] Immens, *The Pious Communicant*, p. 183.

[24] The text of the Form of Administration is contained in the appendix of Immens, *The Pious Communicant*, pp. 241–248.

[25] Immens, *The Pious Communicant*, p. 185.

and repent from our sinful ways there is abundant pardon in the cross of Christ. All who repent of their sins are therefore invited to take their place at the Lord's Table. This is the Invitation.[26]

Immens sees the Invitation as an invitation to accept Christ. That is, he sees it in evangelistic terms. This is particularly clear from the typology he uses. As we find it in Proverbs 9:1-6, the minister is the maidservant of the Lady Sophia, that is, Holy Wisdom, sent out to invite the simple to a great feast. Wisdom has prepared her festal board with meats and choice wines and has now sent out her ladies in waiting, that is, the ministers of the Gospel, to announce that all is ready. So it was when Jesus told his parable of the wedding feast (Matt. 22:1-14). The preachers were to go out to the highways and hedgerows to invite all kinds of people to enter into the kingdom and receive the Gospel. So it was in more than one of the parables of Jesus. The people must prepare for the feast and put on their festal garments. We cannot be sure when the Bridegroom will come, but then the messenger comes, warning us to get ready, and this the wise virgins do. The wise virgins are those who are prepared for communion with Christ. The faithful pastor is the one who sees to it that all is in readiness. All is in readiness and those chosen of God enter into the wedding feast of the Lamb and take their place at the Table.

C. Communion Meditation

A third feature of the Reformed communion service which we find Immens developing is what is usually called the communion meditation—a relatively short, informal inspirational message delivered by the minister presiding at the communion service. In the seventeenth and eighteenth centuries the main sermon delivered at the communion service was called the action sermon.[27] The

---

[26] Immens, *The Pious Communicant*, p. 190. See also, pp. 202, 204, and 205.

[27] As yet I have not found an explanation of this term. In Scotland, at least, its use seems fairly general.

15: Dutch Pietism

action sermon preaches the heart of the gospel to the Christian congregation. It was preached toward the beginning of the service. The communion meditation, on the other hand, was preached primarily to a small group gathered around the Table immediately before sharing the bread and the wine, and a discrete communion meditation was given for however many communion tables the size of the congregation necessitated.

The communion meditation as Immens understood it would not be necessary for a mature congregation. It ought to be sufficient for the more mature congregation to meditate on the words of Christ when he instituted the sacrament. The pietists, however, whether they were in The Netherlands or the Highlands, put considerable emphasis on meditation. Obviously Immens was afraid most communicants would not be able to come up with suitable meditations to occupy their minds while sitting at the table, so he felt an obligation to provide a suitable communion meditation. This, of course, for a larger congregation would lengthen the service considerably. Immens' thought on this subject is, however, easily understood.

For most congregations, there is a real need to encourage devotion. Ministers need to encourage their congregations by observations designed to excite faith. This is pietism at its most obvious. "They must address the weeping Marys who see not Jesus, though he be present with them at the table, saying, Why weep ye? Whom seek ye?"[28]

We notice two things here. First we see that the great importance given to the subjective experience of participating in the sacrament was becoming much more important than the objective observance of the rite. It is not the sign of the broken bread and the poured out wine or the sign of sharing a meal, but rather the word of the preacher which is operative. Here we see the pietist concern to stimulate the religious emotions busily at work.

For Immens the Supper is indeed a means of grace, but one

---

[28] Immens, *The Pious Communicant*, p. 190.

gets the impression that the heavy weight is still borne by the Word. "These [words] may, by some animating observations, which God may put in the mouths of his servants, be quickened, and obtain new life and strength: and even those who may be in some measure suitably, actually exercised, may be benefited: it may please the Lord to bless what may be spoken, in such a manner, that their souls may be still more quickened."[29] It is, to be sure, God who through his Holy Spirit puts our souls in the proper frame of mind. God uses our emotions to feed us spiritually.

According to Immens, it is when we are seated at the Lord's Table that it may please God to give us a strong sense of the immediate presence of himself. Perhaps this is the sort of thing the Apostle Paul meant by "being lifted up to the third heaven" (2 Cor. 12:1f.).[30] That is not, however, the way God ordinarily deals with us. Nevertheless, God does give us a foretaste of the heavenly banquet at his Table. This we can objectively count on regularly, but at times God grants this subjectively as well. We feel it in our hearts. It was this personal experience that made Dutch pietism such a strong religious movement.

Pietism, whether in The Netherlands or on the American frontier, or in South Africa for that matter, gave everyday Christians an abiding sense of the presence of God. In the celebration of Holy Communion this sense of the divine presence became more intense. Here one was united to Christ in his death and in his resurrection. One joined with God's people as one sat at the Lord's Table in the household of faith. For Dutch pietism this was a profound experience. This is what becomes so very evident as we read this work of Peter Immens.

---

[29] Immens, *The Pious Communicant*, p. 190.

[30] Immens, *The Pious Communicant*, p. 195.

D. Covenant Renewal

The fourth feature of the Reformed communion service as Immens presents it is that at its center it is an act of covenant renewal. From its very beginning, the Reformed Church has found the biblical doctrine of the covenant most helpful in coming to an understanding of both baptism and the Lord's Supper. Having become disenchanted with the sacramental theology of Scholasticism, the Reformers turned to what they found taught in Scripture about baptism being a sign and a seal of the covenant of grace, the broken bread a promise of God's provision, and the cup of the Lord's Supper being the new covenant in Christ's blood. We have spoken of this at length. But as we have proceeded it has become increasingly evident that the Reformed communion service, at its center, is a service of covenant renewal.[31]

If that is so, then at the very center of the sacrament of Holy Communion is the idea that it is a thanksgiving for God's mighty acts of redemption in Christ, especially for the incarnation, the atonement, the resurrection, and the establishment of his eternal kingdom. It is a thanksgiving that the kingdom has come. In fact, it can simply be called the eucharist, as we find it in 1 Corinthians 10:16. This is basic to the biblical understanding of covenant renewal as we have shown above. Immens makes this very clear:

> Consider also the object of the Lord's Supper. It was instituted to keep in remembrance the death of Christ, and to shew it forth until he come. Now how are we to shew forth the death of Christ?—not only by a pious calling it to our minds, whilst we are at the table, but by a constant, sincere, and faithful acknowledgment of the love which he hath manifested to sinners by a return of love to him on our part, which is evidenced by words and actions in the whole tenour of our walk and conversation.[32]

---

[31] Immens, *The Pious Communicant*, p. 208.

[32] Immens, *The Pious Communicant*, p. 208.

The "return of love" is the thanksgiving. That is, the essence of thanksgiving is a recounting of all God has done to free us from sin and death. When the Christian Church celebrates its eucharist, that is, its sacrament of Holy Communion, it fulfills the feast of Passover as it was decreed by Moses.[33] It not only recounts the history of salvation, it meditates on it. It jubilates over it and becomes part of it.

Immens frequently makes the point that every day in our prayers and meditations we should renew our covenant vows so that we keep fresh our devotion to Christ.[34] Even at that, however, the renewing of our covenant vows at the celebration of Holy Communion is of special solemnity. This is made particularly clear when at communion the whole congregation rises and recites together the Apostles' Creed.[35]

E. Appropriate Thanksgiving

A fifth concern of the Reformed communion service that we find in Immens' lecture is that we render appropriate thanks to God. Covenant renewal ultimately entails thanksgiving. It is this which refreshes us in hope. We have already spoken at some length about this, but we have more to say here, particularly in regard to some of the more objective features of Immens' teaching.

The first thing our Dutch pietist is concerned about seems to be the Sunday evening service following a communion. However, what Immens seems to be ultimately aiming at is a Monday thanksgiving service such as we find in the more highly elaborated Scottish communion seasons. Whether Immens had a Monday thanksgiving service at his own church in Zeeland at the time we hesitate to say, but he was obviously writing for people who were presented with several possibilities. Immens obviously thought it important enough to preach a whole sermon devoted to the obligations of those who

---

[33] Immens, *The Pious Communicant*, p. 209.

[34] Immens, *The Pious Communicant*, p. 216.

[35] Immens, *The Pious Communicant*, pp. 216–217.

15: Dutch Pietism

participate in the sacred meal. He had quite a few words for the "pious communicant," enough for the Sunday evening service, to be sure, and enough for a Monday service as well.

There is another very important subject we need to address, and that is what Peter Immens has to tell us about the traditional Reformed communion psalmody. First he mentions Psalm 103:1–13. This is probably the second most often sung psalm at communion. Psalm 23—which, strangely enough, Immens does not mention at all—is the most often sung. The psalms he does mention, however, are particularly appropriate for the end of the service. First off he mentions Psalm 116:12–13 (KJV):

> What shall I render unto the LORD
>   for all his benefits toward me?
> I will take the cup of salvation
>   and call upon the name of the LORD.

This is an eloquent psalm of thanksgiving. It is often used as the hymn of thanksgiving following baptism as well as communion. Or, again Immens would use Psalm 95:1–2 (KJV):

> Come, let us sing unto the LORD;
>   let us make a joyful noise to the rock of our salvation.
> Let us come before his presence with thanksgiving,
>   and make a joyful noise before him with psalms.

Making a joyful noise, mentioned twice in this psalm, would seem to have in mind the use of drums and tambourines, pipes and horns, lyres and harps. The praise of God is not limited to the human voice. There were those in The Netherlands who would forbid instrumental music in church, but there were also those who cultivated the organ and the bell tower, as anyone who has spent any time in The Netherlands will fondly remember.

Turning to Psalm 105 Immens is very brief, quoting only the first three verses. Psalm 105 is a psalm which I find especially appropriate for the communion service.

> Give thanks unto the LORD, call upon his name,
> make known his deeds among the people;
> Sing unto him, sing psalms unto him:
> > talk ye of all his wondrous works.
> Glory ye in his holy name.
> (Psalm 105:1–3a, KJV)

This is a long psalm but it is a thanksgiving for the history of salvation and it recounts at length the mighty acts of God for our salvation. Many other psalms, Immens allows, would be appropriate as well, but these he singles out as being especially appropriate.

The point that Immens makes most clearly is that the conduct of the pious communicant after a communion Sabbath should reflect the high solemnity of the occasion. Believers are above all obligated to express this gratitude by a holy walk. This is, of course, rather obvious, and the typical pietist preacher more than likely would draw it out at length.[36] But there is something else that Immens says that shows particular insight. Gratitude also involves an acknowledgment of the mercies of God. "We confess this with the heart to God, when we recount to him all his dealings with us, and praise him for all his wondrous works."[37] This is why we find in Scripture so many psalms which recount a history of God's mighty works. Recounting holy history plays a major role in our worship. The historical psalms were often sung in the worship of the Temple.

An important part of this thanksgiving that should follow the communion is remembering our relationship to God as our Father. If we are to remember our special relation to God as children of our Father we are encouraged and given confidence in his service. In the same way we are to recount in appreciation the redemptive works of Christ whereby we have been freed from the power of sin. A Reformed theology of worship is resolutely trinitarian. It puts in high relief the atoning death of Christ and his victorious resurrection. No less does it celebrate the sanctifying work of the

---

[36] Immens, *The Pious Communicant*, p. 207.

[37] Immens, *The Pious Communicant*, p. 214.

Holy Spirit. As we have said again and again, worship is the work of the Holy Spirit in the body of Christ to the glory of the Father. The covenantal dimension of our communion is once more called to mind. We are to give thanks that in this sacrament the covenant has been renewed once more. We have been restored to an intimate personal relationship with the one eternal God.[38]

By the beginning of the eighteenth century the Reformed church had produced a highly developed eucharistic piety. It was markedly different from the eucharistic piety of the age of the Reformation. We are only beginning to appreciate the spirituality of this age. We cannot, of course, recover the piety of our long-gone ancestors. We cannot go back to pietism, but then, neither do we have to follow the dictates of post-modernism. If at the beginning of the twenty-first century we still want to be Reformed, we must shape our worship according to Scripture.

THEODORUS JACOBUS FRELINGHUYSEN

Well-schooled in the pietism of the Lower Rhineland, Theodorus Frelinghuysen (1692–1747) arrived in New Amsterdam as a missionary to organize a church for the Dutch colonists in what today we call New Jersey.[39] He was sent out by the Classis of Amsterdam, arriving in New Amsterdam, by now New York, in 1720. There were already a number of flourishing Dutch congregations in both New Amsterdam and Albany, as well as several settlements along the Hudson. The young missionary was perhaps overly impressed with the importance of his position and quickly provoked the opposition of the Dutch ministers already in the field.[40]

---

[38] Immens, *The Pious Communicant*, p. 223.

[39] For biographical information on Frelinghuysen, see: Frelinghuysen, *Forerunner of the Great Awakening*; Tanis, *Dutch Pietistic Calvinism in the Middle Colonies*; and Robert Eells, *Forgotten Saint: The Life of Theodore Frelinghuysen: A Case Study of Christian Leadership* (Lanham, MD: University Press of America; and Palos Heights, IL: Trinity Christian College, 1987).

[40] For a collection of his sermons, see Frelinghuysen, *Forerunner of the Great Awakening*.

The Dutch colony in New York was prospering even under English rule and it was in the process of expanding into the valley of the Raritan, upriver from New Brunswick. The ministers decided to give their newest colleague responsibility for the new settlements in the Raritan Valley, figuring it would keep him out of their hair.

Even in New Jersey Frelinghuysen did not get along too well with his Dutch colleagues. He did, however, get along with his English-speaking colleague, the pastor of the English-speaking Presbyterian church in New Brunswick, Gilbert Tennent. Gilbert Tennent was about ten years younger than Frelinghuysen. His congregation was made up largely of Scottish Presbyterians who under the Duke of Cumberland had been put in prison for holding conventicles in their homes and refusing to follow the *Book of Common Prayer*. Tennent, who had been trained by his father at the Log College on the Neshaminy, came under the strong influence of Dutch pietism.

As time went along the two pastors of New Brunswick, Frelinghuysen and Tennent, made common cause with George Whitefield, Jonathan Edwards, and the Great Awakening. So it happened that Dutch pietism became an important root of the Great Awakening.

16

THE GREAT AWAKENING
AND JONATHAN EDWARDS

It was a full generation before the Revolution that American Christianity began to take on its own character.[1] This Great Awakening was well named. It was not a mission program like the missionary journeys of the Celtic monks. Nor was it a doctrinal reform like the Protestant Reformation. It was an awakening, a quickening, a sudden enlivening of a very conventional and traditional church. No one founded it or organized it. It was, as Jonathan Edwards put it in *A Faithful Narrative*, "a fresh outbreak of God's grace, an outpouring of the Holy Spirit that gave new life to the Christian church in the American Colonies."[2]

Our focus in this chapter is very particular, namely, how did the sacrament of Holy Communion fit into this revival which sud-

[1] On the Great Awakening generally, see: Mark A. Noll, *A History of Christianity in the United States and Canada* (Grand Rapids, MI: Eerdmans, 1992), pp. 91–113; Edwin S. Gaustad, *The Great Awakening in New England* (New York: Harper, 1957); Herman Harmelink, "Another Look at Frelinghuysen and His Awakening," *Church History* 37 (December 1968): 423–438; C. F. Lodge and E. Martin, "The Crisis of the Church in the Middle Colonies, 1720–1740," in *Interpreting Colonial America: Selected Readings*, ed. James Kirby Martin (New York: Dodd and Mead, 1973); Charles H. Maxson, *The Great Awakening in the Middle Colonies* (Chicago: University of Chicago Press, 1920); Perry Miller and Alan Heimert, eds., *The Great Awakening: Documents Illustrating the Crisis and its Consequences* (Indianapolis: Bobbs-Merrill, 1967); Harry S. Stout, *The New England Soul: Preaching and Religious Culture in Colonial New England* (New York: Oxford University Press, 1986); and James Tanis, *Dutch Calvinistic Pietism in the Middle Colonies: A Study in the Life and Times of Theodorus Jacobus Frelinghuysen* (The Hague: Martinus Nijhoff, 1967).

[2] For a modern edition of Edwards' description of the Great Awakening, see: Jonathan Edwards, *A Faithful Narrative of the Surprising Work of God*, found in Jonathan Edwards, *The Great Awakening*, The Works of Jonathan Edwards, vol. 4, ed. C. C. Goen (New Haven and London: Yale University Press, 1972).

denly fell on American Christianity? We wish we had more information, but none of the leaders of the Great Awakening left us a treatise on eucharistic theology. Furthermore, we have no liturgical text which reports on just how the sacrament of Holy Communion might have been celebrated at First Church in Boston, one of the Congregational churches in New Haven, or the Presbyterian Church in Trenton, New Jersey. The best that we have is Increase Mather's response to Solomon Stoddard's innovations.[3] What has been most helpful has been a number of communion sermons which have come down to us, but even at that we wish we had far more than we have. Specialists in eighteenth century church history might yet come up with more detailed information. Therefore, we simply report on what we have been able to learn up to this point.

JONATHAN EDWARDS

If I am to be completely honest about it, I always found the writings of Jonathan Edwards (1703–1758) on the sacrament of Holy Communion rather disappointing.[4] While on many subjects I am perfectly happy to recognize Edwards as America's great theologian, I found his eucharistic theology rather incomplete.[5] Most of what he has to say concerns the subject of the relationship of the sacrament to church discipline. The subject is treated at length in

---

[3] See Increase Mather, *The Order of the Gospel, Professed and Practiced by the Churches of Christ in New England* (Boston: B. Green and J. Allen for Nicholas Buttolph, 1700).

[4] For biographical information on Edwards, see: George M. Marsden, *Jonathan Edwards: A Life* (New Haven: Yale University Press, 2003); and Iain H. Murray, *Jonathan Edwards: A New Biography* (Edinburgh: Banner of Truth Trust, 1987).

[5] Two works treating Edwards' theology include: John H. Gerstner, *The Rational Biblical Theology of Jonathan Edwards, in three volumes* (Powhatan, VA: Berea Publications, 1993); and Sang Kyun Lee, *The Philosophical Theology of Jonathan Edwards* (Princeton, NJ: Princeton University Press, 1988). A recently released work on Edwards' eucharistic theology has come to our attention: William M. Schweitzer, *God is a Communicative Being: Divine Communicativeness and Harmony in the Theology of Jonathan Edwards*, T. & T. Clark Studies in Systematic Theology (Edinburgh: T. & T. Clark, 2012).

his polemic against Solomon Williams.[6] This is a rather peripheral issue in the teaching of the church on the sacrament of the Lord's Supper.[7] Edwards has not left us a work treating the central issues of the Lord's Supper. There is no treatise on either the real presence or the eucharistic sacrifice. He has left us no eucharistic liturgy like that of John Knox nor a series of preparatory sermons such as so many Reformed preachers have produced. The best we have is a few isolated sermons which were preached at a communion service. Even in these sermons our premier American theologian seems obsessed with the subject of worthy participation.[8] As Edwards presents it, the sacrament of Holy Communion is apparently above all a penitential discipline. All too frequently the text for these sermons is, "Let a man examine himself, and so let him eat of that bread, and drink of that cup" (1 Cor. 11:28, KJV).

I have tried several times to do a brief study of Edwards' understanding of the sacrament of Holy Communion, but I have been thwarted by a lack of primary source material. What little information I could find simply suggested that he looked at it much the way his colleagues did. It was all very vague. There is no doubt about it. The position of Edwards was completely orthodox. It is just that his teaching at this point seemed to be at

---

[6] Much of the literature on Edwards' eucharistic theology centers on the controversy over the Half-Way Covenant in Northampton. See Alan D. Strange, "Jonathan Edwards and the Communion Controversy in Northampton," *Mid-America Journal of Theology* 14 (2003): 57–97; and Robert G. Pope, *The Half-Way Covenant: Church Membership in Puritan New England* (Princeton, NJ: Princeton University Press, 1969). For the writings of Edwards on the subject, see Jonathan Edwards, *Ecclesiastical Writings*, The Works of Jonathan Edwards, vol. 12, ed. David D. Hall (New Haven and London: Yale University Press, 1994). This includes his *The Humble Inquiry*, pp. 165–348, *Misrepresentations Corrected*, pp. 349–504, and *"Narrative of Communion Controversy,"* pp. 505–619. The introduction by the editor, David D. Hall, is especially helpful. See David D. Hall, "Editor's Introduction," *Ecclesiastical Writings*, pp. 1–90.

[7] To be sure, the Puritans generally gave great importance to church discipline, but the actual sacrament was another matter.

[8] For a recent article discussing this problem, see Oliver Crisp, "Jonathan Edwards and the Closing of the Table: Must the Eucharist be Open to All?" *Ecclesiology* 5/1 (2009): 48–68.

the root of the problem of a certain shyness about celebrating the sacrament of Holy Communion that has, alas, become typical of American Protestantism. For far too many of us, the sacrament is more penitential than eucharistic.

It never occurred to me that the problem might be that a sizable collection of Edwards' eucharistic sermons might never have gotten to the publishing house, but that seems to be what happened. Recently a collection of previously unpublished communion sermons appeared edited by Don Kistler. This collection of nine sermons had been buried in archives somewhere and those who were interested in Edwards' sacramental teaching had not gotten the full picture. Let us look first at four sermons commonly available in the Yale edition of Edwards' works, and then we will look at four sermons from the recent volume of sermons on the Lord's Supper.

A. COMMUNION AS SELF-EXAMINATION

Here is another communion sermon on 1 Corinthians 11:26. Edwards begins by opening up this much-used text. In the First Epistle to the Corinthians the Apostle Paul brings to the attention of the Corinthian Church that there were some serious problems with the way they observed the Lord's Supper.[9] They were celebrating the Lord's Supper as a feast in the same way so many of the mystery religions and religious fraternities of antiquity observed their rites. They came to have a party rather than a memorial of the atoning death of Christ.[10]

What is very clear is that the mistaken approach of the Corinthians ignored the covenantal dimension of the Supper. The Lord's Supper of its very essence was a matter of the fellowship or communion of the whole body of Christian believers. Those

[9] Jonathan Edwards, "Self-Examination and the Lord's Supper," found in Jonathan Edwards, *Sermons and Discourses, 1730–1733*, The Works of Jonathan Edwards, vol. 17, ed. Mark Valeri (New Haven and London: Yale University Press, 1999), pp. 264–272, hereinafter Edwards, *Sermons, 1730–1733*.

[10] Edwards, *Sermons, 1730–1733*, p. 265.

of the church who had the leisure would come early and eat most of the food that had been prepared so that by the time the poorer members of the church came there was nothing left. Besides, they drank to the point of intemperance. Had they forgotten that the Supper was instituted on the eve of Christ's passion? This meal should be approached with serious intentions. "But let a man examine himself, and so let him eat of that bread, and drink of that cup. For he that eateth and drinketh unworthily, eateth and drinketh damnation to himself, not discerning the Lord's Body" (1 Corinthians 11:28–29).[11] As Edwards understood it, the Corinthians mistook the sacred food as common bread and wine. They were not able to distinguish this sacred meal from the common meals they took for physical nourishment. They failed to recognize that through this meal they entered into a special relationship with their brothers and sisters in Christ.[12] This insensitivity to the deeper meanings of the sacrament is the worst kind of irreverence.

From this exposition Edwards draws the following doctrine: "Persons ought to examine themselves of their fitness before they presume to partake of the Lord's Supper, lest by their unworthy partaking, they eat and drink damnation to themselves."[13] Edwards comments that here in this ordinance the dying love of Christ is both exhibited and offered to us. To be sure, Edwards reminds us, we are all far from being worthy of this offer. Here, of course, we notice the difference between the Reformed teaching on the eucharist and the memorialist understanding common to much of the American Protestant approach to the Lord's Supper. In the sacrament, union with Christ is not merely remembered. It is offered to us as well. It is here that Reformed Protestantism goes beyond the nominalist understanding of the sacrament taught by John Wycliffe.[14]

---

[11] Here and in the remainder of this study Scripture is quoted as in the Yale edition of Edwards' works.

[12] Edwards, *Sermons, 1730–1733*, p. 265.

[13] Edwards, *Sermons, 1730–1733*, p. 266.

[14] Edwards, *Sermons, 1730–1733*, p. 266.

The purpose of this sermon is to urge Christians to approach the Lord's Table in a spirit of self-examination and humility. Our preacher is quite explicit about what he means by this.[15] First one should examine whether one is living a moral life, or perhaps whether one indulges any immoral practice or lust. Edwards allows no distinction between major sins and minor sins. Such things should be renounced and abandoned before coming to the Lord's Table. To make his point, Edwards reminds us again of the Passover typology. For the Jews it was the case that those who were ritually unclean were not allowed to partake of the feast.

Again those who would be fit to approach the Lord's Table should reflect on whether or not they are serious about abandoning their sinful ways. It is particularly important to examine oneself as to whether one harbors any ill feelings towards one's neighbors, any spirit of jealousy or revenge, or envy. One must seriously resolve to lay aside such divisions and party spirit as the Corinthians had allowed to sour their fellowship.[16]

> Such a spirit in a man renders a man unfit and makes the ordinance void as to him in the same manner as the having leaven in a house rendered the Passover void. Leaven typified any wickedness, but especially malice and hatred. It fitly represented this by reason of its sourness; . . .[17]

If members of the congregation have quarrels with one another, they should resolve them before coming to the Lord's Table.

Finally, people should examine themselves as to their real reasons for coming to the Lord's Table. With this, of course, our preacher returns to his text. The Epistle to the Corinthians gives much attention to just exactly this subject, namely, the importance of nourishing the spiritual unity of the congregation. It is Chris-

---

[15] Edwards, *Sermons, 1730–1733*, p. 267.

[16] Edwards, *Sermons, 1730–1733*, p. 268.

[17] Edwards, *Sermons, 1730–1733*, p. 269.

tian love that builds up the congregation and it is this that the sacrament both exhibits and offers. "Those that worthily partake, they eat and drink eternal life; that is, their eating and drinking will be profitable to their souls and tend to their salvation, and the promise of eternal life is sealed to them."[18] The covenantal dimension of Edwards' doctrine is clear enough, for he goes on to say, "Persons, when they come into the church, they promise [to own the covenant]. And every participation in this ordinance is the most solemn renewal and sealing of those promises possible, for this ordinance is a seal on both parts."[19] There was nothing wrong with Edwards' eucharistic doctrine. It fits in well with the teaching of the standard Reformed preachers of the seventeenth and eighteenth centuries. There was nothing unique about it, either. It was just that it got overshadowed by a combination of situations and problems that threw it off balance.

There are, however, several sacramental sermons which do give us a picture of a more balanced understanding of the sacrament of Holy Communion.

B. Communion as Feast

Behind this pietistic concern for a eucharistic discipline we are, in fact, able to find sermons giving us a more traditional Puritan communion piety. A particularly rich sermon in this regard is a sermon preached sometime late in 1728 or perhaps early in 1729. The title of the sermon is "The Spiritual Blessings of the Gospel Represented by a Feast."[20]

The text for the sermon is Luke 14:16, "Then said he unto

---

[18] Edwards, *Sermons, 1730–1733*, p. 270.

[19] Edwards, *Sermons, 1730–1733*, p. 271.

[20] Jonathan Edwards, "The Spiritual Blessings of the Gospel Represented by a Feast," found in Jonathan Edwards, *Sermons and Discourses, 1723–1729*, The Works of Jonathan Edwards, vol. 14, ed. Kenneth Minkema (New Haven and London: Yale University Press, 1997), pp. 280–296. Hereinafter Edwards, *Sermons, 1723–1729*.

him, A certain man made a great supper and bade many."[21] True to Puritan plain style rhetoric, our preacher begins by putting his text in context. He explains that it was often the custom in ancient times to hold feasts in the evening and so it was that a prominent leader of the Pharisees gave a feast and as part of the entertainment for the evening Jesus delivered a discourse. To open up his subject he told a parable. The point of this parable is that, "The spiritual blessings of the gospel are fitly represented by a feast."[22] Edwards brings in a parallel text to make his point, quoting from Revelation 3:20, "'If any man hear my voice, and open the door, I will come in, and sup with him, and he with me.'"[23]

We find this theme often in Scripture. The feast is spoken of in very literal terms and yet the spiritual meaning is quite clear. We find this in Isaiah 25:6, "'and in this mountain shall the Lord of Hosts make unto all the people a feast of fat things, a feast . . . of wines on the lees well refined.'"[24] Again Edwards finds this theme in that great text of the Wisdom theology: "Wisdom hath builded her house, she hath hewn out her seven pillars: She hath killed her beasts; she hath mingled her wine; she hath also furnished her table . . ." (Proverbs 9:1–2, KJV). Likewise the same theme is found in the parable of the prodigal son, where the return of the lost son is celebrated with the killing of the fatted calf (cf. Luke 15:23).[25]

Edwards points to the fact that this was the whole point of those major feasts of the Old Testament: the feast of Passover, the feast of Tabernacles, and the feast of the Ingathering. Edwards tells us that these feasts were "typical" of the great gospel feast.[26] That is, they were types and foreshadows of the wedding feast of the Lamb.

In the great feast to which all these types point God is the host

---

[21] Edwards, *Sermons, 1723–1729*, p. 280.
[22] Edwards, *Sermons, 1723–1729*, p. 281.
[23] Edwards, *Sermons, 1723–1729*, p. 281.
[24] Edwards, *Sermons, 1723–1729*, p. 281.
[25] Edwards, *Sermons, 1723–1729*, p. 281.
[26] Edwards, *Sermons, 1723–1729*, p. 281.

and it is he who makes the provision. It is he who invites the guests. Sinners are the invited guests and believers are those who accept the invitation. It is Christ who purchased the dainties on which we feed and it is the Holy Spirit who is the entertainment, filling us with love, joy, and peace. This is the meat and drink for which Christ gave himself. Alluding to John 4:14, Edwards tells us that this is the water that Christ gives and which shall be in us a well of water springing up unto eternal life. "The faith and love and hope which a believer exercises, answers to the accepting of the invitation of those that are invited to a feast, and their coming to it, and sitting at God's table and eating and drinking those good things with which he entertains them."[27] Here we find very traditional Puritan imagery for the usual Puritan understanding of the Lord's Supper. Particularly we notice the reference to sitting at the table.

At this point the sermon begins to enumerate the different ways in which the provisions of the gospel are represented by a feast.[28] In the first place we must observe the tremendous expense of this feast. Some are sunk so low in their depravity that they are recovered only with great effort. The suffering of the Son of God to redeem sinners was most dear to the Father, and yet it was grace served to sinners free of cost. Second, the value of this feast as we find it in Job 28 is far above much fine gold. It is more precious than onyx and sapphires, coral and rubies.[29] It is costly for God and yet free for us. There is no point in our endeavoring to pay back to our host the cost of precious dainties. We are freely invited because God wants to show his liberality. God invites us freely as we have it in Isaiah 55:1, "'Come, and buy wine and milk without money and without price.'"[30] We find the same thing in Revelation 22:17, "'And the Spirit and the bride say, Come. And let him that

---

[27] Edwards, *Sermons, 1723–1729*, p. 282.
[28] Edwards, *Sermons, 1723–1729*, p. 282.
[29] Edwards, *Sermons, 1723–1729*, p. 283.
[30] Edwards, *Sermons, 1723–1729*, p. 283.

heareth say, Come. And let him that is athirst come. And whosoever will, let him take the water of life freely.'"[31] All that is required of us is to accept the invitation, sit down at the table, and eat and drink.[32] Again Edwards recalls that passage from the Wisdom tradition, Proverbs 9:2–5: "'Wisdom hath killed her beasts; she hath also mingled her wine; she hath also furnished her table. She hath sent forth her maidens: she crieth upon the highest places of the city, Whoso is simple, let him turn in hither: as for him that wanteth understanding, she saith unto him, Come, eat of my bread, and drink of the wine which I have mingled.'"[33] As we find it in Revelation 3:20, once more, "Christ promises that he will come in, and sup with us, and we shall sup with him, if we only hear his voice and open the door."[34]

There is a third sense of comparison. A feast fitly represents the gospel because it "nourishes the soul as food does the body. Christ Jesus, as applied by the Spirit of God in our enlightening, effectual calling and sanctification, is the only nourishment of the soul."[35] This is what we find in the story of that manna that fed the children of Israel in the wilderness. We find this taught in Leviticus 21:6, which speaks of the sacrifices being the "bread of God." As Christians we understand this typologically, as we find in John 6:38, where Jesus says, "'I am the bread of life.'"[36] As I see it, this is a major characteristic of Reformed eucharistic theology. Wisdom theology has strongly influenced the eucharistic theology of the Reformed churches.

The communion is then appropriately compared to a feast because of the excellency of it. A feast characteristically serves fine food. There are always delicacies, rare game and fowl, spiced

---

[31] Edwards, *Sermons, 1723–1729*, p. 283.
[32] Edwards, *Sermons, 1723–1729*, p. 283.
[33] Edwards, *Sermons, 1723–1729*, pp. 283–284.
[34] Edwards, *Sermons, 1723–1729*, p. 284.
[35] Edwards, *Sermons, 1723–1729*, p. 284.
[36] Edwards, *Sermons, 1723–1729*, p. 284.

sweets and rich sauces. It is properly called the bread of heaven and the food of angels (Psalm 105:40). Moreover, this is a royal feast as we find it in Matthew 22. There the feast is a wedding feast for the king's son.

Edwards' fifth point is that gospel provisions are appropriately compared to a feast because of their abundance and variety.[37] In Christ we have every provision for the soul and the body. There is every sort of thing we need to make us happy and this goes both for those of simple taste and those of more cultivated appetites. There is no asceticism here. Edwards obviously respects the needs of both the intellectual and the artist, the craftsman and the businessman. There is a fascinating variety in the blessings of God.

Next we notice that this gospel feast is marked by friendship.[38] "There is the nearest union and a holy friendship between Christ and believers."[39]

The seventh characteristic of this feast is the communion of the saints. This has always been a special concern of Reformed eucharistic doctrine. Just as the sacred meal is to be understood as an *eucharistia*, so it is to be understood as a *koinonia*. Edwards brings to full force this New Testament concept. The sacred meal is a fellowship, a communion. In this sacred meal believers have communion with Jesus and with each other because they share the same food.[40]

The eighth and final point Edwards wants to make is that the provisions of the gospel are to be compared to a feast because of its joy. To support this point he brings up again a number of the biblical images he has already explored as a sort of summary statement. He speaks of the invitation of Isaiah 55:12, where we are invited to delight in fatness as well as the feast given by the father at the return of his prodigal son. Everyone around was invited to come, to sing,

---

[37] Edwards, *Sermons, 1723–1729*, p. 285.
[38] Edwards, *Sermons, 1723–1729*, p. 286.
[39] Edwards, *Sermons, 1723–1729*, p. 286.
[40] Edwards, *Sermons, 1723–1729*, p. 287.

to dance, and to feast. Our preacher once again reminds us of the invitation to come to the wedding feast of the Lamb.[41]

We notice in this sermon the considerable influence of the nuptial typology. The Song of Songs plays an important role in Reformed eucharistic theology, as we have already noticed and as we will notice again. Never losing sight of the importance of remembering the atoning death of the Savior when celebrating the sacrament, Edwards is equally emphatic in remembering at the sacrament the invitation to the wedding feast of the Lamb. It is a joyful feast observed on the Lord's Day celebrating the resurrection of Christ.

Edwards' sermon now turns to application.[42] He makes the point that since we have spoken of the Wisdom of Christ in representing the grace of God in the observing of a feast we need to speak of the sacrament as the sealing of a covenant of friendship. In the sacrament the promises of God are sealed to us. This dimension of the sacrament Edwards sees foreshadowed or typified in the story of the covenantal feast observed by Isaac and Abimelech in Genesis 26:30.[43] This story shows us how "God doth as it were invite [us] to his own table and sits down with us. He receives [us] into his house and family, and feasts us at his own table."[44]

We notice here also that we have not only a covenantal union with Christ but also his abiding presence. Christ was not only present with his disciples at the Last Supper but he is with us whenever we observe this ordinance. As Edwards sees it, ". . . he sits with his people in every sacrament."[45]

Edwards' understanding of the sacrament as an invitation to enter into the household of faith is of particular importance:

---

[41] Edwards, *Sermons, 1723–1729*, p. 288.
[42] Edwards, *Sermons, 1723–1729*, p. 288.
[43] Edwards, *Sermons, 1723–1729*, p. 288.
[44] Edwards, *Sermons, 1723–1729*, p. 288.
[45] Edwards, *Sermons, 1723–1729*, p. 289.

"God sends forth his messengers, and calls many such to his houses, and washes them from their filthiness and clothes them with white raiment, adorns [them] with robes as king's children and makes them to sit down at his table."[46] Here Edwards, however, feels a need to warn his congregation that this invitation is now open but we should beware lest we tarry too long in accepting it. The time may soon come when the door which is open now will be closed.[47]

The sermon gives much attention to how the Christian must accept this invitation by living the Christian life.[48] If you would at the last day enter into the great feast then in this life you must strive to bear the image of Christ and share his likeness. You must learn patiently to bear the cross.[49]

C. COMMUNION AS THE MEMORIAL OF CHRIST'S ATONING SACRIFICE

Reformed theologians have often had a much more profound sense of the meaning of memorial than is usually recognized. In this sermon Edwards was primarily concerned to affirm the doctrine of the atonement which Deism was beginning to find offensive.[50] The Enlightenment found the doctrine of the deity of Christ offensive but it also found the whole idea of a substitutionary atonement an insult to the dignity of man. The sacrament of Holy Communion which had as its purpose to show forth the death of Christ in the breaking of the bread and the pouring of the wine made very explicit the centrality of the doctrine of the vicarious atonement.[51]

While we find it significant that Edwards recognized that the

---

[46] Edwards, *Sermons, 1723–1729*, p. 289.

[47] Edwards, *Sermons, 1723–1729*, p. 290.

[48] Edwards, *Sermons, 1723–1729*, p. 294.

[49] Edwards, *Sermons, 1723–1729*, p. 295.

[50] Jonathan Edwards, "The Sacrifice of Christ Acceptable," found in Edwards, *Sermons, 1723–1729*, pp. 440–457.

[51] On Edwards' theological concern in this sermon, see Minkema's introduction to this sermon. Edwards, *Sermons, 1723–1729*, pp. 437–439.

sacrament does indeed emphasize the doctrine of the vicarious atonement, our primary concern in studying this sermon is to get a glimpse of the basic theological assumptions of Edwards' eucharistic piety. For this purpose the sermon before us is most helpful. Like the sermon we have just studied, it is rich in its use of the traditional eucharistic typology. It especially develops the Old Testament types involving the sacrificial system in the Law of Moses as it is interpreted in the Epistle to the Hebrews. In this, of course, Edwards is following the lead of Martin Luther's *Babylonian Captivity of the Church*.

The sermon before us takes its text from Psalm 40:6-8: "Sacrifice and offering thou didst not desire; mine ears hast thou opened: burnt offering and sin offering hast thou not required. Then said I, Lo, I come: in the volume of the book it is written of me, I delight to do thy will, O my God: yea, thy law is within my heart."[52] This is one passage among many in the Old Testament which makes clear the insufficiency of the sacrificial system as it was observed in the Temple of Jerusalem. "Sacrifice and offering thou didst not desire . . . ," as the text has it. We find the same thought in Psalm 51:16, "For thou desirest not sacrifices; else would I give it: thou delightest not in burnt offering."[53] Again we see the same thought in Micah 6:6-8 and Jeremiah 7:22-23. The point is that God will have from us obedience rather than sacrifice. So, then, of what value were these sacrifices and why was it that God had regard to these sacrifices as he did to the sacrifice of Abel (cf. Genesis 4:4)? The first reason the sacrifices were acceptable to God was that they were done in obedience. The second was that these sacrifices were a remembrance of human sin, and the pain and death wrought by our sin.[54] In Hebrews 10:3 we read that the sacrifices

---

[52] The sermon before us is entitled "The Sacrifice of Christ Acceptable," and is included in Edwards, *Sermons, 1723–1729*, pp. 440–457. As is our custom for these sermons, the Scripture lessons are as quoted in the text. This opening text is contained on p. 440.

[53] Edwards, *Sermons, 1723–1729*, p. 440n.

[54] Edwards, *Sermons, 1723–1729*, p. 447.

of the Day of Atonement were a continual remembrance, year by year, of the sin of Israel. Our preacher then elaborates these different sacrifices offered on their required occasions.

A third purpose served by these sacrifices was to show the necessity of offering satisfaction for the wrong deeds of the people. The people were taught that justice had to be satisfied by the meting out of a penalty. Sacrifices made clear that without the shedding of blood there was no remission of sin, as is taught in the Epistle to the Hebrews (Hebrews 9:22). Edwards brings out at considerable length the typology of sacrifice and atonement as we find it in the Epistle to the Hebrews.[55] These sacrifices also taught God's willingness to be reconciled. The sacrificial system taught not only God's passion for justice but also his abounding mercy. Above and beyond all this, the sacrifices have a "typical" purpose, that is, they serve as types and foreshadows of far more profound mysteries. "They are full of gospel doctrine."[56]

Still, it is clear from both the New Testament and from numerous places in the Old Testament itself that the sacrifices of the Law never took away sin. As much as they may have served a purpose in God's plan and as much as God may have commanded them in the Law of Moses, they did not remove sin. On the other hand, the sacrifice of Christ on the cross, in and of itself, did atone for the sin of the elect.

With this the sermon turns to meditating on the perfections of the sacrifice of the cross. It is a beautiful meditation for those approaching the celebration of the sacrament, and it is just this sort of meditation that the piety of the Reformed churches expected from those who participated in the sacred meal.

The heart of the sermon meditates on how it is that the sacrifice of Christ is in itself most holy.[57] While it is admitted again

---

[55] Edwards, *Sermons, 1723–1729*, p. 447.
[56] Edwards, *Sermons, 1723–1729*, p. 448.
[57] Edwards, *Sermons, 1723–1729*, p. 449.

and again that the sacrifices of the Law never really took away sin and therefore had to be offered repeatedly, "the sacrifice of Christ is properly most holy; there is a transcendent holiness in it, and therefore it must be very acceptable to God."[58]

The sacrifice of Christ was most holy because, as we find it in Isaiah 53:10, Christ made his soul an offering for sin. He gave himself not the body of another or the body of a beast, but rather he himself was a perfect sacrifice. He was without blemish and without sin, something that could not be said of any other offering, either man or beast.[59] This offering was not only perfectly holy because he was spotless, but infinitely holy because he was the Son of God. He was in and of himself divine. He was not only faultless but divinely perfect, the source of all that is good and right. It is that which gives this sacrifice an infinite value in the sight of God. Edwards goes on to speak most profoundly. "The divine nature of Christ is that altar that sanctifies the gift, supposed to be typified by the altar in the tabernacle and temple: which altar had no real holiness, for what holiness can there be in stones or brass? Now this altar so sanctifies the gift, that it gives it an infinite holiness."[60]

The sacrifice of the cross was actually propitiatory because the Son delighted to vindicate the Father.[61] Christ despised the pain and the suffering that he might vindicate the holiness, the justice, and the mercy of God, and in his own willingness and compassion he made satisfaction for the injury humanity had done to God. Moreover, he offered up his own soul, so he offered a proper sacrifice because it was his own to dispose of. "He voluntarily subjected himself to this extreme suffering because he delighted to do God's will, which likewise showed an infinite regard to God and his commands, that he would obey it in so suffering; which also rendered that act

---

[58] Edwards, *Sermons, 1723–1729*, p. 449.
[59] Edwards, *Sermons, 1723–1729*, p. 449.
[60] Edwards, *Sermons, 1723–1729*, p. 450.
[61] Edwards, *Sermons, 1723–1729*, p. 450.

of his an act of transcendent holiness. The sacrifices under the law were offered by God's people in obedience."[62] Edwards goes on at some length meditating on the virtue of the cross. This meditation is outwardly an argument for the doctrine of the atonement but even more it is a meditation on the grace of God as it is revealed in the sacrifice of the cross. It is in its highest sense worship.

A particularly moving passage in this sermon tells us how Christ's sacrifice was not only propitiatory but meritorious. The votive sacrifices of the Law of Moses were performed not only to satisfy divine justice but also to obtain God's favor. "They were for a sweet savor to God, to procure his favors: this was often the end of those sacrifices that were vows . . . . So the blood of Christ was not only a price to pay a debt, but it was also a price to buy positive blessings with. Christ hath purchased the church with his blood (Acts 20:28); the purchased possession is purchased by Christ's blood."[63]

The typology found in the Epistle to the Hebrews has always been especially dear to Reformed piety. It shows at particular length the meaning of the sacrifice of the Day of Atonement in understanding the meaning of the sacrifice of the cross and especially in explaining the uniqueness of Christ's sacrifice. Christ's sacrifice is once and for all time.[64] It is complete and sufficient. It is on this that the communicant meditates as he or she approaches the holy Table. Sermons of this sort were preached frequently in the celebration of communion in Reformed churches.

D. Communion as Glorying in the Savior

Another "sacrament sermon" we find from Edwards is one preached in 1729.[65] The title is "Glorying in the Savior." The

---

[62] Edwards, *Sermons, 1723–1729*, p. 450.

[63] Edwards, *Sermons, 1723–1729*, p. 454.

[64] Edwards, *Sermons, 1723–1729*, p. 455.

[65] Jonathan Edwards, "Glorying in the Savior," found in Edwards, *Sermons, 1723–1729*, pp. 460–470. See the introduction by Minkema, pp. 458–459.

text is taken from Isaiah 45:25, "In the Lord shall all the seed of Israel be justified, and shall glory."[66] What interests us about this sermon is its understanding of glorying. To glory in something is the opposite of being ashamed of something. This we get from the introduction of the sermon.[67] The prophecy of Isaiah from which Edwards draws his text tells of a day in which the true seed of Israel will come to value their spiritual heritage. They will be faithful to their God. They will delight and glory in their God who, unlike the pagan gods, can save them in time of trouble. Isaiah prophesies that they will glory in the saving power of their God. Edwards gives us a definition of glorying. "To 'glory' is for a person to express his high esteem of his own advantages of excellency, honor or happiness above others."[68] This is generally taken in a negative sense. It often implies a foolish boasting, but in our text it is taken quite positively. When the psalmist says, "My soul makes its boast in the Lord," it is quite positive (cf. Psalm 34:2). The Apostle Paul uses it in a positive sense, "'Let him that glorieth, glory in the Lord'" (1 Cor. 1:31).[69]

Edwards opens up his text by suggesting several ways in which we should glory in Christ. First our preacher tells us that Christians should have "a humble and joyful sense of mind of the great privilege and happiness they have above others."[70] It is appropriate that those who enjoy such high privileges be sensible of such privileges. "It becomes them to admire their own happiness, and their sense of it should excite exultation of heart and joy of soul."[71] Joy is one of the spiritual gifts bestowed upon Christians. It witnesses to the glory of God, and exercises true piety and devotion. Joy is a major component of the worship that is in spirit and in truth.

---

[66] Edwards, *Sermons, 1723–1729*, p. 460.
[67] Edwards, *Sermons, 1723–1729*, p. 460.
[68] Edwards, *Sermons, 1723–1729*, p. 463.
[69] Edwards, *Sermons, 1723–1729*, p. 463.
[70] Edwards, *Sermons, 1723–1729*, p. 463.
[71] Edwards, *Sermons, 1723–1729*, p. 464.

Second, it is appropriate that this joy be manifested or expressed. It should be manifested in our behavior, but also in divine songs. Here it is clear that Edwards has in mind not only the psalms but the canticles as well. He mentions the songs of "Moses, Deborah, and Hannah and the blessed Virgin."[72] In fact, Edwards makes a special point of saying that the exercising of spiritual joy in exalting the Savior is especially appropriate at the Lord's Supper. According to Edwards that was one of the reasons Christ instituted the Lord's Supper. "'Twas designed partly for this end, that we might, by celebrating this ordinance, give testimony of our sense of our own happiness."[73]

To glory in Christ is to boast in his excellencies and beauty, to tell of his transcendent glory as the bridegroom in the Song of Solomon marvels at the beauty of the bride. It is to speak of the mighty acts of deliverance, to recount his victories, especially his mighty acts of redemption. It is to boast of our relation to him. He is our God. He is our Savior. He is our Redeemer. It is to glory in the promises of Christ.[74] To glory in Christ is to glory in his name and his honor. As we find it in Psalm 115:1, "'Not unto us, O Lord, not unto us, but unto thy name give glory, for thy mercy, and for thy truth's sake.'"[75] The believer wants to honor Christ that all might recognize his good and devote themselves to his service.[76]

The sermon goes on at some length glorying in Christ as King of kings, exulting in his grace and goodness, and delighting in his kingdom. The sermon inspires the congregation to glory in the Savior and finally sums it all up by exhorting the congregation to "attend on this ordinance of the Lord's Supper with the spirit of true glory."[77]

---

[72] Edwards, *Sermons, 1723–1729*, p. 464.
[73] Edwards, *Sermons, 1723–1729*, p. 464.
[74] Edwards, *Sermons, 1723–1729*, p. 464.
[75] Edwards, *Sermons, 1723–1729*, p. 465.
[76] Edwards, *Sermons, 1723–1729*, p. 465.
[77] Edwards, *Sermons, 1723–1729*, p. 469.

The more of these sacramental sermons I read, the more positively impressed I become. They are profoundly moving! My American literature professor from many years ago would never have believed it.

E. Communion as Union with Christ

Very recently a popular edition of nine sermons on the sacrament of Holy Communion by Jonathan Edwards came to my attention.[78] Regrettably it is not a scholarly edition. It comes to us in modern diction rather than the quaint style of eighteenth-century English. Even at that, we are grateful to the editor for making these sermons available. One gets the impression from the conclusion of the ninth sermon that someone a long time ago had made a collection of these nine sermons on the sacrament of the Lord's Supper.[79] This new edition of Edwards' eucharistic sermons puts Edwards' thought in a much better light. They give us a much more profound impression of Edwards' eucharistic theology than could be deduced from the material previously available. It is not that the recently published sermons have something new. It is rather that they support and amplify teachings that standing alone might seem eccentric. In these sermons Edwards makes especially clear his teaching that in communion we experience union with Christ. It is union with Christ that is at the heart of Edwards' eucharistic theology. Let us look at three sermons that make Edwards' teaching particularly clear.[80]

---

[78] Jonathan Edwards, *Sermons on the Lord's Supper*, ed. Don Kistler (Orlando, FL: The Northampton Press, 2007). Actually it was my friend and colleague, Terry Johnson, pastor of the historic Independent Presbyterian Church of Savannah, Georgia, who put it under my nose and insisted I read it immediately.

[79] Edwards, *Lord's Supper*, p. 157.

[80] Apologies to Dan Ledwith who, as one of my students at Princeton Theological Seminary, tried to get me interested in the eucharistic theology of Jonathan Edwards. Mr. Ledwith is now pastor of a Congregational Church in Massachusetts. I should have let him write that paper on Edwards' eucharistic theology long ago.

F. Communion as Seal

The first sermon we will look at has the title, "The Lord's Supper Was Instituted as a Solemn Representation and Seal of the Holy and Spiritual Union Christ's People Have with Christ and One Another."[81] The text is taken from 1 Corinthians 10:17, "For we being many are one body and one bread, for we are all partakers of that one bread." The sermon was preached in January of either 1750 or 1751.

The sermon begins by explaining that one of the leading problems among the Christians of Corinth was that some of the members would participate in feasts held in pagan temples. The Apostle Paul insists on the inappropriateness of such a practice. For Christians, participation in the Lord's Supper is nothing less than union with Christ. This is developed in four points. First of all is the Christian's union with Christ—something the Apostle Paul frequently emphasizes. We find it expressed with particular clarity in Romans 12:5, "We being many are one body in Christ." Again we find this in 1 Corinthians 12:20, "Now we are many members but yet one body." Then again in verse 27, "Now you are the body of Christ and members in particular."[82]

The second point Edwards makes is that not only are we united together in the one body of Christ, but we are also united one with another. The two go together, union with Christ and union with other Christians.

Next Edwards points out that this is a high and strict union. Just what Edwards means by "a high and strict union" is not at first clear to those of us who speak the English of the twenty-first century, but it seems that what Edwards wants to convey is that it is a very profound union. Edwards knows the theological literature. He knows the church has for centuries spoken of the nature of our

---

[81] Whether or not Edwards gave it this title is not clear. Edwards, *Lord's Supper*, pp. 70–78. Scripture passages are as quoted in the sermon.

[82] Edwards, *Lord's Supper*, p. 71.

union with Christ and how it is brought about by participation in the sacrament of communion. What Edwards says here is that this union is very real. He is addressing the doctrine of the real presence. We find this in Ephesians 5:30, where the Apostle Paul speaks of the mystery of the union of husband and wife.[83] It is a profound union like the union between husband and wife. This high union is very personal but it is also spiritual and vital. There have been those who have denigrated Reformed eucharistic theology as being vitalist, or perhaps dynamistic, not appreciating what Reformed theology really has to say on this subject.[84]

The fourth point is that this union with Christ and with other Christians is both exhibited and manifested by participation in the Lord's Supper. Basic to this union with Christ is a union of hearts.[85] This union of hearts between the believer and his Lord is the basis of a union of hearts between Christians one with another. This union of hearts knits us together into one family of the children of God. This basic affirmation—that Holy Communion should be understood as union with Christ—can be expressed in a number of biblical figures. Christ is the head of the body and we are all members of the one body. It can also be expressed by the figure of the Temple built on the rock or again it can be expressed by the nuptial metaphor. Christ is the bridegroom and the church is the bride. One can also speak of the vital union between Christ and the believer.[86] Here we are speaking of the pneumatic dimension of the sacrament. Believers are given the Spirit of Christ, which gives them spiritual power.

From here Edwards goes on to speak of communion as a solemn representation and seal.[87] In the celebration of the sacrament

---

[83] Edwards, *Lord's Supper*, p. 71.

[84] See chapter 3 on the subject of the Wisdom dimension of Calvin's eucharistic theology.

[85] Edwards, *Lord's Supper*, p. 72.

[86] Edwards, *Lord's Supper*, p. 73.

[87] Edwards, *Lord's Supper*, p. 74.

we behold the family of God gathered around the Lord's Table enjoying the benefits our Father has provided for us. The minister breaks bread and pours out the wine to show us the passionate love of Christ for us in going to the cross of his free will. But there is more. The Lord's Supper is a seal. This is elaborated at length showing how seals confirm a promise or make a document legal. A seal is also of significance because it assures us that a covenant has been ratified by the signatories.[88]

That the sacrament is a seal is, of course, an important aspect of Reformed eucharistic theology. Then, going further, we need to realize it is a seal in both directions. It is a seal of the promises of God and it is a seal of the believer's vows of faith. Here Edwards' covenantal understanding comes through loud and clear. The sacrament is also a seal and assurance on the part of the communicants that they come to this table to accept Christ and that they wish to join themselves to Christ.[89] Here Edwards makes particularly clear what we will find generally among the preachers of the Great Awakening, that the sacrament of Holy Communion has a distinct evangelistic dimension.

G. Communion with Christ's Body and Blood

We turn now to another sermon in this newly discovered collection. It has as a title, "The Sacrament of the Lord Is the Communion of the Body and Blood of Christ."[90] The sermon was preached in August of 1745. The text is, "The cup of blessing which we bless, is it not the communion of the blood of Christ?"[91]

For those interested in sacramental theology this sermon is especially important. It gives particular attention to the Greek word *koinonia* and how it is to be understood. As Edwards under-

---

[88] Edwards, *Lord's Supper*, p. 75.
[89] Edwards, *Lord's Supper*, p. 76.
[90] Edwards, *Lord's Supper*, pp. 79–96.
[91] Edwards, *Lord's Supper*, p. 79.

stands it, this Greek word is to be translated by the English word "communion." In English-speaking Reformed churches this seems to be the preferred term for the sacrament. This was especially the case in the eighteenth century.

Communion means partaking or enjoying some good or some benefit together with others. Sometimes the word *koinonia* is translated by "communion" and sometimes by "fellowship." We must go on to ask very specifically what is meant by communion of the body and blood of Christ.[92] There are two things to be considered here—what we partake of and with whom we partake. We partake of the body and blood of Christ as we find it in this text. Here we are obviously speaking of the atonement accomplished on the cross when our Savior offered up his body and blood to atone for our sin. When it comes to the matter of with whom we partake, surely it is to be with other Christians.

Having established that this sacred ordinance is a Christian communion in which there is a sensible representation of the communion as well as a memorial of it, we need to make the following points.[93] It is a joint partaking of the body and blood of Christ, as it is represented in this sacred ordinance. There are all kinds of gospel truths represented in this sacrament. The minister is a representation of the Lord himself, while the body and blood of Christ are represented by the bread and wine. The suffering of Christ is represented by the breaking of the bread and the pouring of the wine. "Christ's freely offering and giving . . . is here represented."[94] The vicarious passion of Christ is, to be sure, a central focus of eucharistic meditation. For the Deist, of course, this would become a major problem with the sacrament, but Edwards, it is clear, is a staunch supporter of the traditional piety. Believers receiving Christ are also represented. By faith the soul

---

[92] Edwards, *Lord's Supper*, p. 80.

[93] Edwards, *Lord's Supper*, p. 80.

[94] Edwards, *Lord's Supper*, p. 81.

accepts Christ, feeds on Christ, and receives him as its refreshment, its strength and comfort.[95]

We notice at this point a particularly rich passage on Edwards' eucharistic theology:

> Here is represented believers' union with Christ by which they have communion; here is represented for us circumstances of happiness, entertainment, and joy in that the Lord's Supper represents a feast. It represents the present happiness, as it were, a feast; it represents future happiness in heaven. Here is some representation of the blessed society above. That happiness is compared to a feast.[96]

Surely we recognize the eschatological dimension of these lines. This is obviously important for Edwards just as it had been for Calvin. It is this union with Christ that is at the heart of Edwards' eucharistic theology. It is here that he understands the dimension of presence.

As we find it in this sermon, the dimension of presence is closely linked with the dimension of covenant. For the Reformed theologian, it is important to remember that the sacrament of Holy Communion is a seal of the covenant of grace. As we have already noticed, it is a seal both on our part and on Christ's part. It affirms and confirms God's promise to us and our promise to God. Tacking down this point Edwards leaves us a great line, "Christ sealing the covenant with His blood is the greatest seal that ever was."[97]

H. Communion with Christ

Let us move on to another sermon which treats the subject more fully. This sermon has the title, "Christians Have Communion with

---

[95] Edwards, *Lord's Supper*, p. 81.

[96] Edwards, *Lord's Supper*, p. 82.

[97] Edwards, *Lord's Supper*, p. 84.

Christ."[98] Much of the material we discovered in the above sermon we find elaborated at greater length here. Edwards puts a strong emphasis on the sacrament of the Lord's Supper bringing us into communion with Christ. To enter this communion with Christ is the purpose of life. "We are called by the gospel to communion with Christ."[99] In his introduction Edwards puts it this way, "When we say that saints have communion with God, what is principally meant is that they are partakers with God of His holiness and happiness."[100] A good part of the sermon is devoted to opening up this basic point.

Edwards begins his explication by asserting first that Christians have communion with Christ in being partakers with him of his righteousness and of the benefit of his obedience and perfect sacrifice.[101] Christians are partakers with Christ of the benefits of his sacrifice. His sacrifice justified not only himself but us as well.

Secondly, we participate in his relation to the Father. Because Christ is the Son of God we become the sons of God. Here Edwards dwells heavily on Johannine theology. Edwards quotes the Gospel of John, "'But as many as received Him, to them gave He power to become sons of God, even to them that believe on His name'" (John 20:17), and "'For the Father Himself loveth you because ye have loved Me, and have believed that I came out from God'" (John 16:27).[102]

Edwards continues. Christians have communion with Christ in that they partake of the same Spirit. "This is indeed the main thing wherein a believer's communion with Christ consists: they have the fellowship of the Spirit; they drink into the same Spirit with Christ."[103] But then Edwards goes on to say that, by partak-

---

[98] Edwards, *Lord's Supper*, pp. 134–150.

[99] Edwards, *Lord's Supper*, p. 136.

[100] Edwards, *Lord's Supper*, p. 136.

[101] Edwards, *Lord's Supper*, p. 140.

[102] Edwards, *Lord's Supper*, p. 141.

[103] Edwards, *Lord's Supper*, pp. 141–142. Though it may sound odd to our ears, ". . . drink into the same Spirit" follows the diction of the KJV (1 Cor. 12:13).

ing of the same Spirit, Christians are made partakers of the same comfort and spiritual joy. That is why the Spirit of Christ is therefore called the Comforter.[104] In the same way Christians who are united to Christ show the peace of God, as we again find it in the Gospel of John. "Peace I leave with you, my peace I give unto you" (John 14:27, KJV).

Edwards' final point is that Christians have communion with Christ in glory. We partake of Christ's heavenly glory.[105] Christ as a conquering general has returned home through the gates of heaven and even now leads us into the City of God. Christians have communion with Christ in his rule and his dominion, and to be sure we have communion with Christ in his resurrection, as the Apostle puts it so emphatically in the sixth chapter of Romans. "For if we have been planted together in the likeness of his death, we shall be also in the likeness of his resurrection" (Rom. 6:5, KJV).[106]

What is particularly clear here is Edwards' doctrine of the spiritual presence. In fact, one gets the impression that, in this sermon, Edwards has done a particularly good job of expounding Calvin's doctrine of the spiritual presence. Here we have about as good a job of setting forth the Calvinist position as I know. Like Calvin, Edwards has left Scholasticism behind and has tried to speak of this mystery in terms of the biblical vocabulary.

One cannot do better than quote from the sermon itself:

> Lastly, there is a spiritual society between Christ and believers that is founded in their common partaking of benefits. And they are called to converse with Christ: they express their love and admiration of Him, and dependence upon Him and delight in Him, and their desires to Him with a sense of His presence in meditation, in prayer and in praises. They often look to Him, lifting up their hearts to Him.

---

[104] Edwards, *Lord's Supper*, p. 143.
[105] Edwards, *Lord's Supper*, p. 144.
[106] Edwards, *Lord's Supper*, p. 145.

And Christ is wont to meet with and mutually to communicate Himself to them. At such times, He will manifest Himself to them, and will by His Spirit make known His friendship and love, and teaches them and counsels and comforts them, as it were, by an inward spiritual work. [107]

We American Protestants have not appreciated the mysticism of the Great Awakening. It is very clear in David Brainerd's *Journal*, but we find it here in Jonathan Edwards as well. Here it suddenly becomes very clear that in the prayer and praises, in the meditation and the reading and preaching of the Word of God, and above all, in the celebration of the Lord's Supper, Jonathan Edwards had regularly experienced holy communion.[108]

Again and again Edwards had known in the simple worship of New England the presence of God. What is becoming more and more evident is that the communion sermons of Jonathan Edwards are among the spiritual treasures of Reformed piety.

With sermons like these the Puritan communion services of the eighteenth century would appear to have truly been feasts of praise and thanksgiving for God's mighty works of creation and redemption. These sermons show quite explicitly the festal nature of these celebrations. They are thoroughly Christocentric, with their strong emphasis on the doctrine of the atonement. The importance of the sacrificial typology from the Epistle to the Hebrews as well as the nuptial typology of the Song of Solomon maintains a balance between the epicletic nature of the sacrament and the eucharistic nature of the sacrament. It is both Passover and manna in the wilderness. It is both Last Supper and wedding feast of the Lamb. What we find in these eucharistic sermons of Jonathan Edwards is clear evidence of a very full eucharistic theology.

---

[107] Edwards, *Lord's Supper*, p. 145.

[108] On the question of celebrating the sacrament each Lord's Day, see Jonathan Edwards, *Some Thoughts Concerning the Present Revival of Religion in New England*, found in Edwards, *The Works of Jonathan Edwards*, 4: 522.

17

THE GREAT AWAKENING
Other Voices

It was Gilbert Tennent, New Jersey's pastor-theologian, who gave us the most profound look at the sacrament of Holy Communion and how it fit into the worship of the Great Awakening.[1] We find in Gilbert Tennent what we had hoped to find in Jonathan Edwards. Eventually Edwards came through for us, but Tennent deserves a certain priority all the same. Only very recently has the importance of Gilbert Tennent for the history of sacramental theology been realized.[2]

George W. Robertson helpfully brought together a number of sermons that Gilbert Tennent preached at "sacramental solemnities" and pointed out for us a clear and consistent sacramental doctrine.[3]

---

[1] On Gilbert Tennent in general, see Milton J. Coalter, Jr., *Gilbert Tennent, Son of Thunder* (New York: Greenwood Press, 1986); and Samuel L. Logan, "Tennent, Gilbert (1703–1764)," *Dictionary of American Christianity*, ed. Daniel G. Reid, Robert D. Linder, Bruce L. Shelley, and Harry S. Stout (Downers Grove, IL: InterVarsity Press, 1990), pp. 1164–1165.

[2] The doctoral thesis of George Robertson has opened up a whole new chapter in the history of Reformed sacramental theology. See George W. Robertson, *Sacramental Solemnity: Gilbert Tennent, the Covenant and the Lord's Supper*, PhD dissertation, Westminster Theological Seminary, 2007.

[3] These sermons, as Robertson lists them, are as follows:
   1. "The Espousals," preached in New Brunswick in 1735 (Zenger, NY)
   2. "The duty of Self-Examination, considered in a Sermon on 1 Cor. 11.28" (October 22, 1737)
   3. "The Unsearchable Riches of Christ considered," (August, 1737)
   4. "Sermons preached on Sacramental Occasions" (Boston, Draper, 1739)
   5. "Brotherly Love Recommended by the Argument of the Love of Christ: a Sermon Preached at Philadelphia, January 1747–8. Before the Sacramental Solemnity. With some Enlargement" (Philadelphia: B. Franklin, 1748)
   6. A sermon on Matthew 22:2 (July 1755)
   7. A sermon on Romans 3:25–26 (July 1755)

GILBERT TENNENT[4]

Noted for his classical learning and his evangelical fervor, Gilbert Tennent (1703–1764) was, along with Jonathan Edwards, one of the leaders of the Great Awakening. In addition to being an evangelist he was a man of genuine theological convictions. As Milton J. Coalter has recently pointed out, it was Tennent's theological discipline that helped turn the Great Awakening into a creative theological force. With thinkers like New England's Jonathan Edwards, Virginia's Samuel Davies, and New Jersey's Gilbert Tennent, the Great Awakening became a cohesive spiritual force, which gave unity to the American colonies in the generation before the Revolution. It is easy to understand why all this has made Gilbert Tennent a popular subject for historians. But there are other dimensions to this fascinating figure. A recent manuscript discovery makes it clear that Gilbert Tennent was a significant preacher of Christian piety. For those who have been trying to search out a Protestant spirituality for our day he has much to offer.

Gilbert Tennent was born in Ireland in 1703, the same year in which both John Wesley and Jonathan Edwards were born. He came to America as a boy with his father, William, and was taught theology by his father at the Log College on the banks of

---

8. Love to Christ," a sermon on Canticles 2:3 (1757)
9. A sermon on Canticles 4:16 (1757)
10. A sermon on Canticles 4:16 (1757)
11. A sermon on Jeremiah 13:15–17 (June 1758)
12. A sermon on Isaiah 1:19, 20 (June 1758)
13. A sermon on 1 John 5:21 (October 1759)
14. A sermon on Isaiah 48:9–11 (November 1759)
15. A sermon on Malachi 3:17–18 (n.d.)
16. A sermon on 2 Chronicles 20:26–29 (n.d.)
17. "Thanksgiving and Praise Included" (n.d.)
18. A sermon on Psalm 27:4 (n.d.)
19. A sermon on Psalm 84:11 (n.d.)

See the bibliography in Robertson, *Sacramental Solemnity*.

[4] This section is taken from Hughes Oliphant Old, "Gilbert Tennent and the Preaching of Piety in Colonial America: Newly Discovered Tennent Manuscripts in Speer Library," *The Princeton Seminary Bulletin*, 10/2 (1989): 132–137.

the Neshaminy. It was this Log College that was the forerunner of Princeton University. In 1726 Gilbert Tennent became pastor of the Presbyterian church in New Brunswick, New Jersey. There under the influence of Theodorus Jacobus Frelinghuysen, pastor of the Dutch Reformed church in New Brunswick, he began to preach revival.[5] Within ten years his ministry was attracting considerable attention as New Jersey's Raritan Valley became one of the seedbeds of the Great Awakening. It was then that John Wesley's disciple George Whitefield began his tour of the area, and for some time the two men worked together. In 1743 Tennent was called to Philadelphia to become pastor of a new congregation which had come into being because of Whitefield's preaching. This soon became, under Tennent's leadership, Second Presbyterian Church. The church grew, and in time Tennent was clearly one of the most prominent ministers in the Middle Colonies. It was inevitable, therefore, that he should be called upon to be a trustee of the College of New Jersey. It was the students of his father's Log College and their friends who were the driving force behind the college. Princeton was, in effect, the fruit of the Great Awakening.

From its very beginning the Princeton tradition was dedicated to learning and piety. Even if as things developed the learning tended to eclipse the piety, it did not start out that way. That was what made the difference between the Princeton tradition and the pietism of the Continent. European pietism tended to separate the religion of the head from the religion of the heart. The emphasis of Jonathan Edwards, Samuel Davies, and Gilbert Tennent was to give equal importance to piety and learning. The piety we find in the sermons of Gilbert Tennent was a very learned piety.

It was rather typical of eighteenth-century religious leaders that their most important writing took the form of a sermon rather than a theological treatise. This is not unique to the eighteenth century.

---

[5] Interestingly enough, the Frelinghuysen family has continued its influence on the state of New Jersey. A member of the family is active in politics to this day.

Bernard of Clairvaux chose to develop his theology in his magnificent series of sermons on the Song of Solomon. They may be sermons but they are commonly regarded as the *Summa theologica* of Cistercian theology. One could also mention the *Theological Orations* of Gregory of Nazianzus and the *Hexaemeron* of Basil of Caesarea. In the eighteenth century there were several major religious thinkers who chose to make their sermons their primary channel of expression. John Wesley is the best-known example. His fifty standard sermons give the classic formulation of his thought. Another theological masterpiece of eighteenth-century theology is found in the sermons of Samuel Davies, the Great Awakening preacher of colonial Virginia. Up until the Civil War Davies' three volumes of sermons were regarded as one of the most literate expressions of American religious thought. Jonathan Edwards also wrote much of his thought in sermonic form. As the late Paul Ramsay put it, sermon writing was the workbench of the eighteenth-century theologian. It is not surprising, then, that Tennent's thought was expressed primarily in his sermons. The eighteenth century was, after all, a century devoted to the experiential. As theologians of that day like to put it, they were interested in "experimental religion."

A. Preaching Piety in Colonial America

The largest collection of Tennent's sermons is a series of something more than 160 sermons on a microfilm produced by the Presbyterian Historical Society.[6] In his lifetime more than eighty of Tennent's sermons were published. Many of these were published as individual sermons or in small collections of two or three, a good number of these being the sermons he preached on public occasions. We have two sermons, for instance, that he preached before the governor of the colony of West Jersey on the occasion of a public fast day. Sermons on public occasions were an important part of the preaching activity of the ministry in colo-

---

[6] The Presbyterian Historical Society microfilm collection is located in Philadelphia.

nial America, but they were not the most important part. It was, however, these sermons that tended to get published. As Henry Stout has pointed out, the ministers of colonial America were interested in shepherding society, but they were not as one-sidedly preoccupied with that subject as the published sermons have led us to imagine.[7] At the beginning of the Great Awakening several of Tennent's evangelistic sermons were published. Of particular interest among these is *Sermons on Sacramental Occasions,* published in Boston in 1739.[8] These sermons show how clearly the revivals of eighteenth-century America were connected to the celebration of the sacraments. The most famous, or perhaps infamous, sermon Tennent preached was "The Danger of an Unconverted Ministry." To Tennent's embarrassment the sermon was often reprinted. It made him look like a firebrand, and he really was not anything of the sort. The longest series of sermons Tennent published was a series of twenty-three on the *Westminster Shorter Catechism*, published in Philadelphia in 1744.[9] Particularly interesting in this series of catechetical sermons is the way Tennent has followed the pattern of Thomas Watson, whose sermons on the *Westminster Shorter Catechism* were highly valued in the seventeenth century.[10] However much Tennent may have been influenced by pietism at the beginning of his ministry, the solid framework of his theology was put together with timbers from the classic Puritan theologians of the late seventeenth century, such as Thomas Watson, Stephen Charnock, and Samuel Willard. Both Tennent and Edwards were deeply concerned with the theological issues of the revival they had experienced, and in fact that concern wrote itself deeply into American Christianity and has not yet been completely erased.

---

[7] Stout, *The New England Soul*, pp. 4–5.

[8] Gilbert Tennent, *Sermons on Sacramental Occasions* (Boston: J. Draper, 1739).

[9] Gilbert Tennent, *Twenty-three Sermons on the Chief End of Man* (Philadelphia: W. Bradford, 1744).

[10] A modern edition of this work is: Thomas Watson, *A Body of Divinity* (London: Banner of Truth Trust, 1965).

Tennent, like Edwards, was a theologian evangelist.

It is not, however, in the published sermons that we discover Gilbert Tennent as a teacher of the discipline of the Christian life. It is in these manuscript sermons that never made their way through the printing press that this becomes most clear. Many of the manuscript sermons that were commonly known up to this point treat the subjects of piety and personal devotion, but this group is particularly rich on this subject.

Communion with God was frequently an important subject in the Puritan pulpit. The sacrament of the Lord's Supper was frequently called simply Communion. The whole Song of Solomon typology implied the celebration of the sacrament.

The fourth sermon in the series is preached on a text from the Song of Solomon, "Awake, O north wind; and come, thou south; Blow upon my garden, that the spices thereof may flow out" (Song 4:16, KJV). The message Tennent draws from the text is that just as a gardener cares for a garden, so God cares for the church. Taking the image of the garden, the preacher ranges through the whole of the Song of Solomon to elaborate the image. Among the observations he makes are the following: a garden is a piece of land chosen and set apart for the use of the owner just as the church and every member of it are chosen and set apart for God's purposes. As a garden must be watered regularly, so God's people must often be spiritually refreshed by the dew of Hermon. A garden, Tennent explains, goes through different seasons. There is the summer with its warm south winds and winter with its cold north winds. Both are necessary to the growth of the garden. The church must experience its times of hardship and temptation if it is to experience its times of growth and fruitfulness. Much of this seems to have been inspired by John Flavel's *Husbandry Spiritualized*.[11] Flavel was an English Puritan who was read widely in America and seems to have been par-

---

[11] John Flavel, *Husbandry Spiritualized: The Heavenly Use of Earthly Things*, found in John Flavel, *The Works of John Flavel*, vol. 5 (Edinburgh and Carlisle, PA: The Banner of Truth Trust, 1982).

ticularly appreciated by Gilbert Tennent.

Next Tennent turns to explaining the blowing of the wind as the work of the Holy Spirit in the church. The graces of the Spirit are many and varied, just like the variety of spices mentioned in the Song of Solomon. We read of nard, saffron, myrrh, and frankincense. It is the blowing of the wind that allows the fragrances to perfume the garden. Without the work of the Holy Spirit grace is not exercised, and it is the exercising of grace that glorifies God, comforts our souls, and edifies our neighbors. It is the exercising of spiritual gifts by the prompting of the Holy Spirit that supports us in the performing of Christian service and strengthens us in times of suffering. Quite contrary to what we are often told, eighteenth-century theologians had a strong doctrine of the Holy Spirit, especially when it came to teaching on the means of grace and the sacraments.

The influence of Richard Sibbes, another great Puritan divine, is clearly discernible in this sermon.[12] Sibbes had preached a series of sermons on the Song of Solomon early in the seventeenth century. Tennent's interpretation of the text follows Sibbes very closely. As each aspect of this imagery is developed, one is led to an ever greater appreciation of how God works in our lives. Tennent uses Solomon's magnificent imagery to assure us that, both by the hand of providence and by the working of the Holy Spirit, God is constantly active in our lives. This is a sermon, as so many sermons on the Song of Solomon down through the centuries, that speaks of our constant communion with God.

The fifth sermon is on the love of the Christian for Christ. The Latin title he gave the sermon was simply *De amore christo*, "Love to Christ." It, too, is developed from a text of the Song of Solomon, "Because of the savor of thy good ointments thy name is as ointment poured forth, therefore do the virgins love thee" (Song 1:3, KJV). As Tennent understands the text, it means that Christians love Christ

---

[12] Richard Sibbes, *Bowels Opened: or, Expository Sermons on Canticles IV. 16, V. VI*, found in vol. 2, *Works of Richard Sibbes*, ed. Alexander B. Grosart (Edinburgh and Carlisle, PA: Banner of Truth Trust, 1983).

because of the anointing he has received. He has been anointed with the oil of gladness above his fellows. On him has been poured out all the graces of God's Spirit. As in the previous sermon, Tennent does a beautiful job of relating the imagery of his text to other passages of Scripture that develop the same imagery. He has a sensitivity to the poetic use of language and understands the importance of the development of poetic imagery in Scripture. The heart of this sermon is Tennent's teaching on the nature of true love for Christ. True love for Christ is the fruit of faith: "We love him because he first loved us." It is not only that Christ's love causes our love, but that his Spirit spread abroad in our hearts draws out our love to him. It is also because of Christ's love for us that our love for him grows. Our love is more and more increased by enjoying communion with him. It is interesting to compare the way Tennent interprets this verse to the commentary of Matthew Henry. Henry was the most beloved expositor of American Presbyterians for generations. While Tennent's interpretation runs along similar lines, it is not primarily dependent on Henry. On the other hand, both Henry and Tennent follow the same general approach to the Song of Solomon found in the notes of the Geneva Bible. While we do not have a commentary on the Song of Solomon from Calvin, the notes of the Geneva Bible are about as close to the Genevan Reformer as we can get.

The tenth sermon in this collection develops the same theme of love to Christ. It is apparently a sermon that was preached at a communion service. Tennent has given a Latin title to the sermon, *De nuptiis cum Christo*. It is drawn from the parable of the wedding feast of the king's son in the twenty-second chapter of Matthew. Quite appropriately the imagery of the Song of Solomon is used to develop the parable. At some length Tennent speaks of the excellence of the love of Christ to us and why we should accept his invitation to the wedding feast. It is in effect an essay on the spiritual riches that Christ the bridegroom bestows upon his bride. Nuptial imagery was often used by the Puritans to develop their understanding of Christian piety. Thomas Shepard's long treatise *The Parable of the Ten Virgins*, one of the first theological works written in America, is one of the best examples.[13] Typical of the Great Awakening, Tennent's sermon is designed to inspire the religious affections. The new insights Jonathan Edwards had put down in his masterful treatise *Religious Affections* obviously influenced Gilbert Tennent. Finally, the sermon is concluded by an invitation to the Lord's Supper: "Sinners, if you marry him all is yours. All his riches are yours forever. If you are in debt even a thousand talents, he has enough to pay all. All he asks is your consent. Will you come to the King's supper? Will you embrace him, accept him for your all? What do you say? What answer shall I return to the great king who sent me to you?" This beautiful sermon is the clearest possible evidence for the fact that eighteenth-century American Presbyterians had a very strong sacramental dimension to their evangelistic preaching. It was at the Lord's Supper that they preached the central message of the Gospel. At the Lord's Supper, they expected the faithful to pledge their faith to Christ and renew the vows of the covenant.

It is easy to understand why sermons such as these have received little attention in the last couple of generations. The "spiritual exegesis" of the Song of Solomon was commonly regarded with suspicion. It may have been beautifully developed in the days of Bernard of Clairvaux, and John Calvin may have defended it against Sebastian Castellio, but for most exegetes of the mid-twentieth century the classic Christian interpretation of the Song of Solomon was hopelessly out of date. Be that as it may, the Puritans had developed a whole theology of Christian love on the basis of the nuptial imagery of both the Old and New Testaments. Richard Sibbes, Thomas Shepard, and John Cotton only begin the list of great Puritan divines who worked out a theology of the love of God based on the

---

[13] Thomas Shepard, *Parable of the Ten Virgins Opened and Applied*, vol. 2 of *The Works of Thomas Shepard*, 3 vols. (Boston: Doctrinal Tract and Book Society, 1852; Reprint, New York: AMS Press, Inc., [1852] 1967).

imagery of the wedding feast. All this, of course, is very traditional material in the whole history of Christian spirituality. Tennent's sermons are variations on very classical themes.

Gilbert Tennent was a remarkably well-rounded preacher. He had an astounding spiritual vitality, a trait he has bequeathed to the whole of American Christianity. An important component of that vitality was its vigorous piety. The newly discovered manuscripts make it very clear that love for Christ was at the heart of the piety he preached. For many Americans today the search for spirituality has led to some rather exotic places. It probably never occurred to them that some real gems could be mined in New Jersey.

B. The Sacrament as Assurance of the Love of Christ

One of the major contributions of George Robertson's study is his discussion of the place of the sacrament of communion in the Christian life as it has been understood in the Calvinist tradition.[14] He wants to show us that Tennent's teaching is in no way a novelty. It goes back to the Reformation. Robertson organizes Tennent's approach to the sacrament under five points. First, the sacrament is a sign and seal of the promise of the gospel. It is also a major function of the sacrament to bring us into union with Christ. The sacrament also serves as a dramatization of the gospel. This is followed by a sense in which the sacrament of communion is a sacrifice of thanksgiving. Finally, the sacrament acts to bring us into the bond of love that unites us together in the fellowship of the church. Let us look at each point one at a time.

First of all, Tennent would understand the sacrament to be a sign and a seal of the promises of the gospel.[15] The celebration of the sacrament promotes and supports our assurance of salvation. It heightens our worship when we respond to God's grace. Even

---

[14] See Robertson, *Sacramental Solemnities*. See note 2 (p. 633).

[15] Robertson, *Sacramental Solemnities*, pp. 226–247.

more, our meditations on Christ's sacrifice encourage us to holiness of life. This is why it is important to arrive at a communion service well prepared to enter fully into the celebration. At this point, Robertson calls on Cotton Mather's *A Companion for Communicants* of 1690.[16] To those interested in the history of Christian worship this reference to Cotton Mather is particularly interesting. To begin with, it is interesting because it shows that the piety of evangelical Protestantism quite widely understood that one should prepare for a "sacramental occasion," but also because it shows that the Reformed ministers throughout the American colonies knew and read each others' theological works.[17]

To define the sacrament as a sign and seal of the promises of God is characteristic of the Reformed confessions of faith. The statement is, of course, based on Romans 4:11, which defines circumcision as the sign and seal of God's promise to Abraham. This passage might be said to have had a formative influence on early sixteenth-century sacramental theology. To define the sacrament as a sign and a seal of God's promises is also to embark on a covenantal understanding of the sacrament. We notice that Robertson claims Tennent's theology of the sacraments as a covenantal theology of the sacraments, as the title of his thesis suggests.

Secondly, Robertson would identify union with Christ as a major function of the sacrament. Here, of course, the Reformed tradition finds strong support in much contemporary New Testament research. The point is that the Christian life is a life in Christ. Whether understood in a Pauline sense or a Johannine sense, union with Christ is of the essence of the doctrine of the real presence. This is particularly true with Calvin. When it comes to Bullinger and his development of covenantal theology it comes

---

[16] Robertson, *Sacramental Solemnities*, p. 158.

[17] We regret that we could not include a more thorough study of this work. Cotton Mather, *A Companion for Communicants: Discourses on the Nature, the Design, and the Subject of the Lords Supper; with Devout Methods of Preparing for, And Approaching to that Blessed Ordinance* (Boston, 1690).

out very clearly. One can, of course, speak of a covenantal union and one can also speak of a mystical union, and, as I read Robertson, I get the impression that Tennent has both in mind. This is particularly the case when Tennent uses the imagery of the Song of Solomon, as he does so frequently.

George Robertson claims that another function Reformed theologians attributed to the sacraments was as a dramatization of the gospel. When I first read this I was more than put off, but, then, as this term "dramatization" appeared chapter after chapter in George Robertson's work, I began to see his point, though what Robertson says here can easily be misunderstood. The sacrament is an event that shows forth the Lord's death until he comes. What I think Robertson means by this is that in the sacrament we act out the gospel. We receive the blessings of the gospel from God, our loving Father, and we share them with our brothers and sisters in Christ. For myself, I would prefer the word "show forth" rather than "act out" or "dramatize," but, as I said, Robertson makes his point. The sacrament is not just a visualization of the gospel but an experiencing of the gospel as well.

The eighteenth century put a lot of emphasis on experiencing. It was, after all, the century of both Jonathan Edwards and John Wesley. We have ever since Augustine heard about the sacraments making the gospel visual rather than merely audible. In fact, today we hear this a little bit too much, but that is another matter. On the other hand, it is not just a matter of hearing; it is a matter of seeing and feeling and even tasting. It is the total experience. Neither radio nor television is enough. One needs to be there to worship in its fullest. One needs to be there and take part for it to be real worship.

A fourth function Robertson finds in Tennent's celebration of the sacrament of communion is that it serves as a sacrifice of thanksgiving. It returns to God the thanks that we owe to him for all the blessings of our creation and redemption. Let there be no confusion here between a propitiatory sacrifice and a sacrifice of praise and thanksgiving. We do not observe communion that we might receive the blessings of God but rather *because* we have received the blessings of God.

The doctrine of the eucharistic sacrifice is one of the major points of division between Protestants and Catholics. Protestants insist that there is a great difference between a propitiatory sacrifice and a eucharistic sacrifice. It was a propitiatory sacrifice that Christ offered on the cross, but it is a sacrifice of praise and thanksgiving that we offer daily before the throne of grace. The continual sacrifice is a sacrifice of praise and thanksgiving. The propitiatory sacrifice is the sacrifice Christ offered on the cross once and for all. Strictly speaking the eucharistic sacrifice is a sacrifice of thanksgiving. That is what the Greek word *eucharistia* means. Common usage, however, takes "eucharistic" to refer to anything having to do with the sacrament of the Lord's Supper. Hence, one speaks of "eucharistic vestments" or "eucharistic doctrine." The phrase "eucharistic sacrifice" can properly mean one thing to Protestants and quite another to the Catholics. We can be well assured Tennent had the two straight.

A proper Protestant doctrine of the eucharistic sacrifice understands that the communion service is an act of thanksgiving, a memorial of sacred history. To celebrate the eucharist properly is to give great attention to the prayers, the hymns, and the psalms that are a major feature of the service. It is with praise and thanksgiving that we recount the history of salvation. It is to celebrate and give thanks for all the blessings of creation and providence, for our redemption and sanctification, and for the hope of victory in the end.

Finally, the purpose of celebrating the sacrament of Holy Communion is to enter into the bond of love that unites us together in the fellowship of the Church. Here, again, the covenantal dimension of the sacrament comes through loud and clear. A covenantal theology of the sacrament is equally concerned with the sacrament as union with Christ on the one hand and fellowship with the brethren on the other. This is one reason that, for

Tennent, the Invitation is such an important part of the liturgy. Evangelism is essential to worship. As Robertson points out so clearly, one of the beautiful things about Tennent's eucharistic preaching is that evangelism and worship are kept in balance.

C. THE SACRAMENT AS MYSTICAL EXPERIENCE

One of the great sermons in the history of the American Church was preached by Gilbert Tennent in New Brunswick, New Jersey, in the year 1735. It was one of the initial sermons of the Great Awakening. The title of the sermon was, "The espousals, or a passionate perswasive to a marriage with the Lamb of God, wherein the Sinners Misery and the Redeemers Glory is unvailed in. A sermon upon Gen. 24:49. Preach'd at N. Brunswyck, June the 22nd, 1735."[18] One immediately jumps to comparing it to Jonathan Edwards' even more famous sermon, "Sinners in the Hands of an Angry God." What a contrast! Edwards' sermon is more frequently quoted as one of the initial sermons of the Great Awakening. While Edwards' sermon was intended to scare the hell out of everyone, Tennent's sermon invites us to a wedding feast, the wedding feast of the Lamb. In short, it is an invitation to partake of the sacrament of Holy Communion, a foretaste of the heavenly wedding feast.[19]

As our study of the sacrament of Holy Communion in the piety of the Reformed Church has proceeded, we have noticed how often the sacrament has been understood in terms of the wedding feast. We spoke of this particularly in regard to the Dutch pietist, Jodocus van Lodenstein, and to Samuel Rutherford, the Scottish representative to the Westminster Assembly. In the sermon before us the preacher frequently compares the covenant of

---

[18] Gilbert Tennent, *The espousals, or a passionate perswasive to a marriage with the Lamb of God, wherein the Sinners Misery and the Redeemers Glory is unvailed in. A sermon upon Gen. 24:49. Preach'd at N. Brunswyck, June the 22nd, 1735* (New York: Printed by J. Peter Zenger, 1735). Hereinafter, Tennent, *Espousals*. Thanks is given to Princeton Theological Seminary for assistance in obtaining a copy of this sermon.

[19] Tennent, *Espousals*, pp. 4–5.

grace to the marriage covenant. What we find particularly interesting here is that Tennent shows us with the greatest clarity how the sacrament of communion fits into the Great Awakening. A century later in the American revivals of the nineteenth century the sacraments just don't figure in unless the revivals are under the auspices of the Baptists or the Campbellites.

Part of the genius of this sermon is the choice of text, namely, the story of Abraham sending one of his most trusted servants, Eliezar of Damascus, to find a wife for his son Isaac. The story is told at considerable length in the twentieth chapter of Genesis.[20] Tennent comments in detail and then explains that he intends to treat the story typologically. This would have been the normal approach for his day. As Tennent sees it, Eliezar is a type of the minister of the gospel. It is the responsibility of the minister to woo the congregation for his Lord. Just as Eliezar was supposed to win the assent of Rebecca, so the minister of the gospel is supposed to win his congregation to Christ, so that they leave the land of sin and come to be the bride of Christ. This may be a bit complicated for the modern congregation, but an eighteenth-century congregation would have received it as a masterly stroke of interpretation.[21] One may well object that it is more of an allegorical interpretation, but the Presbyterians of New Jersey knew their Bibles well enough to follow their preacher. At least, they did in those days.

Tennent tells his congregation that his purpose in preaching is to bring those in his congregation into a marriage covenant with the great God.[22] He wants to awaken them to their absolute need of union to and communion with Christ.[23] Tennent is very realistic. He reminds his congregation that part of the marriage covenant is self-denial and taking up the cross, but on the other

---

[20] Tennent, *Espousals*, pp. 4–6.

[21] Tennent, *Espousals*, p. 7.

[22] Tennent, *Espousals*, p. 11.

[23] Tennent, *Espousals*, p. 12.

hand this union with Christ is a union of the deepest intimacy. It is to experience "the kisses of the King." It is to have his love spread about in our hearts. It is to be able to say as we find it in the Song of Solomon, "My beloved is mine, and I am his: he feedeth among the lilies" (Song of Solomon 2:16, KJV). It is to know by experience what it is to be sealed by the Spirit and to cry, *Abba, Father*. Language like this is the language of mysticism. Whether one reads it in David Brainerd or Richard Sibbes or Bernard of Clairvaux it is the language of a very distinct kind of piety.

This sermon is a preparatory sermon.[24] That is, it is meant to prepare people to receive the sacrament of Holy Communion. More properly, it is an "action sermon," the sermon preached at the communion service. When we consider this, we realize that Tennent has a very mystical understanding of communion. It is union with Christ to which the congregation is invited. Mysticism as Tennent seems to understand it is a heightened sense of the presence of Christ. It is knowing Christ to be present as the two disciples on the road to Emmaus finally knew him to be present as they shared a supper together at that inn along the way, or as Elijah knew Christ to be present in the still, small voice. It is as Christ himself promised at his ascension that he always would be with us.

At one point Tennent exhorted his congregation, ". . . consider what this happiness which Christ offers to those who are willing to be espoused to him contains."[25] There is freedom from every evil, from every sin, from every punishment for sin or fear of punishment for sin. There is freedom from every corruption. There is freedom from every temptation either from the Devil himself or from wicked men. There is freedom from all imperfections. ". . . Their faith will be turned into sight, there will be no more doubtings of the goodness of their State, the continuance of their Father's love . . ."[26] Pick-

---

[24] Tennent, *Espousals*, p. 32.

[25] Tennent, *Espousals*, p. 35.

[26] Tennent, *Espousals*, p. 36.

17: The Great Awakening
Other Voices

ing up from the Apostle Paul, Tennent reminded his congregation, *"Here we see darkly as in a Glass, but there we Shall see Face to Face.* I Cor. 13. 12. In this *Vission* of God, *the Understandings* of the Glorified will be Entertain'd with the noblest Discoveries of Truth, which is their proper Good. They shall be inexpressibly delighted with beholding the charming Glories of the divine *Nature*, the transcendent beauties of his *Word*, and the surprizing Harmony of his Works."[27]

Gilbert Tennent, like Jonathan Edwards and Samuel Davies, was surely one of the masters of the American pulpit. Tennent was typical of the colonial period. He was part and parcel of the eighteenth century, the homiletical counterpart of Haydn and Mozart. His art is lyrical and intricate. Tennent's congregation must have thrilled as their preacher uttered these lines concerning the kingdom of God: "There the blessed Jesus seated on a Throne of great Glory, adorned with all his mediatorial Beauty and Excellency, will be rapturously Admired, and reverently ador'd, by all the shining Ranks of prostrate Saints and Seraphims, and the Honours of his dying but victorious Love perpetually Sung with the sweetest Accents by all the heavenly Hosts. *Rev. 5. 9. Rev. 14. 1.-4.*"[28]

This is not a short sermon and our preacher comes up with his homiletical ecstasies more than once. We notice particularly the climax of his Invitation:

> Behold, poor sinners the Stately glorious and joyful Triumphs of *Emanuel's* Country! Look how the Rivers of pious Love and perpetual Joy of pure peace and perfect Pleasure rove in endless circles through the whole Land! See there is the Tree of Life, the Bread of heaven, the Angel's Manna! Sinner, look eastward, westward, northward, and southward, all this will God give thee, if thou wilt be but espoused to his Son, the blessed Lord Jesus.[29]

What is very clear from this sermon is that evangelism is seen as an

---

[27] Tennent, *Espousals*, p. 37. Scripture is as quoted by Tennent.

[28] Tennent, *Espousals*, p. 38.

[29] Tennent, *Espousals*, p. 39.

invitation to take part in the sacrament of communion. Communion is the goal of evangelism. As things began to develop in the next century and a half, this sacramental goal was more and more neglected. Preparatory services were obviated because evangelism lost its sacramental conclusion. It was no longer connected with the regular worship of the church.

What we find very positive in Gilbert Tennent is that evangelistic preaching builds up to communion. He preaches repentance and offers reconciliation and that reconciliation takes the form of communion with God and fellowship with the neighbor. We will never understand the Great Awakening if we only read "Sinners in the Hands of an Angry God." Tennent's sermon, "The Espousals" did, in fact, balance Edwards' sermon. It was Tennent's sermon that won New Jersey to the Great Awakening.

There is another matter to consider here. As is well known the Dutch Reformed pastor at New Brunswick, Theodorus Jacobus Frelinghuysen, strongly influenced Tennent. Could it be that this whole emphasis on the wedding feast as a type of the sacrament may well go back to the sacramental mysticism of Jodocus van Lodenstein and the mysticism of Dutch Calvinism?

One of Tennent's strong points was his mysticism. Scholars are beginning to notice this more and more. For Tennent union with Christ was one of the major purposes of the sacrament. Surely this sermon shows us something of the mystical dimension of Tennent's religious experience. Let us not forget, however, that the mystical element of the Great Awakening was generally very strong. It was in 1745 that Newark Presbytery ordained David Brainerd to be a missionary to the Indians in New Jersey and Pennsylvania. David Brainerd was one of the classic mystics of American Christianity. Brainerd died in the home of Jonathan Edwards, and it was Edwards who published his meditations. This sermon is full of the sort of mysticism Brainerd expressed. It was in Cranbury, New Jersey, that Brainerd established one of his Native American congregations. Mysticism was not some exotic expression of medieval religion for Tennent and his contemporaries. It was an important element in the religious experience of mid-eighteenth-century Reformed Protestantism. The communion services Tennent presided over were charged with a mystical sense of union with Christ and the bond of love uniting the congregation.

SAMUEL DAVIES

The apostle of the Great Awakening in Virginia, Samuel Davies (1723–1761) was eventually chosen to be president of Princeton University.[30] A powerful preacher, he is often thought of as one of the outstanding orators of Colonial America.[31] The three volumes of his sermons which have come to us are today regarded as classics of American homiletical literature.[32] Here is a man who, like Jonathan Edwards and Gilbert Tennent, stands as one of the fathers of American Christianity.

Unlike John Willison or Matthew Henry, Samuel Davies never devoted any particular attention to the Lord's Supper. We have no theological treatise on the subject from him, nor do we have any devotional writings as we have from Willison. We do not even have

---

[30] For a study of the life and ministry of Samuel Davies, see: George N. Pilcher, *Samuel Davies: Apostle of Dissent in Colonial Virginia* (Knoxville, TN: University of Tennessee Press, 1971). See also Wesley M. Gewehr, *The Great Awakening in Virginia, 1740–1790* (Durham, NC: Duke University Press, 1930); Hughes Oliphant Old, *The Reading and Preaching of the Scriptures in the Worship of the Christian Church*, vol. 5, *Moderatism, Pietism, and Awakening* (Grand Rapids, MI: Eerdmans, 2004), pp. 154–167; and Louis B. Weeks, "Davies, Samuel," in *Dictionary of Christianity in America*, ed. Daniel G. Reid, Robert D. Linder, Bruce L. Shelley, and Harry S. Stout (Downers Grove, IL: InterVarsity Press, 1990), pp. 342–343.

[31] It was from Davies that Patrick Henry learned the art of oratory. The Henry family regularly attended Davies' church in Hanover County, Virginia.

[32] The three volumes of Davies' sermons first appeared shortly after his death. An edition published by the Presbyterian Board of Publication appeared in 1854. A reprint of this is currently available from Soli Deo Gloria as Samuel Davies, *The Sermons of the Rev. Samuel Davies*, 3 vols., reprint of the 1854 edition (Morgan, PA: Soli Deo Gloria Publications, 1995). Hereinafter, Davies, *Sermons*.

a complete series of sermons for a sacramental season as we have from so many Reformed pastors. We have to rely on three sermons. The three sermons do not appear to be connected. One appears to be a preparatory sermon while the others appear to have been preached at a celebration of the Supper. What this means is that Samuel Davies gives us an idea of what a typical colonial American pastor understood by the sacrament of the Lord's Supper. We find much of the same material in these three sermons of Samuel Davies as we find in Willison, or Henry, or even Calvin. What Davies lacked in uniqueness he more than makes up for in showing us what was typically taught in the colonial American pulpit on the subject of the Lord's Supper.[33] Sad to say, the sermons include no dates. At several points the preacher addresses his listeners as Virginians; therefore it would seem that they were the product of his regular pastoral ministry in Hanover County, Virginia. If this supposition is correct, it means they would have been preached in the 1750s.[34]

The first of these sermons bears the title, "The Christian Feast."[35] For our purposes it is by far the most helpful of the three sermons because it intends to be an instruction in the purpose of participation in the service. It is the traditional preparatory sermon preached on the Sunday immediately before a "Sacramental Sunday," as the expression went. There may have been additional preparatory services during the week, but they are not specifically mentioned. On the other hand, the itinerant nature of Davies' ministry in Virginia may not have allowed for weekday services.

The text Davies chose for this preparatory sermon tells us much about how our preacher understood the sacrament. The apostle Paul in the first of his letters to the Corinthians speaks of Christ's sacrifice in terms of the Jewish feast of Passover.

---

[33] I think the eucharistic sermons of Davies are the key to understanding the eucharistic theology of the colonial American church.

[34] It could be argued that the first of these sermons was preached in Princeton, due to its more comprehensive nature.

[35] Davies, *Sermons*, 2:141–173.

17: The Great Awakening
Other Voices

Then the apostle urges the Corinthians, "Therefore let us keep the feast, not with old leaven, neither with the leaven of malice and wickedness; but with the unleavened bread of sincerity and truth."[36] The point the sermon makes is that those who intend to keep the Christian feast must prepare for that feast by ridding themselves of the leaven of sin. For our purposes what is most interesting is that the Christian sacrament is understood in terms of the Jewish Passover. Davies observes that the Lord's Supper "has the same place under the gospel dispensation which the passover had under the law."[37]

The passover typology has always been very important in the development of the Reformed understanding of the Lord's Supper as well as the rites observed in its celebration. ". . . for though that feast is no more to be observed, yet that which was signified by the paschal Lamb is now come to pass: *Christ our passover is sacrificed for us*, and the ordinance of his supper is appointed as a sacred feast, in commemoration of him, and our deliverance by him, as the passover was commemorative of the deliverance from Egypt, . . ."[38] The choice of the text implies the passover typology.

Even more, the choice of the text assumes that the Lord's Supper is to be understood as one of the biblical signs found throughout Scripture sealing a covenant. Typologies were important to Davies, and he briefly surveys a number of them. As the tree in the Garden of Eden signified the covenant with Adam or as the rainbow after the flood was a sign of the covenant with Noah or as circumcision sealed the covenant with Abraham, or, finally, as Passover sealed God's promise to deliver God's people from Egypt, so baptism and the Lord's Supper are the signs and seals of the New Covenant, the covenant of grace established in the death and resurrection of Jesus Christ. It is typical of God's way of dealing with us that he often adds

---

[36] Davies, *Sermons*, 2:141.

[37] Davies, *Sermons*, 2:141.

[38] Davies, *Sermons*, 2:142.

to his Word "sensible signs and significant actions."[39] Because we are material, physical beings we need tangible signs and confirming spiritual truths. Obviously for Davies the typological nature of the sacraments was a key to their understanding. Davies is not unusual in this; it was rather typical for Reformed theology of the time.

Getting down to the body of the sermon we find that Davies speaks of the Lord's Supper in terms of five theological terms: memorial, sacrament, covenant, communion, and evangelism.

A. Memorial

The Lord's Supper "was intended as a memorial of the sufferings of Christ for his people."[40] About this Jesus himself was quite emphatic. "*This do in remembrance of me.*" Davies is quite clear that the text does not simply intend mental recollection. He has already made clear in his introduction that it is an action, a significant action. Zwingli had, of course, made the same point. Davies tells us, "That we are to remember him particularly and principally as suffering for our sins, is evident from his words in distributing the elements, *This is my body which is broken for you*. Here a moving emphasis is laid upon his body being broken; broken, crushed, and mangled with an endless variety of sufferings. So again, *This cup is the New Testament in my blood, which is shed for you*. Hence it is evident this ordinance was appointed as a memorial of a suffering Saviour; and it is under this notion that we are particularly to remember him. We are to *show the Lord's death*, says the apostle; his death which was the consummation of his sufferings, *till he come again* to visit our world in a very different and glorious manner."[41] The celebration of the Lord's Supper in Reformed churches has always made a point of breaking the bread and pouring the wine in the sight of the people. The elements themselves speak of the passion of Christ. The grain has been through

---

[39] Davies, *Sermons*, 2:144.

[40] Davies, *Sermons*, 2:144. Italics are in the original.

[41] Davies, *Sermons*, 2:145.

the mill and the wine through the press, but, even more, the bread is broken and the wine poured out. This is essential to the sign. Yet, it is not suffering alone that we remember. Reformed churches have always made a point that the Supper be celebrated on the Lord's Day, that is, the Day of Resurrection. Not only that, but the Supper is understood as a sign, even a foretaste of the wedding feast of the Lamb, the heavenly celebration that the Lamb who suffered here on earth triumphed over the grave and awaits us in heaven as risen Lord. All this Davies makes very clear when he tells us, "*We are to show the Lord's death . . . till he come again* to visit our world in a very different and glorious manner."[42]

Davies compares the Lord's Supper to the gift that one might give to a friend when one departs for a long journey. But such a gift is a memorial until one returns. As we have seen, this eschatological dimension of the Lord's Supper is very strong in seventeenth and eighteenth-century Reformed eucharistic devotion. This is evident from the many communion sermons preached on the wedding feast of the king's son or the various texts from the Song of Solomon or the book of Revelation.

For the eighteenth century the religious affections were of the utmost importance. We are not at all surprised to hear Davies insist, "This remembrance of a suffering Saviour must be attended with suitable affections."[43] We should approach this ordinance with a suitable sense of repentance and humility as well as "an ardent love and gratitude for his dying love to us."[44] This gratitude should express itself in thanksgiving for his goodness and mercy and the "dedication of ourselves to him and his service forever."[45] Participation in this sacrament is for those who "place all their dependence on him only; who feel his love constraining them, and are

---

[42] Davies, *Sermons*, 2:145.

[43] Davies, *Sermons*, 2:145.

[44] Davies, *Sermons*, 2:146.

[45] Davies, *Sermons*, 2:146.

determined to 'live no more to themselves, but to him that died for them, and rose again.'"[46]

It hardly needs to be said that all this interest in the suffering and death of Jesus only makes sense because of the resurrection. With the resurrection it was made clear that God had accepted the sacrifice. The suffering was not simply one more tragedy, but ultimate victory. It was therefore that it was celebrated on the Lord's Day, the day of resurrection.

B. Sacrament

The second point Davies makes is, "The Lord's supper was appointed as a badge of our Christian profession, and of our being the disciples of Jesus Christ."[47] Our colonial American theologian seems to be well aware of Tertullian, the ancient Christian theologian from North Africa, and his explanation of the Latin word *sacramentum*. Zwingli had given great weight to the thoughts of Tertullian and, as we have seen, the basic thoughts of Tertullian were often recounted by Reformed theologians. Davies does not specifically mention Tertullian by name, but the ideas are recognizable all the same.

As Davies puts it, "We openly profess that we are not ashamed of the cross or the religion of the despised Nazarene, but publicly avow our relation to him before the world. This perhaps may be intended by that expression of St. Paul, *showing the Lord's death*. We show, profess, and publish to all the world the regard we have even to his ignominious death. We may look upon this ordinance as an oath of allegiance to Jesus Christ."[48] Again we recognize the thought of Tertullian. Baptism was understood this way as was the reciting of the Creed. As Tertullian had explained it, the Creed was nothing less than the vows of faith made at baptism. In more biblical language, they would be referred to as the covenant vows. Tertullian's expla-

---

[46] Davies, *Sermons*, 2:146.

[47] Davies, *Sermons*, 2:147.

[48] Davies, *Sermons*, 2:147.

nation contributed substantially to the covenantal understanding of baptism and the Lord's Supper. Even more, it reflected the New Testament understanding of both baptism and the Lord's Supper.

Davies continues this thought by telling us, "And hence probably it was first called [*sacramentum*] a sacrament; which probably signifies an oath, and particularly that kind of oath which the Roman soldiers took to their generals, in which they engaged to be faithful to their leaders, and to fight for their country, and never desert its cause."[49] Obviously Davies has far more in mind about the sacrament of the Lord's Supper than a memorial of someone who tragically died seventeen hundred years before. To understand the sacrament as an oath of allegiance is to see the sacrament not only as a memorial of Christ but, even more, as a commitment to him.

Davies follows his argument even further by quoting much the same thought from another ancient North African theologian, Augustine. The edition of Davies' sermons before me gives the words of Augustine in quotation marks and provides the Latin text in a footnote.[50] The translation runs as follows:

> Ye know, my beloved, that the soldiers of this world, who receive but temporal rewards from temporal masters, do first bind themselves by military sacraments or oaths, and profess that they will be faithful to their commanders; how much more, then, ought the soldiers of the eternal King, who shall receive eternal rewards, to bind themselves with the heavenly sacraments or oaths, and publicly profess their fidelity to him![51]

---

[49] Davies, *Sermons*, 2:147.

[50] Davies, *Sermons*, 2:148. His footnote tells us that Augustine's quotation is found in "August. [Augustine] Oper. [*Opera Omnia* (Complete Works)] Tom [Volume] x. p. 984." Davies, when he was president of Princeton, was the first to catalogue all of the university's books, and in that catalogue, which Davies had published, we find a Latin folio edition of Augustine's complete works in ten volumes, printed in "Basil" in 1556. This means Princeton owned a later printing of the Froben Edition text edited by Erasmus and printed in Basel, Switzerland. This is most likely the very copy from which Davies read and quoted.

[51] Davies, *Sermons*, 2:147–148.

Davies comments, "Now if we receive the sacrament of the Lord's supper in this view, we assume a badge or mark of distinction from the rest of the world, and openly profess ourselves his disciples. We take a solemn oath of allegiance to him, and swear that we will be his faithful servants and soldiers to the end of life."[52] Zwingli, Bucer, and Calvin were all well aware of the significance of Tertullian's rediscovery for the recovery of eucharistic faith and worship.[53] They well understood that Augustine had built on Tertullian, and their insights were obviously kept fresh in the minds of Reformed pastors well into the eighteenth century.

The reciting of the Creed played an important role not only in the Lord's Supper service of Zurich but in that of Geneva as well. The reciting of the Creed both at baptism and at the Lord's Supper was characteristic of Reformed worship until very recently.

C. Covenant

The third point of Davies' sermon is, "We may consider this ordinance of the Lord's supper as a seal of the covenant of grace, both upon God's part and upon ours."[54] Here, too, we have an insight which goes back to the early years of the Reformation. The recovery of a covenantal theology of the sacrament, as we have pointed out, played a large role in the eucharistic thought of both Oecolampadius and Bullinger. It can be traced back to Luther, but it was Oecolampadius and especially Bullinger who really developed it. Calvin, as we have said, assumed it, and yet he was not the one who really worked it out.

Davies in a few words puts the covenantal dimension of the Lord's Supper very simply and clearly. "Every sacramental institution seems to partake of the general nature of a seal; that is, it is

---

[52] Davies, *Sermons*, 2:148.

[53] On the influence of Tertullian on the first generation of Reformers, see Hughes Oliphant Old, *The Patristic Roots of Reformed Worship* (Zurich: Theologische Verlag Zurich, 1975), pp. 283–289.

[54] Davies, *Sermons*, 2:149.

a sensible sign for the confirmation of a covenant or contract."[55] What is interesting about this passage is that it shows us how much Davies and his generation of Reformed theologians looked to the long tradition of biblical signs to understand the Christian sacraments, such as the sign of the rainbow given to Noah, the sign of circumcision given to Abraham, and the sign of Passover given to Moses. Again we see that the typological dimension of the sacraments was cherished by Reformed theologians. So many of the prophets had given signs to seal the promises they had been sent to proclaim. It was in terms of these signs of the covenant that Reformed theologians have again and again understood the sacrament of the Lord's Supper. To make his point that the Lord's Supper is a seal of the covenant Davies appeals to the fact that the apostle Paul calls circumcision a sign and a seal:

> This St. Paul expressly asserts, with regard to circumcision, when he says, that "Abraham received the sign of circumcision, a seal of the righteousness of faith." Rom. iv. 11. And Christ asserts the same thing concerning the ordinance now under consideration: *This cup*, says he, *is the New Testament*, or covenant, *in my blood*; that is, it is a ratifying sign or seal of the covenant of grace, which is founded in my blood.[56]

This passage from Romans was very helpful to the Reformers when they had tried to find a way to understand the sacraments in terms of biblical theology rather than in terms of Scholastic philosophy. The passage made clear how it is that we are justified by faith, and yet the sacraments do have a very significant role in our redemption; the sacraments become signs and seals of the salvation that comes by faith. The sacraments do not save us. We are saved by the grace of God working through faith. The sacraments are a sign of that grace and a seal of the promise of salvation through faith.

As Davies understands it the words of institution as we find

---

[55] Davies, *Sermons*, 2:149.

[56] Davies, *Sermons*, 2:149. Italics in the original.

them in 1 Corinthians 11:25 say much the same thing as Romans 4:11 when they tell us that the cup is the new covenant in his blood. What this means is that to drink of the cup is to receive the sign and the seal of the covenant of grace. To make this clear Davies gives us a thumbnail sketch of covenant theology. He tells us that God deals with the human race through covenants or contracts. One might say he deals with us through a charter or constitution. God is one party to these covenants, man is the other, and Christ is the mediator. The terms of the covenant are that out of his love for us, his creatures, he is willing to restore sinners to the life for which God had originally created us. In view of the atoning sacrifice of his Son he is willing to bestow pardon for all our sin, the blessings of this life, and the gift of eternal life upon all those who truly desire to know God and serve him according to his word. For our part we are to receive and submit to Jesus Christ as our Lord and Savior. We are to believe in him with all our hearts, repent of our sin, and devote ourselves to Christ's service. "This is the substance of that happy contract: and of this the Lord's supper is a seal as to both parties."[57]

The question is, does this covenant really need to have a sign or a seal for it to be valid? Is it not enough for the covenant to be proclaimed and for us to receive it by faith? To this question Davies answers, "On God's part this covenant can receive no intrinsic confirmation. He has plainly declared it in his word; and no oaths or confirming signs can add any intrinsic certainty to his declaration."[58] An honest man's word is as good as his bond, as it is often said. How much more is it true of the Word of God? God's Word needs no external authority or proof. It is its own authority, simply because it is God's Word. Yet from the human standpoint a sign is necessary. The weakness of human flesh makes signs necessary. It is for the sake of our human weakness that God regularly confirms his Word with signs and wonders.

---

[57] Davies, *Sermons*, 2:150.

[58] Davies, *Sermons*, 2:150.

So it is from the human side of things that sacraments are signs and seals which make clear our participation in the covenant:

> As our part in receiving these elements, we signify our hearty consent to the covenant of grace, and, as it were, set our seal to it to confirm it. The language of that speaking action is to this purpose; "I cordially agree to the plan of salvation through Jesus Christ revealed in the gospel; and in token thereof I hereunto affix my seal. As I take this bread and wine before many witnesses, so I openly and avowedly take and receive the Lord's Jesus as my only Saviour and Lord . . . ."[59]

D. COMMUNION

Next our colonial American preacher presents the Lord's Supper as communion. It is both intended as an experience of communion among fellow Christians with each other and as communion with God. Behind this word "communion" in the original Greek text is the word *koinonia*. Davies does not mention the Greek word, but it is clear that he is well aware of its characteristic range of meaning. In our common parlance today we usually speak of the fellowship of Christians, meaning the sharing of a common life together, while when we want to speak of our relationship with God we tend to speak of communion with God; yet, behind the two is that basic Greek word, *koinonia*.

First Davies speaks of communion as fellowship with the saints. He notices that this doctrine is so important that it is expressed in the Apostles' Creed, or, as Davies puts it, "the common creed of the Christian church."[60] When we say the Creed we profess our belief in the communion of the saints. Davies gives us a definition of the communion of the saints, "By the communion of the saints, I mean that mutual love and charity, that reciprocal acknowledgment of each other, that brotherly intercourse and fellowship,

---

[59] Davies, *Sermons*, 2:150–151.
[60] Davies, *Sermons*, 2:151.

which should be cultivated among them as children of the same father, in the same family, and as members of the same society, or mystical body."[61] We should notice that the first thing Davies says is that the communion of the saints has to do with mutual love and charity. The communion of the saints is a supportive fellowship, a fraternal sharing, a family relationship, and a social union. Typical of the eighteenth century it is more a matter of the heart than the head. It is not primarily intellectual or cognitive, but rather it is thoroughly experiential and relational.

We also notice that it is in accordance with this understanding of the communion of the saints that Davies explains the practice of sitting around the table. In America, the typical Reformed Church arranged the pews in such a way that the congregation was seated around the communion table. In some cases a special table was set up for the occasion and chairs were put around the table, but in other places the pews were arranged around the table and no rearrangement of the furniture was necessary. However the furniture may have been set up, the point was that the congregation received the bread and wine sitting at or around the table. The important thing was that the sign of sharing a meal needed to be preserved. Davies makes the point, "Our sitting down at the same table, partaking of the same elements, and commemorating the same Lord, are very expressive of this communion, and have a natural tendency to cultivate and cherish it. In such a posture we look like children of one family, fed at the same table upon the same spiritual provisions."[62] The typology of the household of faith is clearly significant for Davies.

Davies notes that the sacrament of the Lord's Supper is often called "the communion." He points out that it is called by this name in 1 Corinthians 10:16–17, "'The cup of blessing which we bless, is it not the communion of the blood of Christ?' that is,

---

[61] Davies, *Sermons*, 2:151.

[62] Davies, *Sermons*, 2:151–152.

Is it not a token and pledge of our joint share and communion in the blessings purchased by his blood? 'The bread which we break, is it not the communion of the body of Christ?' that is, Is it not a sign of our common right to the happy effect of the suffering of his body?"[63]

Davies follows this allusion to 1 Corinthians 10:16–17 with a reference to a simile so often used in the ancient church. Just as a loaf of bread is made of many grains of wheat, so the church becomes one body made up of many members. To make sure, however, that this simile is not misunderstood, he adds a caution, stressing that this union is a social union, "one sacred body politic."[64] What Davies understands this text to speak about is not some sort of monolithic, ontological union in which we all lose our identity. He obviously understands it as a covenantal bond. It is a social bond, held together by a covenant.

Second, Davies wants to speak of our communion with God. "In this ordinance God maintains communion with his people, and they with him."[65] Communion is not a private devotion of the individual soul with the creator, but a devotion of the covenant community with him who granted the covenant and thereby established the covenant community. Christian worship is essentially social. We worship God together as a people. "This is a communion of a more divine and exalted kind than the former." The communion we have with one another is an essential presupposition of the communion we have with God. It is in our joining together that we enter into God's presence. It is often "mentioned in Scripture as the privilege of the people of God. *Our fellowship*, says St. John, *is with the Father, and with his Son Jesus Christ.* I John i.3."[66] It is this which we hear in the Apostolic Benediction which

---

[63] Davies, *Sermons*, 2:152.

[64] Davies, *Sermons*, 2:152.

[65] Davies, *Sermons*, 2:154.

[66] Davies, *Sermons*, 2:154.

often concludes the service of worship.[67]

Davies gives us a definition of this communion between God and his people. He understands it partly in terms of the communication between God and his people and partly in terms of the community of property and sharing of goods. There is a material side to this and there is a spiritual side. "He communicates his love and the influences of his Spirit to them; and they pour out their hearts, their desires, and prayers before him. He draws near to them, and revives their souls; and they draw near to him, and converse with him in prayer, and in other ordinances of his worship."[68] This is what is meant when it is said that God dwells among his people. In 1 Corinthians 6 we even read that our bodies are the temples of the Holy Spirit (1 Cor. 6:16–19). As children of the same Father, we are joint heirs of the same inheritance. The relation between God and his people is often seen as being as close as the relation between husband and wife. This conjugal relation is drawn out at considerable length, "Here again the conjugal relation may be a proper illustration. As the wife is entitled to the inheritance of her husband, and he is answerable for her debts and obligations, so Christ made himself answerable in behalf of his people, for all their debts to the law and justice of God; and they are entitled to all the blessings he has purchased. Oh what a gracious and advantageous exchange is this for us!"[69] As we see here, the typology of the Song of Solomon constantly recurs.

The sign of sharing a meal is central to the celebration of the sacrament. Davies is quite emphatic about this. "Now the Lord's Supper is a very proper emblem of this communion, and a suit-

---

[67] Here is one of the few evidences I know of which attests to the use of the Apostolic Benediction at the close of an American Protestant service of worship. Most of the evidence suggests the Aaronic Benediction was the benediction most frequently used.

[68] Davies, *Sermons*, 2:154–155.

[69] Davies, *Sermons*, 2:155.

able means to cultivate it. It is the place where Christ and his people meet, and have their interviews. He, the great Master of the feast, feeds them at his own table, upon his own provisions, in his own house, and they eat and drink, as it were, in company with him; and thus it is a social entertainment between them."[70] The diction of the mid-eighteenth century is a bit unusual here, but what Davies intends is abundantly clear. The visual sign of sharing table fellowship makes very clear to us that God has welcomed us into a family-like relation to himself and to our brothers and sisters in Christ. It is an intimate and familiar relationship that we have with God as we gather about this table.

If there is to be a real communion with God, then there must be a real presence of God at this table. Davies tells us, "There he favours them with his spiritual presence, and gives them access to him; and they draw near to him with humble boldness, and enjoy a liberty of speech and conversation with him."[71] The sign of sharing a meal with Christ and sitting at table with the Savior makes clear the reality of the presence. That was as true in colonial Virginia as it had been in the Upper Room or beside the Sea of Galilee.

But communion is more than presence. It is a sharing as well. "There, under the elements of bread and wine, he makes over to them his body and blood, and all the blessings purchased by his sufferings; and they receive them with eager desire; they cast their guilt and unworthiness upon him, and give themselves to him, in return for his richer gifts to them."[72] This is central to the meaning of that New Testament word *koinonia*, which we translate by the English word "communion." Samuel Davies does understand his New Testament Greek! We not only enjoy his presence, he shares with us and we share with him. "There is a solemn exchange made between them of guilt for righteousness, of misery for happiness,

---

[70] Davies, *Sermons*, 2:155–156.

[71] Davies, *Sermons*, 2:156.

[72] Davies, *Sermons*, 2:156.

of the curse for a blessing, of life for death."[73] This exchange is essential to communion. The sign of this exchange is the sharing of a meal, a family meal. Sitting together about the table, we are all served and we all serve. "And of all this, his appointing and their receiving this ordinance, and, as it were, sitting down together at one table, like husband and wife, or parent and children, is a very proper emblem and representation."[74]

Very interestingly, Davies makes a remark at this point which reveals that his high vision of the sacrament of the Lord's Supper was the common experience of many in his congregation. He says, "I doubt not but some of you, upon such occasions, have enjoyed the pleasures of communion with him, which gives you a high esteem for this sacred feast, and clearer ideas of its design, than is the power of any language to afford."[75] In eighteenth-century colonial America the celebration of the Lord's Supper was indeed the Christian feast, a regularly recurring high point in the Christian life.

When Samuel Davies organized his Presbyterian congregation in Hanover County, Virginia, it was the Episcopal Church which was the established church of the colony. The Episcopal Church had retained the practice of going forward, kneeling at the altar, and receiving the bread and the wine from the hands of the clergy. The Reformed practice of sitting about the table to receive the sacrament from other members of the congregation would have been considered a novelty. Davies put a great emphasis on the sign of sitting about the table because he was a firm supporter of the value of this solidly Protestant liturgical practice.

E. Evangelism

The sermon we have just studied is a most comprehensive sermon. Surely there were many more things which our colonial Ameri-

---

[73] Davies, *Sermons*, 2:156.

[74] Davies, *Sermons*, 2:156.

[75] Davies, *Sermons*, 2:156–157.

17: THE GREAT AWAKENING
OTHER VOICES

can preacher might have said on the subject. One sermon would hardly exhaust his thoughts, as comprehensive as that sermon might be. A sermon which beautifully complements the sermon we have just studied is Sermon 55, "The Gospel Invitation."[76] It is interesting because it brings out the evangelistic dimension of the Lord's Supper.

The sermon is well named. It is an invitation to receive the gospel. It is preached on Jesus' parable, the wedding feast of the king's son (Luke 14:21–24). Once again we see that this parable was frequently used as the sermon text for the celebration of the Lord's Supper in Reformed churches of the seventeenth and eighteenth centuries. Surely the reason for this is not only that it expresses the evangelistic dimension of the sacrament but its eschatological dimension as well. In Reformed churches of the period the Lord's Supper was understood as a foretaste of the wedding feast of the Lamb, an invitation to the heavenly banquet. To participate in the sacrament was received as a sign that one would enter into the eternal kingdom of Christ and all his saints. The introductory paragraph to the sermon puts it very well:

> So vast and various are the blessings proposed to our acceptance in the gospel, that they can never be fully represented, though the utmost force of language be exhausted for that purpose in the sacred writings. Among other lively images, this is one in my context, where the gospel is compared to a feast, a marriage-feast of royal magnificence. The propriety and significancy of this representation are obvious at first sight; for what is more rich and elegant, and what more agreeable to mankind, than such an entertainment![77]

Davies, being a careful expositor of Scripture, spends some time explaining the primary sense of the passage as we find it in the Gospel of Luke. Jesus wants to make clear to the Jews of his day

---

[76] Davies, *Sermons*, 2:627–643.

[77] Davies, *Sermons*, 2:627.

that the Gentiles are to be included in the kingdom. It is not, however, this message that our preacher wants to get across. It is an accommodated sense of the passage that Davies wants to unfold to his congregation.[78]

One point which is very clear from Davies' sermon is what those blessings of the gospel are which are represented by a marriage feast, or, to use the old terms of traditional theology, what is the *res* of the sacrament. First, it is pardon for sin, for thousands, even millions of the most aggravating sins.[79] Second, it is the influence of the Holy Spirit. Here we come to that basic concern of Reformed theology to make clear the work of the Holy Spirit. It is "the influences of the Holy Spirit to sanctify our depraved natures, to subdue our sins, and implant and cherish in our hearts every grace and virtue."[80] It is the Holy Spirit working in our hearts which gives us "freedom from the tyranny of sin and Satan, and favorable access to the blessed God."[81] This is beautifully put, but even more an indication of the rich development of the pneumatic dimension of Reformed eucharistic theology.

Davies is equally perceptive in his insights on the work of the Holy Spirit in effecting eucharistic communion. It is through the Holy Spirit working in our hearts that we have sweet communion with God through Jesus Christ, even in this world. This is surely an important aspect of the blessing of the Supper. The sign of the shared meal makes this most clear. The *res* of the sacrament is ultimately communion with God the Father and with our brothers and sisters in Christ. Again we notice that the household of faith typology is strong. In the Supper there are "the reviving communications of divine love, to sweeten the affections of life; and the constant

---

[78] Davies, *Sermons*, 2:632.

[79] Davies, *Sermons*, 2:631.

[80] Davies, *Sermons*, 2:631.

[81] Davies, *Sermons*, 2:631.

assistance of divine grace to bear us up under every burden, and to enable us to persevere in the midst of many temptations . . ."[82]

Again the eschatological dimension of the sacrament comes out strongly when Davies tells us the blessings of the sacrament include, "a title to heaven, and all its inconceivable joys." The Lord's Supper is a sign and a seal of the wedding feast of the Lamb; it is in the preaching of the gospel that we are invited, and, in receiving it by faith, our place is reserved. Even more it is an appetizer, an *hors d'oeuvre* which intimates the delicacies yet to come. "In short," Davies tells us, the Supper is a sign and seal of "complete salvation in due time, and everlasting happiness equal to the largest capacities of our nature."[83]

Another point which is very clear from this sermon is that what we really do at the Lord's Supper is receive Christ as our Savior. We accept the gospel. "The duty represented by complying with an invitation to a marriage feast, in this parable, implies our embracing the gospel as true, . . ."[84] Here is where we commit ourselves to Christ; here is where the decision is made; here is where we make the vows of the covenant and become participants in the covenant community.

The evangelistic intention of the sermon becomes even clearer as our preacher continues. Davies tells his congregation that he is one of those servants whom the king has sent out to the poor and the crippled and the blind to urge them to come into the feast. "Where are the poor, the maimed, the halt, and the blind? In quest of you I am sent; and I am ordered to bring you in. And will ye refuse? Come, ye poor! accept the unsearchable riches of Christ. Come, ye blind! admit the healing light of the Sun of Righteousness. Ye halt and maimed! submit yourselves to him, who, as a Physician, can heal what is disordered, and as a Creator can add what is wanting.

---

[82] Davies, *Sermons*, 2:631.

[83] Davies, *Sermons*, 2:631.

[84] Davies, *Sermons*, 2:633.

Come, ye hungry, starving souls! come to this feast . . ."[85]

To be sure, the invitation is offered to his congregation in Hanover County, Virginia. It is offered to all of them, of course. Yet, it is an invitation that has been offered to countless men and women for seventeen hundred years now. Here we find, however, a most interesting fact. Davies is quite explicit that it is offered not only to the white planter, the artisans, shoemakers, and blacksmiths, but to the "negroes" as well. He assures them that there are seats in heaven reserved for them. He urges them to enter into the banquet! "Come then, let this feast be adorned with your sable countenances, and furnished with guests from the savage wilds of Africa."[86]

Samuel Davies is famous for his contribution to American education. When one mentions this it is usually his work in establishing Princeton University, but Davies was also an enthusiastic supporter of education for black people. Davies, however, was above all an evangelist, and it was because he was fundamentally an evangelist that he did so much for education. Like Billy Graham at the end of the twentieth century, he was an inclusive evangelist, believing that the King had sent his servants out into the highways and hedgerows, the inner cities and backwoods of the world, to issue the invitation into the kingdom to every human being—poor people, tax collectors, black slaves, "rednecks," and, yes, even the lily-white planters of Tidewater Virginia. To celebrate the sacrament of the Lord's Supper as Christ intended it to be celebrated is to invite everybody in.

More must be said, however. It is not the social problems of this world which is our ultimate concern. The invitation is to a transcendent life. What Davies brought up in this sermon was destined to be a major concern of American Christianity. Black people heard the invitation and they slowly began to accept it. In the course of time, they accepted it with enthusiasm and began

---

[85] Davies, *Sermons*, 2:636–637.
[86] Davies, *Sermons*, 2:640.

to enter into communion not only with the Father but with the brethren as well. To read this invitation as Davies made it in the middle of the eighteenth century only makes us realize the eternal significance of liturgical tradition.

18

NEW SCHOOL CONGREGATIONALISM

The Great Awakening had peaked by the time Timothy Dwight had become president of Yale. The time had come to look for a new revival. As Lyman Beecher saw it, the new president of Yale was the one who was to bring in a second Great Awakening. Beecher may have exaggerated Dwight's role, but it is certainly true that Dwight's ministry marked the beginning of a new era in the piety of American Protestantism. This is certainly evident in two sermons on the Lord's Supper found in the systematic theology Dwight's students published shortly after his death in 1817: *Theology, Explained and Defended, in a Series of Sermons*.[1]

Rather early in his ministry, Dwight began to have trouble with his eyesight. The trustees of Yale provided him with an amanuensis—a particularly gifted young man named Nathaniel Taylor. Eventually the young theologian became Timothy Dwight's successor. Nathaniel Taylor, then, did much to mature the theology of New England. Between the two of them, Dwight and Taylor, Yale enjoyed some fifty years of consistent theological leadership.

What we find most interesting is the way that these New Englanders came to understand the celebration of the sacrament subjectively, that is, they understood participation in the sacrament to be a subjective experience. To be sure there is the objective experience, but more important is the subjective experience that we feel in our hearts. What we find here in Dwight and Taylor is not so very different from what we find in the German theologian

---

[1] Timothy Dwight, *Theology, Explained and Defended, in a Series of Sermons*, 5 vols. (Middletown, CT: Clark and Lyman for Timothy Dwight, New Haven, 1818–1819).

Friedrich Schleiermacher (1768–1834). We notice, in fact, that these men were contemporaries. Here, again, we are dealing with the religious affections of admiration, gratitude, humility, obedience, brotherly love, and goodwill to all people. The symbols that are laid out before us and even held out and offered to us inspire our religious affections, our devotions, and our resolutions to live a more profoundly Christian life. For the New Englanders, the celebration of Holy Communion is above all the sharing of a sacred meal that nourishes us in godliness.

TIMOTHY DWIGHT

Timothy Dwight (1752–1817) was born in Northampton, Massachusetts, the son of a prominent businessman in Northampton and Mary, the third daughter of Jonathan Edwards.[2] God had blessed Jonathan Edwards with a large family of one son and ten daughters. Timothy Dwight was the elder brother of a large family. His father, also Timothy, was one of twelve children, while he and his wife, Mary Edwards, brought ten children into the world. Not only was Timothy Dwight the Elder a prosperous farmer, he was also a merchant and served as a major in the Connecticut Regulars. The name Timothy Dwight was perpetuated for several generations.

As one looked at it in those days, Edwards' daughter married well. But, then, she was not only the daughter of Jonathan Edwards, she was also the great granddaughter of Solomon Stoddard, the

---

[2] For biographical information on Timothy Dwight, see: Charles E. Cuningham, *Timothy Dwight, 1752–1817* (New York: Macmillan Company, 1942); William C. Dowling, "Timothy Dwight," in *American National Biography* (Oxford and New York: Oxford University Press, 1999); John R. Fitzmeir, *New England's Moral Legislator: Timothy Dwight, 1752–1817* (Bloomington: Indiana University Press, 1998); John R. Fitzmeir, "Dwight, Timothy," in *Dictionary of Christianity in America*, ed. Daniel G. Reid, Robert D. Linder, Bruce L. Shelley, and Harry S. Stout (Downers Grove, IL: InterVarsity Press, 1990), pp. 370–371; Albert H. Freundt, Jr., "Dwight, Timothy," in *Encyclopedia of the Reformed Faith*, ed. Donald K. McKim (Louisville: Westminster John Knox Press; and Edinburgh: Saint Andrew Press, 1992), p. 112; Kenneth Silverman, *Timothy Dwight*, (New York: Twayne Publishers, 1960); and Annabelle S. Wenzke, *Timothy Dwight (1752–1817)* (Lewiston, NY: E. Mellen Press, 1989).

minister who had founded the church at Northampton. Northampton, when the church was planted there, was on the frontier of New England. It was on the shores of the Connecticut River, upstream from New Haven. Furthermore, the Connecticut River is the largest river in New England, connecting Northampton, Hartford, and finally New Haven, where the colony of Connecticut had been founded in 1662. At New Haven the Connecticut empties into Long Island Sound. There was no question about it: in 1795, when Timothy Dwight was named president of Yale, he was profoundly connected with New England Congregationalism.

Theologically Timothy Dwight was very much concerned to stamp out the influence of the Enlightenment. He particularly opposed what he called the French apostasy, but he was also very critical of David Hume and several of the English philosopher-theologians of the day. His lectures at Yale were regarded as sermons that defended orthodox Christianity. It was these sermons that inspired the Second Great Awakening. That, at least, was the way Lyman Beecher, one of his most popular students, regarded the work of his mentor.[3] Those who regarded the teaching of Dwight favorably tended to think of it as the "New Divinity" rather than the same old gospel. Still, it was quite opposed to the Unitarianism so prevalent in Boston. Looking at Dwight's New Divinity today we quickly recognize it as an American version of pietism, a second installment of the gospel preached by Jonathan Edwards.

A particularly interesting facet of Dwight's ministry is his support of the American Board of Commissioners for Foreign Missions. The often told story of how an Hawaiian islander ended up weeping on the steps of the Yale University Chapel begging the Congregational Church of New England to send missionaries to his home in the islands of the Pacific is well known. It was all part of the New Divinity.

It was while Timothy Dwight was professor of theology at

---

[3] See Fitzmier, "Dwight, Timothy."

Yale that we begin to notice a growing neglect of the sacrament of Holy Communion in the devotional life of American Protestantism. We see this in certain circles more than in others, but it seems to have taken place sometime between 1790 and 1830. It is most clearly documented in the sacramental sermons of Timothy Dwight, and, yet, what we find in Timothy Dwight seems to be more a sort of resistance to the current trend. It is not as though Dwight was promoting this neglect. As we will see, the grandson of Jonathan Edwards could come up with some very profound insights regarding the sacrament. It was just that other things were taking the place of the sacrament Christ had instituted. There were other influences that seem to have promoted this change as well. Among those influences was the Enlightenment, which had little interest in formal religious rites or ceremonies.

One has to admit that Timothy Dwight shows no great enthusiasm for the sacrament of the Lord's Supper.[4] He recognizes that it has played a major role in the worship of the Christian Church. He has not, however, left us a major work on the subject. All we have is two sermons which appear in the appropriate place in his systematic theology. Whether they were real sermons preached to a live congregation is not clear. Neither of the sermons appears to be a preparatory sermon. In fact, the communion seasons so popular in Scotland during the eighteenth century just don't seem to play a significant role in New England at the beginning of the nineteenth century. As vital as Jonathan Edwards' communion sermons so obviously were, Edwards' grandson seems to have lost contact with the tradition.

Having said this, let us look at Timothy Dwight's definition of the Lord's Supper.[5] "It is a symbolical religious service, instituted by Christ as a commemoration of his death. The symbols

---

[4] I have spent quite a bit of time looking for some primary sources on this subject, especially in the works of Joseph Bellamy and Samuel Hopkins, with no success.

[5] Quotations will be taken from Timothy Dwight, *Theology Explained and Defended, in a Series of Sermons*, 5 vols. (London: Reprinted for W. Baynes, 1822). Source taken from www.archive.org, accessed November 25, 2011.

18: NEW SCHOOL CONGREGATIONALISM

are bread broken, and wine poured out, denoting the breaking of His body and the effusion of His blood upon the cross."[6]

Dwight goes on to describe the service as follows: "The bread is to be broken and the wine poured out by a minister of the gospel only; and by him both are to be distributed to every member of the church who is present. . . . Before the administration of each of these elements, a prayer is to be made; in which the blessing of God is to be implored upon the celebration of the ordinance, and thanks are to be given to him . . ."[7] We notice that Dwight gives special attention to two elements in the communion prayer, namely, the communion invocation and the eucharistic prayer proper, that is, the thanksgiving for God's mighty acts of creation and redemption. ". . . Thanks are to be given to him, for his mercy and goodness generally, and particularly as displayed in the interesting event which is commemorated. The whole service is to be concluded with singing a psalm or hymn by the communicants."[8] One notices very carefully that Dwight follows the New Testament account, "and when he had given thanks he broke it" (cf. Matthew 26:26; Mark 14:22; Luke 22:19). The eucharistic prayer, that is, the prayer of thanksgiving, is at the heart of the service. Again one notices that the singing of the psalm or hymn at the conclusion of the sacred meal is a major part of the service.

Another thing we notice very carefully is that not only is this service frequently called the "eucharist," but also it is frequently called a "sacrament." As previously mentioned, this is a Latin word which refers to the oath given by a soldier on entering into his military service. In the Lord's Supper we make a promise to devote our lives to the service of God. The biblical word for this aspect of the service is "covenant." In taking part in the sacred meal we enter into a covenant relationship. Dwight certainly

---

[6] Dwight, *Theology Explained*, 4:328.

[7] Dwight, *Theology Explained*, 4:328–329.

[8] Dwight, *Theology Explained*, 4:328.

understood the point, but it was not a primary concern of his understanding. He was much more interested in understanding the Lord's Supper as a symbolic service that teaches us the nature of Christ's redemptive work.[9]

As Dwight understands it, the design of the Lord's Supper is to "represent the great sacrifice of Christ on the cross."[10] Dwight goes on to say, "The truth here declared is sufficiently evident from the breaking of the bread, and pouring out of the wine; and completely from the words of Christ; This is my body which is broken for you. 1 Cor. 11:24. And this is my blood of the New Testament which is shed for many. Mark 14:24."[11] What seems to interest Dwight is that in the Lord's Supper we go beyond what is heard with the ear. In the sacrament we are dealing with what is seen and felt. And yet it is in "a certain sense."

In the Lord's Supper this truth becomes evident more intensely than in any other religious ordinance. The breaking of the bread and the pouring out of the wine exhibit the sacrifice of Christ with a special force, a special liveliness. The effectiveness of this sacrament goes beyond even the Passover.

> All the parts of this service are perfectly simple, and are contemplated by the mind without the least distraction or later. The symbols are exact and most lively portraits of the affecting original; and present to us the

---

[9] Quite understandably, Dwight seems more influenced here by the eucharistic theology of John Wycliffe than that of Ulrich Zwingli. Tertullian had a strong influence on the theologians of Zurich because of the edition of Tertullian published by Beatus Rhenanus. One of the pastors of Zurich, Konrad Pellikan, had written the preface to that edition. It was from the Swiss Reformers that the sixteenth-century Reformation learned about the original meaning of the word *sacramentum*. It is still an open question as to whether Wycliffe was aware of Tertullian's contribution to the development of the Christian theological uses of the term in its earliest development. Eventually I would like to write an essay on Wycliffe and the sources of his eucharistic theology. It is becoming clear to me that the Reformers of Zurich had a very different approach than the English Reformer John Wycliffe.

[10] Dwight, *Theology Explained*, 4:330.

[11] Dwight, *Theology Explained*, 4:330.

> crucifixion and the sufferings of the great subject of it, as again undergone before our eyes.[12]

This is a rather strong statement and perhaps we should understand it in terms of Dwight's often used refrain, "in a certain sense." "We are not barely taught; we see and hear, and of consequence feel, that Christ our Passover was slain for us, and died on cross, that we might live."[13] Quite obviously for Dwight, the Lord's Supper exhibits to us the atonement which this divine person has accomplished for mankind. With the same intensity this sacred service exhibits to us our depravity, our justification by the grace of God, and generally the whole teaching of the doctrine of the church regarding the reconciliation of an apostate humanity to his offended Creator. "In this solemn ordinance, these truths are in a sense visible. The guilt of sin is here written with a pen of iron and with the point of a diamond. Christ in a sense ascends the cross; is nailed to the accursed tree; is pierced with the spear; and pours out his blood to wash away the sins of men. Thus in colors of life and death we here behold the wonderful scene in which was laid on him the iniquity of us all."[14] That this sacred feast is observed on the Lord's Day makes visible to us the resurrection. It is a foretaste of the wedding feast of the Lamb and the hope of eternal life. When the church comes together in this sacred assembly it demonstrates the communion of the saints and the fellowship of the body of Christ.[15]

As Dwight saw it, another of the purposes for which Christ instituted the sacrament of the Lord's Supper was to unite Christians in a "known, public, and efficacious, bond of union."[16] This is surely more than the "mere memorial" New England Congre-

---

[12] Classical Protestantism would never go along with this, and Dwight even might have backed away from it on second thought. Dwight, *Theology Explained*, 4:330.

[13] Dwight, *Theology Explained*, 4:330–331.

[14] Dwight, *Theology Explained*, 4:332. Notice the repetition of "in a sense."

[15] Dwight, *Theology Explained*, 4:338.

[16] Dwight, *Theology Explained*, 4:339.

gationalists are accused of teaching. What we clearly have is a covenantal dimension of the sacrament. Christians appear at the table of Christ in a body; as members of Christ who is the head of the body. They appear as members of one another. They appear as being professors of the Christian faith united in one faith, one hope, and one baptism. In the celebration of communion we are united in one system of doctrine and one code of behavior, one discipline and one common pilgrimage and one final home.[17] Even more significantly Dwight understands the sacrament of Holy Communion to be a visible and affecting pledge of Christ's love to his followers.

Still another reason this sacrament was given to us is that these signs of broken bread and poured out wine might stir up our religious affections. Dwight's grandfather, Jonathan Edwards, wrote one of the classics of American theology on this subject, namely, *On the Religious Affections*. This classic underlined the importance of observing religious rites with sincerity. Dwight's approach to communion, we can therefore expect, gives considerable importance to feeling the deepest emotions suggested by the rites.

"Our hearts should be stirred by the loveliness of virtue as well as the odiousness of sin, the threatenings of the law as well as the invitations and promises of grace. This invigorates our faith. It forms new resolutions."[18] Here Dwight's eloquence is impressive. There is no question but that Edwards' great contribution to Reformed theology was to appreciate the role of the emotions in our religious experience. Here we see a good example of this.

At this point Dwight turns to addressing himself to the question of the qualifications required of those who intend to participate in the sacred rite.[19] Dwight begins with a discussion of the typological background of the questions. Here, too, covenant theology is treated at length. The children of Israel were required to enter into

---

[17] Dwight, *Theology Explained*, 4:340.

[18] Dwight, *Theology Explained*, 4:342.

[19] Dwight, *Theology Explained*, 4:342.

covenant with God and by doing this they were entitled to all the covenantal privileges of the people of God. They avouched themselves to the LORD. That is, they made a vow to be God's people, to walk in his ways, and to keep his statutes. This swearing is in effect to enter into covenant with God. Furthermore these words contained a command to exercise truth and righteousness in this sacramental transaction. "That Christians, in making this profession, . . . are bound to act with sincerity, and to exhibit before the eye of God truth in the inward parts."[20] Here Dwight's pietism comes through loud and clear. It is the inward devotion that really counts.

It is in this discussion of the qualifications of the communicants that we today find the biggest problem with our Puritan heritage. Somehow the net result far too often was that few people in the pew dared approach the sacred Table because they were afraid that they did not have the worthiness demanded to approach it. Assurance of salvation was discussed endlessly and in the process grace, at times, fell out of sight. This, of course, began to be a problem long before the Reformation and even back to the patristic age. Both Chrysostom and Augustine complained about it.

So, then, how are we to approach the sacred Table? We are to draw near with admiration.[21] This disposition is indicated by the injunction, *Do this in remembrance of me.* We are not directed here to observe the sacrament with indifference but rather we are to engage ourselves in this rite with the most profound solemnity and most sincere affection and respect. "We are to remember Christ in this ordinance with ADMIRATION. Everything pertaining to the character of this glorious person is fitted to awaken this emotion of the mind."[22] Here we find the heart of the New School eucharistic theology. To participate in the service is to express one's admiration and devotion for the mystery of Christ's eternal deity, his incarnation,

---

[20] Dwight, *Theology Explained*, 4:343.

[21] Dwight, *Theology Explained*, 4:348.

[22] Dwight, *Theology Explained*, 4:348.

his life and ministry in this world, his love for mankind, his passion and death, his propitiatory sacrifice, his resurrection, his exaltation, and his sitting at the right hand of the Father. At the sacramental Table the whole character of Christ is brought before our eyes. At this point Dwight makes several points that would seem very close to the medieval doctrine of the repetition of the sacrifice.[23]

Our second response is to approach the Lord's Table with gratitude.[24] Whenever human culture has advanced to any degree of civilization, we have a recognition of this emotion. All peoples recognize the need to express the debt we owe to those who have advanced our way of life. So it is particularly with the emotion of gratitude. Here, again, we detect the influence of Timothy Dwight's distinguished grandfather, Jonathan Edwards. The Hebrew word of thanksgiving, *yadah*, is a particularly profound word. It recounts the history of salvation, acknowledges the depth of gratitude that is owed to the Savior, and rejoices in the good that has been conferred.

Dwight then teaches that we should approach the Lord's Table with humility.[25] Dwight takes up the text of the Apostle Paul, "God commendeth his love to us, in that, while we were yet sinners, he gave his Son to die for us."[26] It is not as though we learned the law and statutes of the Bible and kept them and thereby earned the blessings of God. It is far more that our frailty and our failures have proven we are not fit for God's kingdom and therefore God had to save us because there was no other way. The emotion of humility comes quite easily to those who have any inclination or sensitivity to the right, the good, and the fair. Here is one place, of course, where our Puritan forefathers were even more than realistic. In the Reformed tradition it is very clear that we must all approach the Lord's Table in a spirit of humility and repentance. While the piety

---

[23] Dwight, *Theology Explained*, 4:348.

[24] Dwight, *Theology Explained*, 4:350.

[25] Dwight, *Theology Explained*, 4:353.

[26] Cite as quoted in Dwight, *Theology Explained*, 4:353.

of New England never developed the preparatory service so avidly maintained by the Scots, it did insist that the worthy communicant should be sure that he or she be attired in the proper garments for a wedding feast. This would be done in one's prayer and devotion on Saturday evening by each individual in his or her prayer closet, as well as in following the prayers of the minister.[27]

When we come to the Lord's Table we are bound to offer most vigorous resolutions of obedience.[28] To participate in a communion service is to make a profession of faith, to offer oneself up to Christ to be our Lord and Savior. Here faith runs as a river through our lives. Here heart and head move in the same direction. This is the sort of religious affection that pietism would have from us. Here Dwight comes in very powerfully for the sincerity of our profession. The ultimate test is the saying of Jesus, "If you love me, keep my commandments" (cf. John 14:15).

To take part in the communion service is the deepest form of religion. It is the ultimate subjectivity. It is to enter into a relationship and even more it is to experience conversion. It is to cross over the bridge from a self-centered life to a God-centered life. But of one thing we must be fully aware—it is done in faith and in hope.

Dwight's next point is that "we are required to appear at the table of Christ with brotherly love."[29] Where there is faith and hope there must also be love. Faith, hope, and love, these three, are the essence of the Christian life. It is at the Lord's Table that Christians appear most intimately and yet most publicly. "They sit around one table, united in one covenant; commune in one worship; celebrate in one crucified Saviour; and, through him, are by

---

[27] See Charles E. Hambrick-Stowe, *The Practice of Piety: Puritan Devotional Practices in Seventeenth-Century New England* (Chapel Hill: Published for the Institute of Early American History and Culture, Williamsburg, Virginia, by the University of North Carolina Press, 1982).

[28] Dwight, *Theology Explained*, 4:356.

[29] Dwight, *Theology Explained*, 4:356.

adoption the children of one common Father."[30]

As Dwight reads it, the commandment to love one another as we find it in the Gospel of John was given immediately after the first celebration of the Lord's Supper. There is a most logical connection between the two. The commandment to love one another is acted out in the sacred rite. Our love, however, is not limited to the members of the Christian community. It is not limited to one another but is to spread out to all our fellow men.[31] It is here that our New England theologian brings in the question of presence. As he sees it, Christ is present at every celebration of Holy Communion. He is seated with us at the Table demonstrating the subjective reality pointed to by the objective rite.

New England theologians profoundly appreciated the subjective dimension of religious experience. Rationalism never sensed the inner reality of Christian doctrine. It rarely felt the power of faith. Nor did it understand the comfort of hope, but there is one more thing Dwight would like to consider and that is the motives of participating in the sacrament. Above all we celebrate Holy Communion because Christ commanded his disciples to do just that. The authority of Christ to demand the observance of this rite is rooted and granted in his divine authority. Furthermore, if we honor our Creator in our hearts at all we realize that it was the Son who was sent by the Father to gather in the faithful.[32] The Unitarianism so popular in early nineteenth-century New England found no support in the pulpit of Timothy Dwight. Those who would honor their Creator must worship as directed by the Son.

Surely one of Dwight's concerns was that the honoring of God be not only in public worship but also in the secret recesses of our hearts. Who can meditate on the passion of Christ, his mercy and generosity, and not sense the appropriateness of honoring him who

---

[30] Dwight, *Theology Explained*, 4:356.

[31] Dwight, *Theology Explained*, 4:358.

[32] Dwight, *Theology Explained*, 4:360.

18: New School Congregationalism

suffered and died for us? No one who knows the sacred history can hold back the exercises of devotion that the Church has for centuries offered to God Almighty each Lord's Day.

It is the heart worship of the believing congregation that Dwight addresses:

> If then we celebrate this ordinance in obedience to his command, we shall celebrate it in remembrance of Christ, with a design to honour him in our own hearts, and in the sight of others. When we call to find who it is to whom we render this honour, what he has done and what he has suffered for our sakes; what is the character of those for whom all this was done; and what is the nature, the number, and the magnitude, of those blessings which these sufferings have procured for his followers; we cannot fail to perceive, that not authority only, but benevolence also, benevolence operating in the most glorious manner, demands our obedience to this injunction of the Redeemer. Every ingenuous feeling of man is here addressed in the most forcible manner. The authority for which this precept proceeds, is the highest. The beneficence which enforces it, is unrivalled. Reverence for this authority, and gratitude for this beneficence, combine their obligatory power to produce in mankind a faithful and cheerful obedience to this precept.[33]

For Dwight a proper celebration of the sacrament demands much meditation. This, of course, goes back to John Calvin as well as plenty of other Reformed theologians. The sort of celebration Dwight has in mind cannot be rushed or hurried. Discerning the Lord's body takes time. As Dwight saw it, in the living out of his incarnation, Christ addresses our hearts, our inner being. Here we have a thoroughly pietistic approach to worship. In actual practice, the leisurely celebrations Dwight advocates might not be all that different from the celebrations of the Erskines after all.

Another beautifully pietistic passage follows a little further on:

---

[33] Dwight, *Theology Explained*, 4:359–360.

> To bring this subject home to your hearts, behold your Redeemer nailed to the cross. For whom was his body broken? For whom was his blood poured out? Who were the lost beings whom he came to seek and to save, and for whom he gave his life a ransom? On whose account was he forsaken of his Father? For whom did he give up the ghost, and descend to the grave? Whose sins did he wash away? For whom did he shut the gates of perdition, and open the door of endless life? Those who are now before me are the immortal, guilty, ruined beings for whom all this was done. You are the very sinners whom he came to redeem from the sins of this life, and the sorrows of that which is to come. To you he now proffers all the blessings of his mediation: the forgiveness of sin; the renovation of the soul; the hope, the peace, and the joy, which flourish with undecaying beauty in a pious mind; the guidance, the support, and the consolations, of his own Spirit; and an interest in his everlasting love. You, he wished, he labours, to constitute sons, and kings, and priests, to God our Father; and holds out to your acceptance crowns of immortal glory.[34]

Here, again, we find the same devotional intensity we found in the Erskines, or John Willison, or the Dutch pietists.

Let us look at another passage which expresses a thoroughly pietist expression of Christ's presence at the sacrament:

> Let the hearts of Christians burn within them, while Christ meets them at his table, and converses with them on all the agonies of the cross, on all the wonders of redeeming love, and on all the glories of that happy world to which he is gone before to prepare a place for their final residence. Let them listen with transport while he declares to them, If I go and prepare a place for you, I will come again and receive you unto myself, that where I am ye may be also, and let them exclaim, Amen, even so; come, Lord Jesus.[35]

---

[34] Dwight, *Theology Explained*, 4:360.

[35] Dwight, *Theology Explained*, 4:361.

18: New School Congregationalism

Particularly interesting is what Dwight has to say about the benefits of the sacrament. They are shown to us as we follow the service. At the Lord's Table we are provided with spiritual food. We are united to our brothers and sisters in Christ. We are shown our place at the wedding feast of the Lamb. We are given a taste of the glories to come. Here brotherly love is kindled into a flame. Sharing in the sacrament, like the other means of grace, exercises our faith, stimulates our devotion, and makes our devotion more ardent. At Holy Communion the religious affections purify our devotion, correct our thoughts, and stimulate our charity and benevolence. We experience an evangelical refreshment, a heavenly rapture.

Toward the end of Dwight's treatment of the sacrament of Holy Communion in his five volume systematic theology we find a few pages under the heading of REMARKS.[36] What we apparently have here are some notes on the subject of Holy Communion which the editor of Dwight's systematic theology found in the papers of our New England theologian, but which had not come down in the sermons originally preached. We find nothing new here, but we do find some hints for explaining why American Protestantism lost interest in the sacrament of Holy Communion in this very creative period.

First of all, Dwight wants to insist on the wisdom of this institution. The sacrament of communion was indeed established by Christ himself and it is "peculiarly worthy of the all-perfect mind."[37] From the way this passage reads, it sounds like Dwight is arguing with somebody. It sounds like he is admonishing the church of his day because he feels that the sacrament is being neglected. Strongly influenced by the rationalism of the eighteenth century, the sacrament seemed to many of those in the pew much too dreary.

Here we find Dwight arguing that communion teaches us "the

---

[36] Dwight, *Theology Explained*, 4:365–367.

[37] Dwight, *Theology Explained*, 4:365.

purification of our affections, and the amendment of our lives."[38] The sacrament is of value because it appeals so powerfully to the senses, the imagination, and the heart, and at the same time enlightens us in the happiest manner. Timothy Dwight obviously understands the sacrament from the standpoint of pietism and yet he feels some concern to respect the demands of the Enlightenment.

The second admonition we have here is the importance of preparing ourselves for the celebration of the sacrament. As far as I can discover, we have nothing in New England resembling the preparatory services in The Netherlands or Scotland, but apparently Dwight thinks of this as something that needs to be developed. Then we notice that Dwight argues for more frequent celebrations of the sacrament. He is obviously critical of the more infrequent celebrations of the Presbyterians in the middle and southern states.[39]

Furthermore, we find that Dwight argues for the solemnity of the celebration. Perhaps we have a hint here that Dwight is not too positively impressed by the enthusiasm of the frontier revivals such as those of Charles Finney. Apparently Dwight has not dwelt with the practical problem that it is hard to argue for more frequent celebrations on one hand and greater solemnity on the other. It is hard to get the congregation to come for preparatory services and at the same time to come to a celebration every Lord's Day. My elders once made me aware of this very practical problem.

NATHANIEL WILLIAM TAYLOR

The Great Awakening was history by the time Nathaniel Taylor (1786–1858) had become the leading theologian of Connecticut Congregationalism. New School theology was very much aware that it had pioneered a trail for American Christian thought and one usually takes great pains to make clear the uniqueness of the New School. On the subject of eucharistic piety, however, we are sur-

---

[38] Dwight, *Theology Explained*, 4:365.

[39] Dwight, *Theology Explained*, 4:366.

prised to find that one of the best statements of Reformed thought is to be found in the works of Nathaniel Taylor. This is surprising because we have but a single sermon from him on this subject.

Nathaniel Taylor was named for his grandfather, a widely respected pastor.[40] He was born in New Milford, Connecticut, in 1786. In 1807 he graduated from Yale. Five years later he became pastor of First Congregational Church in New Haven. This was the most prestigious pulpit in the state of Connecticut. One presumes he was an impressive young preacher to have been entrusted with that pulpit. Then ten years later he was appointed Timothy Dwight Professor of Didactic Theology at Yale. For the next thirty-six years he was a major voice in the American church. At the time, he represented the continuity of New England Theology. He began his work at Yale as amanuensis for Timothy Dwight, who was rapidly losing his eyesight. It was only after Taylor's death that his students published a selection of his works.[41]

So here we are with only one sermon on which to base our impressions of Taylor's teaching on the function of Holy Communion. If nothing else the scarcity of source material would seem to suggest that in New England Congregationalism the sacrament of Holy Communion had lost much of its importance. There is only one thing that makes us hesitate to draw this conclusion—the

---

[40] For biographical information on Nathaniel Taylor, see: "Taylor, Nathaniel William," in *The Encyclopedia Britannica*, 11th ed., 32 vols. (New York: Encyclopedia Britannica, 1911), 26:472; John R. Fitzmier, "Taylor, Nathaniel William," in *Dictionary of Christianity in America*, pp. 1161–1162; Earl William Kennedy, "Taylor, Nathaniel William (1786–1858)," in *Encyclopedia of the Reformed Faith*, p. 361; Sidney Earl Mead, *Nathaniel William Taylor (1786–1858), A Connecticut Liberal*, reprint of the 1942 edition (Hamden, CT: Archon Books, 1967); and Douglas A. Sweeney, *Nathaniel Taylor, New Haven Theology, and the Legacy of Jonathan Edwards* (Oxford and New York: Oxford University Press, 2003).

[41] Nathaniel W. Taylor, *Practical Sermons* (New York: Clark, Austin, and Smith, 1858). Two more volumes appeared the following years: Nathaniel W. Taylor, *Lectures on the Moral Government of God*, 2 vols. (New York: Clark, Austin and Smith, 1859) and Nathaniel W. Taylor, *Essays, Lectures, etc., upon Select Topics in Revealed Theology* (New York: Clark, Austin and Smith, 1859).

one eucharistic sermon which has come to us is particularly rich. Someone in the Congregational Church of New England must have been exploring the deeper issues of eucharistic theology.

The first hint that there is more going on here than most theologians have up to this point imagined is the rather unusual text Taylor has chosen for this sermon. He has chosen Psalm 4:6–7 (KJV):

> There be many that say, Who will show us any good?
>   Lord, lift thou up the light of thy countenance upon us.
> Thou has put gladness in my heart,
>   more than in the time
>   that their corn and their wine increased.

Introducing his sermon our preacher tells us that he would like to speak about what we are to understand by the light of God's countenance, and why the Christian desires it above all earthly good.[42]

Quite simply then what Taylor understands by the sacrament of Holy Communion is to enter into the presence of God. The light of God's presence is nothing less than to enjoy the religious affections. It is to know the favor of God. It is to behold the face of God and to experience the warmth and friendliness of the Almighty.[43] We notice here that Taylor is very careful to guard the typical Reformed teaching on the sufficiency of Scripture. It is not that the Christian needs to receive some unique doctrine or to go through some initiatory rite.[44] One gets the impression that Taylor is concerned to guard against those who would replace the sacrament of the Lord's Supper with the anxious bench or the "new methods."

For Taylor, as for the typical Reformed theologian, Christian faith is built on the promises of God. When presented in the ministry of Word and sacrament they are received by faith; they are

---

[42] Taylor, *Practical Sermons*, p. 75.

[43] Taylor, *Practical Sermons*, p. 76.

[44] Taylor, *Practical Sermons*, p. 77.

the basis of the religious affections.[45] The religious affections: love, hope, assurance, faith, and faithfulness, need to be exercised, and so they are in the ordinary means of grace. In the experience of every Christian there are seasons of darkness.[46] For the true Christian these times pass as God's grace beams upon us again.[47] There are many Christians who witness this experience. One wonders if Taylor had read David Brainerd or even perhaps the Spanish mystics. How many Christians have those triumphant discoveries of the power of the blood of Christ to wash us and cleanse us of all our sin, evil desires, and inward pollution.

Here we have from the systematic theologian what we found a couple generations before in the journals of David Brainerd, a real New England mysticism, a real Puritan mysticism. It is through prayer and meditation that we come to exercise the religious affections. Taylor tells us that the true Christian manages "by prayer, by meditation, by self-consecration, and by other exercises of devotion, to come near to God, even to his seat."[48] The true Christian understands what it is for God "to break forth on the soul with a clear manifestation of the perfections of his Godhead, and to impart to it a serenity 'mild as the zephyr and more rapturous than song.'"[49]

The religious affections serve as an assurance of the verity of our familiarity with God. In this state of mind there is between the soul and God a delightful fellowship with God.[50]

This union with God is particularly noticed in the fact that the true Christian is devoted to the same hopes and purposes set forth by the Almighty. Devotedness and submission to the will of God makes us one with him.[51] Included in these religious affections is

---

[45] Taylor, *Practical Sermons*, p. 78.
[46] Taylor, *Practical Sermons*, p. 80.
[47] Taylor, *Practical Sermons*, p. 81.
[48] Taylor, *Practical Sermons*, p. 82.
[49] Taylor, *Practical Sermons*, p. 82.
[50] Taylor, *Practical Sermons*, p. 84.
[51] Taylor, *Practical Sermons*, p. 85.

an adoring jog in the Creator's designs and an assimilation in his character and, above all, union in emotion that is nothing less than heavenly happiness. This is the oneness for which the Savior prayed, "As thou, Father, art in me, and I in thee, that also they may be one in us" (John 17:21, KJV).[52] One immediately recognizes, of course, the language of Christian mysticism as it is to be found all the way back through Christian history.

Taylor is particularly eloquent when he comes to speak of the religious affections pouring into our souls the hope of heaven.[53] It is when we meditate on God's promises that we become aware of God as he truly is. This brings us to an assurance of God's love, God's favor, and God's protection. For the Christian, it is important to long for that clear vision of God in the exercise of holy affections. It is this which imparts to the Christian the peace of God which passes all understanding, as the apostle Paul so profoundly put it. Or, again to use the terminology of the apostle Peter, "He who commanded the light to shine out of darkness hath shined in our hearts" (cf. 1 Pet. 2.9).

We notice here how staunchly Trinitarian Taylor is at this point. He clearly affirms the doctrine of the atonement as well as the divinity of Christ as the congregation approaches the Lord's Table. It is God in Christ that we approach as we come to this sacred Table. Come to the very throne of grace, expecting manifestations of the love of Christ. Expect here to be filled with the religious affections, lively faith, and ardent love. Meet here your God and Savior, for here he will lift up upon you the light of his countenance.

---

[52] Taylor, *Practical Sermons*, p. 86.

[53] Taylor, *Practical Sermons*, p. 87.

19

OLD SCHOOL PRESBYTERIANISM

The heyday of the Great Awakening was long past. America had become a prosperous, rapidly growing country, locked in a battle over expansion and slavery. The church was divided as well, reflecting the strains of pietism, revivalism, and ceremonialism against the traditional Calvinism of the colonial period. The Enlightenment had taken its toll. American theology was at a crossroads, and with it, its understanding of Holy Communion.

CHARLES HODGE

It would be hard to exaggerate the importance of Charles Hodge (1797–1878) for the shaping of nineteenth-century American Protestantism.[1] He was both its leading theologian and the distilled essence of its character. Hodge was above all a biblical scholar, exegete, and commentator, but he was also a systematic theologian, producing a three-volume systematic theology. Even more, he was a competent linguist, having studied his theology in Latin and discussed it in both German and French, not to mention English.

Charles Hodge was born in Philadelphia in the days when that city was the center of American intellectual life. His father

---

[1] For biographical information on Hodge, see: W. Andrew Hoffecker, *Charles Hodge: The Pride of Princeton* (Phillipsburg, NJ: Presbyterian and Reformed, 2011); Mark A. Noll, "Hodge, Charles (1797–1878)," in *New Dictionary of Theology*, eds. Sinclair B. Ferguson and David F. Wright (Downers Grove, IL, and Leicester, UK: InterVarsity Press, 1988), pp. 312–313; see also David B. Calhoun, *Princeton Seminary*, vol. 1, *Faith and Learning, 1812–1868* (Edinburgh and Carlisle: Banner of Truth Trust, 1994), pp. 103–124.

was a Scotch-Irish physician who regrettably died before his son was a year old. His mother raised him in comfortable, genteel circles. He married Sarah Bache, the great granddaughter of Benjamin Franklin. Franklin, of course, had been the most prominent citizen of Philadelphia for many years.

A. Princeton's Systematic Theologian

It was in 1815 that young Hodge graduated from the College of New Jersey in Princeton. He continued his education at Princeton Theological Seminary, which had only recently been founded by Archibald Alexander. Alexander became the surrogate father of this brilliant and promising young man, who up to this time had been raised by his widowed mother.

Soon after graduating from the seminary he was appointed to the faculty. In 1826, however, he left for Europe where he spent his time looking into the religious thought of the day. He acquainted himself with the religious philosophy of Friedrich Schleiermacher at the University of Berlin. He studied New Testament with Wilhelm Hengstenberg, the orthodox Lutheran biblical apologist. At Halle he made himself familiar with the pietist revival of August Tholuck. Hodge's theological curiosity was unbounded. Nevertheless Hodge was very cautious when it came to the heady theology he discovered in Germany. Even at that, he came home three years later with a whole library and standing orders with a number of leading book sellers in Berlin and London.

He devoted himself to writing a series of commentaries on several of the Pauline epistles, namely Romans, First and Second Corinthians, and Ephesians. These commentaries are still recognized as being of particular value. Hodge was careful in his research and clear in his exposition. One of Hodge's major contributions was his direction of the theological journal, *Biblical Repertory and Princeton Review*. He himself wrote many of the articles, giving informed and balanced reactions to a wide variety of religious issues of his day. Hodge was inclined toward an intelligent conservatism. On the one hand he was firmly opposed to the revivalism of Charles Finney and on the other the High Church ceremonialism of the Oxford movement. His defense of Calvinistic orthodoxy was polite, well-balanced, and consistent. As James W. Stewart put it, Hodge wrote "scholarly defenses of the Reformed doctrines of original sin and atonement" and advocated "Scottish common sense realism." He was suspicious of "Horace Bushnell's romanticism and Ralph Waldo Emerson's transcendentalism."[2]

Charles Hodge was very much a family man. He and his first wife Sarah Bache had seven children. Their son Archibald Alexander Hodge succeeded his father as professor of systematic theology at Princeton. A few years after the death of his first wife Charles Hodge married Mary Stockton, a daughter of Princeton's most prominent family. Richard Stockton had been a signer of the Declaration of Independence. The stately manor house of the Stockton family, Morven, was across the street from the seminary.

B. THE MEANS OF GRACE

Charles Hodge, like most other American Presbyterians in the middle of the nineteenth century, was brought up on the *Westminster Shorter Catechism*, and he was a meticulous follower of the Westminster Standards. The fact that he begins his chapter on the sacraments by reminding us that the *Catechism* teaches us that the means of grace are the Word, prayer, and sacraments, should tip us off to the bedrock of his sacramental theology.[3] Therefore we are hardly surprised when he begins this section by reminding us that the sacrament of Holy Communion is a means of grace. That was the teaching of the *Westminster Shorter Catechism* and that

---

[2] James W. Stewart, "Hodge, Charles (1797–1787)," *Encyclopedia of the Reformed Faith*, ed. Donald K. McKim (Louisville: Westminster John Knox Press, and Edinburgh: Saint Andrew Press, 1992), p. 175.

[3] Charles Hodge, *Systematic Theology*, vol. 3, reprint (Grand Rapids, MI: Eerdmans, 1973), 3:466f.

is where Hodge starts. The *Catechism* goes on to define a sacrament as ". . . an holy ordinance instituted by Christ; wherein, by sensible signs, Christ and the benefits of the New Covenant are represented, sealed, and applied to believers."[4]

Taking up the question of the nature of the sacraments, Hodge spends quite a bit of time looking at the Latin word *sacramentum*. The meaning of the word has always been something of a problem. It is not, of course, a biblical word, and during the Middle Ages one lost track of why the church has come to use the word the way it has. Elsewhere we have discussed this at considerable length. The Reformers of Zurich had been able to make some giant steps forward in discovering the meaning of the word through the discovery of some ancient manuscripts of Tertullian, who did so much to shape Christian Latin. As I've noted already, the original meaning of the word *sacramentum* is a vow of allegiance made by a soldier entering military service.[5] For this reason it was particularly appropriate to speak of baptism as a *sacramentum*. Later, then, it was applied to other religious rites. Hodge comes up with several quotations from Augustine that elucidate the meaning of the word in the Latin-speaking Church at the end of the patristic age.[6] Hodge also discusses how the Latin Vulgate used the word *sacramentum* to translate the Greek *musterion*, or mystery, in a number of important passages.[7] The erudition of Hodge is really impressive. The point that Hodge is obviously moving toward is that a sacrament is a sacred sign. It is a visible sign of a mystery that is beyond the visual and the tangible. Summing up his discussion he puts it this way:

> Baptism and the Lord's Supper are admitted to be sacraments. They are (1.) Ordinances instituted by Christ. (2.) They are in their nature significant, baptism of cleansing; the Lord's Supper of spiritual nourishment.

---

[4] Hodge, *Systematic Theology*, 3:487.
[5] Hodge, *Systematic Theology*, 3:486.
[6] Hodge, *Systematic Theology*, 3:485.
[7] Hodge, *Systematic Theology*, 3:486.

19: OLD SCHOOL PRESBYTERIANISM

> (3.) They were designed to be perpetual. (4.) They were appointed to signify, and to instruct; to seal, and thus to confirm and strengthen; and to convey or apply, and thus to sanctify, those who by faith receive them.[8]
>
> We especially want to notice the word "significant." It is the nature of the sacraments to signify. Sacraments have a message. This is of their essence.

At this point Hodge turns to the efficacy of the sacraments. It is a most interesting passage Hodge has left us here. He begins by addressing himself to the original position of Zwingli, as he sees it, and the position later taken by the Remonstrance, that is, the position of the followers of Arminius.[9] The problem with this position is that it denies that the sacraments are means of grace. As the Arminians see it, the sacraments may be signs of divine teachings. They may teach us and they may remind us but they do not in themselves convey divine grace. The term "means of grace" is then, from an Arminian point of view, misleading.

The clear teaching of the Reformed church, according to Hodge, is that the sacraments really are means of grace. This teaching we find again and again in the classic Reformed confessions of faith and catechisms. Hodge puts it this way:

> ... the sacraments are real means of grace, that is, means appointed and employed by Christ for conveying the benefits of his redemption to his people. They are not, as Romanists teach, the exclusive channels; but they are channels. A promise is made to those who rightly receive the sacraments that they shall thereby and therein be made partakers of the blessings of which the sacraments are the divinely appointed signs and seals.[10]

What this specifically means when speaking of the Lord's Supper is that God forgives us our sins in spite of our inability to deserve

---
[8] Hodge, *Systematic Theology*, 3:487.
[9] Hodge, *Systematic Theology*, 3:498.
[10] Hodge, *Systematic Theology*, 3:499.

that forgiveness. It means that the Holy Spirit transforms us so that we really do become the men and women God intended us to be. Furthermore, this all comes about through the work of God in our hearts. To put it in the words of Hodge himself, ". . . the efficacy of the sacraments is due solely to the blessing of Christ and the working of his Spirit."[11] It is not a matter of the minister being a miracle worker or the liturgy being a magical formula. It is because Christ has instituted this memorial and because the Holy Spirit is at work within us to bring about what the sign depicts. As I have tried to make the point ever since my doctoral thesis, the key to understanding Reformed worship is the doctrine of the Holy Spirit. Here is one important place where the teaching of Hodge closely follows that of Calvin.

One thing is very clear in the chapter Hodge gives us on the means of grace. Nothing is said that might indicate that the sacraments are of greater importance than the Word. He points out quite clearly that nothing is said in Scripture that would lead us to place the sacraments above the Word in communicating to us the benefits of redemption. Quite to the contrary, "tenfold more is said in Scripture of the necessity and efficiency of the Word in the salvation of men, than is therein said or implied by the power of the sacraments."[12] It is at this point, in sacramental theology in general, that Hodge finds himself on controversial ground. He gives us very careful distinctions between the Reformed position, the Roman position, and the Lutheran position. He quotes Cardinal Bellarmine, the seventeenth-century Jesuit theologian, as well as another Jesuit, a contemporary of Hodge, the Italian Giovanni Perrone, at considerable length. All this, of course, is in Latin.

It is, however, when he comes to discussing the necessity and the validity of the sacraments that Hodge is most convincing. Hodge cannot go along with the absolute necessity of the sacra-

---

[11] Hodge, *Systematic Theology*, 3:500.

[12] Hodge, *Systematic Theology*, 3:502.

ments as the Roman Catholics or the Lutherans understand it. As Hodge understands it, it is the role of the Holy Spirit that prevents us from adopting an *ex opere operato* approach to the sacraments.[13]

As Hodge sees it, what is really at issue here is ritualism. Does Christianity offer us salvation through ceremonial? That was what the Hellenistic mystery religions offered late antiquity and from time to time it has seemed that Christians have been tempted to follow the same approach. For Hodge the Christian antidote is John 4:24 (KJV), "God is a spirit: and they that worship him must worship him in spirit and in truth." In the last analysis, Hodge affirms, we are justified by faith, not by the observance of rites.[14]

One place where we find Hodge quite helpful is his recognition of the significance of the *Consensus Tigurinus*. Tigurinus, for those who might not be in on all the mysteries of Renaissance geography, is the Latin name for Zurich. There was an important development between the position of the earliest Reformed theologians, Zwingli and Oecolampadius, and the position reached by the later Reformed theologians, Bullinger and Calvin.[15] Bullinger was successor to Zwingli as pastor of the city of Zurich. He was a young erudite Christian Humanist of irenic temperament. In discussion with Calvin, the two men were able to reach an agreement that the sacraments are not only signs but also seals. This *Consensus Tigurinus* has ever since been regarded as the Reformed position rather than the earlier position of Zwingli and Oecolampadius.[16]

For some reason Hodge does not even mention Bucer. Be that as it may, Bullinger and Calvin in the *Consensus Tigurinus* were able to

---

[13] Hodge, *Systematic Theology*, 3:509–514.

[14] Hodge, *Systematic Theology*, 3:521–523.

[15] Regrettably this study has not been able to focus on the earliest attempts of Reformed theologians to understand the sacraments. There is much to be studied on the teachings of Zwingli, Oecolampadius, Bucer, and a number of others.

[16] In my opinion the Reformer of Basel, John Oecolampadius, has yet to be carefully studied. It may be the case that the position of Oecolampadius was simply influenced by late medieval mystics such as John Tauler.

agree that the sacraments were not only signs but also seals. This, at least, is the way Hodge understood it.[17] The sacraments of baptism and communion, then, are not only signs; they are *effective* signs.

C. THE RITE OF COMMUNION

The contribution of Charles Hodge was to present American Protestantism with a classic statement of traditional Christianity in an age that took great pride in having revolutionized human civilization. The nineteenth century understood itself as the modern age, or, at least, that is the way the people saw it. They had progressed far beyond the traditional, but what Hodge wrote was traditional. Here was a Christian faith that had established itself in a new and free land. It had survived the ravages of the Enlightenment and the blasphemies of Unitarianism and was forging into the frontier of a new land. In the excitement of all this, Hodge and his colleagues at Princeton reaffirmed the historic verities of the Reformed faith. Charles Hodge, as John Mackay one time put it in a sermon I heard at Miller Chapel, was a spiritual Isaac. He dug again the wells his father Abraham had dug before him. Charles Hodge was a man of faith but a man of inherited faith. He was brought up in a tradition and he was faithful to that tradition. His faith was inherited and yet it was vigorous and creative. Charles Hodge set the landmarks in a new land where the landmarks still had to be set.

When Charles Hodge wrote his chapter on the sacrament of Holy Communion in his *Systematic Theology*, the old preparatory and thanksgiving services were disappearing. For a couple of centuries the tradition in the various Reformed churches was to spend the better part of a week preparing to participate in the communion service. We have spoken of how Calvin prepared his congregation for the celebration of Easter Communion by preaching through the passion narrative. We have spoken of Johann Kaspar Lavater, who did this in eighteenth-century Zurich as did Jodocus van Lodenstein

---

[17] Hodge, *Systematic Theology*, 3:517–518.

19: OLD SCHOOL PRESBYTERIANISM

and Willem Teellinck in The Netherlands. The devotional intensity of the Scottish communion seasons was proverbial.

By the time of the American Civil War the preparatory service was more and more a vestigial rite. One asks why a rite, once so devoutly observed, could so rapidly disappear. It may well be because it developed so phenomenally into the camp meetings of the American frontier that those who had grown up in more settled religious communities came to have an aversion to these frontier brethren and their long, protracted meetings. The analysis of John Williamson Nevin so often repeated may give us a good clue as to what happened to the preparatory service. The piety of the settled church and the piety of the frontier church are inevitably quite different. However that may be, when Hodge wrote his systematic theology the preparatory service was definitely on the wane.

The end result, far too often, was that the celebration of the sacrament left the faithful faced with a spiritual ambiguity. They all too clearly knew a hungering and a thirsting for the things of God and at the same time they were all too aware of their spiritual failures. To resolve all this between eleven o'clock and twelve noon on Sunday morning seemed an impossible task. Add to this the confessional wrangling over the miracle of transubstantiation and the real presence and the average American Protestant of a century ago found the role of the sacrament rather obscure. One thing is clear: the importance of Holy Communion to the piety of nineteenth-century American Presbyterians plummeted. It became an occasional rite, observed three or four times a year. The plummeting of the importance of the sacrament of Holy Communion in the piety of American Protestantism is no doubt largely to be explained by Unitarianism, or, perhaps more correctly, by Deism.

Nevertheless, let us look at a number of features of the chapter on the Lord's Supper that we find in the *Systematic Theology* of Charles Hodge.[18] It is without doubt a major source document for

---

[18] For Hodge on the Lord's Supper, see Hodge, *Systematic Theology*, 3:611f.

the eucharistic piety of American Protestantism. The basic passages of Scripture are quoted at length. These include the passage on the institution of the Lord's Supper as it is found in Matthew (Matt. 26:26–28), then the parallel passages in Mark and Luke (Mark 14:22–24 and Luke 22:19–20), then the two passages in the Apostle Paul's First Epistle to the Corinthians (1 Cor. 10:15–17) describing the sacrament as participation in Christ, and then the passage in the following chapter recounting the story of the institution of the sacrament as the Apostle Paul had received it (1 Cor. 11:23–29). From these passages Professor Hodge draws his teaching on the Lord's Supper in his usual simple and straightforward manner.

The first thing Hodge takes from these passages is that the sacrament of the Lord's Supper "is a divine institution of perpetual obligation."[19] The subject is introduced by a long discussion of the variety of names that have been used for the sacrament going back to the ancient church. Hodge is obviously interested in church history. In fact, we notice that he has a broad interest in the history of the Greek church, the Syriac church, and the Latin church, both of ancient times and modern times. Hodge was a man of broad interest. He was not only well read but well traveled. Hodge gives particular attention to the names used to describe this ordinance in Greek and Latin: "eucharist," "liturgy," "mystery," "synaxis," "sacrament," and "mass."[20] The point of this seems to be the argument that the church has indeed, all down through its history, perpetuated this ordinance. The church has done what Christ ordained in the institution of the sacrament. It has continued in century after century, in land after land, to observe this ordinance in memory of the death and resurrection of Christ.

The next thing Hodge takes up is the elements of the sacraments.[21] That the elements are bread and wine would seem to

---

[19] Hodge, *Systematic Theology*, 3:612.

[20] Hodge, *Systematic Theology*, 3:613–614.

[21] Hodge, *Systematic Theology*, 3:615–617.

19: Old School Presbyterianism

be quite obvious from the text, but over time controversies have arisen. Should the bread be common bread or should it be unleavened bread? At the Last Supper, since it was both the feast of Passover and the feast of unleavened bread, Jesus and the disciples would have used unleavened bread, but the universal practice of the Church until the eleventh century was to use leavened bread. At that time the Western Church began to use little wafers of unleavened bread. The controversy continues between the Eastern and Western Churches to this day. As Hodge saw it, the issue can easily be regarded as *adiaphora*, that is, as indifferent.[22]

It is the same way with the question of whether one should mix water with the wine. Apparently the wine used in antiquity was very strong and we can assume that at the Last Supper Jesus would have mixed water with the wine. Nowhere, however, does the biblical text demand this and from time to time there have been controversies about this. Again Hodge sees this as *adiaphora*, that is, indifferent, a question of no great importance.[23] Hodge does tell us, however, that during the Reformation under the reign of Edward VI the first *Prayer Book* of 1549 had a rubric directing that a little bit of pure water be mixed with the wine, but that with the second *Prayer Book* this rubric was removed and has not been reintroduced. One is constantly amazed at Professor Hodge's erudition on such fine points.

Much more significant is the section which follows. Here Hodge treats the sacramental actions.[24] Reformed theologians have usually treated this subject at length when discussing the Lord's Supper in terms of systematic theology. It is not the elements of bread and wine that are so important as it is what is done with them. It is the eucharistic actions that are of first importance. As Hodge understands it, there are three things involved here: the

---

[22] Hodge, *Systematic Theology*, 3:615.

[23] Hodge, *Systematic Theology*, 3:616–617.

[24] Hodge, *Systematic Theology*, 3:617–619.

blessing, the breaking, and the giving.[25] Different theologians have divided this up differently. A generation ago Gregory Dix was particularly well known for his fourfold shape of the liturgy.[26] First he speaks of the fact that Jesus took the bread. He finds in this the offertory.[27] Then second Dix finds that Jesus gave thanks. This, of course, would be the eucharistic prayer. Next he broke the bread, and finally he gave the bread to his disciples. We noticed in an earlier chapter that the eighteenth century Scottish pastor John Willison had spoken of a sixfold shape of the liturgy.

Hodge is not too convincing at this point. There were obviously several prayers here, as contemporary biblical scholars would point out. They were *berakoth*, that is, blessings, or, more exactly, prayers of thanksgiving. We will have more to say about this in a moment. Here we will simply note that the second action according to Hodge is the breaking of the bread, while the third is the giving of the bread and the wine to the disciples.

Let us at this point look more carefully at the first of these eucharistic actions outlined by Hodge, namely, the blessing of the elements of bread and wine. Hodge tells us that this is "the introductory and consecrating prayer."[28] He continues by telling us that it has a threefold object. The first object is to give thanks to God for the gift of his Son, whose atoning death was about to be celebrated. Sad to say, Hodge is very brief and very vague at this point. One would hope that the prayer would open up in a hymnic fashion God's saving purposes in this prayer, recounting the mighty works of God for our salvation. All we get, however, is that the prayer should put the congregation in a suitable frame of mind to receive the saving benefits of the gospel.[29]

---

[25] Hodge, *Systematic Theology*, 3:619.

[26] Gregory Dix, *The Shape of the Liturgy* (London: Adam & Charles Black, 1975).

[27] This seems a bit farfetched, but it fits into Hodge's theology.

[28] Hodge, *Systematic Theology*, 3:617.

[29] Hodge, *Systematic Theology*, 3:618.

19: Old School Presbyterianism

One wishes that Hodge had elaborated just what he had in mind here. He is very specific as to what he does not mean. With the aid of the most recent biblical scholarship one might well find it appropriate to offer up a *berakah*, that is, a thanksgiving for God's mighty acts of creation and redemption, such as we find in Psalms 103, 104, and above all in Psalm 105. In such a prayer one would recount the history of salvation. That is what we find in so many of the great eucharistic prayers of the ancient church, such as the prayer of the liturgy of St. Basil and the eucharistic prayer of the *Apostolic Constitutions*. This is much the same thing as we find in the eucharistic prayer of John Knox. It is the prayer of John Knox that for many years I have used as my model. This approach to the eucharistic prayer makes good sense theologically, as we find in 1 Timothy 4:4, where we are told that by giving thanks for God's gifts we consecrate them to our use. So it is that in giving thanks for the history of salvation we consecrate it for our salvation and number ourselves in the household of faith who have moved from death to life.

Hodge would have us regard as the third purpose of this prayer to be the consecration of the elements.[30] The Puritans had discussed this at some length, especially after the criticism Bucer wrote in his *Censura* of the whole concept of blessing things instead of people. Richard Baxter had written a very fine eucharistic epiclesis for his *Reformed Liturgy* of 1661. There was, to be sure, definitely more than one Puritan point of view here. Hodge clearly opts for one point of view rather than the other.

Let us move on to the second of the three eucharistic actions Hodge outlines, namely, the breaking of the bread. Presumably the same thing would hold for the pouring of the cup. Hodge makes the point that it is not the elements of bread and wine alone that make the sacrament but rather what is done with them. It is the broken bread that signifies the crucified and sacrificed body of Christ. It is the poured out wine that signifies the life of Christ

---

[30] Hodge, *Systematic Theology*, 3:618.

poured out for our salvation.[31] It was in the middle of the nineteenth century when the Unitarians were vigorously attacking the whole idea of a vicarious atonement that American Protestants were beginning to realize the importance of showing the centrality of the traditional doctrine of the atonement. The enlightened religion of the Deists had its effect on the popular religiosity of the day. The whole idea of sacrifice, expiation, and atonement so powerfully evoked by the rite of the sacrament seemed to be so primitive. Those in the congregation who were influenced by Unitarianism tended to avoid the sacrament. The rites of the communion service were obviously strong arguments for the traditional doctrine. Hodge reminds us of the text of 1 Corinthians 10:16, "The bread which we break." It is not just the bread but the bread broken. Again it is clear from Acts 2:42 that the sacrament is sometimes simply called "the breaking of bread."[32] As Hodge sees it, much of the significance of the rite is lost when separate wafers are distributed. Furthermore, Hodge points out that the significance of the rite is included when Jesus directs us to bless, break, and distribute the bread in remembrance of him. The eucharistic action is just as important as the eucharistic elements and the eucharistic words.

Our systematic theologian goes on to speak of the third of the eucharistic actions, the giving or sharing of the bread and wine. The eucharistic actions not only celebrate the atoning sacrifice of Christ, but the sharing of God's gifts one with another. It is the sharing, the *koinonia* of the loaf and of the cup, that makes clear the meaning of the meal. It is important to the significance of the rite that one begin with one loaf of bread and that one divide up that loaf. It speaks to us of the unity of believers.[33] Simply placing the wafer on the tongue of the communicant is not sufficient. It is important that the communicant reach out with his or her hand and receive it. It is the

---

[31] Hodge, *Systematic Theology*, 3:619.

[32] Hodge, *Systematic Theology*, 3:619.

[33] Hodge, *Systematic Theology*, 3:619.

same way with taking first the bread and then the wine. The biblical texts make it clear that these are two distinct actions, the sharing of the bread and the sharing of the wine. Hodge would no doubt have found the modern practice of intinction quite insufficient. Again we notice that Hodge seems to be rather well informed as to how these variations in the ritual developed.

Having treated these questions of the eucharistic acts at greater length than most Reformed authors are accustomed to, our systematic theologian takes up the design of the Lord's Supper. By this Hodge means the purpose of the sacrament. Jesus instituted the sacrament as a memorial of his death, and not simply to the fact that his death occurred. Rather, the fact is that Christ's death occurred as an atoning sacrifice. At this point Hodge is very specific.

> It is, therefore, just as certain that Christ died upon the cross as that Christians everywhere celebrate the Lord's Supper. It is not only, however, the fact of Christ's death, which this sacrament thus authenticates; but also its design. Our Lord declared that He died as a substitute and sacrifice. "This is my body which is given for you;" or, as the Apostle reports it, "broken for you." "This is my blood of the New Testament, which is shed for many for the remission of sins." Redemption, therefore, is not by power, or by teaching, or by moral influence, but by expiation.[34]

The use of the word "expiation" here leaves no question but that Hodge firmly supports a high doctrine of the atonement. The polemic against the Unitarians can hardly be overlooked. But notice how he continues:

> It is this truth which the Lord's Supper exhibits and authenticates. Still further, as Christ affirms that his body was to be broken and his blood shed for the remission of sin, this from the nature of the case involves on his part the promise and pledge, that the sins of those who receive and trust Him, shall certainly

---
[34] Hodge, *Systematic Theology*, 3:621–622.

> be forgiven. The sacrament thus becomes not only a sign but also a seal.[35]

Here, of course, we notice not only the strong doctrine of the atonement but also the strong covenantal understanding of the sacraments. The sacrament is a sign of a divine promise. It confirms God's Word. Again we quote Hodge directly:

> As, therefore, the truth revealed in the Word has the highest power that can belong to truth in its normal influence on the human mind; so even the natural effect of the truths symbolized and authenticated in the Lord's Supper, is to confirm the faith of the believer.[36]

This passage is quite clear in itself, but it must be understood along with the traditional Reformed emphasis on the work of the Holy Spirit in the observance of the sacraments. Here ever since Oecolampadius and Bucer and Calvin, Reformed theologians have felt the influence of the Eastern Orthodox theologians.

Again we quote Hodge very specifically:

> But as the natural or objective power of the truth as revealed in the Word is insufficient for conversion or sanctification without the supernatural influences of the Spirit, so the truths set forth in the eucharist avail nothing towards our salvation unless the Spirit of all grace gives them effect. On the other hand, as the Word when attended by the demonstration of the Spirit, becomes the wisdom and power of God unto salvation; so does the sacrament of the Lord's Supper, when thus attended, become a real means of grace, not only signifying and sealing, but really conveying to the believing recipient, Christ and all the benefits of his redemption.[37]

A covenantal understanding of the Lord's Supper makes the point that, by sharing in the sacred meal, we participate in Christ.

---

[35] Hodge, *Systematic Theology*, 3:622.

[36] Hodge, *Systematic Theology*, 3:622.

[37] Hodge, *Systematic Theology*, 3:622.

Hodge quotes from 1 Corinthians 10:16–17, "The cup of blessing which we bless, is it not a participation in the blood of Christ?" Here Hodge inserts the Greek word *koinonia* in the text. Nothing could make clearer what Hodge has to say. He is talking about what a number of modern New Testament scholars have called Christian mysticism.[38] This is rather surprising when we look at Hodge through the great cloud of stereotypes that usually obscure the figure of Princeton's classic theologian. Slowly I am beginning to realize that Hodge was a man of far greater breadth than those who have so superficially criticized him have imagined.

Let us continue our look at this brief study of the design of the sacrament of the Lord's Supper. We read this very concise statement: "In the Lord's Supper, therefore, the believer receives Christ. He receives his body and blood."[39] This is the basic point Hodge wants to make, but our theologian opens this up further. He explains that the effect of this union with Christ is twofold. First we are united in one body in the sense that we become members of the Church, and second Christ dwells within us. Here Hodge opens up passages from the Gospel of John and the Epistle to the Galatians. Hodge, we remember, was first of all an exegete. It is in the end as an exegete that he commends himself to us. Finally we have to say that the design of the Lord's Supper is to enter into communion with Christ. It is to unite us both to Christ and to each other.[40]

Next we must take a look at Hodge's section on the qualifications for the Lord's Supper.[41] Surely one of the most difficult aspects of the sacrament of Holy Communion for devout members of the Reformed church is the question of worthy participation. The Reformed church has very often stressed the importance of a scrupulous preparation so much that the more devout have hesitated

---

[38] Hodge, *Systematic Theology*, 3:622.

[39] Hodge, *Systematic Theology*, 3:622.

[40] Hodge, *Systematic Theology*, 3:623.

[41] Hodge, *Systematic Theology*, 3:623–626.

to actually participate. This, to be sure, is not a problem unique to nineteenth-century Dutch Calvinists or Scottish Presbyterians. John Chrysostom complained of it in fourth-century Antioch and Augustine in fifth-century North Africa. On the other hand, one might well ask if the opposite problem is beginning to appear at the beginning of the twenty-first century here in America.

A careful reading of Hodge shows that he is really quite moderate in this matter. He is far more moderate, at least, than Jonathan Edwards in the middle of eighteenth-century New England.

Hodge does make a very strong case for the importance of preparing oneself for participation in the sacrament. The apostle Paul makes a point of this in 1 Corinthians 11:28 (KJV), "Let a man examine himself and so let him eat of that bread, and drink of that cup." As Hodge sees it, one of the reasons we celebrate the sacrament is to make a profession of our faith. "It is plain from the preceding account of the nature and design of this sacrament, that it is intended for believers; and that those who come to the table of the Lord do thereby profess to be his disciples."[42] As Hodge sees it, those who come to the Lord's Table must have a competent knowledge of Christ and the gospel. They must believe the record God has provided of the saving work of his Son. What Hodge has in mind is that communicants must understand the catechism, namely, the teaching of the church on the nature of our salvation in Christ. Hodge has in mind an explicit faith, not merely an implicit, vague, or general faith.[43] It is not necessarily the case that one must have assurance of saving faith, but one must at least sincerely hunger and thirst for faith. Hodge does not expect the communicant to be sinless, but at least one must yearn for holiness, hate the traces of sin still remaining in one's life, and come to the Lord's Table seeking release from all sin still remain-

---

[42] Hodge, *Systematic Theology*, 3:623.

[43] Hodge, *Systematic Theology*, 3:624.

19: OLD SCHOOL PRESBYTERIANISM

ing. One may have doubts, but one must labor to resolve them.[44]

Hodge is very careful in the matter of fencing the Table. He admits there is no way of guaranteeing the purity of the church and assuring that the unworthy are prevented from participation. We cannot judge the consciences of others and in the end we have to leave that to God. On the other hand, Hodge says, ". . . those who act unworthily of their Christian profession should be subjected to the discipline of the Church."[45] What we find strange here is that in all this there is no mention of the preparatory services which had played such a major role in the eucharistic piety of so many Reformed churches of an earlier time.

D. Controversies Over Eucharistic Doctrine

Finally we turn to what Hodge has to say about the doctrinal controversies between the Reformed, the Lutherans, and the Roman Catholics on the doctrine of the real presence.[46] The way the subject is presented is of particular interest. It makes us aware that what we have here is not the work of a pastor so much as the work of an academic theologian. Hodge speaks more as a systematician than as a pastor. Even at that, Hodge is quite understandable.

The following points should be noticed. First of all, Christ is truly present, but the presence is far more profound than merely a matter of locality. Christ is present like the sun is present although in heaven. We know the sun is present when we feel its warmth. Second, Christ's presence is a matter of faith. It is by believing that we eat the flesh of Christ and drink his blood as we find it in John 6. Third, it is through the work of the Holy Spirit in our hearts that Christ is present. Fourthly, then, Christ is present to the communicant because Christ enlivens us, and gives us new life, clearer understanding, deeper faith, and spiritual power. We come

---

[44] Hodge, *Systematic Theology*, 3:625.

[45] Hodge, *Systematic Theology*, 3:625.

[46] Hodge, *Systematic Theology*, 3:626f.

to the Lord's Table to be fed with spiritual food. Hodge supports the tradition of the Reformed church in insisting, lastly, that those who come to the Lord's Table without faith take nothing away but the guilt of profaning the things of God.[47]

Opening up these points, Hodge gives us a long systematic analysis of a large number of Reformed confessions of faith and catechisms. This is a magnificent piece of work because in effect it presents us with a history of the Reformed doctrine of the sacrament of communion from the earliest attempts to rethink this doctrine such as the *Confession of Faith* that Zwingli presented to the city council of Zurich in 1523 to its most developed and mature statements as they are found in the *Heidelberg Catechism* and the *Second Helvetic Confession*. The thoroughness of the good professor's research is admirable. He tells us of the *Confessio Tetrapolitana*, the *Confession of Basel*, and the *First Helvetic Confession*, as well as a number of Zwingli's studies such as the *Expositio Christiana Fidei* written just before Zwingli's death and published by Bullinger in 1536.[48]

Hodge moves on then to treat the teaching of Calvin. It is, of course, quite different from the teaching of Zwingli. Historians of Christian doctrine have long recognized this.[49] Hodge goes on to speak of a number of confessional documents that reflect the eucharistic doctrine of Calvin, such as the *Gallican Confession*, the *Belgic Confession*, and the *Scots Confession* of 1560.[50] Very important here is the *Zurich Consensus (Consensus Tigurinus)* agreed upon by the ministers of both Zurich and Geneva.[51] Then he gives several pages to a discussion of the eucharistic theology of the *Heidelberg Catechism* and several more pages to the *Second Helvetic Confession* of 1565.[52] He even discusses the *Thirty-Nine Articles* of the Church of

---

[47] Hodge, *Systematic Theology*, 3:643f.

[48] Hodge, *Systematic Theology*, 3:626–628.

[49] Hodge, *Systematic Theology*, 3:628–631.

[50] Hodge, *Systematic Theology*, 3:630.

[51] Hodge, *Systematic Theology*, 3:631–633.

[52] Hodge, *Systematic Theology*, 3:634–636.

19: OLD SCHOOL PRESBYTERIANISM

England approved by Elizabeth I in 1562.[53] Having given us this extensive review of the development of Reformed eucharistic theology Hodge tries to sum up the central message of the Reformed churches on this vigorously controverted subject.

First of all it needs to be made clear that the Reformed churches have consistently taught a doctrine of the real presence. The question is how this presence is to be understood. "God is present with his people when He controls their thoughts, operates on their hearts, and fills them with the sense of his nearness and love."[54] One has often charged the Reformed with holding a doctrine that locates Christ's presence in the imagination. It is not all in the head or only in the head, but Hodge is quite clear:

> Christ is present when He thus fills the mind, sheds abroad his love in our hearts by the Holy Ghost given unto us; and not only communicates to us the benefits of his sufferings and death, that is, the remission of our sins and reconciliation with God, but also infuses his life into us. Nothing is plainer from Scripture than that there is this communication of life from Christ to his people.[55]

Here Hodge brings several passages of Scripture traditionally brought to bear on the question by Reformed theologians, namely, Galatians 2:20, "I live; yet not I, but Christ liveth in me," and Colossians 3:4, which tells us that Christ lives within us.[56] Similarly, the passage in John 6 tells us that Christ is the vine and we are the branches. It is a solid teaching of Scripture that believers receive their life from Christ. "This, again, is a presence to us and in us which is not imaginary, but in the highest sense real and effective."[57]

There is no question but that Charles Hodge has helped us

---

[53] Hodge, *Systematic Theology*, 3:636–637.

[54] Hodge, *Systematic Theology*, 3:638.

[55] Hodge, *Systematic Theology*, 3:638.

[56] Scripture is as quoted in Hodge, *Systematic Theology*, 3:638.

[57] Hodge, *Systematic Theology*, 3:638.

understand and appreciate the role of the sacrament of Holy Communion in the Christian life, and yet somehow we find the systematic theology of Hodge not nearly as helpful as the sermons that have so often come down to us from preachers such as James Waddel Alexander, the Erskine brothers, or John Willison, to name just a few. Scholastic theology does not explain the mysteries nearly as well as the biblical types, the type of the Passover, the type of the wedding feast or the type of the manna in the wilderness.

Especially interesting in the writings of Charles Hodge on the subject of the sacrament of communion is the breadth of his reading. One notices, for instance, that Hodge gives attention not only to Calvin but Zwingli as well. He quotes a number of the earliest Zwinglian confessions. The *First Helvetic Confession* as well as the *Confessio Tetrapolitana* are taken into account. He gives particular attention to the *Consensus Tigurinus*. Hodge has obviously studied both the *Belgic Confession* and the *Scots Confession* of 1560 as well as the doctrinal statement of the Reformed Church of France. The intention of Hodge is evidently to show the breadth and comprehensiveness of Reformed sacramental theology.

The more one studies Charles Hodge, the more one is impressed with the breadth of his interest and the thoroughness of his reading. His years in Germany gave him a good introduction to classic Lutheran eucharistic theology. On the other hand, he had spent some time with Tholuck at Halle where there was a neo-pietistic revival in progress. Even more impressive is this young American's exploration of the thought world of the University of Berlin. Neander and Schleiermacher were in those exciting days trying to reconcile the differences between the Lutheran and the Reformed, hammering together a sort of pan-Protestantism, as it has been termed. At the same time various philosophical movements popular in early nineteenth century Germany were complicating the discussion. Hodge briefly deals with Olshausen

19: OLD SCHOOL PRESBYTERIANISM

and then a bit further on with Ebrard.[58] Apparently he did not find these thinkers too helpful.

E. REVIEW OF NEVIN'S *MYSTICAL PRESENCE*

For the story of the sacramental piety of the Reformed churches in America, the review Charles Hodge wrote of Nevin's *Mystical Presence* in the *Biblical Repertory and Princeton Review* has been especially important.[59] The first reviews that appeared shortly after Nevin's publication were very positive. Notable among these positive reviews was one from Johannes Ebrard, a pastor of the Church of Basel in German-speaking Switzerland, who had given much attention to the subject of worship in the Reformed church.[60]

Another very positive review came from young Phillip Schaff, a church historian sent to America by the Basel Mission to support the establishment of German Protestantism in America.[61] One reason Hodge's review attracted so much attention is that Hodge made it clear that one of the major faults of Nevin's book was that he had succumbed entirely too much to German philosophy. Whether the influence of the idealism of Hegel or the subjectivism of Kant, the slur was regrettably broadsided. Hodge, although he had studied both in Halle and Berlin, gives the impression of being xenophobic.[62]

Somehow I can't quite believe that Hodge was really xenophobic any more than I can believe that Nevin was inclined toward Socinianism. We may indeed have an example here of the unwillingness of American theologians to learn from German theologians.

---

[58] Hodge, *Systematic Theology*, 3:650f.

[59] Charles Hodge, "Review of Nevin's *Mystical Presence*," in *Biblical Repertory and Princeton Review* 20/2 (1848).

[60] Hodge, "Review of Nevin's Mystical Presence."

[61] Phillip Schaff, it should be noted, was also commended to the German-speaking Protestants in America by Krummacher.

[62] On the influence of idealism and subjectivism, see "Hegelianism," in *Encyclopedia Britannica*, 15th ed., 29 vols. (Chicago: Encyclopedia Britannica, Inc., 1994), 5:798–799; and "Kantianism," in *Encyclopedia Britannica*, 6:726–727.

I will admit that I find the review written by Hodge half-baked. It was Theodore Appel who said that Hodge simply did not do his homework when he sat down to write the review.[63] In the providence of God the genius of Hodge and the creativity of Nevin both have an essential place in an American theology of worship.

What is really at issue here is that this was one of those times when Hodge should have given his most careful effort to evaluating a very important book and failed to recognize it. But then, he was not the last theologian, or the last scholar of any field for that matter, to have made this mistake. What is regrettable is that Hodge never did leave us a major statement on eucharistic theology. It is somewhat the same situation that we noted with Jonathan Edwards. We do not have a great statement of the eucharistic teaching of Jonathan Edwards but we do have some great sermons from him. Even more, we have some great sermons from Gilbert Tennent. So it is with Hodge. It is really James Waddel Alexander who has left us the best statement of Old School Presbyterian eucharistic piety. He may not have treated all the theological loci we would have liked, but it is a beautiful statement nevertheless.

JAMES WADDEL ALEXANDER

From the pulpit of James Waddel Alexander (1804–1859), the elder son of Archibald Alexander, we have a number of eucharistic sermons.[64] The sermons have come down to us without any date or indication of where they might have been preached. These sermons do not form a series but are rather a random selection made post-

---

[63] Theodore Appel, *The Life and Work of John Williamson Nevin* (New York: Arno Press and the New York Times, 1968), pp. 280–281. See also Darryl G. Hart, *John Williamson Nevin: High Church Calvinist* (Phillipsburg, NJ: Presbyterian and Reformed, 2005).

[64] For biographical information on James Waddel Alexander, see Hughes Oliphant Old, *The Reading and Preaching of the Scriptures in the Worship of the Christian Church*, vol. 6, *The Modern Age* (Grand Rapids, MI: Eerdmans, 2007), pp. 248–250; Calhoun, *Princeton Seminary*, 1:286–87; and James Waddel Alexander, *The Life of Archibald Alexander*, reprint (Harrisonburg, VA: Sprinkle Publications, 1991).

humously. They are, however, exemplary of the Reformed eucharistic sermon.[65] These sermons are hymns of praise to God, like the eucharistic prayer in the Liturgy of St. Basil so greatly beloved in the Eastern Orthodox churches. They exalt God's name, magnify his attributes, and delight in his awesome presence. They are doxological expressions as much akin to prayer as to preaching. In fact, they are prayer and sermon at the same time.

There is no attribute, however, in which Alexander so elaborately delights than the attribute of love. The eucharistic preaching of James Alexander abounds in praise for the love of God. The editor of the collection has therefore entitled the collection, *God is Love*. For Alexander the Supper is the sacrament of the love of God because love is the ultimate attribute of God. The first sermon in the series shows us that the eucharist is the celebration of God's love.[66]

The third sermon, "The Two Natures of Christ," is a veritable Christological hymn.[67] This is particularly noteworthy because it was preached in a day when the Unitarians boasted that the orthodox could not produce a single text of Scripture that stated unambiguously that Jesus is truly God. Eucharistic sermons as we find them in preachers like J. W. Alexander are a type of doxological preaching. They hallow God's name, as all of our worship should. We notice this particularly in this sermon on the two natures of Christ.

The Lord's Supper is a memorial of the crucifixion of our Lord.[68] Here our preacher leads his congregation in a meditation on the passion of Christ, which brings before our eyes once more the final outpouring of God's love for a fallen humanity. As our preacher vividly recounts the details of that passionate story our emotions are understandably stirred. But our preacher has even

---

[65] The text studied is taken from James Waddel Alexander, *God is Love*, reprint of *Sacramental Discourses*, published in 1860 (Edinburgh and Carlisle, PA: Banner of Truth Trust, 1985), hereinafter Alexander, *Sacramental Discourses*.

[66] "God is Love," found in Alexander, *Sacramental Discourses*, pp. 7–27.

[67] Alexander, *Sacramental Discourses*, pp. 57–85.

[68] See "The Crucifixion," in Alexander, *Sacramental Discourses*, pp. 115–141.

at that restrained himself from a theatrical dramatization of that story which aims at stirring up the emotions of the congregation. We have no Jesuit "spiritual exercises" here. Alexander puts it quite clearly, "I have accomplished my purpose of giving a simple narrative of our Lord's death on the cross; being that particular event, which of all others he selected to be commemorated by a sacramental ordinance, by all disciples, through all ages."[69] That memorial, however, is not enough. It must be viewed with the eyes of faith. The congregation must view it as God's mighty act for our salvation. We approach the table aright "when we remember our Lord. . . . The broken bread aids the remembrance; it is Christ's broken body. The fruit of the vine, the cup of blessing which we bless, aids the remembrance—it is the new testament in his blood."[70] There must be an eye of faith that sees through the outward sign of broken bread and poured out wine.

Art has been called in to melt the affections. Alexander as professor of *belles lettres*, apparently has given some thought to the Christian use of art.

In the sermon, "Christ Bearing Our Sins," we have another example of the sermon being a memorial of Christ's propitiatory work, his wondrous work of redemption.[71] Of particular interest in this sermon is his review of a number of passages of Scripture which make a point of this, such as Isaiah 53,[72] Galatians 3:13, and Romans 5:8, " . . . while we were yet sinners, Christ died for us."[73] Apparently the central theme of Alexander's communion sermons, when viewed as a whole, is the memorial of God's redemptive love in the sacrifice of the cross. He emphasizes the necessity of the cross, the uniqueness of the cross, the sufficiency of the cross, and

---

[69] Alexander, *Sacramental Discourses*, p.128.

[70] Alexander, *Sacramental Discourses*, pp. 128–129.

[71] Alexander, *Sacramental Discourses*, pp. 171–201.

[72] Alexander, *Sacramental Discourses*, p. 190.

[73] Alexander, *Sacramental Discourses*, p. 191.

he emphasizes it over against the Unitarian denial of it. What is interesting here is that Alexander argues for the doctrine of the substitutionary atonement over against Unitarianism by pointing to the obvious significance of the signs of broken bread and poured out wine. Unitarianism taught many church members in the nineteenth century to keep their distance from the communion table. Deism also was very much offended by the sacrament of communion.

One has to say that the memorial Christ left was the Supper, not the crucifix. Our preacher is quite eloquent at this point. The Supper is the closest sight we will ever have in this life of the redeemer. No crucifix, no icon will give us a closer view of Christ's redemptive act or any view of Christ himself than this Supper.

A. The Supper as the Hallowing of God's Name

It is at the celebrating of the Supper that we most profoundly glorify God's name. The first sermon in the series has the title, "God is Love" and its text is taken from the First Epistle of John 4:8, 16. "He that loveth not knoweth not God; for God is love . . . and we have known and believed the love that God has for us. God is love; and he that dwelleth in love dwelleth in God, and God in him."[74] It is to recognize in the broken bread and the poured out wine as it is placed before us on the Lord's Table a sacrament of God's love. To meditate on this sacred food as we have been taught will lead us to an affection towards God, a remembrance of Christ, and a communion with the brethren as is proper at the sacramental feast. To gaze on this bread and wine is to realize that God is our Father who cares for the needs of his children. It is to recognize the providence of God. It is to perceive that the Supreme Excellence is benevolent. Neither philosophers of ancient Greece nor the Deist of our own day know anything of the love of the Father.

While Alexander is not one to press the claims of natural theology, he figures we as Christians, once we understand the basic

---

[74] Alexander, *Sacramental Discourses*, pp. 9–27.

truth of the gospel, can understand quite clearly the works of creation and providence. With the sacramental feast before us we understand that God is Truth; God is righteousness; God is power. We understand even better than the philosophers do the attributes of God. "Especially after we have the key placed in our hand by Scripture, we walk through the mighty halls of the universal palace with amazement and thankfulness rising at every step."[75] As our preacher goes over the attributes of God, his preaching becomes magnificently doxological. He hallows God's name, taking up the language of the Psalm of David:

> O Lord how manifold are thy works;
>   In wisdom hast thou made them all.
> The whole earth is full of thy riches.[76]

> O that man would praise the Lord
>   For his goodness and for his wonderful works
>   To the children of men.[77]

At the Lord's Supper we see the bread and wine before us as a sign and a promise of the divine benevolence. The bread and wine on the table prepared for us is not a cold god, a naked power, a brute force, or a monolithic unity. It is a kindly force, a creative being. The wisdom from on high is nourishing. It is a loving wisdom, patiently waiting to be loved. The justice of God is not blind nor is it an unattainable ideal, but a full generous source of every blessing. It is a feast prepared for us. Wisdom has built her house; she has prepared her feast (Prov. 9:1–2).

To those who have yet to be instructed by the gospel, neither nature, creation, nor providence speaks of love. All the wondrous works are dumb without the Gospel. "We might take some angel-guide and voyage from orb to orb, through all the stellar paths, yet

---

[75] Alexander, *Sacramental Discourses*, p. 19.

[76] Psalm 104:24, as quoted by Alexander, *Sacramental Discourses*, p. 19.

[77] Psalm 107:21, as quoted by Alexander, *Sacramental Discourses*, p. 19.

see no trace of mercy. As sinners we could catch no sight of compassion or promise of pardon. All these belong to the innermost glory of the heart of God which is revealed by the Word."[78] We notice that Word is capitalized. It is the Word who is Christ that Alexander has in mind, "This is my body broken for you." It is the mystery of the feast prepared for us that assures us of the ultimate benevolence of the eternal. "That is to say; the manifestation to us that God is love is in God's sending his Son. Here is the principal shining forth of the hidden glory of the Divine Nature."[79]

It is in the celebration of the Lord's Supper that we encounter the reality of God's attributes. It is only here that in this life we can appreciate God's wisdom, power, justice, and patience. It is here that we can begin to glorify his name. "While we were constrained to admit that the contemplation of nature is insufficient to assure us of God's mercy and grace to sinners, or fully to instruct us concerning his benevolence, it is nevertheless true, that after we have learnt these lessons at the cross, and thus discovered the key to nature's hieroglyphic, we may return to survey the works of infinite wisdom and power as the works of him who is also infinite love. Then the prospect changes."[80] The sacrament makes evident the harmony of God's attributes. The sacrament gets us beyond the philosophy of the ancient Greeks and the rationalism of the modern Unitarian. "It is no longer the same cold orphaned universe, 'Old things are passed away, behold all things are become new; and all things are of God who hath reconciled us to himself by Jesus Christ.'"[81] At this point our preacher's sermon magnifies God's name, "The pure vault of wintry honor looks down with its starry countenance all serenely radiant in love. The fragrance of forests and the blush of summer flowers now come to us as from a Redeemer. And every breath of

---

[78] Alexander, *Sacramental Discourses*, p. 20.

[79] Alexander, *Sacramental Discourses*, p. 20–21.

[80] Alexander, *Sacramental Discourses*, p. 23.

[81] Alexander, *Sacramental Discourses*, pp. 23–24.

mercy in daily things is a whisper of grace, from one who died for us."[82] The eucharist glorifies God's name, magnifies his attributes and manifests his true nature as nothing else in human experience. Here are the visible body and blood of Jesus. It is the nearest view, this side of heaven, into the majesty of divine perfection.

In another eucharistic sermon Alexander makes the point that there is happiness glorifying the name of God. To celebrate the Lord's Supper is to enter into a fellowship of adoration, love, and praise. In the late 1850s when these sermons were preached there was much concern about revival, but Alexander would draw us to something higher than the revival that was understood at the time. He dreamed of a revival of the spirit of worship in which whole assemblies would be touched with an appreciation of a present God. Common worship is more than individualistic devotion. It is a sanctified harmony. It is corporate experience of profound awe; it is a joining together in rapturous joy. It is not an idle dream but the faith of the church that at last the time will come when all God's people will finally be gathered together in a renewal of the spirit of worship. Then God's praise will ascend with such richness that a day in God's courts will be better than a thousand elsewhere.

B. The Supper as the Memorial of the Incarnation

Alexander's eucharistic preaching glories in the orthodox doctrine of the person of Christ. At the Supper Christ is to be proclaimed as true God and true man. We find this particularly in his sermon, "The Two Natures of Christ."[83] The sermon takes as its text Romans 9:5, "whose are the Father's and of whom, as concerning the flesh, Christ came; who is over all God blessed forever. Amen."[84]

There is no question but that the sermon has a strong polemical tone to it. It is not surprising because in 1850, Unitarianism

---

[82] Alexander, *Sacramental Discourses*, p. 24.

[83] Alexander, *Sacramental Discourses*, p. 59–85.

[84] Scripture as quoted by Alexander, *Sacramental Discourses*, p. 59.

19: OLD SCHOOL PRESBYTERIANISM

had reached its zenith. It is over against the background of the increasing popularity of Unitarianism that we must understand this sermon. This is clear from the opening lines of the sermon, "We are sometimes challenged by Unitarianism to produce any text, in which Christ is distinctly said to be God. Here is just such a text. *Christ is God over all blessed forever.* The words bear no other meaning. You may deny that the book is true and authoritative, but once you receive the New Testament, you are constrained to the profession that *Christ is God.*"[85]

Perhaps a sermon with such obvious polemical intent should not be admitted to a discussion of the doctrine of the Lord's Supper. But on the other hand Alexander, a man well known for being of an irenic and moderate nature, has a brilliant insight here. The celebrations of the Lord's Supper, as it has been celebrated since New Testament times, is a proclamation of the orthodox doctrine of the person and work of Christ. To preach Christ as true man and true God is at the heart of the celebration of the Eucharist, it is of the essence of the sacred feast. The feast before us is nothing less than the wisdom from on high. We have been invited to eat at the table Wisdom has prepared, to taste of her bread and drink of her wine (Prov. 9:5). As we find it in the Gospel of John, it is not Moses who feeds us the bread of heaven but the Father in heaven (John 6:32). It is Christ himself who is the bread of life. It is Christ, true God and true man, who gives life to the world. It is therefore that Alexander calls us to behold Christ prepared on the table before us as the spiritual food the Father provides for us. Here we see quite clearly why the popularity of eucharistic devotion plummeted so dramatically in the nineteenth century. The eucharist was at odds with the fundamental teachings of Unitarianism. The Lord's Supper affirmed everything the Unitarians denied.

Alexander would have us behold Christ at the Lord's Table and behold him as true God and true man. He develops this at

---

[85] Alexander, *Sacramental Discourses*, p. 59.

length. The Word was made flesh as we find it at the beginning of the Gospel of John. "Throughout the Gospel account we find both natures remaining in mysterious union, yet perfectly distinct. The Lord Jesus Christ, 'being the eternal Son of God, of one substance and equal with the Father, in the fullness of time became man, and so was, and continueth to be, God and man, in two entire distinct natures, and one person forever.' This is the clear New Testament account."[86] Not only are we to behold the Christ on whom we feed as true God, we are to behold him as true man. As we find it in Paul's Epistle to the Galatians, God sent forth his Son made of a woman. Christ is just as truly man as he is God. As is made clear in the Gospel of Luke, the infant Savior was at one and the same time son of Mary and Son of God. Here again our preacher develops this at length.

There is another aspect of this which is of particular interest, and that is that Alexander would have us come to the Lord's Table and contemplate not only Christ as true God and Christ as true man, but Christ as one person, bringing together the divine and the human. There is no mixing or confusing of the two natures. Neither does the divine overcome the human nor the human corrupt the divine. Alexander understands the Chalcedonian Christology. He continues, "And on the other hand, this divinity and this humanity, equally precious to our faith, exist in one Christ, sole and undivided; one glorious Person, whose name is Wonderful, and whose like is not in the universe. This has been the doctrine of the Catholic Church for hundreds of years."[87] Here is one point, our preacher insists, where Catholics and Protestants agree.

Unitarians would probably not admit it, but the sacrament of the Lord's Supper, properly understood, is a powerful refutation of their doctrines. What we find most important here is that Alexander, one of the more prominent American evangelical preachers

---

[86] Alexander, *Sacramental Discourses*, pp. 65–66.

[87] Alexander, *Sacramental Discourses*. p. 67.

of the mid-nineteenth century, regards the memorial or, perhaps better, the *anamnesis*, of the incarnation as one of the focal points of the celebration of the Lord's Supper. One notices through the centuries how often the eucharistic prayers of the past elaborately recount the doctrine of the person of Christ, just as in this sermon of James Alexander. One thinks especially of the eucharistic prayer of the *Apostolic Constitutions* or even more that of St. Basil. Alexander's eucharistic sermon on the two natures of Christ, like these ancient eucharistic prayers, celebrate the sacrament of the Lord's Supper in remembrance of our Lord Jesus Christ, Son of God from all eternity, Son of Man forever and ever.

C. The Supper as Memorial of Christ's Redemptive Sacrifice

In his eucharistic sermons Alexander frequently treats the Supper as the *anamnesis* of Christ's redemptive sacrifice. One might even go so far as to say that this is characteristic of the old Princeton eucharistic theology. It is clearly the most frequently treated subject. Let us begin by looking at the sermon "The Crucifixion."[88] The sermon begins by a full recounting of the story of the crucifixion as it is found in the gospels. He recounts the story very soberly. The point our preacher wants to make is that the purpose of the sacrament is to remember the story. This is why the Supper is a memorial or *anamnesis*.

Having recounted at length the story of the crucifixion, Alexander tells us why he has done this. "I have accomplished my purpose of giving a simple narrative of our Lord's death upon the cross; being that particular event, which of all others he selected to be commemorated by a sacramental ordinance, by all disciples, through all ages; until he shall come again . . . ."[89] There may be much else that is to be remembered at the Lord's Supper, but this is its primary intent. This may not be overshadowed or neglected

---

[88] Alexander, *Sacramental Discourses*, pp. 115–141.

[89] Alexander, *Sacramental Discourses*, p. 128.

without doing violence to our Lord's intention. At the Last Supper Jesus made this very clear. He indicated that the bread was in remembrance of his broken body and the cup a memorial of the pouring out of his blood for the remission of sins. Taking the bread and wine together we perceive "that we approach this table aright, when we remember our Lord—when we remember him as shedding his blood for remission—that is when we remember him as an expiatory oblation."[90] To be sure, the bread and the wine aid our memory. Mere bread and wine, however, do not make a sacrament. Faith has to look through and beyond the broken bread and poured out wine and see the Lamb of God who takes away our sin. One cannot help but note the similarity to Luther here. To truly celebrate the sacrament we must encounter our Savior. As Alexander puts it so vividly, "There must be an eye of faith to look through and beyond the element and see Jesus Christ, visibly set forth, crucified among us."[91]

Sacraments are signs to be understood. They are more than just food and drink. They point us to a higher reality and that higher reality is the atoning death of the Son of God. The sacrament both exhibits and seals the covenant of grace, which opens to us this saving virtue. Applying all this to the congregation gathered around the table, Alexander says, "All which brings us again to the important truth, that in partaking we must bend all the perceptions of the soul on a single point, Christ on the cross— . . . Christ pouring forth his blood as the basis of that New Covenant which gives to many remission of sins. To this centre or focal point of all theology, I invite your regards this day."[92]

True to the tradition of the Reformed communion sermon this sermon is an invitation to accept Christ as Lord and Savior. "The voice of Jesus from the accursed tree, calls to you in bewailing but

---

[90] Alexander, *Sacramental Discourses*, pp. 128–129.

[91] Alexander, *Sacramental Discourses*, p. 129.

[92] Alexander, *Sacramental Discourses*, pp. 129–130.

gracious accents, 'Look unto me and be saved, all ye ends of the earth.' Look then. Come hither with me beloved disciples . . . come hither and draw more closely around the cross."[93] To remember Christ's death on the cross, to remember it rightly, is to hear from the Crucified the invitations to turn from the world and its ways and follow the Savior. It is to follow him into a new life, a life of devotion to God and service to the neighbor. To rightly celebrate the Supper is to hear the love of God addressed to us. We need no greater proof that it is eternal love that calls us to follow Christ. "Greater love hath no man than this, that a man lay down his life for his friends" (John 15:13, KJV). "Can you doubt God's love?"[94] It is the members of his congregation, our preacher insists, who are intended in this invitation. "The message of the cross is a message to you, and offered to universal acceptance, to your personal acceptance."[95]

This sermon is not only an invitation to remember but also an invitation to both faith and repentance. It remembers the cross because the cross is the basis of the New Covenant, but it also invites faith because it is by faith that we lay hold of the New Covenant and enter into it. It is through repentance that we advance in the life of the New Covenant and so more and more die unto sin and live unto righteousness. "Faith 'discerns the Lord's body;' faith receives it. Faith feeds upon it. The lively emblems of this holy table are helps to faith."[96] Even more, the eucharistic meal is that these symbols are, "not a sign merely, but a seal, of divine appointment pledging unto us . . . all the loving kindness and covenant grace purchased by the death of Christ."[97]

Another sermon, "Christ Bearing our Sins," speaks at length of the eucharist as the memorial of Christ's sacrifice.[98] Once again,

---

[93] Alexander, *Sacramental Discourses*, p. 130.
[94] Alexander, *Sacramental Discourses*, p. 131.
[95] Alexander, *Sacramental Discourses*, p. 131.
[96] Alexander, *Sacramental Discourses*, p. 135.
[97] Alexander, *Sacramental Discourses*, pp. 135–136.
[98] Alexander, *Sacramental Discourses*, pp. 173–201.

Alexander is concerned to object to the corrupting influence of the Enlightenment, which by the middle of the nineteenth century had weakened orthodox Christian theology quite considerably. The Unitarians found the idea that Christ should have died for us an especially objectionable doctrine. A substitutionary atonement was objectionable to any who had been influenced by Deism and, as Alexander points out again and again, the sacrament of the Lord's Supper, especially as it was understood by classical Protestantism, hardly fits into a Deistic approach to worship. In short, Alexander, typical of the Old School, took the sacrament very seriously, whereas the New School tended to give little attention to it.

The text Alexander chooses makes plain the vicarious nature of the cross. "Who his own self bare our sins in his own body on the tree" (1 Pet. 2:24, KJV). The heart of the sermon gives us five ways in which we are to understand that Christ bore our sins.

First, Christ bore our nature. "It was the all-essential preliminary to his whole work. To be our Head, he became bone of our bone. 'The Word was made flesh.' It is the greatest and most precious of mysteries."[99] We find this again and again in these eucharistic sermons of this Old School preacher. The celebration of the Lord's Supper is the occasion for remembering the cardinal doctrines of the Christian faith, especially those doctrines concerning the person and work of Christ. In this sermon, the doctrine of the incarnation is mentioned first, but it is sort of a preface to the doctrine of the atonement.

Second, *"Christ actually endured pain."*[100] The whole time of his earthly life from his birth in a stable to his crucifixion on the cross was one humiliation after another. The troubles of his childhood, the opposition to his ministry, the rejection of the scribes and Pharisees to his teaching, his agony in the garden, his torture, his thirst on the cross and his burial in the earth. It was one insult after

---

[99] Alexander, *Sacramental Discourses*, pp. 180–181.

[100] Alexander, *Sacramental Discourses*, p. 182.

another. All this he endured, yet without sin.

Third, that Jesus suffered for our sins is one of the most obvious teachings of Scripture. Alexander goes through a whole list of texts starting with Isaiah 53, "He hath borne our grief and carried our sorrows." "He was wounded for our transgressions; he was bruised for our iniquities." From Romans 5:6 he quotes, "Christ died for the ungodly" and from 1 Corinthians 15:3, "Christ died for our sins."[101] He adds another half dozen texts to make his point. This sermon is indeed an *anamnesis* of Christ's vicarious suffering. What is particularly to be noted in these texts is that Christ suffered for our sins. He bore "our sins in his own body on the tree" (1 Pet. 2:24, KJV).

Fourth, Christ bore our sins in the sense that he bore the penalty of our sins. This has been the historic witness of the church down through the centuries. There is nothing novel or artificial about this teaching. It is quite simple. "We were to have been punished. Christ was punished for us. We were to have died. Christ died for us. It is the plain signification of the expression often repeated in Scripture; 'Christ died for us,' that is, died in our stead."[102] Here our preacher supports the Old School position at length.

Finally our preacher comes to his fifth point, *"Christ so bore our sins as to remove from us all their penal consequences and secure our salvation.* By that suffering, he exhausted the penalty, and discharged the debt."[103]

Here we have a profound insight into the eucharistic piety of the Old School. The congregation, gathered about the Lord's Table, listens to this portrayal of God's redemptive work in Christ, recognizes that Jesus the very Son of God has been sent by the Father to call a rebellious and sinful people to himself. Here is the preaching of the gospel at its epicenter. Here God's elect are called to enter into the great banquet, the wedding feast of the Lamb. The faithful come to the Supper. There they see how God

---

[101] Alexander, *Sacramental Discourses*, p. 183.

[102] Alexander, *Sacramental Discourses*, p. 185.

[103] Alexander, *Sacramental Discourses*, p. 192.

can be just and yet the justifier of the ungodly that believe in Jesus.

Here at the Lord's Table, the sum and substance is presented to us. The history of our salvation in Christ is recounted. The signs of the covenant are on the table before us. "Christ is visibly set forth, crucified in the midst of us. We are beside the altar, and before us is the bleeding Lamb of propitiation."[104] This sermon very powerfully makes the point that the sacrament of the Lord's Supper is the memorial of the Lamb of God who takes away the sin of the world. Just as the Passover was a memorial of redemption from Egypt, so the Supper is a memorial of our redemption from this world. For this prominent Old School preacher the Supper is clearly to be understood in terms of all the imagery found in Scripture. For the Lord's Supper, just as for Passover, the sacrifice of the Lamb was central to the imagery.

D. THE SUPPER AS *AGAPÉ*

Having made the point that the breaking of the bread and the pouring of the wine are an obvious memorial of the redemptive suffering of Christ we move on to another central point. In this sacrament we gather around a table and share a meal with one another. The earliest attempts to reshape the celebration of communion back in the age of the Reformation show a concern to bring into focus the significance of sharing a meal together. The basic sign of sharing a meal is right at the center of a true celebration of the Lord's Supper. Even more, the earliest documents produced by the ancient Church refer to the sacrament as an *agapé*, a Feast of Christian Love. The Lord's Supper was called an *agapé* because to participate in it was to experience God's love for us on the one hand and to share it with our neighbors on the other. What is essential to understand is that God's love, as it is revealed in the cross of Christ, is the source of the love which binds us together in the bond of love which we experience at the Lord's Table.

---

[104] Alexander, *Sacramental Discourses*, p. 193.

19: Old School Presbyterianism

In Alexander's sermon, "God is Love," the text taken is two verses from the First Epistle of John: "He that loveth not, knoweth not God; for God is love. . . . And we have known and believed the love that God hath for us. God is love; and he that dwelleth in love dwelleth in God, and God in him" (1 John 4:8, 16).[105] In his interpretation of this passage, Alexander points to the admonition of the beloved Apostle, "Beloved, let us love one another." Then the Apostle adds, "for love is of God." (1 John 4:7, KJV). Alexander then interprets this with a quick metaphor, "Here he traces the flood to the fountain." Then he goes on to explain, "In other words, love is divine, and proceeds from the very nature of God."[106] That God is love is revealed in the incarnation. As we find it in the succeeding verse, "In this was manifested the love of God toward us, because that God sent his only begotten Son into the world, that we might live through him."[107] It is this line that is descending from God to men, and shows us more of God than all works and all symbols. Strictly speaking, we have no direct vision of God unless we have a vision of love when we sit together at the Lord's Table and experience the love of the brethren. When we sit at the Lord's Table we are to see and love God's image in those around us.

It is in discovering the love of God as it was manifested in the person of Jesus that we are transformed and the image of God is renewed in us. In the sacrament, we discover this redemptive love and are enabled more and more to pass it on to our neighbors. Our preacher calls the congregation to the table:

> Behold, my brothers, the holy stream which circulates around the eucharistic table; love in God to believers—love in believers to God—love in brothers to brothers; all comprised in the higher law, God is love. We are in the spot, of all others, where such affections may be best awakened and promoted, for we are at the cross.

---

[105] Alexander, *Sacramental Discourses*, p. 9.

[106] Alexander, *Sacramental Discourses*, p. 13.

[107] Alexander quoting I John 4:9. Alexander, *Sacramental Discourses*, p. 14.

> Here is the sacrifice of propitiation, in sacramental emblem. Here are the body and the blood of Jesus, in visible commemoration. Here is the nearest view, vouchsafed to us this side of heaven, into the secret majesty of Divine perfection.[108]

In another sermon, "God's Great Love to Us," Alexander tells us that God's love to us is the blessing of blessings.[109] It is the source of all subordinate blessings. God's love is the source of the love of others toward us as well as the source of our love toward others. "Give any soul assurance of God's perpetual love, and you crown that soul with bliss."[110] The very sign of the Lord's Table in the house of our Heavenly Father, sitting around it to be nourished by the bread of life and the cup of salvation, makes it clear that the love of the Father is the source of the love of the brethren. If it is true that we love him because he first loved us, it is also true that we love each other because he first loved us.

A particularly moving sermon in this series has the title, "The Hymn of the Eucharist."[111] Not surprisingly, it draws our attention to the little text at the end of the story of the Last Supper as it is focused in the Gospel of Matthew, "And when they had sung a hymn, they went out into the Mount of Olives" (Matt. 26:30).[112] It is a good sermon on the subject of worship in general although it specially concerns the subject of the sacrament of the Lord's Supper. It makes the point that, for a Christian celebration, communion hymnody is especially appropriate because it fosters harmony in the congregation. Singing unites us in the bond of love. Alexander points out that as the psalms are sung, all voices are united with a unity emulating the unity of heaven. This is a great privilege and attunes the heart to joining this heavenly worship.

---

[108] Alexander, *Sacramental Discourses*, pp. 26–27.

[109] Alexander, *Sacramental Discourses*, pp. 31–55.

[110] Alexander, *Sacramental Discourses*, p. 36.

[111] Alexander, *Sacramental Discourses*, p. 131.

[112] Alexander, *Sacramental Discourses*, p. 89.

19: OLD SCHOOL PRESBYTERIANISM

As this Old School Presbyterian understands it, worship could achieve no higher goal than to become "a fellowship of adoration, love and praise."[113] What a new face this would put on our solemn gatherings, if whole assemblies solidly united in heart and soul as one man, were touched with an apprehension of the presence of God, and not only individually but jointly, sending up a volume of sanctified harmony. Sometimes it would be in tender supplication, sometimes in profoundest awe, sometimes in rapturous joy but all together and all in accord, not a heart unmoved, not a voice silent!

The *agapé* feast of the early Christian church was understood as a foretaste of a heavenly feast yet to come. It was therefore that they celebrated Communion. The bond of love that they celebrated in the church here on earth was an intimation and assurance of the bond of love that they would experience in the last day. Then, in that glorious day, "there will be such a renewal of the spirit of worship, as in a thousand places the voice of joy shall be in the tabernacles of the righteous. Then shall God's praise—highest employment of human tongues—ascend with such richness and volume, that a day in God's courts shall be better than a thousand."[114]

E. THE SUPPER AS SIGN AND SEAL OF THE NEW COVENANT

For Reformed Protestantism the covenantal dimension of the Lord's Supper is of major importance. This means that we understand the celebration of the communion to be a transaction. It is not just a statement or a visible word. It is that, to be sure, but beyond that, it is a participation in an act. It is becoming part of a community. It is exercising our membership in the body of Christ. It is joining the church and continuing to take part in the fellowship of the church. This approach to the sacrament is made especially clear in Alexander's sermon, "Communion in Christ's Body

---

[113] Alexander, *Sacramental Discourses*, p. 110.

[114] Alexander, *Sacramental Discourses*, p. 111.

and Blood."[115] The text for the sermon is 1 Corinthians 10:16 (KJV), "The cup of blessing which we bless, is it not the communion of the blood of Christ?" The sermon is not based on a text so much as it is on a passage, namely, the tenth chapter of Paul's First Epistle to the Corinthians. This chapter in its entirety makes especially clear the covenantal dimension of the Lord's Supper.

The intention of the Apostle Paul in his letter to the Corinthians is to warn them of the dangers of participating in pagan culture. To be a Christian is to come out of the pagan culture and leave it behind and to enter into a new Christian community, the kingdom of God. To be a Christian is to take part in the life of the Christian community. The problem was that too many Corinthians were trying to live in both communities at the same time. Paul urges his converts to make up their minds. If they are going to come to church and participate in the Lord's Supper, they could not continue to go to feasts held by their friends in pagan temples. Paul's argument here tells us much about how the New Testament church regarded the sacrament of the Lord's Supper.

Paul begins his discussion of the problem of participation with an appeal to the Old Testament types of the Christian sacraments of baptism and the Lord's Supper. These include the baptism of the children of Israel in the Red Sea, and their being fed in the wilderness by the gift of manna from heaven and drinking from the rock. Paul's point is that the sacraments are not magical rites which automatically confer salvation. Here Alexander follows the traditional Protestant exegesis. They, as other Old Testament sacraments, were sacred acts in which the faithful became engaged in the sacred community. By participation in these sacred services one becomes a member of the people of God.

For Alexander, the key word here is "participation" or, as it is translated in the text of the King James Version, "communion." Our preacher reminds us that the original Greek word is a very

---

[115] Alexander, *Sacramental Discourses*, p. 233–260.

19: OLD SCHOOL PRESBYTERIANISM

rich word and has considerable depth of meaning. The word is so important theologically that it has been transliterated into English, "*koinonia.*" The word, *koinonia*, can be translated by "participation" or "fellowship," by "communion" or even by "sharing." The passage Alexander has chosen to bring the whole chapter into focus uses the word twice, "the cup of blessing which we bless, is it not communion in the blood of Christ. The bread which we break is it not communion in the body of Christ."[116]

Alexander goes on to develop the meaning of *koinonia* here by pointing out that Paul is not focusing on just the communion of one individual Christian with Christ. He is talking about much more. In Communion, we partake in common with many others. This is particularly clear in the Old Testament type. "The Israelites were all under the cloud, and all passed through the sea."[117] But then as Paul goes on developing his argument, he tells us, "for we being many are one loaf, and one body: for we are all partakers of that one loaf."[118] The covenantal dimension of the sacrament is very strong here. Alexander makes it even stronger, reminding us of the patristic interpretation which one finds in so many of the Fathers of the ancient church. "As many grains of wheat, ground and kneaded and compacted, form the unity of a simple loaf of bread . . . thus many believers, joined to Christ, and joined to each other, form one corporate structure of Christian community."[119] Alexander finds two leading thoughts here. Believers have communion with Christ and they have communion with each other. The Lord's Supper is in truth an *agapé*, a manifestation of the way the love of God brings us into love for the brethren. As Alexander himself puts it, "Believers have communion or participation or fellowship, with Christ; and that, in this, they have fellowship with

---

[116] First Corinthians 10:16 as quoted in Alexander, *Sacramental Discourses*, p. 233.
[117] First Corinthians 10:1 as quoted in Alexander, *Sacramental Discourses*, p. 239.
[118] First Corinthians 10:17 as quoted in Alexander, *Sacramental Discourses*, p. 239.
[119] Alexander, *Sacramental Discourses*, p. 239.

one another. And this is set forth, by vivid emblem, in the one loaf of the sacrament, and the one cup of blessing."[120]

At this point Alexander turns to the subject of how it is that we participate. We participate by faith. Here Alexander is at his most forceful. Alluding to the prologue of the Gospel of John he says, "To as many as received him, to them gave he authority to become sons of God, even to them which believe on his name. That is, faith receives. Faith makes Christ ours."[121] It is by faith that we participate in the body of Christ. It is by faith that we have communion with the risen and ascended Christ. In the end what that means is that through faith Christ is ours. It is by faith that Christians gather around the Lord's Table and break bread one with another and pass the cup from one hand to the next. In doing this "the blessings of the covenant are proffered and received."[122] Not only does the sacrament offer the promises of the gospel, it seals them as well. This sealing is the work of the Holy Spirit, who assures us of the truth of these promises and begins to bring about their fulfillment.

At the very heart of the Reformed communion service is the making or the renewing of the covenant vows. The first time one participates, the new communicants are usually prepared formally by the minister in some sort of communicants class or by some sort of catechetical instruction. This may well be summed up by the congregation reciting together the Apostles' Creed. For most communicants it is a matter of renewing the covenant vows in a very personal and informal way. But every time we celebrate the Lord's Supper we hear the covenant promises offered once again to us. They are held out to us with generous hands and so we should receive them to our spiritual nourishment and eternal enjoyment.

---

[120] Alexander, *Sacramental Discourses*, p. 239.

[121] Alexander, *Sacramental Discourses*, p. 244.

[122] Alexander, *Sacramental Discourses*, p. 245.

19: Old School Presbyterianism

F. The Supper as Foretaste of the Wedding Feast of the Lamb

We have often noticed that the preachers of the Reformed Church seem to preach on texts from the Revelation of John with considerable frequency. J. W. Alexander has left us a fine eucharistic sermon on Revelation 19:12–13, "His eyes were a flame of fire, and on his head were many crowns; and he had a name written that no man knew but himself and he was clothed with a vesture dipped in blood: and his name is called the Word of God."[123] The sermon is quite simply an *anamnesis* of the glorified Christ.

Our preacher points out to us how the Scriptures present the glorified Christ to us. While the Revelation of John is chiefly concerned to show us "the great warfare and victory of the glorious future," we have surely noticed that it also brings into view "some tokens and signal remembrances of the humiliation and the atonement."[124] In the very crown we are made to see the cross. Again and again we see in the memorial of the crown the memorial of the cross as well. Alexander demonstrates his point with a long list of passages throughout the whole book of Revelation. The Revelation begins with an ascription of praise to "him that loved us and washed us from our sins in his own blood, and hath made us kings and priests . . . ."[125] Here we find both the humiliation and the exaltation, both the cross and the crown. A bit further on in chapters four and five we are shown that great service of heavenly worship engaged in praise and adoration. It is a magnificent vision of the victory of God's people and yet, in the very center, on the very throne of God, we see the Lamb that was slain. In the very center of heaven are both the cross and the crown. We are told of the throng of white-robed saints and then discover in chapter seven that they serve God

---

[123] "Christ's Cross and Crown." Alexander, *Sacramental Discourses*, pp. 341–366. Scripture is as quoted by Alexander.

[124] Alexander, *Sacramental Discourses*, p. 341.

[125] Revelation 1:5 as quoted in Alexander, *Sacramental Discourses*, p. 342.

night and day. Their glistening white robes are white because they have been washed in the blood of the Lamb. Once again we find closely joined together, the cross and the crown.

For Alexander, Christ's victorious reign is in consideration of his death. The cross is the purchase of the crown. The truth we find in Revelation we find as well in Paul's Epistle to the Philippians, which tells us that Christ "became obedient unto death, even the death of the cross; wherefore also God hath highly exalted him, and given him a name which is above every name" (Phil. 2:9).[126] It is the same theme we have found in Isaiah 53. "It is because of this that he comes even to the marriage supper, with a vesture dipped in blood. The mediatorial exaltation of Jesus Christ is all in consequence of his mediatorial humiliation . . ."[127]

For Alexander, the imagery of the wedding feast so strong in Reformed eucharistic piety implies the idea of the consummation of the love of Christ for his bride. This obviously is a beautiful image and few of us would have a problem with preaching it. There is another dimension to this image which, however, we might not be quite so prepared to develop. The Lord's Supper is a memorial to the Last Day, the Day of Judgment. To celebrate this feast is to remember the vengeance of the Lion of Judah. It is to tramp out the vintage where the grapes of wrath are stored. Here we must remember that other image from the prophet Isaiah, "I have trodden the winepress alone and of the people there was none with me; for I will tread them in mine anger and trample them in my fury; and their blood shall be sprinkled on my garments, and I will stain all my raiment."[128] As Alexander sees it, this refers to the punishment Christ shall inflict on his most obstinate enemies. To be sure, it is Christ as bridegroom that is the primary image here, but the idea of Christ as judge should not be overlooked.

---

[126] Alexander, *Sacramental Discourses*, p. 344.

[127] Alexander, *Sacramental Discourses*, p. 345.

[128] Alexander, *Sacramental Discourses*, p. 352.

There are so many passages of Scripture which speak of Christ as judge. Alexander reminds us of Psalm 2 and its warning against the plots of the kings of the earth and its rulers in their haughty rejection of the Lord's anointed. Will not the Lord hold them in derision and break them like a potter's vessel? John in the Revelation sees the destruction of Babylon, the wicked city that corrupted the word of the prophets and rejected the apostles. No saint can do other than rejoice at the fall of Babylon and all her poisonous offspring. "I suppose there never was a true believer who did not rejoice with Christ in his heavenly recompense and exaltation."[129]

This sermon first remembers Christ in both his divinity and humanity, having portrayed him as crucified for our sins and victorious over all the devices of Satan and as judge on the Last Day. It now remembers Christ in his mercy seeking us all to come to him as Lord and Savior, to acknowledge his Lordship and to give to the King of kings and Lord of lords the service that is due. To remember him aright is to acknowledge him as Lord.

BENJAMIN BRECKINRIDGE WARFIELD

No one who has ever seen the twinkle in the eye of Benjamin Breckinridge Warfield's portrait that hangs at Princeton Seminary will ever doubt that he is one of the patriarchs of American Christianity. He was a genius with paternal warmth, a saint among the scholars.

Benjamin Breckinridge Warfield (1851–1921) was born in the Kentucky Bluegrass, the son of a wealthy farmer in some of the most beautiful farming country in America.[130] His mother was the

---

[129] Alexander, *Sacramental Discourses*, p. 360.

[130] For biographical information on Warfield, see: W. Andrew Hoffecker, "Warfield, Benjamin Breckinridge," in *Dictionary of Christianity in America*, (Downers Grove, IL: InterVarsity Press, 1990), pp. 1234–1235; Roger Nicole, "Warfield, Benjamin Breckinridge," in *Encyclopedia of the Reformed Faith*, ed. Donald K. McKim (Louisville: Westminster John Knox Press; and Edinburgh: Saint Andrew Press, 1992), pp. 390–391; and Noll, "Warfield, Benjamin Breckinridge," in *New Dictionary of Theology*, pp. 716–718.

daughter of Robert Breckinridge, a theologian of some distinction, who actually produced a two volume systematic theology. It should also be noted that Robert Breckinridge is sometimes identified as the founder of Old School Presbyterianism and a champion of abolition. He was professor at the theological seminary in Danville, Kentucky, and it was no doubt for him that Breckinridge Hall at Centre College was named. This bit of incidental intelligence is of interest to me because I spent my freshman year of college in Breckinridge Hall.

Warfield was sent off to college at Princeton where he was one of the last students of James McCosh, so famous for his Scottish common sense philosophy. After college he went to Princeton Seminary and there he drank in the urbane conservatism of Charles Hodge, who, like McCosh, was finishing up his last years. After his formal education he traveled in Europe. Returning to America he taught New Testament at Western Theological Seminary in Allegheny, Pennsylvania. Finally he was called to Princeton to succeed A. A. Hodge as professor of didactic and polemic theology.

While Warfield's theological contributions are widely recognized, these were more in terms of journal articles, book reviews, and lectures to his students rather than in terms of volumes of systematic theology or theological monographs. He did produce a two volume polemic against perfectionism.[131] A volume of his chapel talks, published posthumously, proved much more popular.[132] Several collections of his works have been published. There is a ten volume collection of his complete works, and also a two volume edition of selected works.[133] Warfield was not so much a

---

[131] Benjamin B. Warfield, *Perfectionism*, 2 vols. (New York: Oxford University Press, 1931). A more modern, one-volume edition was published: Benjamin B. Warfield, *Perfectionism*, ed. Samuel G. Craig (Philadelphia: Presbyterian & Reformed, 1958).

[132] Benjamin Breckinridge Warfield, *Faith and Life* (Edinburgh and Carlisle, PA: Banner of Truth Trust, 1990).

[133] Benjamin Breckinridge Warfield, *The Works of Benjamin B. Warfield*, 10 vols. (Grand Rapids, MI: Baker Book House, 1991); and Benjamin Breckinridge Warfield, *Selected Shorter Writings*, ed. John E. Meeter, 2 vols. (Phillipsburg, NJ: Presbyterian and Reformed Publishing Co., 1970, 1973).

19: Old School Presbyterianism

systematic theologian as he was an apologist. The title of his chair was professor of didactic and polemic theology. The title seems a bit awkward today, but it was the title of the chair when Charles Hodge occupied it. He was supposed to be a theologian specializing in apologetics; that is what he was hired to do, to put it bluntly.

There was another aspect to this. The organ of communication which was given to him was Princeton's theological journal. For some reason it changed its name from time to time. In Warfield's earlier days it was called the *Presbyterian and Reformed Review*. Later it changed its name to the *Princeton Theological Journal*.[134] Under Warfield this journal was dedicated to the defense of classical Augustinian Calvinism. It was the antithesis of the Unitarianism taught at Harvard and the New School Calvinism being taught at Yale. Of particular concern to this journal was the subject of the inspiration of holy Scripture. Warfield was the champion of inerrancy in a day when it had few serious defenders. Sad to say, Warfield has left us only the briefest treatments of Reformed eucharistic theology. This is especially regrettable because Warfield did leave us so much on the subject of piety. What we do have from him is therefore all the more valuable.[135] Let us look at three of the most helpful publications that Warfield has left us.

A. "Communion in Christ's Body and Blood"

First, we have the chapel sermon "Communion in Christ's Body and Blood."[136] The sermon takes up the question of the eucharistic sacrifice so often debated between Protestants and Catholics.

---

[134] Under Charles Hodge it was called *Biblical Repertory and Princeton Review*. See: John W. Stewart, "Hodge, Charles (1797–1878)," in *Encyclopedia of the Reformed Faith*, pp. 174–176.

[135] From Glen J. Clary we do have a very fine paper, "The Eucharistic Theology of Benjamin Breckinridge Warfield," written as his final paper at Erskine Theological Seminary for the class Theology of Worship in Contemporary Discussion, Summer, 2008.

[136] Warfield, *Faith and Life*, pp. 222–230.

Luther himself in the *Babylonian Captivity of the Church* had identified the doctrine of the eucharistic sacrifice as one of the major errors of the Roman Catholic Church at the end of the Middle Ages. The doctrine of the eucharistic sacrifice is not often treated in the pulpit, probably because it was thought of as too problematic or too negative. It needs to be treated nevertheless.

Warfield takes as his text, 1 Corinthians 10:16–17: "The cup of blessing which we bless, is it not a communion of the blood of Christ? The bread which we break, is it not a communion of the body of Christ? Seeing that we, who are many, are one bread, one body: for we all partake of the one bread."[137] Here Warfield, not to our surprise, begins by insisting that we interpret our text from its historical context. The Corinthians lived in a world where people were very familiar with ritual sacrifice. Both among the heathen of the Hellenistic world and among faithful Jews there were daily sacrifices.[138] These sacrifices so often observed in both Hellenistic society and in the Jewish world would offer up a sacrificial animal and then from the body of that animal would prepare a feast that was eaten by the worshipers. The Apostle Paul specifically mentions this further on in this epistle. From such feasts the faithful Christian dare not partake. Such an act makes one a participant in the worship of idols.[139] We find the same principle in the sacrifices of the Jews. The Apostle Paul goes on to say, "Consider Israel after the flesh. Are not those who eat the sacrifices, communicants in the altar?" (cf. 1 Cor. 10:18). By sharing the sacrificial feast one shares in the religious benefits of the feast.[140]

This is certainly the way we are to understand the feast of Passover. The Lord's Supper is to be understood as the Christian

---

[137] Scripture is as quoted by Warfield, *Faith and Life*, p. 222.
[138] Warfield, *Faith and Life*, pp. 222–224.
[139] Warfield, *Faith and Life*, p. 225.
[140] Warfield, *Faith and Life*, p. 226.

continuation of Passover.[141] Driving in this point at considerable length, Warfield sums it up:

> How simple, how significant, the whole is, when once it is approached from the historical point of view. The Lord's Supper is the continuation of the passover feast. The symbol only being changed, it is the passover feast. And the eating of the bread and drinking of the wine mean precisely what partaking of the lamb did then. It is communion in the altar. Christ our Passover is sacrificed for us; and we eat the passover whenever we eat this bread and drink this wine in remembrance of Him. In our communing thus in the body and the blood of Christ we partake of the altar, and are made beneficiaries of the sacrifice He wrought out upon it.[142]

Warfield goes on to point out that when we gather at the Lord's Table we find not simply bread and wine, but bread broken for us and wine poured out. This is not simply a feast; it is a sacrificial feast. It is no mere church supper here!

There is a second point to be found in our text. To participate in this meal is to become part of the church. There is one loaf of bread and we become one by all participating in that one loaf.[143] This is one of the reasons we so often call the Lord's Supper the communion. To use the term "communion," of course, emphasizes the covenantal dimension of the sacrament.

> Another lesson which our text to-day brings us is that the root of our communion with one another as Christians lies in our common relation to our Lord. We are "many," says the Apostle; that is what we are in ourselves. But we "all"—all of this "many"—are "one"— one body, because there is but one loaf and we all share from that one loaf. Christ is one and we come into relations of communion with one another only through our common relation with Him. The root

---

[141] Warfield, *Faith and Life*, p. 227.
[142] Warfield, *Faith and Life*, pp. 228–229.
[143] Warfield, *Faith and Life*, p. 230.

of Christian union is, therefore, the uniqueness, the solity of Christ. There is but one salvation; but one Christian life; because there is but one Savior and one source of life; and all those who share it must needs stand side by side to imbibe it from the one fountain.[144]

B. THE SACRIFICIAL FEAST

Let us look at another short essay on the Lord's Supper that has come down to us.[145] The title of this essay suggests that Warfield intends this as a summary statement of his teaching rather than an occasional sermon as seems to be the case with the sermon we have just studied. Basic to Warfield's doctrine is the confidence that Jesus deliberately chose to institute the sacrament of communion in the course of the observance of Passover. The Christian sacrament is the continuation of the Jewish feast. He puts it very clearly, "Nothing can be more certain than that he deliberately chose the Passover Meal for the institution of the sacrament of his body and blood."[146]

Warfield shows the similarity between Passover and the Lord's Supper as we find it in the Gospels and in the report of the Apostle Paul in 1 Corinthians 11. Warfield speaks of the typical character of the paschal lamb. That is, the paschal lamb is the type of Christ, the Lamb of God who takes away the sin of the world. The Lamb is there both at Passover and at the celebration of the Christian sacrament. In both, the same Lamb is fed upon.

Warfield was rather unique in his day for his willingness to find the origins of Christian worship in the worship of the Temple and the worship of the synagogue. Joachim Jeremias has done much to clear up that question since 1901 when Warfield wrote this. It is also the case that Warfield's clairvoyance on this question was supported by his pioneering study of the *Didaché*, which had

---

[144] Warfield, *Faith and Life*, p. 230.
[145] Warfield, "The Fundamental Significance of the Lord's Supper," *Selected Shorter Works*, 1:332–338.
[146] Warfield, *Selected Shorter Works*, 1:332.

19: OLD SCHOOL PRESBYTERIANISM

only recently been rediscovered.[147]

Warfield tells us concerning the Lord's Supper, "It is not something entirely different from the Passover—or even wholly separate from it—now put into its place, to be celebrated by Christians instead of it. It is much rather only a new form given to the Passover, for the continuance of its essential substance through all time."[148] At the heart of the new Christian celebration of Passover was the indication that this new feast follows the sacrifice of the passover lamb. Jesus himself took the bread and said, "This is my body broken for you." He took the cup and said, "This cup is the New Covenant poured out for many for the remission of sins" (cf. 1 Cor. 11:24–25). This was a propitiatory sacrifice that Jesus was to offer on the cross. Not only was the broken bread and poured out wine a reminder that Passover was a sacrifice; it was a thanksgiving that this sacrifice avails for our salvation. This sacrifice was once for all offered up and once for all received on high. It never needs to be offered up again.

There is a difference between the offering up of a sacrifice on the altar and the sharing of the sacrificial feast which follows that sacrifice. The eucharist is the thanksgiving feast that follows the atoning sacrifice of the Lamb of God. Warfield fully understands the historic Protestant objection. He fully understands the objection to the doctrine of the eucharistic sacrifice registered by Luther in his *Babylonian Captivity of the Church*.

If liberal Protestants at the end of the nineteenth century were offended by the biblical understanding of sacrifice and wanted to hear no more of propitiatory sacrifices, Warfield wants to make very clear that all this is deeply written into the most sacred of Christian rites. No Christian worship can be conceived without it. This does not mean, however, that we should return to offering a so-called eucharistic sacrifice day by day, as was the practice at the end of the

---

[147] See Clary, "Warfield's Eucharistic Doctrine."

[148] Warfield, *Selected Shorter Writings*, 1:333.

Middle Ages. We do not want to find ourselves in the position of the priests of the Temple who, to follow the words of the Epistle to the Hebrews, offered again and again the same sacrifices that can never take away sins (cf. Heb. 9–10). Warfield puts it very well:

> That is the fundamental significance of the Lord's Supper. Whenever the Lord's Supper is spread before us we are invited to take our place at the sacrificial feast, the substance of which is the flesh and blood of the victim which has been sacrificed once for all at Calvary; and as we eat these in their symbols, we are—certainly not repeating his sacrifice, nor yet prolonging it—but continuing that solemn festival upon it instituted by Christ, by which we testify our "participation in the altar" and claim our part in the benefits bought by the offering immolated on it. The sacrificial feast is not the sacrifice, in the sense of the act of offering: it is, however, the sacrifice, in the sense of the thing offered, that is eaten in it: and therefore it is presuppositive of the sacrifice in the sense of the act of offering and implies that this offering has already been performed.[149]

C. Sitting at the Lord's Table

A most significant essay on the means of celebrating Holy Communion was published in the *Journal of the Presbyterian Historical Society*.[150] It appears to be the last thing Warfield wrote on the sacraments.[151] This article is particularly interesting because to my knowledge there is so little available on the subject.

Warfield tells us that the question was debated vigorously for three weeks at the Westminster Assembly. It seems that the English Congregationalists preferred to pass the bread and wine

---

[149] Warfield, *Selected Shorter Works*, 1:337.

[150] Benjamin Breckinridge Warfield, "The Posture of the Recipients at the Lord's Supper," *Journal of the Presbyterian Historical Society* (June, 1920). Reprinted in Warfield, *Selected Shorter Writings*, 2:351–369.

[151] Clary, "Warfield's Eucharistic Doctrine."

19: OLD SCHOOL PRESBYTERIANISM

through the pews while the Scottish Presbyterians liked to set up special tables for a sacramental occasion. The communicants in both cases sat to receive both the bread and the wine. The discussion apparently got quite intense and no one would give any ground.

Equally as well known is the story of John Knox and the so-called Black Rubric. At the time of the *Prayer Book* of 1549, the *First Prayer Book* of Edward VI was still being printed. John Knox, who had been appointed by the King to preach the gospel throughout England, got the ear of Archbishop Cranmer and convinced him that the rubrics of the new *Prayer Book* should specifically forbid communicants from bowing down before the consecrated host and receiving it with adoration. Rubrics are usually printed in red, hence the word "rubric," but this rubric, because of the rush and confusion at the printer's office, was mistakenly printed in black, hence, the Black Rubric. This got the discussion off to a rather sinister start. Cardinal Grindal had pointed out in a recent Catholic tract the act of kneeling before the host implied its worship. Now that the Catholic cardinal had pointed out that kneeling before the host could be understood as an act of worship, the Protestants became scandalized that they were being required by the new prayer book to commit idolatry. Finally Queen Elizabeth coming to the throne in 1558 insisted on receiving the bread and wine "devoutly kneeling." What really angered the Protestants was the Queen's insistence on claiming the authority to decide the matter.

For generations the question of posture at the Lord's Supper became a hot issue. In Scotland particularly it became a symbol of the authority of the church to govern itself. Scotland followed John Knox, and the Church of Scotland decided for sitting at the Lord's Table. In England, on the other hand, it was one of those little things the Queen used to demonstrate royal supremacy. It was not surprising, then, that Thomas Cartwright and the Cambridge Presbyterians made this one of their primary issues in their

Admonition to Parliament in 1572.[152]

In the American colonies there were definite differences between how the New England Calvinists celebrated the Lord's Supper and how the Scotch-Irish Presbyterians observed it. The communion season held by Gilbert Tennent in New Brunswick, New Jersey, was obviously of the Scottish sort and yet, as we have noticed above, the communion sermons preached by J. W. Alexander do not seem to have been preached at a communion season. On the other hand, Warfield tells of the Presbyterian Church of New Hartford, New York. It was obviously organized by a group of New England Congregationalists. According to the Plan of Union, however, they organized themselves as a Presbyterian church because they were in western New York. This was followed through consistently when it came to the manner of posture at the Lord's Table. The congregation sat at a table or tables especially put up for the occasion. Whether there were preparatory services is not reported. Look again!

Warfield had evidently done quite a bit of research on this matter of posture at the Lord's Table.[153] He learned from Phillip Schaff that at the time of the Reformation Zwingli initiated the first Reformed communion season of the Zurich church by having the communicants sit to receive the bread and wine. The old gilded altarpieces had been removed and large wooden tables were put in their place. The bread and wine were served on wooden plates and in large wooden cups. The Zurich Reformer tried to make the celebration of the Lord's Supper look as much like a meal in someone's home as he could.[154]

Standing, however, prevailed in Geneva. Communicants went forward to a large table in the choir of the church. The minis-

---

[152] See Walter H. Frere, ed., *Puritan Manifestoes: A Study of the Origin of the Puritan Revolt* (London: Published for the Church Historical Society by S. P. C. K., 1954).

[153] See, Warfield, "The Posture of the Recipients at the Lord's Supper."

[154] Warfield, "The Posture of the Recipients at the Lord's Supper."

ters stood behind the table and reached across the table both the bread and then the wine. The ministers served the bread while the deacons served the wine. As Warfield has it, the system was preserved in French Huguenot churches in his day. The communicants would stand in a circle around the table and pass the bread and the cup from person to person around the table.[155]

In recent times, Warfield tells us, there has been a real change among American Presbyterians and this change, according to Warfield, was largely brought about by Thomas Chalmers in St. John's Church in Glasgow. He built it into a very large church and when the sacrament was observed it took a long time to see that all were served. To accommodate the large congregation the pews were arranged around the Table. The minister sat behind the Table and the elders to the right and to the left with the pews in front. The bread and the wine were then passed through the pews.

As Warfield saw it, and I certainly agree with him, posture at the Lord's Table is *adiaphora*, that is, it is indifferent. On the other hand, and here I also find myself in agreement with Warfield, it is helpful to celebrate the rite in such a way that it makes clear the meaning of the sign that seals the covenant. The rite should look like a meal—a festal meal.

Warfield found himself in agreement with Chalmers' suggestion that the whole church be arranged in such a way that it suggested that the entire congregation was gathered around the Table. The minister would stand directly behind the Table while the elders would flank the Table to the right and the left and the pews would be arranged in front of the Table. This would not work too well with the neo-Gothic architecture so popular in those days, but changes in architectural style were occurring rapidly in the nineteenth century. More and more churches were building their sanctuaries so that both the pulpit and the communion table were in the midst of the congregation rather than down a long nave to a

---

[155] Warfield, "The Posture of the Recipients at the Lord's Supper."

chancel at the far end. The strength of Warfield's suggestion here is that it gives the congregation a sense of being a congregation. Instead of seeing nothing more than the backs of peoples' heads, one has more of a feeling of being a fellowship, a sacred assembly gathered around the Lord's Table. What Warfield would suggest is that we arrange our churches in such a way that we are always seated at the Table, not only to partake of the sacred meal, but to listen to the reading and preaching of the Word and to join together in prayer.

To conclude this chapter on Old School Presbyterianism, let us take another look at the portrait of Benjamin Breckinridge Warfield in Stevenson Lounge at Princeton Seminary. The benevolent smile of that grand old patriarch, the twinkle of his eye, and the curl of his beard are the key to Old School Presbyterianism. The subject for which he is famous is the subject of Protestant piety, neither a world-denying piety nor a heavenly-transcendent sort of piety. He taught a serious sort of piety that knew what it meant to bear the cares of the world and to be at home with its mysteries. If we are to understand Warfield's teaching on the sacrament of the Lord's Supper we first have to read Warfield's two volumes entitled simply, *Perfectionism*. The mystery in the end is a matter of presence.

20

THE AGE OF ROMANTICISM

It was romanticism that filled Princeton with its gothic towers and cloistered walks. That romanticism might be thought of as a theological movement may come as a surprise, but when one thinks about it one hardly has any problem regarding Sir Walter Scott and Alfred Lord Tennyson alongside the High Church movement. Romanticism very definitely had its effect on the worship of the Christian Church. James Hastings Nichols made that very clear in his study on Nevin and the Mercersburg theology.[1] Romanticism was a reaction against rationalism, put very simply. As a philosophical movement it began to realize that religion has its own reasons, or, to put it another way, that the heart has its own rationality. No one preached the gospel of romanticism more passionately than John Henry Newman from the pulpit of St. Mary's in Oxford. It was those sermons of Newman that lit the fuse that eventually set off the whole liturgical renewal movement.

JOHN WILLIAMSON NEVIN

There was something unique about the sacramental piety of Old School Presbyterianism. It was evangelical, to be sure, but it also had a strong sense of the church. It understood the value of the regular worship of the church, its institutions, and its order. That was one of the things that made it different from the more lib-

---

[1] James Hastings Nichols, *Romanticism in American Theology: Nevin and Schaff at Mercersburg* (Chicago: University of Chicago Press, [1961]). See also James Hastings Nichols, *The Mercersburg Theology* (New York: Oxford University Press, 1966).

eral Congregationalism of New England. In New Jersey, western Pennsylvania, the Valley of Virginia, and the Piedmont of the Carolinas, Presbyterians took a different route from those who went out from Connecticut, through the Mohawk Valley, and into Ohio. These Presbyterians developed a markedly different sort of Reformed Christianity, known as Old School Presbyterianism, which as time went along became very dear to many.[2] The leaders of the Old School Presbyterianism included men such as Archibald Alexander in Lexington, Virginia, Father Rice in Danville, Kentucky, and Charles Washington Baird, among others, but particularly one thinks of John Williamson Nevin (1803–1886), who was a distinct voice for the recalling of American Reformed churches to a more classical Protestantism.[3]

Nevin really typifies a whole movement, although he is a particular example which sets him apart from the other examples of this movement such as Horace Bushnell, Charles Hodge, and James Henley Thornwell, who also were part of this clear movement toward a more classical Christian piety. The movement as a whole rejected Unitarianism on one hand and revivalism on the

---

[2] My interest here is far from being merely objective. A few years ago a trunk was discovered in the attic of my grandfather, Robert Nevin Oliphant. The trunk had been gotten for him when he was sent off to Mercersburg Academy sometime around 1880. What this old trunk indicates to me is why I have such a passion for the subject of worship.

[3] For biographical material on Nevin see: Theodore Appel, *The Life and Work of John Williamson Nevin* (Philadelphia: Reformed Church Publication House, 1889); Stephen R. Graham, "Nevin, John Williamson (1803–1886)," in *Dictionary of Christianity in America*, ed. Daniel G. Reid, Robert D. Linder, Bruce L. Shelley, and Harry S. Stout (Downers Grove, IL: InterVarsity Press, 1990), pp. 807–808; Howard Hageman, "Nevin, John Williamson (1803–1886)," in *Encyclopedia of the Reformed Faith*, ed. Donald K. McKim (Louisville: Westminster John Knox Press; Edinburgh: Saint Andrew Press, 1992), pp. 255–256; Darryl G. Hart, *John Williamson Nevin: High-Church Calvinist* (Phillipsburg, NJ: Presbyterian and Reformed Publications, 2005); Jack Martin Maxwell, *The Liturgical Lessons of Mercersburg*, ThD thesis, Princeton Theological Seminary, 1969; and Jack Martin Maxwell, *Worship and Reformed Theology: The Liturgical Lessons of Mercersburg*, Pittsburgh Theological Monograph Series (Pittsburgh: Pickwick Press, 1976).

20: THE AGE OF ROMANTICISM

other. These men set their sights on a thoroughly biblical Christianity which maintained its continuity with both the ancient church and the Reformation of the sixteenth century. It is our assumption that Nevin is to be understood as part of this larger Old School movement. It is beside Hodge that we should see Nevin, rather than in opposition to him.

Nevin was born on the family farm near Shippensburg, Pennsylvania, just north of the Mason-Dixon line.[4] The country is filled with prosperous farms. It is an area of gently rolling hills, but only a few miles to the west, the Appalachian Mountains begin to rise more sharply. Scarcely a generation or two before, the Scotch-Irish settlers had been given the land in the hope they would keep the Indians from bothering the Mennonites and the Quakers east of the Susquehanna River. These "plain people," as they were called, were pacifists. The Scotch-Irish, on the other hand, were pretty good Indian fighters. By the time Nevin was born, the Indians were no longer a problem, and the Scotch-Irish culture was well established. As a boy John Nevin went to the old Middle Spring Presbyterian Church every Sabbath where he heard its systematic expository preaching of the Bible in the morning and the preaching of the catechism in the afternoon. More than likely, during the week the church served as the schoolhouse and the preacher was the schoolmaster.

For a week in the spring, after the roads had thawed, and then perhaps again in late fall, after the crops were in, there would be a communion season. Every member of the congregation would come together for a week of preaching, at which time several ministers would take their turn in the pulpit. On Sunday this season would reach its climax and the sacrament would be celebrated, followed by a thanksgiving service in the afternoon or perhaps the next day. Immediately we recognize the Scottish communion season we

---

[4] Here the information on Nevin is taken from Hart, *John Williamson Nevin: High-Church Calvinist*; and Richard E. Wentz, *John Williamson Nevin: American Theologian* (New York and Oxford: Oxford University Press, 1997).

have spoken of at great length in earlier chapters.⁵ It was an orderly system that nourished the faithful who lived out over the countryside enjoying the blessings of God, making their land fruitful, glorifying God and enjoying him forever, as the catechism put it.

By 1803 central Pennsylvania was no longer frontier territory and the Middle Spring Presbyterian Church was hardly a mission station. It was a settled church where spiritual needs were cared for by a well-educated ministry. It was not at all the same situation the church was in at Cane Ridge, Kentucky, in 1802, where Alexander Campbell's famous revival broke out, or even in northern New York where Charles Finney began to experience revivals a few years later.⁶

It was in 1821 that young Nevin was sent off to college. That he should have gone to Union College seems a bit strange, but then he went to Princeton Seminary which was still in its infancy. Archibald Alexander was in his prime, and still filled with the enthusiasm of the frontier. Nevin did well at Princeton. In fact, when young Charles Hodge was sent off to study in Germany for two years, Nevin was appointed as his substitute. Hodge returned and Nevin was offered a position teaching theology at Allegheny Theological Seminary in Pittsburgh. Later on this seminary was better known as Western Theological Seminary. It is now Pittsburgh Theological Seminary. In the meantime Nevin's father had died and Nevin took in his mother and two younger brothers, establishing a home for them in Pittsburgh for the next eleven years.⁷ The eleven years in

---

⁵ See Leigh Eric Schmidt, *Holy Fairs: Scottish Communions and American Revivals in the Early Modern Period* (Princeton, NJ: Princeton University Press, 1989).

⁶ For a discussion of the theological forces at work during this period, see George M. Marsden, *The Evangelical Mind and the New School Presbyterian Experience* (New Haven: Yale University Press, 1970).

⁷ If I have been correctly informed, the next younger brother was Ethelbert, who went on to become professor of music at Harvard, and one of the founders of American musicology. He was every bit as prominent in his field as the older brother was in theology. What interests me, however, is that the youngest of the three brothers married an Oliphant, the sister of my great grandfather. Now it happened that my great grandfather had ten sons, the seventh of whom he named for his brother-in-law, Robert Nevin. So it was that my grandfather was

20: THE AGE OF ROMANTICISM

Pittsburgh welded Nevin quite firmly to western Pennsylvania, the heartland of Scotch-Irish Presbyterianism.

The Scotch-Irish Presbyterians had a sense of heritage. They knew themselves to be the heirs of a great Christian tradition. We will see this with Charles Washington Baird, who was clearly the child of western Pennsylvania Presbyterianism but was also strongly aware of his French Huguenot heritage.[8] Again we see the same thing with Archibald Alexander, who bought the theological library of the Dutch Reformed pastor of Somerville, New Jersey. Of the very essence of Old School Presbyterianism was its sense of transcending a merely national heritage. Being Anglican might be strongly related to being English, or being Lutheran might be strongly related to being German. Being Reformed, however, was a different matter. Plenty of the Reformed were English or Scottish or Dutch. One could be French and still be Reformed or one could be German and Reformed as well. Nevin very particularly exemplified this principle of Reformed spirituality.

In 1840 Nevin was called to the faculty of the German Reformed Church in Mercersburg, Pennsylvania, not far from his birthplace just outside of Shippensburg.

It was in 1835 that Charles Finney published his work on revivalism. It popularized what has since become known as the Second Great Awakening. It had come about a century after the Great Awakening led by Jonathan Edwards and Gilbert Tennent. Not everyone was positively impressed with the revivals of the Second Great Awakening. John Williamson Nevin was among those who published his objections. We should note, however, that his objections were not the same as those of the Unitarians and the followers of the Enlightenment. Rather, they came from the

---

Robert Nevin Oliphant. My grandfather was even sent off to Mercerburg Academy, if the family tradition has it right. That must have been around 1880.

[8] See my article on Charles W. Baird in *American Presbyterians*: Hughes Oliphant Old, "*Eutaxia, or, The Presbyterian Liturgies: Historical Sketches*, by Charles W. Baird, 1855," in *American Presbyterians* 66/4 (Winter, 1988): 260–263.

side of more classical Reformed orthodoxy.[9]

A few years later Nevin published his study of Reformed eucharistic theology under the title, *The Mystical Presence*.[10] This was indeed a major statement, although it provoked much controversy. After a long study of the Reformers of the sixteenth and seventeenth centuries in which he quotes such Reformers as Calvin, Bullinger, Ursinus, Beza, and a host of others down even to the Westminster Standards, Nevin charges the heirs of the Reformed tradition in his day with having lost sight of the original vision of the Reformers' eucharistic theology.[11]

As Nevin sees it, it is this myopia of the heirs of the Reformed tradition in regard to its sacramental piety which had led to the aberrations of revivalism. It is because our sacramental practice has become confused that these "new methods" have arisen. Four points in particular might be noted.

First, we have failed to recognize the uniqueness of the Lord's Supper among the different ordinances of worship. We put too much emphasis on the Supper as the Word made visible, implying that the Supper gives us nothing beyond what the Word has already given us. Nevin says:

> In the old Reformed view, the communion of the believer with Christ in the Supper is taken to be *spe-*

---

[9] See Hart, *John Williamson Nevin*, p. 88–103, for a discussion of Nevin's objections. For the text of Nevin's arguments, see John Williamson Nevin, *The Anxious Bench* (Chambersburg, PA: Printed at the Office of the "Weekly Messenger," 1843); reprint ed. Augustine Thompson (Eugene, OR: Wipf and Stock Publishers, 2000).

[10] John Williamson Nevin, *The Mystical Presence: A Vindication of the Reformed or Calvinistic Doctrine of the Holy Eucharist* (Philadelphia: J. B. Lippincott & Co., 1846); reprint ed. Augustine Thompson (Eugene: OR: Wipf and Stock, 2000). There is an even newer version of this work, which we have not been able to use for this volume: John Williamson Nevin, *The Mystical Presence: and the Doctrine of the Reformed Church on the Lord's Supper*, ed. Linden J. DeBie, general ed. W. Bradford Littlejohn (Eugene, OR: Wipf & Stock Publishers, 2012.)

[11] The following study is based on the reprint of the 1846 edition of Nevin, *The Mystical Presence*, as above. For a thoughtful interpretation of Nevin's understanding of the Lord's Supper, see Maxwell, *Worship and Reformed Theology*.

> *cific* in its nature, and *different* from all that has place in the common exercises of worship. The sacrament, not the elements, of course, separately considered, but the ordinance as the union of element and word, is held to be such an exhibition of saving grace, as is presented to the faith of the church under no other form. It is not simply the word brought to mind in its ordinary force. The outward is not merely the occasion by which the inward, in the case, is made present to the soul as a separate existence; but inward and outward, by the energy of the Spirit, are made to flow together in the way of a common life; and come thus to exert a peculiar, and altogether extraordinary power, in this form, to the benefit of the believer.[12]

To make his point he quotes several lines from John Owen. To be sure Nevin is not speaking of the elements of bread and wine alone, but the sacrament as a whole—the words, the actions, and the elements of bread and wine all together. The perception that the words, the acts, and the elements all go together is, as Nevin says, one of the basic emphases to Reformed eucharistic piety. We made a special point of this above in regard to John Knox who insisted that seeing the bread broken and the wine poured, the gathering of the congregation around or at the table, sitting at the table and sharing the sacred meal one with another, were essential to a full celebration of the sacrament.

Second, we have failed to maintain a sense of the mystical nature of the sacrament of the Lord's Supper. What Paul says of marriage, "This is a great mystery" (cf. Ephesians 5:32), can also be said of the Lord's Supper. Something happens when we celebrate the sacrament. We might almost say that what happens is miraculous, a transformation operated by the Holy Spirit in which we are joined together in the fellowship of the church as members of the body are joined together to its head. This is the covenantal fellowship whereby we are joined together into one body.

---

[12] Nevin, *Mystical Presence*, p. 105.

> In the old Reformed view, the sacramental transaction is a *mystery*; no, in some sense an actual *miracle*. The Spirit works here in a way that transcends, not only the human understanding, but the ordinary course of the world also in every other view. There is a form of action in the sacraments, which now belongs indeed to the regular order of the life that is comprehended in the church, but which as thus established still involves a character that may be denominated "supernatural," as compared with the ordinary constitution, not only of nature, but even of the Christian life itself.[13]

Calvin himself tells us that this covenantal fellowship so unites us to Christ that we become bone of his bone and flesh of his flesh. This is the mystery; this is the miracle. Here we see what Nevin means by his title *Mystical Presence*. Again, he quotes Calvin to support his point: "'In the sacred Supper, then, we acknowledge it a *miracle*—transcending both nature and our own understanding—that Christ's life is made common to us with himself, and his flesh given to us as aliment [that is, food or nourishment].'"[14] What the Holy Spirit does in the course of the celebration of the sacrament is to unite us to Christ, nourishing us with his passion.[15] Right at this point we probably need to admit that Nevin's language here must have been very hard for even the more theologically perceptive reader in the mid-eighteen hundreds, let alone the average churchgoer.

Third, according to Nevin, "The old Reformed doctrine includes always the idea of an *objective force* in the sacraments. The sacramental union between the sign and the thing signified is real."[16] Under the influence of the Enlightenment, Reformed eucharistic theology had become increasingly subjective. This is in contrast with the Reformers, who had made it clear very early

---

[13] Nevin, *Mystical Presence*, p. 106.

[14] Nevin, *Mystical Presence*, p. 106.

[15] Nevin does not footnote his source here but he more than likely has Ephesians 5 in mind.

[16] Nevin, *Mystical Presence*, p. 108.

20: The Age of Romanticism

in the Reformation that, while they insisted that the Supper was a sign, they did not mean that it was an empty sign. This was stated very significantly at the *Wittenberg Concord* in 1535. The Reformed view has always insisted that the sacrament "not only signifies, but *seals*" the covenant.[17] We have to admit that Nevin is not always as clear as we would like. For his day, however, he was remarkable.

> The sacramental transaction certifies and makes good the grace it represents, as actually communicated at the time. So it is said to *exhibit* also the thing signified. The thing is *there;* not the name of the thing only, and not its sign or shadow; but the actual substance itself. "The sacrament is not picture," says Calvin, "but the true, veritable pledge of our union with Christ."[18]

Much the same thing is said today by the heirs of the Puritans, but what they really have in mind is a very subjective experience. Sad to say, Nevin laments, we begin to find this in Edwards, in Hopkins and Bellamy, right down to Timothy Dwight and Dr. Dick.[19]

Finally Nevin gives us his fourth point. "According to the old Reformed doctrine the invisible grace of the sacrament, includes a real participation in his *person*. That which is made present to the believer, is the very life of Christ himself in its true power and substance."[20] Nevin's point here is well taken. This is surely an element in Calvin's eucharistic theology. More importantly, however, is that it sounds quite similar to what a number of contemporary scholars have called the "in Christ" mysticism of the Apostle Paul. Nevin puts it this way:

> The doctrine proceeds on the assumption that the Christian salvation stands in an actual union between Christ and his people, mystical but in the highest sense

---

[17] Nevin, *Mystical Presence*, p. 109.

[18] Nevin, *Mystical Presence*, p. 109.

[19] Nevin, *Mystical Presence*, pp. 112f. The reference to Dr. Dick seems to refer to Dr. John Dick, professor at United Presbyterian Divinity Hall in Glasgow.

[20] Nevin, *Mystical Presence*, p. 111.

> real, in virtue of which they are as closely joined to him, as the limbs are to the head in the natural body. They are in him, and he is in them, not figuratively but truly; in the way of a growing process that will become complete finally in the resurrection.[21]

Surely Nevin has caught an important dimension of sixteenth-century eucharistic theology. Nevin would probably have been better understood if he had put this in a more biblical terminology, but more than one theologian has had that problem. This is especially the case with Reformed eucharistic theology. The Reformed understanding of the Lord's Supper is really based on biblical theology rather than systematic theology or, more specifically, Scholastic systematic theology. When Reformed theologians try to explain the Lord's Supper in terms of Scholasticism they rarely come off too well. If they stick to the biblical terminology they do much better. Here we find the same thing. If Nevin had spoken of all this in terms of covenant he might have been better understood.

Let us turn now to Nevin's formulation of what he means by the mystical presence. Nevin presents his position in a number of theses. We shall look at the most important of these one by one.[22]

"1. *The human world in its present natural state, as descended from Adam, is sundered from its proper life in God by sin, and utterly disabled in this character for rising by itself to any higher position.* The fall of Adam was the fall of the race."[23] We notice here as throughout that Nevin's theology is in no way watered down by the Enlightenment.

"3. *By the hypostatical union of the two natures in the person of* Jesus Christ, *our humanity as fallen in Adam was exalted again to a new and imperishable divine life.*"[24] As Nevin sees it, the race could only be saved if this salvation was brought about in it rather than outside

---

[21] Nevin, *Mystical Presence*, p. 111.

[22] Nevin, *Mystical Presence*, p. 160. The reader will notice that Nevin's actual theses are printed in italics.

[23] Nevin, *Mystical Presence*, p. 160.

[24] Nevin, *Mystical Presence*, p. 161.

it. It had to lay hold of its organic universal character. "Such an inward salvation of the race required that it should be joined in a living way with the Divine Nature itself, as represented by the everlasting Word or Logos, the fountain of all created light and life."[25] We notice here that Nevin is appropriating what we have called the Wisdom dimension of Calvin's eucharistic theology.

"5. *The Christian salvation, then, as thus comprehended in Christ, is a new life, in the deepest sense of the word.* Not a doctrine merely for the mind to embrace. Not an event simply to be remembered with faith, as the basis of piety in the way of example or other outward support."[26] Nevin is concerned to avoid both a mere doctrinal orthodoxy and a sentimental moralism. The rationalism of his day had tended to reduce the eucharist to a rite in which one remembered all one's sins and pled for the forgiveness of God. It was this sort of eucharistic piety Nevin wanted to get beyond.

"6. *The new life of which Christ is the Source and Organic Principle, is in all respects a true human life.* It is in one sense a divine life. It springs from the Logos. But it is not the life of the Logos separately taken. It is the life of the Word made flesh, the divinity joined in personal union with our humanity."[27] Surely one of the strengths of Nevin's attempt to understand the sacrament is his determination to understand it in terms of a completely orthodox Christology. Nevin insists that the new humanity is completely human. It is descended from Adam, but through communion with Christ it is man better than man ever was before. This new life is, "Not a new humanity wholly dissevered from that of Adam; but the humanity of Adam itself, only raised to a higher character, and filled with new meaning and power, by its union with the Divine Nature."[28]

"7. *Christ's life, . . . rests not in his separate person, but passes over to his people; thus constituting the* church, *which is his body, the fullness of him*

---

[25] Nevin, *Mystical Presence*, p. 162.

[26] Nevin, *Mystical Presence*, p. 163.

[27] Nevin, *Mystical Presence*, p. 164.

[28] Nevin, *Mystical Presence*, p. 164.

who fills all in all."[29] Central to Nevin's eucharistic theology is his doctrine of the church. A covenantal understanding of the sacrament would, of course, lead in this direction. We have already seen this in the eucharistic theology of John Owen. If we understand the Lord's Supper in terms of covenant renewal then it is only natural that we should understand the Supper as nourishing our participation in the Church. This nourishing is not mechanical but rather organic. It unfolds in the course of history. It grows; it develops. "Christ goes not forth to heal the world by outward power as standing beyond himself; he gathers it rather into his own person."[30] As individuals we are inserted into his person. That is how we are born again from above. The new life grows in us more and more until it is completely developed, but that is only on the last day in the resurrection. Here, of course, we are talking of the Reformed doctrine of sanctification. It is in regard to sanctification that we understand the Lord's Supper as the food which nourishes the new life.

"8. *As joined to Christ, then, we are* one *with him in his life, and not simply in the way of a less intimate and real union.*"[31] Here, of course, we find Nevin particularly close to Calvin. We have spoken of this above in regard to the Wisdom dimension of Calvin's eucharistic theology. Here Nevin seems very close to certain modern New Testament scholars who find in the Apostle Paul an "in Christ" mysticism. The new life that we have been brought into by regeneration

> is deeper than all thought, feeling, or exercise of will. Not a quality only! Not a mere relation! A relation in fact, as that of the iron to the magnet; but one that carries into the center of the subject a form of being which was not there before. Christ communicates his own life substantially to the soul on which he acts, causing it to grow into his very nature. This is the *mys-*

---

[29] Nevin, *Mystical Presence*, p. 164.

[30] Nevin, *Mystical Presence*, p. 164.

[31] Nevin, *Mystical Presence*, p. 165.

tical union—the basis of our whole salvation, the only medium by which it is possible for us to have an interest in the grace of Christ under any other view.[32]

To speak of the Lord's Supper bringing about a mystical union may be perfectly understood in some circles, but in western Pennsylvania before the Civil War it was a bit exotic. From a strictly biblical point of view, of course, it makes sense to speak of the church as the body of Christ. Proof texts abound! The historic doctrine of the church from the New Testament down to our own day is very clear that the church is the body of Christ.

"9. *Our relation to Christ is not simply parallel with our relation to Adam, but goes beyond it, as being immeasurably more intimate and deep.* Adam was the first man; Christ is the archetypal man, in whom the true ideal of humanity has been brought into view."[33] Nevin would very carefully guard himself from any doctrine of fusion with or between the divine nature and the human nature. Like Peter Martyr Vermigli before him, he was aware that the Scholastic theologians had gotten very close to this error. Nevin also carefully guards himself against any doctrine of *theosis* as it developed in Byzantine theology.

"10. *The mystical union includes necessarily a participation in the entire humanity of Christ.*"[34]

"11. *As the mystical union embraces the whole Christ, so we, too, are embraced by it not in a partial but whole way.*"[35] It is here, of course, that Nevin makes such a point of sticking with both Nicene orthodoxy and Chalcedonian orthodoxy. For the following several theses Nevin turns his attention to the polemic between the Lutherans and the Reformed as well as the Catholics and the Reformed showing the difference between the real presence, transubstantia-

---

[32] Nevin, *Mystical Presence*, p. 165.
[33] Nevin, *Mystical Presence*, pp. 165–166.
[34] Nevin, *Mystical Presence*, p. 166.
[35] Nevin, *Mystical Presence*, p. 167.

tion, and consubstantiation. We skip over these and resume with his thesis concerning the Holy Spirit.

"16. *The union of Christ with believers is wrought by the power of the* HOLY SPIRIT."[36] We are born again by the Holy Spirit. We are nourished in the new life by the same Holy Spirit. It is by the Holy Spirit that we are in Christ and he is in us. Nevin, ever watchful that his eucharistic theology be trinitarian, insists that it is the Holy Spirit, proceeding from the Father and the Son, which is the form in which and by which the new creation is upheld. The root of this new creation, however, is none other than Jesus Christ. What I think all this means is that the Christian is by the work of the Holy Spirit no longer a lonely creature but a man in communion with God and with his brothers and sisters in Christ. He is a member of the church, the body of Christ. Here, it seems to me, Nevin has understood Calvin well.

"17. *Christ's life is apprehended on the part of his people only by* FAITH. The life itself comes to us wholly from Christ himself, by the power of his Spirit."[37] That is, it is taken hold of by faith, and this faith is faith in Christ, not faith in the Holy Spirit, as some charismatics seem to preach today. We should never speak of the empowering of the Spirit as though the Holy Spirit has replaced Christ.

"19. *'A sacrament is a holy ordinance instituted by* Christ; *wherein, by sensible signs,* Christ *and the benefits of the new covenant are represented, sealed, and* applied *to believers.'* Thus the Westminster Shorter Catechism, echoing the voice of the whole Reformed Church, as it had sounded throughout Christendom for a century before!"[38] Nevin had a way of always getting back to the Westminster Standards. He had learned the *Westminster Catechism* as a child and it had stuck with him even as he transferred to the German Reformed Church. The point that he wants to make here is that it takes more than

---

[36] Nevin, *Mystical Presence*, p. 173.

[37] Nevin, *Mystical Presence*, p. 174.

[38] Nevin, *Mystical Presence*, pp. 176–177.

signs to make a sacrament. The other part of the sacrament is the invisible grace that is signified by the signs. Sacramentally, or mystically, they are joined together. "The sign and the thing signified are, by Christ's institution, mysteriously bound together, so as to form in the sacramental transaction one and the same presence."[39] Going back to the *Westminster Shorter Catechism* Nevin underlines the words, "Christ and the benefits of the new covenant." The "and" is important. First Christ and then the benefits. Because we are joined to Christ, the benefits of the new covenant are ours.

Nevin moves on to another question from the *Westminster Shorter Catechism*. "20. *The Lord's Supper is a sacrament, wherein, by giving and receiving bread and wine according to Christ's appointment, his death is showed forth, and the worthy receivers are, not after a corporal and carnal manner, but by faith, made partakers of* his body and blood, *with all his benefits, to their spiritual nourishment and growth in grace.*"[40] Here we are at the heart of what Nevin has to say. We notice particularly that what he has to say is drawn out of the *Westminster Catechism*.

> Here are sensible signs—bread and wine solemnly given and received. Here also we have the invisible grace—Christ and his benefits. To make the case clearer, it is Christ's "body and blood, with all his benefits"; the first, of course, as the basis and medium of the last. The visible and invisible are different, and yet, in this case, they may not be disjoined. They flow together in the constitution of one and the same sacrament. Neither of the two is the sacrament, abstracted from the other. The ordinance holds in the sacramental *transaction;* which includes the presence of both, the one materially, for the senses, the other spiritually, for faith. Christ's body is not in or under the bread, locally considered. Still, the power of his life in this form is actually exhibited at the same time in the mystery of the sacrament. The one is as truly and really present in the institution as the other. The elements are not

---

[39] Nevin, *Mystical Presence*, p. 177.

[40] Nevin, *Mystical Presence*, pp. 177–178.

> simply significant of that which they represent, as serving to bring it to mind by the help of previous knowledge. They are the pledge of its actual presence and power. They are bound to it in mystical, sacramental union, more intimately, we may say, than they would be if they were made to include it in the way of actual local comprehension. There is far more, then, than the mere commemoration of Christ's death. Worthy receivers partake also of his body and blood, with all his benefits, through the power of the Holy Spirit, to their spiritual nourishment and growth in grace.[41]

This is what Nevin means by the mystical presence. In the observance of the sacrament we are joined to the crucified, risen, and ascended Christ. He is present. We dwell in him and he dwells in us. We are united to his body. We are made alive with the new life of his Spirit.

"21. *The sacrament of the Lord's Supper has reference directly and primarily to the atonement wrought out by Christ's death on the cross.*"[42] By the mid-nineteenth century the Unitarians were vigorously bringing into question the idea of a substitutionary atonement. Nevin shows no interest in following in their train. It is not just Christ who is shown forth to be received but the Christ whose crucified body and poured out blood were offered up as a sacrifice. On the other hand we find no interest in seeing in the celebration itself a sacrifice. Nevin stays carefully away from any suggestion of a doctrine of a eucharistic sacrifice or a liturgical oblation.[43] At one point Nevin says, "We need no new atonement; but we do need to fall back perpetually on the one sacrifice for sin, which Christ has already made upon the cross."[44] Here Nevin is as clear as he could possibly be.

"22. *As the medium, however, by which we are thus made partakers of the new covenant in Christ's death, the Holy Supper involves a real communication*

---

[41] Nevin, *Mystical Presence*, p. 178.

[42] Nevin, *Mystical Presence*, p. 178.

[43] Nevin, *Mystical Presence*, p. 178.

[44] Nevin, *Mystical Presence*, p. 179.

with the person of the Savior, now gloriously exalted in heaven."[45] Here Nevin brings us back to the covenantal dimension of the sacrament. What the sacrament is all about is the covenantal fellowship. For Nevin this covenantal fellowship is, "a real life union with Christ, powerfully wrought in our souls by the Holy Spirit."[46] Having drawn his understanding of the Lord's Supper out of the *Westminster Catechism*, he now turns to drawing it out of the *Heidelberg Catechism*.[47] Finally, he claims support from the great Puritan theologian John Owen.

Nevin really makes a very impressive case for his "mystical presence." Point by point he seems to understand much of what the Reformers of the sixteenth century taught regarding the Lord's Supper, both from the standpoint of eucharistic theology and eucharistic piety.

The biggest problem with Nevin's famous work, *The Mystical Presence*, is that his language throws people off. It sounds a bit too medieval—too magical. Even worse was his wavering along the road to Rome at one point and his attempt to come up with a "High Church" Reformed liturgy. It all seemed like ecclesiastical romanticism. If read with a generous spirit, however, what he has to say in regard to eucharistic theology rings true. He helped many American Protestants recover a sacramental realism that for generations had been compromised by the subjectivism of the age.

CHARLES WASHINGTON BAIRD'S *PRESBYTERIAN LITURGIES*

If John Williamson Nevin's message did not quite get to the ear of those for whom it was intended there were others who had very similar concerns who reached a more receptive audience.

---

[45] Nevin, *Mystical Presence*, p. 179.

[46] Nevin, *Mystical Presence*, p. 179.

[47] Nevin, *Mystical Presence*, p. 180.

Charles Washington Baird was still a young man when he published his study of Presbyterian liturgies.[48] Baird's work won the approval of Charles Hodge.[49] When, as a rookie pastor, I first began to study the subject of how I was supposed to conduct the communion service, the first book I came upon was Baird's *Presbyterian Liturgies*, which I found in the Theological Book Agency of Princeton Theological Seminary.[50]

Charles Washington Baird was one of those who helped stem the disintegration of worship wrought by the revivalists of the early nineteenth century.[51] A Presbyterian of the Old School background, he found the new methods of frontier revivalists irreverent and disorderly. Although he was born of frontier stock, Baird was

---

[48] The first edition of Baird's work bears the title *Eutaxia*: Charles Washington Baird, *Eutaxia, or, The Presbyterian Liturgies: Historical Sketches* (New York: M. W. Dodd, 1855). The second edition, however, was entitled *The Presbyterian Liturgies*.

[49] Charles Hodge, "Letter of appreciation to C. W. Baird," in *Correspondence: Feb. 15, 1845–Aug. 28, 1860*, ed. William McKendree Scott, Archives of Speer Library at Princeton Theological Seminary, 1845–1860.

[50] The edition I found was Charles Washington Baird, *The Presbyterian Liturgies: Historical Sketches* (Grand Rapids, MI: Baker Book House, 1957). I also want to mention that about ten years ago I was teaching a course at Reformed Theological Seminary in Orlando, Florida, and one of my students discovered a copy of the first edition of *Eutaxia, or, The Presbyterian Liturgies*. I encouraged him to study his newfound treasure in more detail. I had published an article in 1988 in *American Presbyterians* on Baird and the background of his work. My student published his work, receiving a prize in church history for it. Cf. Bruce H. Benedict, "Charles W. Baird: An American Presbyterian Retrospective," paper submitted to Mr. John R. Muether, Assistant Professor of Church History and Librarian, Reformed Theological Seminary–Orlando, The Aiken Taylor Award for American Presbyterian Church History presented by The Historical Center of the Presbyterian Church of America, 2003 (St. Louis: PCA Historical Center, 2003).

[51] The following study of Baird and his work is an amplified edition of my study which appeared in *American Presbyterians*: Hughes Oliphant Old, "*Eutaxia, or, The Presbyterian Liturgies*, by Charles W. Baird, 1855," *American Presbyterians* 66/4 (Winter, 1988): 260–263. It was more than twenty years ago that I was asked to write this study of Charles W. Baird's *Eutaxia*. It had always been my intention to expand this article. With the growing weakness of my eyesight, I will simply have to deliver the original article here. As I see it, Baird's work is an important foundation stone of American Protestant worship.

20: THE AGE OF ROMANTICISM

hardly a redneck. At the time of his birth in 1828, his father was master of the Latin school in Princeton.[52] From the time he was seven years old he lived in Paris and then Geneva, where his father represented the Foreign Evangelical Society, an organization dedicated to the support of the Protestant cause in the Catholic countries of Europe. By the time young Baird returned to America to pursue his education at the University of the City of New York and Union Theological Seminary, he was a cosmopolitan young gentleman. In 1855, when Baird published *Eutaxia*, he was not yet thirty years old, but he had traveled widely and could see the worship of American Protestantism in a broad perspective.[53]

Baird's Old School roots were important in shaping his ideas on worship. When the Scotch-Irish Presbyterians crossed the Appalachians they had in their church a strong anchor in historic Christian culture. Charles Baird's father, Robert Baird, had been brought up in Fayette County, up the Monongahela River from Pittsburgh, right in the heartland of Old School Presbyterianism.[54] As a teenager he was sent off to school in Uniontown wearing his mother's homespun. There he was the student of the Reverend James Dunlap, an eloquent preacher who delighted in the study of the Greek New Testament. Dunlap was a great lover of the Greek

---

[52] For further biographical detail, see Benedict, "Charles W. Baird."

[53] The first edition in 1855 appeared without the author's name, merely referring to Baird as a minister of the Presbyterian church. The following year it was published in London by Thomas Binnie, a leading Congregational minister, but with a different title: Charles Washington Baird, *A Chapter on Liturgies: Historical Sketches*, intro. Thomas Binnie (London: Knight and Sons, 1856). In 1957, Baker Book House republished Binnie's edition under the title *The Presbyterian Liturgies*. In this article references to *Eutaxia* are to the 1957 edition, and will be referred to as C. W. Baird, *Eutaxia*. The name *Eutaxia* comes from the Greek text of 1 Cor. 14:40, "but all things should be done decently and in order."

[54] Henry M. Baird, *The Life of the Rev. Robert Baird, D.D.* (New York: Anson D. F. Randolph, 1966), pp. 9f. Hereinafter, H. M. Baird, *Robert Baird*. Henry M. Baird was professor of history at the University of the City of New York and the brother of Charles. Henry also wrote a biographical sketch of his brother for *Memorials of the Rev. Charles W. Baird* (New York and London: G. P. Putnam's Sons, 1888). Hereinafter H. M. Baird, *Charles Baird*.

and Latin classics and he imparted a classical education to his students. Robert Baird went off to Washington College in 1816 where he imbibed the serious learning of a frontier college. There academic lectern and church pulpit were not too clearly distinguished. Godliness and learning went hand in hand. In the Presbyterianism of western Pennsylvania, the fact that one lived on the frontier did not necessarily mean one had left culture on the other side of the Appalachians. Robert Baird was only one example of an important, but often overlooked, American phenomenon which one might call frontier gentility. For this frontier gentility, the worship of the church was an important tie to a learned and orderly Christian tradition. Revivalism may have appealed to many on the frontier, but there were others like Robert Baird who preferred the simple dignity of Old School Presbyterian worship.

If our young liturgical scholar had been strongly influenced by the frontier heritage of his father, he was just as strongly influenced by the background of his mother. In 1824 Fermine Du Buisson and Robert Baird were married in Philadelphia. She was a young woman of French Huguenot ancestry and her son came to cherish his mother's heritage, producing a book on Huguenot history later in his life.[55] In 1835 the family moved to France, and living there for a good number of years only deepened the family's appreciation of their French Protestant heritage. The final end of the old regime in 1830 had brought with it a Protestant emancipation in France. Once again the Huguenots were free to hold public worship and the mission which had brought Robert Baird to Paris was a mission of encouragement to the Protestants of France. The young Charles must have heard the stories of Protestant heroism from house guests and family friends as his father went about strengthening the bond of fellowship between American and French Protestantism. One of the things which makes

---

[55] Charles Washington Baird, *History of the Huguenot Emigration to America* (New York: Dodd, Mead & Co., 1885).

20: THE AGE OF ROMANTICISM

Eutaxia such interesting reading is its delight in the heritage of the French Reformation, a heritage which was especially dear to Charles Baird because of his maternal lineage.

Charles Baird's life in Europe brought him in contact with diverse strands of liturgical life even if it was only a matter of hearing his father's experiences. As time went along his father's ministry in Europe blossomed. He was received at several royal courts with enthusiasm, even being honored with an invitation to the wedding of the Czar's daughter, the Archduchess Olga, a service of worship which must have presented the Russian Orthodox liturgy in all its splendor. Baird was in Russia to encourage the temperance movement and to arrange to have Bibles distributed by the American Bible Society.[56] He charmed the Czar as a frontier gentleman of good breeding and excellent education. From the King of Prussia Baird got a warm reception and the theologians of the University of Berlin found him even more interesting. In Germany he imbibed the Pan-Protestantism of the disciples of Schleiermacher. August Neander, the church historian, encouraged Baird to write a history of the American church. A German translation was produced for which Neander wrote an introduction.[57] At one point Robert Baird took the whole family on an extended trip to Italy. He was concerned to establish a relationship with the Waldensians. The trip to Italy made quite an impression on the family and eventually young Charles, once he had graduated from seminary, returned as pastor of a congregation of Americans in Rome. Italian unification had not yet been achieved during Baird's pastorate in Rome, and the city was presided over

---

[56] On Robert Baird's impressions of Russian Orthodox worship, cf. H. M. Baird, *Robert Baird*, pp.160–161.

[57] *Religion In America* was first published in Scotland in 1844. An American edition and a German translation appeared the same year: Robert Baird, *Religion in America* (New York: Harper & Brothers, 1844). An enlarged edition appeared in America in 1856: Robert Baird, *Religion in America* (New York: Harper & Brothers, 1856). For further details, see H. M. Baird, *Robert Baird*, pp. 203–207.

by the papal court. There the young American minister observed Roman Catholic worship in what for an American Protestant must have been its most exotic form.[58]

If Charles Baird's *Eutaxia* reflects a broad experience of Christian worship, it also reflects a historical ability far in advance of other Americans writing on the subject of worship in that day. Baird's major contribution was that he presented to American Protestants a series of liturgical texts from the sixteenth and seventeenth centuries which showed that classical Reformed Protestantism had a very definite liturgical tradition. The variety of liturgical texts presented is remarkable. We find three services from Calvin's Geneva: the Lord's Day service, the communion service, and the service for daily prayer. We find the Lord's Day service and the communion service of John Knox, Richard Baxter's *Reformed Liturgy*, the liturgy of the Dutch Reformed Church in America, and the liturgy of the German Palatinate. He devoted a chapter to the liturgy used by the early Puritans, and even tells us something of the liturgy of the Reformed Church of Hungary. For a work produced in America before the Civil War, one is amazed that Baird's interest extends far beyond the bounds of an Anglo-Saxon heritage. If Baird had done nothing more than present the American church with this broad spectrum of Reformed liturgical texts, his work would have been significant.

But Baird did more. He set these documents in their historical context. His footnotes mention source documents for the Reformation such as Theodore Beza's *Histoire ecclesiastique*.[59] He is able to point to a number of passages in the works of Calvin which illuminate the actual liturgical texts. For example, he knows the

---

[58] On the impressions of the Baird family of the Holy Week services in Rome, cf. H. M. Baird, *Robert Baird*, pp. 146–148.

[59] Baird mentions the *Registre du Conseil d'Etat*, then available only in the archives of Geneva. On the other hand, the three hundredth anniversary of the Genevan Reformation in 1836 had stimulated a number of historical studies, with which Baird was acquainted. See C. W. Baird, *Eutaxia*, pp. 15, 17, and 26.

20: THE AGE OF ROMANTICISM 773

passage in Calvin's commentary on Job which tells us how daily prayer was celebrated. He is able to interpret the practice of the Reformed Church of France by passages from the Acts of the National Synod.[60] He was familiar with the work of French Protestant historians who were his contemporaries.[61]

Baird's knowledge of the sources of German Reformed worship is more limited. Young Charles was apparently with his father on at least some of his trips to Germany, for he speaks of his own observation of German liturgical practice.[62] Unlike the French texts which he presents in his own translation, the text he gives us of the liturgy of the Palatinate is the translation which appeared in the *Mercersburg Review*. On the other hand, Baird has obviously studied August Ebrard's *Reformiertes Kirchenbuch*, the pioneering work of German Reformed liturgical renewal.[63]

For the early liturgical traditions of Scotland Baird was quite successful in finding significant documents for their interpretation.[64] He found, for instance, a letter written by John Knox on

---

[60] Baird makes considerable use of this material, which he finds in John Quick, *Synodicon in Gallia Reformata* (London: Printed for T. Parkhurst and J. Robinson, 1692).

[61] He quotes, for instance, from the *Bulletin de la Société de l'histoire du Protestantisme Français*; from Pierre André Sayous, *Études littéraires sur les écrivains français de la Réformation* (Paris: G. Fischbacher, 1881); from Guillaume de Félice, *Histoire des Protestants de France* (Paris and Toulouse, 1850; English translation, New York, 1851); and from the biographical dictionary of Eugène and Émile Haag, *La France Protestante*, 9 vols. (Paris and Genève: J. Cherbuliez, 1846–1859).

[62] C. W. Baird, *Eutaxia*, p. 130.

[63] J. H. August Ebrard, *Reformiertes Kirchenbuch* (Zurich: Meyer und Zeller, 1847). This work contains much historical material on which Baird has drawn, e.g., C. W. Baird, *Eutaxia*, pp. 35, 211, 213, 222, 224, and 254. Baird knew at least three modern European languages: French, Italian, and German. H. M. Baird, *Charles Baird*, p. 2.

[64] Baird had apparently read widely among the works of John Knox. He mentions a collection of his works published by the Presbyterian Board of Publications in Philadelphia in 1842, and another edited by W. M'Gavin in Glasgow in 1844. In addition to this he studied David Calderwood's massive *The History of the Kirk of Scotland* (1678; Edinburgh: Printed for the Wodrow Society, 1842–1849). He studied two collections of documents relating to the Scottish Reformation: William Dunlop's *A Collection of Confessions of Faith, Catechisms, Directories, Books of*

how worship should be celebrated. He correctly perceives the great importance of Knox's account of the troubles at Frankfurt for the history of Christian worship. Baird also studied Thomas M'Crie's pioneering biography of the Scottish Reformer. M'Crie did an outstanding work of retrieving Knox from the odium with which English historiography was determined to becloud him. Having M'Crie's more balanced appreciation of the Scottish Reformation to guide him, Baird was better able to appreciate the liturgical work of Scotland's leading Reformer.

As we would expect, Baird's *Eutaxia* is a product of the Age of Romanticism. It abounds in vignettes of John Calvin's being carried into the gothic Cathedral of St. Pierre for Easter communion just before his death, the heroic resistance of the Huguenots in the Cevennes mountains celebrating the Reformed liturgy in secret, and English Puritans on trial before the Anglican hierarchy for staunchly maintaining the liturgical traditions of Geneva. That was the sort of thing that inspired readers in 1855.[65] Romanticism had a very particular appeal in America. The frontier had been conquered and now people craved culture and refinement. They wanted to know about their heritage. The Bairds, typical of Old School Presbyterians, had kept in touch with their historic roots. They had never lost the sense of *Eutaxia*, of doing things decently and in order. If on the frontier many Americans had lost their sense of tradition and now wanted to recover it, Charles Baird knew where it was to be found.

Liturgical reform in the nineteenth century was the child of romanticism.[66] This was true of the liturgical reforms of Mer-

Discipline, etc. . . . (Edinburgh: James Watson, 1719) and *A Compendium of the Laws of the Church of Scotland,* ed. W. Steuart (Edinburgh, 1837–1840).

[65] Charles Baird was born and brought up in Fayette County, Pennsylvania, the same county in which my great great grandfather was brought up. One only need look at my ancestors' names to realize the influence of romanticism. My great great grandfather's name was Fidelio Hughes Oliphant. He had a sister named Juliet and brothers named Orlando and Ethelbert. I could go on, but you see the point.

[66] Nichols, *Romanticism in American Theology*, pp. 5–26. On Baird, see pp. 290f.

20: THE AGE OF ROMANTICISM

cersburg as well as those of the Oxford Movement back in England. The uniqueness of Baird's work becomes apparent when we compare it with these other reforms. The most obvious difference between Baird and the Mercersburg School was that Baird brought into focus a much larger picture of the worship of classical Protestantism. Baird made the liturgical traditions of Geneva and the French Huguenots accessible to English-speaking Protestants, but then, balancing this, Baird affirmed the English Puritans as important witnesses to the Reformed liturgical tradition.

The liturgical reforms of the Oxford Movement were even further removed from those proposed by Charles Baird. The Oxford Movement was a movement which turned away from the Protestant heritage altogether. Deploring democracy, and being Tories through and through, the Oxford Movement blamed the revolutions which began the nineteenth century on the Reformation and dreamed of a return to the Middle Ages. Romanticism all too often depended on history that was worse than faulty. Too much of it was simply dreamed up—like Wagner's operas or Sir Walter Scott's novels. The Oxford Movement was nationalistic and regarded Protestantism as a German invasion. Baird, on the other hand, was inspired by the faith of the Protestant Reformers. He knew the Reformation well enough to admire it, and he recognized the Reformers as the source of a characteristically American Christianity to which he was deeply committed.

What sets Charles Baird off from many of his contemporaries was that he was an American of cosmopolitan taste who was proud of his own tradition. He provided American Protestants with a timely vision of their liturgical heritage. He made clear that American Protestantism had its own catholicity. Baird made the point that worshiping God decently and in order was the proper delight of classical Protestantism.

21
VICTORIAN EVANGELICALISM

We find a very distinct type of piety in Great Britain in the nineteenth century. It was an era in which the British Empire ruled vast territories from Canada to India, from Gibraltar to Australia. In the days of Queen Victoria her subjects could boast that the sun never set on the proud Union Jack. It was an age which sent missionaries to the most remote provinces of China, to the islands of Tonga, and even to Uganda and the headwaters of the Nile. As Horton Davies used to point out, British Christians were totally absorbed by the missionary movement except for a few isolated Tories distracted by the High Church movement. The celebration of the sacrament of the Lord's Supper was just not a major concern. There were, however, some exceptions to the growing neglect of the sacrament of Holy Communion in Evangelical circles, and it is to some of these exceptions that this chapter is devoted.

THOMAS CHALMERS

Thomas Chalmers (1780–1847) was the first moderator of the Free Church of Scotland. He was one of the prophets of evangelical Protestantism. A profound intellect, he was also a man of warm, humble piety. Few leaders of the Christian church have so well exemplified the teaching of Jesus himself.[1]

---

[1] For biographical material on Chalmers, see: Stewart J. Brown, *Thomas Chalmers and the Godly Commonwealth in Scotland* (Oxford and New York: Oxford University Press, 1982); Thomas Chalmers, *Letters of Thomas Chalmers* (Edinburgh: Banner of Truth Trust, 2007); A. C. Cheyne, ed. *The Practical and the Pious: Essays on Thomas Chalmers (1780–1847)* (Edinburgh: Saint Andrew Press, 1985); and Wil-

Born in Anstruther, Fifeshire, Thomas Chalmers manifested an amazing facility in mathematics from an early age. At the age of eleven he entered the University of St. Andrews and there applied himself with single-hearted devotion to mathematics. As a teaching assistant, he drew great crowds of students to his lectures. His brilliance so provoked the jealousy of the professorial staff that the university had to officially forbid him to teach. Eventually, however, he was reinstated. The Presbytery of St. Andrews, on the other hand, licensed him to preach at Kilmany and for awhile he both preached to his congregation and lectured at St. Andrews, this time focusing on chemistry. Chalmers had an amazing ability to concentrate on different subjects, both scientific and philosophical, simultaneously.

About this time Chalmers, being faced with a number of personal problems, deepened his devotion to his religious commitments, going through a profound experience of conversion which had obviously been inspired by the growing evangelical movement. The passion of his preaching was widely noticed, and in 1815 he was called to the pastorate of the Tron Church in Glasgow, one of the old established parish churches of Scotland's second largest city. It was at the Tron Church that Chalmers preached his remarkable series of apologetical sermons on astronomy.[2]

A titan in his day, Thomas Chalmers was one of those who shaped what we call evangelical Protestantism. He had at the same time both a keen sense of the importance of personal piety and a realistic appreciation of the practical needs of the city. In addition to being a theologian he was also a sociologist and a natural scientist. He wrote significant works on economics and cosmology.[3] His life

---

liam Hanna, *Life of Thomas Chalmers*, ed. James C. Moffat (Cincinnati: Moore, Anderson, Wilstach & Keys; New York: Newman & Ivison, 1853).

[2] On these sermons, see Hughes Oliphant Old, *The Reading and Preaching of the Scriptures in the Worship of the Christian Church*, vol. 5, *Moderatism, Pietism, and Awakening* (Grand Rapids, MI: Eerdmans, 2004), pp. 514–519.

[3] Among the important works of Chalmers are: *The Christian and Civic Economy of Large Towns*, 3 vols. (Glasgow: Chalmers & Collins, 1821–1826); *On Political Economy, in Connexion with the Moral State and Moral Prospects of Society* (New York: Daniel

and thought have been well documented.[4] Sad to say, we do not find among this extensive literary legacy a work specifically dedicated to the sacrament of Holy Communion. About as much as we can find is a couple of communion sermons. Chalmers is, however, known to have been responsible for significantly reshaping the way the sacrament was celebrated during his pastorate in Glasgow. From the somewhat meager sources available, the following things can be said about Dr. Chalmers' approach to the observance of the Sacrament.

A. Holy Communion as Covenant Renewal

First, Chalmers' approach was fundamentally covenantal. Here he was in essential agreement with the historic Reformed position. He viewed the liturgical act as an act of covenant renewal. This is made abundantly clear in the second of two sermons we have from Chalmers.[5] The text of the sermon is 2 Corinthians 6:17–18 in which we find an obvious statement of the covenant, "I will receive you, and will be a Father unto you, and ye shall be my sons and daughters, saith the Lord Almighty" (KJV). Here in 2 Corinthians 6 the Apostle Paul alludes to the covenant as it is formulated in 2 Samuel 7:14. There are, of course, a number of parallel passages which open up this text (e.g., Lev. 26:12 and Jer. 31:33).

To sit down at the Lord's Table and partake of the bread and the wine is to partake of the New Covenant. As Jesus himself put it, "This cup is the new covenant in my blood." It is not merely to

---

Appleton, 1832); and *A Series of Discourses on the Christian Revelation: Viewed in Connexion with the Modern Astronomy* (Glasgow: Printed for John Smith and Son, 1817).

[4] See William Hanna, *Memoirs of the Life and Writings of Thomas Chalmers, D.D., LL.D*, 4 vols. (Edinburgh: Thomas Constable and Co.; London: Hamilton, Adams, and Co., 1852). In addition there are several collections of his works: Thomas Chalmers, *Posthumous Works of the Rev. Thomas Chalmers, D.D., LL.D*, ed. William Hanna, 9 vols. (New York: Harper & Brothers, Publishers, 1849); Thomas Chalmers, *The Select Works of Thomas Chalmers*, 4 vols. (New York: R. Carter, 1848); Thomas Chalmers, *Sermons and Discourses* (New York: Robert Carter, 1844); and Thomas Chalmers, *The Works of Thomas Chalmers*, 25 vols. (Glasgow: William Collins, [1836–1842]).

[5] Chalmers, Sermon XIX, *Posthumous Works*, 6:291f.

remember Christ's death but much more to partake of the benefits and the saving power of Christ's redemptive sacrifice. It is to be united to Christ who both died for us and rose for us. As Chalmers sees it, we sit down at the Lord's Supper and share the bread and wine as a profession of faith.[6] We are not just remembering Christ's death; we are taking our place at his Table in his house. One notices as the nineteenth century progresses and the High Church movement develops that very little is said of the covenantal dimension of the sacrament.

B. HOLY COMMUNION AS INVITATION TO ACCEPT CHRIST

In both of the communion sermons Chalmers has left us, there is a strong element of invitation; that is, the preacher invites his listeners to accept Christ as Lord and Savior. In Sermon VIII we find Dr. Chalmers concluding his sermon with these words: "On this day, then, devoted to the celebration of a Saviour's love, let the desponding Christian find comfort to his soul. . . . He [Christ] addresses, without exception, the language of invitation and encouragement."[7] To make his point he calls on the famous invitation of the Savior himself, "Come unto me all ye that labor and are heavy laden and I will give you rest" (Matt. 11:28, KJV). Here in the conclusion of the sermon we hear the very word of Christ, the son of God, inviting the truly repentant to leave this world behind and follow him into the kingdom of God.[8] Let us note that this is the essence of the evangelical Protestant approach to the celebration of the sacrament of Holy Communion. It is an invitation to accept Christ.

When we turn to the other communion sermon that has come down to us we find the same thing. The preacher finds in the communion service the "inviting voice of God Himself."[9] In offering

---

[6] Chalmers, Sermon VIII, *Posthumous Works*, 6:96.

[7] Chalmers, Sermon VIII, *Posthumous Works*, 6:104.

[8] Chalmers, Sermon VIII, *Posthumous Works*, 6:104.

[9] Chalmers, Sermon XIX, *Posthumous Works*, 6:298.

us the bread and the wine and a place at his Table, "He condescended to put Himself into the attitude of a petitioner, and implore the return of sinners, and ply them with the assurances of His willingness to welcome them back again."[10]

Further on in this same sermon we find Dr. Chalmers making a very clear invitation to reaffirm the covenant: "I should like you to enter from this moment into a firmer, and a faithfuller, and a more closely felt alliance with that living intercessor who is now looking over you."[11] The word "alliance" here is clearly a synonym for "covenant." What we have here in this celebration of the sacrament of Holy Communion is an act of covenant renewal. It is not simply a memorial of Christ's death. Evangelical Protestantism as we see it developing in Great Britain early in the nineteenth century gave a particularly important place to the celebration of the sacrament and at the very center of that celebration was the invitation to reaffirm the covenant.

C. Holy Communion as Eucharist

The importance of thanksgiving to the biblical concept of worship is expressed by the fact that often one uses a form of the word as it is found in the Greek New Testament, namely "eucharist." Some might find the use of this "loan word" a bit pretentious and so we usually avoid it, but on the other hand when we use it we recognize that there is something special about the biblical concept of thanksgiving.

At the very heart of a covenantal understanding of worship is the recital of God's mighty works of creation and redemption. This centrality of the history of salvation is of the essence of worship. The liturgy of the feast of tabernacles is a good example:

> "A wandering Aramean was my father; and he went down into Egypt and sojourned there, few in num-

---

[10] Chalmers, Sermon XIX, *Posthumous Works*, 6:299.
[11] Chalmers, Sermon XIX, *Posthumous Works*, 6:304.

ber; and there he became a nation, great, mighty, and populous. And the Egyptians treated us harshly, and afflicted us, and laid upon us hard bondage. Then we cried to the LORD the God of our fathers, and the LORD heard our voice, and saw our affliction, our toil, and our oppression; and the LORD brought us out of Egypt with a mighty hand and an outstretched arm, and with great terror, with signs and wonders; and he brought us into this place and gave us this land, a land flowing with milk and honey." (Deuteronomy 26:5–9)

But we also find it in a number of psalms such as Psalms 78, 104, 105, and 136. The reason this reciting of holy history is so important is that in giving thanks for the past we invoke God's help for the future. Thanksgiving and hope are essentially related. The assurance of God's redemptive and sanctifying power is strengthened when we remember what God has done in the past.

With Sermon VIII, Chalmers intended to inspire in his listeners the most appropriate sentiments for approaching the Lord's Table. First of all he wants to speak of thanksgiving.[12] At length our preacher expatiates on the appropriateness of thanksgiving to God for his wondrous works of creation. Chalmers elaborates the hope for a Savior preached by the prophets. The Christian should approach the Lord's Table with thankfulness for the atonement wrought on Calvary.[13] Thanksgiving for the atonement is at the heart of the service! No less central, to be sure, is the thanksgiving for the resurrection.

If for Chalmers Communion is a remembrance of God's mighty acts of redemption, it is also a foretaste of the glories of heaven. As we sit about his Table here on earth we are given an intimation of the wedding feast of the Lamb. It is, as we have so often seen, a solid biblical principle of worship that the remembrance of God's faithfulness in the past is an invocation of God's

---

[12] Chalmers, Sermon VIII, *Posthumous Works*, 6:93.
[13] Chalmers, Sermon VIII, *Posthumous Works*, 6:94.

faithfulness in the time to come. To celebrate this sacred feast is to nourish sentiments of hope.[14]

D. Holy Communion as Sitting at the Father's Table

We have spoken at length of the Scottish communion seasons of the eighteenth century as they were celebrated by such devout and pious ministers as John Willison, Robert Walker, and the Erskine brothers. We have noticed that these services were very careful to give each communicant a place at the Lord's Table. Special tables were set up running down the aisles connected to the head table behind which the minister and the elders sat. Typically it would take six or seven sittings and with each sitting there would be a brief communion "address," as they were called, in which the minister would speak of the significance of the broken bread and poured out wine. The communicants would then eat the sacred food and return to their seats.

All this could take quite a bit of time and typically the service could go on for hours. Great crowds could present themselves, especially since the usual practice was to offer but one communion Sabbath a year. Chalmers fully described the practical logistics of these communion seasons to the Synod of Glasgow in the process of defending his innovative celebrations of the sacrament.[15] The communion seasons, so profoundly celebrated in the village churches of the eighteenth century, had become a mob scene in the crowded cities of the nineteenth century. It was for purely practical reasons that Chalmers had re-arranged the serving of the bread and wine to the communicants in their pews. This innovation was resisted by some, but within a few years, most congregations had decided for what was called "pew communion."[16] The reason the change was

---

[14] Chalmers, Sermon VIII, *Posthumous Works*, 6:102.

[15] Chalmers' defense before the Synod is presented in Hanna's *Memoirs*, vol. 2.

[16] See Benjamin B. Warfield, "Posture of the Recipients . . . ," in *Selected Shorter Writings*, vol. 2, ed. John E. Meeter (Phillipsburg, NJ: Presbyterian & Reformed Publishing, 1973).

so readily accepted was that it was far more practical. It shortened the service significantly. But even more, it evoked the sign of the sharing of a meal in the house of the Father. This sign of sharing a meal in the household of faith had always been a primary concern of Reformed eucharistic piety. It is firmly based on the parables of Jesus (Matt. 22:2–14; Matt. 25:1–13) and thoughtfully opened up by Calvin in his *Short Treatise on the Lord's Supper*.[17]

When Chalmers defended his innovation before the Synod of Glasgow, he appealed to the text of the *Book of Common Order* which John Knox himself had put together for the Church of Scotland in 1560. Pew communion witnesses very clearly to the dimension of fellowship or *koinonia* in the celebration of the sacrament. As we receive the bread and the wine from one neighbor, we pass it on to another neighbor. As we have seen, Timothy Dwight makes this point quite explicitly, but this is just the sort of thing Thomas Chalmers as an evangelical would have found especially interesting.

This was all part of Chalmers' evangelical sociology. The reason he started St. John's Church in Glasgow was that he recognized the need of the Church to be sensitive to the concerns of the city. Glasgow was one of those burgeoning cities created by the Industrial Revolution. Scots had left their idyllic villages in the Highlands and Islands of western Scotland and in the beginning of the nineteenth century were crowding into Glasgow. They worked on the docks, building the ships that brought in the trade and treasures of the great commercial empire. These shipwrights and dock workers lived in the most crowded of tenements. The churches were crowded, too. They might have been big enough for the little gothic town of the late sixteenth century, but the teeming Victorian city of Glasgow was another matter. On a communion Sabbath twice as many people crowded into those little parish churches. A parish of ten thousand people was typical. The old system was just not adequate for the huge crowds, and yet there was a theological insight that needed

---

[17] For a discussion of Calvin's *Short Treatise*, see chapter 2 of this volume.

to be preserved. Pew communion fulfilled both requirements.

In his defense before the Synod of Glasgow, Chalmers made clear what a lot of others were beginning to realize. The old communion seasons with great numbers of communicants, crowded conditions, and awkward tables made any kind of reverence all but impossible. The situation on the Virginia frontier at about this time was similar. It was the protracted meetings in Kentucky and the Carolinas which killed the Scottish communion seasons here in America. The boisterous celebrations of the frontiersmen made many think twice about the old way of celebrating communion.

One more thing needs to be said. Dr. Chalmers was not the inventor of pew communion. There were others who had practiced it in Scotland. More than that, however, was the fact that pew communion was the long accepted practice in Zurich and German-speaking Switzerland. It goes back to Zwingli himself. Apparently English Congregationalists practiced it as well as New England Congregationalists. By the middle of the nineteenth century, James Alexander was using pew communion at Fifth Avenue Presbyterian Church in New York City, although he had strong roots in the Valley of Virginia. In 1800 that was still the frontier. His communion sermons preached in New York show no sign of the old communion seasons of eighteenth century Scotland.

E. Holy Communion and the Sign of the Lord's Day

Surely one of the most remarkable teachings of Chalmers on Communion is that when we approach the Lord's Table we should mingle the sacramental and the sabbatical.[18] Dr. Chalmers reminds us that the early Christians made a point of celebrating the Lord's Supper on the first day of the week. They did not choose to celebrate their sacrament on the day of the crucifixion, that is, on Friday, or even on the day the Lord's Supper was eaten, namely on Thursday, but rather they chose the first day of

---

[18] Chalmers, Sermon XIX, *Posthumous Works*, 6:304.

the week, that is, Sunday. So we should celebrate the memorial of Christ's death on the memorial of the resurrection, that is, on Sunday, the Lord's Day, the day the tomb was found empty.

In Scotland, great attention was given to the observance of the Christian Sabbath. This concern was fundamental to Scottish piety. Chalmers' phrase about mingling the sacramental and the sabbatical makes its point if one is familiar with the pious lingo of Scotland, even if it sounds a bit quaint. The Lord's Day and the Lord's Supper and the Lord's Cup and the Lord's Table peculiarly belong together.

ROBERT DALE

Robert Dale (1828–1895), a Congregational minister in Birmingham, was rather well known for his eucharistic doctrine, but it was apparently considered a bit eccentric for most Congregational churches.[19] Dale has left us a treatise on eucharistic doctrine, *The Doctrine of the Real Presence and of the Lord's Supper*.[20] One of the most interesting features of Dale's essay is that he is writing about the sacrament at the end of the nineteenth century and is very much concerned not to admit to anything that might seem superstitious.

As we would expect from the title of this work, what we have here is a formal doctrinal treatise. Significantly he begins with a long history of eucharistic doctrine. The place he begins, however, is the early Middle Ages. At great length he unwinds the story of how the doctrine of transubstantiation began to develop. We learn all about Ratramnus, Paschasius, Rabanus Maurus, Berengarius, and Peter Lombard. At considerable length our learned English Protestant shows us the weaknesses of the doctrine so insisted upon by medieval Catholicism. Typically Protestant, he makes very clear how the

---

[19] On Robert Dale, see: Alfred William Winterslow Dale, *The Life of R. W. Dale of Birmingham* (London: Hodder and Stoughton, 1898); and Horton Davies, *From Newman to Martineau, 1850–1900*, vol. 4, *Worship and Theology in England*, 5 vols. (Princeton, NJ: Princeton University Press, 1961–1975), pp. 322–333.

[20] Found in Robert W. Dale, *Essays and Addresses*, 3rd ed. (London: Hodder and Stoughton, 1901), pp. 298f.

doctrine of transubstantiation does not explain the essential passages of Scripture. One notices time and again that the Catholic theologian on which he depends is the famous Counter-Reformation theologian, Cardinal Bellarmine. It is very clear, however, that Dale is not only arguing with the Catholic doctrine of transubstantiation but also, and perhaps even more forcefully, against the High Church Anglican doctrine of the real presence. As far as Dale is concerned, there is really very little difference between them.

Then, as we read on we find that Dale is also very critical of other Evangelicals who have gone to the opposite extreme. He tells us that most recently his fellow Independent theologians have deserted even the great preachers of the Commonwealth, such as Baxter, Owen, and Watson. Dale dismisses them as extreme Zwinglians. Alas, Dale does not seem to know much about Zwingli's position, let alone the position of Bucer or Bullinger. When he gets down to describing the Protestant position he quotes Turretin at length and says not a word about Calvin. The biggest problem with Dale's treatise is that the whole covenantal dimension of the sacrament is ignored.

CHARLES HADDON SPURGEON

It was the heyday of evangelicalism when C. H. Spurgeon (1834–1892) preached at London's Metropolitan Tabernacle.[21] Every word that came down from his pulpit was put into print, flooding the market from New York to New Zealand. Charles Haddon Spurgeon was the most famous preacher in the English-speaking world.[22] The man was full of paradoxes. He never had the advan-

---

[21] For biographical material on Spurgeon, see: Arnold Dallimore, *Spurgeon: A New Biography* (Edinburgh: Banner of Truth Trust, 1995); and Lewis A. Drummond, "Charles Haddon Spurgeon," found in *Baptist Theologians*, eds. Timothy George and David S. Dockery (Nashville: Broadman Press, 1990).

[22] For more information on Spurgeon and communion, see: Charles H. Spurgeon, *Twelve Sermons on the Lord's Supper* (Grand Rapids, MI: Baker Book House, 1994); and Michael Walker, "Charles Haddon Spurgeon (1834–1892) and John Clifford (1836–1923) on the Lord's Supper," *American Baptist Quarterly* 7/2 (1988): 128–150.

tages of a theological education and yet his learning was prodigious. His grandfather had been a Congregational minister and young Charles spent hour upon hour in his grandfather's library thoroughly absorbing the literary legacy of the Puritans.

Surely one of the paradoxes in Spurgeon's ministry was that although he was famous as a practitioner of the art of preaching as well as the most well-known homiletical theoretician among British evangelicals, he was a vigorous promoter of celebrating Holy Communion each Lord's Day. He often expressed his conviction on this subject. For instance, in a sermon on the dimension of table fellowship he tells us that it is his custom to observe the sacrament every Sabbath day as a number of others in his congregation regularly do and have done for many years. In this, he tells us, they enjoyed the nearest communion with Christ they had ever known and again and again blessed his name for this ordinance.[23]

As far as I know Spurgeon is the only one of the great evangelical preachers of the nineteenth century who voiced such a strong opinion on the subject of Holy Communion. There were others, to be sure, who may have had longings in this direction, but to my knowledge he is the only one who was able to bring it about. Princeton's homiletician, Andrew Blackwood, published a volume of the communion sermons of Spurgeon, and it was that volume which inspired this chapter.

Others have obviously been similarly inspired. Christian Focus Publications has published another volume enlarging the collection published by Blackwood.[24] The book bears the title, *Till He Come: A Collection of Communion Addresses*.[25] Notably this collection contains a number of sermons expounding verses from the Song of Solomon. This is particularly interesting to me because

---

[23] Charles Haddon Spurgeon, *Charles H. Spurgeon*, ed. Andrew W. Blackwood (New York: Fleming H. Revell, 1949), p. 90. Hereinafter Spurgeon, *Sermons*.

[24] Spurgeon, *Sermons*, p. 90.

[25] Charles Haddon Spurgeon, *Till He Come: A Collection of Communion Addresses* (Fearn, UK: Christian Focus Publications, 2003).

it supports my thesis that the frequency of Spurgeon's eucharistic sermons on texts from the Song of Solomon and the Revelation of John suggests a strong doctrine of the real presence.

Spurgeon's eucharistic theology deserves a volume in itself. That is a worthy project, but I am afraid my failing eyesight will never allow me to do it. Permit me, however, to sketch out a few thoughts about what might be covered in such a volume.

A. THE LORD'S TABLE

An especially informative sermon on Spurgeon's eucharistic doctrine has the title, "Christ and His Table Companions." It takes as its text Luke 22:14, "And when the hour was come, He sat down, and the twelve apostles with him."[26] The sermon begins by pointing out that there are but two New Testament sacraments and they are both very simple and straightforward.[27] They are best understood when looked at most simply. With the Lord's Supper we should take very seriously the obvious fact that Jesus sat at table with his apostles as one of the most basic dimensions of the ordinance. The table fellowship involved in the celebration of the Lord's Supper is basic to its meaning. It is one of the most obvious elements in the eucharistic symbolism. Reformed theologians have consistently pointed this out, from Bucer's *Grund und Ursach* down to the present.

Spurgeon gives us a word picture of the Last Supper.[28] It took place in a large upper room with a table in it. Nothing is said of an altar; it is simply a table. Nor is it suggested by the gospels that anyone knelt down before it. The apostles sat at a table. No doubt they sat at the table in the oriental manner, that is, half-reclining, half-sitting. Furthermore, this sitting was around the table.[29]

---

[26] The above sermon is taken from Spurgeon, *Till He Come*, pp. 187–200. Scripture quotations are as the preacher read them.

[27] Nineteenth-century Baptists avoided the word "Sacrament," preferring the word "ordinance."

[28] Spurgeon, *Till He Come*, p. 188.

[29] Spurgeon, *Till He Come*, p. 188.

The sort of meal the apostles shared with Jesus implies a certain intimacy. There were many followers of Jesus who were not yet disciples. That the apostles shared this meal with Jesus implied a sacred bond.[30] The point is that when we participate in the Lord's Supper we become the table companions of our Lord Jesus Christ. As Spurgeon sees it, the most obvious meaning of the sign of the Lord's Supper is that Christ invites us to sit with him at his table and share his bread and his wine with him. "All the Lord's believing people are sitting, by sacred privilege and calling, at the same table with Jesus, for truly, our fellowship is with the Father and with His Son Jesus Christ. He has come into our hearts, and He sups with us, and we with Him; we are His table-companions, and shall eat bread with Him in the kingdom of God."[31]

There is more to be said, and here Spurgeon begins to think of the Lord's Supper as a covenant sign. To be table companions implies "mutual fidelity," as Spurgeon puts it.[32] The sharing of a meal together is the sealing of an implied covenant. According to Spurgeon, "Having eaten together, they were under bond to be faithful to one another."[33] If you are really the friends of Christ, you may be well assured in eating this bread and sharing this cup that Christ has pledged himself to be faithful to you. "He has received you as his honoured guests, and fed you upon His choicest meats, and therefore He does as good as say to you, 'I will never leave you.'"[34] But there is another pledge of fidelity here, and that is the covenantal bond between believers one with another. The covenant begins with God's faithfulness to us and moves on to our faithfulness to God and to one another as well.[35]

---

[30] Spurgeon, *Till He Come*, p. 190.
[31] Spurgeon, *Till He Come*, p. 191.
[32] Spurgeon, *Till He Come*, p. 191.
[33] Spurgeon, *Till He Come*, p. 191.
[34] Spurgeon, *Till He Come*, p. 192.
[35] Spurgeon, *Till He Come*, p. 192.

B. Communion with Christ

First Corinthians 10:16–17 seems to be the fundamental text for Spurgeon's understanding of Holy Communion:

> The cup of blessing which we bless, is it not the communion of the blood of Christ? The bread which we break, is it not the communion of the body of Christ? For we being many are one bread, and one body: for we are all partakers of that one bread. (KJV)

This text is generally very important for Protestant eucharistic theology and it is the reason the sacrament is so frequently called "communion." The Puritans who taught Spurgeon theology could be rather sticky about words. We notice, for example, that Spurgeon much prefers the word "ordinance" to the word "sacrament." For Spurgeon the word "communion" has two faces. It speaks of communion with God and it speaks of communion with the brethren, that is, the members of the church.[36] The word "communion" is the word used by the King James Version to translate *koinonia*, a word that in Greek means fellowship. *Koinonia* refers to something that is shared or held in common. The church is a *koinonia* because we belong together. Fellowship is an experience that is shared.

In this passage, the Apostle Paul explains that the cup that we share at the communion service is in reality a sharing in the blood of Christ. In the same way the loaf of bread which we share makes us participants in the body of Christ. To share in the communion is to receive Christ. It is to accept him as Savior. It is to become a member of the church and to reaffirm our membership in the church as often as we take it. The fact that it is shared is of the essence of its meaning. That is the special significance of the word *koinonia*. This is fairly easy to understand when we are speaking of the church as a fellowship of men and women who share the same faith, the same sense of values, and the same moral code. What is

---

[36] Spurgeon, *Sermons*, p. 122.

more difficult to understand is that in the sharing of this sacred meal we share in the history of salvation, in the incarnation in the atoning sacrifice on the cross, the breaking of Christ's body, the shedding of Christ's blood, the resurrection, and the ascension into heaven. By sharing in this meal we take our place in the spiritual exodus out of this world unto the Father. Even more, as Spurgeon sees it, our fellowship, or communion, is with the Father and with his Son Jesus Christ, inspired and enlivened by the Holy Spirit.

Spurgeon is concerned right from the first to make clear that we enjoy union with Christ and with his church in order to enjoy communion. Union with Christ is the basis of communion.[37] "We must be one with Christ in heart, and soul, and life."[38] This union is the basis of communion. "Communion is ours by personal intercourse with the Lord Jesus. We speak with him in prayer and He speaks with us through the Word."[39] Spurgeon's understanding of communion is much broader than the communion that comes from participation in the bread and wine at the Lord's Table, however. It is the personal relationship that is continual for the devout. We have communion with Christ when we share his thoughts and purposes. We have communion with Christ when we share his emotions, his likes and dislikes, and even his tears.[40] Spurgeon is particularly eloquent at this point. Our preacher goes on in considerable detail speaking of how we have communion with Christ when we continue his work, even when we share in his sorrows and when we shed a sympathetic tear.[41]

For Spurgeon it is above all at the Lord's Supper that we take Christ to be our Savior.[42] "By our sincere reception of Jesus into our hearts an indissoluble union is established between us and the

---

[37] Spurgeon, *Sermons*, p. 122.
[38] Spurgeon, *Sermons*, p. 122.
[39] Spurgeon, *Sermons*, p. 123.
[40] Spurgeon, *Sermons*, p. 124.
[41] Spurgeon, *Sermons*, p. 125.
[42] Spurgeon, *Sermons*, p. 127.

Lord, and this manifests itself in the mutual communion. To as many as receive Him, to them He has given this communion, even to them that believe in his name."[43]

Having looked at one dimension of the sacrament—communion with Christ—we need to look at communion with fellow Christians.[44] There is, of course, a real joy to be shared as Christians join together in witnessing to our common faith and, even more, to our common hope. Here of course is one of the heights of communion. When Christians join together in hymns of praise, in praying the psalms together, and bearing witness to the power of Christ's atoning sacrifice in proclaiming that Christ is risen, we experience the highest reaches of Christian worship. Spurgeon had a high sense of the importance of hymnody and psalmody to Christian worship. We find this particularly in his sermon "The Memorable Hymn."[45] Communion with fellow Christians is the basis of our missions of mercy, our care of the sick, our support of those in mourning, and our care of the poor. There is a strong source of communion with fellow Christians in sharing with each other the stories of how God has delivered us in crises we have gone through.[46]

C. Communion with the Brethren

Another sermon that gives us an important insight into Spurgeon's teaching on communion is drawn from Luke 22:14, "and when the hour was come he sat down and the twelve apostles with him." The title of the sermon is, "Christ and His Table Companions."[47]

We have already looked at this sermon once before, but there is more to be said.[48] Spurgeon begins by making the point that at

---

[43] Spurgeon, *Sermons*, p. 127.

[44] Spurgeon, *Sermons*, p. 127.

[45] Spurgeon, *Sermons*, pp. 31f.

[46] Spurgeon, *Sermons*, p. 130.

[47] Spurgeon, *Sermons*, p. 79.

[48] See above, section A.

the celebration of the Last Supper the apostles sat down together at a table to share a meal. It was, of course, a very special meal, that is, the Feast of Passover. The fact that Jesus and his disciples should have shared this meal together implied a particularly close relation between them. There were many people who might be counted as followers. They might have not had much more than a casual interest in the teaching of Jesus and in time there were certain of these followers that Jesus drew closer into fellowship and regarded as disciples. They would have had a deeper commitment to the teachings of Jesus, but the twelve that gathered around the table in the Upper Room had been admitted into a much deeper level of fellowship. Up to this point they were called servants, but now Jesus calls them friends.[49]

One can be a follower for some time before really becoming a disciple. One can sit at the feet of the Master and learn his doctrine and the principles of his way of life before coming to trust the Master and really follow his way of life. There comes a time, however, when one makes a commitment to the Master and is invited to sit at the table with him. This is more than mere friendship.[50] This is what is happening here. To be invited to share the Passover feast with Jesus was to be admitted to the closest degree of fellowship, the most intimate communion.

There is another point to be made here. What is implied, first of all, is mutual fidelity.[51] "This was the seal of an implied covenant."[52] Here, of course, Spurgeon puts in the clearest possible terms classic Reformed eucharistic teachings. The sacrament of Communion is a sign and a seal of the covenant of grace. This is the terminology of the Westminster Standards. At this table we pledge ourselves to be faithful to one another. We pledge ourselves

---

[49] Spurgeon, *Sermons*, p. 81.
[50] Spurgeon, *Sermons*, p. 83.
[51] Spurgeon, *Sermons*, p. 84.
[52] Spurgeon, *Sermons*, p. 84.

to be faithful to Christ, but, even more importantly, Christ pledges himself to be faithful to us.

At the very heart of the Reformed teaching on the Lord's Supper is this covenantal understanding of what is really going on at this celebration. The sacrament of Holy Communion has as its purpose the nourishing of the covenant. Baptism is the establishing of the covenant and Communion is the renewing of the covenant. It involves the renewing of our covenant vows and the encouraging and supporting of our faith, our love to God and one another and our hope in the life to come.

D. The Paschal Psalms

Communion for Spurgeon was a particularly appropriate place for the congregation to join together in the singing of hymns and especially psalms. He mentions this in more than one of his communion sermons.

In his sermon "The Memorable Hymn," Spurgeon takes Matthew 26:30 as his text: "And when they had sung a hymn they went out into the Mount of Olives."[53] For Spurgeon the most interesting thing about this text is that it indicates that Jesus had indeed been following the Jewish Passover Seder. Jesus was concerned to fulfill completely the traditions of worship that Moses had established.[54] For Reformed theologians seeing the Lord's Supper as the fulfillment of Passover has always been of the highest importance. Even Zwingli, who is usually accused of having a sort of minimalist understanding of the sacrament, directed that singing or reciting the first of the Passover psalms should be used at the conclusion of the service. We find this in the *Zurich Service Book* of 1525.

As Spurgeon understood it, Psalms 113 and 114 were sung at the beginning of the service and Psalms 115–118 were sung at the end of the service. Our preacher takes us through these psalms,

---

[53] Spurgeon, *Sermons*, p. 31.

[54] Spurgeon, *Sermons*, p. 32.

showing us how they might have spoken to Jesus as he approached the cross.[55] Think what it must have meant to Jesus to sing in Psalm 118, "Bind the sacrifice with chords, even unto the horns of the altar." For Jesus these psalms must have been prophetic. For the disciples singing, the Passover psalms must have helped them remember the deliverance of their fathers from the land of bondage. It must have helped them remember the whole history of being freed from the bondage of Egypt and their entry into the Promised Land. So, for the Christian, singing at the Lord's Supper must spur our remembrance of the freedom we have in Christ.[56]

So now, as Spurgeon instructed his congregation, is the time for us to come and sing our Passover hymn. Let us sing a hymn that is solemn, but not as at a funeral. "Let us sing softly, but none the less joyfully. These are not burial feasts; those are not funeral cakes which lie upon this table and yonder fair linen cloth is no winding sheet. 'This is my body,' said Jesus, but the body so represented was no corpse; we feed upon a living Christ."[57] The feast we observe is a joyful feast. It is on the Lord's Day that we feast. We do not approach it as serfs on our knees but as freedmen to serve Christ in drinking wine which gladdens our hearts. Sitting around the table as free men now is the time to sing, "The Lord is my shepherd I shall not want. He maketh me to lie down in green pastures: He leadeth me beside the still waters."[58] Spurgeon had no intention of advocating exclusive psalmody, but he nevertheless learned the fullness of Christian prayer from the Psalms. All these emotions of lamentation, supplication, festal shouts, and solemn resolves belong to a celebration of Holy Communion.

---

[55] Spurgeon, *Sermons*, p. 32.
[56] Spurgeon, *Sermons*, p. 37.
[57] Spurgeon, *Sermons*, p. 38.
[58] Spurgeon, *Sermons*, p. 39.

21: Victorian Evangelicalism

E. The Real Presence of Christ

Spurgeon's sermon, "Real Contact with Jesus" opens up the question of just exactly what we mean by the real presence.[59] Our preacher takes the story of the woman who was healed from a debilitating disease by simply touching Jesus. The title of the sermon, "Real Contact with Jesus" is an immediate tipoff that the preacher wants to talk about the doctrine of the real presence. At one point he puts it this way:

> Jesus said, " Somebody hath touched me," from which we observe that in the use of means and ordinances we should never be satisfied unless we get into personal contact with Christ so that we touch him as the woman touched his garment.[60]

Spurgeon used the phrase "means and ordinances" because, as a Baptist, he was very hesitant to use the word "sacrament." What he means by "means and ordinances" is Word, prayer, and sacrament. A bit further on he says, "First, then, when in the use of all means and ordinances let it be our chief aim and object to come into personal contact with the Lord Jesus Christ."[61] There are far too many people who come into church Sunday by Sunday, but do not enter into a real personal communion with Christ. "There is no inward touching of the blessed Jesus."[62] As Spurgeon understands it, there is an "ordinance" of grace for you who have gone into the very arms of Christ.

This is great preaching, but it certainly makes communion a very subjective sort of experience. As the sermon progresses it becomes clear that what Spurgeon has to say about communion he also says about prayer and the reading and preaching of Scrip-

---

[59] Spurgeon, *Sermons*, pp. 64f.
[60] Spurgeon, *Sermons*, p. 64.
[61] Spurgeon, *Sermons*, p. 65.
[62] Spurgeon, *Sermons*, p. 66.

ture. Unless you have this kind of personal relationship, the whole thing has been a "mere dead performance, without life or power."[63] This seems like a very nominalist sort of piety, that coming to Christ is "a very different thing from coming to the Lord's Table."[64]

From this point on the sermon becomes an invitation to "put out the hand of faith and touch Christ."[65] There is no question about it; this is a great sermon. From a theological standpoint it makes an important distinction between the rite that one goes through and the faith that transcends the rite. Spurgeon is distinguishing the formal rite from the religion of the heart and, having done that, he presses on to speak of the divine power which is behind this formal rite. The text specifically says that Jesus perceived that virtue had gone out from him. Our preacher says, "The woman in the crowd did touch Jesus, and, having done so, she received virtue from him."[66] This word "virtue" is a theologically hot word especially when one is discussing the eucharistic theology of the Reformed faith. One often blames Calvin's eucharistic theology with being "virtuistic." What that means is that when Christ is understood to be present in and through the observance of the sacred supper, the power of God is present and active. It is like the brightness and warmth of the sun in heaven and yet felt and experienced among us.

There is a real objectivity to the communion that we celebrate as God transforms our lives and lifts us up out of the spiritual doldrums and blesses us with "the heights of ecstatic worship."[67] Spurgeon was no nominalist, but he was a mystic. His mysticism, however, was of a thoroughly biblical sort.

---

[63] Spurgeon, *Sermons*, p. 67.
[64] Spurgeon, *Sermons*, p. 70.
[65] Spurgeon, *Sermons*, p. 70.
[66] Spurgeon, *Sermons*, p. 72.
[67] Spurgeon, *Sermons*, p. 73.

F. Christ's Presence and the Work of the Holy Spirit

It has long been my contention that the key to Reformed eucharistic theology is the doctrine of the Holy Spirit. I made that clear in my doctoral thesis some forty years ago.[68] Spurgeon treats that subject in a sermon on John 14:18, "I will not leave you comfortless: I will come to you."[69] First of all our preacher notes that the margin reads, "I will not leave you orphans; I will come to you." Putting this text in context our preacher tells us these are the words of Jesus as he spoke them to his disciples in the Upper Room. What Jesus was telling them was that he was going to leave them, but knowing the fears that must have been in their hearts he wanted to calm their hearts and so he assured them that they would not be left alone in this wild and crazy world. In Spurgeon's paraphrase of this discourse, Jesus promises them that he may be absent to them in the flesh but he will be present to them in a far more efficacious manner. He will be present to them spiritually.[70] Furthermore, "'I will come to you spiritually, and you shall derive from My spiritual presence even more good than you could have from My bodily presence had I still continued in your midst.'"[71]

Spurgeon goes into some length elaborating the meaning of the devastation that an orphan experiences. It is a powerful devastation. Nothing can make up for it. Only one devastation is anything like the devastation of an orphan and that is the devastation of a widow. For the Christian, however, there is a power beyond this terrible loss. Christ has bestowed upon us his Holy Spirit and through his Holy Spirit he is always present. Best of all "his spiri-

---

[68] See Hughes Oliphant Old, *The Patristic Roots of Reformed Worship* (Zurich: Theologischer Verlag Zurich, 1975).

[69] Spurgeon, *Sermons*, pp. 105f.

[70] Spurgeon, *Sermons*, p. 105.

[71] Spurgeon, *Sermons*, p. 106.

tual presence is quite as blessed as his bodily presence."[72] This is a moving sermon. Our preacher makes a special point of assuring us that "since the Holy Spirit has been given us we have richer fare and are more indulged with spiritual comforts than believers were before the bodily presence of the Master had departed."[73]

As these sermons of Spurgeon began to soak in, I realized that Spurgeon understood better than anyone of more recent times what Bucer, Oecolampadius, and, above all, Calvin meant by a spiritual presence. Jean-Jacques von Allmen used to make the point that the spiritual presence meant a presence accomplished or brought about by the Holy Spirit. This is certainly true, but Spurgeon understood what this meant and was able to convey it with an ecstatic flavor theologians rarely achieve. It is in the end the preacher's calling to give wings to words and that Spurgeon did.

> It is most for your profit that you should receive the Spirit of truth, not through the golden vessel of Christ in His actual presence here, but through the poor earthen vessels of humble servants of God like ourselves. At any rate, whether we speak or an angel from heaven, the speaker matters not; it is the Spirit of God alone that is the power of the Word, and makes that Word to become vital and quickening to you. Now, you have the Spirit of God. The Holy Spirit is so given, that there is not a truth which you may not understand. You may be led into the deepest mysteries by His teaching.[74]

G. Presence and Mysticism

On the subject of mysticism I have had conflicting views for a long time. I have always wanted to do a very thorough study of the eucharistic theology of John Oecolampadius. I suspect he was much more formed by Rhenish mysticism than we usually imagine. One thing is clear, Oecolampadius was not simply a "me too"

---

[72] Spurgeon, *Sermons*, p. 108.
[73] Spurgeon, *Sermons*, p. 109.
[74] Spurgeon, *Sermons*, p. 110.

reflection of Zwingli. Be that as it may there is no question but that Spurgeon was a mystic. Where he got it from is beyond me. For a man who read as widely as Spurgeon did there is no telling. We have already spoken of decidedly mystical elements in the eucharistic theology of Gilbert Tennent. The treasure chest of Reformed eucharistic reflection is surprisingly rich. The puzzle is, are we going to find John Williamson Nevin and Charles Haddon Spurgeon whistling the same tune?

Spurgeon's sermon "Mysterious Visits" suggests a strong mystical element in the eucharistic theology of our champion of Victorian evangelicalism. He takes his text from Psalm 17, "Thou hast visited me in the night."[75] We get the impression that the sermon was preached at a regular communion service. We read in the introduction, "To you who gather with me about the communion table, I will speak of my own experience nothing doubting that it is also yours."[76] Whatever experiences one might have had of this sort, it should be very clear that such experiences can only be understood as the work of the Holy Spirit. One might charge Spurgeon with illuminism here but I think this would be a mistake. We notice, however, that Spurgeon quotes from Job, "'I have heard of thee by the hearing of the ear, but now mine eye seeth thee. Wherefore I abhor myself, and repent in dust and ashes'" (Job 42:5–6, KJV). Our preacher comments, "We can read of God and hear of God, and be little moved; but when we feel His presence, it is another matter."[77]

The sermon goes on to speak of a number of mystical experiences spoken of in the Bible, such as Paul's Damascus Road experience and Paul himself being lifted up to third heaven (cf. Acts 9:1–8; 2 Cor. 12:1–4). This encourages our preacher to speak of his own experience. "Believe me, there are such things as personal

---

[75] Spurgeon, *Sermons*, p. 151.
[76] Spurgeon, *Sermons*, p. 151.
[77] Spurgeon, *Sermons*, p. 152.

visits to His people. He has not left us utterly. Though He be not seen bodily by bush or brook, nor on the mount, nor by the sea, yet doth He come and go, observed only by the spirit, felt only by the heart. Still He standeth behind our walls. He showeth himself through the lattices [Song of Solomon 2:9]."[78] The biblical allusions in these lines are superb. Those who know their Bibles quickly pick up the allusions to the burning bush, the Brook Cherith, the appearance of Jesus on the Sea of Galilee in John 6, the Transfiguration, the Damascus Road experience, and other passages. The mysticism we find here is very similar to what is found in Ralph Erskine a century before.

Spurgeon does not often get polemical, but here he does. He clearly attacks the Roman Catholic understanding of the real presence. What they advocate is a corporeal presence of the Lord Jesus. In that sense the only real presence of Jesus is in heaven. As a Reformed theologian Spurgeon speaks quite clearly, "but we firmly believe in the real presence of Christ which is spiritual and yet certain. By 'spiritual' we do not mean unreal: in fact, the spiritual takes the lead in real-ness to spiritual men. I believe in the true and real presence of Jesus with His people: such presence has been real to my spirit. Lord Jesus, Thou Thyself hast visited me. As surely as the Lord Jesus came really as to His flesh to Bethlehem and Calvary, so surely does He come really by His Spirit to his people in the hours of their communion with Him. We are as conscious of that presence as of our own existence."[79]

For Spurgeon, the presence of Christ with his people is a comprehensive presence or, perhaps, a plenary presence. We experience it in the reading and preaching of Scripture. As we find it in the *Didaché*: "Where his Word is preached, there is he present." We find it in baptism: "Lo, I am with you always." We find it in prayer: "When two or three are gathered together in my name,

---

[78] Spurgeon, *Sermons*, p. 155.

[79] Spurgeon, *Sermons*, p. 157.

there I am with them." We find it when we gather together at the Lord's Table. Worship is communion with Christ. It is both objective and subjective. We know it in our hearts, but we know it very objectively as well. Yes, but at times, at least, to use Ralph Erskine's expression, as a sort of Bethel experience we realize that God himself was there although we did not realize it.

22

HENRY VAN DYKE
AND THE BOOK OF COMMON WORSHIP

The *Book of Common Worship* is a major document for the study of twentieth-century Reformed worship.[1] It has never been for Presbyterians what the *Book of Common Prayer* has been for Episcopalians. It has, however, had a very definite place in the piety of American Presbyterians, especially among those who like to be thought of as "High Church Presbyterians."[2] The *Book of Common Worship* is the expression of a particular age. It has a very particular character and was shaped by a distinct historical figure by the name of Henry van Dyke.

HENRY VAN DYKE: A MAN OF LETTERS

Henry van Dyke (1852–1933) was a man of letters and, in his day, he was one of America's most highly regarded men of letters. The Avalon edition of his works includes eighteen volumes of poems, essays, short stories, and sermons.[3] His essays on literary criticism

---

[1] Our study is based on the following three versions: 1906, 1932, and 1946. *The Book of Common Worship* (Philadelphia: Presbyterian Board of Publication and Sabbath-school Work, 1906); *The Book of Common Worship*, revised (Philadelphia: Presbyterian Board of Christian Education, 1932); and *The Book of Common Worship* (Philadelphia: Published for the Office of the General Assembly by the General Division of Publication of the Board of Christian Education of the Presbyterian Church in the United States of America, 1946). Quotations will come from the 1946 edition, hereinafter, *Book of Common Worship* (1946).

[2] For an analysis of the three editions of the *Book of Common Worship*, see David Rodney Bluhm, *Trends of Worship Reflected in the Three Editions of the Book of Common Worship of the Presbyterian Church in the United States of America* ([Pittsburgh]: s.n., 1957?).

[3] The Avalon edition refers to van Dyke's collection of his printed works. It is named for his home, Avalon, formerly on the corner of Bayard Lane and what is

were highly regarded, as were his fishing stories.

I was brought up to call Henry van Dyke "Cousin Henry." My grandmother was a Chambers, and both the van Dykes and the Chambers are old New Jersey families. I can't tell you just how we are related, but when I was taken down to Princeton to begin my studies at the seminary my grandmother pointed out Avalon, the van Dyke home on Bayard Lane. At that point my grandmother solemnly told me that Cousin Henry had died just a few days before I was born. It was almost as though I had been charged to continue his work.

Henry van Dyke was a minister and the son of a minister.[4] His father was the pastor of suburban Philadelphia's Germantown Presbyterian Church when he was born. Henry van Dyke, Sr., was a rather prominent minister who had done much to repair the divisions between Old School and New School Presbyterianism. Young Henry started his higher education in the Brooklyn Polytechnic Institute. His father had been called to a church in Brooklyn, New York, and this no doubt facilitated his studies there. Then young Henry went on to Princeton to study English literature and theology. His studies at Princeton were followed by two years of travel in Europe. He studied in Berlin under Dorner, an experience which made him wary of liberal Protestantism. His first experience as a pastor was in Newport, Rhode Island, where he was pastor of a Congregational Church. Then in 1883 he was called to be pastor of New York City's Brick Presbyterian Church.

---

now Paul Robeson Place in Princeton. I inherited these volumes from my uncle, A. C. Oliphant, a cousin of van Dyke's. Henry van Dyke, *The Works of Henry van Dyke*, Avalon edition, 18 vols. (New York: Charles Scribner's Son, 1920–27).

[4] For information on the life of Henry van Dyke, see the biography by his son, Tertius van Dyke, *Henry van Dyke, a Biography* (New York: Harper, 1935); William Herman Box, *A Study of the Preaching of Henry van Dyke* (n. p., 1955); Hugh T. Kerr, ed., *Sons of the Prophets: Leaders in Protestantism from Princeton Seminary* (Princeton, NJ: Princeton University Press, 1963); and John R. Wiers, "van Dyke, Henry," in *Dictionary of Christianity in America*, ed. Daniel G. Reid, Robert D. Linder, Bruce L. Shelley, and Harry S. Stout (Downers Grove, IL: InterVarsity Press, 1990), p. 1211.

There he won a reputation for his highly literate sermons. In New York he attracted a congregation of cultured, professional people who were familiar with the movements and interests of the day. He had won such a high reputation as a preacher that in 1902 he was elected Moderator of the Presbyterian General Assembly.

Van Dyke was a great supporter of causes. One of his causes was conservation, and to him and others of like persuasion we owe the national park system. Yellowstone National Park was one of his favorite causes. He wrote an important article for *Harper's* on the wasting of our gifts through soil erosion in the wheatlands of the Red River Valley.[5] Van Dyke firmly believed that God reveals himself in nature. His hymn, "Joyful, joyful, we adore thee," written in 1907, was one of the most frequently sung hymns of the twentieth century. It well expresses van Dyke's literate, optimistic gospel.

> Joyful, joyful, we adore thee,
> God of glory, Lord of love;
> Hearts unfold like flowers before Thee,
> Opening to the sun above.
> Melt the clouds of sin and sadness,
> Drive the dark of doubt away;
> Giver of immortal gladness,
> Fill us with the light of day.

The high point of van Dyke's career as a literary critic came while he was still a young man when he published his study of Alfred Lord Tennyson. Van Dyke regarded Tennyson as the third great English poet along with Milton and Shakespeare. Tennyson was still alive and had attained a venerable age. The great poet invited the young critic to visit him in England and van Dyke accepted. It was a rich reward.[6] One thing is very clear; Van Dyke's appreciation for Tennyson identifies him as a disciple of romanticism.

---

[5] See "Biography of Henry Van Dyke," accessed April 22, 2009, www.poemhunter.com/henry-van-dyke/biography/.

[6] For a longer version of this story, see "Biography of Henry van Dyke."

Another cause heavily supported by Henry van Dyke was liberal democracy. He had been a classmate of Woodrow Wilson at Princeton. Wilson at one point named him ambassador to The Netherlands. Van Dyke pressed for America's entering the First World War on the side of France and eventually became so well known for his support of the approaching war that he had to resign his diplomatic post. To make his point he joined the armed services and became a Navy chaplain. His poem supporting France as the cradle of American democracy was so well known that often American school children were required to memorize it. Van Dyke was a real francophile and at one point was named professor of American literature at the University of Paris. The American poet-preacher was rewarded by his second homeland with a street named after him in the neighborhood of the Arc de Triumphe in Paris.

Henry van Dyke was often involved in very political causes. Several times the Democratic Party published papers which van Dyke had written. In 1917 he wrote an important article, "Fighting for Peace," and then in 1919 he followed it with an equally important article, "What Peace Means."[7]

After the war he settled down in his beautiful home on Bayard Lane in Princeton. As professor of English literature at Princeton his essays on literary criticism carried considerable weight, and he was a spokesman for the culture of the day. He had accomplished much and was recognized for his achievements.

For us it is of particular interest that van Dyke himself considered his greatest accomplishment to be the *Book of Common Worship*, and, indeed, he deserves much of the credit for this book. If it was to Thomas Cranmer that much of the credit goes for the English *Book of Common Prayer*, it is to Henry van Dyke that much of the credit goes for the American *Book of Common Worship*. One thing has to be admitted, however. Van Dyke was better at literary criticism than he

---

[7] "Fighting for Peace" was published separately in New York by Charles Scribner's Sons in 1917. "What Peace Means" was published in New York by Fleming Revell in 1919. Both articles are included in van Dyke, *Works*, vol. 11.

was at Reformed theology. Even more, it has to be said that he understood his own age better than he understood his Reformed theological heritage. Perhaps it was a matter of an overly optimistic enthusiasm for the gradually developing ecumenical spirit of Princeton. The ecumenical spirit was at flood tide at Princeton back in those days. There were a number of Presbyterians who were dreaming of a union of Presbyterians and Episcopalians. This plan of union even came to a vote. The Presbyterians approved it but it was too much for the Episcopalians. There were many who said van Dyke's prayer book was the first step to a union of the two denominations. When the Episcopalians turned it down the movement cooled rapidly. The *Book of Common Worship* never received general acceptance in the Presbyterian Church the way van Dyke had hoped.

A. Van Dyke's Communion Service: The High Tide of Romanticism

Let us look in some detail at the communion service of the *Book of Common Worship*.[8] First of all, we have to agree with the critics of this prayer book that it looks like a slightly re-arranged version of the Anglican *Book of Common Prayer*. It even starts out with that classic collect from the Sarum rite:

> Almighty God, unto whom all hearts are open, all desires known, and from whom no secrets are hid: Cleanse the thoughts of our hearts by the inspiration of Thy Holy Spirit, that we may perfectly love Thee, and worthily magnify Thy holy name; through Christ our Lord. *Amen.*[9]

This is to be followed by the Ten Commandments and the singing of the *Kyrie*:

> Lord have mercy.

---

[8] On the other hand, we have to submit to the discipline of brevity. The bulk of literature on the subject constrains us.

[9] *The Book of Common Worship* (1946), p. 155.

Christ have mercy.
Lord have mercy.

After that we find the Anglican Prayer of Humble Access taken directly from the *Book of Common Prayer*:

> Ye who do truly and earnestly repent of your sins, and are in love and charity with your neighbors, and intend to lead a new life, following the commandments of God, and walking from henceforth in His holy ways: Draw near with faith, and take this Holy Sacrament to your comfort; and make your humble confession to Almighty God.[10]

The strong dependence on the Anglican *Prayer Book* is once again obvious in the unison Prayer of Confession.

> ALMIGHTY God, Father of our Lord Jesus Christ, Maker of all things, Judge of all men; We acknowledge and confess our manifold sins; Which we, from time to time, most grievously have committed; By thought, word, and deed; Against Thy divine majesty. We do earnestly repent; And are heartily sorry for these our misdoings; The remembrance of them is grievous unto us. Have mercy upon us; Have mercy upon us, most merciful Father; For Thy Son our Lord Jesus Christ's sake; Forgive us all that is past; And grant that we may ever hereafter serve and please Thee in newness of life; To the honor and glory of Thy name; Through Jesus Christ our Lord. Amen.[11]

Strangely enough, while Henry van Dyke may have gotten much of this material from the Anglican *Prayer Book*, the Anglican *Prayer Book* itself got much of this material from Reformed sources, namely from the *Strasbourg Psalter*. Some of this material the Reformers seem to have gotten in turn from Prone, a late medieval preaching service popular in the German Rhineland. Eventually

---

[10] *The Book of Common Worship* (1946), p. 156.

[11] *The Book of Common Worship* (1946), p. 156.

some of this material has to be traced back to medieval and patristic sources. This strong dependence on historic source material was quite typical of the Age of Romanticism. This was the era in which Princeton was being filled up not only with gothic chapels but gothic dormitories and refectories.

On the other hand the psalmody so important in Reformed worship has pretty much dropped from sight. A verse or two in the opening sentences are gathered from the Psalms. The singing of a whole metrical psalm would be much more in keeping with the Reformed tradition. What is particularly regrettable is that the Reformed tradition of the communion psalms has left no trace on van Dyke's service. We do not find any indication that Psalm 23, "The Lord is my shepherd," should be sung at communion, or Psalm 133, "How good and pleasant it is when brothers dwell together in unity," or Psalm 24, "Lift up your heads, O ye gates," or Psalm 84, "How lovely is your dwelling place, O Lord of Hosts."

As regards the beginning of the service we get the impression that some pretty standard Reformed traditions have been replaced in some cases word for word by Anglican formularies. One suspects that the desire for the joining of the two denominations is playing a strong role. The communion service proper begins with the Invitation, a collection of Scripture verses inviting the faithful to participate in the sacrament.

> BELOVED in the Lord, hear what gracious words our Saviour Christ saith unto all that truly turn to Him:
>
> Come unto Me, all ye that labor and are heavy-laden, and I will give you rest.
>
> Take My yoke upon you, and learn of Me; for I am meek and lowly in heart: and ye shall find rest unto your souls.
>
> I am the Bread of Life: he that cometh to Me shall never hunger; and he that believeth on Me shall never thirst. Him that cometh to Me I will in no wise cast out.

> Blessed are they which do hunger and thirst after righteousness: for they shall be filled.[12]

After the Invitation, there is a hymn. During the singing of the hymn the elders uncover the table and take their places. With this the minister recites the Words of Institution as they are found in 1 Corinthians 11:

> I have received of the Lord that which also I delivered unto you, That the Lord Jesus the same night in which He was betrayed took bread: and when He had given thanks, He brake it, and said, Take, eat: this is My body, which is broken for you: this do in remembrance of Me. After the same manner He took the cup, when He had supped, saying, This cup is the New Covenant in My blood: this do ye, as oft as ye drink it, in remembrance of Me. For as often as ye eat this bread, and drink this cup, ye do show the Lord's death till He come.[13]

At this point the rubrics direct that the presiding minister should lay his hand on the plate and the chalice: "I take these Elements of bread and wine, to be set apart from all common uses to this holy use and mystery; and as He gave thanks and blessed, let us draw nigh unto God, and present unto Him our prayers and thanksgivings."[14] With this van Dyke would begin his version of the eucharistic prayer. We will take up the subject of the eucharistic prayer in a moment, but first we need to look very carefully at what has happened in this Invitation. A tremendous change has taken place. In the first place we see nothing here that might be called a fencing of the table, or, to use the more ancient term, a dismissal of the catechumen. Theologically what is going on is that those who have heard the gospel preached are now invited to receive Christ. Revivalism made this the focus of the service rather than the actual communion. For the frontier camp meetings the Invitation had become the altar call. On

---

[12] *The Book of Common Worship* (1946), pp. 159–160.

[13] *The Book of Common Worship* (1946), p. 160.

[14] *The Book of Common Worship* (1946), pp. 160–161.

the other hand, the High Church movement ritualized this Invitation as Henry van Dyke has done here. Instead of being invited to receive Christ we are invited to participate in the mystery, that is, in the sacrament. What was so clear in Gilbert Tennent has been totally obscured in the *Book of Common Worship*.

Even more importantly, we have here a setting apart of the elements. Here the bread and wine are set aside by a declaration of the minister rather than by a prayer of invocation. Is this supposed to be an epiclesis? Perhaps it is just one of those compromises that committees inevitably come up with. As it appears in van Dyke's service what we have here is an epiclesis. This striking phrase, "set aside from a common to a sacred use," is found in the *Westminster Directory*. There, however, it quite unambiguously takes the place of an epiclesis. The phrase may possibly go back to Peter Martyr Vermigli who had the theological subtlety to come up with something like that. Still more significantly we notice that the Words of Institution have been taken out of the Eucharistic Prayer to make it clear that the words of Christ concerning his body and blood are to be understood as the Words of Institution, not some sort of consecration formula.

Now let us look at the Eucharistic Prayer. We mean by this quite simply the prayer of thanksgiving over the bread and wine on the Lord's Table. The text of the Words of Institution is quite plain. Jesus took bread and gave thanks; then when the meal came to an end Jesus took the cup and gave thanks, or, as some passages have it, he blessed it. The two mean the same thing. Among the Jews, *giving thanks* for food is the same as *blessing* it. Over the centuries much ink has been spilled over this subject. Just exactly what its function is and how it should be formulated has been the topic of many a learned treatise. We therefore approach the subject on cat's paws.

Basically van Dyke's Eucharistic Prayer is made up of eight paragraphs with an introductory invocation and a concluding doxology. The first paragraph is a paragraph of thanksgiving for the creation, followed by a paragraph of thanksgiving for the works of redemption. Then we find a paragraph of thanksgiving for the institution of the sacrament. The fourth paragraph is the memorial or commemoration. Here the similarity to the Roman mass is obvious. This is followed by the epiclesis or invocation of the Holy Spirit, then the oblation and after that several brief intercessions. The whole is concluded by an elaborate doxology and the Lord's Prayer.

What we have here is essentially what the High Church liturgiologists considered a correct Eucharistic Prayer. What the High Church movement meant by that was a eucharistic prayer which followed the patterns of the fourth and fifth-century liturgies of Basil of Caesarea, the *Apostolic Constitutions*, and the sacramentaries of Leo the Great and Gregory the Great. The liturgical scholarship of the Neo-Gothic Age was elaborate and fastidious, as anyone who has walked through the Princeton Graduate School will recognize. One easily recognizes the similarity of van Dyke's Eucharistic Prayer to the Eucharistic Prayer of the *Apostolic Constitutions* and several other ancient rites. By the time van Dyke got into the subject, nineteenth-century liturgiologists knew quite a bit about the liturgies of the ancient church.

Having made this point, let us look at van Dyke's prayer more closely.[15] He introduces the Eucharistic Prayer with the *Sursum corda*:

> The Lord be with you.
> *And with thy spirit.*
> Lift up your hearts.
> *We lift them up unto the Lord.*
> Let us give thanks unto our Lord God.
> *It is meet and right so to do.*

To be sure the *Sursum corda* goes back at least to the early third century. It is found in the *Apostolic Traditions* of Hippolytus, which may or may not recommend it. Hippolytus was a rather contentious elder in the Church of Rome. At one point he set himself up

---

[15] Again we feel constrained by the discipline of brevity, even though much work by very distinguished scholars has been invested in this subject.

as the true bishop of Rome and organized himself as a rival pope. Apparently he was a good preacher, but a naïve theologian. His understanding of the sacrament of Holy Communion verged on being magical. How it was that his liturgy got preserved is not at all clear. Be that as it may, Calvin following him, saw the theological significance of the *Sursum corda*.[16] Its whole point is to emphasize the transcendent dimension of the Sacrament. All that we do at this sacred table is a heavenly mystery. The main trouble with the *Sursum corda* is that it turns the prayer into a ritual. It turns it into an *opus operandi* rite and makes the whole sacrament seem like a matter of hocus pocus—a matter of magic. We have said this before, but it needs to be said again.

The Eucharistic Prayer continues with an invocation calling on God's name using a number of the biblical names for God:

> It is very meet, right, and our bounden duty that we should at all times and in all places give thanks unto Thee, O Holy Lord, Father Almighty, Everlasting God; who didst create the heavens and the earth and all that in them is; who didst make man in Thine own image and whose tender mercies are over all Thy works.[17]

The prayer, like so many prayers in the *Book of Common Worship*, revels in archaic language. "It is very meet, right, and our bounden duty" may be eloquent, but it is terribly archaic. One hesitates to fuss over the archaic language. Of much more interest is what follows. The prayer develops into a prayer of thanksgiving for God's mighty works of creation, the creation of the heavens and the earth, and the creation of man in the image of God.

At this point the minister is to insert one of the Proper Prefaces, ten of which are given, and they too are very similar to those in the Anglican *Prayer Book*. In most cases the version in the Angli-

---

[16] It was probably William Farel who came up with what is often called the Reformed *Sursum corda*.

[17] *The Book of Common Worship* (1946), p. 161.

can *Prayer Book* was simply translated from the Latin, probably by Thomas Cranmer.

There was a time when the material in these Proper Prefaces made up the main bulk of the Eucharistic Prayer. Even in the days of Basil the Great it was expected that the celebrant would extemporize a hymnic recital of God's mighty acts of creation and redemption. As the fervor of Christian worship cooled in the fifth and sixth centuries this hymn of thanksgiving became shorter and shorter. For the Western rites they were carefully formulated by such men as Pope Leo, Pope Gelasius, and finally Pope Gregory the Great. The Prefaces, like the collects of these liturgical artists, became classics, and even in the age of the Protestant Reformation, they were translated into English. Some of them were probably translated by Thomas Cranmer himself. Here the Anglican *Prayer Book* is at its best. Even at that, van Dyke's *Book of Common Worship* revises these prefaces to lighten the theological language. The Preface for Christmas found in the Anglican *Prayer Book* reads:

> Because thou didst give Jesus Christ, thine only Son, to be born as at this time for us: who, by the operation of the Holy Ghost, was made very man, of the substance of the Virgin Mary his mother; and that without spot of sin, to make us clean from all sin. Therefore with Angels, etc.[18]

While the Preface in the *Book of Common Worship* reads:

> And especially at this time we praise Thee, because Thou didst give Jesus Christ Thine only Son to be born for us of Mary, that through Him we might have power to become the sons of God. Therefore, with angels, etc . . .[19]

While it is clear that van Dyke's committee has edited these Pref-

---

[18] Quotations from the Anglican Prayer Book are taken from *The Book of Common Prayer* (New York: The Church Pension Fund, 1945), p. 77.

[19] *The Book of Common Worship* (1946), p. 166.

aces with a heavy hand, it is also clear that they are based on the Anglican prayers. The fact that these Prefaces go back to the Gregorian, or Gelasian, or Leonine Sacramentaries was just the sort of thing that excited the romanticism of nineteenth century America. These prayers would fit perfectly into the Princeton University Chapel. That was the whole tactic of so many Christians in the Age of Romanticism. The patina of antiquity somehow was supposed to commend the Christian faith to the almost converted.

Let us return to the subject of the first paragraph of the Eucharistic Prayer of van Dyke's *Book of Common Worship*. We need to notice that gradually over the history of the Church this hymnic recital of God's mighty works of redemption has been whittled down. The Eucharistic Prayer originally was supposed to be one long reciting of sacred history. We have examples of this in the eucharistic prayers of St. Basil or the eucharistic prayer found in the *Apostolic Constitutions*. Both of these go back to the mid-fourth century, but one could go back to several of the Psalms, such as Psalm 78, Psalm 105, or Psalm 136, for example. The recounting of sacred history was a major component of biblical worship.

Van Dyke's Eucharistic Prayer continues with the *Sanctus* sung by the whole congregation. Here, again, we have a very ancient prayer that goes far back in the history of the church and even into the synagogue in pre-Christian times. Again what we have here is a highly ritualized prayer that supports an *opus operandi* approach to prayer. The particular function of the *Sanctus* should be to remind us of the heavenly dimension of our worship. We worship here on earth but we worship in the company of the heavenly host. As it appears in these two prayer books, however, the prayer becomes ritualized so that it seems more like an incantation.

As some commentators suggest, the *Sanctus* seems to be misplaced, or maybe it is the Proper Preface that is misplaced. It would seem more obvious that the *Sanctus* would follow the thanksgiving for the creation. Well, that is the way liturgical tradition develops. The final argument is simply, "This is the way we have always done it." For romanticism that was enough.

The object of thanksgiving again changes as this eucharistic prayer remembers God's mighty acts of redemption in Christ. Christ took our nature upon himself and suffered death upon the cross for our redemption. There he made a full, perfect, and sufficient sacrifice for the sins of the whole world. Here, at least, a thoroughly Protestant concern is clearly expressed. Classical Protestantism has always been concerned to emphasize that the sacrifice of Christ was once and for all.

Now the prayer shifts its focus once again. It thanks God for the institution of the sacrament. This makes up the third paragraph of the prayer. The sacrament is to be a perpetual memorial of Christ's death until he comes. Therefore we remember his incarnation and holy life, his passion and precious death, his resurrection, his glorious ascension, and his continual intercession.

What we find troubling here is that van Dyke's prayer races over the subject of the history of redemption. ". . . Thou, of Thy great mercy, didst give Thine only Son Jesus Christ to take our nature upon Him, and to suffer death upon the cross for our redemption; who made there a full, perfect, and sufficient sacrifice for the sins of the whole world . . ."[20] That having been said, the prayer turns our attention to Christ's command that the church observe a memorial of his death and sacrifice until he comes again. The prayer then makes clear that the church now observes this memorial by remembering Christ's sacrifice. This is done by setting forth the gifts of bread and wine as the sacrifice we have been called upon to make. Here is the Oblation, if I understand the text correctly. It is a sacrifice of bread and wine offered up in memory of Christ's sacrifice on the cross.

Here, sad to say, the prayer misses completely the teaching of classical Protestantism. It certainly contradicts what Luther

---

[20] *The Book of Common Worship* (1946), p. 162.

taught in the *Babylonian Captivity of the Church*, what Calvin and Bullinger taught in the *Zurich Consensus*, and what is taught in the Westminster Standards. It may be beautiful literature, but as theology it is misleading.

Following the Oblation is the Epiclesis, the fifth paragraph of the prayer:

> And we most humbly beseech Thee, O merciful Father, to bless and sanctify with Thy Holy Spirit both us and these Thy gifts of bread and wine, that the bread which we break may be the communion of the body of Christ, and the cup of blessing which we bless, the communion of the blood of Christ.[21]

We have already spoken of the minister's declaration that the bread and wine are hereby set aside from a common to a sacred use. Apparently this epiclesis is another approach to the same concern, namely, the consecration of the elements.

Here we get the impression that van Dyke's prayer opens the door to the most primitive views of transubstantiation. The wording, however, is sufficiently ambiguous that one is not exactly nailed down to any one understanding. What does it mean for the bread to be the communion of Christ's body or the wine to be the communion of the blood of Christ? For the Apostle Paul communion in the body and blood of Christ is a strong statement of a covenantal understanding of the sacrament. To share in the meal is to participate in the covenant community. Even before we ask that question we find ourselves wondering what it means to bless and sanctify the bread and wine. The Westminster Standards have used the phrase "to set aside from a common to a sacred use." As I figure it this is a very good interpretation. It claims some sort of consecration but steers clear of any sort of magic. As I have said before, I suspect the phrase goes back to Peter Martyr Vermigli, but I am not finished with him yet.

---

[21] *The Book of Common Worship* (1946), p. 162.

The final paragraph of this Eucharistic Prayer is the most puzzling of all. We read:

> And here we offer and present unto Thee ourselves, our souls and bodies, to be a reasonable, holy, and living sacrifice; and we beseech Thee mercifully to accept this our sacrifice of praise and thanksgiving, as, in the communion of all the faithful in heaven and on earth, we pray Thee to fulfill in us, and in all men, the purpose of Thy redeeming love.[22]

One immediately recognizes, of course, the allusion to Romans 12:1–2 (KJV): "I beseech you therefore, brethren, by the mercies of God, that ye present your bodies a living sacrifice, holy, acceptable unto God, which is your reasonable service." How this phrase got into the Anglican *Prayer Book* is rarely recognized. It is my hypothesis that it was originally from Martin Bucer.[23] Bucer had used the prayer in Strasbourg until 1536 when, inspired by the *Wittenberg Consensus*, he removed it, but the prayer had found its way into Hermann von Wied's proposed liturgy for Cologne, and there Cranmer had found it.

The question is whether the Eucharist is to be understood as the sacrifice of praise and thanksgiving because the consecrated bread and wine are offered up as a sacrifice, or whether it is the recounting of the history of salvation that is offered up as a prayer of thanksgiving and hymn of praise. What the Apostle Paul had in mind in Romans 12:1–2 is the living of the Christian life. This, of course, is consistent with the whole tradition of the Christian interpretation of Micah 6:8 (KJV), "He hath shewed thee, O man, what is good; and what doth the Lord require of thee, but to do justly, and to love mercy, and to walk humbly with thy God?" Romans 12:1–2 does not teach us that the sacrament of Holy Communion is a sacrifice of praise and thanksgiving, but rather

---

[22] *The Book of Common Worship* (1946), p. 162.

[23] See, Hughes Oliphant Old, *The Patristic Roots of Reformed Worship*, American edition (Black Mountain, NC: Worship Press, 2004), pp. 86–87.

that the sacrifice of the true Christian is to do justice, to love mercy, and to walk humbly with God.[24]

The prayer is concluded with a doxology: "Through Jesus Christ our Lord, by whom, and with whom, in the unity of the Holy Spirit, all honor and glory be unto Thee, O Father Almighty, world without end. *Amen.*"[25] The Lord's Prayer is at this point recited by the whole congregation.

Again the minister takes up the Words of Institution, but this time acts them out as he goes:

> According to the holy institution of our Lord Jesus Christ, and in remembrance of Him, we do this: For in the night in which He was betrayed, HE TOOK BREAD,
>
> *Here the presiding Minister shall take the Bread into his hands*
>
> And when he had blessed, and given thanks, HE BRAKE IT,
>
> *Here he shall break the Bread*
>
> And said, TAKE, EAT: THIS IS MY BODY WHICH IS BROKEN FOR YOU: THIS DO IN REMEMBRANCE OF ME. AFTER THE SAME MANNER ALSO, HE TOOK THE CUP
>
> *Here he shall raise the Cup*
>
> Saying: THIS CUP IS THE NEW COVENANT IN MY BLOOD: THIS DO YE, AS OFT AS YE DRINK IT, IN REMEMBRANCE OF ME.[26]

Here, again, there is a major departure from the historic Reformed tradition. Nothing is said about pouring the cup in van Dyke's service. Van Dyke's service, on the other hand, speaks of raising the cup. This sounds like a gesture of offering or oblation. Nothing

---

[24] See my article, "John Calvin and the Prophetic Criticism of Worship," in *John Calvin and the Church: A Prism of Reform*, ed. Timothy George (Louisville: Westminster John Knox Press, 1990).

[25] *The Book of Common Worship* (1946), pp. 162–163.

[26] *The Book of Common Worship* (1946), p. 163.

could be further off the mark for a Reformed celebration, unless it be what follows. After this the *Agnus Dei* is recited:

> O LAMB OF GOD, WHO TAKEST AWAY THE SINS
> OF THE WORLD:
> HAVE MERCY UPON US.
> O LAMB OF GOD, WHO TAKEST AWAY THE SINS
> OF THE WORLD:
> GRANT US THY PEACE.[27]

That all this is printed in capital letters certainly implies that it is understood as a formula of consecration. Nothing, of course, could be more at odds with traditional Reformed theology. The inclusion of the *Agnus Dei* is copied directly from the medieval Roman mass. Here the romanticism of the *Book of Common Worship* is running full force. Whether it is mediated by the Anglican *Prayer Book* I hesitate to say, but however directly or indirectly it may have come, there is no question that it is theologically dependant on a doctrine of the real presence that most American Presbyterians would find superstitious. To say or sing the *Agnus Dei* at this point in the service makes of this hymn a liturgical acclamation hailing Christ who, through the reciting of the words of Christ, is now present on the altar. We have to admit that we have a hard time understanding how it ever came about that a committee of Presbyterians would adopt this service.

After the people have received the communion there is the Post-Communion Thanksgiving:

> ALMIGHTY and everliving God, we most heartily thank Thee that in Thy great love Thou hast fed us at Thy Table with this spiritual food, and hast assured us of Thy goodness toward us; and that we are members of the mystical Body of Thy Son, the blessed company of all faithful people, and heirs of Thine everlasting kingdom. And we beseech Thee, O Heavenly Father, so to assist us with Thy grace that we may continue

---

[27] *The Book of Common Worship* (1946), p. 163.

in this holy fellowship, and live henceforth to Thy glory; through Jesus Christ our Lord, who liveth and reigneth, and is worshiped and glorified, with Thee, O Father and the Holy Spirit, world without end. *Amen.*[28]

Here, again, van Dyke has copied the prayer from the Anglican *Prayer Book.*[29]

Interestingly enough, however, here is one of those prayers found in the Anglican *Prayer Book* that from a theological standpoint is thoroughly Reformed. Like the Prayer of Confession at the beginning of the service it appears to have been modeled ultimately on the prayer of Bucer.

B. An Alternative Order for Liberal Protestantism

One of the most interesting aspects of the *Book of Common Worship* is that it offers a second order for the celebration of the sacrament of Holy Communion. It appears to be the work primarily of Henry van Dyke.[30] We probably have to say that it is not so much a liberal

---

[28] *The Book of Common Worship* (1946), p. 164.

[29] See *The Book of Common Prayer*, p. 83.

[30] There is a story told in our family which sums up, at least for me, the theology of Henry van Dyke. As the modernist-fundamentalist controversy was at its most aggravated, J. Gresham Machen was supplying the pulpit of First Presbyterian Church in Princeton. As my cousin Helen Gibbons told the story, every Sunday he was fulminating tar and feathers in the pulpit and serving it from the communion table. One Sunday it got a bit too rancorous and Cousin Helen stood up in the middle of the sermon and said to Henry van Dyke, who was sitting behind her, "Henry, I am not ill. I am sick." Henry van Dyke, at that point in his life, had a reputation for the discriminating use of words. Cousin Helen, accompanied by her husband, Cousin Herbert, walked home, a short distance of three blocks. Henry van Dyke must have joined them, because he would have had to pass Greenholm, the Gibbons home, on the way to Avalon, the van Dyke home. Somehow a number of other Princeton theologians who were offended by Machen's preaching found themselves at the Gibbons home as well and Cousin Helen found herself serving coffee and cinnamon toast to this impromptu theological symposium meeting in her husband's study. The story was continued by my cousin, Mila Gibbons, who must have been about fifteen years old at the time. Mila was taking a fresh supply of cinnamon toast up to her father's study. When she entered the room the subject was the doctrine of the virgin birth. Henry

Protestant interpretation of the sacrament of the Lord's Supper as it is an attempt to soft peddle the doctrines which liberal Protestants found objectionable. The most obvious example of this tendency in the work of van Dyke generally is his version of the Prayer of Confession. The prayer, of course, in its basic inspiration goes back to Bucer. Cranmer's version as it is found in the *Book of Common Prayer* of 1549 makes very clear the Christian abhorrence of sin.

> Almighty GOD, father of our Lord Jesus Christ, maker of all things, judge of all men, we acknowledge and bewail our manifold sins and wickedness, which we from time to time, most grievously have committed, by thought, word and deed, against thy divine majesty, provoking most justly thy wrath and indignation against us; we do earnestly repent and be heartily sorry for these our misdoings; the remembrance of them is grievous unto us, the burden of them is intolerable: have mercy upon us, have mercy upon us, most merciful father, for thy son our Lord Jesus Christ's sake, forgive us all that is past, and grant that we may ever hereafter, serve and please thee in newness of life, to the honor and glory of thy name: Through Jesus Christ our Lord.[31]

Van Dyke's prayer lightens the burden considerably. Most of us brought up in Presbyterian churches will know it by heart:

> MOST holy and merciful Father; We acknowledge and confess before Thee; Our sinful nature prone to evil and slothful in good; And all our shortcomings and offenses. Thou alone knowest how often we have sinned; In wandering from Thy ways; In wasting Thy

---

van Dyke was summing up his views when Mila heard him say, "When it comes to the virgin birth, I am not the least bit interested in the clinical aspects of the story." For the author of *The Other Wiseman* there was obviously more to Christmas than the Scopes trial would seem to imply. On the other hand, when it came to theology Cousin Henry was imprecise and rather vague.

[31] This prayer is taken from Bard Thompson, *Liturgies of the Western Church* (Philadelphia: Fortress Press, [1961] 1980), p. 260. The spelling and some of the punctuation has been modernized.

gifts; In forgetting Thy love. But Thou, O Lord, have mercy upon us; Who are ashamed and sorry for all wherein we have displeased Thee. Teach us to hate our errors; Cleanse us from our secret faults; And forgive our sins; For the sake of Thy dear Son. And O most holy and loving Father; Help us, we beseech Thee; To live in Thy light and walk in Thy ways; According to the commandments of Jesus Christ our Lord. *Amen.*[32]

Van Dyke's prayer is indeed a confession of sin. It is just that it does not grovel in it.

Let us look at another prayer in this alternative service. It is the first prayer in the communion service proper:

> O GOD, who by the life and death and rising again of Thy dear Son has consecrated for us a new and living way into the holiest of all: Cleanse our minds, we beseech Thee, by the inspiration of Thy Holy Spirit, that, drawing near unto Thee with a pure heart and conscience undefiled, we may receive these Thy gifts without sin, and worthily magnify Thy holy name; through Jesus Christ our Lord. *Amen.*[33]

The prayer apparently intends to take the place of some kind of fencing of the table. It certainly brings in the imagery of entering into the holy of holies, but it has to be admitted that the seriousness of sin is passed over rather awkwardly in spite of the traditional phraseology.

When one thinks about this service over against the whole history of Reformed communion services, one is struck by the fact that very little is said about self-examination, meditation on our guilt, and our sin. The *Book of Common Worship* does allow for a preparatory service, but I have never known of such a service ever being observed except when I tried to hold one in my first church. As for the actual Eucharistic Prayer itself we must say about the same thing. Much

---

[32] *The Book of Common Worship* (1946), p. 12.
[33] *The Book of Common Worship* (1946), p. 171.

classical imagery is used. There is the *Sursum corda*, the *Sanctus*, the Epiclesis and the Oblation from the various medieval and ancient rites, but the operative lines come straight from liberal Protestantism. We notice the same thing with the Prayer of Thanksgiving for the works of creation following the *Sursum corda*:

> It is very meet, right, and our bounden duty that we should at all times give thanks unto Thee, O Lord, our Heavenly Father, for all Thy bounties known and unknown; but chiefly are we bound to praise Thee for Thy great love wherewith Thou hast drawn us to Thyself in Christ and made us to sit in heavenly places with Him, who is our Peace.[34]

Here we detect the pen of Henry van Dyke. "Thou has drawn us to Thyself in Christ and made us to sit in heavenly places with Him, who is our Peace." It is a great line, but again it is theologically vague. For a church that has for centuries taught the importance of the doctrines of creation and providence, the *Book of Common Worship* substitutes "all Thy bounties known and unknown!" Creation is completely sidestepped. Again very traditional language is brought in with the *Sursum corda* and the *Sanctus*, but the doctrinal language is missing. Good traditional literature seems more important than sound doctrine.

The commemoration is again a bare bones confession of the redemptive work of Christ:

> Most gracious God, the Father of our Lord Jesus Christ, whose once offering up of Himself upon the cross we commemorate before Thee: We earnestly desire Thy Fatherly goodness to accept this our sacrifice of praise and thanksgiving: . . .[35]

Van Dyke's commemoration is specifically identified as the sacrifice of praise and thanksgiving. That the memorial of Christ's pas-

---

[34] *The Book of Common Worship* (1946), p. 172.
[35] *The Book of Common Worship* (1946), p. 172.

sion is a sacrifice of praise and thanksgiving we can go along with. It is just that this Eucharistic Prayer would also call the offering of the bread and wine a sacrifice of praise and thanksgiving and even the sacrifice of ourselves as the eucharistic sacrifice.

Another curious feature of van Dyke's alternative order is that it gives us a thumbnail outline of eucharistic doctrine that is quite different from the way van Dyke and his committee actually understood it. The minister is to admonish the congregation:

> As we draw near to the Lord's Table to celebrate the Holy Communion of the body and blood of Christ, we are gratefully to remember that our Lord instituted this Sacrament:
>
> For the perpetual memory of His dying for our sakes and the pledge of His undying love;
>
> As a bond of our union with Him and with each other as members of His mystical Body;
>
> As a seal of His promises to us and a renewal of our obedience to Him;
>
> For the blessed assurance of His presence with us who are gathered here in His name;
>
> And as a pledge of His coming again.[36]

This is probably a pretty good statement of the way a fairly well informed, traditional Presbyterian understood the sacrament of Holy Communion toward the middle of the twentieth century. This is not, however, the direction in which van Dyke and his committee is moving. This obvious contradiction is probably to be explained by the way committees work. But, then, the Anglican *Book of Common Prayer* is filled with similar ambiguities. Both horns of the dilemma are put side by side. That was what held the Elizabethan Settlement together—studied ambiguity. Studied ambiguity may be the glue of Anglicanism. Reformed theologians, however, tend to find it uncomfortable at best.

---

[36] *The Book of Common Worship* (1946), p. 169.

What is rather strange is that as this thumbnail sketch of eucharistic doctrine has it, nothing is said about a eucharistic sacrifice. The Eucharistic Prayer before us, however, misses no opportunity to speak of the sacrifice of praise and thanksgiving, the sacrifice of ourselves, our souls and our bodies, and even the identity of the bread and wine as a sacrifice. At every point where the Anglican *Book of Common Prayer* speaks of sacrifice, this supposedly Presbyterian rite echoes it. Henry van Dyke's rite is far more Anglican than Presbyterian. What one misses in the eucharistic prayers of the *Book of Common Worship* is a full and generous recital of the history of redemption. This should be the most prominent feature of the Eucharistic Prayer. That, after all, is why it is called the Eucharistic Prayer. It is first and foremost a prayer of thanksgiving.

To a serious theologian the eucharistic prayers of the *Book of Common Worship* are a scandal. They are shaped not by eucharistic doctrine but by the spires and gargoyles of romanticism. They express a theology of worship that no informed Presbyterian believed, but they did fit in with the chapels Ralph Adams Cram kept building.

The Post-Communion Thanksgiving of this alternative order is a particularly important prayer. There is much in it that is very commendable. It is a prayer which expresses a concern for the communion of the saints, the mystical presence of Christ at the Supper, and the covenantal union of the members of the body.

> WE GIVE Thee thanks, O Lord, for Thy rich mercy and invaluable goodness, vouchsafed to us in this sacred Communion, wherein we have assurance that we are very members of the mystical Body of Thy Son, and heirs through hope of Thine everlasting kingdom. So enrich us by Thy continual grace that the life of Jesus may be made manifest in our mortal body, and Thy kingdom be furthered through all such good works as Thou hast prepared for us to walk in.
>
> O Almighty God, who has built Thy Church upon

the foundation of the apostles and prophets, Jesus Christ Himself being the head cornerstone: Grant, we beseech Thee, that, being gathered together in unity by Thy Holy Spirit, Thy Church may manifest Thy power among all peoples to the glory of Thy name; through Jesus Christ our Lord, who liveth and reigneth with Thee and the same Spirit, one God, world without end.

Eternal Light, immortal Love, we bless Thy name for all Thy servants who have kept the faith and finished their course and are at rest with Thee. Help us to abide in their fellowship and to follow their example, that we with them may sit down at the marriage supper of the Lamb, which is in heaven. *Amen.*[37]

These prayers express a dimension of eucharistic theology not often found in the history of Reformed theology. Here liberal Protestantism, quite in the spirit of romanticism, has reached back to the piety of the Middle Ages which had developed an elaborate cult of the saints. These Post-Communion Prayers appreciate the continuity of the church from age to age and pray to God for the insight and strength to continue the ministry Christ himself has commissioned the church to continue.

Strangely enough what we find most interesting about the alternative order is the new and fresh material which it offers. Too often, however, it comes up with traditional material made to sound like Elizabethan liturgical prose. These three prayers are fresh and original. They speak to their day but they are masked by the literary forms of an age long passed. The sort of romanticism van Dyke brought to Princeton sounds much like the proposals of Nevin a generation before. We find it all carefully spelled out in an article found in the *Princeton Review* in 1888, written by none other than Henry van Dyke's father.

---

[37] *The Book of Common Worship* (1946), pp. 174–175.

C. The *Book Of Common Worship* in Retrospect

Let me take a few paragraphs to reflect on this work. There are times when the minister wants to get out the *Book of Common Worship* and read it. One of those times, I discovered early in my first pastorate, is when a minister is asked to conduct a funeral for someone who is unknown to the minister or else has only the loosest connection with the church. When that happened to me, I was happy to have the *Book of Common Worship* to read out the prayers and the Scriptures that were provided. On the other hand, when doing the funeral of the mother of one of my elders who had finally been released after months of painful illness, as the attentive pastor I felt I must have something specially prepared.

It is the same way with weddings. Sticking to the book saved me once from a pretty bizarre ceremonial some bride's mother wanted to introduce. Sticking to the book is certainly not always wrong, and I suppose many ministers most often use the *Book of Common Worship* for weddings and funerals. It is well suited to that purpose. It takes no effort or preparation from the minister and it is dignified and intelligent. For those who listen carefully it does have a solid Christian message.

Besides this, it has been around awhile. People recognize it when they see it, at least if they have attended the Presbyterian Church for any length of time. People recognize it when they hear it. It sounds like church almost as much as the sound of the King James Bible. This is a positive accomplishment, especially in those circles where what is wanted is civil religion. Conventional religious rites have their place, especially for military chapels and college graduations. That, however, is not what is supposed to be going on at a celebration of the sacrament of Holy Communion. The Old School Presbyterian communion season was a pretty intense sort of occasion. Henry van Dyke was of an entirely different temperament. Civil religion was just fine with him. He was, after all, a Navy chaplain for a time. The book was also a convenient size and could easily be carried in processions or held in one's hand at the graveside.

The biggest problem with the *Book of Common Worship* was that most serious Presbyterians or Congregationalists, German or Dutch Reformed, expect more from their minister than read prayers. We regard leading in prayer as an important part of the gospel ministry. Samuel Miller had made that very clear in his manual on public prayer back in the days when Princeton Seminary was founded. The great Elizabethan Puritan, William Perkins, had opened up this line of thought in his famous *Art of Prophesying*, pointing out that it was not only important for the prophet to proclaim the Word of God to the people but just as much it was the prophet's ministry to offer up the prayers of the people to God. As the times change, so do the needs of the people, and it is important for the minister to discern these changes. The great example of the Puritan approach to public prayer was the book by Matthew Henry, whom we treated at considerable length in chapter 12. That the minister should give an appreciable amount of time to prepare to lead the congregation in public prayer is surely one of the basic principles of Reformed worship.

What one misses in the communion service of the *Book of Common Worship* is a comprehensive and straightforward prayer of thanksgiving for God's mighty acts of creation and redemption. This Eucharistic Prayer would be said over the bread and wine as a recounting of the history of salvation, the memorial Christ himself instituted. It should be a prayer in the tradition of Matthew Henry and Samuel Miller. Improvisation they had developed into an art. It was carefully premeditated and yet spontaneous and free flowing when actually offered up in the course of the service of worship. That was the art of leading in prayer.

One thing which is very clear about the *Book of Common Worship* is that it was never entrusted to the hands of the people as was the Episcopalian *Book of Common Prayer*. The *Book of Common Worship* always remained a book of the professional clergy. To use what would probably be a more popular term, the *Book of Common Worship* is a service book. It never had anything like the authority behind it that the *Book of Common Prayer* had. The *Book of Common Prayer* was vigorously promulgated by King Edward VI, enforced by Queen Elizabeth I, and down almost to our day had the authority of the state behind it. It also had the authority of the hierarchy of the Church of England. That, however, was not the case with the *Book of Common Worship*. Not even the most enthusiastic supporters of the *Book of Common Worship* were able to get the General Assembly to go along with anything more than a commendation for voluntary use.

The best way we can describe what the *Book of Common Worship* did to the communion service was simply to formalize it. For American Presbyterians, Holy Communion had been for more than two hundred years a major event in the life of the congregation, requiring special preaching and services of prayer lasting over several days. With the communion service in the *Book of Common Worship*, it is all pretty much cut and dried so that if the minister does not preach too long it can all be done in the space of an hour. It is sort of like what happened to Christian worship in the Age of Justinian. It was codified. Reformed worship got its Code of Justinian, so to speak.

Apparently there were a few holdouts in the matter of preparatory services and there were plenty of ministers who customarily cut out large parts of the service or who improvised parts here and there, but essentially one did not really have to give much thought to celebrating Communion. One just read most of it out of the book. The unfortunate thing about it was that interest in the sacrament plummeted during this period. This was especially the case during the middle of the twentieth century. The *Book of Common Worship* became a crutch for American Presbyterians. It was a great resource for those who did not have time to bother about sacramental niceties. Presbyterian ministers were interested in other things in the Fifties, Sixties, and Seventies.

One of the most unhappy developments of the *Book of Common Worship* was its complete surrender to the neo-gothic religious mystique. It tended to be more influenced by romanticism than anything more theological. The Anglican High Church movement seems to have influenced the *Book of Common Worship* as much as anything else. That was true of Nevin as well as of van Dyke. The *Book of Common Worship* was a reaction against the frontier revivals, but it reacted in a definitely High Church direction. Yet, with all these problems there was one important contribution of the two communion services in Henry van Dyke's *Book of Common Worship*. The services conveyed a sense of reverence and awe that for Presbyterians is essential to worship. They may not be solidly Reformed in their theology, but the language at least is classic. The flow of the service is dignified.

To be honest, I have to admit my ambiguity at this point. Recently one of my cousins up in Princeton died, and I had been asked to do the funeral at the Princeton University Chapel. Although her father had been a Presbyterian minister she didn't get to church very often. The cousin was a Christian, to be sure, but also a prominent member of the arts community in Princeton. She was a dancer and presided over a rather avant garde dance studio. The family and I decided to read the service out of Henry van Dyke's prayer book. That was what we did, and it was perfect. And, yet, that night I had a hard time getting to sleep. Had Old School Presbyterianism completely dried up and blown away?

To be sure a funeral is one thing and a service of Holy Communion is quite another, and it is the service of Holy Communion that is the subject of our inquiry. It is just that that particular experience of using the *Book of Common Worship* held in the Princeton University Chapel brought together a lot of my conflicting thoughts. Yes, there are some real values in the *Book of Common*

Worship, but there are also glaring problems.

As best as I can figure it, the communion service we find in the *Book of Common Worship* is not Reformed at all. It misses the covenantal understanding of the sacraments taught by the sixteenth-century Reformers. Furthermore, it ignores the service envisioned by the *Westminster Directory*. It particularly falls short of the tradition of conceived prayer so profoundly developed by Matthew Henry, Isaac Watts, and Samuel Miller. The basic problem is quite simple. Reformed theology and romanticism just don't fit together too well. John Calvin and Alfred Lord Tennyson are never going to feel too comfortable with each other. Or, to put it another way, it is going to take the grace of heaven to reconcile Sir Walter Scott and John Knox.

23

JEAN-JACQUES VON ALLMEN
AND THE ECUMENICAL APPROACH

It is only after considerable hesitation that I write on this subject, in which I have been so personally involved.[1] I will obviously treat it more subjectively, but then, on the other hand, there is a special value to that as well. Whenever we speak of worship, we are bound to be subjective about it. Jean-Jacques von Allmen I regard as my Doctor Father, and to him I owe great respect.[2]

Somehow I got a double dose of the ecumenical movement. John Alexander Mackay, one of the leaders of the ecumenical movement, was the theologian I admired most when I was at Princeton in the mid-fifties. He was prominent in a very different phase of the ecumenical movement. He was so Scottish and so Reformed and so passionate as a missionary to the Third World. Von Allmen was different. He was a man who lived on the border. He was born in Lausanne and brought up in Basel, a German-speaking city. He attended the French-speaking Protestant church. He was self-consciously a French-speaking person. Neuchâtel is a French-speaking town, but ten minutes down the railroad track is Canton Bern, just as clearly German-speaking. I never heard

---

[1] Between 1966 and 1971 I studied the history of Christian worship under Jean-Jacques von Allmen. I first went over to Europe in 1964 and studied in Tübingen for two years, then moved to Neuchâtel where I lived for the next three years. Following von Allmen's advice I then studied in Paris and finally I spent two years in Basel as his student.

[2] For biographical material on von Allmen, see the introductory essay in Albert du Pury, ed., *Communio Sanctorum: Mélanges offerts à Jean-Jacques von Allmen* (Geneva: Labor et Fides, 1982); and "Jean-Jacques von Allmen," www.puritanboard.com/f18/jean-jacques-von-allmen-32420/, accessed October 7, 2012.

von Allmen speak German, but he must have been fluent in it. As a child he must have picked it up on the streets. Besides that, lectures in the theological faculty of Basel are in German. He read German theologians all the time, but still he always spoke French. One time he told me, "Oh, you don't have to read all that German theology. It is too morose." He didn't mean that literally, of course, but he had his own set of cultural hang-ups.

A BORDER THEOLOGIAN

Von Allmen's theological education was strongly under the influence of both Karl Barth and Oscar Cullmann. They were at the center of the theological world in which he was brought up. This might not have come out when he spoke in an international context, but in the lectures he gave and the stories he told in a more intimate context, it came out again and again. For von Allmen, Basel was home—just across the Rhine from Germany and just at the end of the street car line from France.

It was in 1936, while von Allmen was still a teenager, that he was sent to spend some time in England. This is the sort of thing Swiss families still do with their children if they want them to be in either the business or academic world. They send them off to live with friends or relatives who live in England or some other country where they will learn another language. That year in England was a turning point for von Allmen. The Church of England really excited him. He loved the pageantry. He found his home church back in Switzerland drab by comparison. From that point on von Allmen was a closet Anglican.

Interestingly enough he started his theological education at the Free Church seminary in Lausanne. It was in 1936 that he began his theological studies—just before the war. I do remember that from time to time he made negative remarks about the evangelicals of Canton Vaud. Perhaps his mother was Vaudois, but otherwise I have not been able to discover von Allmen's connection to

23: JEAN-JACQUES VON ALLMEN AND THE ECUMENICAL APPROACH

Lausanne. The distinct impression I got from almost three years of hearing his lectures was that it was in Basel that he really studied theology. He did, however, do his doctorate in Neuchâtel, but this is probably due to the fact that the von Allmen family from generations back was Neuchatelois. Each Swiss citizen is the citizen of his ancestral canton. I remember Madame von Allmen showing me a magnificent seventeenth-century armoire one time and explaining that it had come down in the von Allmen family and that the von Allmen family had lived in Neuchâtel a long time. That is the way things work in Switzerland. The Second World War was well underway when he received his degree in theology in 1941.

Following the usual Swiss pattern, von Allmen did his internship in a small church in the Val-de-Travers, then filled a number of other posts. He was a bit longer at Liniers on the Lake of Neuchâtel. For a while he was pastor of the French-speaking church of Lucerne, a small city in the heart of Inner Switzerland where the thickest Schweitzer Deutsch is spoken.

For von Allmen the writing of his doctoral thesis was an opportunity to dig deeply into the history of the Church of the Canton of Neuchâtel.[3] He wrote on the great Neuchatelois preacher, Jean-Frédéric Ostervald, who in the late seventeenth century opened up the Church of the Canton of Neuchâtel to the influences of Anglican moderatism as it was developed by such men as Archbishop Tillotson.[4] He defended his thesis at Neuchâtel in 1948. Anglicanism remained a continuing influence in von Allmen's thought for the rest of his life. Von Allmen was always a great supporter of episcopacy, and began to work this out in his doctoral thesis.

It was in 1958 that von Allmen was called to be professor of

---

[3] Jean-Jacques von Allmen, *L'Église et ses fonctions d'après Jean-Frédéric Ostervald: Le problème de la théologie pratique au début du XVIIIme siècle* (Neuchâtel and Paris: Delachaux et Niestlé, 1947).

[4] Hughes Oliphant Old, *The Reading and Preaching of the Scriptures in the Worship of the Christian Church*, vol. 5, *Moderatism, Pietism and Awakening* (Grand Rapids, MI: Eerdmans, 2004), pp. 34–38.

practical theology. His understanding of the field of practical theology has always had a profound influence on me. I remember one time he put it most lucidly: Practical theology begins with the doctrine of the Holy Spirit and works itself out in the doctrine of the church. Von Allmen was one of those twentieth-century theologians who gave special attention to the doctrine of the church. But, then, from the doctrine of the church von Allmen would move to the doctrine of the ministry, sacramental theology, and finally to the worship of the church, that is, to liturgy. One notices that von Allmen has left us major works on each of these subjects.[5]

One of the most revealing things I remember about my work with von Allmen was the subjects he assigned me for my preliminary exams. First of all he wanted me to study the *Lumen gentium* of the Second Vatican Council. He wanted me to read all those classics of modern liberal Catholicism that were still hot off the press, the works of Yves Congar, Jean Daniélou, Henri de Lubac, Antoine Chavasse, Jean Leclercq, and Lucien Cerfaux. Second, he wanted me to study the doctrine of the ministry in the *Second Helvetic Confession*, the doctrine of the sacraments in the Gospel of John, and finally the place of icons in Christian worship. He was all in favor of icons and was perfectly willing to understand them as the Orthodox churches do today. How a student of Barth could go along with the Russian Orthodox theology of icons is a mystery to me, but that was von Allmen. It was a tremendously interesting course of study that he set for me, but it was also a good catalogue of the subjects that most occupied his own mind. Surely this is why he never lost my interest.

It was only after I had been in Neuchâtel for a while that I

---

[5] For an introduction to von Allmen's works on worship and the ministry, see Jean-Jacques von Allmen, *Preaching and Congregation*, trans. B. L. Nicholson (Richmond: John Knox Press, [1962]); Jean-Jacques von Allmen, *Prophétisme sacramentel: neuf études pour le renouveau et l'unité de l'Église* (Neuchâtel: Delachaux et Niestlé, 1964); Jean-Jacques von Allmen, *Le saint ministère* (Genève: Centre protestant d'études, 1965); and Jean-Jacques von Allmen, *Worship: Its Theology and Practice* (New York: Oxford University Press, 1965). For a complete bibliography see, du Pury, *Communio Sanctorum*.

began to realize that there was considerable opposition to von Allmen's "ecumenical tendency." Several Neuchâtel pastors made sure I understood that von Allmen certainly did not speak for the majority of Swiss Reformed pastors. It was just that von Allmen had brought such vitality to the theological faculty at Neuchâtel that most people were willing to put up with some of his catholicising ideas. Ever since von Allmen's appointment to Neuchâtel the place had taken off, but still there was real uneasiness about his teaching. As one of the other faculty members put it to me one time, There is an old proverb, "A leaning wall will eventually fall in the direction in which it leans." But from 1966 to 1971 when I was in Neuchâtel, ecumenical feelings were at their height.

An important facet of von Allmen's ministry was his involvement with the World Council of Churches. As a member of the Faith and Order Commission he found himself at the highest level of ecumenical discussion. He often spoke about the discussions that were current at the time. I remember particularly his report of his visit to Brazil. It must have been about 1970. What he had found particularly interesting was the charismatic churches of Brazil. He was very much inspired by them. Particularly interesting to him was that they really had an episcopate. A charismatic pastor functioned as a bishop. At least, that was how it looked in Brazil. For von Allmen that was a very positive point.

From 1972–1974 my beloved Doctor Father served as director of the Ecumenical Institute at Tantur in Jerusalem. I was not in direct personal contact with him at the time. Indirectly I heard that he was enjoying it with his usual *joie de vivre*. Von Allmen's most popular publication is, without doubt, his Bible dictionary, *La vocabulaire biblique*, which made him well-known to biblical scholars around the world.[6] It had been translated into a good number of languages, and that made him especially appropriate for the post in Jerusalem.

---

[6] Jean-Jacques von Allmen, ed., *La vocabulaire biblique* (Neuchâtel: Delachaux et Niestlé, 1954).

Still another dimension of our theologian's ministry was his editing of the collection *Bibliographie*, published by Delachaux et Niestlé.[7] This collection includes over fifty titles, many having to do with the concerns of the ecumenical movement, and especially ecumenical worship. One notices particularly Jean de Watteville's book on the eucharistic sacrifice, F. J. Leenhardt's study of the doctrine of transubstantiation, Oscar Cullmann's book on the worship of the ancient church, and Max Thurian's apologetic for the eucharistic memorial. These books all have in common an attempt to reclaim a more Catholic understanding of worship. Essentially, what von Allmen believed was that the reformed Catholicism advocated by liberal French theologians of the time would eventually win over the whole of Christianity.

THE ECUMENISM OF TAIZÉ

An important dimension of my studies at Neuchâtel was participating in the retreats at Taizé. Taizé is just across the French border from Neuchâtel, a couple of hours by car. A group of theological students from Neuchâtel had organized the first retreat I went on. I was still struggling to understand French, but I brought home a lot of the literature from Taizé, and in the following months, I studied it carefully. I listened to the tapes I purchased at Taizé until I had them down by heart. It was a good way of getting my French devotional vocabulary straight. For a student of John Mackay it soon became most apparent that the twentieth century offered more than one approach to ecumenism.

A few months later I returned to Taizé alone, this time prepared to stay several weeks. I must have spent a total of two months at Taizé while I was a student at Neuchâtel. At the time the brothers at Taizé understood themselves as Christians from various traditions—Lutheran, Anglican, Reformed, Roman

---

[7] Jean-Jacques von Allmen, *Bibliographie J. J. Von Allmen, 1939–1957* [i.e. 1967] (Neuchâtel: Delachaux et Niestlé, 1968).

23: Jean-Jacques von Allmen and the Ecumenical Approach

Catholic, and Orthodox—living together in a community that they regarded as prophetic of the ecumenical church that was to come. They did not think of themselves as a Reformed monastic community as is sometimes suggested. Nevertheless, they sort of hinted around that they were what they thought Reformed was really supposed to be. They had their own approach to being "truly Reformed."

There were a few things, however, that were troubling. If the brothers wanted to build the ecumenical church of the future, why did they make such a point of their continuing the tradition of Cluny? Cluny, the greatest monastic community of medieval France, was just a few miles down the road. The mobs of the French Revolution had torn it down stone by stone two hundred years ago. The romanticism of Taizé was undeniable. Liturgically considered, the worship of Taizé is best described as stripped down, modernized Catholicism with a few nods to Eastern Orthodoxy. The only thing that Taizé had adopted from a Protestant liturgical tradition was a Bach prelude or postlude on a portable organ.

One of the highlights of my visit to Taizé was an interview with Max Thurian. I had read the English translation of his study on the eucharistic memorial as well as Brevard Childs' rebuttal. I found Childs more convincing. Thurian had made a major departure from classical Reformed eucharistic theology, as far as I could see. Still, I appreciated the interview. A few years later, however, the wall fell in the direction it was leaning, as one of my professors at Neuchâtel had said it would. Max Thurian converted to Catholicism.

Before Brother Max made his departure from Protestantism I noticed that von Allmen was becoming more and more critical of Taizé and especially of the founder of Taizé, Roger Schutz. My opinion at the time was that it was a personal antipathy. I think von Allmen would have celebrated the Lord's Supper pretty much the way it was celebrated at Taizé if he had had the opportunity, and yet I don't think von Allmen liked Schutz.

In addition, von Allmen was not terribly interested in a revival of monasticism. He was married at the age of twenty-four, as soon as he got a job. Anyone who knew the von Allmens realized they were a particularly happy couple. An interesting aspect of their life together was that von Allmen and his wife celebrated the eucharist in their home every Sunday. They celebrated it together, just the two of them. In time, if I have it right, he thought better of the practice. That, at least, was the context in which he confessed it to me. One thing was clear; he was genuinely concerned that I had not yet found a wife. Such was his fatherly care for his students. Another thing that should be said is that von Allmen was never too interested in the Neo-Platonism that was often such a strong component of the new "ecumenical faith." I never remember him endorsing Lenten fasting. On the other hand, the rediscovery of the theology of Origen by Jean Daniélou was in full bloom when I was in Neuchâtel. Von Allmen, however, enjoyed life too much to be a real ascetic.

ESSAY ON THE LORD'S SUPPER

Von Allmen in his *Essay on the Lord's Supper* gives an important statement of the "ecumenical" approach to a celebration of the Lord's Supper.[8] Here we must underline that what we are dealing with is not an attempt at defining a "Reformed" understanding of the sacrament so much as an "ecumenical" understanding. In a French-speaking theological world, of course, this "ecumenical" discussion will have to be largely with Roman Catholics. In America, however, we can have a significant ecumenical discussion without the Catholics. The question for von Allmen seemed to be to what extent the Protestant protests are still salient. During the period in which I studied with von Allmen, he never imagined the almost total rejection of the ecumenical movement, first by Pope John Paul II and

---

[8] Von Allmen, *The Lord's Supper* (London: Lutterworth Press, 1969).

now by Pope Benedict XVI.[9] The very long pontificate of John Paul was a crippling blow to the ecumenical movement as von Allmen saw that movement. In fact, it was probably a mortal blow. Be all that as it may, let us turn to von Allmen's *Essay on the Lord's Supper*.

The title of von Allmen's *Essay on the Lord's Supper* is carefully chosen. An essay is a short, informal attempt to treat a subject. An essay is very different from a treatise which intends to give a complete, formal treatment of a subject. The title suggests that the author sees himself as striking out into uncharted territory. He is not attempting to redefine the Reformed doctrine of the Lord's Supper but rather to sketch out the dimensions of a new ecumenical approach to the sacrament. As von Allmen sees it, this new ecumenical approach is called for because the latest scholarship has called into question much of the older literature on the subject.[10] Hans Lietzmann's *Messe und Herrenmahl* had recently been published suggesting that the sacrament was pretty much the creation of the church from two different sources.[11] On the other hand, Joachim Jeremias was beginning to show that the Lord's Supper was indeed a celebration of Passover.[12]

For a student of Cullman it is not surprising that von Allmen is quite content to find the sacraments in the New Testament. Still one is a bit surprised to find that, for a student of Barth, von Allmen figures the Scriptures alone do not provide sufficient grounds for developing our observance of the Sacrament. For von Allmen it is quite clear that our approach should have both a biblical and an ecclesiastical dimension. At this point it is evident that von

---

[9] Von Allmen may have died before John Paul II's rejection of the ecumenical movement had become quite clear.

[10] Von Allmen, *The Lord's Supper*, p. 10.

[11] Von Allmen, *The Lord's Supper*, p. 11. The actual work is available as Hans Lietzmann, *Messe und Herrenmahl: eine Studie zur Geschichte der Liturgie* (Bonn: A. Marcus und E. Weber's Verlag, 1926). A translation was later made: Hans Lietzmann, *Mass and Lord's Supper: A Study in the History of the Liturgy*, trans. Dorothea H. G. Reeve (Leiden: E. J. Brill, 1979).

[12] Von Allmen, *The Lord's Supper*, p. 12.

Allmen's approach is indeed ecumenical rather than Reformed. Reformed theologians have been insistent that our worship is to be reformed according to Scripture alone.

One of von Allmen's arguments which came through frequently in his lectures is that the New Testament church maintained a *disciplina arcana*, as did the Hellenistic mystery religions.[13] Early Christians did not talk about their mysteries with those who were not members and therefore the New Testament does not tell us very much about the Lord's Supper. If that is the case, how could we expect to find in the New Testament enough material to develop a eucharistic liturgy or a doctrinal explanation of the sacrament? Either directly or indirectly von Allmen was much too much influenced by Odo Casel's *Das christliche Kultmysterium*.[14]

As I have already suggested, von Allmen is really a closet "High Church" Anglican. There are, to be sure, plenty of Anglicans who are Reformed, but in the course of time there were Anglicans who wished to develop a compromise between Reformed and Catholic, and one of the places which we begin to find this is in the doctrine of Scripture and tradition. It was John Whitgift, archbishop of Canterbury during the reign of Elizabeth I, who insisted that Scripture is not sufficient to draw up and regulate the worship of the Church. One had to depend on the tradition of the church as well. Whitgift accused the Puritans of following the Anabaptists in invoking the regulative principle. Whitgift's exaggeration of the Reformed approach to worship has been attempted by friend and foe alike. Be that as it may, the position of the Reformed churches has always been that it is Scripture alone that is to guide the church in shaping its worship. Rather curiously von Allmen tries to get around the theological impasse by telling us that our worship should be both ecclesial and biblical.[15] All von Allmen gives

---

[13] Von Allmen, *The Lord's Supper*, p. 13.

[14] Odo Casel, *Das christliche Kultmysterium* (Regensburg: F. Pustet, 1948).

[15] Von Allmen, *The Lord's Supper*, p. 19.

us is a slight tampering with terminology. It is hardly a substantial compromise. The old impasse still stands.

Von Allmen's ecumenical approach is called for because, as he sees it, there have been important advances made in biblical research. In one respect, of course, he is right. There have been important steps forward, but this does not necessarily make for greater agreement in the matter of eucharistic theology. Von Allmen read widely in the biblical studies that were so prolifically produced in the mid-twentieth century. It was during the flowering of von Allmen's ministry that Gerhard Kittel produced his great *Dictionary of the New Testament* and von Allmen would have read all this when it came out.[16]

A. THE NEW BIBLICAL PHILOLOGY

Von Allmen's use of the newer biblical research is exemplified by his explanation of the meaning of the *anamnesis*, "remembrance." This is an important word for eucharistic theology. Jesus tells us that when we observe the Lord's Supper we are to do it in remembrance of him.[17] Somehow, in the way von Allmen reads the research of his day, this means that in the celebration of the sacrament of Holy Communion "the church offers to God in the broken bread and in the cup of the New Covenant the very symbols of Christ's sacrifice."[18] Here, too, we notice a major departure from classical Reformed theology. To be sure, there is a sense in which the Prayer of Thanksgiving so central to the rite is a sacrifice. Prayer is always a sacrifice of praise and thanksgiving. The Scriptures make this very

---

[16] Von Allmen, *The Lord's Supper*, p. 24. Kittel's work began around 1932 and was finished after he died in 1948. Gerhard Kittel and Gerhard Friedrich, eds., *Theologisches Wörterbuch zum NeuenTestament*, 10 vols. (Stuttgart: W. Kohlhammer, 1932–1979). The work was translated beginning in 1964: Gerhard Kittel and Gerhard Friedrich, eds., *Theological Dictionary of the New Testament*, trans. and ed. Geoffrey W. Bromiley, 10 vols. (Grand Rapids, MI: Eerdmans, 1964–1976).

[17] Von Allmen, *The Lord's Supper*, p. 23.

[18] Von Allmen, *The Lord's Supper*, p. 28f.

clear (see Psalm 50:14 and 23, Hebrews 13:15, and 1 Peter 2:5, etc.). The offering of the bread and cup is another matter entirely, and this goes back to the bedrock of the Protestant theology of worship—Luther's *Babylonian Captivity of the Church*.

Because von Allmen read everything and because he was committed to a very inclusive ecumenism, his written works are often contradictory. On the question of the eucharistic sacrifice he can discuss such different authorities as Joachim Jeremias, Pierre Benoît, and Alan Richardson.[19]

B. THE BYZANTINE DOCTRINE OF THE HOLY SPIRIT

As von Allmen saw it there was no more pressing component of an ecumenical eucharistic theology than a strong doctrine of the Holy Spirit. Von Allmen's teaching on this subject I always found most helpful. My impression is that von Allmen's interest in the doctrine of the Holy Spirit was fueled by quite a bit of personal contact with the Russian Orthodox community in Paris. At the time I was doing my doctoral studies with von Allmen in Neuchâtel, Boris Bobrinskoy was also doing his studies with von Allmen, and I got the impression that the two were very close. As a result, I made a point of reading a lot of material on Eastern Orthodox theology.

For von Allmen the function of the *epiclesis* in the Byzantine liturgy was a major emphasis. He defined the epiclesis as, "the Prayer which calls on the Holy Spirit to act so that the Supper really becomes what Jesus Christ intended when he instituted it."[20] One easily understands why the Byzantine theologians were so offended by the Western theologians when they discovered that their mass had no *epiclesis*. It looked to them like a weakening of the doctrine of the Trinity.[21] The work of the Father was men-

---

[19] Von Allmen, *The Lord's Supper*, p. 29.

[20] Von Allmen, *The Lord's Supper*, p. 30.

[21] Von Allmen, *The Lord's Supper*, p. 33.

tioned in the canon as was the work of the Son, but the work of the Holy Spirit was not. Von Allmen figured that this was one of the wrongs which a true ecumenical compromise should set right. In fact, much of von Allmen's ecumenical synthesis is concerned with justifying several of the historic causes of the Eastern Orthodox churches. Here is one of those places where von Allmen's mastery of the history of Christian worship becomes evident to those who have read the extensive literature. Von Allmen may seem a bit obscure to many at this point, but it is because he has taken part in a discussion to which most of us have had little access.[22]

C. Baptismal Discipline

It is at this point that we should by all means bring in von Allmen's particular concern for the recovery of pre-baptismal catechetical disciplines. Baptism, as von Allmen sees it, must be preceded by a thorough course of catechetical instruction and the maintaining of an acceptable Christian life for a certain period of time. In other words, von Allmen was in staunch opposition to infant baptism.[23] Here, of course, the influence of Karl Barth is evident. As with Barth it is not that infant baptism is invalid so much as it is unwise.

Von Allmen's ecumenical compromise was to give something to the evangelicals and radical Protestants, as he regarded them. In the same way he wanted to include Brazilian charismatics. This may sound a bit strange to us that one so devoted to "High Church" causes should so strongly oppose infant baptism, but it is to be explained by the influence of Karl Barth, on one hand, and a concern to be fair to all sides in his ecumenical passion to include all parties. Von Allmen was above all a fair and generous man, and his vision of the ecumenical church went all the way from the Armenian Orthodox to Brazilian Pentecostals. My Doctor Father would not have been happy with today's situation. As

---

[22] Von Allmen, *The Lord's Supper*, p. 34.
[23] Von Allmen, *The Lord's Supper*, p. 37.

I remember it, von Allmen was embarrassed by the way Markus Barth had developed his father's teaching on baptism. He figured that Markus had done away with sacraments in general. He was also embarrassed that his colleagues presented their infant children for baptism. No one seemed to be following Karl Barth's suggestion! Here von Allmen very definitely veered away from classical Reformed teaching. In regard to von Allmen's appreciation of the charismatics, however, not too many ecumenical theologians felt positively toward them.

D. Episcopacy

Von Allmen's confidence that episcopacy was of the essence of the church was one of the first things communicated by his lectures. His emphasis on episcopacy was so strong that, if I remember correctly, he regarded episcopacy as a presupposition of the ecumenical movement.[24] This was not one of those things which in the course of the ecumenical movement could be compromised or modified. My impression was that von Allmen was rather hard-nosed on this point, although being hard-nosed was not characteristic of von Allmen. Looking back on it today I am beginning to realize that without this "High Church" approach to episcopacy the Catholics would never go along with the ecumenical movement, and the whole thing would be lost. Now, of course, we realize von Allmen was right. Episcopacy does seem to be a requirement of the ecumenical movement.

Von Allmen figured that as early as Ignatius of Antioch the church recognized that episcopacy was essential to the existence of the church.[25] As von Allmen saw it, every flock must have a shepherd or it is not a flock. Every family must have a father or it is a collection of orphans gathered around a widow. Every bishop

---

[24] The literature at the time ran rather strongly in that direction, as I remember.
[25] Von Allmen, *The Lord's Supper*, p. 46.

23: Jean-Jacques von Allmen and the Ecumenical Approach

(or overseer) must have a charge.[26] This hierarchical structure is of the essence of the eucharistic celebration, as von Allmen sees it. One time von Allmen and I were discussing this privately and I told him he might be able to sell some nineteenth-century English Tories on something like that but an American Presbyterian, never. With a good-natured poke, he responded, "How do you think it goes over in the free county of Neuchâtel?" Von Allmen had high hopes that his ecumenical vision was destined to come to fruition.

What is surprising is that von Allmen sees this patriarchal, or, even better, hierarchal, structure as of the essence of the eucharist. If I have understood von Allmen correctly, the versicles that are so important to "High Church" liturgy demonstrate this patriarchal structure. It is therefore that the versicles are essential to an ecumenical liturgy:

> Lift up your hearts.
> We lift them up unto the Lord...
> Let us pray...

As von Allmen saw it, it is when clergy and laity cooperate that the eucharistic sacrifice is most rightly offered up.[27] My personal opinion is that what we really find in Ignatius of Antioch is a very clear example of the influence of the Neo-Platonic concept of hierarchy having a very strong influence on the organizational structure of the sub-apostolic church.

E. The Supper as Fraternal Communion

Here is one place where von Allmen's ecumenical approach to the sacrament picks up a strong Reformed emphasis. As our Swiss theologian puts it, "The Supper is a two-fold communion: it unites Christ and the Church; it unites Christians to one another. These two aspects are indissoluble, the latter being determined and also

---

[26] Von Allmen, *The Lord's Supper*, p. 44.
[27] Von Allmen, *The Lord's Supper*, pp. 47–48.

implied by the former."²⁸ Communion is first of all communion between Christ and the church. We find this two different ways in the New Testament. We find it as communion *with* Christ and we find it as communion *in* Christ. The story of Jesus sharing a meal with the two disciples at the inn at Emmaus is an example of communion with Christ as well as the text from Revelation 3:20 where Jesus promises that when we open the door to his knock he will come in and eat with us and we with him. In 1 Corinthians 10:16, however, the Apostle Paul speaks of communion in Christ. "The cup of blessing which we bless, is it not a participation in the blood of Christ? The bread which we break, is it not a participation in the body of Christ?" (1 Cor. 10:16, RSV). Von Allmen then goes on to interpret this text by telling us that "Paul does so because for him the intention of the Supper is to incorporate believers into Christ himself."²⁹

It is at this point that von Allmen makes two very important observations. In the first place here is one example where the New Testament really nails down its doctrine of the real presence. If Christ is not really present at the meal, how can we speak of sharing a meal with him? Von Allmen supports this with a quotation from none other than John Calvin, "To deny that true communion with Jesus Christ is offered to us in the Supper is to make the holy Sacrament inane and ineffective, which is an abominable blasphemy unworthy of being listened to."³⁰

Interestingly enough it is in this context that von Allmen brings up the subject of the sacrament of communion being a foretaste of the wedding feast of the Lamb.³¹ What von Allmen seems to be unaware of is that in the seventeenth and eighteenth centuries Reformed preachers very frequently treated the wedding feast

---

[28] Von Allmen, *The Lord's Supper*, p. 55.
[29] Von Allmen, *The Lord's Supper*, p. 56.
[30] Von Allmen, *The Lord's Supper*, p. 56.
[31] Von Allmen, *The Lord's Supper*, p. 57.

typology at the celebration of the sacrament. Here is but another example of how little von Allmen seems to be aware of Reformed sacramental doctrine and piety after the Age of the Reformation.

It is in this same context that von Allmen brings up the covenantal understanding of the sacrament. What he says is, "The Supper is a Sacrament of the New Covenant."[32] Sharing in the sacrament forges a covenantal unity between all the members of the church. This is obviously not a particularly strong concern in von Allmen's ecumenical understanding of the sacrament. It cannot be said, however, that it is absent. A Reformed understanding of the sacrament would offer a much more highly developed covenantal understanding of the sacrament. It is right here, if nowhere else, that it becomes obvious that von Allmen's understanding of the Lord's Supper is not Reformed. His lack of appreciation of the value of infant baptism is quite consistent with this. No doubt von Allmen would agree that there is a covenantal dimension to both sacraments. It is just that the covenantal dimension is not very strong.

F. Spiritual Food

It is in chapter IV that von Allmen takes up the question of "the dialectic between what comes from God and what is offered to Him."[33] This is certainly one of von Allmen's major theological interests. Interestingly enough he admits that it is one of those issues in which a Reformed theologian feels most ill at ease. Apparently, and we will see this as we go along, it is one of the aspects that von Allmen himself is most uncomfortable with in regard to Reformed eucharistic theology.

Von Allmen is particularly interested in the eucharistic doctrine found in the bread of life discourse in the sixth chapter of the Gospel of John. Here Scripture puts very clearly what it is that is the gift of God when we receive the Lord's Supper. The Sup-

---

[32] Von Allmen, *The Lord's Supper*, p. 59.
[33] Von Allmen, *The Lord's Supper*, p. 75.

per is "a gift of Living Bread."[34] That is, the gift is Christ himself. It is Jesus Christ who is the bread of life that is come down from heaven which gives life to the world. We find the same thing at several points in the New Testament where the manna is identified as the type of the eucharistic bread.[35] Von Allmen says that the manna makes it possible for the Gospel of John to speak of the eucharist as the gift of the living bread.

We also find in the New Testament that what God gives us in the sacrament is spiritual food and drink. We find this particularly in 1 Corinthians 10: 1–3. The water from the rock and the manna from heaven are called spiritual. That is, they have a pneumatic significance.[36] It was at this point that von Allmen always appealed to the Eastern Orthodox doctrine of the Holy Spirit. Spiritual presence means presence through the Holy Spirit. John 4 was always brought into the discussion here. "God is a Spirit, and those who worship him must worship him in Spirit and truth" (John 4: 23).

At some length, von Allmen discusses the question of what the gospels really mean by that phrase in the Lord's Prayer, "Give us this day our daily bread." As von Allmen sees it, the phrase really has to do with the sacrament of the Lord's Supper. It is the bread of the great feast at the end of history, the bread of tomorrow, the bread of heaven. The food we receive at communion is really a foretaste of the wedding feast of the Lamb.[37] As von Allmen saw it, all these terms used in the New Testament to speak of the sacred food are in complete agreement. They tell us that the living Christ is present at the Supper. He then quotes Calvin: "'The bread of the Lord . . . is sanctified to represent for us and to dispense to us the body of Christ."[38] It is here that von Allmen would find his

---

[34] Von Allmen, *The Lord's Supper*, p. 75.

[35] Von Allmen, *The Lord's Supper*, p. 76.

[36] Von Allmen, *The Lord's Supper*, p.77.

[37] Von Allmen, *The Lord's Supper*, p. 78.

[38] The quotation is not identified, however. Von Allmen, *The Lord's Supper*, p. 78.

doctrine of the real presence of Christ. I don't think he does a particularly good job here. I have heard him do a much better job on this subject.

G. Eucharistic Sacrifice

Once again von Allmen's attention turns to the question of the eucharistic sacrifice. We have spoken of the downward movement, what God gives to us. Now our ecumenical theologian wants to stress the upward movement, the sacrificial movement.[39] This should be understood in terms of the glorification of Christ. At one and the same time we should speak here of his elevation on the cross, his entrance into the heavenly temple as High Priest, his session at the right hand of the Father, and his intercession for the saints.

At this point von Allmen launches into a long argument to the effect that the whole ancient church speaks continually of the eucharist in terms of sacrifice. The use of sacrificial terminology is continual in the literature of the ancient church. He quotes Alan Richardson, an Anglican theologian of the mid-fifties.[40] The impression one gets from reading this is that Richardson's statement is to be regarded as incontrovertible, but then no sooner does he finish this withering blast than he states from the other side that it must remain beyond discussion that the sacrifice of Christ is unique. Here von Allmen becomes very critical of a number of Catholic eucharistic devotions. Von Allmen then sets himself to reconciling the dilemma.

To make sense out of this dilemma von Allmen insists that in the Supper Jesus instituted a memorial, or *anamnesis*, of his sacrifice.[41] If I remember correctly, von Allmen had great respect for Alan Richardson. He followed him on numerous points, especially on the cardinal points of Anglican "High Church" theology, but

---

[39] Von Allmen, *The Lord's Supper*, p. 86.
[40] Von Allmen, *The Lord's Supper*, p. 87.
[41] Von Allmen, *The Lord's Supper*, p. 90.

here he obviously thought Richardson had been a bit reckless. The point was that much of the sacrificial phraseology was metaphorical. At one point, von Allmen says, the Fathers spoke of the eucharist as a sacrifice by analogy. This was its intended understanding, but in time it became familiar and people forgot it was by way of analogy.[42] One has to say that this explanation is hardly going to satisfy the serious Catholic theologian. The chances that Catholic theologians would accept this as an acceptable compromise are exceedingly remote. Von Allmen then continues his argument to assert that in time, when Christians were no longer confronted by pagan and Jewish sacrifices, misunderstandings easily arose.[43] Christians nevertheless must always use this sacrificial phraseology because Jesus himself made a sacrament of his sacrifice.

Today, of course, much of the Protestant discomfiture with a sacrificial interpretation of the sacrament really comes out of the Deist objection to the idea that Christ's death on the cross was an atoning sacrifice. For the Unitarians nothing could be a greater stumbling block than the sacrament of Holy Communion. The vicarious atonement is in the heart of it. "This is my body broken for you . . . This cup is the New Covenant in my blood poured out for many for the remission of sins." The classical Protestant objection to the doctrine of the eucharistic sacrifice is quite different from the Deist or Unitarian objection.

Protestants usually are willing to speak of a sacrifice of praise and thanksgiving. For most Reformed theologians the life of prayer is a continual sacrifice. Works of mercy are thought of as spiritual sacrifices, and yet there is a basic difference between Christian worship and Jewish worship, as it is expressed so clearly in Hebrews 9 and 10. The priests of the Temple stood daily at their altar and offered their multitude of sacrifices, whereas for the Christian, Jesus, the anointed Son of God, offered up on the cross one sacrifice. This

---

[42] Von Allmen, *The Lord's Supper*, p. 90.
[43] Von Allmen, *The Lord's Supper*, p. 91.

sacrifice was complete and sufficient to atone for the redemption of the whole human race. This is the classical Protestant concern. We find it again and again, from Luther's *Babylonian Captivity of the Church*, the *Second Helvetic Confession*, the *Heidelberg Catechism*, the sermons of Jean Daillé, and, to be sure, the Westminster Standards.

The question is, does von Allmen end up compromising this basic Protestant insight? I think it has to be said that he does. At one point von Allmen says, "Indeed what we have seen of the Supper as sacrifice is decisive enough to enable us to say that the Supper suffers the amputation of one of its component elements if it is deprived of its sacrificial significance."[44] Whatever might be said about von Allmen's compromise here, there is no question but that he is not aiming at a Catholic understanding but at an ecumenical understanding. He is equally critical of much of Catholic eucharistic piety.

As one who proudly claims to be von Allmen's student, I figure that where we are now is at the threshold of a new and more intense study of the Reformed heritage of Christian worship. We have heard long enough about the poverty of our liturgical tradition. Yes, that is part of the story, but only part. There are plenty of riches to it as well. That, sad to say, is what the liturgical scholars of the twentieth century overlooked. It is to be hoped that the Reformed Church of the twenty-first century will rediscover some of the classics to which this volume has pointed.

WILLY RORDORF

One of the things that needs to be said about Jean-Jacques von Allmen is that he had a way of gathering about himself men of imagination and ability. Von Allmen was the man of vision who made the theological faculty of Neuchâtel a very small but very good theological faculty for several years. How much I learned from Henri-Philippe Menoud, professor of New Testament at

---

[44] Von Allmen, *The Lord's Supper*, p. 95.

Neuchâtel, and, even more, from Willy Rordorf! It was really from von Allmen that I learned what Rordorf was beginning to hammer together about the *Didaché*. It was von Allmen who had the wisdom to put Rordorf in a position that would allow him to spend most of his time doing research on an evangelical understanding of the early church fathers.[45]

Surely the best course I ever took in my academic career was Rordorf's seminar on Tertullian. I spent all term preparing for that course. Rordorf had me do a paper on Tertullian and worship. What an exercise! Von Allmen knew what he was doing. He saw where I was going and he saw what Rordorf was doing, and in both cases he gave us the opportunity to work on our projects.

Only von Allmen would have given me the opportunity to write a thesis on *The Patristic Roots of Reformed Worship*. He told me that I would have a difficult time proving my point, but he surely wanted me to succeed. He encouraged me even though it was clear that he had a different vision of what worship should look like. That encouragement was the mark of a truly great teacher.

---

[45] It was von Allmen himself who told me how he had to argue for the appointment of Rordorf to Neuchâtel. Rordorf's family came from Zurich in German-speaking Switzerland.

CONCLUSION

To sum up, in the centuries that followed the Reformation, profound insights came to light in the eucharistic piety of the Reformed church, but, in the twentieth century, these insights were largely forgotten or ignored. It is to be hoped that in the twenty-first century these insights will be rediscovered and appreciated.

But now the question is, *Where do we go from here?* From a pastoral standpoint this question is most pressing, and it is from that standpoint that I want to write. I have been pastor of two churches for a total of eighteen years. In both these churches I had as a conscious goal of my ministry the deepening of the congregation's experience of Holy Communion. In each case I think there was clear progress made in this direction.

What I have to say on where we should go from here comes out of very practical experiences. I want to talk about things that worked and things that didn't work. Even more, these thoughts well up from thinking over how I might have done it better. Again and again we had to settle for something that was less than ideal. For the first six years of my pastorate in Indiana I had to try to lead worship in a tin-roofed quonset hut. We eventually got our white clapboard meetinghouse. What a difference that move made! No one has to go any further to convince me of the importance of the architectural setting of Christian worship.

What I want to talk about at this point has more to do with rites than doctrine. This may seem eccentric, but I think that is where we are right now. We need to be more specific about our liturgy. We need to give more thought to our forms of worship. So what, then, do I have to say about how we might go about deepening the experience of Communion? Let me make some concrete suggestions.

One assumes, of course, that the first thing which has to be in place for our service of worship is the preaching of the gospel. In the beginning was the Word, as the Gospel of John starts out. Jesus began his ministry by preaching for three years before he sealed that ministry by sharing the Passover feast with his disciples. Even before that there was the ministry of John the Baptist and the preaching of the prophets. The Reformed understanding of Holy Communion is that it is the sign and the seal of the promises of the covenant of grace, proclaimed in the reading and preaching of Scripture. When all is said and done the preaching comes first. The Supper depends on it. The Supper seals the preaching.

Reformed worship should be reformed according to Scripture. Contemporary biblical scholarship has made much progress in helping us to understand what the Scriptures do, in fact, tell us about worship. Archbishop Whitgift had it wrong! The Bible does tell us much about how we should worship. In fact, the Bible is a great mine filled with precious gems yet to be brought to light. This should be sort of obvious, but let us not make the mistake of ignoring the obvious. Having said that, let me outline a list of concrete things I think we should aim toward.

First of all I think we should very slowly move toward recovering a regular Lord's Day celebration of the sacrament. This is not the sort of thing that can suddenly be instituted. With my church in Indiana we went from once a year to about ten times a year. That took ten years.

Second, I think we need to work on developing at the center of our communion celebrations a true Eucharistic Prayer, a prayer of thanksgiving for God's mighty acts of creation and redemption. I used to give quite a bit of time to preparing a Eucharistic Prayer on the days we observed Communion, especially for a Christmas or Easter celebration. There were certain things I figured should always be mentioned, such as thanking God for the atoning sacrifice of Christ and his gift of new life in the resurrection. I always mentioned the incarnation and ascension. At the center was the remembering of Christ's high priestly ministry at the right hand of the Father. But, then, I came up with a few new things that God had in his grace poured out upon us. One time I might mention Christ's healing ministry or another time his sending out the apostles to continue his work. I figured the Scriptures have very carefully told us what to do when we celebrate communion. We read that Jesus took the bread and wine and then gave thanks. As time went along I more and more found myself inspired by the great thanksgiving psalms such as Psalm 105, Psalm 136, and Psalm 78.[1]

Logically, I suppose, all sorts of things could be included in this hymn of thanksgiving, such as a thanksgiving for creation as in Psalm 104 or a thanksgiving for God's mighty acts of redemption from Adam to Christ. One time I might mention the ministry of the patriarchs and another time the wisdom of the prophets. I often gave special attention to giving thanks for the pouring out of the Holy Spirit on the day of Pentecost. This Eucharistic Prayer ought to be offered in a festal spirit of victory over sin and death and in a spirit of entering into the consummation of history. Far too many of our Reformed communion services have had a funereal air. They seem more appropriate to Good Friday than to Easter.

Here, then, is another reform I would recommend. We should be sure to celebrate Communion on Easter Sunday. I made a big thing about celebrating Communion on Easter. The Maundy Thursday communion service had been what my congregation expected year after year. I convinced them that if it was only on Maundy Thursday that they celebrated the Supper then the whole thing conveyed the wrong message. So we added the Easter cel-

---

[1] For examples of Eucharistic Prayers formulated over the years, see Hughes Oliphant Old, *Leading in Prayer: A Workbook for Ministers* (Grand Rapids, MI: Eerdmans, 1995).

ebration and made it a real feast, and I think everybody got the point. From then on our Easter Communion became the Christian celebration of Passover, a passage from death to life. Easter became the high point of our worship, the festive outpouring of our praise and thanksgiving for God's grace in the past and a foretaste of eternal glory.

Another closely related reform that I would recommend is that when we receive new members we do it at a communion service. The old Presbyterian terminology was that when we "joined" the church we became "communicant members." That is, we were admitted to the Lord's Table. This should especially be the case when we receive the communicants' class. Once this becomes the established practice it should be much easier to understand what is really going on when we observe the Sacrament. We are making a public profession of faith and thereby joining the church.[2]

Using the same line of reasoning I think we need to emphasize that the vows made when new members are received are our covenant vows, the confession of Christian faith. This applies to reciting the Apostles' Creed at the communion service as well. For each participant the very act of participation is a profession of faith, and that is the reason we recite the Creed at a full celebration of the Sacrament.

Somewhere in the service there should be prayers of confession and supplication. I used Charles W. Baird's translation of the prayer from the *Genevan Psalter* with the Assurance of Pardon. For a while I tried to revive a Thursday evening preparatory service, but that didn't work. What did work was the reviving of Sunday evening vespers. There we gave ample attention to both psalm

---

[2] For further information on the relationship of receiving communion and making a profession of faith, see Hughes Oliphant Old, *The Shaping of the Reformed Baptismal Rite in the Sixteenth Century* (Grand Rapids, MI: Eerdmans, 1992), pp. 179–200, which constitutes chapter 7, "Catechetical Instruction." For a historical treatment of the subject, see Hughes Oliphant Old, *Worship, Reformed According to Scripture*, revised and expanded edition (Louisville: Westminster John Knox Press, 2002), pp. 109–146.

Conclusion

prayer and prayers of lamentation, confession, and repentance. It was the same way with the ministry of intercessory prayer when we revived daily morning prayer. Daily morning prayer put a strong emphasis on intercessory prayer.

Perhaps the most difficult part of the communion service for me to understand has been the Invitation. I think the problem developed over time. For too long I had heard it called the "fencing of the Table." At this point too many ministers of otherwise sound Reformed training would spend ten minutes or more belaboring the theme of who should and who should not participate. The congregation was given to understand that participation must be on cat's paws. Fairly early in my academic studies of this subject I learned that historically, at least by the fourth century, this part of the service was called "the dismissals." That helped smooth out the problem, at least a little bit. For awhile I simply left it out. Then I began to realize that what was really going on at this point in the service was that people were being invited to participate in the sacred meal and thereby make a profession of faith. The person I learned this from was none other than Gilbert Tennent. Next I discovered it was all through the Scottish tradition, particularly in Andrew Thomson. Then I returned to Calvin's *Genevan Psalter* and found the same thing. It was there all the time, of course. I just had not seen it.

Somewhere toward the beginning of the communion service proper there should be a Communion Invocation. It should not be substituted for the Eucharistic Prayer but rather be offered after the minister and the elders have been seated at the Table. Here is the place to use that classic line from the *Westminster Directory*, "set aside these elements of bread and wine from a common to this sacred use." It would also be appropriate to remember the long discussion in the history of Christian doctrine of the place of the *epiclesis*. The *epiclesis* as the Greek church would have it is the prayer that the Father would pour out the Holy Spirit on these gifts and on this congregation and transform them into the body of Christ. We don't have to decide for the Greek church or the Latin church at this point, but it would be worth expressing the importance of the pouring out of the Holy Spirit to our worship. Richard Baxter had that one down pretty well. There is no reason, however, that every communion service should have to touch on every theological base on its way to home plate.

Another prayer that I consider of particular importance is the unison Prayer of Dedication after the congregation has been served the bread and wine. I have always used the one from the *Genevan Psalter*. This prayer, of course, goes back to Bucer. As I see it the importance of this prayer is that it brings out more fully the meaning of the biblical concept of thanksgiving. The Hebrew word *yadah* not only means "to thank" but also to confess the obligation it lays upon those who have received God's grace. That obligation is to dedicate one's life to the service of God. In thanksgiving, finally, we give ourselves. This is a primary dimension of the rite of the sacrament. We find this again and again in the Psalms. When we cry to God for help and God hears our prayers, then we owe to him our service, our very lives, for all eternity.

Recently I have been asked by several to comment on the practice of intinction that has become increasingly popular among those influenced by the liturgical renewal movement in the Roman Catholic Church. As it fits into Catholic attempts to reform worship, I think it is a positive step forward. It is another matter when it comes to the worship of the Reformed churches. The main problem with intinction, as I see it, is that it weakens the sign of sharing a meal with our brothers and sisters in Christ in the house of the Father. It ends up looking like the old practice of "going forward" to the altar and kneeling down at the altar rail to taste the sacred food. Nothing could be less Reformed.[3]

Intinction mangles the original shape of the covenant meal. The Christian sacrament as Jesus himself observed it was a meal

---

[3] See chapter 6, where I discuss the two prayer books of Edward VI.

Conclusion

with the blessing of bread at the beginning, and a blessing of the wine at the end. The prayers that go with Holy Communion are essential to its nature. There is an invocation and a memorial of holy history. There is a confession of sin and a profession of faith. There is a thanksgiving and a dedication of our lives to God. There are psalms of praise and finally the sealing of the covenant meal.

Of the essence of Reformed worship is that it should be according to Scripture, as we read three times alone in the *Didaché*. There are certain things Scripture tells us Jesus did at this sacred meal. We should, as faithful ministers, do them as well. Our worship should be "in the same manner" also. Such worship glorifies God.

For those of us who are particularly delighted by liturgical archeology I have a suggestion. One might revive the Scottish traditions of communion psalmody. At the beginning of the service one might sing Psalm 23, then, as the elders come forward and find their places around the Table, one might sing the last verses of Psalm 24, "Lift up your heads, O ye gates." One time I heard Theophilus Taylor, one of the most venerable Reformed Presbyterian preachers of the mid-fifties, preach on Psalm 133, "Behold, how good and pleasant it is when brothers dwell together in unity." According to him this was a long time favorite communion psalm among the Reformed Presbyterians. There are several metrical versions of Psalm 116 that are especially appropriate for the communion service. For the end of the service the opening verses of Psalm 103 are almost universal, "O Thou my soul, bless God the Lord." But then for Easter there is nothing more appropriate than the Passover Psalms, especially Psalm 118 (KJV), "This is the day which the Lord hath made; we will rejoice and be glad in it . . . Blessed be he that cometh in the name of the Lord."

I would like to say just a word about the architectural setting of Reformed worship. It is not the style that concerns me so much. Be it a gothic cathedral like St. Pierre in Geneva or a white clapboard meetinghouse like the Congregational Church in Old

Lyme, Connecticut, or, for that matter, one of those masterpieces of modern architecture built by the Reformed Church in Switzerland, what I would urge is an arrangement that would promote the visual image of a group of people sharing a meal together. There should be a large wooden table so that the participants can be gathered around it and each participant both receive the sacred food from a neighbor and serve that food to a neighbor.

One more important thing needs to be mentioned, and that is the deacons' collection. The deacons' collection should be taken after the congregation has shared the bread and wine. This is done for theological reasons. The deacons' collection is not to be confused with the offertory of the mass which had highly developed sacrificial interpretations. On the other hand, it should be made quite clear that the giving of alms and the support of the ministries of mercy are an essential part of the celebration of the sacrament of Communion. That almsgiving is a part of the sacrament of Communion is made clear both by the preface of Calvin's communion service with the French refugees in Strasbourg and by the *Westminster Directory*.

The study of the history of Christian worship has been my life work. It has been a fascinating study, always opening itself up to richer treasures. The best is yet to come. Our worship here is but a foretaste of the wedding feast of the Lamb.

BIBLIOGRAPHY

à Brakel, Wilhelmus. *The Christian's Reasonable Service.* Translated by Bartel Elshout. 4 volumes. Grand Rapids, MI: Reformation Heritage Books, 1992.

"Admonition to the Parliament." Found in *Puritan Manifestos.* Edited by W. H. Frere and C. L. Douglas. London: SPCK, 1954.

Alexander, James Waddel. *God is Love.* Reprint of *Sacramental Discourses*, published in 1860. Edinburgh and Carlisle, PA: Banner of Truth Trust, 1985.

———. *The Life of Archibald Alexander.* Reprint. Harrisonburg, VA: Sprinkle Publications, 1991.

Allen, Thomas. *The Call of Christ unto Thirsty Sinners to Come to Him and Drink of the Waters of Life.* 4th edition. Boston: Printed by J. Allen for Eleazar Phillips, 1710.

Appel, Theodore. *The Life and Work of John Williamson Nevin.* Philadelphia: Reformed Church Publication House, 1889.

———. *The Life and Work of John Williamson Nevin.* New York: Arno Press and the New York Times, 1968.

Archer, Stanley. *Richard Hooker.* Boston: Twayne, 1983.

The Articles of Religion. As found in *The Book of Common Prayer According to the Use of the Episcopal Church* (proposed). The Church Hymnal Corporation and The Seabury Press, 1977.

Augustine. *On the Holy Trinity.* The Nicene and Post-Nicene Fathers, first series, volume 3. Grand Rapids, MI: Wm. B. Eerdmans Publishing Co., 1976.

Baillie, Donald. *The Theology of the Sacraments.* New York: Charles Scribners and Sons, 1957.

Baird, Charles Washington. *A Chapter on Liturgies: Historical Sketches.* Introduction by Thomas Binnie. London: Knight and Sons, 1856.

———. *Eutaxia, or, The Presbyterian Liturgies: Historical Sketches.* New York: M. W. Dodd, 1855.

———. *History of the Huguenot Emigration to America*. New York: Dodd, Mead & Co., 1885.

———. *The Presbyterian Liturgies: Historical Sketches*. Grand Rapids, MI: Baker Book House, 1957.

Baird, Henry M. *The Life of the Rev. Robert Baird, D.D.* New York: Anson D. F. Randolph, 1966.

———. *Memorials of the Rev. Charles W. Baird*. New York and London: G. P. Putnam's Sons, 1888.

Baird, Robert. *Religion in America*. New York: Harper & Brothers, 1844.

———. *Religion in America*. Enlarged edition. New York: Harper & Brothers, 1856.

Baker, J. Wayne. "Erastianism." In *The Oxford Encyclopedia of the Reformation*, 2:59–60. Edited by Hans J. Hillerbrand. 4 volumes. New York: Oxford University Press, 1996.

———. *Heinrich Bullinger and the Covenant: The Other Reformed Tradition*. Athens: Ohio University Press, 1981.

Barker, William S. *Puritan Profiles, Fifty-four Puritans: Personalities Drawn Together by the Westminster Assembly*. Fearn, UK: Christian Focus Publications, 1996.

Barucq, André. *Le livre des Proverbs*. Paris: Gabalda, 1964.

Battles, Ford Lewis. Translator and editor. *The Piety of John Calvin*. Grand Rapids, MI: Baker Book House, 1978.

Baxter, Richard. *The Autobiography of Richard Baxter*. London and Toronto: J. M. Dent & Sons, Ltd., 1925.

———. *A Christian Directory: or, A Summ of Practical Theologie*. London: Printed by Robert White, for Nevill Simmons, 1673.

———. *The English Nonconformity, as Under King Charles II, and King James II*. London: Printed by Tho. Parkhurst, 1690.

———. "The Order of Celebrating the Sacrament of the Body and Blood of Christ." In *The Reformed Liturgy*. Contained in Richard Baxter, *A Christian Directory*. Reprint. Ligonier, PA: Soli Deo Gloria Publications, 1990.

———. *The Practical Works of Richard Baxter*. 4 volumes. Ligonier, PA.: Soli Deo Gloria Publications, 1990–91.

———. *The Reformed Liturgy*. Found in Richard Baxter. *The Practical Works of Richard Baxter*, 1:923–948. 4 volumes. Ligonier, PA.: Soli Deo Gloria Publications, 1990- 91.

———. *The Reformed Pastor*. Edited by Hugh Martin. London: SCM Press, 1956.

———. *The Reformed Pastor.* Edinburgh and Carlisle, PA: Banner of Truth, 1974.

———. *The Saints' Everlasting Rest.* Evansville, IN: Sovereign Grace Book Club, 1950.

———. *The Saints' Everlasting Rest.* Edited and introduced by John T. Wilkinson. Vancouver: Regent College Publications, 2004.

Beeke, Joel R. "Ebenezer and Ralph Erskine: Their Lives and Their Preaching." In Ebenezer Erskine. *The Beauties of Ebenezer Erskine.* Selected by Samuel McMillan. Introduction by Joel R. Beeke. Grand Rapids, MI: Reformation Heritage Books; and Fearn, UK: Christian Focus Publications, 2001.

———. "The Dutch Second Reformation." In Wilhelmus à Brakel. *The Christian's Reasonable Service.* Translated by Bartel Elshout. 4 volumes. Grand Rapids, MI: Reformation Heritage Books, 1992.

———. *The Quest for Full Assurance: The Legacy of Calvin and His Successors.* Edinburgh and Carlisle, PA: Banner of Truth Trust, 1999.

Beeke, Joel R. and Mark Jones, eds. *A Puritan Theology: Doctrine for Life.* Grand Rapids, MI: Reformation Heritage Books, 2012.

Beeke, Joel R. and Randall J. Pederson. *Meet the Puritans.* Grand Rapids, MI: Reformation Heritage Books, 2006.

Begrich, Joachim. *Studien zu Deuterojesaja.* Reprint. Munich: Theologische Bücherei, 1963.

Benedict, Bruce H. "Charles W. Baird: An American Presbyterian Retrospective." Paper submitted to Mr. John R. Muether, Assistant Professor Church History and Librarian, Reformed Theological Seminary–Orlando. The Aiken Taylor Award for American Presbyterian Church History presented by The Historical Center of the Presbyterian Church of America, 2003. St. Louis: PCA Historical Center, 2003.

"Benefices." *Encyclopedia Britannica.* 11th edition, 3:725–26. 32 volumes. Chicago: Encyclopedia Britannica, 1910.

Beyer, Klaus. *Semitische Syntax in Neuen Testament.* SUNT I. Göttingen: Vandenhoeck & Ruprecht, 1962.

Beyer, Ulrich. *Abendmahl und Messe: Sinn und Recht der 80. Frage des Heidelberger Katechismus. Beiträge zur Geschichte und Lehre der Reformierten Kirche.* Neukirchen-Vluyn: Neukirchener Verlag des Erziehungsvereins, 1965.

Bicknell, Edward John. *A Theological Introduction to the Thirty-Nine Articles of the Church of England.* London and New York: Longmans, 1955.

Bieder, Werner. "PNEUMA in Sapientia." *Theologisches Wörterbuch zum neuen Testament*, 6:369–70. Edited by Gerhard Kittel and Gerhard Friedrich. 9 volumes. Stuttgart: W. Kohlhammer Verlag, 1964.

Bierma, Lyle D., et al. *An Introduction to the Heidelberg Catechism: Sources, History, and Theology*. Grand Rapids, MI: Baker Academic, 2005.

Billings, J. Todd. *Calvin, Participation, and the Gift: The Activity of Believers in Union with Christ*. Oxford: Oxford University Press, 2007.

"Biography of Henry Van Dyke." www.poemhunter.com/henry-van-dyke/biography/. Accessed April 22, 2009.

Black, J. William. *Reformation Pastors: Richard Baxter and the Ideal of the Reformed Pastor*. Carlisle [UK]: Paternoster Press, 2004.

"Black Rubric." *Oxford Dictionary of the Christian Church*. Edited by F. L. Cross. Oxford: Oxford University Press, 1974.

Blaikie, William Garden. *The Preachers of Scotland*. Edinburgh: T. & T. Clark, 1888.

Blench, J. W. *Preaching in England in the Late Fifteenth and Sixteenth Centuries: A Study of English Sermons, 1450-c.1600*. New York: Barnes and Noble, 1964.

Bluhm, David Rodney. *Trends of Worship Reflected in the Three Editions of the Book of Common Worship of the Presbyterian Church in the United States of America*. [Pittsburgh]: s.n., 1957?.

Boisset, Jean. *Sagesse et sainteté dans la pensée de Jean Calvin*. Paris: Presses universitaires de France, 1959.

The Book of Common Prayer. New York: The Church Pension Fund, 1945.

The Book of Common Worship. Philadelphia: Presbyterian Board of Publication and Sabbath-school Work, 1906.

The Book of Common Worship. Revised. Philadelphia: Presbyterian Board of Christian Education, 1932.

The Book of Common Worship. Philadelphia: Published for the Office of the General Assembly by the General Division of Publication of the Board of Christian Education of the Presbyterian Church in the United States of America, 1946.

Boot, Izak. *De Allegorische Uitlegging van het Hooglied, voornamelijk in Nederland*. Woerden: Zuiderduijn, 1971.

Booty, John E. "The Book of Common Prayer." In *The Oxford Encyclopedia of the Reformation*, 1:189–193. Edited by Hans J. Hillerbrand. 4 volumes. New York: Oxford University Press, 1996.

―――. *The Godly Kingdom of Tudor England: Great Books of the English Reformation.* Wilton, CT: Morehouse-Barlow Co., 1981.

Borgen, Peder. *Bread from Heaven: An Exegetical Study of the Concept of Manna in the Gospel of John and the Writings of Philo.* Leiden: Brill, 1965.

Bornert, René. *La réforme protestante du culte à Strasbourg au XVIe siècle (1523–1598): approche sociologique et interprétation théologique.* Leiden: E. J. Brill, 1981.

Bovard, William John. *The Preaching of Ebenezer Erskine: His Contributions to the Evangelical Pulpit of Today.* Pittsburgh: n.s., 1961.

Box, William Herman. *A Study of the Preaching of Henry van Dyke.* N. p., 1955.

Braun, François-Marie. *Jean le théologien: les grandes traditions d'Israël et l'accord d'Écritures selon le quatrième évangile.* Paris: Gabalda, 1964.

Brecht, Martin, Klaus Deppermann, Ulrich Gäbler, and Hartmut Lehmann. *Geschichte des Pietismus.* 2 volumes. Göttingen: Vandenhoeck & Ruprecht, 1995.

Bremer, Francis J., and Tom Webster. *Puritans and Puritanism in Europe and America: A Comprehensive Encyclopedia.* Santa Barbara, CA: ABC-CLIO, 2006.

Brienen, T. *De Predeking van de Nadere Reformatie. Een Onderzoek nnar het gebruik van het klassifikatiemethode binnen de predeking van de Nadere Reformatie.* Amsterdam: Uitgeverij Ton Bolland, 1974.

Brienen, T., K. Exalto, et al. *De Nadere Reformatie. Beschrijving van haar voornaamste vertegenwoordigers.* 'S-Gravenhage: Uitgeverij Boekencentrum B. V., 1986.

―――. *Theologische Aspecten van de Nadere Reformatie.* Zoetermeer: Uitgewerij Boekencentrum, 1993.

Brightman, Frank Edward. *The English Rite: Being a Synopsis of the Sources and Revisions of the Book of Common Prayer.* 2 volumes. London: Rivingtons, 1915.

Bromiley, Geoffrey W. *Thomas Cranmer, Theologian.* New York: Oxford University Press, 1956.

Bromiley, Geoffrey W., editor. *Zwingli and Bullinger.* Library of Christian Classics, volume 24. Philadelphia: The Westminster Press, 1953.

Brown, Dale W. *Understanding Pietism.* Grand Rapids, MI: Wm. B. Eerdmans Publishing Co., 1978.

Brown, Raymond. *The Gospel according to John.* Garden City, N. Y.: Doubleday Company, 1966.

Brown, Stewart J. *Thomas Chalmers and the Godly Commonwealth in Scotland.* Oxford and New York: Oxford University Press, 1982.

Bruce, Robert. *The Mystery of the Lord's Supper*. Translated and edited by Thomas F. Torrance. Richmond: John Knox Press, 1958.

Bucer, Martin. *Martin Bucers Deutsche Schriften*. Edited by Robert Stupperich. 5 volumes. Gütersloh: Gütersloher Verlagshaus Gerd Mohn; Paris: Presses Universitaires de France, 1960.

———. *Martini Buceri Opera Latina*. Volume 15, *De Regno Christi*. Edited by François Wendel. Paris: Presses Universitaires de France; Gütersloh: C. Bertelsmann Verlag, 1955.

———. *On the Ceremonies of the Anglican Church: A Critical Examination*. Found in Edward Charles Whitaker, editor. *Martin Bucer and the Book of Common Prayer*. Alcuin Club Collection, volume 55. Great Wakering: Mayhew-McCrimmon, 1974.

Buchanan, Colin, ed., *The Savoy Conference Revisited: The Proceedings Taken from the Grand Debate of 1661 and the Works of Richard Baxter*. Cambridge, UK: Grove Books, Ltd., 2002.

Burroughs, Jeremiah. *An Exposition of the Prophecy of Hosea*. Reprint. Beaver Falls, PA: Soli Deo Gloria Publications, 1989.

———. *Gospel Worship, or, the Right Manner of Sanctifying the Name of God*. Edited by Don Kistler. Ligonier, PA: Soli Deo Gloria Publications, 1990.

———. *The Rare Jewel of Christian Contentment*. Reprint. London: Banner of Truth Trust, 1964.

———. *The Saints' Happiness*. Reprint. Beaver Falls, PA: Soli Deo Gloria Publications, 1989.

Busser, Fritz. "Bullinger and 1566." In *Controversy and Conciliation: The Reformation and the Palatinate, 1559–1583*. Edited by Derk Visser. Allison Park, PA: Pickwick Publications, 1986.

Calamy, Edmund. *An Abridgement of Mr. Baxter's History of His Life and Times*. London: Printed for J. Lawrence, etc., 1713.

Calderwood, David. *The History of the Kirk of Scotland*. 1678. Edinburgh: Printed for the Wodrow Society, 1842–1849.

Calhoun, David B. *Princeton Seminary*. Volume 1, *Faith and Learning, 1812–1868*. Edinburgh and Carlisle: Banner of Truth Trust, 1994.

Calvin, John. *Calvin's Commentaries*, Translated by A. W. Morrison. 12 volumes. Grand Rapids, MI: Wm B. Eerdmans Publishing Company, 1989.

———. *Commentaire de M. Jean Calvin sur l'Epistre de sainct Iaques*. Paris (?): Jean Crespin, 1550.

———. *Commentaire de M. Iean Calvin sur l'Evangile selon sainct Iean, Traduit du latin*. Paris (?): Robert Stephanus, 1553.

———. *Commentaire sur l'epistre Canonique de S. Iean*. Geneva: Girard, 1551.

———. *Commentaires de Jean Calvin . . . tome deuxième, Évangile selon saint Jean*. Edited by M. Réveillaud. Geneva: Labor et Fides, 1968.

———. *Commentarii in Epistolas Canonicas, unam Petri, unam Joannis, unam Iacobi, Petri alteram. Iudae unam*. Paris (?): Jean Crespin, 1551.

———. *Commentary on the Book of Psalms by John Calvin, Translated from the original Latin and collated with the Author's French Version*. Tranlsated by James Anderson. 5 volumes. Edinburgh: The Calvin Society, 1845. Photolithographic reproduction. Grand Rapids, MI: Wm. B. Eerdmans Publishing Co., 1949.

———. *The First Epistle of Paul to the Corinthians*. Translated by John W. Fraser. *Calvin's New Testament Commentaries*. Grand Rapids, MI: Wm. B. Eerdmans Publishing Co., 1989.

———. *Galatians, Ephesians, Philippians and Colossians*. Translated by T. H. L. Parker. Calvin's New Testament Commentaries. Grand Rapids, MI: Wm. B. Eerdmans Publishing Co., 1965.

———. *The Gospel According to St. John, part two 11–21, and the First Epistle of John*. Translated by T. H. L. Parker. Calvin's New Testament Commentaries. Grand Rapids, MI: Wm. B. Eerdmans Publishing Co., 1988.

———. *A Harmony of the Gospels Matthew, Mark and Luke, and The Epistles of James and Jude*. Translated by A. W. Morrison. *Calvin's New Testament Commentaries*, volume 3. Grand Rapids, MI: Eerdmans, 1989.

———. *In Evangelium secundum Iohannem Commentarius*. Geneva (?): Robert Stephanus, 1553.

———. *In librum Psalmorum, Iohannis Caluini commentarius*. Geneva (?): Robert Stephanus, 1552.

———. *Institutes of the Christian Religion*. Edited by John McNeill. Translated by Ford Lewis Battles. Library of Christian Classics, volumes 20–21. Philadelphia: The Westminster Press, 1960.

———. *Institutes of the Christian Religion* (1536). Translated and edited by Ford Lewis Battles. Grand Rapids, MI: Wm. B. Eerdmans Publishing Co., 1986.

———. *Ioannis Calvini opera quae supersunt omnia*. Edited by William Baum, Edward Cunitz, and Edward Reuss. 59 volumes. Corpus Reformatorum, vols. 29–87. Brunswick and Berlin: C. A. Schweiske, 1863–1900.

———. *Le Livre des Pseaumes exposé par Iehan Caluin* . . . . Paris (?): Conrad Badius, 1552.

———. *Opera selecta*. Edited by Petrus Barth and Dora Scheuner. 5 volumes. Munich: Chr. Kaiser, 1926–1959.

———. *Petit traité de la Sainte cène de notre Seigneur Jésus Christ*. La Haye: Imprimerie de J. Roering, 1844.

———. *Sermons on the Saving Work of Christ*. Selected and translated by Leroy Nixon. Grand Rapids, MI: Baker Book House, 1980.

———. *Short Treatise on the Lord's Supper*. Library of Christian Classics, volume 22. Philadelphia: Westminster Press, 1954.

———. *Theological Treatises*. Library of Christian Classics, volume 22. Philadelphia: Westminster Press, 1954.

———. *A Treatise on the Sacraments of Baptism and the Lord's Supper*. Edinburgh: John Johnstone, 1837.

———. *Treatises on the Sacraments, Catechism of the Church of Geneva, Forms of Prayer, Confessions of Faith*. Translated by Henry Beveridge. Fearn, UK: Christian Focus Publications, 2002.

"Calvin, John." In *The Oxford Encyclopedia of the Reformation*, 1:234–240. 4 volumes. New York and Oxford: Oxford University Press, 1996.

Cameron, Nigel M. de S., editor. *Dictionary of Scottish Church History and Theology*. Edinburgh: T. & T. Clark; and Downers Grove, IL: InterVarsity, 1993.

Campi, Emidio, editor. *Petrus Martyr Vermigli: Humanismus, Republicanismus, Reformation*. Geneva: Droz, 2002.

Carson, John L. and David W. Hall, editors. *To Glorify and Enjoy God: A Commemoration of the 350th Anniversary of the Westminster Assembly*. Edinburgh and Carlisle, PA.: The Banner of Truth Trust, 1994.

Casel, Odo. *Das christliche Kultmysterium*. Regensburg: F. Pustet, 1948.

Chalmers, Thomas. *The Christian and Civic Economy of Large Towns*. 3 volumes. Glasgow: Chalmers & Collins, 1821–26.

———. *Letters of Thomas Chalmers*. Edinburgh: Banner of Truth Trust, 2007.

———. *On Political Economy, in Connexion with the Moral State and Moral Prospects of Society*. New York: Daniel Appleton, 1832.

Bibliography

―――. *Posthumous Works of the Rev. Thomas Chalmers, D.D., LL.D.* Edited by William Hanna. 9 volumes. New York: Harper & Brothers, Publishers, 1849.

―――. *The Select Works of Thomas Chalmers.* 4 volumes. New York: R. Carter, 1848.

―――. *A Series of Discourses on the Christian Revelation: Viewed in Connexion with the Modern Astronomy.* Glasgow: Printed for John Smith and Son, 1817.

―――. *Sermons and Discourses.* New York: Robert Carter, 1844.

―――. *The Works of Thomas Chalmers.* 25 volumes. Glasgow: William Collins, [1836–1842].

Cheyne, A. C., editor. *The Practical and the Pious: Essays on Thomas Chalmers (1780–1847).* Edinburgh: Saint Andrew Press, 1985.

Childs, Brevard. *The Book of Exodus.* Philadelphia: Westminster Press, 1975.

Christ, Felix. "Jesus Sophia." In *Abhandlungen zur Theologie des Alten und Neuen Testaments*, 57 (1960).

"Church of Scotland." Http://everything2.com/title/Church+of+Scotland. Accessed 7/30/2012.

Clary, Glen J. "The Eucharistic Theology of Benjamin Breckinridge Warfield." Written as his final paper at Erskine Theological Seminary for the class Theology of Worship in Contemporary Discussion, Summer, 2008.

―――. "Ulrich Zwingli and the Swiss Anabaptists: Sola Scriptura and the Reformation of Christian Worship." In *The Confessional Presbyterian*, volume 6. Rowlett, TX: Reformation Presbyterian Press, 1006.

Coalter, Milton J., Jr. *Gilbert Tennent, Son of Thunder.* New York: Greenwood Press, 1986.

Cocksworth, Christopher J. *Evangelical Eucharistic Thought in the Church of England.* Cambridge, UK: Cambridge University Press, 1993.

Coffey, John. *Politics, Religion and the British Revolutions: The Mind of Samuel Rutherford.* Cambridge, UK: Cambridge University Press, 1997.

Collinson, Patrick. *The Elizabethan Puritan Movement.* Berkeley: University of California Press, 1967.

―――. *English Puritanism.* London: Historical Association Pamphlet, 1983.

―――. "Vestiarian Controversy," *Oxford Encyclopedia of the Reformation*, 1:231–232. 4 volumes. Edited by Hans J. Hillerbrand. New York and Oxford: Oxford University Press, 1996.

A Compendium of the Laws of the Church of Scotland. Edited by W. Steuart. Edinburgh, 1837–1840.

The Confession of Faith: The Larger and Shorter Catechisms. Edinburgh: The Free Church of Scotland, 1976.

The Confessions of Faith, Catechisms, Directories, Form of Church-Government, Discipline, etc., of Public Authority in the Church of Scotland. Glasgow: Printed by Robert and Thomas Duncan for the Church of Scotland, 1771.

Conzelmann, Hans. *Der erste Brief an die Korinther.* Göttingen: Vandenhoeck & Ruprecht, 1969.

———. "Wisdom in the N. T." *The Interpreter's Dictionary of the Bible.* Supplementary volume. Nashville: Abingdon Press, 1984.

Coolidge, John S. *The Pauline Renaissance in England: Puritanism and the Bible.* Oxford: Clarendon, 1970.

Corda, Salvatore. *Veritas Sacramenti: A Study of Vermigli's Doctrine of the Lord's Supper.* Zurich: Theologischer Verlag, 1975.

Cottrell, Jack. *Covenant and Baptism in the Theology of Huldreich Zwingli.* ThD. dissertation. Princeton, NJ: Princeton Theological Seminary, 1971.

Cragg, Gerald Robertson. *Puritanism in the Period of the Great Persecution, 1660–1688.* Cambridge, UK: Cambridge University Press, 1957.

Crenshaw, James L., editor. *Studies in Ancient Israelite Wisdom.* New York: Ktav Publishing House, 1976.

———. "Wisdom in the O. T." *The Interpreter's Dictionary of the Bible.* Supplementary volume. Nashville: Abingdon Press, 1984.

Crisp, Oliver. "Jonathan Edwards and the Closing of the Table: Must the Eucharist be Open to All?" *Ecclesiology* 5/1 (2009): 48–68.

Cuningham, Charles E. *Timothy Dwight, 1752–1817.* New York: Macmillan Company, 1942.

Cypris, Ottomar Frederick . *Basic Principles: Translation and Commentary of Martin Bucer's* Grund und Ursach, *1524.* Th.D dissertation for Union Theological Seminary in the City New York, 1971. Ann Arbor: UMI Dissertation Services, 2003.

Daillé, Jean. *XXI sermons de Iean Daillé, sur le X. Chapitre de la I Epitre de S. Paul aux Corinthiens: prononcez à Charenton, l'an 1664, 1665, 1666.* Genève: Iean Ant. & Samuel de Tournes, 1668.

———. *Exposition de l'institution de la S. Cene: rapportée par Saint Paul en sa I. Epitre aux Corinthiens: en xix sermons.* Genève: Iean Ant. & Samuel de Tournes, 1664.

———. *Sermons sur le Catéchisme des Eglises Reformées*. Genève: Pour le Societé de Libraires, 1701.

Dale, Alfred William Winterslow. *The Life of R. W. Dale of Birmingham*. London: Hodder and Stoughton, 1898.

Dale, Robert W. *The Doctrine of the Real Presence and of the Lord's Supper*. Found in *Essays and Addresses*. 3rd edition. London: Hodder and Stoughton, 1901.

———. *Essays and Addresses*. 3rd edition. London: Hodder and Stoughton, 1901.

Dallimore, Arnold. *Spurgeon: A New Biography*. Edinburgh: Banner of Truth Trust, 1995.

Davies, Horton. *Like Angels from a Cloud: The English Metaphysical Preachers, 1588–1645*. San Marino: Huntington Library, 1986.

———. *From Cranmer to Baxter and Fox, 1534–1690*. Volume 1 of *Worship and Theology in England*, 3 volumes. Grand Rapids, MI: Eerdmans, 1996.

———. *From Newman to Martineau, 1850–1900*. Volume 4 of *Worship and Theology in England*, 5 volumes. Princeton, NJ: Princeton University Press, 1961–1975.

Davies, John Hamilton. *The Life of Richard Baxter of Kidderminster*. London: W. Kent, 1887.

Davies, Samuel. *The Sermons of the Rev. Samuel Davies*. 3 volumes. Reprint of the 1854 edition. Morgan, PA: Soli Deo Gloria Publications, 1995.

Dawley, Powel M. *John Whitgift and the Reformation*. New York: Charles Scribner, 1954.

de Félice, Guillaume. *Histoire des Protestants de France*. Paris and Toulouse, 1850. English translation, New York, 1851.

de Reuver, Arie. *Sweet Communion: Trajectories of Spirituality from the Middle Ages through the Further Reformation*. Translated by James A. DeJong. Grand Rapids, MI: Baker Academic, 2007.

de Vrijer, Marinus Johannes Antoinie. *Lodenstein (Uren met Lodenstein)*. Baarn, Netherlands, 1947.

Debelius, Martin. *Der Brief des Jakobus*. Edited by H. Greaven. 11th edition. Göttingen: Vandenhoeck & Ruprecht, 1964.

Denny, Joanna. *Anne Boleyn: A New Life of England's Tragic Queen*. Philadelphia: Da Capo Press, 2006.

[Dick, Rev. John]. Http://freestgeorges.blogspot.com/2008/08/teaching-theology-for-140-years-xi.html. Accessed September 21, 2012.

di Gangi, Mariano. *Peter Martyr Vermigli, 1499–1562: Renaissance Man, Reformation Master*. Lanham, MD: University Press of America, 1993.

DiLella, Alexander A. and Patrick W. Spehan. *The Wisdom of Ben Sira*. The Anchor Bible Commentary, volume 39. New York: Doubleday, 1987.

The Directory for the Publick Worship of God. New York: Reprinted for Robert Lenox Kennedy, 1880.

The Directory for the Publick Worship of God. Found in *Westminster Confession of Faith*. Inverness, UK: Printed by John C. Eccles for the Publications Committee of the Free Presbyterian Church of Scotland, 1976.

A Directory for the Publique Worship of God, Throughout the Three Kingdoms of England, Scotland, and Ireland. London: Printed for Evan Tyler, Alexander Fifield, Ralph Smith, and John Field, 1644.

The Directory for the Worship of God. Found in *The Constitution of the Presbyterian Church in the United States of America*. Philadelphia: Published for the General Assembly by the Board of Christian Education of the Presbyterian Church in the U.S.A., 1955.

Dix, Gregory. *The Shape of the Liturgy*. London: Adam and Charles Black Ltd., 1975.

Dodd, C. H. *The Interpretation of the Fourth Gospel*. Cambridge: At the University Press, 1958.

Donnelly, John Patrick and Joseph C. McLelland, editors. *The Peter Martyr Library*, volumes 1–9. Kirksville, MO: Thomas Jefferson University Press: Sixteenth Century Journal Publishers, 1994–.

Doolittle, Thomas. *A Treatise Concerning the Lord's Supper*. Edited by Don Kistler. Morgantown, PA.: Soli Deo Gloria Publications, 1998.

"Doolittle, Thomas." In the *Oxford Dictionary of National Biography*, 16:561. Edited by H. C. G. Matthew and Brian Harrison. 60 volumes. Oxford and New York: Oxford University Press, 2004.

"Thomas Doolitle (1630–1707)." www.monergism.com/directory/link_category/ Puritans/Misc-Puritans/Thomas-Doolitle/. Accessed April 7, 2011.

Doran, Suzan. *Elizabeth I and Religion: 1558–1603*. London and New York: Routledge, 1994.

Douglas, Brian. "Nicholas Ridley, c. 1500–1555, Bishop of London." http:// web.mac.com/brian.douglas/Anglican_Eucharistic_Theology/Blog/ Entries/2006/5/28_Nicholas_Ridleyc1500_-_1555Bishop_of_London. html. Accessed June 17, 2009.

———. "Richard Hooker, 1554–1600, Anglican Divine." http://web.mac.com/brian.douglas/Anglican_Eucharistic_Theology/Blog/Entries/2006/5/24_Richard-Hookerc._1554–1600Anglican-Divine.html. Accessed 9/1/2008.

Dowling, William C. "Timothy Dwight" In *American National Biography.* Oxford and New York: Oxford University Press, 1999.

Drummond, Lewis A. "Charles Haddon Spurgeon." Found in *Baptist Theologians.* Edited by Timothy George and David S. Dockery. Nashville: Broadman Press, 1990.

du Pury, Albert, editor. *Communio Sanctorum: Mélanges offerts à Jean-Jacques von Allmen.* Geneva: Labor et Fides, 1982.

Duffy, Eamon. *The Stripping of the Altars: Traditional Religion in England, 1400–1580.* New Haven: Yale University Press, 1992.

Dunlop, William. *A Collection of Confessions of Faith, Catechisms, Directories, Books of Discipline, etc.* Edinburgh: James Watson, 1719.

———. *A Compendium of the Laws of the Church of Scotland.* Edited by W. Steuart. Edinburgh, 1837–1840.

Dwight, Timothy, *Theology, Explained and Defended, in a Series of Sermons.* 5 volumes. Middletown, CT: Printed by Clark and Lyman for Timothy Dwight, New Haven, 1818–1819.

———. *Theology Explained and Defended, in a Series of Sermons.* 5 volumes. London: Reprinted for W. Baynes, 1822. Source taken from www.archive.org, accessed November 25, 2011.

Ebrard, J. H. August. *Reformiertes Kirchenbuch.* Zurich: Meyer und Zeller, 1847.

Edwards, Jonathan. *Ecclesiastical Writings.* The Works of Jonathan Edwards, volume 12. Edited by David D. Hall. New Haven and London: Yale University Press, 1994.

———. *A Faithful Narrative of the Surprising Work of God.* Found in Jonathan Edwards, *The Great Awakening.* The Works of Jonathan Edwards, volume 4. Edited by C. C. Goen. New Haven and London: Yale University Press, 1972.

———. "Glorying in the Savior," Found in Jonathan Edwards, *Sermons and Discourses, 1723–1729.* The Works of Jonathan Edwards, volume 14. Edited by Kenneth Minkema. New Haven and London: Yale University Press, 1997.

———. *The Humble Inquiry*. Found in Jonathan Edwards, *Ecclesiastical Writings*. The Works of Jonathan Edwards, volume 12. Edited by David D. Hall. New Haven and London: Yale University Press, 1994.

———. *Misrepresentations Corrected*. Found in Jonathan Edwards, *Ecclesiastical Writings*. The Works of Jonathan Edwards, volume 12. Edited by David D. Hall. New Haven and London: Yale University Press, 1994.

———. "Narrative of Communion Controversy." Found in Jonathan Edwards, *Ecclesiastical Writings*. The Works of Jonathan Edwards, volume 12. Edited by David D. Hall. New Haven and London: Yale University Press, 1994.

———. "The Sacrifice of Christ Acceptable," Found in Jonathan Edwards, *Sermons and Discourses, 1723–1729*. The Works of Jonathan Edwards, volume 14. Edited by Kenneth Minkema. New Haven and London: Yale University Press, 1997.

———. "Self-Examination and the Lord's Supper." Found in Jonathan Edwards, *Sermons and Discourses, 1730–1733*. The Works of Jonathan Edwards, volume 17. Edited by Mark Valeri. New Haven and London: Yale University Press, 1999.

———. *Sermons on the Lord's Supper*. Edited by Don Kistler. Orlando: The Northampton Press, 2007.

———. *Some Thoughts Concerning the Present Revival of Religion in New England*. Found in Jonathan Edwards, *The Great Awakening*. The Works of Jonathan Edwards, volume 4. Edited by C. C. Goen. New Haven and London: Yale University Press, 1972.

———. "The Spiritual Blessings of the Gospel Represented by a Feast." Found in Jonathan Edwards, *Sermons and Discourses, 1723–1729*. The Works of Jonathan Edwards, volume 14. Edited by Kenneth Minkema. New Haven and London: Yale University Press, 1997.

Eells, Hastings. *Martin Bucer*. New Haven: Yale University Press, 1931.

Eells, Robert. *Forgotten Saint: The Life of Theodore Frelinghuysen: A Case Study of Christian Leadership*. Lanham, MD: University Press of America; and Palos Heights, IL: Trinity Christian College, 1987.

Ella, George. "Henry Bullinger: Shepherd of the Churches." In *The Decades of Henry Bullinger*. Edited by Thomas Harding. Grand Rapids, MI: Reformation Heritage Books, 2004.

Elshout, Bartel. *Pastoral and Practical Theology of Wilhelm à Brakel*. Grand Rapids, MI: Reformation Heritage Books, 1997.

Elton, Geoffrey R., et al. "Cranmer, Thomas." In *The New Encyclopedia Britannica*, 3:713–715. 15th edition. 29 volumes. Chicago: Encyclopedia Britannica, Inc., 1994.

Emerson, Everett H. *English Puritanism from John Hooper to John Milton*. Durham, NC: Duke University Press, 1968.

Emery, Pierre-Yves. *Le sacrifice eucharistique selon le théologiens réformés français du XVIIe siècle*. Neuchâtel: Delachaux et Niestlé, 1959.

Encyclopædia Britannica. s.v. "Thomas Wilcox." Encyclopædia Britannica Inc., 2012. http://www.britannica.com/EBchecked/topic/643485/Thomas-Wilcox (accessed May. 23, 2012).

Engelberts, W. J. M. *Willem Teellinck*. Amsterdam, 1898.

"Erskine, Ebenezer." *The Encyclopedia Britannica*. 11th edition, 9:754–755. 32 volumes. New York: Encyclopedia Britannica, 1910.

Erskine, Ebenezer. *The Beauties of Ebenezer Erskine*. Selected by Samuel McMillan. Introduction by Joel R. Beeke. Grand Rapids, MI: Reformation Heritage Books; and Fearn, UK: Christian Focus Publications, 2001.

———. *The Rainbow of the Covenant Surrounding the Throne of Grace, Being the Substance of Some Sermons, Preached at the Sacrament of Muckart, June 23, 1728*. Belfast: James Magee, 1780.

———. *Sermons Upon the Most Important and Interesting Subjects*. Philadelphia: John M'Culloch, 1792.

———. *The Whole Works of the Late Rev. Mr. Ebenezer Erskine: Consisting of Sermons and Discourses on the Most Important and Interesting Subjects in Three Volumes*. London: William Baynes, 1799.

———. *The Works of Ebenezer Erskine*. Glasgow: Free Presbyterian Publications, 2001.

Erskine, Ebenezer and Ralph. *A Collection of Sermons from Various Important Subjects and on Divers Occasions*. London: Edward Dilly, 1757.

"Erskine, Ralph." In *The Encyclopedia Britannica*. 11th edition, 9:755–756. 32 volumes. New York: Encyclopedia Britannica, 1910.

Erskine, Ralph. *Gospel Sonnets, or Spiritual Songs: To Which Is Prefixed an Account of the Author's Life and Writings*. Pittsburg: Luke Loomis & Co., 1831.

———. *The Life and Practical Works of the Reverend Ralph Erskine*. Xenia, OH: Board of the Calvinistic Book Concern, 1844.

———. *Select Sermons of Ralph Erskine*. Volume 1. London: Houlston and Wright, 1863.

———. *The Sermons and Other Practical Works: Consisting of About One Hundred and Fifty Sermons, Besides His Poetical Pieces*. Glasgow: Printed by J. Bryce, 1777–1778.

———. *Sermons and Other Practical Writings: To Which Is Prefixed a Short Account of the Author's Life and Writings*. Glasgow: Robert Urie, 1765.

———. *The Works of Ralph Erskine*. 8 volumes. Glasgow: Free Presbyterian Publications, 1991.

Fant Jr., Clyde E., *20 Centuries of Great Preaching*. 12 volumes. Waco, Texas: Word Books, Publisher, 1971.

Ferguson, Sinclair B., Graham S. Harrison, Michael A. G. Haykin, Robert W. Oliver, and Carl R. Trueman. *John Owen: The Man and His Theology*. Phillipsburg, NJ: Presbyterian and Reformed Publishing Co., and Darlington, UK: Evangelical Press, 2002.

Figgis, Neville J. "Erastus and Erastianism." *Journal of Theological Studies* 2 (1901): 66–101.

Fincham, Kenneth and Nicholas Tyacke. *Altars Restored: The Changing Face of English Religious Worship, 1547–c.1700*. Oxford: Oxford University Press, 2007.

Finlayson, Michael George. *Historians, Puritanism, and the English Revolution*. Toronto and Buffalo: University of Toronto Press, 1983.

The First and Second Prayer Books of Edward VI. New York: E. P. Dutton, 1949.

Fitzmeir, John R. "Dwight, Timothy." In *Dictionary of Christianity in America*. Edited by Daniel G. Reid, Robert D. Linder, Bruce L. Shelley, and Harry S. Stout. Downers Grove, IL: InterVarsity Press, 1990.

———. *New England's Moral Legislator: Timothy Dwight, 1752–1817*. Bloomington: Indiana University Press, 1998.

———. "Taylor, Nathaniel William." In *Dictionary of Christianity in America*. Edited by Daniel G. Reid, Robert D. Linder, Bruce L. Shelley, and Harry S. Stout. Downers Grove, IL: InterVarsity Press, 1990.

Flavel, John. *Husbandry Spiritualized: The Heavenly Use of Earthly Things*. Found in John Flavel. *The Works of John Flavel*, volume 5. Edinburgh and Carlisle, PA: The Banner of Truth Trust, 1982.

Florijn, H. "Immens, Petrus." In *Biografisch Lexicon voor de Geschiedenis van het Gereformeerd Protestantisme*. Volume 5. Edited by C. Houtman e.a. Kampen: Kok, 2001, 275–276.

Frantz, Adolf. *Die Messe im deutschen Mittelalter, Beiträge zur Geschichte der liturgie und des religiösen Volkslebens.* Darmstadt: Wissenschaftliche Buchgesellschaft, 1963.

Fraser, Donald. *The Life and Diary of the Reverend Ebenezer Erskine, of Stirling: Father of the Secession Church, to Which is Prefixed a Memoir of His Father, the Rev. Henry Erskine, of Chirnside.* Edinburgh: W. Oliphant, 1831.

Frelinghuysen, Theodorus Jacobus. *Forerunner of the Great Awakening: Sermons of Theodorus Jacobus Frelinghuysen (1691–1747).* Edited by Joel Beeke. The Historical Series of the Reformed Church in America, no. 36. Grand Rapids, MI: Wm. B. Eerdmans Publishing Co., 2000.

Frere, Walter H., editor. *Puritan Manifestoes: A Study of the Origin of the Puritan Revolt.* London: Published for the Church Historical Society by S. P. C. K., 1954.

Freundt, Albert H., Jr. "Dwight, Timothy." In *Encyclopedia of the Reformed Faith.* Edited by Donald K. McKim. Louisville: Westminster John Knox Press; and Edinburgh: Saint Andrew Press, 1992.

Fritsch, Charles T. *The Book of Proverbs.* The Interpreter's Bible. Volume IV. New York & Nashville: Abingdon Press, 1955.

Gaffin, Richard B., *Calvin and the Sabbath: The Controversy of Applying the Fourth Commandment.* Fearn, UK: Christian Focus Publications, 1997.

Gärtner, Bertil E. *John 6 and the Jewish Passover.* Lund: C. W. K. Gleerup, 1959.

Gasquet, Francis Aidan. *Edward VI and the Book of Common Prayer.* London: J. Hodges, 1891.

Gaustad, Edwin S. *The Great Awakening in New England.* New York: Harper, 1957.

Gebbie, D. Douglas. "The Church and State in Scotland." In *A Historical Introduction to the Works of William Cunningham.* www.presbyterianreformed.org/articlesbooksShow.php?articlesID=1. Accessed 7/30/2012.

Gemser, Berend. *Sprüche Solomons.* In *Handbuch zum alten Testament.* 2nd edition. Tübingen: J. C. B. Mohr (Paul Siebeck), 1963.

Gerrish, Brian A. *Grace and Gratitude: The Eucharistic Theology of John Calvin.* Eugene, OR: Wipf & Stock Publishers, 2002. First published in 1993 by Fortress Press.

Gerstner, John H. *The Rational Biblical Theology of Jonathan Edwards, in three volumes.* Powhatan, VA: Berea Publications, 1993.

Gewehr, Wesley M. *The Great Awakening in Virginia, 1740–1790.* Durham, NC: Duke University Press, 1930.

Gilbert, M. "L'Eloge de la Sagesse (siracide 24)." *Revue théologique de Louvin* V (1974): 326–348.

Goebel, M., and S. D. van Been. "Lodenstein, Jodocus van." In *Realencyklopädie für protestantische Theologie und Kirche*, 11:572–574. Edited by J. J. Herzog. 24 volumes. Leipzig: J. C. Hinrichs, 1896–1913.

Goehler, Albert. *Calvins Lehre von der Heiligung*. Munich, 1934.

Gordon, Bruce and Emidio Campi, editors. *Architect of the Reformation: An Introduction to Heinrich Bullinger*. Grand Rapids, MI: Baker Academic, 2004.

Graham, Stephen R. "Nevin, John Williamson (1803–1886)." In *Dictionary of Christianity in America*. Edited by Daniel G. Reid, Robert D. Linder, Bruce L. Shelley, and Harry S. Stout. Downers Grove, IL: InterVarsity Press, 1990.

Green, Ian. "Review of Kenneth Fincham and Nicholas Tyacke, *Altars Restored*, and Christopher Haigh, *The Plain Man's Pathways to Heaven*." In *The English Historical Review*, 74/508:677–701.

Greschat, Martin. "Bucer, Martin" *The Oxford Encyclopedia of the Reformation*, 1:221–224. Edited by Hans J. Hillerbrand. 4 volumes. New York: Oxford University Press, 1996.

———. *Martin Bucer: A Reformer and His Times*. Louisville: Westminster John Knox Press, 2004.

Griffiths, John, editor. *The Homilies: Appointed to be Read in Churches*. Hereford: Brynmill, 2006.

Haag, Eugène and Émile. *La France Protestante*. 9 volumes. Paris and Genève: J. Cherbuliez, 1846–1859.

Hageman, Howard. "Nevin, John Williamson (1803–1886)." In *Encyclopedia of the Reformed Faith*. Edited by Donald K. McKim. Louisville: Westminster John Knox Press; Edinburgh: Saint Andrew Press, 1992.

Haigh, Christopher. *The Plain Man's Pathways to Heaven: Kinds of Christianity in Post-Reformation England, 1570–1640*. Oxford: Oxford University Press, 2007.

Hall, Joseph H. "General Synod of the Associate Reformed Presbyterian Church." In *Dictionary of Christianity in America*. Downers Grove, IL: InterVarsity Press, 1990.

Haller, William. *Elizabeth I and the Puritans*. New York: Cornell University Press, 1964.

———. *The Rise of Puritanism; or, the Way to the New Jerusalem as Set Forth in Pulpit and Press from Thomas Cartwright to John Lilburne and John Milton, 1570–1643*. New York: Columbia University Press, 1947.

Hambrick-Stowe, Charles E. *The Practice of Piety: Puritan Devotional Practices in Seventh-Century New England*. Chapel Hill: Published for the Institute of Early American History and Culture, Williamsburg, Virginia, by the University of North Carolina Press, 1982.

Hanko, Herman. *The History of the Free Offer*. Chapter 6, "The Marrow Controversy." Grandville, MI: Theological School of the Protestant Reformed Churches, 1989. www.prca.org/pamphlets/Free%20Offer/chapter6.htm. Accessed 7/25/2012.

Hanna, William. *Life of Thomas Chalmers*. Edited by James C. Moffat. Cincinnati: Moore, Anderson, Wilstach & Keys; New York: Newman & Ivison, 1853.

———. *Memoirs of the Life and Writings of Thomas Chalmers, D.D., LL.D.* 4 volumes. Edinburgh: Thomas Constable and Co.; London: Hamilton, Adams, and Co., 1852.

Harding, Thomas, editor. *The Decades of Henry Bullinger*. Grand Rapids, MI: Reformation Heritage Books, 2004.

Harman, Allan. *Matthew Henry: His Life and Influence*. Fearn, UK: Christian Focus Publications, 2012.

Harmelink, Herman. "Another Look at Frelinghuysen and His Awakening." *Church History* 37 (December 1968): 423–438.

Hart, Darryl G. *John Williamson Nevin: High-Church Calvinist*. Phillipsburg, NJ: Presbyterian and Reformed Publications, 2005.

Hartog, Jan. *Geschiedenis van de Predikkunde in de Protestantsche Kerk van Nederland*. Utrecht: Kemink & Zoon, 1887.

Hauggaard, William P. *Elizabeth and the English Reformation: The Struggle for a Stable Settlement of Religion*. London: Cambridge University Press, 1968.

Hedegard, David. *Seder R. Amran Gaon*. Lund: A. B. Ph. Lindstedts Universitetsbokhandel, 1951.

"Hegelianism." In *Encyclopedia Britannica*, 5:798–799. 15th edition. 29 volumes. Chicago: Encyclopedia Britannica, Inc., 1994.

Heppe, Heinrich. *Geschichte des Pietismus und der Mystik in der reformierten Kirche*. Leiden: Brill, 1879.

Heidelberg Catechism. In *The Constitution of the Presbyterian Church: Part I, The Book of Confessions*. Louisville: The Office of the General Assembly, 2004.

Heidelberg Catechism, 1563–1963:400th Anniversary Edition, The. New York: United Church Press, 1962.

Helm, Paul. *Calvin and the Calvinists*. Carlisle, PA: Banner of Truth Trust, 1982.

Henry, Matthew. *An Account of the Life and Death of Mr. Philip Henry.* London: Printed for Tho. Parkhurst and John Lawrence, 1698.

———. *A Church in the House: or, Family Religion.* New York: American Tract Society, [1824?].

———. *The Communicant's Companion: or Instructions and Helps for the Right Receiving of the Lord's Supper.* Morris-town, NJ: Printed by Henry P. Russell, 1809.

———. *The Communicant's Companion : or Instructions and Helps for the Right Receiving of the Lord's Supper.* Volume 1 of *The Complete Works of the Rev. Matthew Henry . . . (His Commentary Excepted).* 2 volumes. Reprint of the 1855 edition. Grand Rapids, MI: Baker Book House, 1979.

———. *An Exposition of All the Books of the Old and New Testaments.* Six volumes. Edinburgh: Printed by and for Colin Macfarquhar, 1772.

———. *An Exposition of the Shorter Catechism.* Edinburgh: J. Lowe, 1857.

———. *Life and Times of the Rev. Phillip Henry, M. A., Father of the Commentator.* New York: R. Carter, 1849.

———. *Matthew Henry's Commentary on the Whole Bible.* Peabody, MA: Hendrickson Publishing Co., 1991.

———. *A Method for Prayer.* Philadelphia: Towar, J. & D.M. Hogan, and Thomas Kite, 1831. Reprint edited by J. Ligon Duncan III. Greenville, SC: Reformed Academic Press, 1994.

Heppe, Heinrich. *Geschichte des Pietismus und der Mystik in der reformirten Kirche, namentlich der Niederlande.* Leiden: E. J. Brill, 1879.

Hodge, Charles. "Letter of appreciation to C. W. Baird." In *Correspondence: Feb. 15, 1845–Aug. 28, 1860,* ed. William McKendree Scott, Archives of Speer Library at Princeton Theological Seminary, 1845–1860.

———. "Review of Nevin's *Mystical Presence.*" In *Biblical Repertory and Princeton Review* 20/2 (1848).

———. *Systematic Theology.* Volume 3. Reprint. Grand Rapids, MI: Wm. B. Eerdmans Publishing Co., 1973.

Hoffecker, W. Andrew. *Charles Hodge: The Pride of Princeton.* Phillipsburg, NJ: Presbyterian and Reformed, 2011.

———. "Hodge, Charles (1797–1878)." In *Dictionary of Christianity in America.* Edited by Daniel G. Reid, Robert D. Linder, Bruce L. Shelley, and Harry S. Stout. Downers Grove, IL: InterVarsity Press, 1990.

———. "Warfield, Benjamin Breckinridge." In *Dictionary of Christianity in America*. Edited by Daniel G. Reid, Robert D. Linder, Bruce L. Shelley, and Harry S. Stout. Downers Grover, IL: InterVarsity Press, 1990.

Hoffman, John Charles. "Pietism." In *New Catholic Encyclopedia*, 11:355. 17 volumes. Washington, D.C.: Catholic University of America Press, 1968.

Hopf, Constantin. *Martin Bucer and the English Reformation*. Oxford: B. Blackwell, 1946.

Holifield, E. Brooks. *The Covenant Sealed: The Development of Puritan Sacramental Theology in Old and New England, 1570–1720*. New Haven: Yale University Press, 1974.

Hooker, Richard. *Of the Laws of Ecclesiastical Polity*. Edition Keble, 1865. As quoted in Brian Douglas. "Richard Hooker, 1554–1600, Anglican Divine." http://web.mac.com/brian.douglas/Anglican_Eucharistic_Theology/Blog/Entries/2006/5/24_Richard-Hookerc._1554-1600Anglican-Divine.html. Accessed 9/1/2008.

Hudson, Winthrop S. *The Cambridge Connection and the Elizabethan Settlement of 1559*. Durham, NC: Duke University Press, 1980.

Immens, Peter. *The Pious Communicant Encouraged and Directed in What He May Approach the Holly Supper, Acceptably to God and Profitably to Himself in a Series of Lectures*. Translated by John Bassett. New York: Isaac Collins and Son, 1801.

———. *True and False Assurance*. Grand Rapids, MI: Free Reformed Church, 19–.

———. *De godvruchtige avondmaalganger*. Groningen: R. Boerma, 1900.

Isbell, S. "Rutherford, Samuel." In Nigel M. de S. Cameron, editor. *Dictionary of Scottish Church History and Theology*. Edinburgh: T. & T. Clark; Downers Grove, IL: InterVarsity Press, 1993.

James, Frank A., III, John Patrick Donnelly, and Joseph C. McLelland, editors. *The Peter Martyr Reader*. Kirksville, MO: Truman State University Press, 1999.

"Jean-Jacques von Allmen." www.puritanboard.com/f18/jean-jacques-von-allmen-32420/. Accessed October 7, 2012.

Jenkins, Gary W. *John Jewell and the English National Church: The Dilemma of an Erastian Reformer*. Aldershot, UK: Ashgate Publishing Company, 2006.

Jenny, Markus. *Die Einheit des Abendmahlsgottesdienstes*. Zürich and Stuttgart: Zwingli Verlag Zürich, 1968.

Jeremias, Joachim. *The Eucharistic Words of Jesus*. New York: Charles Scribner's Son, 1966.

Jewel, John. "Sermon preached at Paul's Cross." Found in John Jewel. *The Works of John Jewel*. Edited by John Ayre. The Parker Society edition. Cambridge: Printed at the University Press, 1845.

Johnson, Dale W. and Richard G. Kyle. *John Knox: An Introduction to His Life and Works*. Eugene, OR: Wipf and Stock, 2009.

Jones, Norman L. "Elizabethan Settlement." In *The Oxford Encyclopedia of the Reformation*, 2:36–38. Edited by Hans J. Hillerbrand. 4 volumes. New York: Oxford University Press, 1996.

———. *Faith by Statute: Parliament and the Settlement of Religion, 1559*. London: Royal Historical Society; and Atlantic Highlands, NJ: Humanities Press, 1982.

Jungmann, Joseph Andreas. *The Mass of the Roman Rite: Its Origins and Development*. Translated by Francis A. Brunner. 2 volumes. New York: Benziger, 1950–1955.

Kaegi, Werner. *Erasmus ehedem und heute, 1469-1969*. Basel: Helbing and Lichtenhahn, 1969.

"Kantianism." In *Encyclopedia Britannica*, 6:726–727. 15th edition. 29 volumes. Chicago: Encyclopedia Britannica, Inc., 1994.

Kapic, Kelly M. *Communion With God: The Divine and the Human in the Theology of John Owen*. Grand Rapids, MI: Baker Academic, 2007.

Kemp, Charles F. *A Pastoral Triumph: The Story of Richard Baxter and His Ministry at Kidderminster*. New York: Macmillan Co., 1948.

Kennedy, Earl William. "Taylor, Nathaniel William (1786–1858)." In *Encyclopedia of the Reformed Faith*. Edited by Donald K. McKim. Louisville: Westminster John Knox Press; and Edinburgh: Saint Andrew Press, 1992.

Ker, John. *The Erskines: Ebenezer and Ralph*. Edinburgh: James Gemmell, 1881.

Kerr, Hugh T., editor. *Sons of the Prophets: Leaders in Protestantism from Princeton Seminary*. Princeton, NJ: Princeton University Press, 1963.

Ketley, Joseph, editor. *The Two Liturgies, A.D. 1549 and A.D. 1552*. Cambridge: Printed at the University Press, 1844.

Kidner, Derek. *An Introduction To Wisdom Literature: The Wisdom Of Proverbs, Job & Ecclesiastes*. Downers Grove, IL: InterVarsity Press, 1985.

Kittel, Gerhard. *Theological Dictionary of the New Testament*. Translated and edited by Geoffrey W. Bromiley. 10 volumes. Grand Rapids, MI: Wm. B. Eerdmans Publishing Co., 1964–1976.

Kittel, Gerard and Gerhard Friedrich, editors. *Theologisches Wörterbuch zum Neuen Testament*. 9 volumes. Stuttgart: W. Kohlhammer Verlag, 1964.

Kittelson, James M. *Wolfgang Capito, from Humanist to Reformer*. Leiden: E. J. Brill, 1975.

Kirby, Torrance, Emidio Campi and Frank A. James, III, editors. *A Companion to Peter Martyr Vermigli*. Leiden and Boston: Brill, 2009.

Kirby, W. J. Torrance. *Richard Hooker, Reformer and Platonist*. Aldershot, UK and Burlington, VT: Ashgate Publications, 2005.

Kirby, W. J. Torrance, editor. *Richard Hooker and the English Reformation*. Dordrecht and Boston: Kluwer Academic Publishers, 2003.

Kleinknecht, Hermann. "PNEUMA." *Theologisches Wörterbuch zum neuen Testament*, 6:343–357. Edited by Gerhard Kittel and Gerhard Friedrich. 9 volumes. Stuttgart: W. Kohlhammer Verlag, 1964.

Knappen, Marshall Mason. *Tudor Puritanism: A Chapter in the History of Idealism*. Chicago and London: The University of Chicago Press, 1970.

Knowles, Nigel. *Richard Baxter of Kidderminster*. Bewdley: Star and Garter, 2000.

Knox, John. *The Forme of Prayers and Ministration of the Sacraments*. Geneva, 1556.

"Knox, John." *Oxford Dictionary of the Christian Church*. Edited by F. L. Cross. Oxford: Oxford University Press, 1974.

Knox, Ronald A. *Enthusiasm: A Chapter in the History of Religion*. London: Oxford University Press, 1950.

Koch, Ernst. *Die Theologie der Confessio Helvetica Posterior*. Neukirchen-Vluyn: Neukirchener Verlag des Erziehungsvereins GmbH, 1968.

Kolfhaus, Wilhelm. *Christusgemeinschaft bei Johannes Calvin*. Neukirchen: Krs. Moer, 1939.

Koopmans, Jan. *Das altkirchliche Dogma in der Reformation*. Munich, 1955.

Kraus, Hans-Joachim. *Psalmen*. 2 volumes. Biblischer Kommentar altes Testament. Neukirchen Kreis Moers: Neukirchener Verlag, 1961.

Krusche, Werner. *Das Wirken des Heiligen Geistes nach Calvin*. Göttingen: Vandenhoeck und Ruprecht, 1957.

Kuntz, John Kenneth. "The Canonical Wisdom Psalms of Ancient Israel, their Rhetorical, Thematic, and Formal Dimensions." *Essays in Honor of James Muilenberg*. Edited by Jared T. Jackson and Martin Kessler. Pittsburgh: The Pickwick Press, 1974.

Lachman, David C. "Andrew Mitchell Thomson." In *Dictionary of Scottish Church History and Theology*. Edited by Nigel M. de S. Cameron. Edinburgh: T. & T. Clark, 1993.

Lake, Peter. "Admonition Controversy," *Oxford Encyclopedia of the Reformation*, 1:7. Edited by Hans J. Hillerbrand. 4 volumes. New York and Oxford: Oxford University Press, 1996.

———. *Anglicans and Puritans? Presbyterianism and English Conformist Thought from Whitgift to Hooker.* London: Allen & Unwin, 1988.

———. "Cartwright, Thomas." *Oxford Encyclopedia of the Reformation*, 1:269–70. Edited by Hans J. Hillerbrand. 4 volumes. New York and Oxford: Oxford University Press, 1996.

———. *Moderate Puritans and the Elizabethan Church.* Cambridge and New York: Cambridge University Press, 1982.

———. "Whitgift, John." *Oxford Encyclopedia of the Reformation*, 4:270–71. Edited by Hans J. Hillerbrand. 4 volumes. New York and Oxford: Oxford University Press, 1996.

Lamont, William M. *Puritanism to Nonconformity.* 2 volumes. New York: Harper, 1848–49.

Lee, Sang Kyun. *The Philosophical Theology of Jonathan Edwards*. Princeton, NJ: Princeton University Press, 1988.

Leith, John H. *Calvin's Doctrine of the Christian Life*. Louisville: Westminster John Knox, 1989.

Lietzmann, Hans. *Mass and Lord's Supper: A Study in the History of the Liturgy*. Translated by Dorothea H. G. Reeve. Leiden: E. J. Brill, 1979.

———. *Messe und Herrenmahl: eine Studie zur Geschichte der Liturgie*. Bonn: A. Marcus und E. Weber's Verlag, 1926.

Lillback, Peter. *The Binding of God: Calvin's Role in the Development of Covenant Theology*. Grand Rapids, MI: Baker Academic; Carlisle, UK: Paternoster, 2001.

Lindberg, Carter, editor. *The Pietist Theologians: An Introduction to Theology in the Seventeenth and Eighteenth Centuries*. Malden, MA: Blackwell Publications, 2005.

Loades, David M. "Ridley, Nicholas." In *The Oxford Encyclopedia of the Reformation*, 3:431–432. Edited by Hans J. Hillerbrand. 4 volumes. New York and Oxford: Oxford University Press, 1996.

———. *The Oxford Martyrs*. Bangor, Gwynedd: Headstart History, 1992.

Loane, Marcus L. *Makers of Puritan History*. Edinburgh: Banner of Truth, 2009.

Locher, Gottfried W. *Huldrych Zwingli in neuer Sicht*. Zürich and Stuttgart: Zwingli Verlag Zürich, 1969.

———. *Zwingli's Thought: New Perspectives*. Leiden: E. J. Brill, 1981.

Lodge, C. F., and E. Martin. "The Crisis of the Church in the Middle Colonies, 1720–1740." In *Interpreting Colonial America: Selected Readings*. Edited by James Kirby Martin. New York: Dodd and Mead, 1973.

Logan, Samuel L. "Tennent, Gilbert (1703–1764)." *Dictionary of American Christianity*. Edited by Daniel G. Reid, Robert D. Linder, Bruce L. Shelley, and Harry S. Stout. Downers Grove, IL: InterVarsity Press, 1990.

Luther, Martin. *Works*. 6 volumes. Philadelphia: Muhlenberg Press, 1930–1943.

Lytle, Guy Fitch, III. "Articles of Religion." In *The Oxford Encyclopedia of the Reformation*, 1:80–83. Edited by Hans J. Hillerbrand. 4 volumes. New York: Oxford University Press, 1996.

Maag, Karin, editor. *Melanchthon in Europe: His Work and Influence Beyond Wittenberg*. Grand Rapids, MI: Baker Books, 1999.

MacCulloch, Diarmaid. *Boy King: Edward VI and the Protestant Reformation*. New York: Palgrave, 2001.

———. *The Later Reformation in England, 1547-1603*. New York: Palgrave, 2001.

———. *Thomas Cranmer: A Life*. New Haven: Yale University Press, 1996.

MacEwen, Alexander R. *The Erskines*. Edinburgh and London: Oliphant, Anderson & Ferrier, 1900.

MacGregor, Geddes. *The Thundering Scot*. Philadelphia: The Westminster Press, 1957.

Mack, Burton. *Logos und Sophia, Untersuchungen zur Weisheitstheologie im hellenistischen Judentum*. SUNT, 10. Göttingen: Vandenhoeck und Ruprecht, 1973.

Maclean, Iain S. "The First Pietist: an Introduction and Translation of a Communion Sermon by Jodocus van Lodenstein." In *Calvin Studies VI*. Edited by John Leith. Davidson, NC: Calvin Colloquium, 1992.

Macleod, John. *Scottish Theology in Relation to Church History Since the Reformation*. Edinburgh and Carlisle, PA: Banner of Truth Trust, 1974.

Mann, Jacob and Isaiah Sonne. *The Bible as Read and Preached in the Old Synagogue*. 2 volumes. New York: KTAV Publishing House, 1971, and Cincinnati, Ohio: Hebrew Union College, 1966.

Manschreck, Clyde L. *Melanchthon: The Quiet Reformer*. New York: Abingdon Press, 1958.

Marsden, George M. *The Evangelical Mind and the New School Presbyterian Experience.* New Haven: Yale University Press, 1970.

———. *Jonathan Edwards: A Life.* New Haven: Yale University Press, 2003.

Marshall, Rosalind K. *John Knox.* Edinburgh: Berlinn, 2008.

Mather, Cotton. *A Companion for Communicants: Discourses on the Nature, the Design, and the Subject of the Lords Supper; with Devout Methods of Preparing for, And Approaching to that Blessed Ordinance.* Boston, 1690.

Mather, Increase. *The Order of the Gospel, Professed and Practiced by the Churches of Christ in New England.* Boston: B. Green and J. Allen for Nicholas Buttolph, 1700.

Mauser, Ulrich W. *Christ in the Wilderness.* SBT 39 (1963).

Maxson, Charles H. *The Great Awakening in the Middle Colonies.* Chicago: University of Chicago Press, 1920.

Maxwell, Jack Martin. *The Liturgical Lessons of Mercersburg.* ThD thesis. Princeton Theological Seminary, 1969.

———. *Worship and Reformed Theology: The Liturgical Lessons of Mercersburg.* Pittsburgh Theological Monograph Series. Pittsburgh: Pickwick Press, 1976.

Maxwell, William D. *John Knox's Genevan Service Book.* Westminster: Faith Press, 1965.

Mayor, Stephen. "The Teaching of John Owen Concerning the Lord's Supper." *Scottish Journal of Theology* 18 (1965): 170–181.

McCormack, Bruce L. "Union with Christ in Calvin's Theology: Grounds for a Divinization Theory?" In *Tributes to John Calvin: A Celebration of His Quincentenary*. Edited by David W. Hall. The Calvin 500 Series. Phillipsburg, NJ: Presbyterian and Reformed Publishing, 2010.

McCoy, Charles S. and J. Wayne Baker. *Fountainhead of Federalism: Heinrich Bullinger and the Covenant Tradition.* Louisville: Westminster John Knox Press, 1991.

McDonnell, Kilian. *John Calvin, the Church, and the Eucharist.* Princeton, NJ: Princeton University Press, 1967.

McGinn, Donald J. *The Admonition Controversy.* New Brunswick, NJ: Rutgers University Press, 1949.

McIntosh, John R. "Willison, John." In *Dictionary of Scottish Church History and Theology*. Edited by Nigel M. de S. Cameron. Edinburgh: T. & T. Clark, 1993.

McKane, William. *Proverbs, a New Approach.* Philadelphia: Westminster Press, 1975.

McKee, Elsie Anne. *John Calvin on the Diaconate and Liturgical Almsgiving.* Geneva: Librairie Droz, 1984.

McKim, Donald K. "Calvin's View of Scripture." *Readings in Calvin's Theology.* Grand Rapids, MI: Baker Book House, 1984.

———. *Ramism in William Perkins' Theology.* New York: Peter Lang, 1987.

McLelland, Joseph C. *The Visible Words of God: An Exposition of the Sacramental Theology of Peter Martyr Vermigli, A.D. 1500–1562.* Grand Rapids, MI: Wm. B. Eerdmans Publishing Co., 1957.

McNair, Philip Murray Jourdan. *Peter Martyr in Italy: An Anatomy of Apostasy.* Oxford: Clarendon, 1967.

M'Crie, Thomas. *The Life of John Knox.* Glasgow: Free Presbyterian Publications, 1976.

Mead, Sidney Earl. *Nathaniel William Taylor (1786–1858), A Connecticut Liberal.* Reprint of the 1942 edition. Hamden, CT: Archon Books, 1967.

Meyer, Rudolf. "MANNA." *Theologisches Wörterbuch zum neuen Testament,* 4:466f. Edited by Gerhard Kittel and Gerhard Friedrich. 9 volumes. Stuttgart: W. Kohlhammer Verlag, 1964.

Miller, Perry, and Alan Heimert, editors. *The Great Awakening: Documents Illustrating the Crisis and its Consequences.* Indianapolis: Bobbs-Merrill, 1967.

Miller, Ross J. "Calvin's Understanding of Psalm Singing as a Means of Grace," and "Music and the Spirit: Psalm Singing in Calvin's Liturgy." Found in *Calvin Studies VI.* Edited by John H. Leith. Papers presented at the Sixth Colloquium on Calvin Studies at Davidson College. Davidson, NC: Colloquium on Calvin Studies, 1994.

M'Kerrow, John. *History of the Secession Church.* Edinburgh: Oliphant, 1839.

Moore, George Foot. *Judaism in the First Centuries of the Christian Era.* 2 volumes. New York: Schocken Books, 1971.

Morgan, Irvonwy. *The Nonconformity of Richard Baxter.* London: Epworth Press, [1946].

Mowinckel, Sigmund. *The Psalms in Israel's Worship.* Translated by D. R. Ap-Thomas. 2 volumes. New York and Nashville: Abingdon Press, 1962.

Muilenburg, James. "The Book of Isaiah," Chapters 40–66. *Interpreters Bible,* volume 5. New York and Nashville: Abingdon Press, 1956.

Muller, Richard A. "The Foundation of Calvin's Theology: Scripture as Revealing God's Word." *The Duke Divinity School Review* 44 (1979).

Muller, Richard A. and Rowland S. Ward. *Scripture and Worship: Biblical Interpretation and the Directory for Public Worship*. Phillipsburg, NJ: Presbyterian and Reformed Publishing, 2007.

Murphy, Roland E. "A Consideration of the Classification 'Wisdom Psalms'." *Vetus Testamentum*, Sup. 9, pp. 156–167.

———. *Seven Books of Wisdom*. Milwaukee: Bruce Publishing Co., 1960.

Murphy, Terence R. "Book of Homilies." In *The Oxford Encyclopedia of the Reformation*, 1:194–195. Edited by Hans J. Hillerbrand. 4 volumes. New York and Oxford: Oxford University Press, 1996.

Murray, Iain H. *A Scottish Christian Heritage*. Edinburgh: The Banner of Truth Trust, 2006.

———. *Jonathan Edwards: A New Biography*. Edinburgh: Banner of Truth Trust, 1987.

———. *A Scottish Christian Heritage*. Edinburgh: The Banner of Truth Trust, 2006.

Nestingen, James Arne. "Gnesio-Lutherans." In *Oxford Encyclopedia of the Reformation*, 2:177–180. Edited by Hans J. Hillerbrand. 4 volumes. New York: Oxford University Press, 1996.

Nevin, John Williamson. *The Anxious Bench*. Chambersburg, PA: Printed at the Office of the "Weekly Messenger," 1843. Reprint edited by Augustine Thompson. Eugene, OR: Wipf and Stock Publishers, 2000.

———. "Introduction." In *The Commentary of Dr. Zacharias Ursinus on the Heidelberg Catechism*. Fourth American Edition. Cincinnati: Elm Street Printing Company, 1888.

———. *The Mystical Presence: A Vindication of the Reformed or Calvinistic Doctrine of the Holy Eucharist*. Philadelphia: J. B. Lippincott & Co., 1846. Reprint edited by Augustine Thompson. Eugene: OR: Wipf and Stock, 2000.

———. *The Mystical Presence: and the Doctrine of the Reformed Church on the Lord's Supper*. Edited by Linden J. DeBie. General editor W. Bradford Littlejohn, Eugene, OR : Wipf & Stock Publishers, 2012.

A New Directory for the Public Worship of God: Found on the Book of Common Order, 1560–64, and the Westminster Directory, 1643–45. Edinburgh: Printed for the Free Church of Scotland by MacNiven and Wallace, 1898.

Nichols, James Hastings. *The Mercersburg Theology*. New York: Oxford University Press, 1966.

———. *Romanticism in American Theology: Nevin and Schaff at Mercersburg*. Chicago: University of Chicago Press, [1961].

Nicole, Roger. "Warfield, Benjamin Breckinridge." In *Encyclopedia of the Reformed Faith*. Edited by Donald K. McKim. Louisville: Westminster John Knox Press; and Edinburgh: Saint Andrew Press, 1992.

Niesel, Willhelm. *Calvins Lehre vom Abendmahl*. Munich: Chr. Kaiser, 1930.

———. *The Theology of Calvin*. English translation by Harold Knight. Philadelphia: The Westminster Press, 1956.

Noll, Mark A. *A History of Christianity in the United States and Canada*. Grand Rapids, MI: Eerdmans, 1992.

———. "Hodge, Charles (1797–1878)." In *New Dictionary of Theology*. Edited by Sinclair B. Ferguson and David F. Wright. Downers Grove, IL and Leicester, UK: InterVarsity Press, 1988.

———. "Warfield, Benjamin Breckinridge." In *New Dictionary of Theology*. Edited by Sinclair B. Ferguson, David F. Wright, and J. I. Packer. Downers Grove, IL and Leicester, UK: InterVarsity Press, 1988.

Null, Ashley, *Thomas Cranmer's Doctrine of Repentance: Renewing the Power to Love*. Oxford and New York: Oxford University Press, 2000.

Nuttall, Geoffrey Fillingham. *Richard Baxter*. Stanford: Stanford University Press, 1965.

Oberman, Heiko A. *The Harvest of Medieval Theology: Gabriel Biel and Late Medieval Nominalism*. Revised edition. Grand Rapids, MI: Baker Book House, 2000.

———. "*Via Antiqua* and *Via Moderna*: Late Medieval Prolegomena to Early Reformation Thought." *Journal of the History of Ideas* 48/1 (Jan–Mar 1987): 23–40.

O'Donovan, Oliver. *On the Thirty-Nine Articles: A Conversation with Tudor Christianity*. Exeter: Paternoster Press, 1986.

Old, Hughes Oliphant. "Biblical Wisdom Theology and Calvin's Understanding of the Lord's Supper." *Calvin Studies VI*. Edited by John H. Leith. Papers presented at the Sixth Colloquium on Calvin Studies at Davidson College. Davidson, NC: Calvin Colloquium, 1992.

———. "Bullinger and the Scholastic Works on Baptism: A Study in the History of Christian Worship." In *Heinrich Bullinger: 1504–1575, Gesammelte Aufsätze zum 400. Todestag*. Zurich: Theologischer Verlag Zürich, 1975.

———. "Calvin as Evangelist: A Study of the Reformer's Sermons in Preparation for the Christian Celebration of Passover." *Calvin Studies VII*. Edited by John H. Leith. Davidson, NC: Calvin Colloquium, 1994.

———. "The Covenantal Dimension of Calvin's Eucharistic Theology." *Calvin Studies XII*. Edited by Michael D. Bush. Due West, SC: Calvin Colloquium, 2006.

———. "Daily Prayer in the Reformed Church of Strasbourg, 1523–1530." *Worship* 52/2 (March 1978): 121–138.

———. "The Eucharistic and Eschatological Dimensions of Calvin's Doctrine of the Lord's Supper." Paper given at the Fourteenth Calvin Colloquium at Due West, SC, in January, 2010.

———. "*Eutaxia, or, The Presbyterian Liturgies: Historical Sketches*, by Charles W. Baird, 1855." In *American Presbyterians* 66/4 (Winter, 1988): 260–263.

———. "Gilbert Tennent and the Preaching of Piety in Colonial America: Newly Discovered Tennent Manuscripts in Speer Library." *The Princeton Seminary Bulletin*, 10/2 (1989): 132–137.

———. "Henry, Matthew." *Dictionary of Major Biblical Interpreters*. Edited by Donald McKim. Downers Grove, IL and Nottingham, UK: InterVarsity Press, 2007.

———. "John Calvin and the Prophetic Criticism of Worship." In *John Calvin and the Church, A Prism of Reform*. Edited by Timothy George. Louisville: Westminster John Knox Press, 1990.

———. *Leading in Prayer: A Workbook for Ministers*. Grand Rapids, MI: Wm. B. Eerdmans Publishing Co., 1995.

———. *The Patristic Roots of Reformed Worship*. Zurich: Theologische Verlag Zurich, 1975. American edition, Black Mountain, NC: Worship Press, 2004.

———. *The Reading and Preaching of the Scriptures in the Worship of the Christian Church*. Volume 3, *The Medieval Church*. Grand Rapids, MI: Wm. B. Eerdmans Publishing Co., 1999.

———. *The Reading and Preaching of the Scriptures in the Worship of the Christian Church*. Volume 4, *The Age of the Reformation*. Grand Rapids, MI: Wm. B. Eerdmans Publishing Co., 2002.

———. *The Reading and Preaching of the Scriptures in the Worship of the Christian Church*. Volume 5, *Moderatism, Pietism, and Awakening*. Grand Rapids, MI: Wm. B. Eerdmans Publishing Co., 2004.

———. *The Reading and Preaching of the Scriptures in the Worship of the Christian Church*. Volume 6, *The Modern Age*. Grand Rapids, MI: Wm. B. Eerdmans Publishing Co., 2007.

———. *The Shaping of the Reformed Baptismal Rite in the Sixteenth Century*. Grand Rapids, MI: Wm. B. Eerdmans Publishing Co., 1992.

———. *Worship, Reformed According to Scripture*. Revised and expanded edition. Louisville: Westminster John Knox Press, 2002.

Orme, William. *The Life and Times of the Rev. Richard Baxter*. 2 volumes. Boston: Crocker & Brewster; and New York: J. Leavitt, 1831.

Ong, Walter, S. J. *The Presence of the Word, Some Prolegomena for Cultural and Religious History*. Minneapolis: University of Minnesota Press, 1981.

Owen, John. *The Correspondence of John Owen (1616–1683): With an Account of his Life and Work*. Edited by Peter Toon. Cambridge: James Clarke, 1970.

———. *The Death of Death in the Death of Christ: A Treatise of the Redemption*. Philadelphia: Green and M'Laughlin, 1827.

———. *An Exposition of the Epistle to the Hebrews*. Edited by W. H. Goold, 7 volumes. Edinburgh and Carlisle, PA: Banner of Truth Trust, 1991.

———. *The Works of John Owen*. Edited by William H. Goold. 16 volumes. London: Banner of Truth Trust, 1965–1968.

Packer, J. I., *A Quest for Godliness: The Puritan Vision for the Christian Life*. Wheaton, IL: Crossway, 1990.

Paul, Robert S. *The Assembly of the Lord: Politics and Religion in the Westminster Assembly and the "Grand Debate."* Edinburgh: T. & T. Clark, 1985.

———. *The Atonement and the Sacraments*. Nashville: Abingdon, 1960.

Payne, Jon D. *John Owen on the Lord's Supper*. Edinburgh and Carlisle, PA: Banner of Truth Trust, 2004.

Payne, Jon D. and Sebastian Heck, editors. *A Faith Worth Teaching: The Heidelberg Catechism's Enduring Message*. Grand Rapids, MI: Reformation Heritage Books, 2013.

Pearson, A. F. Scott. *Thomas Cartwright and Elizabethan Puritanism, 1535–1603*. Cambridge: The University Press, 1925.

Peel, Albert, and Leland H. Carlson. *Cartwrightiana*. Elizabethan Nonconformist Texts 1. London: George Allen and Unwin, Ltd., 1951.

Perkins, William. *The Art of Prophesying*. Revised edition. Edinburgh and Carlisle, PA: Banner of Truth Trust, 1996.

———. *The workes of that famous and worthy minister of Christ: in the universitie of Cambridge*. 3 volumes. London: Iohn Leggatt, 1612–1613.

———. *The Works of William Perkins*. Introduced and edited by Ian Breward. Courtenay Library of Reformation Classics, volume 3. Appleford, UK: Sutton Courtenay Press, 1970.

Philo of Alexandria. *Allegorical Interpretation*. As found in *The Works of Philo*, volume 1. The Loeb Classical Library. 10 volumes. Greek text with English translation by F. H. Colson and G. H. Whitaker. Cambridge, MA: Harvard University Press, 1971.

———. *On the Change of Names*. As found in *The Works of Philo*, volume 5. The Loeb Classical Library. 10 volumes. Greek text with English translation by F. H. Colson and G. H. Whitaker. Cambridge, MA: Harvard University Press, 1971.

Pilcher, George N. *Samuel Davies: Apostle of Dissent in Colonial Virginia*. Knoxville, TN: University of Tennessee Press, 1971.

Pollard, Arthur. *Richard Hooker*. London: Published for the British Council and the National Book League by Longmans, Green, 1966.

Pope, Robert G. *The Half-Way Covenant: Church Membership in Puritan New England*. Princeton, NJ: Princeton University Press, 1969.

Porter, Harry C. *Reformation and Reaction in Tudor Cambridge*. Cambridge, UK: University Press, 1958.

Powicke, Frederick J. *The Life of the Reverend Richard Baxter: 1615–1691*. Boston: Houghton Mifflin Co., 1824.

Prescott, Anne Lake. *Elizabeth and Mary Tudor*. Aldershot, UK: Ashgate Publishing Company, 2001.

Proost, J. "Jodocus van Lodensteyn." *Academic Proeschrift*. Amsterdam, 1880.

Quick, John. *Synodicon in Gallia Reformata*. London: Printed for T. Parkhurst and J. Robinson, 1692.

Rankin, Oliver Shaw. *Israel's Wisdom Literature*. Edinburgh: T. & T. Clark, 1936.

Reicke, Bo. *The Epistles of James, Peter, and Jude*. Anchor Bible. New York: Doubleday, 1964.

Reynolds, Edward. *Meditations on the Holy Sacrament of the Lord's Last Supper*. Found in Edward Reynolds, *The Whole Works of the Right Rev. Edward Reynolds, D.D.*, volume 3. Photolithographic reprint of the 1826 edition. Morgan, PA: Soli Deo Gloria Publications, 1999.

———. *The Whole Works of the Right Rev. Edward Reynolds, D.D.* 6 volumes. London: Printed for B. Holdsworth in St. Paul's Church-yard, 1826.

———. *The Whole Works of the Right Rev. Edward Reynolds, D.D.* Photolithographic reprint of the 1826 edition. 6 volumes. Morgan, PA: Soli Deo Gloria Publications, 1999.

Rice, Eugene F. *The Renaissance Idea of Wisdom.* Cambridge, MA: Harvard University Press, 1958.

Rickey, Mary Ellen and Thomas B. Stroup, editors. *Certaine Sermons or Homilies Appointed to be Read in Churches in the Time of Queen Elizabeth I, 1547–1571: A Facsimile Reproduction of the Edition of 1623 with an Introduction.* Gainesville, FL: Scholars' Facsimiles and Reprints, 1968.

Ridley, Jasper Godwin. *Nicholas Ridley.* London and New York: Longmans, Green, 1957.

———. *Thomas Cranmer.* Oxford: The Clarendon Press, 1962.

"Ridley, Nicholas." In *The Encyclopedia Britannica*, 23:320. 11th edition. 32 volumes. New York: Encyclopedia Britannica, Inc., 1911.

Ridley, Nicholas. *The Works of Nicholas Ridley, D.D. Sometime Lord Bishop of London, Martyr, 1555.* Edited for the Parker Society by the Rev. Henry Christmas. Cambridge: Printed at the University Press, 1843.

Ritschl, Albrecht. *Die Geschichte des Pietismus in der reformirten Kirche.* Bonn: A. Marcus, 1880–1886. Reprinted in Albrecht Ritschl, *Geschichte des Pietismus.* 3 volumes. Berlin: de Gruyter, 1966.

Robertson, George W. *Sacramental Solemnity: Gilbert Tennent, the Covenant and the Lord's Supper.* PhD dissertation. Westminster Theological Seminary, 2007.

Rordorf, Willy. *Sunday.* Philadelphia: Westminster Press, 1968.

Rorem, Paul E. *Calvin and Bullinger on the Lord's Supper.* Bramcote, UK: Grove Books Limited, 1989.

Ross, Kenneth Needham. *The Thirty-nine Articles.* London: Nowbray; New York: Morehouse-Gorham, 1960.

Runia, Klaas. *Het hoge Woord en de Lage Landen: hoe er door de Eeuwen heen in Nederland gepreekt is.* Kampen: J. H. Kok, 1985.

Rupp, Ernest Gordon. "Philip Melanchthon and Martin Bucer." In *A History of Christian Doctrine*, Edited by Hubert Cunliffe-Jones. London: T&T Clark, 2006.

Rutherford, Samuel. *Christ Dying and Drawing Sinners to Himselfe.* Edinburgh: Printed by T. Lumisden and J. Robertson for James Weir, 1727.

———. *Fourteen Communion Sermons*. Preface and notes by Andrew A. Bonar. Edinburgh: J. A. Dixon, 1986.

———. *Fourteen Communion Sermons*. 2nd edition. Glasgow: Charles Glass, 1877.

———. *A Free Disputation Against Pretended Liberty of Conscience*. London: Printed by R. I. for Andrew Crook, 1649.

———. *Letters of the Rev. Samuel Rutherford, With a Sketch of His Life*. Edited by Rev. Andrew A. Bonar. New York: Robert Carter & Brothers, 1851.

———. *Lex Rex, or, The Law and the Prince*. Reprint. Harrisonburg, VA: Sprinkle Publications, 1982.

"Rutherford, Samuel." In *The Encyclopedia Britannica*, 23:940. 11th edition. 32 volumes. New York: The Encyclopedia Britannica Company, 1911.

Ryken, Philip G. *Thomas Boston as Preacher of the Fourfold State*. Carlisle, UK: Published for Rutherford House by Paternoster Press, 1999.

Sayous, Pierre André. *Études littéraires sur les écrivains français de la Réformation*. Paris: G. Fischbacher, 1881.

Scheible, Heinz. "Philipp Melanchthon." In *Oxford Encyclopedia of the Reformation*, 3:41–45. Edited by Hans J. Hillerbrand. 4 volumes. New York: Oxford University Press, 1996.

Schmidt, Leigh Eric. *Holy Fairs: Scottish Communions and American Revivals in the Early Modern Period*. Princeton, NJ: Princeton University Press, 1989.

Schmidt, M. "Pietismus." In *Die Religion in Geschichte und Gegenwart*, 5:370–381. 3rd edition. 6 volumes. Tübingen: J. C. B. Mohr [Paul Siebeck], 1957–1965.

Schneider, John R. "Philipp Melanchthon." In *Dictionary of Major Biblical Interpreters*. Edited by Donald K. McKim. Downers Grove, IL: InterVarsity Press, 2007.

Schweitzer, William M. *God is a Communicative Being: Divine Communicativeness and Harmony in the Theology of Jonathan Edwards*. T. & T. Clark Studies in Systematic Theology. Edinburgh: T & T. Clark, 2012.

Schweizer, Eduard. "PNEUMA bei Johannes." *Theologisches Wörterbuch zum neuen Testament*, 6:436–443. Edited by Gerhard Kittel and Gerhard Friedrich. 9 volumes. Stuttgart: W. Kohlhammer Verlag, 1964.

Scott, Robert Balgamie Young. *The Way of Wisdom in the O. T.* New York: Macmillan, 1971.

Scott, Kenneth B. *Ebenezer Erskine: the Secession of 1733, and the Churches of Stirling*. Stirling, UK: Viewfield Church, 1983.

Second Helvetic Confession. In *The Constitution of the Presbyterian Church: Part I, The Book of Confessions*. Louisville: The Office of the General Assembly, 2004.

Selderhuis, Herman J. *Calvin's Theology of the Psalms*. Grand Rapids, MI: Baker, 2007.

Shepard, Thomas. *Parable of the Ten Virgins Opened and Applied*. Found in volume 2 of Thomas Shepard, *The Works of Thomas Shepard*. 3 volumes. Boston: Doctrinal Tract and Book Society, 1852; Reprint, New York: AMS Press, Inc., 1967.

Sibbes, Richard. *Bowels Opened: or, Expository Sermons on Canticles IV. 16, V. VI*. Found in volume 2, *Works of Richard Sibbes*. Edited by Alexander B. Grosart. Edinburgh and Carlisle, PA: Banner of Truth Trust, 1983.

Silverman, Kenneth. *Timothy Dwight*. New York: Twayne Publishers, 1960.

Simpson, Phillip. *A Life of Gospel Peace: A Biography of Jeremiah Burroughs*. Grand Rapids, MI: Reformation Heritage Books, 2011.

Smits, Luchesius. *Saint Augustine dans l'oeuvre de Jean Calvin*. 2 volumes. Assen: Van Gorcum, 1957.

Solt, Leo Frank. *Church and State in Early Modern England, 1509–1640*. New York: Oxford University Press, 1990.

Spitz, Lewis W. *The Religious Renaissance of the German Humanists*. Cambridge, MA: Harvard University Press, 1963.

Spinks, Bryan. *Two Faces of Elizabethan Anglican Theology: Sacraments and Salvation in the Thought of William Perkins and Richard Hooker*. Lanham, MD: Scarecrow Press, 1999.

Spurgeon, Charles Haddon. *Charles H. Spurgeon*. Edited by Andrew W. Blackwood. New York: Fleming H. Revell, 1949.

———. *Till He Come: A Collection of Communion Addresses*. Fearn, UK: Christian Focus Publications, 2003.

———. *Twelve Sermons on the Lord's Supper*. Grand Rapids, MI: Baker Book House, 1994.

Stewart, James W. "Hodge, Charles (1797–1787)." In *Encyclopedia of the Reformed Faith*. Edited by Donald K. McKim. Louisville: Westminster John Knox Press, and Edinburgh: Saint Andrew Press, 1992.

Stoeffler, F. Ernest. *Continental Pietism and Early American Christianity*. Grand Rapids, MI: Wm. B. Eerdmans Publishing Co., 1976.

———. *The Rise of Evangelical Pietism*. Leiden: E. J. Brill, 1965.

Stout, Harry S. "The Great Awakening." In *Dictionary of Christianity in America*. Edited by Daniel G. Reid, Robert D. Linder, Bruce L. Shelley, and Harry S. Stout. Downers Grove, IL: InterVarsity Press, 1990.

———. *The New England Soul: Preaching and Religious Culture in Colonial New England*. New York: Oxford University Press, 1986.

Stupperich, Robert. *Melanchthon*. Philadelphia: Westminster Press, 1965.

Strange, Alan D. "Jonathan Edwards and the Communion Controversy in Northampton." *Mid-America Journal of Theology* 14 (2003): 57–97.

Strype, John. *The Life and Acts of John Whitgift*. 3 volumes. Oxford: Clarendon Press, 1822.

Sweeney, Douglas A. *Nathaniel Taylor, New Haven Theology, and the Legacy of Jonathan Edwards*. Oxford and New York: Oxford University Press, 2003.

Tanis, James R. *Dutch Calvinistic Pietism in the Middle Colonies: A Study in the Life and Theology of Theodorus Jacobus Frelinghuysen*. The Hague: Martinus Nijhoff, 1967.

"Taylor, Nathaniel William." In *The Encyclopedia Britannica*, 26:472. 11th edition. 32 volumes. New York: Encyclopedia Britannica, 1911.

Taylor, Nathaniel W. *Essays, Lectures, etc., upon Select Topics in Revealed Theology*. New York: Clark, Austin and Smith, 1859.

———. *Lectures on the Moral Government of God*. 2 volumes. New York: Clark, Austin and Smith, 1859.

———. *Practical Sermons*. New York: Clark, Austin, and Smith, 1858.

Taylor, Walter L. *As They Sat at Table: Presbyterian Communion Practices*. D.Min. dissertation. Due West, SC: Erskine Theological Seminary, 2012.

Teellinck, Willem. *Het Geestelyk Cieraet van Christi Brutlofts-Kinderen, ofte de Oractijke des Heylighen Avondtmaels Daer inne*. Middelburg, 1620.

———. *Het Geestelyk Cieraet van Christi Brutlofts-Kinderen, ofte de Oractijke des Heylighen Avondtmaels Daer inne*. 20th edition. Franeker: T. Wever, 1969.

Tennent, Gilbert. *The espousals, or a passionate perswasive to a marriage with the Lamb of God, wherein the Sinners Misery and the Redeemers Glory is unvailed in. A sermon upon Gen. 24:49. Preach'd at N. Brunswyck, June the 22nd, 1735*. New York: Printed by J. Peter Zenger, 1735.

———. *Sermons on Sacramental Occasions*. Boston: J. Draper, 1739.

———. *Twenty-three Sermons on the Chief End of Man*. Philadelphia: W. Bradford, 1744.

Tertullian. *De baptismo liber: Homily on Baptism*. Edited with commentary and translation by Ernest Evans. London: SPCK, 1964.

Thompson, Bard. *Liturgies of the Western Church*. Philadelphia: Fortress Press, [1961] 1980.

Thomson, Andrew. *Lectures, Expository and Practical, on Select Portions of Scripture*. 2 volumes. Edinburgh: Printed for William Blackwood, Edinburgh; and T. Cadell and W. Davies, London, 1816.

———. *Sermons and Sacramental Exhortations by the Late Andrew Thomson, D. D., Minister of St. George's Church Edinburgh*. Edinburgh: Printed for William Whyte & Co., William Collins and M. Ogle, Glasgow; J. Dewar, Perth; and Longman, & Co., London, 1831.

Thurian, Max. *L'Eucharistie, mémorial du Seigneur, Sacrifice d'action de grâce et d'intercession*. Neuchâtel: Delachaux et Niestlé, 1959.

Toon, Peter. *God's Statesman: The Life and Work of John Owen*. Exeter: Paternoster Press, 1971.

Trinterud, Leonard J., editor. Elizabethan Puritanism. New York: Oxford University Press, 1971.

Tulloch, John. *English Puritanism and its Leaders: Cromwell, Milton, Baxter, Bunyan*. Edinburgh: Blackwood, 1861.

van Buren, Paul. *Christ in Our Place*. Edinburgh: Oliver and Boyd, 1957.

van de Poll, G. J. *Martin Bucer's Liturgical Ideas*. Assen: Van Gorcum, 1954.

VanDoodewaard, William. *The Marrow Controversy and the Seceder Tradition*. Grand Rapids, MI: Reformation Heritage Books, 2011.

van Dyke, Henry. *The Works of Henry van Dyke*. Avalon edition. 18 volumes. New York: Charles Scribner's Son, 1920–27.

van Dyke, Tertius. *Henry van Dyke, a Biography*. New York: Harper, 1935.

van Lodenstein, Jodocus. *Geestelyke Opweker voor het Onverloochende, Doode en Geestelose Christendom*. Amsterdam: Andr. Douci, 1732.

von Allmen, Jean-Jacques. *Bibliographie J. J. Von Allmen, 1939–1957* [ie. 1967]. Neuchâtel: Delachaux et Niestlé, 1968.

———. *L'Église et ses fonctions d'après Jean-Frédéric Ostervald: Le problème de la théologie pratique au début du XVIIIme siècle*. Neuchâtel and Paris: Delachaux et Niestlé, 1947.

———. *The Lord's Supper*. London: Lutterworth Press, 1969.

———. *Preaching and Congregation*. Translated by B. L. Nicholson. Richmond: John Knox Press, [1962].

———. *Prophétisme sacramentel: neuf études pour le renouveau et l'unité de l'Église*. Neuchâtel: Delachaux et Niestlé, 1964.

———. *Le saint ministère*. Genève: Centre protestant d'études, 1965.

———. *Worship: Its Theology and Practice*. New York: Oxford University Press, 1965.

von Allmen, Jean-Jacques, editor. *La vocabulaire biblique*. Neuchâtel: Delachaux et Niestlé, 1954.

von Rad, Gerhard. *Wisdom in Israel*. Translated by James D. Martin. Nashville and New York: Abingdon Press, 1972.

Vermigli, Peter Martyr. *The Life, Early Letters and Eucharistic Writings of Peter Martyr*. Introduced and edited by Joseph C. McLelland and Gervase E. Duffield. Appleford, UK: Sutton Courtenay Press, 1989.

Visser, Derk, editor. *Controversy and Conciliation: The Reformation and the Palatinate 1559–1583*. Allison Park, PA: Pickwick Publications, 1986.

———. *Zacharias Ursinus: The Reluctant Reformer, His Life and Times*. New York: United Church Press, 1983.

Walker, Michael. "Charles Haddon Spurgeon (1834–1892) and John Clifford (1836–1923) on the Lord's Supper." *American Baptist Quarterly* 7/2 (1988): 128–150.

Walker, Robert. *Sermons on Practical Subjects, Late one of the Ministers of the High Church of Edinburgh; to which is prefixed a character of the Author by Hugh Blair, D. D.* 5th edition. 3 volumes. Edinburgh: E. Elliot and G. Robinson, 1785.

Wallace, Ronald S. *Calvin's Doctrine of the Christian Life*. Edinburgh: Oliver and Boyd, 1959.

———. *Calvin's Doctrine of the Word and Sacrament*. Reprint. Portland: Wipf and Stock, 1997.

Waltke, Bruce K. *The Book of Proverbs, Chapters 1–15*. Grand Rapids, MI: Eerdmans, 2004.

Walton, Izaak. *The Lives of Dr. John Donne, Sir Henry Wotton, Mr. Richard Hooker, Mr. George Herbert and Dr. Robert Sanderson*. London: Bell and Daldy, 1864.

Walton, Robert C. "Heinrich Bullinger." In *Shapers of Religious Traditions in Germany, Switzerland, and Poland, 1560–1600*. Edited by Jill Raitt. New Haven: Yale University Press, 1981.

Warfield, Benjamin Breckinridge. *Faith and Life*. Edinburgh and Carlisle, PA: Banner of Truth Trust, 1990.

———. *Perfectionism*. 2 volumes. New York: Oxford University Press, 1931.

———. *Perfectionism*. Edited by Samuel G. Craig. Philadelphia: Presbyterian and Reformed Publishing Co., 1958.

———. "Posture of the Recipients at the Lord's Supper" In *Selected Shorter Writings*. Volume 2. Edited by John E. Meeter. Phillipsburg, NJ: Presbyterian and Reformed Publishing Co., 1973. Originally published in *Journal of the Presbyterian Historical Society* (June, 1920).

———. *Selected Shorter Writings*. Edited by John E. Meeter. 2 volumes. Phillipsburg, NJ: Presbyterian and Reformed Publishing Co., 1970, 1973.

———. *The Works of Benjamin B. Warfield*. 10 volumes. Grand Rapids, MI: Baker Book House, 1991.

Watkins, Owen C. *The Puritan Experience*. New York: Schocken Books, 1972.

Watson, Jean L. *Life of Ebenezer Erskine*. Edinburgh: James Gemmell, 1881.

Watson, Thomas. *A Body of Divinity*. London: Banner of Truth Trust, 1965.

Weeks, Louis B. "Davies, Samuel." In *Dictionary of Christianity in America*. Edited by Daniel G. Reid, Robert D. Linder, Bruce L. Shelley, and Harry S. Stout. Downers Grove, IL: InterVarsity Press, 1990.

Weiser, Artur. *The Psalms, A Commentary*. Philadelphia: The Westminster Press, 1962.

Wendel, François. *Calvin, the Origins and Development of his Religious Thought*. Translated by Philip Mairet. New York and Evanston: Harper & Row, 1963.

Wentz, Richard E. *John Williamson Nevin: American Theologian*. New York and Oxford: Oxford University Press, 1997.

Wenzke, Annabelle S. *Timothy Dwight (1752–1817)*. Lewiston, NY: E. Mellen Press, 1989.

Werner, Eric. *The Sacred Bridge, Liturgical Parallels in Synagogue and Early Church*. New York: Schocken Books, 1970.

Westermann, Claus. *Isaiah 40–66, A Commentary*. Philadelphia: The Westminster Press, 1969.

The Westminster Directory: Being a Directory for the Publique Worship of God in the Three Kingdomes. Introduction by Ian Breward. Bramcote: Grove Books, 1980.

Whitgift, John. *The Works of John Whitgift: containing The defence of the answer to the admonition, against the reply of Thomas Cartwright* (1851). 3 volumes. Reprint. New York: Johnson Reprints, 1968.

Whittingham, William. *A Brief Discourse of the Troubles at Frankfort, 1554–1558 AD.* London: Eliot Stock, 1908.

Wiers, John R. "van Dyke, Henry." In *Dictionary of Christianity in America*. Edited by Daniel G. Reid, Robert D. Linder, Bruce L. Shelley, and Harry S. Stout. Downers Grove, IL: InterVarsity Press, 1990.

Wilckens, Ulrich. "SOPHIA". *Theologisches Wörterbuch zum Neuen Testament*, 7:465–475. Edited by Gerhard Kittel and Gerhard Friedrich. 9 volumes. Stuttgart: W. Kohlhammer Verlag, 1964.

Williams, George Hunston. *The Radical Reformation*. Philadelphia: Westminster Press, 1962.

Williams, J. B. *Memoirs of the Life, Character and Writings of the Rev. Matthew Henry.* London, 1828. Reprinted with Henry's biography of his father. Edinburgh: Banner of Truth Trust, 1974.

Willis, Edward David. *Calvin's Catholic Christology: The Function of the So-called Extra Calvinisticum in Calvin's Theology*. Leiden: E. J. Brill, 1966.

Willison, John. *The Afflicted Man's Companion*. In John Willison, *The Practical Works of the Rev. John Willison*. Edited by W. M. Hetherington. Glasgow, Edinburgh, and London: Blackie and Son, [1830].

———. *The Balm of Gilead*. In John Willison, *The Practical Works of the Rev. John Willison*. Edited by W. M. Hetherington. Glasgow, Edinburgh, and London: Blackie and Son, [1830].

———. *Example of Plain Catechising*. In John Willison, *The Practical Works of the Rev. John Willison*. Edited by W. M. Hetherington. Glasgow, Edinburgh, and London: Blackie and Son, [1830].

———. *The Practical Works of the Rev. John Willison*. Edited by W. M. Hetherington. Glasgow, Edinburgh, and London: Blackie and Son, [1830].

———. *A Sacramental Catechism*. Edited by Don Kistler. Morgan, PA: Soli Deo Gloria Publications, 2000.

———. *A Sacramental Directory* (1716); *Five Sacramental Sermons* (1722); and *Sacramental Meditations* (1747). In John Willison, *The Practical Works of the Rev. John Willison*. Edited by W. M. Hetherington. Glasgow, Edinburgh, and London: Blackie and Son, [1830].

———. *Treatise concerning the Sanctification of the Lord's Day*. In John Willison. *The Practical Works of the Rev. John Willison*. Edited by W. M. Hetherington. Glasgow, Edinburgh, and London: Blackie and Son, [1830].

Wisloff, Carl F. *The Gift of Communion: Luther's Controversy with Rome on Eucharistic Sacrifice*. Translated by Joseph M. Shaw. Minneapolis, Minn.: Augsburg Publishing House, 1964.

Won, Jonathan. *Communion with Christ: An Exposition and Comparison of the Doctrine of Union and Communion with Christ in Calvin and the English Puritans*. PhD. dissertation. Philadelphia: Westminster Theological Seminary, 1989.

Wright, David, editor. *Martin Bucer: Reforming Church and Community*. Cambridge and New York: Cambridge University Press, 1994.

Yule, George. *Puritans in Politics: The Religious Legislation of the Long Parliament 1640–1647*. Appleford, UK: Sutton Courtenay Press, 1981.

Zaret, David. *The Heavenly Contract: Ideology and Organization in Pre-Revolutionary Puritanism*. Chicago: University of Chicago Press, 1985.

Ziener, G. *Weisheitsbuch und Johannesevangelium*. Bib 38 (1957), 395–418; and 39 (1958), 37–60.

Zwingli, Ulrich. *On the Lord's Supper*. Found in *Zwingli and Bullinger*. The Library of Christian Classics, volume 24. Edited by G. W. Bromiley. Philadelphia: The Westminster Press, 1953.

———. *Zurich Service Book* of 1525 (*Action or Use of the Lord's Supper*). English text found in Bard Thompson, *Liturgies of the Western Church*. Philadelphia: Fortress Press, 1980.

SCRIPTURE INDEX

GENESIS

20	647–648
28:10-22	553

LEVITICUS

10:3	347

NUMBERS

6:24-26	39

DEUTERONOMY

26	511
26:5-11	31

PSALMS

4:6-7	690
16	492
17	801
19	94–96
23	26
40:6-8	618
73	543
116:12-19	376
138	170–171
144:15	480

PROVERBS

9:1-6	85–86, 98, 292, 460

SONG OF SOLOMON 297, 478–479, 490, 529, 788

2:4	432, 487–488
2:14-17	299–300
4:16	638–642
7:5	539

ISAIAH 526

11	149
40	486, 550
45	622
53	34
55	99
61	567

JEREMIAH

14:8	477–478
31:31-33	38, 256

DANIEL

9	241–242

ZECHARIAH

13:7-9	287–288

MATTHEW

11:28	566
22	640
26:26-28	702
26:30	732

Mark

14:24	54–55, 702

Luke

2	543
14:16	611–612
14:21-24	667
22:14	789, 793
22:19	3, 702
24:50	39

John

	176
6	98–99
14:18	799
17:20-23	62–64

Acts

2:42	40

Romans

4:11	659
5:7-8	577
8	131
9:5	722

1 Corinthians

10:1-3	852
10:15-18	58–64, 412, 662–663, 702, 734, 742, 791
11:17-34	407–408
11:24-26	3, 66, 164
11:25	660
11:26	19, 608
12	150
13	34

2 Corinthians

6:17-18	779

Galatians

5	150

Ephesians

1:9	74
5	60–61

1 Timothy

4:4-5	510

Hebrews

	621
3:7-8	481–482
9	159
9-10	415
13:15	161

James

	90–93

1 John

	88–90
4:8, 16	731

Revelation

	789
3:1-6	534
3:20	434
8:17	559
19:7-14	302
19:12-13	737

SUBJECT INDEX

A

Adam 761–763
ad fontes ('to the sources') 225
Admonition of 1570 327–330
adoption 485
adoration of the host 224
Agnus Dei 27, 822
Alexander, James W. 716–718
alms, collection of 40
altars 201–203
Anabaptists 48, 76
anamnesis. See remembrance
Anglo-Genevan Psalter 241, 244, 250, 255
Apostles' Creed 28–29, 152, 520, 661, 860
Apostolic Constitutions, The 26, 198–199, 814
Arminianism 283
Art of Prophesying, The 231–232
assurance of pardon 23, 183–184, 243, 860
atonement 140, 410, 617, 706, 707, 728, 766
Augustine, St. 75, 130, 358, 657

B

Baird, Charles W. 7, 768–774
baptism 538, 847–848
Barth, Karl 836, 847–848
Basil, St. 26, 814
Battle of Kappel 313
Baxter, Richard 365–368
benediction 39–40
biblical theology 387
Black Rubric 188, 747
body of Christ 59
Book of Common Order 239–240, 512, 523, 784
Book of Common Prayer 183, 186–187, 200, 805, 810, 827, 832
Book of Common Worship 805, 808–809, 828, 830–832
Brainerd, David 650, 691
Brakel, Wilhelm à 587–588
bread of life 852–853
bread of life discourse 97–106
breaking of the bread 273, 705–706
Brethren of the Common Life 588
bride of Christ 540–541
Bruce, Robert 259–262
Bucer, Martin 4, 25, 125, 203–214, 820, 862
Bullinger, Heinrich 4, 48–49, 313–315, 658
Burroughs, Jeremiah 346–349
Byzantine church 125

C

Calvin, John 4–5, 308
 sermons 141–148
 views on Lord's Day 17–18
Cambuslang Revival 475
Campbell, Alexander 7
Capito, Wolfgang 4, 17
Cartwright, Thomas 328
catechetical sermons 414
Chalmers, Thomas 777–779
Charles I 283, 288
Charles II 283, 366
Childs, Brevard 841
Christian's Reasonable Service, A 587–588
Chrysostom, John 358
church discipline 32, 348–349
church members, reception of 860
Church of England 181–183
clerical vestments 208
commemoration 62
Communicant's Companion, A 442–443
communion 445–447, 503–504, 630, 661–666, 734, 743, 790–791, 793, 797, 850. *See also* fellowship
communion invocation 29–30, 153–154
communion meditation 596–597
communion of the saints 679, 828
communion seasons 145–146, 473–474, 477, 531–532, 676, 753, 783
communion table 248, 360–362, 514–515, 662, 748, 783
communion with God 45–46, 68–69, 397, 541

community of believers 59–60
Companion for Communicants, A 643
confession of faith 152
confession of sin 241
Consensus Tigurinus 4, 132–133, 192, 699
consubstantiation 266
conviction 482
corporal presence 193
covenant 457–458, 462–463, 480, 491, 494, 616, 658–661, 677, 735, 779, 794
Covenanters 497, 532
covenant renewal 553, 599–600, 762
covenant theology 43, 45–47, 48, 256, 351, 395, 496–497, 658, 680, 708, 762, 779
Cranmer, Thomas 189–192, 205–206, 816
Cromwell, Oliver 386–387
Cullmann, Oscar 836

D

Daillé, Jean 405–407
Dale, Robert 786–787
Davies, Samuel 651–653
deacons' collection 864
Death of Death in the Death of Christ, The 385
Deism 617, 701
de Labadie, Jean 587
devotional practices 459–460
dismissal 350
divine institution 333, 352, 702
Dix, Gregory 257, 507–508
Doolittle, Thomas 377–384
Dwight, Timothy 673–676

SUBJECT INDEX

E

Eastern Orthodoxy 846–847, 852
Easter Sunday 859
Ecclesiasticus 85, 99
ecclesiology 838
ecumenicalism 839, 842
Edwards, Jonathan 3, 606–608, 633, 682
Edward VI 182–183, 200, 205
efficacy of sacraments 129, 697
elements 162, 164, 265, 362–363, 413, 470, 500, 506, 702, 720, 726, 765, 813
  distribution of 361–362, 512
Elizabethan Settlement 183, 215
Elizabeth I 181, 213–215, 219–220
empowerment of believers 107–108
English Reformation 182
Enlightenment 112–114, 573, 617, 675
episcopacy 848–849
Erastianism 181, 189, 214, 588
Erskine, Ebenezer 531–534
Erskine, Ralph 531–532, 549–550, 802
eschatology 173–174, 176, 286, 434, 494–495
Essay on the Lord's Supper 842–843
eucharist 781.
  See also thanksgiving
eucharistic prayer 194, 210–211, 249–250, 362, 373, 677, 813–814, 814, 858
eucharistic sacrifice 194, 645–646, 741
eucharistic theology 801
Eutaxia 769, 772, 774–775

evangelism 136, 153–154, 577, 650, 667–668, 780
experiential religion 135

F

faith 128, 173, 322, 343, 546, 718, 736
feast 449, 612, 664, 730
feast days 24, 212–213
Federal theology 49
feeding upon Jesus Christ 107–108, 114, 119–120, 131, 154, 271, 274, 561
fellowship 148, 429, 445, 679.
  See also communion
fencing of the table 246, 348–349, 595, 681, 711, 812, 861. *See also* invitation to the Lord's Supper
Field, John 327
First Prayer Book 188
Five Sacramental Sermons 477–478
Flavel, John 638
Frederick III 308
Frelinghuysen, Theodorus 603, 650
French Evangelical Psalter 39, 170
frequency of celebration 357–358, 379–380, 419–420, 433, 688, 701, 788

G

Genevan liturgy 13–14, 166–167
Genevan Psalter 4, 13, 15, 174, 356, 419, 523, 595, 860
Geneva, Reformation in 14–15
German Mass 39–40
gestures 209

glorying 622–624
Gnesio-Lutherans 307
God
  faithfulness 555–556
  fatherhood 52
  glorifying 719
  unity of 63–64
Golden Chain, The 233
Gospel Worship 346–347
grace 437
Great Awakening (First) 5, 605–606, 633, 635, 647, 673
Great Awakening, Second 675, 755–756
Gregory the Great 814

H

Heidelberg Catechism 307, 308–312, 767
Henry, Matthew 5, 441–442, 831
Henry VIII 190, 199
Hippolytus 814
Hodge, Charles 693–695
holiness 485, 537
Holy Spirit 125, 262, 267, 275–278, 310, 339, 344–346, 369–370, 410, 482, 485, 525–527, 639, 668, 711, 764–765, 799–800, 846–847, 852, 859, 862
  gifts of 148–150
Hooker, Richard 227–230
hope 173
hymnody 4

I

Ignatius of Antioch 848
Ignatius of Loyola 46
Immens, Peter 590–591
incarnation 271, 288, 300–301, 453, 510, 761
intinction 862–863
invitation to the Lord's Supper 31–32, 246–247, 350, 359–360, 460, 572, 594–595, 669–670, 812, 861. *See also* fencing of the table
invocation 240, 677

J

Jesus Christ
  anointing 639
  ascension 108, 145–146, 176, 483
  as wisdom 86–87
  as Word of God 88–89
  blood 382–383, 412
  cross 352, 619–621, 725, 737
  glorified 737, 853
  Lamb of God 559–560, 737
  offices 402, 545, 570
  person 723–724, 759, 760
  resurrection 294–295, 453, 489
  sacrifice 853
  suffering 728–729
Jewel, John 217–226

K

kerygma. *See* proclamation
Knox, John 239, 254–255, 512, 522, 705, 747, 773
koinonia 68–69, 300, 397, 413, 435, 445, 504, 627–628, 661, 709, 735, 791. *See also* fellowship

L

Lamb of God 103, 105
Latin (as language of mass) 223

Subject Index

Laud, William 283
Leo the Great 814
Lex Rex 284
liturgy 151–154
Log College 634
logos 86, 95, 761–762
Lombard, Peter 315
Lord's Day 16–17, 489–490.
 See also Sabbath
Lord's Prayer 52–53, 245
Lord's Supper
 as communal meal 33–34
 benefits of 128–129, 428, 467–469
 definition 676, 696
 in Geneva 15–16
 on feast days 19
 visual aspects 465–466
love feast 408, 489, 733
love for Jesus Christ 640–641
love of God 389, 581, 717, 731
Luther, Martin
 Babylonian Captivity of the Church 46
 Treatise on the New Testament, that is the Mass 47

M

manducatio impiorum 194
manducatio spiritualis.
 See feeding upon Jesus Christ
manna 101–102, 235
Marot, Clément 4
Marrow Controversy 533–534
Marshall, Stephen 355–356
Mary I (Queen) 182
Mary Magdalene 293–295
mass (Roman Catholic) 15–16, 25, 163, 174, 236–237, 814
Mather, Cotton 643
Maundy Thursday 859

McCosh, James 740
means of grace 597, 695
meditation 463–465, 515–516, 685
Meditations on the Holy Sacrament 331, 333
Melanchthon, Philipp 306–307
memorial 58, 64, 66, 69, 234–235, 654–655, 717, 818
Mercersburg theology 751, 775
mercy ministry 864
Miller, Samuel 831
missionary movement 777
mystery 73–74, 264, 319, 757–758
mysticism 588, 759, 762, 800–802

N

Nadere Reformatie 430, 586
National Covenant 283, 491, 497
natural revelation 95–96
natural sacraments 76–77
Neander, August 771
Nestorianism 212
Nevin, John Williamson 7, 701, 715–716, 751–756, 801
New Divinity 675, 741
New England theology 673
Newton, John 575
Nominalism 230, 376

O

Oecolampadius, John 4, 73–74, 658, 800
 Testament of Jesus Christ 47–48
old covenant sacraments 78, 317
Old School Presbyterianism 751–752, 833

opus operandi 128, 135, 815
Owen, John 384–387
Oxford Movement 775–776

P

parable of the great feast 291–292
pardon for sin 668
Passover 67, 69, 103–106, 140, 311, 410, 488, 493, 511, 743–745, 795, 860
pastoral prayer 26–28, 185–186, 244–245
Patristic literature 224–226
peace 469
penance 418
penitence 384
penitential discipline 607
Pentecost 146–147
Perkins, William 230–238, 586, 831
perseverance of the saints 419
pietism 381, 437, 476, 518, 531, 559, 675
  Dutch 422, 585–586
piety 459–460, 680, 691–692, 701, 777
Pious Communicant, The 591
posture during Lord's Supper 747–748
pouring of the wine 273
prayer 356–357, 463, 498
prayer and fasting 589, 591, 593
prayer for illumination 244
prayer of confession 22–23, 183–184, 824, 860
prayer of consecration 371–372, 704
prayer of dedication 36–38, 168, 255–257, 522, 862
prayer of intercession 26–27, 437

prayer of thanksgiving 162–163, 165, 166–167, 168, 337, 363, 522, 831, 845
preaching 858
  lectio continua 207, 576
preaching, eucharistic 138–147
preaching, expository 576
preparation for the Lord's Supper 358–359, 378–379, 380–382, 417–418, 588–589, 709
preparatory sermons 259, 280, 286, 424, 431, 608, 648, 652
preparatory services 688, 700, 832
Presbyterianism 531
Presbyterian liturgies 768–769
presence of God 539
private masses 223
proclamation 70, 136, 391, 393, 454–455, 656
professing of faith 393, 710
promises of God 50–51, 52, 391, 557
Protestant Scholasticism 229–230
psalmody 4, 19–21, 38–39, 166, 601, 795–796, 811, 863
The Psalms
  of praise and adoration 20
  of thanksgiving 31, 169, 523, 859
  Passover 38, 795
  recounting God's acts 36, 817
  sung during Communion 34, 601–602
  wisdom 82–83, 92–96
Puritans 5, 325

R

Rationalism 684, 761
Realism 230

Subject Index

real presence of Jesus Christ 109, 177, 262, 276, 278–280, 296–297, 340–343, 364, 416–417, 492, 631–632, 665, 686, 711, 766, 787, 797–798, 850
redemption 493, 718, 818
Reformed Liturgy, The (Baxter) 366–368
regulative principle 225
Religious Affections, The 641
remembrance 311, 342, 374, 389, 409–410, 452, 725, 729, 845
Remonstrants 422
repentance 281
revivalism 755–756, 812, 833
Reynolds, Edwards 330–332
Rhenish Reformers 46, 48–49, 58
Ridley, Nicholas 187–188, 199–203
Roman Catholic abuses 221–224
Romanticism 751, 774, 807, 817, 833
Rutherford, Samuel 282–285

S

Sabbath 388, 858. *See* Lord's Day
sacrament 656–658
 definition 443, 499
Sacramental Catechism, A 495
Sacramental Directory, A 475
Sacramental Discourses (Owen) 386–387
Sacramentarians 312, 503
sacramentum 72, 75–77, 347–348, 444, 696
sacrifice of thanksgiving 160–161
sacrifices 159–160, 618–619, 745, 854
sanctification 117–118, 552, 762

Savoy Conference 367
Schaff, Phillip 715, 748
Schleiermacher, Friedrich 771
Scholasticism 46–47, 229, 262, 314, 335, 406
Scotland 531
Scottish common sense philosophy 695, 740
Scottish Psalter 574
Seceeders 534
Second Helvetic Confession 315–324
Second Prayer Book 187
self-examination 23–24, 280, 351, 418, 428, 461, 516, 592, 609–610, 683, 710, 825
Sermons on Sacramental Occasions 637
sermons, theological 635
Short Treatise on the Lord's Supper 132, 137, 157–158, 166, 419, 784
Sibbes, Richard 639
sign and seal 46, 133, 173, 193, 316, 333, 411–412, 458, 501, 626–627, 642–643, 659, 858
signs 77, 132–133, 263–266, 417, 429, 500, 506, 654, 659, 765
sin 538
sola scriptura 225
Song of Simeon 169
Spener, Philipp 587
spiritual food 235, 322–323, 413, 470–471, 712
spiritual gifts 301
Spurgeon, Charles Haddon 787–788
Strasbourg German Mass 3
Strasbourg liturgy 14, 22, 167
Strasbourg Psalter 184, 810
substance 61
substance and accidents 417

substance of Jesus Christ 110–111, 318
suffering 301
sufficiency of Scripture 318
Sursum Corda 27, 174, 815

T

Taylor, Nathaniel 673, 688–691
Teellinck, Willem 422–429
Ten Commandments
  in worship 23
Tennent, Gilbert 6, 633–642, 801, 861
Tertullian 71–72, 75, 152, 225, 312, 347, 444, 502, 656, 856
thanksgiving 66–67, 67, 157–159, 253, 394, 428, 447–448, 485, 509–510, 522–523, 600–601, 644, 682, 782, 822
thanksgiving sermons 145, 550
theosis 485, 763
Thirty-Nine Articles 214–217
Thomson, Andrew 573–576
Thurian, Max 841
transubstantiation 191, 193, 236, 787
Travers, Walter 227
Treatise on the Laws of Ecclesiastical Polity 228
typology 42, 48, 69, 296, 396–397, 460, 488, 653

U

union with Jesus Christ 53–54, 62, 109, 131, 208, 229, 263–264, 269, 272, 321, 338–339, 400, 505, 536–537, 590, 609, 625–626, 643, 648–649, 763
Unitarianism 684, 701, 706, 719, 722–724, 741
unity of Christians 625
Ursinus, Zacharias 305–308

V

van Dyke, Henry 805–809
van Lodenstein, Jodocus 3, 429–438
Vermigli, Peter Martyr 218, 254, 307
Victorian Age 801
virtuistic 798
visible Word 270, 644
vivification 115–120
Voetius, Gisbertus 587
von Allmen, Jean-Jacques 835–840
vows 498–499

W

Walker, Robert 563–565
Warfield, Benjamin Breckinridge 739–741
wedding feast of the Lamb 175–176, 286, 302, 426, 592, 612, 646–647, 738, 850
Westminster Assembly 283
Westminster Directory for Public Worship 5, 355–357, 363
Westminster Directory for Worship 509
Westminster Shorter Catechism 503, 570, 637, 695, 764
Whitgift, John 228, 328, 844
Wilberforce, William 575
Wilcox, Thomas 327
Willison, John 5, 474–476
wine 703
wisdom 81, 84–85, 292, 490
Wisdom School 81, 82, 87, 93, 111

wisdom theology 86–87, 95, 122, 614, 761
witness of sacrament 56
Wittenberg Concord 266, 759
word and sacrament 708
  joint administration 25
Words of Institution 32, 821–822
  1 Corinthians 11 and 55–58, 246, 378, 595, 812
worship 454, 733
  typological aspects 21–22
Wycliffe, John 193

Z

Zurich Service Book 3, 38, 65
Zwingli, Ulrich 4, 48, 65–66, 72–73, 76, 193, 233, 313, 314–315, 654, 748